Regionalization of the Law of the Sea

Regionalization of the Law of the Sea

PROCEEDINGS

Law of the Sea Institute
Eleventh Annual Conference
November 14–17, 1977

University of Hawaii
Honolulu, Hawaii

Edited by Douglas M. Johnston

Ballinger Publishing Company • Cambridge, Massachusetts
A Subsidiary of J.B. Lippincott Company

This book is printed on recycled paper.

International Standard Book Number: 0-88410-075-8

Library of Congress Catalog Card Number: 78-15357

Printed in the United States of America

Library of Congress Cataloging in Publication Data

Law of the Sea Institute.
Regionalization in the law of the sea.

1. Maritime law–Congresses. 2. Regionalism (International organization)–Congresses. I. Johnston, Douglas M. II. Hawaii. University, Honolulu. III. Title.
JX4408.L37 1978 341.44'8 78-15357
ISBN 0-88410-075-8

Contents

List of Tables

Foreword

It is with pleasure and pride that the state of Hawaii welcomes you to this first conference of the Law of the Sea Institute held in its new home in Hawaii. We in this state have long been aware of the global significance of the law of the sea and of the role of this Institute in shaping the philosophy and evolution of this body of international law. The state of Hawaii, through the University of Hawaii and with the support of our state legislature, has undertaken the sponsorship of the Institute because of our belief that major changes in the future will be determined by ocean developments in the Pacific: by ocean developments in the coastal zones of the major continents on the Pacific Rim and the economic zones of the major island nations in the western and southwestern Pacific, in the waters surrounding the island and archipelagic domains of the south and central Pacific, and in that vast ocean regime beyond the limits of national jurisdiction. A few decades ago the Pacific nations were widely separated not only by miles of ocean but by time. Weeks and months could and did elapse before interaction, commerce, and communication could take place among the nations of this vast community. But today no nation is an island, and no island is remote. High-speed container ships move large cargoes swiftly and economically. People are transported in a matter of hours by high-speed aircraft, and satellites carry communications instantaneously and at low cost.

It is our hope that while you are here you will gain an appreciation of the cosmopolitan community that is Hawaii and also an appreciation of its desire to contribute to the world community. It is our hope that you will also obtain a deeper understanding of the relationship between island communities and the sea. Our forebears on these islands lived on the sea and drew their support from it. Over the years, this dependence was lessened, but now, once again, the importance of the sea is being reasserted. In the very near future, we shall derive substantial energy from the ocean by thermal energy conversion. We shall extract valuable metals from the manganese nodules of the deep Pacific. We shall extract fertilizer and nutrients from the deep ocean for mariculture and aquaculture. We shall develop the fishing, coral, and sand resources of the reefs and their adjacent waters. We shall speed from island to island in modern forms of stable ocean ferries.

Utilization of these resources of the ocean will require management. At the same time, the ocean environment must be protected, and the responsibility for the resource management and environmental protection of the ocean must be placed with the people who occupy the lands that these oceans surround. As we look over the vast Pacific, we see many legal regimes and newer ones proposed for this management. For many island nations an archipelagic doctrine seems most appropriate, providing as it does management control over archipelagic waters and maintaining at the same time traditional passage through straits and international waterways. For some island communities, separated by vast stretches of ocean, it may be more appropriate to claim a separate economic zone for each individual island. In either case, there is a common fundamental principle that the management of the ocean cannot be separated from the management of the land. This principle is independent of the sovereign status of the islands, whether they be, as in Hawaii, an oceanic archipelago of a continental state, or whether they be a territory in trust, or islands such as the Line Islands, whose sovereignty is yet in contention. The development of this philosophy, in which equitable and fair regimes can be developed in each region, regardless of the complexity of sovereignty, is a role which this Institute can well fulfill.

The development of a philosophy for the broad ocean area is of equal importance. Today this area is of interest primarily because of the manganese nodules. Tomorrow it will be of interest because of the tropical belt of geothermal energy and biological productivity that stretches across the wide Pacific. The United Nations has struggled, as yet unsuccessfully, with the problem of establishing an international system for the management of the deep seabed. Such a regime may set a precedent for the resources of the waters above as well as for other, still undiscovered, resources of the deep ocean floor. Development of a philosophy for the broad ocean that takes fully into account both the common heritage of mankind and the rights and responsibilities of island states, including those surrounded entirely by international waters, is yet another role for your Institute to fulfill. This challenge will require much study, a deeper understanding of the ocean than we now have, but above all it will require a sense of goodwill and community. In Hawaii we call this sense of goodwill and community the "spirit of Aloha." It is our earnest hope that you will come to share in that spirit in this Conference and that you will carry it with you in your future endeavors. Mahalo and Aloha!

It is now my privilege to introduce our keynote speaker. The Honorable Patsy

Mink is a daughter of Hawaii. She was born on the island of Maui and her schooling was here in these islands, latterly at the University of Hawaii. Her legal studies carried her to the mainland, where she received her Jurisdoctorate at the University of Chicago. She returned to these islands and quickly entered local politics and state politics. First she became a territorial representative, then a territorial senator and then a state senator in the State House in Hawaii. In 1964 she was elected the U.S. Representative to Congress from Hawaii and served in that capacity for twelve years. During that time she played an active and vital role in the law of the sea. She was a member of the Congressional Advisory Group on the Law of the Sea and was a frequent visitor at the sessions of UNCLOS III and at the earlier preparatory sessions. In 1976 she entered the Democratic primary for the United States Senate in the state of Hawaii. This entry opened the way for your speaker to enter the Democratic primary and I entered as a candidate for the House of Representatives. We both conducted vital and dynamic campaigns. The voters of the state of Hawaii determined that I could best serve the state and the nation as director of the Law of the Sea Institute! Similarly, the voters of the state of Hawaii determined that our speaker could best serve the nation as assistant secretary of state!

John Craven
Director
Law of the Sea Institute

Opening Address

The Honorable Patsy T. Mink
Assistant Secretary of State for Oceans and
Environmental and Scientific Affairs

It is indeed an honor and privilege to be asked to offer opening remarks at this convocation of the Eleventh Annual Conference of the Law of the Sea Institute, convening for the first time in its new abode, my home state of Hawaii. Obviously, as the only island state of the Union, our affinity and rapport with the sea are intense, and intimate. We are indeed pleased to have this important Institute here in Hawaii, and I offer Dr. Craven my warmest congratulations for his personal efforts in this regard.

The theme you have chosen as the focus of your deliberations and discussions at this Conference, "Regionalization of the Law of the Sea," is a most timely one. As you know, the United States has placed great emphasis upon the negotiation and conclusion of a law of the sea treaty. Our policy has been based upon the belief that a comprehensive treaty, fairly, openly, and collectively negotiated, could best provide the necessary conditions to effectively manage the resources of the oceans. Such a treaty must provide the framework for mutual stability, cooperation, and harmony in the realm of ocean space. We have sought through these negotiations to bring forth a new era in ocean relations, which would accentuate global maritime interdependence, and which would enhance and safeguard the common heritage of mankind.

I would be less than candid if I did not state that the Administration is concerned that our most fundamental expectations and precepts concerning this important attempt at universal cooperation now seem in jeopardy. At the last session, the Conference moved forward, both procedurally and substantively, on many issues pertaining to Committees II and III and the establishment of an institutional mechanism for dispute settlement. However, the principle of full, fair, and open discussion was not adhered to in the negotiations on the important issue of deep seabed mining, resulting in a product, to quote my good friend and colleague, Ambassador Elliot Richardson, which was "fundamentally unacceptable to the United States."

As a result, we are now conducting within the government a serious and searching review of our interests and the balance among them and whether these interests can be protected in the type of negotiations which have taken place to date.

Thus, your planned consideration, analysis, and scrutiny of regionalism and its relationship to the law of the sea is timely, appropriate, and consonant with the review now being undertaken within the Administration.

Be assured, however, that even if the law of the sea negotiations were not so troubled, we in the Administration would still view your Conference as a most important undertaking. Although our policies have strongly favored principles of universality, regional arrangements have always figured prominently in our expectations for a new law of the sea. In fact, recognition of this essential relationship has led the United States and other advocates of the universal treaty process to initiate and support numerous provisions in the law of the sea context pertaining to regional initiatives and organizations. Both the Revised Single Negotiating Text (RSNT) and the more recently issued Informal Composite Negotiating Text (ICNT) contain numerous provisions for regional cooperation in respect to marine scientific research, technology transfer and training, management and conservation of living resources, access to living resources by landlocked and geographically disadvantaged states, and protection and preservation of the marine environment. Whether a universal treaty is concluded or not, we would welcome and encourage regional arrangements as entirely appropriate—indeed as major institutions through which the United States and others could seek to promote and enhance not only their own mutual interests, but also the interests of the entire international community in sound resource management and environmental quality.

Some would argue that regional arrangements are alternatives to a comprehensive UNCLOS III treaty. I would argue, however, that they should be supplementary. Whether there is such a treaty or not, regional arrangements will fulfill major functions. They can provide an important and peaceful means by which to promote and safeguard a wide range of interests in the oceans. They can create both the opportunity and means to facilitate multilateral cooperation and communication and thus reinforce the concept and reality of mutual interdependence in marine affairs. They can establish the institutional basis for political, economic, environmental, and resource accommodation in ocean affairs, and thereby institutionalize procedures for forming and implementing joint initiatives, decisions, and policies. And obviously, in the unhappy event that there is no negotiated international law of the sea agreement, cooperative regional arrangements will be considered, should the reformulation of United States oceans policy become necessary.

Lest I be misunderstood, I want to state clearly that, in my opinion, regionalism as both a concept and practice would be most useful and successful as a corollary to a comprehensive law of the sea convention. The negotiation of a generally acceptable treaty would have a profoundly positive influence on states' attitudes toward multilateral cooperation and collaboration, including support for functionally oriented regional organizations and agreements. Conclusion of a law of the sea treaty would provide proof that states can and will resolve their differences; can and will find avenues for compromise even when important national interests are involved; can and will temper their nationalism and propensity toward unfettered sovereignty when overriding community interests and values are at stake. The conclusion of a treaty would demonstrate, quite simply, that we—the society of nations—have both the will and capacity for building a stable structure of peace and community.

Certainly changing circumstances and policies have precipitated a new urgency for regional cooperation. For example, the establishment of 200-mile fishery zones, including our own, has provided a great challenge. Although regional arrangements existed in many areas, extension of jurisdiction has created a need to revise many important multilateral fishery arrangements. For example, a new organization is currently being negotiated to replace the Eastern Pacific Tuna Treaty, of which the Inter-American Tropical Tuna Commission is the primary institutional embodiment. The IATTC's Atlantic counterpart, the Atlantic Tuna Commission, remains a viable and functioning management tool, which may, pending further consultations and the conclusion of an acceptable agreement among the parties concerned, assume expanded regulatory authority for additional migratory species, specifically skipjack and yellowfin tuna. In the North Pacific, the United States has deposited a Notice of Intent to terminate its obligations under the International Convention for the High Seas Fisheries of the North Pacific Ocean (INPFC) due to its incompatibility with our national fishery legislation. However, efforts are now underway to amend that treaty so as to bring it into conformity with national fisheries zones. We have also begun netotiations to establish a regional body to replace the International Convention for the Northwest Atlantic Fisheries (ICNAF). The successor organization will probably focus on scientific cooperation and stock studies, as well as the multilateral management of fish stocks beyond 200 miles in the Northwest Atlantic area. Lastly, I would mention that the United States will be participating in a meeting called by the South Pacific Forum next week to discuss the creation of a regional fisheries agency.

Just as a promising potential exists for the development of effective regional fishery arrangements, especially with regard to transboundary or migratory stocks, a similar potential exists, in the opinion of many, for greater collaborative arrangements in respect to marine scientific research on both a bilateral and multilateral basis. As compared to regional fishery arrangements, our previous efforts have been less intense and vigorous in this area. However, because of the generally restrictive orientation of the scientific research provisions of the ICNT and the overall importance that we and other nations attach to marine science, both for the common good and as a national activity, we in the Administration are contemplating a comprehensive examination and review of the entire range of potential options that we might pursue to enhance United States' and international marine scientific programs. We are reasonably confident that ways and means can be devised to facilitate access for the marine scientific community through cooperative bilateral and multilateral arrangements. If we are to continue to unlock the mysteries of the oceans, if we are to continue ongoing and long-term research activities, a reasonable accommodation between the interests of science and national sensitivities must be found.

Regionalism, I believe, is the companion of interdependence, an explicit recognition that there are emerging issues that extend beyond the capabilities of individual nation-states. Given this recognition, our common interests and perceptions about the value of cooperative actions will lead to effective regional arrangements, open to all states willing to embrace these concepts. Of course, there are certain principles from which regional arrangements cannot derogate. For example, the freedom of navigation, overflight and associated activities beyond narrow territorial seas, and passage through straits are principles of universal application that cannot be impaired by unilateral or regional arrangements.

It is my hope that our future endeavors to conclude regional arrangements will be creative as well as supportive of our international goals governing the use of our oceans and their resources. Your conference, I know, will point toward new consideration, new ideas, new dimensions, and will expand the continuing ever-important debate and dialogue about the law of the sea and its considerations.

Part I

Regionalization and its Consequences at UNCLOS III

Chairman
Douglas M. Johnston
Dalhousie University

Perhaps I might first take just a few minutes to explain that the theme of this Conference was designed by the Board with nothing particular in mind. It is not intended to be an evidence of pessimism on the part of the Board, looking to the future outcome of UNCLOS III. There are pessimists on the Board, but also optimists, and both would be likely to agree that whatever the outcome of that global Conference is likely to be, we can be sure at least that much will remain to be done at regional levels. We would have to expect, treaty or no treaty, that many innovations will be introduced by the nations of the world within various regional settings. We can also expect, unfortunately, that within certain regions there may be disputes, even conflicts perhaps, in the years ahead.

As you can see from the program, we have tried to devote special attention this year to the problems of the Pacific region. Therefore, we are especially delighted to have as many Pacific visitors here as we do. But despite the Pacific focus of the program, we have succeeded, I think, in attracting a genuinely global representation to this year's annual Conference.

It is my great pleasure to introduce my friends and colleagues on this morning's panel. I suspect they are all known to you by name, if not in person, but protocol requires that I pretend otherwise and introduce them to you. Immediately on my right is Professor Lewis Alexander. Professor Alexander is from the University of Rhode Island, and I hope he will allow me to say that he is the father of marine geographers in the world. Professor Alexander, as most of you must know, is one of the founders of the Law of the Sea Institute. For a number of years he was the director of the Institute and in every session from the beginning he has been a fruitful and constant participant. We look forward with great pleasure to his paper. He will be followed immediately by Dr. Dolliver

Nelson. Dr. Nelson was for many years reader in international law at the London School of Economics in England. In recent years he has been a senior member of the United Nations Secretariat at the Law of the Sea Conference. Among other responsibilities he is secretary to the Drafting Committee and as such has a very close inside view of the United Nations Conference. Since the Drafting Committee is now involved in the current textual revisions at UNCLOS III, we have special reason for looking forward to his presentation. Last on the program, but in no other sense, is Professor Richard Bilder from the University of Wisconsin. Professor Bilder is one of the leading international lawyers in the United States, and indeed in the world, and has shown his versatility in a variety of fields of scholarship, not only the law of the sea but in international environmental law, conflict management, and many others. This is a particularly appropriate combination of interests to be represented in one person at a conference such as this. We look forward with great pleasure to hearing all three of these speakers.

Chapter One

Regionalism at Sea: Concept and Reality

Lewis Alexander
University of Rhode Island

The theme of this Conference is marine regionalism, that is, the management of the oceans and their resources at the regional level. For several reasons it is important that we address ourselves at this time to the regional concept. The first is that with the increasing complexities of ocean use we have found that for many purposes unilateral management is not effective. This is true even though, through the imposition of economic zones, we are in the process of extending the exclusive rights of coastal states to cover over one-third of the world ocean. But the inadequacies of global management have also been made apparent through the difficulties experienced in such fields as pollution control, commercial fisheries, and marine technology transfer. We are now poised for a thrust to the deep seabed to exploit its manganese nodules, and here again the issue is raised whether either extreme of management—unilateral or global—will be sufficient to make the exploitation system work. Also, at this time, we find ourselves at what may be a critical juncture in the Third Law of the Sea Conference. Increasingly, the question is raised, what might be the consequences of failure to achieve a new oceans treaty? One aspect of this, to my mind at least, could be an exacerbation of some of the already difficult relationships existing between the developing and developed worlds. Problems of North-South interactions might well impact on the willingness of developing countries to enter, voluntarily and meaningfully, into various types of marine regional arrangements with the major maritime states.

If neither the unilateral nor the global approach appears practical for a number of issues involving ocean management, we are left with the third alternative, regional action—a process that can take place at any one of a number of organizational levels. Regional action may turn out to involve only three or four states in an operation, or alternatively it may encompass whole continents. The compilers of the various negotiating texts apparently recognized early on the inexactness of regional terminologies, so that even if some parts of the Informal Composite Negotiating Text emerge to become incorporated into a new oceans treaty we would be left with relatively few guidelines as to how to handle regional and subregional matters. So one basic point with respect to marine regionalism is that its precepts cannot be handed down from above but must be built up slowly through experience. Data from all types of regional actions must be gathered if we are to develop generalizations for purposes of comparison, modeling, or prediction.

It is necessary also to recognize the basic fragility of existing marine regional arrangements. The coming of the exclusive economic zone presages a period of intense nationalism before many viable regional mechanisms emerge—a fact already evidenced by the fate of several fisheries organizations. At this stage one can only guess what forms of regional systems will eventually develop from this era of ocean nationalism. But I would offer one suggestion. Among the most lasting and successful of marine regional arrangements are those that have counterparts on land, in the form of economic, political, or social integration units. The experiences of the European Economic Community and of the Eastern European Socialist group afford proof of this statement.

Another point is that the viability of future marine regional organizations may depend to a considerable extent on patterns of development aid and assistance. Regional cooperation in the abstract may at times be far less compelling to national officials, particularly in developing countries, than is cooperation that is coupled with some form of outside aid. Such aid could come from the United Nations Development Program (UNDP), from one of the UN specialized agencies, or from a single donor nation, and could be in the form of direct development grants or of assistance in the planning and implementation of regional programs.

THE MARINE REGIONAL CONCEPT

Forms of Marine Regions

Having briefly considered several parameters of the regions issue, we turn now to a more detailed treatment of the regional concept itself. Assessing marine regionalism on a global and comprehensive scale is not a simple exercise, in part because of the various forms the regional concept takes with respect to the sea, and also because of the complex relationships existing between regional and other issues both within and beyond the ocean policy system. As a first step in the assessment process, marine regionalism should be seen in a meaningful perspective.

We are really dealing here with two elements—regions and regional arrangements or organizations. A region is a geographical phenomenon, that is, an area of the earth surface that is differentiated from other areas by one or more criteria. By contrast, the term "regional arrangements" is taken as referring to mechanisms designed to implement various types of cooperative activities among states, particularly those in a contiguous geographic area. These arrangements may exist in the form of agreements, treaties, institutions, or simple working groups. The interactions between regions and regional arrangements form an integral part of the subject matter of regional analysis.

A region is an intellectual concept, created by the selection of certain features that are relevant to an areal interest or problem. It is a geographic generalization whose distinguishing criteria are chosen by the compiler of the region in order to serve a stated objective. Once a region has been so designated, its validity is related to its ability to carry out the tasks for which it was designed. Some regions, of course, are more universally recognized than others. The Mediterranean Sea, for example, is a physical region, defined by its peculiar coastal configuration, and clearly separated from other maritime basins.

Any region may be subdivided into various subregions. The boundaries of a region or subregion may be sharp, as is often the case with jurisdictional areas, or they may be indistinct. Where, for example, are the inland boundaries of the subregions referred to as coastal zones; where are the southern limits of the Arctic? Since regions are intellectually derived, they may be interpreted differently by different observers.

One advantage of regions is that they can serve as frameworks for collecting and assessing data, or for distributing benefits. They may also be of value with respect to the planning and management of programs. And mutual activities taking place within a region may in time lead to the creation of what is often termed "regional consciousness" on the part of all or some of the inhabitants.

With respect to the marine environment there are several forms of marine regions. One is a physical region, which is differentiated from other areas on the basis of coastal configuration. The major semi-enclosed seas of the world form physically defined regions; these, in turn, contain subregions, such as the Adriatic and Aegean Sea of the Mediterranean, or the Gulf of Thailand off the South China Sea. Some geographers would divide the ocean basins into physical regions, such as the Northeast and Northwest Atlantic, and the North Pacific.

A second form of marine region is what might be called "management regions," representing situations where there is a well-defined management problem, capable of being handled as a discrete issue. The annual range of a migratory species, for example, might form the basis for a management region. In some cases, management regions conform to physically defined regions or subregions. For many fisheries and pollution control purposes, the Mediterranean, a physically defined marine region, can also serve as a management region.

A third form is operational regions, that is, sites of one or more regional arrangements. These may be defined, for example, by the limits of competence of a regional fisheries commission or council, or by the terms of an international treaty such as that for the Antarctic. The limits of an operational region may correspond with those of a management or physically defined regional unit. But the differences in the regional connotations of the three categories are important for planning and implementation purposes.

Up to this point we have dealt with regions of the ocean. But the terms "region" and "regional" are also used with respect to groups of countries that have similar interests in ocean matters. One of the most noted of these groups was created twenty-five years ago in South America when the CEP countries agreed to common policies on 200-mile limits. More recently we have read of a "regional law of the sea" for such areas as Western Europe and Africa. In the Informal Composite Negotiating Text the terms "region" and "regional" are applied to groups of landlocked and geographically disadvantaged states.

One form of such "marine-oriented" region is that which focuses on major seaports or other coastal facilities. Some ports are truly regional in scope, serving the waterborne trade of several countries. Among such ports are Dar es Salaam, Lourenco Marques, and Abidjan in Africa; Rotterdam and Genoa in Europe; and Singapore inSoutheast Asia. In addition, service areas may develop on land for such activities as ocean data storage and analysis, or marine education and training.

Marine Regional Arrangements

Turning from regions per se to regional arrangements in the oceans, a first point to note is that such arrangements are set up to handle particular problems, and that only through an understanding of the problems themselves can proper evaluations be made of the corresponding regional systems. The problems or issues to be resolved represent the first of what might be seen as four components of the regional arrangements syndrome. The other components are structure and functions of the regional organization, regional processes, and the impact of regional activities on other phenomena.

Problems. The principal problems that are addressed at this time by marine regional systems are associated with the activity areas of fishing, scientific research, environmental control, and military uses. Other activity areas for which regional solutions might be suitable are shipping, surveying and monitoring, marine education and training, and development assistance. Multi-use problems, involving two or more activities in the same area, may also require a regional or subregional approach. In time, ocean mining and the production of energy from the sea might be developed on a regional scale.

Structure and Functions. The structures of marine regional arrangements vary from agreements for collective action by states to highly sophisticated institutions that are involved in data collection and analysis, decision making, and decision implementation. Some units are affiliated with specialized agencies of the United Nations. Membership is generally open to all interested parties, although there are cases of restrictions, as in conventions focusing on the Black and Baltic Seas. Despite the structure adopted for a particular organization, management problems may arise because of differences among participating states in terms of operational standards for such activities as measurement and research, information storage and retrieval, report writing, and accounting procedures.

The functions of marine regional organizations also vary considerably. Some are concerned with information exchange, data gathering, and coordination of programs. Others go on to establish standards and allocate costs and benefits. In some fisheries arrangements, mutual enforcement provisions are included. And finally, there is at least one regional unit, the International Council for the Exploration of the Sea, that is concerned with the "operational" tasks of research analysis and development.

Regional Processes. A third category in the list of components of marine regional systems concerns regional processes. These processes involve integration and disintegration, growth and decline of the organization, and the establishment of linkages between one regional system and others within the same geographic area. Integrative forces would include (1) the existence of other international arrangements among the member states, which would tend to reinforce the regional consciousness of the participants; (2) the perception by member states of the existence or promise of a favorable cost/benefit ratio so far as participation in the regional organization is concerned; and (3) a strong leadership role by some state or international organization. Among the disintegrative forces would be (1) political, territorial, ideological, or other differences among states; (2) unequal costs and benefits to member countries of the organization; and (3) nonmembership of one or more states within the geographic region. Some insight into these forms of process may be gained through the study of regional integration theory. Such theory has to date been concerned largely with complex organizations on land, so it might be that the relevance of theoretical findings there to marine-related phenomena may be small.

Another component of "regional process" is the linkage between one regional system and others within the same area. What are the correlations, for example, between regional marine science efforts such as IOCARIBE, in the Caribbean, and regional fisheries activities as exemplified by WECAFC? One agency that has been considering the linkage question is UNEP, whose 1976 "Blue Plan" for the Mediterranean Basin recognizes the area as an ecological community and calls for an overall framework for national action with respect to a variety of marine-related activities.

Impact of Regional Activities. A final element of regional arrangements involves their effectiveness with respect to the problems that they were designed to handle. Some regional fisheries organizations have been relatively unsuccessful, in part because the organizations lack true management functions and powers. Almost all of the existing marine regional organizations have been recently created and their impacts are only beginning to be felt.

Perspectives on the Regional Concept

It is apparent from the preceding materials that there are a number of ways to examine the marine regional concept and that each perspective will yield certain advantages. Following is a brief summary of several conceptual approaches.

One is a *geographic area* approach, in which a particular region, such as the North Pacific or the Caribbean, is examined in terms of the problems requiring regional action and of the institutional responses that have or could be made. Such a study could be useful in pointing up linkages among regional systems within the same area.

The *systematic approach* deals with the regional mechanisms themselves, rather than the area. There are here a number of methodologies. One would be to assess the regional arrangements associated with a particular activity, such as fisheries or environmental control, in terms of their structures, functions, and other aspects. Another would be to analyze marine regional mechanisms of all types from the perspective of their management capabilities. Still another methodology would compare regional arrangements at sea with those existing on land. Among the advantages of the systematic approach is that it permits comparative studies of regional systems and contributes to the development of conceptual models.

Third is what might be termed a *national interest approach,* in which the interests of particular states or groups of states toward marine regional arrangements are assessed. How are the ocean interests within a certain state actually defined? How does the state perceive the costs and benefits of participation in a regional system? As a variant of this, one might consider the national ocean interests of groups of states, whether these groups be regional in scope (such as the states of Latin America or Africa) or whether they represent states with common characteristics. Among the latter might be landlocked countries, those with distant-water fishing interests, or states bordering on straits used for international navigation.

There are, of course, other ways of looking at regional issues. One could, for example, view marine regionalism as part of a general world trend toward multistate action regarding common problems, particularly those dealing with the environment and resource use. One could see regional issues in an historical perspective, or seek to ascertain what political precedents exist for current marine regional activities.

The purpose of this discussion of perspectives is not to suggest one approach as being better than others, but rather to point out some of the dimensions of the regional concept. Studies that attempt to embrace the full scope of marine regionalism may have only limited value except for definitional purposes, but a systematic ordering of regional issues within some sort of conceptual framework appears necessary if marine regional analyses are to expand and grow.

FORMS OF EXISTING MARINE REGIONAL ARRANGEMENTS

Turning from the general to the specific, it is instructive to review briefly some of the categories of current marine regional arrangements. Table 1-1 is a list of such regional organizations. While no claim is made for the list's being all-inclusive, it gives some indication of the scope of regional activities in the oceans at this time. The mere listing of titles, of course, provides only a first step in understanding the existing regional processes. Under each title should be included descriptive phenomena such as membership, geographic area covered by the arrangement, organizational structure and functions, and impacts to date on the problems to be resolved.

In terms of activity areas, there are at this time about two dozen regional units associated with *fisheries conservation and management.* A few of these are bilateral in nature, but involve the participation or exclusion of other countries as well. Six regional units are FAO-sponsored; the others are independent. A basic function of regional fisheries has been the collection, compilation, and analysis of data. Some units also recommend conservation measures to their member states. But such measures generally fail to take into account economic factors of the fishery, and in most cases are not binding on member countries. A few regional systems have become involved in allocations of catch. It seems reasonable to expect, with the exception of the International Whaling Commission, that such regulatory functions as the regional fisheries organizations now enjoy will be curtailed, at least in the short term, as a result of what may be an almost universal adoption of 200-mile exclusive fishery zones.

A second category of regional activities involves *scientific research.* A principal initiating agent here is the Intergovernmental Oceanographic Commission of UNESCO. IOC functions not as a project agency but rather as a coordinating group for activities undertaken by individual countries or by UN organizations. Many of IOC's regional scientific activities are under the aegis of IDOE—the International Decade of Ocean Exploration. Among the IOC programs are broad-ranging cooperative studies and investigations, as well as one multipurpose regional unit—IOCARIBE—for the Caribbean and adjacent regions. Independent of IOC are the International Council for the Exploration of the Sea, which is concerned with research and investigation in the North Atlantic, and the International Commission for the Scientific Exploration of the Mediterranean. With the prospects of a consent regime being required for all foreign scientific research in the exclusive economic zone, the role of both global and regional scientific units may before long increase.

One of IOC's units is TEMA, which is concerned with the coordination of

Table 1-1. Regional Organizations

I. Fisheries Conservation and Management

A. FAO-Sponsored

Regional Fisheries Advisory Commission for the Southwest Atlantic (CARPAS)
Fishery Committee for the Eastern Central Atlantic (CECAF)
General Fisheries Council for the Mediterranean (GFCM)
Indian Ocean Fishery Commission (IOFC)
Indo-Pacific Fisheries Council (IPFC)
Western Central Atlantic Fishery Commission (WECAFC)

B. Independent

Baltic Sea Salmon Standing Committee (BSSSC)
Inter-American Tropical Tuna Commission (IATTC)
International Baltic Sea Fishery Commission (IBSFC)
International Commission for the Conservation of Atlantic Tunas (ICCAT)
International Commission for the Northwest Atlantic Fisheries (ICNAF)
International Commission for the Southeast Atlantic Fisheries (ICSEAF)
International North Pacific Fisheries Commission (INPFC)
International Pacific Halibut Commission (IPHC)
International Pacific Salmon Fisheries Commission (IPSFC)
International Whaling Commission (IWC)
Japan–China Joint Fisheries Commission (JCFC)
Japan–Republic of Korea Joint Fisheries Commission (JKFC)
Japanese–Soviet Northwest Pacific Fisheries Commission (JSFC)
Mixed Commission of 1962 (Baltic Sea) (MC)
Mixed Commission for Black Sea Fisheries (MCBSF)
North-East Atlantic Fisheries Commission (NEAFC)
North Pacific Fur Seal Commission (NPFSC)
Permanent Commission of the Conference on the Use and Conservation of the Marine Resources of the South Pacific (PCSP)
Sealing Commission for the Northeast Atlantic (SCNEA)
Sealing Commission for the Northwest Atlantic (SCNWA)
Shellfish Commission for the Skagerrak–Kattegat (SCSK)

II. Scientific Research

A. IOC-Sponsored

Cooperative Study of the Kuroshio and Adjacent Regions (CSK)
Cooperative Investigations in the Mediterranean (CIM)
Cooperative Investigations of the Northern Part of the Eastern Central Atlantic (CINECA)
Southern Oceans Survey (SOC)
Regional Investigation of the El Nino Phenomenon (ERFEN)
IDOE: Environmental Forecasting Program
Investigation of the Subtropical Convergence in the Southwest Atlantic Ocean
Investigation of the Equatorial Undercurrent of the Western Pacific
Sea Surface Current Project
North Pacific Experiment (NORPAX)
International Southern Ocean Studies (ISOS)
Monsoon Circulation Experiment (MONEX)
Joint Air-Sea Interaction Program (JASIN)
Joint North Sea Wave Project (JONSWAP)
Overflow Studies
Mid-Ocean Dynamics Experiment and Test Area (POLYMODE)
IDOE: Environmental Quality Program
Pollutant Transfer

Table 1-1 continued

Geochemical Ocean Sections Study (GEOSECS)
Saronikos Gulf Pollution Study
Controlled Ecosystems Pollution Experiment (CEPEX)
Pollution/Ecology Studies
IDOE: Seabed Assessment Program
Southeast Atlantic Margins
Southwest Atlantic Margins
French-American Mid-Ocean Undersea Study (FAMOUS)
Plate Tectonics and Metallogenesis (Nazea Plate)
Manganese Nodules Project
IDOE: Living Resources–Assessment and Ecology Program
Coastal Upwelling Ecosystems Analysis (CUEA)
Seagrass Ecosystem Study (SES)
LEPOR Programs, not part of IDOE
Variability of the Sea Surface Temperature and Salinity
Fields of the Southwest Pacific and Indian Ocean
Study of North Sea Pollution
Studies of Organic Sedimentary Processes on Shelves, Slopes and the Deep Ocean Floor of the Southwest Pacific
Assessment of the Living Resources in the North Atlantic
Fish Stock Assessment in the South Atlantic
International Tsunami Warning System in the Pacific (ITSU)
IOC Association for the Caribbean and Adjacent Regions (IOCARIBE)

B. Independent
International Council for the Exploration of the Sea (ICES)
International Commission for the Scientific Exploration of the Mediterranean Sea (ICSEM)
Federation of the Institutions Concerned with the Study of the Adriatic Sea (FICSAS)

III. Environmental Control
Agreement for Cooperation in Dealing with Pollution of the North Sea by Oil, 1969
Agreement between Denmark, Finland, norway, and Sweden Concerning Cooperation in Measures to Deal with Pollution of the Sea by Oil (Nordic Agreement), 1971
Convention on the Protection of the Marine Environment of the Baltic Sea Area, 1974
Convention on theProtection of the Environment between Denmark, Finland, Norway, and Sweden, 1974
Convention for the Protection of the Mediterranean Sea Against Pollution (Mediterranean Action Plan), 1976

IV. Military
Treaty for the Prohibition of Nuclear Weapons in Latin America (Treaty of Tlateloco), 1967
Declaration of the Indian Ocean as a Zone of Peace, 1971

V. Regional Development
Indian Ocean Fishery Survey and Development Program
Development of Fisheries in the Eastern Central Atlantic
Development of Fisheries in the Western Central Atlantic
South China Sea Fisheries Development and Coordinating Program (Phase II)
Caribbean Fisheries Training and Development Center
Committee for Coordination of Joint Prospecting for Mineral Resources in Asian Off-Shore Areas (CCOP)
Committee for Coordination of Joint Prospecting for Mineral Resources in South

Table 1-1 continued

Pacific Off-Shore Areas (CCOP/SOPAC)

Others

Antarctic Treaty, 1959
European Agreement for the Prevention of Broadcasts Transmitted from Stations Outside National Territories, 1965
Statement of Indonesia, Malaysia, and Singapore on the Malacca Straits, November 16, 1971

---

training and education in the marine sciences, particularly in the developing countries. Over the past several years TEMA has held a series of regional meetings in such places as Mexico City, Casablanca, Manila, and Cairo. Countries located within the regions served by these cities have been invited to participate in the meetings and work toward the development of joint education and training programs.

Another type of regional arrangement deals with *environmental control.* The lead agency in this area at the global scale is IMCO, the Inter-Governmental Maritime Consultative Organization, which makes recommendations for international action, and drafts conventions and agreements. At the regional level, the primary body is the United Nations Environment Program. Founded in 1972, UNEP is involved in the development of comprehensive action plans for the protection of the marine environment. Like IOC, it coordinates work of other agencies. Its most ambitious program to date is the Mediterranean Action Plan, growing out of the 1976 Convention for the Protection of the Mediterranean Sea against Pollution. UNEP also has plans for the Caribbean/Gulf of Mexico, the Persian (Arabian) Gulf, and the Malacca Straits, and has considered playing an observer's role in some sort of action plan for the Red Sea. There are also regional pollution agreements applicable to the waters off Northwestern Europe.

Since environmental control in the oceans is closely tied in with other activities, such as fishing, shipping and offshore oil exploitation, it would seem that comprehensive regional programs, such as those initiated by UNEP, may prove to be one of the most effective ways for approaching the pollution control and abatement issue.

In another category are the regional *development projects* associated with UNDP, the United Nations Development Program, and with the regional economic commissions of ECOSOC, the Economic and Social Council. UNDP currently supports six regional fisheries development programs; under the aegis of ECOSOC's Commission for Asia and the Pacific are two special units, the Committee for Co-ordination of Joint Prospecting for Mineral Resources in Asian Off-Shore areas (CCOP), and a similar Committee for Joint Prospecting in South Pacific Off-Shore Areas (CCOP/SOPAC). It should be noted with respect to these development arrangements that they are supportive in nature and not involved with actual exploitation or with sharing of the resultant wealth. Even the two Committees for Co-ordination for Joint Prospecting have as their functions promotion, coordination, and the search for possible sources of financial and technical support. Joint activities such as these represent development projects that can contribute over the years to the strengthening of regional bonds and to the possible creation of frameworks for the future establishment of binding regional and subregional systems.

In addition to the major groupings noted here there are other marine regional arrangements that should be mentioned. One involves the naming of the Indian Ocean as a "zone of peace" in 1971 by a UN resolution. In the same year. Indonesia, Malaysia, and Singapore issued a joint statement, calling for a tripartite body to coordinate efforts for the safety of navigation in the Straits of Malacca and Singapore. Yet another regional effort, which was designed to affect both land areas and adjacent offshore waters, was the 1967 Treaty of Tlateloco, which called upon parties to refrain from the testing, use, manufacture, production, possession, or control of nuclear weapons in Latin America. In all three of the cases cited here one might question the actual impacts of these decisions on the uses of the marine environment. Still another marine regional arrangement was the 1965 European agreement on broadcasting from stations outside national territories, which applies to broadcasting stations on objects fixed to or supported by the seabed, and to those onboard ships or aircraft that are outside national territories.

The Antarctic Treaty should also be mentioned. Although it refers primarily to an uninhabited land area, it has several provisions that could be relevant to a regional oceans arrangement as well. For example, the treaty freezes territorial claims to the area, provides for demilitarization and a ban on nuclear explosions, and specifies all waters south of 60°S. lat. as high seas. Since there are no recognized territorial claims on the land mass itself, there can be no internal or territorial waters adjacent to the land, no economic zone, and no nationally claimed continental shelf.

There are other linkages between the Antarctic and general ocean policy matters. Environmentalists may worry about potential polluting of the dense Antarctic waters, fisheries groups may become concerned over unregulated harvesting of the Antarctic krill, while seabed mining spokesmen may wonder whether or not an International Seabed Authority's competence would extend to the maritime areas covered by the Antarctic Treaty. These and other considerations (among them, the relative exclusivity of the treaty itself) clearly tie the Antarctic in with other regional marine issues.

TRENDS IN MARINE REGIONALISM

A final consideration here will concern trends in the marine regional process. Before assessing such trends, some general considerations should be noted, based on the data associated with existing organizations.

One consideration concerns the geographic extent of an operational region, i.e., one covered by a particular arrangement. What happens to states immediately beyond the operational limits? Are they disadvantaged because of their exclusion? Such a situation might arise with respect to fisheries or environmental control arrangements involving the states bordering the Gulf of Guinea or the Arabina Sea. If a neighboring state is excluded will the effectiveness of the arrangement be threatened? Associated with this problem is the case of the "isolated" state that is part of a physical region but remains outside regional systems. Israel, Taiwan, South Africa, or Kampuchea (the former Cambodia) might provide illustrations of this problem.

A second issue involves the levels of "investment" a state makes when participating in a marine regional unit. Does membership require some form of restrictive domestic legislation or other action? Are opportunities for the state foreclosed because of participation? A survey of the costs incurred by countries as a result of inclusion within regional units reveals wide variations with respect both to type and degree of investment. In some cases membership involves only the verbal acquiescence of some individuals of the country's elite with little actual participation.

Considering the wide disparity among the existing regional arrangements the question might logically arise: What do these have in common with one another, other than the fact they relate to the sea and involve two or more countries? Is there any sort of evolutionary pattern among them, so that in terms of management functions they can move from one stage to another along an increasingly regulatory scale? In general terms the answer is that there is a pattern of increasing competence on the part of regional organizations, a pattern that implies growing acceptance of regional jurisdictions on the part of the member states. This process has been apparent in land-based regional mechanisms such as the EEC, with its increased economic integration.

As a corollary to this, a third consideration emerges, namely the interactions between marine and terrestrial regional units. If states are bound together by economic, ideological, or other associations, these ties should serve as centripetal forces for marine-related activities as well. In addition to the EEC and to CMEA in Eastern Europe, there are extant many land-based regional organizations—the Association of Southeast Asian Nations, the South Pacific Commission, the Economic Community of West African States, the League of Arab States, and the Latin American Free Trade Association, to name but a few. It should also be noted in this regard that most marine regional organizations are concerned with the general problems of environmental and resource management, which have strong counterparts on land. There may be lessons to be learned, at least concerning organizational and management techniques, from international river basin development programs, weather modification schemes, and soil control projects. Regionalism at sea should be seen largely as a continuation of a management process that has already been going on for some time on land.

A fourth item concerns regionalism and the landlocked states. Nothing at the Third Law of the Sea Conference has really altered the plight of these countries or provided them with relief from their geographic isolation. Hopefully, regional organizations such as the OAU, the OAS, and the League of Arab States can assist those member countries that are either landlocked and geographically disadvantaged in securing access to the sea and its resources. For some states transit to and from the sea could be enhanced by the development of one or more regional ports, together with adequate overland transport systems to inland areas.

A final generalization concerns the apparent dichotomy in purposes of marine regional systems. Such systems may be both developmental and restrictive. They may work for the benefit of their members and of others associated with the regional organization, in terms of improving environmental quality, enhancing the exploitation of living or nonliving resources, developing member states' economic conditions, helping to resolve regional conflicts involving the sea and its uses, and otherwise enhancing the common good. But along with developmental progress, limited access provisions may be enacted and the advent of the economic zone concept may greatly expand the maritime areas to which such provisions apply. Limitations, for example, may be placed on rights of access of various types of vessels, but such limitations within a regional area may not be uniform with respect to the ships of all states. Such a contingency raises all sorts of difficult questions. What is the price of access to outsiders? Are there one or more "lead" countries within the regional organization that decide on conditions of access? If an arrangement is made for a "nuclear free" zone or a "zone of peace," just what might the parameters be? When used in its restrictive sense, marine regionalism might become a potent political weapon.

Future Trends

Having completed the general considerations, what comments can I make to summarize future trends in marine regionalism? The passage or nonpassage of an oceans treaty will have little direct impact on regional developments because of lack of precision on regionalism in the negotiating texts. But there could be indirect consequences of nonagreement, including the possible conclusion of mini-regime agreements by regional groups, which involve claims to joint ownership of seabed resources in various parts of the ocean beyond national limits.

I doubt that binding regulatory systems will develop in the short term, because of the new offshore jurisdictions coastal states are acquiring and the time needed for most of these states to adjust to new opportunities and needs before participating in constraining regional arrangements. It is to be hoped that for a time 200 miles will be the maximum distance claimed for a coastal state's exclusive rights to offshore waters.

The two types of areas most likely to experience regional organizations in the coming years are semi-enclosed seas and island communities, such as in the western Pacific. The coast of West Africa has also a strong regional potential because of the relative proximity to one another of nearly two dozen coastal and landlocked states. One or more of the geographic areas mentioned above will become multipurpose operational regions; from this, in time, will likely come joint administration arrangements under which one agency is responsible for several separate residual systems.

In conclusion I would note that marine regionalism is the current fad. During the next few years there will be a plethora of regional and subregional organizations coming into existence, some with and some without realistic bases for success. Pressures for regionalism come from three sources. First, already existing organizations, such as the League of Arab States or the South Pacific Commission, will spin off new units. Second, contiguous coastal states will, for one reason or another, decide to form regional arrangements for various purposes as shipping, marine education and training, or joint coastal research activities. Third, existing global agencies, such as IMCO and UNESCO may increasingly turn to regional subdivisions to assist them in carrying out their responsibilities. Already, WMO and UNDP have developed regional centers, and other groups may soon follow. The need will exist for marine regional developments to be monitored by one or more organizations and, where practical, coordinated.

Chapter Two

The Functions of Regionalism in the Emerging Law of the Sea as Reflected in the Informal Composite Negotiating Text[1]

L.D.M. Nelson*
Law of the Sea Secretariat
United Nations

The law of the sea has always been conceived of as positing a legal regime for global application. It was relatively easy to think in those terms, given the fairly small number of international "actors" who until recently played the major role in creating the norms of the law of the sea. Moreover, in a certain sense, this approach paid heed, as it were, to an important principle—the principle of the sovereign equality of states.[2]

Two prime factors have served to weaken this principle of globalism and have been mainly responsible for thrusting to the fore the whole notion of regionalism within the context of the law of the sea: the remarkable expansion of the international community and the appearance of the concept of the exclusive economic zone. It should also be remarked that general technological progress has gone hand in hand with an ever-growing concern with the preservation of the marine environment, a concern that has led to concerted action both on the international and, in particular, on the regional level to halt the degradation of the marine environment.[3]

The emergence of several new states within the international community has had some consequences of direct importance to the notion of regionalism. In the first place, the diversity of maritime interests, which the law of the sea has now to accommodate, has been widened significantly by the emergence of several new states within the world community. Of course, the general indifference that existed among the metropolitan powers with regard to matters concerning the law of the sea as it affected their possessions has rendered this task somewhat more formidable.[4] Attempts are now being made within the forum of the Third

*The views expressed are personal and do not necessarily reflect the official views of the Secretariat of the United Nations.

United Nations Law of the Sea Conference to incorporate some of these interests and situations within a global regime.[5] Nevertheless, the solution to some of the problems posed by the number of maritime situations now exposed to view as a result mainly of decolonization will increasingly be sought on a regional or sub-regional level,[6] since it has always been difficult to establish legal rules of global validity for special cases.

In the second place, several of these new states have swelled the ranks of the developing world and now form a significant part of what has been called the Third World or the Group of 77. As is now well known, the conflict of interests between the Third World (Group of 77) and the developed countries forms the backdrop to the deliberations of the law of the sea that has been taking place in the Third United Nations Law of the Sea Conference in recent years. It seems to the poor countries that, with the law of the sea in a state of flux, they have been presented with an opportunity to narrow the economic and technological gap between themselves and the rich developed world and to eradicate what appears to several of them as the unfortunate consequences of colonialism.[7] This problem, of course, looms large in the transactions of Committee I of the Conference, but it does run like a leitmotif throughout the Conference. Here, too, the notion of regionalism has been invoked to provide at least some solutions to the problem. For instance, Article 203 of the ICNT states in part that: "States shall directly or through competent international or regional organizations, global or regional (a) promote programmes of scientific, educational, technical and other assistance to developing States for the protection and preservation of the marine environment. . . ." Article 276 of the ICNT declares inter alia that "States shall, in co-ordination with the competent international organizations, the Authority and national marine scientific and technological institutions, promote the establishment, especially in developing States, of regional marine scientific and technological research centres in order to stimulate and advance the conduct of marine scientific research by developing States and foster the transfer of technology."[8] The concept of regionalism is thus called in aid in the form of regional organizations and regional centers[9] to help in narrowing the gap between the industrialized world and the Third World, and consequently provide some solution to one of the more challenging contemporary problems.

During the course of the present Third United Nations Law of the Sea Conference the concept of the exclusive economic zone has succeeded in gaining the general acceptance of the member states of the international community. However, no agreement has yet been reached as to the precise juridical nature of the zone. There are two significant problems. One concerns the extent of coastal state competence in the zone; the other relates to the extent to which the interests of landlocked and other geographically disadvantaged states will be accommodated in the exclusive economic zones of their neighbors.[10]

It is this latter issue that directly concerns this inquiry. How far are coastal states prepared to share the resources of their exclusive economic zones with other states, particularly with landlocked states and states that are, in some other respect, geographically disadvantaged by, for instance, possessing short coastlines, being shelflocked, or in certain cases having little resources within their own exclusive economic zone?

In the opinion of some, the general acceptance of the exclusive economic zone will aggravate the inequity already introduced into the law of the sea by the continental shelf doctrine.[11] Now faced with this new development, that is, the emergence of the concept of the exclusive economic zone, the landlocked and other geographically disadvantaged states seek the right to participate on an "equal and non-discriminatory basis" in the exploration and expoitation of both the living and nonliving resources of the neighboring coastal states.[12]

Some members of this group of states support the creation of regional or subregional economic zones where "all States in the region or subregion whether landlocked, geographically disadvantaged or coastal, shall have equal rights to explore and exploit all natural resources of their regional or subregional economic zones".[13]

As it now stands, the ICNT gives landlocked states "the right to participate in the exploitation of the *living* resources of the exclusive economic zones of *adjoining* coastal States on an *equitable* basis."[14] There is no mention here of landlocked states having rights to participate in the exclusive economic zones of coastal states in a subregion or region, though the article does go on to declare that the "terms and conditions of such participation shall be determined by the State concerned through bilateral, subregional or regional agreements ."[15]

A distinction is made between developing and developed landlocked states in that developed landlocked states can only exercise their rights in the exclusive economic zones of adjoining developed coastal states. This distinction is maintained in the text with respect to geographically disadvantaged states.[16]
Only developing geographically disadvantaged states are granted the right to participate on an equitable basis in the exploitation of living resources in the exclusive economic zones of other states in a region or subregion. It is important to observe that in Article 70 where this right is embodied the term "geographically disadvantaged" is not used. Article 70 reads in part:

Article 70

Right of certain developing coastal States in a subregion or region

1. Developing coastal States which are situated in a subregion or region whose geographical peculiarities make such States particularly dependent for the satisfaction of the nutritional needs of their populations upon the exploitation of the living resources in the exclusive economic zones of their neighbouring States and developing coastal States which can claim no exclusive economic zones of their own shall have the right to participate, on an equitable basis, in the exploitation of living resources in the exclusive economic zones of other States in a subregion or region.

> 2. The terms and conditions of such participation shall be determined by the States concerned through bilateral, subregional or regional agreements, taking into account the relevant economic and geographical circumstances of all the States concerned, including the need to avoid effects detrimental to the fishing communities or to the fishing industries of the States in whose zones the right of participation is exercised.

It should be remarked that both Articles 69 and 70 are subject to Articles 61 and 62.[17] It must be presumed that what was primarily intended was to ensure that landlocked and certain developing coastal states have access only to the surplus of the allowable catch.[18] The ICNT gives the coastal state the right to determine the allowable catch of the living resources in its exclusive economic zone[19] and also its capacity to harvest such resources. It shall, through agreements or other arrangements, give other states access to the surplus where it does not have the capacity to harvest the allowable catch.[20] At the heart of these proposals lies the fact that the participation of other states, including landlocked and developing geographically disadvantaged states, in the exploitation of the living resources of the exclusive economic zone depends on the existence of a surplus—the surplus that may exist where the coastal state does not have the capacity to harvest the entire allowable catch.

It is important to mention here in some detail some of the factors that the coastal state has to take into account in granting access to other states. They are *inter alia:* the significance of the living resources of the area to the economy of the coastal state concerned and its other national interests, the provisions of articles 69 (right of landlocked states) and 70 (right of certain developing countries in the subregion or region) and the requirements of developing countries in the region or subregion in harvesting part of the surplus.[21]

The fact that the coastal state can take the significance of the living resources of the area to its economy and its other national interests into account in granting access to other states to its exclusive economic zone gives it a wide discretion in this matter. In the nature of things, it is that kind of factor, it is submitted, that will in the end play a dominant role and such a factor that will be especially strong if a convention on the law of the sea were not to emerge from the Conference. Thus, the question of access will hinge not so much upon the geographically disadvantaged situation of the state seeking participation in the exploitation of the living resources of its neighbor's exclusive economic zone, but on the national needs of the coastal state. It is not surprising that the idea of reciprocity is already emerging as a significant factor in the granting of access.[22]

The maritime problems of landlocked and other geographically disadvantaged states are formidable. It is difficult to envisage solutions that lie outside bilateral, subregional, and regional arrangements.[23] That is not to say, however, that the rights of such states should not be spelled out within the global framework of the proposed convention.[24]

The acceptance of the concept of the exclusive economic zone has not lessened the need for international cooperation for the management of marine resources.[25] The reason, of course, is that "fish swim and do not respect man-made boundaries." There are stocks that fall with the exclusive economic zone of a single coastal state; those whose migratory patterns traverse the exclusive economic zones of two or more coastal states; and those highly migratory species that move freely within and beyond the exclusive economic zones of coastal states and, perhaps, are sometimes to be found always beyond the national jurisdiction of coastal states.[26] The concept of regionalism is of relevance here, since it is by utilizing international organizations, both global and regional, that the international community can best conserve and manage the living resources of the seas. The relevant provisions of the ICNT provide for a form of cooperation between coastal states and global, regional, and subregional organizations for the conservation and management of marine living resources.

For example, Article 61 states *inter alia* that the coastal state and relevant subregional, regional, and global organizations shall cooperate to ensure through proper conservation and management measures that the maintenance of the living resources in the exclusive economic zone is not endangered by overexploitation. States shall also utilize subregional or regional organizations to agree upon measures for the conservation and development of stocks where such stocks occur both within and in an area beyond and adjacent to the exclusive economic zones of two or more states.[27]

In the case of highly migratory species, the coastal states and other states fishing in a region[28] are enjoined to cooperate either directly or through appropriate international organizations in order to ensure the conservation and optimum utilization of such species throughout the region.[29] With regard to the resources of the high seas, states are urged to cooperate in establishing subregional or regional fisheries organizations for the conservation of its living resources.[30]

It is necessary to make some observations on these provisions dealing with the cooperation between states and international organizations with regard to the conservation and management of marine living resources. In the first place, the ICNT does not *expressis verbis* incorporate the idea of using international or regional organizations to promote technical assistance to developing countries for the conservation and management of the living resources of the exclusive economic zone.[31] It may be argued that this role of regional or global organizations is of considerable importance considering the fact that it may include such matters as the assessment of stocks, the economic value of fisheries, and the assessment of the harvesting capacity of coastal states, and so on.[32]

In most instances the text makes reference to both global and regional (and subregional) organizations and rightly does not concern itself with the allocation of responsibilities between the two types of organizations.[33] Nevertheless, it must be remarked that the ICNT, as it now stands, does not seem to envisage a role for global organizations in the management and conservation of highly migratory species,[34] nor, at least as far as Article 118 is concerned, of living resources in areas of high seas.[35] The type of resource that is the concern of these provisions—particularly the provisions dealing with the living resources of the high seas—requires an approach that makes use of both global and regional organizations. In his comments on the global management of highly migratory species, Miles has observed that: "The mobility of the resource combined with the mobility of fleets operating in the Atlantic, Pacific, and Indian oceans produces a need for a truly global approach in both stock assessment and the formulation of management measures."[36]

One of the accepted roles of international organizations is their norm-creating function.[37] They provide fora for achieving uniformity of standards. The ICNT utilizes this standard-setting function of both global and regional organizations, especially with regard to the protection and preservation of the marine environment. A good instance is Article 198, which declares that "States shall co-operate on a global basis and, as appropriate, on a *regional* basis, directly or through competent international organizations, global or *regional,* in formulating and elaborating international roles, standards and recommended practices . . . for the protection and preservation of the marine environment, taking into account characteristic regional features."[38] The same idea runs through the text with respect to the various sources of marine pollution: land-based sources,[39] seabed activities,[40] dumping,[41] and the atmosphere.[42]

The adoption and application of 200-mile exclusive economic zones will undoubtedly create problems for coastal states bordering "enclosed and semi-enclosed seas,"[43] and some important maritime issues are involved in these problems. They include the conservation, management, and allocation of the living resources, the reservation of the marine environment, the delimitation of maritime areas, and even the freedom of navigation.

On the question of living resources, certain states have expressed the view that the establishment of exclusive economic zones in "enclosed and semi-enclosed seas" without taking into account the interest of other littoral states would produce results that were not equitable.[44] On the issue of pollution, there is now general agreement that these marine areas are extremely vulnerable to pollution and thus constitute "special areas" that require the application of stricter pollution standards and a high level of cooperation among the littoral states.[45]

The physical disposition of coastal states in, and the geographical configuration of, these "enclosed and semi-enclosed seas" makes the delimitation of maritime zones especially difficult, and the presence of islands that perhaps constitute a characteristic feature of these maritime regions merely aggravates the problem. It is not surprising, therefore, that some states[46] would like the principle of equity to enjoy pride of place with respect to the delimitation of enclosed or semi-enclosed areas.[47]

The fear of being hemmed in by waters through which there is no longer any freedom of navigation has troubled some states bordering enclosed and semi-enclosed seas. Consequently, they seek to ensure freedom of access in outlets leading to the open seas.[48]

Article 123 of the ICNT, which carries the rubric, "Co-operation of States bordering enclosed or semi-enclosed seas," declares that:

> States bordering enclosed or semi-enclosed seas[49] should co-operate with each other in the exercise of their rights and duties under the present Convention. To this end they shall endeavour, directly or through an appropriate regional organization:
> (a) To coordinate the management, conservation, exploration, and exploitation of the living resources of the sea;
> (b) To coordinate the implementation of their rights and duties with respect to the preservation of the marine environment;
> (c) To coordinate their scientific research policies and undertake where appropriate, joint programmes of scientific research in the area;
> (d) To invite, as appropriate, other interested States or international organizations to co-operate with them in furtherance of the provisions in this article.

There are two salient points which can be made on this provision. In the first place the littoral states of "enclosed or semi-enclosed seas" are not under any obligation to coordinate certain of their maritime policies;[50] they are merely under an obligation to endeavor to coordinate such policies. Thus the text avoids, at least to some extent, imposing "an enclosed or semi-enclosed sea" regime on littoral states that may be unwilling to accept it.

Second, the text has not dealt with the issue of delimitation or the question of the freedom of navigation in these maritime areas. In short, the text seems to have managed to avoid creating a special regime for those zones, a status which, in the opinion of some, invokes such concepts as *mare nostrum* and *mare clausum.*[51]

SOME BRIEF REMARKS ON THE DEVELOPING LAW OF THE SEA AND REGIONALISM

In order to assess properly the place of regionalism in the emerging law of the sea it is necessary to examine the influence that the Conference is exerting on the development of maritime law. For in spite of the fact that its task still remains unaccomplished, the Third United Nations Conference on the Law of the Sea is undoubtedly moulding the structure of the emerging law of the sea.

In evaluating the influence of the Conference on the law, it is useful to take a look at what kind of status, if any, the ICNT possesses in international law. As has already been stated, the text is informal, and is not per se binding on any state. The following analysis of the RSNT,[52] by the delegate from Spain at the sixth session of the Conference, is quite valuable. He observed that:

> The Revised Single Negotiating Text contained three types of regulations. First, there were norms of international law currently in force, which had

> been embodied in conventions or approved through diplomatic channels. Secondly, there were new norms of international law in the process of elaboration which had received broad support and which might be termed norms of an emerging international law. Thirdly, there were other provisions which were broadly criticised and did not reflect the consensus of the international community.[53]

The notion of "broad support" is closely related to, if not identical with, that of consensus. In the opinion of this writer, "broad support" must mean at least support among both developing and developed states[54] as it is hardly conceivable that support by only one of these groups could by itself generate the degree of consensus[55] necessary to ground new norms of international maritime law.

Thus the ICNT contains provisions that embody settled customary law. Instances of such provisions would be those dealing with the regimes of the territorial sea[56] and the high seas. Other provisions of the text are already guiding the practice of states to such an extent that it would be fair to say that they may be termed "norms of an emerging international law." The provisions relating to the exclusive economic zone fall under this category. Finally, it cannot be doubted that there are provisions which have not received broad support. This is especially true of certain basic articles in Part XI (the Area, i.e., the seabed and ocean floor and subsoil thereof beyond the limits of national jurisdiction).

This rationale can also be applied to the concept of regionalism as dealt with in this paper. The text incorporates certain functions of regionalism that in fact already represent to a large extent the practice of states and international organizations or that constitute such a natural development of such practices that they will hardly fail to find general acceptance by states. Such functions as states cooperating with regional organizations to manage and conserve the living resources of oceans or to protect and preserve the marine environment are cases in point. The articles that provide for coordination between states and international organizations, global and regional, for the promotion of programs of scientific and technical assistance to developing countries in matters relating to technical assistance will probably fall under the same category.

On the other hand, the same conclusion cannot be reached with respect to the provision of the text dealing with the accommodation of the interests of the landlocked and geographically disadvantaged in the exclusive economic zones of neighboring states. The issue is as yet unsettled and the likelihood that certain of these provisions may be changed during the course of the negotiations may affect, to a certain extent, their norm-creating potential.

This conclusion is reached in spite of the fact that the concept of the exclusive economic zone has been already generally accepted and has, in fact, been adopted by several coastal states—developing as well as developed—in their national legislation. It may well be that rights such as the rights of participation of landlocked and geographically disadvantaged states in the exclusive economic zone of their neighbors are the kinds of rights[57] that can be created only by the mechanism of the treaty rather than by the process of customary law.

SOME CONCLUSIONS

There are two major conflicts facing the Third United Nations Conference on the Law of the Sea—one arising between the developed and developing world, and the other between the landlocked and geographically disadvantaged states and "the coastal states". It is not without significance that the concept of regionalism has had a part to play in the text in the quest for solutions to these conflicts.

However, it is important that the global dimension of the law of the sea should not be disregarded. This dimension will remain, it is submitted, even if a global convention does not emerge from the present Conference. In this sense there is no question of a global law of the sea being replaced by regional regimes for the oceans. Rather they will complement each other, for there is room for both regimes.

NOTES

1. Referred to hereafter as the ICNT. This text was prepared by the president and chairmen of the three main committees in association with the chairman of the Drafting Committee and the Rapporteur-General. It is informal in character and has the same status as the Informal Single Negotiating Text (SNT) and the Revised Single Negotiating Text (RSNT). It was meant to serve purely as a procedural device and only to provide a basis for negotiation. (See the explanatory memorandum by the President-A/CONF.62/WP.10/Add.l.) Both the Informal Single Negotiating Text and the Revised Single Negotiating Text were prepared by the chairmen of the main committees. Part IV of the Revised Single Negotiating Text was prepared by the president.

2. See Fitzmaurice in the *1955 Yearbook of the International Law Commission,* p. 159, and Waldock, "International Law and the New Maritime Claims," *International Relations* (1956), p. 194.

3. For instances see the Convention on the Protection of the Marine Environment of the Baltic Sea Area (1974), Vol. 13, ILM, p. 546, and the Convention for the Protection of the Mediterranean Sea (1976), Vol. 15, ILM, p. 185.

4. To the same effect see Jean-Claude Douence, "Le droit de la mer en Afrique occidentale," 71 RGDIP (1967), pp. 110–143, on p. 115.

5. An instance of the process of accommodation is the addition of a new criterion for the application of the straight baseline system to those already mentioned in Article 4 of the 1958 Geneva Convention on the Territorial Sea and Contiguous Zone. Article 7(2) of the ICNT, Part II, declares that a coastal state will be entitled to employ the method of straight baselines *inter alia* "where because of the presence of a delta or other natural conditions the coastline is highly unstable," and further points out, that "the appropriate points may be selected along the furthest seaward extent of the low-water line and,

notwithstanding subsequent regression of the low-water line, such baselines shall remain effective until changed by the coastal State in accordance with the present Convention."

6. A distinction ought to be made here between maritime situations that are merely unique, which it would be difficult to accommodate either on a global or regional level, and maritime situations that are perhaps capable of being dealt with on the regional level. An instance of the latter may arise in the case of semi-enclosed seas.

7. This concern is reflected in several parts of the ICNT.

8. See, too, Articles 269, 271, and cf. Article 154(4), which empowers the International Seabed Authority to establish such regional centers or offices as it deems necessary for the performance of its functions. Note that the draft submitted by thirteen developing countries to the Seabed Committee had given the International Seabed Authority the power to make, on the initiative of interested states or in agreement with them, such regional or subregional arrangements, including the establishment of subsidiary organs and regional or subregional facilities, as it deems necessary for the exercise of its functions. (A/AC.138/49)

9. Skolnikoff classifies the functions of international organizations as falling under four categories: service, norm creation and allocation, rule observance and settlement of disputes, and operations. Skolnikoff, "The International Imperatives of Technology," p. 13, cited in Alexander, *Regional Arrangements in Ocean Affairs,* p. 30. Presumably the important function outlined here will fall under the category of service.

10. This term has been used to describe states that, because of geography, stand to gain little, if at all, from the emergence of this new concept. Nevertheless, it seems difficult to find a definition of this term, in spite of the obvious need for one, that would meet with the general acceptance of the Conference. Cf. the president's remarks on its use in certain provisions of the ICNT, where he noted that: "The use of the expression 'geographically disadvantaged States' which appears in various provisions of the text is contingent upon a decision by the Conference regarding the definition of the term." Explanatory memorandum to the ICNT (A/CONF.62/WP.10/Add.l, p.3).

11. Cf. These observations by the Austrian delegate: "The Conference would also have to take into account the fact that many States, as a consequence of their geographical situation or an insufficient level of economic and technological development, or a combination of both factors, were disadvantaged or even totally unable to exercise their rights under the Geneva Conventions." Official Records, Third United Nations Conference on the Law of the Sea (referred to hereafter as Off. Rec.), Vol. I, p. 163.

12. Note, in particular, Articles 2 and 3 of doc. A/CONF.72/L.39, submitted by twenty-two developing and developed landlocked and geographically disadvantaged states to the second session of the Conference. See too, docs. A/CONF.62/C.2/L.35, submitted by Haiti and Jamaica and A/CONF.62/C.2/L.36, submitted by Jamaica. In these latter instances, however, the right to exploit only attaches itself to the "renewable resources." For observations, see, for example, Paraguay, Off. Rec., Vol. II, p. 175; Upper Volta: ibid., p. 174; Haiti: ibid., p. 215; Afghanistan: ibid., p. 216.

13. Article 3 of draft articles submitted by Zambia on July 19, 1977: doc. A/CONF.62/C.2/L.97. See also docs. A/CONF.62/C.2/L.65 (Bolivia and Paraguay) and A/CONF.62/C.2/L.93 (Bolivia). On the question of the delimitation of these regions or subregions, the Zambian draft articles suggest that the Conference should take into account the recommendations of the Secretary-General of the United Nations and the variety of geographical situations.

14. Article 69, italics added.

15. Cf. Article 125, which provides that "the terms and modalities for exercising freedom of transit shall be agreed between the landlocked states and the transit states concerned through bilateral, subregional or regional agreements."

16. It is more correct to speak of "other geographically disadvantaged states" since landlocked states are *par excellence* geographically disadvantaged. However, when the term "geographically disadvantaged states" is used here, it refers to geographically disadvantaged coastal states.

17. Note that in the ICNT, Article 71 makes the provisions of Articles 69 and 70 nonapplicable where the economy of a coastal state is "overwhelmingly dependent on the exploitation of the living resources of the exclusive economic zone."

18. For some critical observations of the drafting of the corresponding provisions in the Revised Single Negotiating Text (RSNT), see C.P. Fleischer, "The Right of a 200-mile Exclusive Economic Zone or a Special Fishery Zone," 14, *San Diego Law Review* (1977), 548–83, at pp. 555–63.

19. Article 61(1).

20. Article 62(2).

21. Article 62(3).

22. The following observations on the United Kingdom Fishery Limits Bill throws this idea of reciprocity into bold relief: "There should be a phasing out of the activities of those countries which have no particular reason to continue fishing within our fishery limits, and which have nothing to offer us in return," Hansard, House of Lords, Volume 378, No. 11, col. 1032. See too, Hansard, House of Commons, Vol. 921, No. 8, col. 1352. Section 201(f) of the USA Fishery Conservation and Management Act of 1976 is to the same effect.

23. Article 255 gives neighboring landlocked and geographically disadvantaged states certain rights, such as rights of anticipation when marine scientific research is being conducted on the exclusive economic zone or on the continental shelf of a coastal state.

24. Note the following observation of Singapore: "Such rights of geographically disadvantaged States should be a basic principle of the Convention and not be left to regional or bilateral agreements." Off. Rec. Volume I, p. 135. To the same effect, see Jamaica: ibid., p. 99.

25. See summary of the discussions of the expert consultation on the future role of FAO in fisheries, of COPI and regional fishery bodies: COFI:C/4/76/4, p.2.

26. Ibid., F.T. Christy, *Disparate Fisheries: Problems for the Law of the Sea Conference and Beyond* (1974), p. 339.

27. Article 53 reads as follows:

"1. Where the same stock or stocks of associated species occur within the exclusive economic zones of two or more coastal States, these States shall seek either directly or through appropriate subregional or regional organizations to agree on the measures necessary to coordinate and ensure the conservation and development of such stocks without prejudice to the other provisions of this Part.

2. Where the same stock or stocks of associated species occur both within the exclusive economic zone and in an area beyond and adjacent to the zone, the coastal State and the States fishing for such stocks in the adjacent area shall seek either directly or through appropriate subregional or regional organizations to agree upon the measures necessary for the conservation of these stocks in the adjacent area."

28. Note that the text states in part that: "The coastal State and other States whose nationals fish in the (sic) region." (Article 64)

29. With respect to anadromous species, Article 66(5) also reflects the regional perspective when it states that "the State of origin of anadromous stocks and other States fishing these stocks shall make arrangements, where appropriate, through regional organizations.

30. Article 118.

31. Cf. in particular, Articles 203 and 276 discussed above on p. 18.

32. See Christy, ibid., p. 343.

33. On this matter the following observations are significant: "In the review of the types of general problems that might be discussed by the Committee on Fisheries, it was stressed that political questions and controversial questions of general economic policy, as well as the actual decision on the implementation of specific management measures, were not the concern of the Committee on Fisheries but were within the responsibility of the appropriate independent regional fishery body. The Committee on Fisheries, and the Department of Fisheries, had, however, an important role in helping to provide the scientific and technical basis for the work of regional fishery bodies, especially those largely composed of developing countries, established within the framework of FAO, and in the study of general principles and techniques of management." Report of the seventh session of the Committee on Fisheries, FAO, Rome, 1972.

34. Article 64.

35. This criticism applies particularly to Article 118, since Article 119 does make provision for exchange of information and so on.

36. Miles, "Organizational Arrangements to Facilitate Global Management of Fisheries," RFF/PISFA Paper 4, Resources for the Future, 1974, p. 19.

37. Skolnikoff, op. cit.

38. Italics added.

39. Article 208(4).

40. Article 209(5).

41. Article 211(4).

42. Article 213(3).

43. Generally, see Alexander, "Regionalism and the Law of the Sea: The Case of Semi-enclosed Seas," *Ocean Development and International Law Journal,* Vol. 2, pp. 151–164.

44. See, for example, Thailand, Off. Rec. Vol. II, p. 275.

45. See, for instance, Iran ibid. p. 273, Italy. Off. Rec. Vol. I, p. 180.

46. See in particular Thailand, Off. Rec., Vol. II, p. 275. See also Iran, ibid., p. 273, Algeria, ibid., p. 277, and doc. A/CONF.62/C.2/6.56 submitted by Turkey.

47. In fact there may be a correlation between the developing trend toward a delimitation of maritime zones based on equity—a trend that is reflected in some states, practice and in the deliberations at the Third Law of the Sea Conference—and the emergence of regionalism in the law of the sea.

48. See Iran, Off. Rec., Vol. II, p. 273; the German Democratic Republic, ibid., p. 276; Israel, ibid., p. 274, and Thailand, ibid., p. 275.

49. Article 122 defines an "enclosed or semi-enclosed sea" as a gulf, basin, or sea surrounded by two or more states and connected to the open seas by a narrow outlet or consisting entirely or primarily of the territorial seas and exclusive economic zones of two or more coastal States."

50. The relevant provision in the SNT did create that kind of obligation. See Article 134, SNT.

51. For some striking observations on this issue, see in particular France, Off. Rec., Vol. II, p. 276.

52. An analysis that can also be applied to the ICNT.

53. Doc. A/CONF.68/SR.79.

54. To what extent this notion applies to the other two main groups in the Conference, i.e., the group of landlocked and geographically disadvantaged states and the "coastal states" is an open question on which evidently much depends.

55. As used in this context, the notion of consensus is somewhat different from that originally intended for this process within the context of the Conference. According to the Gentleman's Agreement of June 27, 1974 "the Conference should make every effort to reach agreement on substantive matters by way of consensus and there should be no voting on such matters until all efforts at consensus have been exhausted." The object was to preserve the interests of the minority at the Conference.

56. Note that on the question of the territorial sea, there seems to be general agreement at the Conference on a breadth of twelve miles for the territorial sea and this has generated the belief among members of the international community that a twelve-mile territorial sea is now a norm of international law

57. Reference here is not to their implementation.

Chapter Three

The Consequences of Regionalization in the Treaty and Customary Law of the Sea

Richard B. Bilder
University of Wisconsin

My assignment is to discuss the consequences of regionalization in the treaty and customary law of the sea. I thought that I might most usefully deal with this topic by briefly commenting on five questions:

1. What are the prospects for regionalism in the law of the sea?

2. What are likely to be the "pros" and "cons" of any further development of regionalism?

3. Does regionalism pose any problems of international law?

4. What are likely to be the broader consequences of any development of regionalism?

5. What, if anything, might we do to increase the likelihood that regionalism will have desirable rather than undesirable consequences for a global system of ocean management?

Clearly, it is difficult to say anything on the topic of regionalism in the law of the sea without drawing on Dr. Alexander's excellent and comprehensive report on *Regional Arrangements in Ocean Affairs,* and that work can be regarded as a continuing footnote to these remarks.

What are the prospects for regionalism in the law of the sea? Are we likely to see a significant increase in regional arrangements in the next few years, and what form are such arrangements likely to take? Let me suggest several points.

First, while regionalism in ocean affairs certainly merits attention and study, I am skeptical that we will see any pronounced and significant trend towards regionalism in the immediate future. The dominant development in the present law of the sea is clearly the move to 200-mile economic zones. I share what I understand to be Dr. Alexander's views that the attention and energies of coastal states will for some time to come be focused primarily on consolidating, administering, and increasing their control within these zones—quite possibly in the direction of converting them into at least functional equivalents to territorial seas—rather than on attempts to deal with ocean problems through regional solutions.

There are, of course, certain problems that coastal nations will probably continue to try to deal with through regional arrangements. These include the management of regional pollution problems, particularly those of enclosed or semi-enclosed seas; the management of certain regional pelagic fisheries; certain regional efforts at scientific inquiry and information gathering; possibly some attempts to establish denuclearized "zones of peace" in certain areas; and perhaps certain regional attempts to deal with areas where jurisdiction is uncertain, such as Antarctica. It is also possible that in a few areas the expansion of coastal state jurisdiction represented by the 200-mile economic zone concept may instigate a search for regional solutions. However, by and large, the expansion of coastal state jurisdiction seems more likely to lead to an increase in unilateral or bilateral efforts to manage ocean problems than to any increased trend toward regional efforts.

Second, whatever trends toward regionalism emerge are unlikely to be strongly affected by the results of UNCLOS III. Indeed it is hard to say whether the success or the failure of the Conference would be more likely to encourage the growth of regionalism. On the one hand, the present provisions of the Informal Composite Negotiating Text contain a number of references to regionalism, which in terms encourage regional arrangements in particular fields such as pollution control, access arrangements for landlocked and geographically disadvantaged states, the management of certain fisheries, marine science and transfer of technology, and so forth. But these provisions are generally vague and would not compel a trend toward regional approaches. On the other hand, failure to reach a global treaty could encourage a search for regional solutions to particular problems as the only short-run alternative to presently unattainable global solutions. But it is also arguable that a failure of UNCLOS III might produce some disillusionment with international cooperation and an increasing emphasis on unilateral or bilateral solutions. I believe that the most realistic expectation is that nations will turn to regional solutions when these seem clearly in their interest, either in terms of inherent rationality or for political or bargaining purposes, and that the basic factors in such decisions will be to a considerable extent independent of whether an UNCLOS III treaty is or is not achieved.

Third, any increase in regionalism in marine affairs may arise less from influences unique to marine problems than as an outgrowth of more general trends toward regionalism and regional organization. Generalized regional organizations and alignments, such as the European Community, the Organization of American States, the Organization of African Unity, and the Arab League are becoming increasingly active. It is in the nature of such organizations to seek to expand regional cooperation and "common policy," in marine affairs as in other matters.

Consequently, it is not unlikely that these regional organizations will show a growing interest and involvement in marine affairs, and attempt to have an increasing influence on law of the sea issues.

Fourth, while it is probable that plurilateral groupings or "blocs" of states will play an important role in post-UNCLOS III marine affairs, these groupings are likely to be based more on a desire by the nations involved to mobilize collective power and bargaining strength in order to secure particular shared objectives than on uniquely regional objectives or a desire to achieve specific regional solutions to regional problems. That is, it is quite possible that we will have to face a law of the sea that is to some extent fragmented among different groupings of states. However, these groupings may not necessarily be explained either in special regional terms or by uniquely regional needs. For example, certain of the present coalitions forged in the UNCLOS III negotiations—a grouping of shipping or naval states concerned with freedom of navigation, a grouping of states concerned with marine science, a grouping of states interested and technically able to participate in the exploitation of deep seabed resources, and so forth—are likely to continue in the post-UNCLOS III world, whatever the outcome of the Conference. In some cases, these groupings may be regionally defined or at least be outgrowths of broader existing regional arrangements. But in many other cases they may not.

Finally, to the extent that regionalism does emerge, it need not be through the clear establishment of express and formal regional arrangements. It is also possible for nations to establish what Douglas Johnston has called an "implicit regionalism" through a coordinated or a unilateral adoption by the states in a particular region of particular common policies or practices. For example, it is possible to visualize situations where all or most of the nations in a particular region refuse to ratify a law of the sea treaty, make the same reservations to such a treaty in the same way, or develop the same practices with respect to particular marine issues.

To the extent that regionalism does develop, is it likely to be a "good" or a "bad" thing? Dr. Alexander and others have pointed out many of these possible implications and their pros and cons.

On the positive side, the following points can be suggested:

First, in some situations, regional approaches appear to offer the easiest, most rational, and most promising solutions to the particular marine problems involved. This is clearly the case where such problems are uniquely regional, as in the case of the pollution of enclosed or semi-enclosed seas such as the Baltic, Mediterranean, or Caribbean, or with respect to the management of certain high seas fisheries. In these cases, only the states in the region are likely to be directly concerned and willing and able to take effective action; the involvement of less concerned outsiders may simply obstruct solutions. It is also true of situations where the existence of strong regional organizations in place, comprised of member states sharing common perceptions and habits of cooperation, can lead to more rapid and effective action.

Second, in the absence of an effective and widely ratified global law of the sea treaty, regionalism may be the highest attainable level of multilateral action—in effect, the best we can hope for. That is, while global cooperation may be preferable, even partial cooperation on a regional basis may be better than the alternative of no cooperation and unilateral approaches. Moreover, regionalism may conceivably simplify and facilitate the eventual achievement of global solutions. It may be easier for a few regional organizations eventually to arrive at common agreements than for a great number of individual states to do so.

Third, regionalism permits experimentation with a diversity of approaches to ocean problems. Attempts by different regional groups to deal with problems in diverse ways can add to our experience of what types of solutions are likely to be most useful in managing ocean problems.

Finally, regional approaches to ocean problems may have desirable side effects. For example, they may help to strengthen general regional organization and regional approaches in other fields, establish broader habits of cooperation, and serve as a catalyst for increasing international integration more generally.

But regionalism also has certain drawbacks and may pose certain dangers.

First, where the nature of the ocean problems involved seem inherently to require global, or at least widely accepted, common approaches, diverse regional approaches may add to the difficulty of finding effective solutions. For example, regional attempts to deal with pollution problems through the establishment of regional vessel-construction standards cannot avoid the potentially disruptive impact of such differential construction standards on a global shipping industry. Indeed, any undesirable developments in ocean management policies may, once they are adopted by regional groups, have added impact and resistance to change. That is, the international community may find it easier to persuade, induce, or coerce an individual nation to yield or to compromise actions, positions, or policies adversely affecting broad community interests than to persuade an entire regional bloc to do so. Moreover, an emphasis on regionalism may divert energies and efforts from the search for more comprehensive global or multilateral solutions.

Second, even where problems are not necessarily global, the most rational and effective basis for multilateral cooperation in seeking solutions may lie in arrangements among states that are not in the same region, or among some but not all states in a region. An attempt at regional solutions to such problems, pressed perhaps by some general regional organization anxious to expand its activities into ocean management, may simply obstruct the development of more meaningful nonregionally based cooperative groupings of nations, or may push nations with differing interests into an inefficient or unworkable regional cooperative mold.

Finally, some regional arrangements may have objectives and effects opposed to the interests of all, or at least particular, nonregional states. For example, certain arrangements might be intended to establish a regional monopoly of particular ocean resources in the region, such as fishery or deep seabed mineral resources, through concerted action designed to exclude nonregional nations from these resources, or to permit access to such resources only to a favored few or on unreasonable or discriminatory conditions. Other arrangements might conceivably be designed to exploit nonregional nations through control by regional states of a particular strait, permitting passage to other nonregional states only on the payment of exorbitant fees or on unreasonable or discriminatory conditions. Indeed, marine regional arrangements might conceivably be used for political purposes by some states in the region in order to discriminate against an unpopular nation or nations in that same region—the possibility of an arrangement of Arab states excluding Israel or of African states excluding South Africa comes readily to mind. As indicated, collective abuses by regional groups may, in view of their added power, be more difficult to remedy than abuses by nations acting individually.

What is the relation of regionalism in the oceans to international law more generally? Does regionalism raise special problems of international law?

Regionalism is a well accepted concept in international law. The role of regional organizations is expressly recognized in the UN Charter and many other international instruments, and there are, of course, a great number of regional organizations, institutions, and other arrangements in existence. Thus, the existence of regional arrangements dealing with ocean problems does not in itself raise international legal problems. Indeed, it is arguable that regional organizations may in some situations properly assert claims or take actions of a nature that might be illegitimate if undertaken by states acting unilaterally—that is, that certain types of collective action by the nations constituting a particular "neighborhood," with respect to problems of their neighborhood, have a certain presumption to legitimacy. Such attitudes were invoked, for example, during the 1962 Cuban Missile Crisis in support of the legality of the OAS resolution authorizing a quarantine on shipment of strategic missiles of Cuba.

Regionalism can generally affect the law of the sea in various ways. Most obviously, the nations of a region, each acting within the scope of its own appropriate jurisdictional competence, may agree to adopt common or collective regulatory or management schemes that directly establish rules within the area of their aggregate regional competence. But regional actions may also generally affect the law of the sea in other ways. For example, if an UNCLOS III treaty is concluded, a concerted policy of nonratification, selective reservation, or agreed interpretation by a particular regional group—for example, the OAS or OAU—could have significant practical effects on the scope, effectiveness, or interpretation of such a treaty. Or, if a treaty is not concluded or widely ratified, a concerted course of practice by a number of nations in a regional group, perhaps organized and supported through their regional organization, could significantly affect the development of customary international law of the sea. Thus, a concerted practice by a number of regional states could go a considerable way toward manifesting the existence of a broader international custom, or toward casting doubt on the continued viability of some inconsistent practice followed by states outside the region, alleged by such other states as constituting customary law. An obvious example is the post-World War II claims of a number of Latin American nations to extensive fisheries limits. This strong regional position clearly had a substantial effect on subsequent developments in this respect, culminating in the concept of a 200-mile economic zone.

But regionalism may be subject to at least some legal constraints.

First, international law, or other international arrangements to which the regional states are parties, appears (at least to some extent) to limit the permissible objectives of regional arrangements. For example, regional nations could not legally pursue objectives inconsistent with their obligations under the UN Charter; under Article 103, the obligations of member states under the Charter prevail in such a case. I am not aware of any "supremacy" clause in the present Informal Composite Negotiating Text of the proposed treaty, but it is possible that such a provision could eventually be incorporated. Again, any regional agreement that was expressly designed to achieve objectives conflicting with certain "peremptory" norms of general international law—that is, norms accepted and recognized by the international community of states as a whole as a norm from which no derogation is permitted—would, under the *jus cogens* principle stated in Article 53 of the Vienna Convention on the Law of Treaties, be invalid. While there is little agreement as to which international norms are in face "peremptory," a regional agreement designed to achieve aggressive aims, for example, or one designed to protect the slave trade, would presumably be contrary to international law and void under this principle. A nonregional state might conceivably use this principle to argue that regional agreements unreasonably conflicting with basic rights of freedom of navigation on the high seas, or designed to appropriate for exclusive use resources generally recognized as the "common heritage of mankind," violate peremptory norms and are invalid.

Second, international law arguably imposes limits on the authority of a regional organization to control conduct by other nonregional states or their nationals outside of those areas or types of conduct that are within the combined separate jurisdictions of the participating regional states and that they consequently might individually control. The question of whether states can somehow gain added legal competence through collective action is, of course, an important one. Certainly, there seems no problem in a group of states aggregating and exercising collectively their separate jurisdictional competencies—for example, by agreeing to a common regime within their combined economic zones, or by agreeing to establish common regulations for vessels of their own nationalities on the high seas. However, there is considerable question as to the authority of a regional organization to establish obligations binding upon other states or their nationals with respect to areas or activities that, even though generally within their geographic region, are not within the specific jurisdictional competence of any of the regional states. This question might be raised, for example, by attempts by a regional organization to establish exclusive rights for its members with respect to a fishery or the exploitation of seabed resources in the international area of the region beyond their combined jurisdictional limits.

My own view is that the most that a regional organization can legally do in such cases is to attempt to exercise moral suasion to obtain compliance by nonmember nations, or communicate a collective political threat against inconsistent action by nonmember nations. This problem is reflected, for example, in Article X of the Antarctic Treaty, which provides that: "Each of the Contracting Parties undertakes to exert appropriate efforts, consistent with the Charter of the United Nations, to the end that no one engages in any activity in Antarctica contrary to the principles or purposes of the present Treaty." Similar language is, of course, employed in Article 2(6) of the UN Charter.

The problem of the legal effect of decisions of regional organizations purporting to limit activities of nonregional nations on high seas within the region was again raised dramatically, if inconclusively, by the OAS resolution imposing a quarantine on the shipment of missiles to Cuba during the 1962 Cuban Missile Crisis. It will be recalled that the Soviet Union denounced this action as "piracy." Of course, outside states may be bound by obligations established by regional arrangements if they either expressly agree to be so bound or if they manifest acquiescence in some other way, as by a consistent course of complying conduct.

Similar limits on the ability of a regional group to impose broad regional rules binding outsiders would seem applicable in situations where nations in a regional area develop special regional customary practices or norms without embodying them in a specific regional agreement. While the International Court of Justice has recognized the concept of regional customary international law, binding upon those states in the region that participated in its formation and possibly modifying as among them some broader rule of customary law, such a regional custom would not bind nonregional states which did not participate in its formation or in some way manifest their acquiescence.

The Antarctic Treaty and the possibility that other types of regional arrangements regarding Antarctica might be concluded raise interesting questions in this respect. In view of the lack of any general agreement concerning recognition of territorial claims by particular nations in Antarctica, no nation, to my knowledge, has made any claim to Antarctic territorial seas or economic zones. Indeed, such claims might arguably be inconsistent with Article IV of the Antarctic Treaty, which provides, *inter alia,* that: "No new claim, or enlargement of an existing claim, to territorial sovereignty in Antarctica shall be asserted while the present Treaty is in force." Conceivably, however, *all* of those nations conducting activities or having potential claims in Antarctica, and all of which are parties to the Treaty, might *collectively,* through some agreement or organization, claim the right to control of such ocean zones. Their theory might be that, while the "division of the pie" among the various nations having claims to and active in Antarctica remains uncertain and is held in obeyance by the treaty, this territorial "pie," and the rights to territorial and economic zone rights associated with territorial claims, are possessed by them collectively as against other nations not participating in the treaty. Of course, recent suggestions that Antarctica should be declared a "common heritage of all mankind" hint that other non-Antarctic nations might be prepared to dispute any such claim.

What, then, can we say as to the consequences of regionalization in the treaty or customary law of the sea? Is regionalism in fact likely to have a significant impact on the law of the sea or to pose serious challenges to a rational and effective system of ocean management?

My belief is that it will not. I have indicated my doubts that there will be any strong trend toward regionalism in the near future, regardless of the outcome of UNCLOS III. To the extent that there is some growth in regional approaches and arrangements, these seem more likely to be a continuation of present trends toward regional solutions to uniquely regional problems, such as the pollution of enclosed or semi-enclosed seas, than to represent any dramatic shift occasioned by developments at UNCLOS III.

Thus, I believe that, by and large, the international community should be able to cope with any likely development in regionalism without undue costs. Hopefully, most such regional arrangements will be directed at providing more rational and effective solutions to regional ocean problems, resulting in a more rather than less effective system of ocean management. To the extent that regionalism does introduce added diversity into the law of the sea, nations have in fact lived with a considerable amount of diversity for a long time, and they can presumably continue to do so—at least so long as they know what the relevant rules are and will be. Indeed, it is possible that regional approaches could result in a net decrease rather than increase in the diversity of rules and management systems governing ocean affairs.

In my view, the threat that regionalism will generally take a highly exclusionary, exploitative, or jurisdictionally expanding form is unlikely to materialize. Coastal states have already achieved their most important objectives through recognition of the concept of 200-mile economic zones. Any additional gains to these states from attempts at further encroachments on ocean freedoms are likely to be marginal at best and may not be worth the political costs or risks involved. Clearly, however—to the extent that regionalism is manifested in exclusionary or exploitative types of arrangements—discriminating against non-regional nations or against regional nations deliberately left out of a regional "club," possibilities for confrontation and conflict will be increased.

Thus, the most significant impact of regionalism may be less in terms of a fragmentation of the law of the sea or the establishment of a diversity of exclusionary regional systems than in a gradual change in the nature and scale of bargaining and law-influencing units through which that law is arrived at, interpreted, and developed. In view of the rapid and dramatic increase that has occurred in recent years in the number of nations—particularly smaller and newer nations—participating in the international system, the trend toward coalition bargaining already manifested in the UNCLOS III negotiations seems likely to continue. As we have seen, many of these coalitions or "blocs" may be regionally based, but many may not. The overriding question may be not simply the impact of regionalism as such or the law of the sea, but the broader impact on the law of the sea and a global system of marine management of an international rule-making process that tends to some increased extent to operate through coalitions of states rather than individual nations.

Finally, what can we do—either through a law of the sea treaty or otherwise—to encourage those aspects of regionalism that seem most useful, to discourage those that seem least useful, and, more generally, to ease any problems for a rational global system of ocean management that regionalism might pose?

First, the international community might seek to establish some kind of broad agreed-upon "ground rules" and general expectations with respect to such matters as the kinds of problems regional arrangements in the oceans should properly be concerned with, the permissible objectives of such arrangements, and the general principles that should govern them. An example of such international "ground rules" in another field is the set of principles relating to inter-governmental commodity arrangements contained in Chapter VII of the Draft International Trade Organization Charter, negotiated in 1946. While the ITO Charter never entered into force, the Economic and Social Council, in its Resolution 30 (IV), recommended that UN members, in negotiating commodity arrangements, adopt as a general guide the principles laid down in Chapter VII, and these have had a significant influence on the form that commodity agreements have taken.

A similar set of "ground rules" covering regional arrangements in the oceans might do various things. For example, as indicated above, the international community could seek broadly to identify those types of problems for which global solutions seem most appropriate and which regional arrangements should not tamper with, as contrasted with those in which regional solutions do seem to have a proper role. Such "ground rules" could seek to establish the principle that regional arrangements in the oceans should be open to participation by all states within the region, without discrimination. They might establish the principle that nonparticipating nations should be entitled to equal treatment in access to privileges or resources covered by the arrangement on the same conditions, without discrimination. They might make it clear that regional arrangements cannot purport to affect the rights of nonparticipating nations in areas beyond the combined jurisdiction of the various nations participating in the arrangement. And so forth. Such "ground rules" could be set out in a law of the sea treaty or in some other form, such as a UN General Assembly or UNCLOS III resolution.

Second, the international community can attempt to establish more viable institutions for integrating regional arrangements into a broader global ocean management framework, and for ensuring that any disputes arising out of a regional arrangements can be settled quickly and in nondisruptive ways. This might involve the establishment of continuing global or interregional coordinating bodies and dispute settlement institutions or other mechanisms.

Finally, we can attempt to strengthen broad community expectations that, in an interdependent world, and more particularly in matters affecting inherently shared resources such as the oceans, neither any single nation nor any single group of nations can legitimately completely "go it alone," ignoring the interests of other states. The obligation of nations to take the interests of other nations into account in determining their policies in such contexts is reflected in the 1974 decision of the International Court in the Anglo-Icelandic *Fisheries Jurisdiction* case, in the work proceeding under the auspices of the General Assembly and UN Environmental Program on Shared Natural Resources, and in a variety of other agreements, resolutions, and statements. If we can achieve broad acceptance of the need for cooperative approaches and of the principle that nations have an obligation to work together to seek to equitably adjust and harmonize their common interests, neither regionalism nor any other problems need pose insurmountable obstacles to achieving a viable system of ocean management.

Discussion and Questions

Douglas Johnston: We have listened to three persuasive presentations, and now is the time to open the hunting season. For those of you who have better eyesight than I have and have discovered fallacies to be exposed and contradictions to be resolved, now is the time to declare yourselves.

Hajim Djalal: It has been said by Dr. Bilder this morning that regional arrangements unreasonably conflicting with the freedom of navigation on the high seas or inconsistent with the principle of common heritage of mankind might be regarded as violating peremptory norms of international law, and thus be deemed invalid. The choice of examples here is, of course, very subjective. One can easily choose other examples of regional arrangements that might be in violation of peremptory norms under the doctrine of *jus cogens.* But let me comment on one point and ask questions on another. With regard to transit through international straits, it should be remembered that Article 16(4) of the 1958 Convention on the Territorial Sea and the Contiguous Zone is still accepted by some states as authority for the view that there can be no suspension of innocent passage of foreign ships through such straits. Now, if there is no convention at UNCLOS III, I am afraid some people would like to go back to that interpretation. So, I would like to say that the general acceptance at this moment of the right of transit passage through straits has nothing to do with peremptory norms of international law. It would be somewhat prejudicial at this stage to view the issue in this light. If UNCLOS III failed, this and other provisions in the 1958 Conventions would be open to interpretation. Second, arrangements that violate the common heritage of mankind on the deep ocean floor are said also to be a possible example of a violation of a peremptory norm of international law.

I would conclude that if regionalism can be in violation of such norms, then unilateral action in this direction is even more likely to be deemed invalid. Am I correct in giving this interpretation?

Richard Bilder: All I was trying to suggest in those remarks on peremptory norms of international law was the possibility of a certain type of argument being raised. Are people likely to make these arguments, and are they going to make them seriously, and is there some chance of their prevailing? I agree that it is difficult to say at this point exactly what a peremptory norm of international law is under the Vienna Convention on the Law of Treaties; and you know how this question would come out in a case before the International Court of Justice. But I think it is realistic to imagine that this type of argument could be made by states. For example, if a regional organization does try to establish control of a particular regional area of the seabed for mining purposes, other nations are likely to complain. Whether they will use this particular legal argument based on the Vienna Convention may be open to doubt, but they will certainly say that the regional organization is acting beyond its jurisdiction, on one ground or another. As the commentator pointed out, the same reaction could be expected in the event of a unilateral statement to the same effect. In short, I was trying to give illustrations of styles of arguments that could be invoked rather than trying to suggest that this is necessarily the present law.

Dennis Earl: I have just a brief question. Mr. Nelson suggests that there were some norms that had achieved a very broad consensus since the discussions began at the conference in 1973, and also that some kinds of norms would not be created through the customary law process but would rather require general acceptance in treaty form. What norms have in fact evolved since 1973, other than the economic zone norm, and what norms specifically would you feel are not appropriate for creation through the customary law process?

Dolliver Nelson: One example of a concept that has emerged at UNCLOS III is that of the twelve-mile territorial sea. I think most states accept the view that the twelve-mile territorial sea is accepted in international law today, and it could only be by custom. On the question of the status of the exclusive economic zone concept, one has to tread very carefully. I think the concept of an exclusive fishing zone up to 200-mile limits has been accepted as a norm, but you know that there are states like Mexico, Guatemala, Haiti, and others that have in fact adopted exclusive economic zones in a sense similar to that of the Conference text, which means they have gone beyond resource-oriented competence to other matters such as marine scientific research and pollution control. Now, is that a part of international law today? It is interesting that there is no uniformity in practice between developing and developed states in regard to the exclusive economic zone. It might be argued that the right of access—a conditional right—

is one of the basic features of the new regime of the economic zone, distinguishing it from the regime of the territorial sea. But a coastal state conceded to have sovereign rights to the resources of the zone might find it difficult to concede that other states have a right of participation. A conflict of views on such a basic question might be fatal to the contention that the concept of the economic zone is established in customary international law. Those rights, in short, that are not yet embodied in state practice seem to me to be the kinds of rights that cannot be adopted by the customary process.

Albert Koers: I have a rather specific question for Mr. Nelson. Regionalism is related to substantive provisions of the ICNT, and we have heard quite a number of very interesting comments on that relationship. However, regionalism is also related, I would say, to the procedural provisions of the ICNT, and I am thinking specifically of the dispute settlement procedures. Now, I would like to have some clarification on that relationship—the relationship between regionalism and the dispute settlement procedures. For example, let us assume that a number of states as members of a regional organization establish a regional economic zone, and then proceed to manage that zone in a way that is contrary to the principles of the ICNT or the new law of the sea convention. Who would be accountable: the states themselves or the regional organization? Of course, it depends on the internal structure of the regional organization, but I may point out that Article 287 of the ICNT, the article on the choice of procedure, seems to apply only to states that are parties to the convention.

Dolliver Nelson: I must first confess that I am not an expert on the dispute settlement procedures of the text, but I have a suspicion the question has to do with the final clauses. What sort of entity will be accepted as having the capacity to ratify or accede to the convention? Would organizations such as the European Economic Communities be covered by this provision in the final clauses? The usual thing is that only states are regarded as parties of general treaties, but there have been some examples of an organization being eligible to become a party. I think there is an example in the recent Mediterranean Convention on Marine Pollution. One of the questions that arises here is whether you can frame the provision in such a way as not to include all sorts of organizations that are not within the contemplation of the conference. This is a question that evidently has to be negotiated. I might add that the final clauses have not yet been discussed by UNCLOS III in any detail.

Abdelkader Abbadi: What I would like to ask is whether regionalism is a feasible and practical solution in the immediate future, or the foreseeable future, and, if not, what is the alternative? Second, what kind of conflicts are expected to be associated with it, if any, and in what manner could they be resolved?

Lewis Alexander: I don't think it is a question of whether regionalism is possible. Regionalism is upon us right now. It is a process, and a functional approach to problem solving. It is here, and I think it is going to remain. In many cases the degree of regionalization will be disappointing, as I pointed out earlier, but this kind of approach will continue to evolve in various ways. As for dispute settlement, I turn that over to the lawyers.

Richard Bilder: Surely there will be conflicts. The best way of taking care of disputes and conflicts is to anticipate them and try to avoid them, so they do not arise; or to lay down some clear principles for taking care of them, when they do arise. One of the possibilities is having clear rules, ground rules, which establish what the relevant organizations can do. Another thing would be to have some kind of supremacy clause in the treaty. In view of what is happening at this Conference, regionalism can involve special kinds of problems, which the present text may not be able to handle under the present dispute settlement provisions. The Conference might be able to supplement these provisions before it is too late.

Part II

Regional Politics in the Management of Marine Resources

Chairman
Judith T. Kildow
Massachusetts Institute of Technology

Judith Kildow: I have had a request from Dr. Kolodkin to begin with a few remarks on this morning's presentations.

Anatoly Kolodkin: Thank you very much. First, I would like to express our gratitude for the invitation of the Institute and the University of Hawaii to visit this unique state, and for the hospitality we have received here. Our cooperation began at the Miami Conference in 1975, continued at Rhode Island, and now for the third time here in Honolulu. At these conferences we have valued the close cooperation of our colleagues from the United States and other countries.

The first comment I have to make is that the ICNT is, in my view, a suitable basis for negotiating a comprehensive convention on the law of the sea. Second, it seems to me that the problem of regionalization is very important and we should not underestimate or diminish its significance. No doubt it has positive features, and positive consequences for the developing and developed countries, including the USSR itself. For example, there is a serious regional problem in the Mediterranean in the field of the environment, and we could not understand why the Soviet Union, Bulgaria, Romania, and Black Sea Congress were not invited to the Barcelona Conference as participants, but only as observers. It seems to me that the Black Sea is a subregional zone of the Mediterranean, and I cannot imagine how there can be full compliance with the provisions of that conference without the Black Sea Congress.

With reference to Professor Bilder's presentation, I would like to stress that we must take into account the need for consistency between all acceptable principles and rules of contemporary international law. Accordingly, regional rules have to be in accordance with generally accepted principles and rules. Second, I am in agreement with my Indonesian colleague, Dr. Djalal, that it is very bad if states take unilateral actions contrary to the emerging consensus of UNCLOS III. Unilateral action by the United States on the seabed would have negative consequences on the Conference. Third, we have in the ICNT very important provisions that create a good balance between the interests of the coastal states and of the international community in the field of navigation: for example, Article 2, which provides that the coastal state may make laws and regulations but "in conformity with the provisions of the present Convention and other rules of international law related to innocent passage through the territorial sea." Some countries propose to delete paragraph 2 of this article, which excludes design, construction, manning, and equipment of foreign ships from the scope of coastal laws and regulations. If this were done, there would be a very bad situation, because in that case these important matters would become subject to the discretion of the coastal states within each region.

I agree with the panelists that the economic zone is one of the main problems of contemporary maritime law. But it seems important to stress that, in accordance with Article 58, the freedoms of the high seas referred to in Article 87 would apply and therefore limit coastal state authority within the economic zone, whatever region the state belongs to. These provisions mean that all states will enjoy the generally accepted rules and principles of contemporary maritime law concerning the freedom of navigation in the economic zone. Allow me also to stress that we are in favor of the provisions of the convention concerning the regulation of scientific research in the economic zone and on the continental shelf, and in my personal opinion it would be acceptable to approve at the Conference the proposal of Mexico. Thank you very much.

Judith Kildow: Now, I would like to go ahead with this afternoon's program. We had hoped to have with us the distinguished ambassadors to the Law of the Sea Conference from Mexico and Trinidad and Tobago, but unfortunately the meeting of the Evansen group diverted their paths from Hawaii to Geneva. However, we are very fortunate to have in Ambassador Castañeda's place someone who has worked very closely with him and is very familiar with the issues and what he would have said to us today. I have also asked his Mexican colleague, with whom he has been working closely, to join us in discussion along with Mr. Nelson. The gentleman who has been so kind as to substitute at short notice for Ambassador Castañeda is Mr. Andrés Rozental, a career foreign service officer for the Mexican government. Educated in the United States, he has been a prominent member of the Mexican delegation to the Seabed Committee and the Third UN Conference on the Law of the Sea. He has been involved in most law of the sea matters in Mexico in recent years as alternate representative to the OAS, representative to IMCO, commissioner to the International Whaling Commission, among other roles. He is very familiar with law of the sea issues in the Caribbean and the Gulf of Mexico.

Chapter Four

Some Brief Considerations on a Caribbean Condominium

Andrés Rozental
Ministry of Foreign Affairs
Mexico

Toward the end of the third session of UNCLOS III, at Geneva in 1975, the notion of a 200-mile exclusive economic zone had already gained sufficient consensus within the Conference to confirm its emergence as a valid institution in international law. In the Caribbean the prospect of the establishment of economic zones by each of the fifteen bordering coastal states, and also by the fifteen island or continental non-self-governing territories, promised to create a maze of overlapping jurisdictions as well as a chaotic mosaic of minute island separations divided between adjacent or opposite land masses.

More than two years have passed since then, and the countries of the Caribbean have neglected to recognize the existence of this problem, despite its inherent potential for conflict. This situation is somewhat surprising, given the fact that some of the Caribbean countries have had a long experience in establishing 200-mile zones. Back in the late 40s and early 50s, four of the Central American nations claimed 200-mile zones with varying degrees of jurisdiction: Panama, Costa Rica, Honduras, and Nicaragua established 200-mile zones, creating the antecedent of the institution we now know as the exclusive economic zone.

I need not repeat here the background of an idea that has remained within the confines of the academic community: namely, the concept of a "matrimonial sea." Indeed it was during a workshop at this very Institute that the idea was born. A lot has been said about the concept of a matrimonial or regional sea, but it has been in general terms. I propose in this short presentation to point out the direction in which the substance of this concept may be developed, so as to raise questions that will have to be debated.

What should a matrimonial sea, or maritime condominium, entail? I can identify the following four main headings: first, the problem of dealing with the living resources of the Caribbean; second, the issue of the utilization of the mineral resources in the seabed; third, the preservation of the marine environment within the semi-enclosed sea; and, finally, the prospects of economic integration that would result from undertaking regional implementation of the new law of the sea in the Caribbean. Later, brief reference will be made to some of the political problems that are likely to develop if the Caribbean coastal nations seriously undertake the implementation of a condominium or matrimonial sea.

Before going any further, I should like to advance the premise of this discussion. Except for one particular aspect of the presentation, we are unwilling to accept the old idea of an "American Mediterranean," consisting of both the Gulf of Mexico and the Caribbean, as a single unit for purposes of regionalization. In the Proceedings of the Law of the Sea Workshop held by this Institute in February 1972, on the subject of Gulf and Caribbean Maritime Problems, Mr. Robert Hodgson explained that for hydrographical reasons the Caribbean and the Gulf of Mexico should be included as part of the so-called American Mediterranean. These reasons, however, do not appear to justify the application of the concept of an American Mediterranean for all purposes, because there is no significant proof of any highly migratory species of living resources that move from the Gulf to the Caribbean or vice versa. The hydrographical nature of the link between these two semi-enclosed seas does, however, seem relevant to the preservation of the marine environment in the region.

As an interesting historical note, it should also be recalled that President Franklin D. Roosevelt, in a Memorandum to his Secretary of State in 1939, proposed the division of the Gulf of Mexico between the United States and Mexico, ignoring entirely the fact that Cuba was also a bordering nation on the Gulf. This may well have been the first case of confusion and misunderstanding about the question of who are the states with vested interests, both direct and indirect, in the Gulf of Mexico.

Why do we feel that the Gulf of Mexico, aside from environmental considerations, should not be considered a part of the Caribbean? We have already mentioned the lack of biological unity. There is a second important reason. Three countries bordering the Gulf of Mexico have already adopted unilateral measures among themselves, implementing the new law of the sea in the area. In 1976, Mexico concluded bilateral agreements, first with Cuba and then with the United States, which incorporated the relevant economic zone provisions of the Revised Single Negotiating Text that emanated from the previous session of UNCLOS III. Early in 1977, the United States and Cuba also negotiated an agreement on this subject. In this way, the utilization of living resources in the Gulf of Mexico has already been taken care of by the three countries that border the area. Additionally, Mexico negotiated the delimitation of its exclusive economic zone with both the United States and Cuba, and a provisional agreement has also been reached more recently between Cuba and the United States on the delimitation of their respective jurisdictional zones.

Thus, for all practical purposes, the Gulf of Mexico is already a closed sea and its problems pertain exclusively to the bordering countries, with the exception of environmental preservation. It is evident that Mexico, the United States, and Cuba will have to adopt cooperative measures in order to protect the marine environment for the internal uses of these three countries within the Gulf, especially with regard to the pollution problems that arise from the exploitation of the nonliving resources of the continental shelf of the United States and Mexico. There may also be a case for treating the Gulf and the Caribbean together for certain environmental purposes, given the importance of the Gulf Stream as the hydrographical link between these (and indeed other) areas, but this appears to be the only justification for considering the two as a single maritime space.

What of the living resources of the Caribbean Sea, on the other hand? In my view, this area has no species that can be described as "highly migratory." Since all of the living resources coexist, ecologically linked in one way or another, and remain within the confines of the Caribbean, I suggest that they should be regarded as "migratory" within the region. In other words, they should be submitted to the same kind of regime as provided for "highly migratory" species by Article 64 of the Informal Composite Negotiating Text. This means that the living resources of the Caribbean should be subjected to a regional regime both for conservation and utilization. Under a regional system—or a "condominium" arrangement—the Caribbean countries might have two alternatives. Either they could consolidate their financial and technical resources in order to exploit jointly all fisheries, within the limits of an agreed conservation program, and distribute the benefits derived therefrom in the same manner as is proposed for the mineral resources of the seabed beyond the limits of national jurisdiction; or, if they prefer to take advantage of the abundance of each individual species within their own economic zones, they might adopt a regional program of surplus allocation and utilization. This second alternative would have the clear advantage of excluding all foreign fleets from the Caribbean, since whatever surplus might result after taking into account the harvesting capacity of all the coastal states would be jointly exploited by all the countries of the region rather than by extra-regional nations. The benefits could then be distributed among the regional participants.

As to the problem of mineral exploitation, I propose that it be completely excluded from any joint regional or condominium approach. When we speak of a matrimonial sea or condominium, we do not attempt to suggest that individual economic zones should be subsumed into a common pool of resources with regional freedom of exploitation as a result. On the contrary, states will insist on the need for individual delimitation of zones precisely, or mostly, because of the question of mineral resources. It would hardly be reasonable at this stage to expect that any of the countries of the area would be willing to abandon or share their sovereignty over these resources. Their exploitation will have to remain within the national jurisdiction of each coastal state.

Any decision by the coastal states of the Caribbean to look at the living resources of the area from a regional point of view will bring enormous benefits and result in positive economic integration of the area. The very idea of pooling resources and sharing capabilities, both financial and technological, will produce positive results. The use of one country's processing plants for the resources obtained on a regional basis will obviate the need for each country to invest in plants of its own. The same may be said of the use of ports, installations, fleet development for specific fisheries, harvesting techniques and, above all, the sharing of scientific knowledge and data for the exploitation of the region's living resources.

But the above considerations might be said to cause some problems of a political nature. The existence within the region of varying political, economic, and social regimes might present serious obstacles to a joint approach to these questions. In spite of the fact that this situation prevails today, we feel that it is of a transitory nature and we should always recognize the dynamic nature of relations among states. We have seen, in the past few years, a complete change in the balance and nature of the relationships among countries of differing ideological persuasions and economic systems. The example of détente, not only between the two superpowers, but between Cuba and the United States, should give us reason for optimism that all interested states, regardless of their political orientation, may look favorably on the proposal for a regional scheme of this kind in the Caribbean.

Commentary

Dolliver Nelson*
Law of the Sea Secretariat
United Nations

[In Chapter Two] I outlined some of the problems that can arise in regionally defined marine areas. Here I will submit an outline of these issues in ascending order–from issues that can be solved easily to those that could possibly create problems in the Caribbean. The first relates to the protection and preservation of the marine environment. The second concerns the problem of the maintenance of freedom of navigation and overflight. The third is concerned with the problem of the delimitation of marine areas; and the fourth, with the conservation and management, and possible allocation, of living resources in the Caribbean. The last two are both very troublesome problems and all I intend to do here is to raise points and not propose solutions. At least I will try not to.

The protection and preservation of the marine environment is clearly an important issue in semi-enclosed seas. The enclosed nature of such maritime areas makes them extremely vulnerable to pollution. Fortunately, in contrast to the Mediterranean, the Caribbean is an area where the waters are perpetually renewed and, therefore, the problem of degradation of the marine environment is not as significant in the Caribbean and not so urgent as is the case in the Mediterranean. Nevertheless, in view of the fact that many of the Caribbean islands depend upon tourism and lovely beaches, it is very important that these islands monitor carefully the level of pollution, especially with the increasing exploitation of offshore areas: for example, in parts of Southeastern Trinidad. Increasing offshore exploitation would definitely pose a threat to the marine environment, but I think, as was made clear by Professor Alexander (Chapter One), UNEP is,

*The views expressed are personal and do not necessarily reflect the official views of the Secretariat of the United Nations.

in fact, very concerned with the question of marine pollution in the Caribbean, and I see no problem here as far as cooperation among the states of the Caribbean is concerned.

The second point relates to the freedom of navigation and overflight. I would not have thought that this issue could present a formidable problem in the Caribbean. The fact is that the straits there are very wide ones, the outlets are very wide, there are many outlets. But I think one should not overlook the problem of freedom of navigation and overflight in the Caribbean. There is always the possibility of the exclusive economic zone regime itself being transformed into something nearer the territorial sea regime. If such a phenomenon were to occur in the Caribbean, it is quite possible that this issue would become very important in the area. This is a rather brief and cursory treatment of the problem—possibly some of the comments from the floor may help us to expand on issues like freedom of navigation and overflight.

The third point is the problem of delimitation of maritime areas. As I mentioned before (Chapter Two), the configuration of most semi-enclosed seas, the very disposition of states within these bodies of water, makes the delimitation of maritime zones especially difficult; and the presence of features such as islands, which perhaps constitute a characteristic feature of these maritime regions, merely aggravates the problem. It is not surprising that certain states in such areas give strong support to the principle of equity since they argue that the application of the equidistance principle could lead to unjust results.

As far as the Caribbean is concerned, there are two significant problems. First, some of these islands face continental land masses. It will be remembered that in the North Sea Continental Shelf Cases of 1969 the suggestion was made that there should be proportionality between length of coastline and the maritime area allocated to a state. If that criterion were to be applied to the Caribbean, the islands of the Caribbean would be in a lot of difficulty, because they just would not be able to provide the coastal facade necessary to create any sort of equilibrium as far as some of the continental states are concerned. So, the concept of proportionality, or the coastal facade theory, may work to the disadvantage of some of the Caribbean territories. Be it noted here that in the recent arbitration between the United Kingdom and France (1977), the Court observed that the notion of proportionality was not a specific principle of customary international law.

Another problem concerns the possibility of overlapping regimes. Suppose you have a situation where the natural prolongation of state A's continental shelf extends beyond the median line separating it from state B. The creation of an exclusive economic zone by state B may well result in the superimposition of one regime above the other. Thus, state A will have the natural prolongation of its territory stretching to about twenty or thirty miles from the coast of state B. State B would have jurisdiction over the superjacent waters up to the median line, whereas state A would exercise jurisdiction over the seabed of the natural prolongation of its continental shelf. Such a phenomenon will not be uncommon, given the volcanic origin of many of the islands, and it can certainly create administrative problems in the area. I think, myself, that the delimitation issue is one which is very important in the Caribbean and one which we shall hear quite a lot of in the future.

The last issue and possibly a very difficult one is the problem of the living resources of the Caribbean—the conservation and management thereof. I think it is useful to recall the story of the exclusive economic zone. As you know, it used to be called the patrimonial sea in Latin America, and one tends to forget that this regime was basically a Third World response to distant water fishing fleets. In other words, this concept actually may not have got off the ground, had it not received the support of the Third World. Here, one of the two motifs of the conference—the conflict of interests between developing and developed worlds—comes into play. The concept was supported by developing countries. The notion of solidarity forced many Third World countries to follow the bandwagon and support the concept, sometimes disregarding their own interests. If you look at the Proceedings of the Santo Domingo Conference, you will see that even then countries like Jamaica and Barbados had their doubts about the concept, simply because they felt that they did not possess worthwhile resources in their exclusive economic zones. At least they felt they would be thrown out of other peoples' exclusive economic zones, expecially from the waters off the continental states of the Caribbean. What has happened, it seems to me, is that states have been taking a position based more on geography than on politics. Geography has made strange bedfellows.

This development has posed a serious problem for the Third Law of the Sea Conference. The fact is that most of the islands of the Caribbean fall in the group of landlocked and geographically disadvantaged states as far as living resources are concerned. Let us now look at what is being offered in the ICNT, in Article 70 particularly, to certain developing coastal states. You will notice that Article 70 is subject to Articles 61 and 62. The point here is that these states possess a right to participate only in the surplus of the allowable catch. Well, in every developing state the objective of having a fisheries industry is to ensure the utilization of the surplus. In other words, the fact of creating a fishing industry is to see that there will be no surplus. That is the whole object of the exercise. Thus, these islands have to face the fact that they may be phased out, if the very objective of a fishing industry is attained.

Before ending, I would like to make a few political points. I am not a politician, but I think I could make some commonsense observations. We know that the extent to which the Caribbean would act as a region in maritime matters would depend on the level of integration in the Caribbean. Regionalism depends not so much on geography, but to a large extent on politics and economics. I am afraid that since the failure of the Caribbean Federation there has generally been a disenchantment with regionalism in the Caribbean—a factor that could influence the type of response the Caribbean states will make to some of their maritime problems. There is another factor. Some of the Caribbean territories are independent; for example, Jamaica, Grenada, Barbados, and Haiti. There are those that are dependent; for instance, Guadeloupe, Martinique, and certain Dutch islands. There are others that enjoy an "associated status" with the United Kingdom; for example, Antigua, St. Vincent, and Dominica. The fact that these islands enjoy such diverse political constitutions also creates some difficulties for effective regional arrangements in the area.

Judith Kildow: Thank you very much, Mr. Nelson. I would like now to introduce Dr. Alberto Szekely, who is here, at my request, on short notice. Dr. Szekely will be responding in part to Mr. Rozental's paper and also to Mr. Nelson's remarks. He is a research fellow at the Institute of Legal Studies at the University of Mexico and legal adviser to the Mexican Undersecretary of Foreign Affairs for law of the sea matters. He has a Ph.D. in international law from the University of London and is a member of the Mexican delegation to UNCLOS III. I would like to present to you Dr. Szekely.

Commentary

Alberto Szekely
Institute of Legal Studies
University of Mexico

Perhaps I might try to identify the aspects of Mr. Rozental's presentation that I think deserve most consideration. First of all, he has brought the idea of the separation of the Gulf and the Caribbean as two different areas except for environmental purposes. One of the important points here is that we already have some implementation of the new law of the sea within the Gulf of Mexico. Events have really overtaken any possibility of other forms of regional action, because there has been intense negotiating activity among the coastal states of the Gulf of Mexico. There is the fact that they have already disposed of the living resources, so to speak, especially the most important ones, through bilateral agreements. Mostly, the surpluses of Mexico have been assigned in this way to the United States and Cuba, largely because these are the countries that have traditionally fished in the Gulf of Mexico. Those surpluses will soon diminish (especially in the very important case of shrimp) and eventually disappear entirely, making the 200-mile zone of Mexico a genuinely exclusive zone. The fact that they have delimited their maritime spaces, albeit on a provisional basis, gives us a clear idea of the independent identity of the Gulf of Mexico, at least from the point of view of the coastal states. They have already implemented some of the provisions that have been informally agreed upon at the Law of the Sea Conference, and we have in fact a new law of the sea being implemented in that region. So, I think that the idea of separating the two areas of the so-called American Mediterranean deserves some comment from the floor, which could really be very helpful in understanding whether this thesis advanced by Mr. Rozental is valid.

Another interesting idea that I think deserves a lot of consideration is his suggestion that because of ecological unity of the living resources of the Caribbean, they should be regarded as if they were migratory species. In other words, all living species in the Caribbean should be subjected to the provision of Article 64 of the ICNT. That would mean that the two objectives of Article 64, namely, conservation and optimum utilization, should be applied through regional arrangements to the living resources of the Caribbean. I see in this interesting suggestion an opportunity to reduce the divisiveness that might arise from different cultural perspectives in the region: differences, for example, between the Anglo and the Latin countries of the Caribbean in interpreting the new law of the sea. For instance, it might seem contradictory to expect that the Central American countries of the Caribbean would be willing to form a pool of resources, to mingle their sovereign rights over the living resources of the Caribbean, when at the same time in the Pacific the same Latin American countries are proposing a system for dealing with true "highly migratory" species, especially yellow fin tuna—which does not really correspond to the more idealistic purposes of Article 64, in the way of regionalism. What I am trying to say is that in the Pacific some Central American countries (e.g., Costa Rica and Mexico) are proposing an international system in which the two objectives of Article 64 will be allegedly fulfilled, but within a system in which national allocations will be the name of the game. That is, in implementing Article 64 in the case of tuna resources in the Pacific, instead of regarding these true migratory species as a common resource, they are dividing them according to the principle of resource adjacency. So it would seem too idealistic to expect that they will be willing to deal with the resources off their Caribbean coasts in a different way: on one side, under a system of national quotas and on the other, under a system of common resources. The Anglo islands of the Caribbean will probably have a different interpretation of Article 64 than the one that the Central American countries have for the highly migratory species in the Pacific. They will probably tend, if the migratory species idea is applied to the living resources of the Caribbean, to look at these resources as a true common resource, and therefore they would probably tend to prefer the first alternative that Mr. Rozental proposed, that is, instead of a joint exploitation of surpluses, a joint exploitation of all resources, regardless of the catch capacity of each country. In any case, I think that the experience of the Central American countries in the Pacific should be taken into account when analyzing their possible attitude toward a condominium in the Caribbean.

Finally, with regard to some of the comments made by Dr. Nelson, I should point out that we are probably spending too much time in dealing with the delimitation problems. If the main subject of this conference is regionalism, I do not think we should spend too much time on delimitation problems, because this is essentially a bilateral problem and not a regional one. Even if the countries of the Caribbean agreed to the idea of a condominium or a matrimonial sea, I think that they would still want to delimit their own exclusive economic zone through bilateral arrangements. Once these bilateral arrangements are concluded, the problem of mineral allocation will be clarified. As Mr. Rozental said, minerals would not be subjected to a regional management system. For the problem of fisheries, I do not think delimitation within a regional concept has much bearing on the subject.

These are some of the points I think should be taken into account in this debate. I think too it is about time to give substance, as Mr. Rozental says, to the concept of a matrimonial sea. I also agree with him that it it not unlikely that some country or group of countries in the Caribbean will eventually take the initiative for regionalizing the administration of the living resources of the Caribbean despite the political obstacles and despite the differences in political persuasions.

Discussion

Edward Miles: What I have to say will follow on some of the points raised by Dr. Nelson, and I will be somewhat skeptical of the possibilities outlined by Mr. Rozental and Dr. Szekely. What we know about distribution of living resources in the Caribbean Basin, particularly if we split the Gulf from the Caribbean, is that most of the resources are distributed along the northern coast of South America. Consequently, in reaction to the proposal of joint exploitation of living resources or regional surplus allocation, I can easily visualize the governments of Guyana, Colombia, Venezuela, and Brazil saying: "It's all very well for Mexico to propose this, since it's not their resources that are to be shared, but we have not the slightest interest in any regional alternatives of that kind." So I don't think that possibility stands a better chance than the proverbial snowball in hell!

To turn to the question of the behavior of the Central American countries that Dr. Szekely raised: Is there any necessary incompatability between the position taken by Central American countries (Costa Rica in particular) vis-à-vis tuna in the Eastern tropical Pacific as opposed to the resources in the Gulf? Not at all. We are dealing with different species, different behavior patterns, and one particularly salient fact is that in recent years there has been a shifting in fishing pattern on the part of the distant water fleets that has resulted in a very significant amount of tuna resources being taken outside of 200 miles. This means that a purely national approach to the allocation problem will result in significant losses for the coastal states and that, in the long run, the only possibility for the coastal states having a voice in the management beyond 200 miles will be a set of arrangements that are quite different from what one may think, looking at the relevant articles in the ICNT.

With respect to the Caribbean, given the biogeography of the island arcs of the Greater and Lesser Antilles, the question of access for Jamaica, Trinidad, and Barbados will be solved only in relationship to the question of what each party has to trade. If the Jamaicans have significant resources which need not necessarily be marine, in relation to Guyana and Colombia, then deals are possible. If they do not, deals are not possible. If Trinidad has significant resources relative to Venezuela and Brazil, the same is true. If they do not, the same is true. In the case of Barbados, with significantly more limited possibilities than either Trinidad or Jamaica, the outlook is very bleak indeed. With respect to economic integration, the outlook is not much better. Trinidad has tried this for some years now, within the context of the Law of the Sea Conference, with a conspicuous lack of success. Here we deal with questions not only of the infrastructure, that is, the low density of interrelationships between the various countries involved, the differences in culture, etc., but also with some very difficult foreign policy objectives of the players involved. In particular, these involve certain rivalries between the major players, and here I would include on the English-speaking side, Guyana, Jamaica, and Trinidad, and on the Spanish-speaking side, Brazil and Venezuela, and in particular the conflicts between Trinidad and Venezuela. The more Trinidad becomes suspicious of Venezuela, it seems the more these suspicions are shared by the Brazilians, and then deals are facilitated between Trinidad and Brazil that seem to be much easier to arrive at than any settlement of outstanding problems between Trinidad and Venezuela. It also seems, or at least so Trinidad claims, that Venezuela has attempted to upset the economic integration applecart arranged between Trinidad, Guyana, and Jamaica for the consolidation of aluminum mining production and processing by offering Jamaica a better deal on the price of energy than Trinidad has, and it seems that Jamaica was more disposed to take the Venezuelan offer. In turn, Trinidadians claimed that the Jamaicans reneged on an agreement, and at this point it seems that the Brazilians became a little more open-handed with the Trinidadians. So there, I think, the second dimension of economic integration goes down the same hole as the first alternative: that is, joint exploitation of living resources or regional surplus allocation.

Now we come to the third and last question: splitting the Gulf from the Caribbean. From the point of view of Mexico, this of course makes good sense, and since the Mexicans are extremely capable negotiators one would not have predicted any other response; in fact, one would have been very greatly surprised if there had been another response. But, from the point of view of the other countries involved in the Greater and Lesser Antilles, this is not necessarily a good idea. If you split the Gulf from the Caribbean, what do they have to trade in terms of regional programs? Very little. If both living and nonliving resources are out, what is left? Environmental protection certainly, scientific research, technical assistance in port development, etc. Where is the money going to come from? The international community? Not likely. The WECAFC and

CARIBE are very weak vessels. Where is the money going to come from? The only possibility is the United States, with which in effect one makes deals for access to do scientific research in return for assistance with environmental protection, resource development, etc. If you split the Gulf from the Caribbean, then from the U.S. point of view it seems to me the situation is much less attractive than if you keep them together, and, therefore, it is very unlikely that you can produce significant amounts of money from U.S. sources, in particular, the Office of Management and Budget and the Congress.

In short, I do not find the proposal very attractive.

Alberto Szekely: You use very convincing arguments to show that joint exploitation of resources in the Caribbean would be a very difficult undertaking, and at the same time, you do not agree with severing the Gulf from the Caribbean only on the basis of environmental action. What else is there, if we do not have joint exploitation of living resources? What other basis do we have to keep them together, other than the environmental one?

Edward Miles: The political one, in the nature of trade-off. Otherwise you have no basis for building long-range alternatives.

Alberto Szekely: I would like to have a more substantial example of what the political basis would be. What would the countries of the region gain by keeping them together? What is the political gain?

Edward Miles: The gain will go to the countries of the Greater and Lesser Antilles, and some gains will flow to the United States. From Mexico's point of view, there are only costs. From the point of view of the countries from the northern part of South America, there are only costs.

Alberto Szekely: You are agreeing then that living resources should not be the basis for keeping them together?

Edward Miles: I would say they *will not*—not should not—be the basis.

Alberto Szekely: Then I really do not identify from your arguments what would be the much stronger reason for keeping them together. One of them, I think we both agree, is regional action for dealing with the preservation of the marine environment in both areas.

Edward Miles: This is the weak one.

Alberto Szekely: Which is the strong one?

Edward Miles: There isn't any.

Alberto Szekely: So you basically agree that they should be separated, because there is no reason to keep them linked?

Edward Miles: You posit an alternative for the Caribbean—what has been called "Caribbean dominion"—and you suggest how this would be achieved, or at least some of the alternatives. The burden of my argument is that those are *not* possible. The only possibility could be if you combined the Gulf and the Caribbean, but then the way in which the trade-offs are distributed, from Mexico's point of view, makes this not a very attractive situation. So that, in terms of my outlook, the recent developments in regional marine arrangements in the Caribbean are not very significant.

Judith Kildow: I think what we have is a basic difference of opinion, based on cultural and national perspectives. Can we have some more questions, please?

Chong-Il Chee: I was intrigued by the term used by Mr. Rozental: matrimonial zone. Some of you may have read the article written by Gardia Amador in 1974, where he makes a distinction in Latin American practice between four kinds of maritime zones: patrimonial, maritime, epi-continental, and territorial. Now I have never head of a matrimonial sea. The situation seems to have changed, perhaps as a result of the women's liberation movement, on behalf of motherhood. Has there been any change in the legal content? Second, in Latin American practice, there are differences in the balance struck between freedom of navigation, freedom of overflight, and so forth, on the one hand, and coastal control in the territorial sea, patrimonial sea, etc., on the other hand. Some sort of uniform standard seems desirable, if state practice is to mature into customary international law. I would appreciate a comment on this from Mr. Rozental or Dr. Szekely. Third, this concept of the prolongation of the land mass, referred to by Dr. Nelson, disturbs me. It does not help as far as I can see. Since the 1969 Continental Shelf Case, there seems to be a movement in the direction of the margin, conceived as part of the regime of the continental shelf.

Andrés Rozental: I will try to answer the question about the term "matrimonial sea," although there is somebody else in this room who knows more about it: that's Professor Alexander, who remembers when the concept first came out. To tell you the truth, it was considered a joke in the beginning. Nowadays the term is sometimes used to refer to an area that might be designated for communal exploitation of adjoining resources, where it would be economically more sensible to work together. It was called "matrimonial" to distinguish it from the "patrimonial sea," which was a popular term for the unshared approach at that time. As regards the comments on the natural prolongation of the land mass, I think Dolliver Nelson, who talked about it earlier, would be in a better position to answer.

Dolliver Nelson: All I was saying was that there are certain instances in the Caribbean where you have a natural prolongation of land territory extending beyond a median line. The consequence of this may be that the median line used for delimiting the exclusive economic zones between the coasts of the two states may not be the same as the line delimiting the seabed area. The consequence of this would surely be that the seabed area would enjoy a different legal regime from the superjacent waters, which may cause a problem. On the point that Dr. Szekely made that delimitation has nothing to do with the semi-enclosed sea, I would remind him that in the debate at Caracas on enclosed and semi-enclosed seas, the delimitation issue was mentioned several times by speakers from a number of countries: Thailand, Iran, Turkey, Algeria, and others. They seem to have believed it had something to do with the nature of these areas.

Chapter Five

Regional Factors in Managing Marine Resources after the Third UN Conference of the Law of the Sea: A European View

Renate Platzöder
Institute for International Affairs
Ebenhausen, Germany, F.R.

Judith Kildow: We are honored to have with us from Germany Dr. Renate Platzöder, who will be presenting a paper on current law of the sea developments in the European Community. She is currently a staff member at the Institute for International Affairs, which is located near Munich, Germany, This institute acts in an advisory role to the federal government in foreign affairs and security matters. She has also been a member of the German Delegation to the Law of the Sea Conference since 1974.

After she finishes her presentation, we have two other panelists who will also be discussing EEC matters. We are happy to have with us Mr. Michael Hardy, legal adviser to the Commission of the European Community, where he deals with legal aspects of the external relations of the Community. Before going to the European Community in 1973, he was with the UN Office of Legal Affairs, where he followed law of the sea topics for many years. He will discuss the external fisheries policies of the EEC. After he is finished, Dr. Albert Koers will discuss the internal fisheries policies of the EEC where there have been a number of important developments recently. Dr. Koers teaches international law at the University of Utrecht, and in addition he is an adviser to the European Commission, particularly on law of the sea and fishery matters. He is also a member of the delegation of the commission to the UN Law of the Sea Conference. So we have a very distinguished panel and I think they will have a number of issues and new ideas to offer you. May I present Dr. Platzöder.

Dr. Renate Platzöder: While preparing my paper, I often wished Europe were a political unity and a mid-ocean archipelago like Hawaii and that the changes in the new law of the sea could be applied to it to the same extent, without being complicated by neighboring state jurisdiction everywhere in the region.

As you all know, the new law of the sea was not initiated in Europe. The revolution of maritime power relationships began in 1945 with two gentle drum beats, when President Truman announced his famous proclamations. They were soon interpreted by Latin American states in a very simple manner, resulting in the 200-mile exclusive economic zone concept. Several years later a new principle of international law was widely agreed upon, the continental shelf principle. Against all logic, which is supposed to be an inherent element of legal thinking, the continental shelves are distributed exclusively among the coastal states according to the length and configuration of their respective coasts. Thus, in Europe, where one can count thirty-five states, only the Soviet Union, Norway, Portugal, Spain, United Kingdom, Iceland, Ireland, and France can claim a substantial portion of the European continental shelf. Nine landlocked states are denied any part thereof. One can draw from this new approach to the law of the sea that the development of the regime for the seabed is based on an archaic concept: there must be losers and winners. There is a minority of states that are more equal than others. This two-class system has since developed. Judged by the Informal Composite Negotiating Text, it has spread like a disease.

Let me give you some examples. There are normal baselines and archipelagic baselines. Two different regimes apply to international straits innocent passage and transit passage. There are high seas freedoms in the exclusive economic zone, which is defined as not being part of the high seas, and there are high seas freedoms on the high seas. Furthermore, two criteria for the delimitation of the continental shelf have been defined: the outer edge of the continental margin criterion and the 200-mile distance criterion. Some coastal states have to share some of their living resources and nonliving resources with certain third states, while others have no such obligation. The coastal states are subdivided into coastal states bordering the enclosed or semi-enclosed seas and coastal states bordering the oceans. There are coastal states that have rights and legitimate interests with respect to resource deposits in the International Seabed Area. And then there is the strange notion of an overall differentiation of developed and developing states to be written into law, sure to petrify a two-class political, economic, and social system. In addition, there is a presumption in favor of the European Socialist states that at least one of them is among four countries that make the greatest contributions to deep seabed mining; and there is another assumption, without any obligation of proof, that at least one of the European Socialist states is among the four major importers of deep seabed minerals. Finally, there is the highly privileged Enterprise of the International Seabed Authority in contrast to the underprivileged position of states parties and other entities engaged in deep seabed mining.

Yet, according to the preamble of the ICNT it is believed that this codification and progressive development of the law of the sea will contribute to the maintenance of international peace and security. How this is to be accomplished on the basis of the ICNT remains to be seen. UNCLOS III has not yet concluded its work, mainly because of the struggle over the so-called common heritage of mankind, which lies beyond the limits of national jurisdiction. Nevertheless, an evolving law of the sea already throws long shadows over the resources within the limits of national jurisdiction. The three informal texts produced by UNCLOS III so far encourage coastal states to extend their jurisdiction over marine resources. Should UNCLOS III fail to conclude a convention, the ICNT or its successor will most probably serve as a guide for the further evolution of the law of the sea. Unfortunately, the marine resources within the limits of national jurisdiction have not been declared part of a regional common heritage. In case UNCLOS III produces a convention that is unbalanced and does not reflect the political and economic realities that prevail outside the United Nations building, the provisions of such a convention will need adaptation to the local and regional conditions and power structures. In Europe at least, the aftermath of UNCLOS III has already begun.

I now shall examine various factors that play, or might play, an important role in managing marine resources in Europe. Maybe I should admit at this stage that I had considerable difficulty in finding factors that might be an incentive to regional management: most factors seem more likely to impede the management of resources. First of all, there is a problem of a general nature. Europe's fundamental political, economic, and social problem has always been a relative lack of natural resources. The various needs and demands usually exceeded the supply of available resources, contributing to national rivalry and competition, and often to bitter conflict throughout the long and stirring history of Europe. The present, relatively peaceful, era is quite an exception.

Second, there are legal factors. As long as the traditional law of the sea, based on a three-mile territorial sea and the high sea freedoms beyond, was applied, the European waters could be considered a common fishing pond. The management of the fishery resources in the Baltic Sea, the North Sea, the Bering Sea, the Northeast Atlantic, the Black Sea, and the Mediterranean Sea was accomplished more or less satisfactorily through bilateral and multilateral arrangements. Due to the fact that a substantial amount of fish is caught within the six- or twelve-mile zone, the extension of exclusive coastal state fishery jurisdiction out to such a limit has drastic consequences. For example, in the North Sea about 50 percent of the total catch comes from waters within twelve miles. According to the provisions of the ICNT, there is no obligation whatsoever to ensure the conservation of such stocks. Another feature of the European fishing pond is that non-European fishermen do not fish there. The introduction of a 200-mile zone is quite a radical measure to redistribute the same fish among the same fishermen. Difficulties arise from the fact that major fishing grounds fall within the 200-mile zone of Iceland and Norway, two countries with a small population (200,000 and 3.9 million respectively). The introduction of the 200-mile zone by Iceland in 1975 not only started a series of 200-mile claims, but also initiated the transfer of conflicts from one European subregion to another.

Several unsettled legal disputes are factors in the management of marine resources in Europe. The Turkish-Greek dispute involves the continental shelf in the Aegean Sea. The situation there is unique. Many Greek islands are located as far as 200 miles from the Greek mainland, even within twenty-four miles of the Turkish coast. Under a six-mile territorial sea, Turkey has five open outlets to the Aegean Sea; under a twelve-mile limit, only two. This problem, mainly a question of access to the sea, is complicated by the fact that substantial oil deposits have been discovered in the Aegean Sea. Greece and Turkey granted exploration and exploitation licenses without agreeing on the delimitation of the seabed. Turkey argues that the Greek islands have no continental shelf of their own. According to the Turkish argument, a great number of Greek islands lie on the natural prolongation of the Turkish coast.

In another dispute, between Sweden and the Soviet Union over the delimitation of the seabed in the Baltic Sea, oil and military interests are at stake. In the middle of the Baltic Sea there is a Swedish island called Goatland. For more than eight years the Soviet Union and Sweden have quarreled over the sea boundary in the vicinity of Goatland. Sweden advocates the equal distance criterion whereby the baseline of the Swedish mainland would serve as a starting point. The Soviet Union is of the opinion that the baselines of the island of Goatland have to be the starting point. The deadlock in these negotiations, and the introduction of a 200-mile fishery zone in the North Sea, led to the Swedish decision to extend her fishing limits in the Baltic Sea on January 1, 1978. According to this Swedish law, the boundary is deemed to lie midway between Goatland and the Soviet coast, with the result that about 45 percent of the Baltic Sea would come under Swedish jurisdiction. So far, Sweden has caught only 10 percent of the annual catch of fish in the Baltic waters.

The Barents Sea is another area of legal conflict. The Soviet Union does not want to see Western fishing vessels and oil rigs in the Barents Sea, since they would obtain a close view of her military activities there. The Soviet port of Murmansk is of extreme importance to the Soviet Union. It is the only ice-free port from which Soviet vessels cna proceed to operational areas in the NATO area without first passing through territorial waters of NATO member-states. Surveyance and control of the relatively narrow, unfrozen passage by foreign states seems to be a nightmare to the Soviet Union even in an era of détente. The Soviet-Norwegian continental shelf negotiations are accompanied by Soviet missile testing in the area under dispute, which is about 160,000 square kilometers in size. This rocket diplomacy has not yet resulted in an agreement on the continental shelf issue, but has stimulated negotiations for an agreement on fisherines in the same area. The draft agreement provides for a gray zone, a zone to be commonly fished and managed. The zone has a rather odd shape, molded as it is by various elements involved in the dispute over the delimitation of the seabed of the Barents Sea: the sector principle, the equidistance criterion, and the outer limit of the Norwegian and Soviet 200-mile zones. There is also a line drawn parallel to the proposed sector line by the Soviet Union, moving the latter considerably to the west. It has to be feared that such a fishery agreement is most likely to project further continental shelf negotiations.

Another problem in the northern region is that of the Spitzbergen archipelago. In the Spitzbergen Treaty of 1921, forty nations confirmed Norway's sovereign rights over the archipelago subject to certain conditions. One is demilitarization. Another condition is that all states parties and their nationals are entitled to exploit the mineral and living resources on equal terms with Norwegian nationals. The crucial questions in the light of the development of the law of the sea are the following: Does the Spitzbergen Treaty apply to the continental shelf of the Spitzbergen archipelago and to its 200-mile zone? The Norwegian position is that the Spitzbergen archipelago has no continental shelf of its own, and the treaty applies only to the territorial waters. The argument is very similar to the Turkish position in respect to the Greek islands in the Aegean Sea. So far, only a few states parties to the Spitzbergen Treaty have declared reservations with respect to the Norwegian position.

A further factor in managing marine resources in Europe is dispute settlement. Judicial decisions have played an important role in the distribution and redistribution of marine resources in Europe. In 1969, the International Court of Justice gave its judgment in the North Sea Continental Shelf Case. Accordingly, the parties concerned—the Federal Republic of Germany, Denmark, and the Netherlands—established their seabed boundaries in the North Sea continental shelf. In 1972, the Court dealt with the Fisheries Jurisdiction Case. Britain and the Federal Republic of Germany had instituted proceedings against Iceland, after Iceland had extended its exclusive fisheries jurisdiction to fifty miles. Iceland questioned the jurisdiction of the International Court of Justice without appearing in court. Consequently, Iceland did not accept the Court's judgment to the effect that the parties concerned were under a mutual obligation to undertake negotiations in good faith for the equitable solution of their differences, and that Iceland was not entitled to exclude unilaterally British and German fishing vessels from the disputed area. Very recently the Court of Justice of the European Communities had to deal with its first fishery case. Ireland claimed a fifty-mile fishery zone and captured a Dutch fishing vessel. According to the Court's judgment, Ireland is not entitled to claim such zones. The court held that the Irish actions were contrary to the European Community's laws and regulations with regard to the establishment of a common fishery zone.

There are also political factors in the management of marine resources, such as these: the political and ideological division of Europe; the U.S.-Soviet relationship; the American interests in Western Europe; the Western European and Soviet relationship; and last, but not least, the Third World. It is evident that an elaborate analysis of these factors would take a few hours, and so I shall confine myself to a few remarks when I come to the second part of my paper.

A fourth category of regional factors in managing marine resources in Europe are the regional intergovernmental organizations: the Council of Europe, the European Free Trade Association, the Nordic Council, and the European Communities. Two of these regional intergovernmental organizations participated in UNCLOS III as observers: the Council of Europe and the European Communities. They already play an important role in managing marine resources. The nine member states of the European Communities agreed in 1976 to the establishment of a common fishery zone. The Parliamentary Assembly of the Council of Europe passed a recommendation presented by the Legal Affairs Committee. The recommendation calls, first, for steps to facilitate the settlement of maritime disputes or conflicts between its members. Second, it proposes a European code for offshore operations to provide for the alignment and harmonization of national provisions governing the conduct of such operations. Third, the recommendation calls for measures to protect the European marine heritage, including the archaeological heritage buried by the sea. The Council of Europe now has twenty member states, Spain being the latest to join the organization. The accommodation of rights and interests of all states in the region or subregion in managing marine resources will certainly need a major effort. In Europe, out of a total of thirty-five states, eighteen states are members of the landlocked and geographically disadvantaged group, the most-hated interest group of UNCLOS III. The provisions of the ICNT in respect to the exclusive economic zone and the continental shelf do not take sufficiently into consideration the interests of this group. To the majority of coastal states, the group is an annoying mishap, and many efforts have been undertaken by developing and developed states to eliminate it as a bargaining bloc. In Western Europe, at least, there is an organization that may be able to deal with this problem, which remains unsolved by UNCLOS III: the Council of Europe. I have noticed, with great surprise, that the group of landlocked and geographically disadvantaged states has been referred to by all speakers here in Honolulu in a positive way.

Under a fifth category of factors in managing marine resources would fall intergovernmental organizations whose scope reaches beyond any precise region, such as the Organization for Economic Cooperation and Development, the North Atlantic Treaty Organization, the Warsaw Pact, and theCouncil for Mutual Economic Assistance. But here too any useful analysis would take another few hours.

The regional zone concept as an alternative to the exclusive economic zone concept has had no significance at UNCLOS III. During the early 1970s, the regional zone concept was discussed among the African states and in the group of landlocked and geographically disadvantaged states. As we all know, the rights and interests of the numerous African states having either no coast or a very short one were sacrificed for the solidarity of the Group of 77, making an exclusive economic zone concept possible. The ICNT contains, however, two major regional approaches with respect to the management of marine resources: namely, the provisions on highly migratory species and those on enclosed and semi-enclosed seas. The ICNT devotes two articles (122 and 123) to the latter. In Europe, the Baltic Sea, the Black Sea, the North Sea, and the Mediterranean

Sea will fall under the definition of Article 122. The seven states bordering the Baltic Sea have influenced the formulation of this definition, but it is not the intention of the Soviet Union that it should be interpreted as including the Mediterranean Sea.

In addition to those two regional approaches, the member states of the European Communities have suggested the inclusion in the convention of a so-called "European Community clause," which in effect is a generally applicable clause providing that customs unions, communities, and other regional economic associations exercising powers in the areas covered by the convention may be parties to the convention. The member states of the European Communities attach great importance to the inclusion of such a clause. According to the Treaty of Rome, the constitution of the European Communities, the member states transferred their competencies in various areas of marine policy covered by UNCLOS III. Therefore, the member states cannot undertake engagements with respect to third states on matters such as fisheries and marine pollution. This legal situation requires that the European Communities become a party to the law of the sea convention, together with the member states. The proposed clause has, unfortunately, not been included in the ICNT, although the European Communities have been recognized as an entity of international law by at least half of the United Nations member states, namely, those that have concluded trade agreements with the European Communities.

One can draw from the law of the sea negotiations the conclusion that incentives to regional or subregional management of marine resources are only a few. Nevertheless, in Europe several attempts at regional management have been made. The North Sea is not only a rich fish pond: it also contains oil and gas. The bordering states of the North Sea have divided the seabed of the North Sea by means of bilateral agreements among one another. The result is that there are "haves" and "have nots" with respect to oil and gas. Britain and Norway came out as the lucky two. Nevertheless, the exploration and exploitation of the North Sea oil and gas was undertaken in an international effort. Extreme weather conditions and other natural features were a challenge to the oil industry. High production costs called for risk sharing. Thus, the North Sea became an international market for offshore technology, investment, and insurance. Nature gave an additional incentive to cooperation and distribution of oil and gas among the bordering states in the North Sea. The rough weather conditions do not permit safe operation of vessels throughout the year. Pipelines had to be installed. The Norwegian Trough, a deep trench off the Norwegian coast, did not permit the laying of pipelines. The oil and gas of the Norwegian Ecofisk field flows through pipelines to Britain and Germany.

Though no regional authority handles exploration, exploitation, and marketing of North Sea oil and gas, the situation can be considered as an example of de facto international regional management. However, the trend is moving backwards. Britain and Norway have set up national oil corporations to control and nationalize oil and gas production and marketing. Relations between the international oil companies and their host government have undergone changes. The need for foreign technology and capital creates some leverage against complete nationalization. In Britain, however, a law was passed providing for subsidies or loans to companies using "Made in Britain" equipment and services. This law has worked especially against the other members of the European Communities. Only very recently, five continental oil companies lodged a complaint with the European Economic Community, saying that such measures are discriminatory and, thus, inconsistent with the Community laws. A justification for the British national attitude is, above all, the oil prices of 1973 to 1974, when governments became aware that they were not in control of energy supplies. Britain, Norway, and France have often expressed the view that the exploitation of oil and gas in their sectors of the continental shelf will have to be conducted in accordance with their own national interests. This basic attitude is the main factor responsible for the failure to establish a common energy supply policy, which could have served as a stimulus to regional management.

Second, the seven coastal states of the Baltic Sea signed in 1973 the Convention on Fishing and Conservation of the Living Resources in the Baltic and the Belts. The Belts are the outlet of the Baltic Sea. The convention came into force one year later. A Baltic fishery commission was established, having its seat in Warsaw. In 1974 the seven coastal states signed the Convention on the Protection of the Marine Environment of the Baltic Sea Area. This convention is not yet in force. The conclusion of these two conventions shortly before UNCLOS III is remarkable. The states concerned intended to influence the law of the sea negotiations and to avoid the application of the evolving 200-mile economic zone concept. The Baltic fishery convention applies to all waters of the Baltic Sea except internal waters. The Swedish decision to claim a 200-mile fishery zone is not primarily intended to impede regional management of the fishery resources in the Baltic Sea. The main purpose seems to have been to secure a bargaining chip in the deep seabed negotiations with the Soviet Union and to obtain a better chance of getting a higher fish quota. The major obstacle to effective regional management of the living resources of the Baltic Sea is the political and ideological division of Europe. The Soviet Union, Poland, and the German Democratic Republic declared themselves in favor of transforming the Baltic Sea into a model zone of peace and good neighborly cooperation. In their view it is not inconsistent with this goal that the Warsaw Pact navies are steadily moving westward.

A third factor is the Mediterranean Sea. The living resources of the Mediterranean Sea are still managed through bilateral agreements. The main problem here is pollution, eighteen states having a total population of about 100 million bordering the Mediterranean Sea. In addition, about the same number of tourists come every year to enjoy the Mediterranean sun and water. The sea, however, is heavily polluted by landbased sources and oil tankers, especially since the reopening of the Suez Canal. In combating marine pollution, the Barcelona Convention signed by twelve states in 1972 is the first achievement. The second step toward cleaning up the Mediterranean Sea followed in October 1977. Under the sponsorship of the United Nations Environment Program, thirteen Mediterranean countries have accepted a complete ban on certain chemicals (plastics, used oil, and radioactive waste) and agreed on a gray list. The discharge of copper, lead, cobalt, and other metals is only allowed under governmental licenses.

Fourth, I come finally to the fishery zone of the European Economic Community. The basic aims of the European Economic Community are for a free movement of goods, the establishment of common customs and tariffs, and the elimination of quantitative restrictions on importation between member states. The Common Market extends to agriculture and trade in agricultural products; free movement of persons, services, and capital; and freedom of establishment of nationals of member states in the territory of another member state. Accordingly, a common market for fishery products was established. The member states agreed on a common structural policy for the fishing industry. In October 1976 the nine foreign ministers of the European Communities decided that the member states bordering the North Sea and the North Atlantic shall declare in a concerted action a common fishery zone. Accordingly, the nine member states now share, since January 1, 1977, a common fishing pond of 200,070 square miles.

The common zone consists legally of separate national zones. According to the act concerning the conditions of accession and adjustment of the treaties, enacted on the occasion of the first enlargement of the European Communities, the member states are authorized until December 31, 1982 to restrict fishing in waters within a six-mile zone to those vessels that have traditionally fished there and that operate from ports in that six-mile zone. In certain areas of Denmark, France, Ireland, and Britain, the six-mile limit may be extended to twelve miles. To put the common fishery zone in effect, an internal regime and a policy toward third states is necessary. So the decision of the Nine to establish a common fishery zone must be considered as quite a bold step. It departs from the usual practice, where first a common denominator is agreed upon and then actions affecting those states are undertaken. In the case of the common fishery zones, the opposite happend. The Nine agreed on a policy toward third states very quickly. The rule is that fishing quotas are only given on a reciprocal basis. The internal regime is still under dispute. The first part of the achievement has been a short-term conservation measure. A total ban on herring fisheries in certain areas of the North Sea has been agreed upon. The Commission of the European Economic Community proposed a cut in the total catch of fish in the zone to 3.9 million tons in 1978. In 1976, 4.5 million tons had been fished. The Commission suggested that only 750,000 tons should be licensed to third states in 1978. Britain, Ireland, Denmark, and the Federal Republic of Germany however, made strong objections to the Commission's proposals. Britain and Ireland insist on a fifty-mile national zone within the common zone. Denmark and the

Federal Republic of Germany do not agree to the proposed quotas. In 1975, German fishermen caught 440,000 tons in the waters which come now under the common fisheries regime. The commission suggested that German fishermen be given a quota of 100,000 in 1978. It is obvious that it would be quite a job for the German administration to explain to their fishermen that 100,000 tons out of 3.3 million is a fair share.

The accommodation of fishing interests in the common zone will depend to a large extent on the Commission's ability to conclude fishery agreements on a reciprocal basis, and fishery agreements on a nonreciprocal basis. As to the first category, it is intended to trade different species, for example, mackerel and cod. The Soviet Union has a big market for mackerel; the European Economic Community a big market for cod. The second category includes fishery agreements such as that concluded between the European Communities and the United States in early 1977. The commission, however, will have to negotiate with African countries. the Lomé Agreement, a trade agreement between the European Economic Community and forty-six developing states, contains a joint declaration on fishing activities providing for fishery development under equal conditions and without distrimination.

The establishment of a common fishery zone must be considered as a positive step in the right direction to regional management of marine resources. The prerequisites are almost perfect—there is a basic treaty aimed at political and economic integration. The treaty is properly institutionalized. There is a common market; there are common funds to facilitate structural changes; there is a court to settle disputes. And last but not least, the European Economic Community is an expanding entity. Greece, Spain, and Portugal have applied for membership. Within the next few years the common fishery zone will be increased by about one million square kilometers. But there are also factors that seem to hamper the management of common fishery zones of the European Economic Community. The waters and the fish involved do not constitute an ideal fishing pond. The zone cuts across the North Sea and across the water of the North Atlantic. The fish do not respect political boundaries; thus, arrangements of the European Economic Community and nonmembers have to be made. Another hampering factor lies in the different political aspirations of the member states. At least one of them tries to dominate at any one moment. Oil, gas, or fish give a state the incentive to dominate. The others are more or less hesitant to put all their eggs in the Community basket. They are not any better.

Chapter Six

External Aspects of the Fisheries Policy of the European Community

Michael Hardy
Legal Adviser
Commission of the European Communities

First, let me say a word about the definition of the Community or Communities involved, since this issue is sometimes a source of confusion. This is the case even in Europe, so it would seem justified to explain this aspect beforehand to a meeting in Hawaii of law of the sea specialists. There are in fact three European Communities—the European Coal and Steel Community (ECSC), the European Atomic Energy Community (Euratom), and the European Economic Community (EEC). They were established separately, under separate treaties, but the institutions involved were merged under further instruments. The main organs therefore—the Commission, the Council, the Parliament, and the Court of Justice—are common institutions, serving all three Communities. For this reason there is a tendency, reflected in the title of the papers by Dr. Koers and myself, to refer to the "European Community" in the singular, without specifying which one, and to cover by so doing the range of institutional measures that may be involved. So far as law of the sea matters are concerned however, it is the European Economic Community (EEC) that is by far the most important. Certainly as regards the fisheries policy, this arises solely under the EEC Treaty; and if any one Community were to be singled out, it would be the European Economic Community. For convenience, and in accordance with fairly widespread practice, however, I have simply referred to "the Community."

The European Community is not an intergovernmental organization as that term is commonly used. It is a *sui generis* body, with powers that are directly applicable to citizens within the Community as well as to member states, powers that in most cases would by their nature normally be exercised only by states.

*The views expressed are put forward in a personal capacity.

The Community legal system exists, as the Court of Justice has emphasized, as a separate legal order, distinct from systems of national law and from the classic interstate arrangements of international law.[1] The common fisheries policy covers both activities in the waters round the coasts of the member states and fishing activities by Community vessels elsewhere—in other words, the exercise of the powers concerned may operate on a territorial basis or according to nationality in a way that is similar to the fisheries policy of a state. The waters in question include, besides those in Europe itself, the waters around Greenland, which is part of Denmark, and those of five French overseas departments: St. Pierre and Miquelon, Guyana, Guadeloupe, Martinique, and Réunion.[2]

Up until 1976 the major step taken by the Community to institute a common fisheries policy—other than the inclusion in the EEC Treaty signed in 1957 of fisheries products in the list of products coming within the common agricultural policy—consisted of the adoption in 1970 of two regulations, Regulation (EEC) No. 2141/70 and Regulation (EEC) No. 2142/70.[3] Regulation 2141/70 set up a common organization of the market in fisheries products, similar to that provided for other agricultural products, and deals chiefly with the operation of price arrangements. The other regulation relates to the conditions under which fishing may be conducted. Article 2 of Regulation 2141/70 provides that equal "conditions of access to and use of" the fishing grounds situated in member states' waters are to be ensured "for all fishing vessels flying the flag of a member state and registered in Community territory." The principle of "equal access" was thus established as the centerpiece of the system, subject to certain exceptions in favor of coastal fishermen that were included in the Act of Accession when Denmark, Ireland, and the United Kingdom entered the Community. Insofar as these arrangements concern the internal side of the common fisheries policy it is not necessary for me to go into them further, since they will be dealt with by Dr. Koers.

The fact that it had been recognized, as a matter of Community law, that access for fishing purposes to waters under the sovereignty or jurisdiction of member states was a Community matter was plainly of the utmost importance when it became clear that the member states would have to extend their fishing limits. In September 1976, in accordance with Community procedures whereby it is the Commission which makes proposals to the Council, on which the Council is then called on to decide, the Commission sent a communication to the Council drawing attention to the need for a Community response to the change which had occurred in fishing conditions, or was about to occur, through the establishment of fishing limits of 200 nautical miles. In order to safeguard the fishing interest of the Community it would be necessary, it was suggested, for member states to extend their limits in the North Sea and the Atlantic, these being the areas in which extensions had already taken place, or been announced, by other states in the region.[4] It was proposed that negotiations should be conducted with third states on a Community basis in respect of the entry of these states into member states' waters where the common fisheries policy applies ("Community waters"), or as regards fishing by vessels of member states in the waters of third states. Community responsibilities would also be engaged in the adaptation of the powers of the various fishery commissions, to which the Community as such would need to become a party. Broadly speaking, three categories of agreements with nonmember countries were envisaged:

1. Agreements with countries where the Community had an interest in fishing in their waters but whose fishermen did not traditionally fish in Community waters. Here the Community would seek to be treated at least as well as any other third country in the allocation of surplus fish stocks.
2. Agreements with countries with which the Community had extensive interlinked fishing interests, suggesting that reciprocal arrangements including, where appropriate, the coordination of measures to conserve fish stocks, would be required.
3. Agreements with countries that fish in Community waters but in whose waters Community fishermen have little interest. The basic objective here would be the progressive phasing out of the current fishing efforts of these countries.

These proposals were accepted by the Council, which adopted a set of resolutions on November 3, 1976 concerning both internal and external aspects of the common fisheries policy. It was agreed that, through concerted action, member states would establish 200-mile exclusive fisheries limits in the North Sea and Atlantic as from January 1, 1977. The Commission was authorized to open negotiations with the various third states in whose waters Community fishermen had an interest in fishing and with those states who wished to continue fishing in Community waters. Since the fishing capacity of the Community was sufficient to enable it to exploit the available stocks in the waters of the member states, the agreements authorizing third states to fish in Community waters would in any case not concern access to surplus stocks, but arrangements relating to access as determined by the coastal authority. Therefore, unless the third state had concluded an agreement with the Community it would not be allowed to fish in waters under the jurisdiction of member states—"no agreement" (or at the least, "no negotiations"), "no fish." In accordance with what seems to have become a standard practice, the agreements themselves were to be of a "framework" character, providing the structure and procedures for the arrangements, without specifying actual fishing quotas. These would be dealt with separately and be the subject of consultations between the parties, following internal deliberations by the coastal state.

Turning now to the negotiations that have been held, the following account is essentially no more than a checklist. It gives some idea, however, of the extent of the activity in which the Community has been engaged over the past year as regards external arrangements, involving a small staff on the Commission side and very frequent (at times daily) meetings of the representatives of the member states, besides the attention given to the internal side of the common fisheries policy and to the Law of the Sea Conference itself. The description can be grouped for convenience under five headings involving respectively: (1) the United States, French Guyana, and Canada; (2) the Scandinavian countries; (3) the USSR, the German Democratic Republic, and Poland; (4) Spain, Portugal, and Yugoslavia; and (5) various African countries.

1. *United States.* An agreement has been concluded between the Community and the United States, which follows the standard U.S. pattern, concerning access by Community fishermen to U.S. waters.[5]
   French Department of Guyana. No agreements have been concluded, but vessels of a number of countries, including the United States, Japan, and the Republic of Korea, have been authorized to fish for shrimp and tuna-like fish off Guyana pursuant to autonomous Community regulations, pending the negotiation of agreements.[6]
   Canada. Negotiations have not yet been concluded on an agreement relating to Community fishing in Canadian waters, although there have been a number of meetings. Provision will also need to be made to cover transboundary stocks in the waters between Canada and Greenland and in respect of fishing off St. Pierre and Miquelon.[7] Unlike the United States, Canada has not insisted on the conclusion of a framework agreement before granting fishing rights, so Community fishing in 1977 has continued, albeit at a reduced level.
2. *Norway.* Negotiations on a framework agreement have been completed and the agreement itself should shortly be concluded. During 1977 Norway has maintained its previous pattern of fishing in Community waters, subject to a quota in the case of herring fishing west of Scotland, and Community vessels have continued to fish, though on a reduced scale, in Norwegian waters. In particular, the Community has accepted quotas in respect of fishing for cod and various other species (haddock, saithe, and Greeland halibut) in the Norwegian zone north of 62° North.[8]
   Iceland. Although there have been several rounds of talks, there have been no formal negotiations with Iceland. Belgium and the Federal Republic of Germany many have continued to fish off Iceland under the terms of existing agreements.
   Faroe Islands. A framework agreement has been drawn up concerning mutual fishing arrangements.[9] Fishing by the Community has continued during 1977, but at a much reduced level for two important species, cod and haddock.
   Sweden. An agreement has likewise been prepared dealing with Swedish fishing in Community waters and making provision for Community fishing in Swedish waters.[10] Sweden has subsequently announced its intention to extend its limits from January 1, 1978.

Finland. Negotiations on a framework agreement have been pursued. Finland does very little fishing in Community waters, however, and has been affected by the general ban on herring fishing in Community waters in the North Sea.[11]

3. *USSR.* The USSR entered into negotiations with the Community in February 1977, at which time the Community granted quotas to USSR vessels on a reciprocal basis, taking account of the possibilities for fishing granted to vessels from member states in USSR waters. After those possibilities in the Barents Sea were reduced in September 1977, the Community limited USSR activities to fishing off Greenland, in execution of an allocation accepted by the Community within the framework of ICNAF.[12]

   German Democratic Republic and Poland. Negotiations were held with these two countries and, pending conclusion of framework agreements, they were allowed to continue fishing, though on a reduced scale. These two countries are unable to offer fishing rights on a reciprocal basis to the Community, however, and the authorization enabling them to carry out fishing activities in Community waters expired on November 30, 1977.[13]
4. *Spain.* Negotiations on a fishing agreement are continuing. The quotas and the number of Spanish boats allowed to fish in Community waters represent a sharp decline from previous figures.[14]

   Portugal. Negotiations with Portugal on a fisheries agreement are less advanced. Portuguese vessels have continued to fish in Community waters, though here too on a lesser scale.[15]

   Yugoslavia. An agreement with Yugoslavia has been proposed, to enable fishing by Italian vessels to continue off the Yugoslav coast.
5. *Guinea-Bissau, Mauretania, and Senegal.* Exploratory talks have been held concerning Community fishing off the coasts of these countries and the Council has agreed that negotiations should be pursued with a view to the conclusion of fisheries agreements. The Lomé Agreement between the Community and the African, Caribbean, and Pacific countries contains a declaration concerning fishing, prepared prior to the general move to 200-mile fishing limits. It may be expected that fisheries will play a larger part when the next Lomé Convention comes to be negotiated.

Turning now to multilateral arrangements, negotiations have taken place during 1977 in order to change the functions and procedures of the existing regional fisheries commissions, the aim being to bring the powers of these bodies into line with the increased limits of national fisheries jurisdiction. In the case of NEAFC, ICNAF, and the Baltic Commission, the Community has taken part in the negotiations and, consistent with its position elsewhere, has proposed that it should become a party to the future arrangements.

Besides regulating the question of access as such of nonmember states, the agreements drawn up and the autonomous regulations adopted also provide for the application of appropriate measures of control. Foreign vessels are required to have a license issued by the Commission, setting out the detailed arrangements (keeping of records, reporting requirements, etc.), the surveillance at sea being done by the patrol boats and aircraft of the member states.

The events that I have outlined are still too recent, and the external aspects of the Community's fisheries policy are in any case too incomplete, for a final assessment to be made of what has and what has not been achieved in this sphere. The passage to the 200-mile zone has occurred—indeed, this was the principal driving force—at a time when stocks were being sharply diminished and there was an overwhelming need for conservation in view of the increase in fishing capacity. Insofar as they were distant water fishing states, the members of the European Communities were bound to see their immediate catches reduced. Fishing possibilities off the coasts of nonmember states have been maintained in most cases, though on a reduced scale, and it may be hoped that these possibilities will be maintained and, as stocks are built up again, increased. The fishing done by third states in Community waters has been very greatly reduced, most evidently so in the case of states in whose waters Community boats do not fish. Vis-à-vis nonmember states, the Community has presented itself as a single coastal state and its capacity to do so has been accepted by others. Since the extension of fishing limits to 200 nautical miles, the Community has, in short, succeeded in acting as a single entity in its dealings with outside parties. It is the use made of the Community's stocks under the internal aspects of the common fisheries policy that is now at the center of attention in the continuing discussions.

NOTES

1. On this aspect see, generally, the reports of the Judicial and Academic Conference, September 27–28, 1976, organized by the Court of Justice of the European Communities, in particular the report by Judge Kutscher, "Methods of Interpretation as seen by a Judge at the Court of Justice," p. 5, especially at p. 30 and following.

2. Fishing activities in the waters of other territories for which Denmark, France, and the United Kingdom are responsible, or by vessels registered in these territories, are the responsibility of these states.

3. Adopted on October 17, 1970, entered into force on February 1, 1971. The two regulations have been replaced, as a codification measure, by Regulations (EEC) No. 100/76 and 101/76. *Official Journal of the European Communities,* 19, L 20 (January 28, 1976): 1, 19. (Subsequent references to the Official Journal are given as "*OJEC.*" For a more detailed description of the two regulations see M. Hardy, "The Fisheries Policy of the European Community," *Law of the Sea: Conference Outcomes and Problems of Implementation,* eds. E. Miles and J.K. Gamble (1977), p. 3, and A. Koers "The External Authority of the EEC in regard to marine Fisheries," *Common Market Law Review* 14, 3 (August 1977): 269.

4. The extension of specific fishing limits is a matter within member state competence. The consequence of any such extension is, however, a matter of concern to the Community. Accordingly, in order to achieve a coherent result it was necessary that the actions of member states should be coordinated.

5. Regulation (EEC) No. 1220/77, *OJEC* No. L 141 (July 9, 1977), p. 1.

6. Regulation (EEC) No. 2159/77, *OJEC* No. L 250 (September 9, 1977), p. 15, and other regulations cited therein; and Regulation (EEC) No. 373/77 (*OJEC*) No. L 53 (February 2, 1977), p. 1. The countries concerned are the Republic of Korea, the United States, Japan, and Sūrinam (for shrimp) and Japan and Venezuela (for tuna-line fish).

7. Under Article 2 of Regulation (EEC) No. 373/77 Canada was authorized during 1977 to make catches equal to the quantities fixed by ICNAF and, as regards the waters off St. Pierre and Miquelon, to the catch possibilities provided for in the 1972 Agreement between France and Canada. *OJEC* No. L 53 (February 2, 1977), p.1.

8. Regulation (EEC) No. 2156/77, *OJEC*, No. L 250 (September 30, 1977), p. 10.

9. Although part of the Kingdom of Denmark, the Faroe Islands are not part of the European Economic Community. Regulation (EEC) No. 2154/77, ibid., p. 4.

10. Regulation (EEC) No. 2161/77, ibid., p. 20.

11. Regulation (EEC) No. 2153/77, ibid., p. 1.

12. Regulation (EEC) No. 2158/77, ibid., p. 13.

13. Regulation (EEC) No. 2155/77, ibid., p. 5.

14. The Community does virtually no fishing in Spanish waters. Regulation (EEC) No. 2160/77, ibid., p. 17.

15. Regulation (EEC) No. 2153/77, ibid., p.1.

Chapter Seven

Internal Aspects of the Common Fisheries Policy of the European Community

Albert W. Koers
University of Utrecht

My assignment today is to bring you up to date in respect of the recent developments within the EEC in relation to its internal common fisheries policy—that is, the policy that is to apply among the EEC member states and their fishermen. We have gone through a difficult period. I can illustrate these difficulties by giving you some dates.

In February 1977 the EEC decided to prohibit fishing for North Sea herring until April 30, 1977. In April the ban on North Sea herring fishing was extended until May 31, 1977. In May the North Sea herring ban was extended until June 30, 1977. In June the ban was extended, with certain modifications, to July 20, 1977. In September the ban was extended until October 31, 1977. And recently, the EEC extended the ban until the end of 1977.

To paraphrase an expression known to all of us, one could say that the recent developments within the EEC in respect of the internal common fisheries policy have been a process of "creeping decision making."

At the 1976 meeting of the Law of the Sea Institute, Mr. Michael Hardy submitted a paper on the EEC's fisheries problems. Therefore, I will limit myself to the developments since that time. However, before going into the substance of these developments, I must at least recall the principle that is at the basis of all current developments, i.e., the principle of equal access. In 1970 the EEC adopted two regulations on fisheries questions dealing mainly with the market for fishery products and with the structure of the fishing industry. However, Article 2 of Regulation 2141/70 required the member states to ensure "equal conditions of access" for all fishing vessels flying the flag of a member state and registered in Community territory to all waters subject to their sovereignty and jurisdiction. Although shortly thereafter this principle of equal access was made subject to a number of derogations, I assume that you will see its implications in relation to the recently established 200-mile fishing zones of the EEC member states: equal access no longer applies just to zones of at most twelve miles from the coast, but to zones of up to 200 miles from the coast.

In October 1976 the European Commission—which, under the EEC's structure, has to make the proposals for the decisions of the Council of Ministers—submitted a set of proposals on the external and internal aspects of the common fisheries policy. Internally, these proposals envisaged: (1) that, at least until 1983, fishing in a zone of twelve miles from the coast would be reserved to the local fishermen (the scope of the derogations of the principle of equal access would thus be extended); and (2) that fishing beyond the twelve-mile limit would be managed through a quota system. Under this quota system a total allowable catch (TAC) would be set for each stock on the basis of scientific information. The catches of nonmember countries in EEC waters would be deducted from the total of the TACs, while the catches of the member states in the waters of nonmember countries would be added. This would then result in a total permissible catch, from which a certain volume would be set aside as a Community reserve, while the remainder would be divided among the member states on the basis of past performance. These proposals were designed to result in a permanent regime.

In November 1976 a special meeting of the EEC Ministers of Foreign Affairs led to the decision to extend fishing limits in the North Sea and the North Atlantic. As to the question of fisheries management, that meeting endorsed the following approach: If no agreement could be reached within the international fisheries commissions (primarily the North-East Atlantic Fisheries Commission, NEAFC) and if the EEC itself would also fail to adopt measures, the member states themselves would take measures, provided that these would be of an interim nature, would avoid discrimination, and would be approved by the European Commission.

Later in November 1976 it was decided that NEAFC should not set TACs and quotas for 1977 with regard to stocks in EEC waters. This was a very important decision, as it meant that the EEC itself had to take the 1977 TAC and quota decisions. As a result, attention shifted from the October proposals for a permanent regime to the need to develop, as rapidly as possible, a 1977 interim regime. Unfortunately, proposals of the Commission for an interim regime were not acceptable to the Council of Ministers and in December 1976 the Council had no choice but to decide that the member states should apply in 1977 the same measures as applied by them in 1976.

Since then the EEC has managed to move beyond that standstill decision, but only in respect of the most critical problems. In February 1977, certain interim conservation measures were adopted. Among these measures were: the prohibition of North Sea herring fishing I mentioned earlier; a prohibition on fishery for herring in the Celtic Sea (until December 31, 1977); a prohibition on the use of factory vessels in EEC waters; a prohibition on fishing with small mesh nets for Norway pout in a certain area (until March 31, 1977, but reintroduced later); and, certain regulations as to by-catches of North Sea herring and demersal species.

Why is it so difficult to develop the internal common fisheries policy? One reason—and probably the most important one—is that the EEC has had to develop this policy under conditions of a serious scarcity in the available fishery resources. EEC fishermen are being banned from the waters of third countries and many stocks of fish in EEC waters are in need of strict conservation measures. Consequently, although from a long-term perspective the common fisheries policy may be a policy to share wealth, it is presently (for all practical purposes) a policy to share scarcity, a policy to share losses. A second reason is that the need to develop the common fisheries policy found the European Commission ill-prepared in terms of organization and staff. A Directorate General for Fisheries was not established until recently and even now not more than ten to fifteen people are involved full time in the internal fisheries problems. A further complicating factor was the decision of November 1976 not to use NEAFC for setting the 1977 TACs and quotas. Whatever else can be said in favor of this decision, one of its effects was that the EEC's decision-making channels became fully involved in the immediate 1977 problems and that relatively little attention could be given to the more permanent arrangements to be established in respect of the internal common fisheries policy.

However, if one looks at the developments during last year from a more general perspective, it is fair to say that at least two things have been accomplished. First, the EEC has managed to avoid any irreparable damage to the stocks. The bans on herring fishing are a case in point. It is highly improbable that such bans could have been established under the old order, i.e., NEAFC. Second, the EEC has also managed to survive a very critical period without irreparable damage to the cooperation among the member states in respect of the common fisheries policy. On the contrary, although the United Kingdom and Ireland have continued to refer from time to time to the idea of 50-mile zones in which fishing would be reserved to their own fishermen, they have not acted to implement such zones. In this context it is of importance that in July the Court of Justice ordered Ireland to suspend certain unilateral measures adopted by Ireland in relation to fishing in waters off the Irish coast.

Let me now turn to the future and give you a brief summary of the various proposals that are presently under consideration within the EEC. First, there is a proposal on the 1978 TACs and quotas. The basic importance of this proposal lies primarily in the method suggested for calculating the quotas of the member states. A distinction is made between: (1) internal stocks–stocks entirely in EEC waters; (2) joint stocks–stocks shared between the waters of the EEC and the waters of a nonmember country with which reciprocal arrangements have been made; and (3) external stocks–stocks outside EEC waters, but open to EEC fishermen. The quota calculations incorporated in this proposal are quite complex. Let me give you an example for internal stocks.

The TAC of an internal stock–determined on the basis of scientific information provided by the International Council for the Exploration of the Sea–is, as a first step, divided among the member states in proportion to the stock's 1976 NEAFC quotas or, if there are no NEAFC quotas, in proportion to its 1976 catches. Then, a separate quota is determined for Ireland (1.67 x Irish 1975 catch), as it is agreed within the EEC that Ireland must have an opportunity to expand its fishing industry. The additional Irish allocation comes from the catch that used to be taken by nonmember countries in EEC waters or, if this is not sufficient, from the quotas of the other member states. As it is also agreed that North Britain has special problems, a third step is to calculate the special needs of North Britain and to obtain an increased allocation for its fishermen, either from a reduction of the catches of nonreciprocal nonmember countries in EEC waters or from the quotas of the member states. Although these quota arrangements are considerably more refined than those in the October 1976 proposals, they have met with considerable opposition in the Council of Ministers.

The second proposal deals with conservation measures of a more technical character (e.g., minimum mesh sizes, minimum fish sizes). The main objective of this proposal is to incorporate the various regulatory measures adopted by NEAFC into EEC law. However, on some points the proposal envisages rules that go beyond the NEAFC rules. It, too, has encountered considerable resistance.

A third proposal is concerned with control. It requires the member states to inspect fishing vessels in their ports and in waters subject to their jurisdiction. It also establishes a system to check compliance with the quotas (by requiring catches to be landed in certain ports, by requiring skippers to maintain certain records and submit certain statements, by establishing a catch data information exchange system, and by setting up a system to close the fisheries when the quotas have been exhausted). This proposal seems broadly acceptable, but its practical effect depends, of course, upon the substantive rules to be controlled.

A fourth proposal sets forth certain measures to adjust the capacity of the fishing industry to the new situation. It would make available financial aids for such things as: the redeployment of fishing vessels; the temporary laying up of fishing vessels; the scrapping of fishing vessels; the reduction of capacity in the processing industry; and information campaigns to promote the consumption of lesser-known species. It is estimated that the cost of such programs for the period 1979 to 1983 would amount to 264 million units of account (pre-1971 dollars) of which the Community would provide 50 percent on condition that the member states provide the other 50 percent.

Finally, I should perhaps mention some proposals of lesser importance. There is, for example, a proposal designed to compensate herring fishermen for their losses as a result of the bans on herring fisheries. There is also a proposal under which the Community would contribute towards the expenses involved in inspecting fishing operations off the Irish coasts and off the coast of Greenland. This proposal is aptly known as the "gunboat regulation."

If the EEC has survived a most difficult period in the development of its common fisheries policy without serious damage and if there are presently several important proposals of the European Commission under consideration, what are the chances of success? My own view is that the situation of creeping decision making will continue for a while. The internal common fisheries policy will not be created on the basis of a number of clear-cut decisions on the fundamental issues. It will rather emerge gradually through numerous decisions on specific points. Consequently, I am not very optimistic about the chances of the present proposals being accepted in toto, but I am fairly optimistic about the ultimate success of the common fisheries policy.

A first ground for my long-term optimism is that the initial difficulties of adjusting to the new situation are gradually being brought under control and that attention has shifted to more permanent arrangements. The stocks are surviving, the fishing industry has begun to adjust itself, and the EEC's decision-making capacity in the area of fisheries is expanding. In terms of internal decisions in effect, the EEC may presently be in about the same situation as last year, but this is not true in terms of experience, knowledge, proposals, and staff. And—most important of all—the political climate has also improved, although there remain very significant differences of opinion among the member states.

Second, the present situation of scarcity of resources in relation to the fishing capacities of the member states is also gradually disappearing, either as the result of the harsh laws of economics or as the result of certain ad hoc measures of the EEC or of the member states. This development will also enhance the chances of success: as I said earlier, it is easier to establish a policy to share wealth than to establish a policy to share scarcity.

Third, it should not be overlooked that the EEC has at its disposal certain instruments that have not yet been really used. I am not only referring to the legal instruments by which the European Commission may force the member states to adhere to the principle of equal access (and, more generally, the principle of nondiscrimination), but also to financial instruments. The Community has financial resources to add to its decisions on the management of the living resources in its waters. It can thus help the fishing industry to overcome the consequences of these decisions. Until now, this instrument has not been used at all.

Finally, developments in respect of the external aspects of the common fisheries policy have been more rapid. These developments make it politically very difficult for the member states to abandon the attempts of establishing an effective internal common fisheries policy.

In conclusion, I would like to say that the EEC is working toward a unique result. When the common fisheries policy will have become a reality, the EEC member states and their fishermen will share a natural resource on a nondiscriminatory basis. I do not know of any other situation in the world where this will also be the case.

LIST OF PRINCIPAL REGULATIONS ADOPTED IN 1977 IN RESPECT OF THE INTERNAL POLICY

1. Council Regulation (EEC) No. 350/77 of February 18, 1977 laying down certain interim measures for the conservation and management of fishery resources. *Official Journal of the European Communities (OJEC)*, 20, L 48 (February 19, 1977): 28
2. Council Regulation (EEC) No. 879/77 of April 26, 1977 amending Regulation (EEC) No. 350/77 laying down certain interim measures for the conservation and management of fishery resources. *OJEC* 20, L 106 (April 29, 1977): 30.
3. Council Regulation (EEC) No. 1057/77 of May 17, 1977 amending Regulation (EEC) No. 350/77 laying down certain interim measures for the conservation and management of fishery resources. *OJEC* 20, L 128 (May 24, 1977): 5.
4. Council Regulation (EEC) No. 1417/77 of June 28, 1977 amending Regulation (EEC) No. 350/77 laying down certain interim measures for the conservation and management of fishery resources. *OJEC* 20, L 160 (June 30, 1977): 20.
5. Council Regulation (EEC) No. 1673/77 of July 25, 1977 amending Regulation (EEC) No. 350/77 as regards the prohibition of fishing for Norwegian pout. *OJEC* 20, L 186 (July 26, 1977): 30.
6. Council Regulation (EEC) No. 2114/77 of September 26, 1977 laying down the interim measures for the conservation and management of North Sea herring. *OJEC* 20, L 247 (September 28, 1977): 1.

7. Council Regulation (EEC) No. 2115/77 of September 27, 1977 prohibiting the direct fishing and landing of herring for industrial purposes other than human consumption. *OJEC* 20, L 247 (September 28, 1977): 2.
8. Council Regulation (EEC) No. 2243/77 of October 11, 1977 prohibiting fishing for Norway pout. *OJEC* 20, L 260 (October 13, 1977): 1.

Discussion and Questions

Judith Kildow: Before opening the floor to questions, I have been asked by all the panelists to express a disclaimer for them that everything they have said here this afternoon is each one's own opinion and not the opinion of the organization each represents. Are there any questions? Dr. Pardo.

Arvid Pardo: I wish to ask any member of the panel whether the European Communities are looking beyond fishery policy to a common policy for utilization of the marine areas that will come under their control as a result of the Law of the Sea Conference, involving navigation, exploitation of energy resources, and so forth.

Michael Hardy: The Community is concerned with other marine activities, for example, steps to prevent pollution, and is a party to several regional conventions on that problem. The Council texts of November 1976 dealt only with the extension of limits for fishing purposes, however, not with the establishment of an economic zone. Accordingly, the question of a general proposal or plan has not really presented itself.

Lewis Alexander: I have two questions. First, I may have missed what you said had happened to NEAFC, which I believe has more members than the Community. Second, does the EEC not have something of a matrimonial sea situation now? As I remember the matrimonial sea proposal, discussed earlier, countries beyond their twelve-mile territorial limits would share a common fishery in the Caribbean, to the exclusion of outsiders or nonlittoral states from the Caribbean.

Albert Koers: With NEAFC, like ICNAF, we are renegotiating the convention. At a recent meeting in London we reached a fair amount of agreement on the basic principles of a new convention, but there will be a further diplomatic conference. The idea is that the Community, as Michael Hardy said, will become a party to the new convention at the exclusion of its members states and, of course, in addition to those other countries that may accede to the new instrument. Now, as to your second question, whether or not we have a matrimonial sea situation, I have heard quite a number of interpretations of that concept, but I think it would not be stretching the matrimonial sea concept too far to say it fits the kind of system we are establishing in the Community.

Edward Miles: I would like to know whether Dr. Koers sees the Community's common fisheries policy as an extension of NEAFC management policy in disguise. If so, why is he optimistic? Most of the stocks in the Northeast Atlantic under NEAFC management are seriously overexploited. The pattern of bargaining that he described and the utilization of NEAFC quotas are not something that can be regarded as very useful. If the Commission intends to continue this kind of pattern without attempting serious reductions in the level of effort, what is the point of the exercise?

Albert Koers: I do not agree with you that what we are doing is NEAFC in disguise. To point to a first difference, the Community has managed, not without difficulty, to impose a ban on herring fishing in the North Sea and Celtic Sea–something that NEAFC never could achieve. NEAFC has been talking about a ban on herring fishing for quite some time, but never managed to reach agreement. Second, I also feel that if you look at the problem of enforcement–and that is a very important issue when you talk about effectiveness–the Community is in a much better position to set up an effective system of enforcement. I am saying this mainly because the Community has the authority, has the competence, to impose obligations directly on the fishermen. The Community does not have to operate through the intermediate level of states. The Community itself can require fishermen, for example, to maintain certain records or report their catch to an appropriate authority. For these reasons the Community is a much more effective management instrument than NEAFC or any other traditional international organization. Now, of course, in certain respects there will be a continuation of existing patterns. For example, as I said briefly in my paper, the Community wishes to use the International Council for the Exploration of the Sea for scientific advice. The Community does not plan to set up its own research organization or research office. So on scientific research the Community may be in a similar situation to NEAFC's, but on management there are certain differences that are important. In my view, however, the Community is making real progress in establishing more effective fishery management.

Dr. Anatoly Kolodkin: Dr. Platzöder mentioned the bilateral negotiations between Norway and the USSR, and referred to the problem of equitable sharing of the continental shelf. I would like to ask her if she recognizes as applicable not only to the shelf but also to the water areas those equitable principles used by the International Court of Justice in the *North Sea Continental Shelf Cases* in 1969. Second, I do not know about the military activity of the Soviet Union in this area because I am not a military expert, but I do know about merchant shipping activity in the area. We do, of course, have a great interest in the negotiations over the Barents Sea and adjacent areas. We are concerned, for example, that Norway might wish to build artificial installations and thereby interfere with our shipping going to and from Murmansk and other areas in the North. Third, the panel was intended to deal with fishery matters, not military ones. But if we were to discuss the peaceful uses of the sea as lawyers, I would want to make a distinction, first of all, between *lex lata*–international law as it now is–and *lex ferenda,* the law that is being proposed. As to the latter, Mr. Brezhnev had proposed several times to withdraw nuclear warships from the Mediterranean. But if this were done by the Soviet Union, it should also be done by the United States and other countries under an international agreement. Thank you very much.

Renate Platzöder: Maybe I will start with the last question. My paper was on "Regional Factors in Managing Marine Resources," but I would refer to the famous phrase of President Amerasinghe that all matters in the law of the sea are interrelated, and certainly there is a relationship or linkage between fishery and military activities. I have never been to Murmansk but I am sure there are shipping activities up there that are not related to military operations. Yet it is a well-known fact that in Murmansk you have a lot of military activity, and if one opens a Norwegian newspaper, one can always read that this is a very sensitive strategic area. I suggested in my paper that it is a nightmare for the Soviet Union that foreigners might be able to watch what is being done up there. I think you confirmed this view.

The first question you asked was whether I would recognize the principles of equitable sharing. Well, I think, from a legal point of view, there are many ways to approach a difficult legal situation. The equitable sharing of fishery resources is a principle that is based on old law, resulting from the principle of the freedom of the high seas, and thus it found its way into the 1958 Fishing Convention. Maybe such a principle can also be transferred to seabed resources. But I am not here to judge what Norway and the Soviet Union are going to agree; I just mentioned in my paper that the oddly shaped fishing zone has had the effect of moving westward the boundary proposed by the Soviet Union in the seabed dispute. If Norway and the Soviet Union agree on such a zone applied to the seabed, that is their business. We would have to accept it.

Odidi Okidi: I have a short, quick question for Mr. Hardy. He mentioned the bilateral agreement now being considered between the EEC and countries like Senegal and mentioned briefly that there might be some law of the sea considerations for negotiation when the next session of the Lomé Convention comes up. I wonder what the EEC countries would have by way of an offer to African countries in general as *quid pro quo* for access to fishing in their waters.

Michael Hardy: I did not mean to suggest in my remarks that when the next Lomé Convention comes to be negotiated the detailed question of right of access be negotiated en bloc between the EEC on the one hand and the ACP states on the other. Questions relating to fisheries, which were very little dealt with the last time, are likely, however, to figure more prominently during the forthcoming discussions, although it is not possible at this stage to say exactly how this will be reflected in the new Lomé Convention.

Part III

Regional Ocean Management: How Feasible in the Developing World?

Chairman
John King Gamble, Jr.
Pennsylvania State University

Perhaps I should begin with an apology. When I first set up this session, I thought we would have at least two representatives from the Third World countries. This did not work out for several reasons. However, we have several people here who will take us to task during the question period, if Third World views are misrepresented.

Without further ado, I would like to introduce Mr. Eiriksson, who has been on loan from the Foreign Ministry of Iceland to the UN Secretariat for the last several sessions of the Conference, and today will speak to us on regional-type arrangements in the Third World. He will be followed by Dr. Barbara Johnson from Victoria, B.C. in Canada, who will deal with the problem of asymmetry in regions that consist of countries at quite different developmental levels. Finally, Professor David Larsen of the University of New Hampshire will add a comment based on recent developments in the Indian Ocean.

Chapter Eight

Some Thoughts on Regional Marine Arrangements in the Developing World

Gudmundar Eiriksson
Ministry of Foreign Affairs
Iceland

I have been asked to present a few thoughts on regional marine arrangements in the developing world. I think that most of us who have been called upon to deal with this topic of regionalism in general terms have found the subject very difficult to approach. On the one hand, a study of regionalism leads one to draw conclusions that are so obvious as hardly to need stating; on the other hand, the subject is so complex, particularly on close inspection, as to defy a general analysis of its characteristics.

I am not sure whether the task is made any simpler by placing emphasis on developing country aspects. There might appear to some to be some merit in considering, for example, whether regional arrangements are more suitable for developing countries than for others, or whether regional arrangements are more likely to be established in developing country regions than in others, or whether the type of marine arrangements established in developing country regions are any different from those in other regions. You will see, as I continue, that it is not really possible to arrive at any definite conclusions on these matters. This does not, perhaps, negate the value of the inquiry. One element, at least, is clear: the greatest growth area for regional concepts will be in the developed world for the time being.

Of course this question is only a subtopic of the general study of the law of the sea from the point of view of developing countries. I think it is difficult to identify more than one or two issues in the law of the sea about which it is possible to conclude upon close analysis that there is a "developing country attitude." One of these is, of course, the question of the International Seabed Area; but even on that question the identity of attitudes is no longer unqualified. In any event, that is the subject that, as presently envisioned, provides the least scope for regional arrangements.

In Chapter Nine, Dr. Johnson will discuss, *inter alia*, those problems that are caused by the presence of developed countries in regions otherwise comprised of developing countries. This category includes many of the developing country regions of the world. In later chapters, papers will be presented on particular regions, such as the South Pacific. Accordingly, I feel that I can indulge in a discussion mainly of concepts and policy on a general level, rather than in a detailed discussion of programs and trends, which might challenge most theoretical constructs.

I have chosen also to center the discussion on the negotiations at the Law of the Sea Conference, and, more specifically, on the present results of the negotiations as manifested in the Informal Composite Negotiating Text.

Focusing on the Law of the Sea Conference places certain limitations on the study and perhaps reduces its usefulness. Certainly no one would contend that the transactions at UNCLOS III are fully representative of what might be called "the real world." Activities are carried out in bodies such as FAO, IOC, and UNEP, as well as in individual regions, which never seem to be taken notice of, even indirectly, at the Conference. Nonetheless, concentration on the Conference makes the study manageable, particularly, since it is, after all, the forum where *policy concerns* are most adequately expressed. But emphasis should be given to the most important feature of the results of the work of the Conference, and that is precisely their global nature. The Conference is well on its way to fulfilling one aspect of its mandate—to adopt *a* convention dealing with *all* matters relating to the law of the sea, bearing in mind that the problems of ocean space are closely interrelated and need to be considered as a whole. Five years ago this seemed an impossible task and it was regarded as inevitable that some major issues must in the end be left to be dealt with in other ways: for instance, on the regional level. It is clear, however, looking at the Informal Composite Negotiating Text, that *globalism* on any issue tends to be the rule, and regionalism the exception, rather than *vice versa.* Please note that I am not here speaking of *internationalism,* which is another concept.

Now I suppose I must say a few words about the difficulties inherent in the definition of the term "region." Clearly there are many different usages, different institutional levels, differing degrees of cooperation, and so forth. It might be tempting initially to distinguish between two types of regional analysis: on the one hand, to look at the arrangements relating to a particular marine region, and on the other hand, to look at the marine activities of the states of a given region.

But, on further consideration, it seems that the difficulty of definition is not a problem facing regionalism *per se* but rather a problem facing a *study* of regionalism: that is, a problem for those trying to establish theories on regionalism by searching for common characteristics. The negotiators at the Law of the Sea Conference are quite aware that the term can have different meanings depending on the circumstances, and the drafting of the composite text is not overly compromised thereby. In the last analysis, in this presentation the term will quite generally be used to refer to arrangements lying intermediate between unilateral or bilateral solutions on the one hand, and global solutions, on the other. I think it is in this sense, at least when it does not clearly refer to a physical region, that it is most often used in the Informal Composite Negotiating Text.

I must confess that I was slightly more ambitious when I first began preparing this paper than the final product probably shows. I thought it appropriate, in fact, to engage in a study of the theoretical aspects of regionalism as analyzed by those writing on international relations and international politics. I thought to seek the answer, in a sense, to the question, not what regionalism can do for the law of the sea, but rather what the law of the sea could do for regionalism. I found this study, of course, quite interesting and found many elements that are familiar to those acquainted with the problems of marine regionalism. I must, however, admit that this was not always, for me, easy reading, and am glad that Dr. Johnson in her paper will be dealing with these matters in a very professional fashion.

But even an amateur can identify a number of factors that make regional marine arrangements, particularly in the developing world, promising areas for study by those interested in the theory of regional integration. In the first place, what is dealt with is a problem area in which there are more limitations on sovereignty and thus a greater tendency toward cooperation than say in the area of customs and tax which unavoidably involve a state's sovereignty. Also, in the developing world marine affairs are in their infancy and cooperation need not require the dismantling or adaptation of existing structures affecting vested interests. Rather, institutions can be designed *ab initio* with cooperation in mind. As a corollory of this, continuing cooperation is encouraged because, first, any success would be identified with the regional arrangement and, second, the withdrawal costs would be greater than if it were possible to revert to a preexisting system.

A lesson might be learned from experience, which shows the difficulty of passing from one level of integration to a higher or more comprehensive level. I am not sure that it will be easy to pass, for example, from consultation to cooperation to common policy, or from a regime dealing only with scientific research to one involving also pollution control or common exploitation of resources.

Disintegrative tendencies also occur in this field, as in others. In some cases, fear of outsiders may unite the countries of a region: this was undoubtedly a factor in the case of the South Pacific Forum states. Equally likely, however, perceptions of interdependence with nonregional states might interfere. No doubt there will continue to be cases of developing states offering fishing rights to extraregional developed states rather than to states in a region that are not able to make competitive bids. It has been pointed out that developing country solidarity is all well and good, but in terms at least of a short-term gain it is often more profitable to do business with developed states. The doctrine of "permanent sovereignty over natural resources," a major unifying principle for developing countries, it moreover essentially a disintegrating element in terms of regionalism.

I should point out that although I am talking about the political aspects of regionalism, I am by no means referring to the regional political groups in the United Nations context: that is, the Asian Group, the African Group, and so on. Of course these groupings remain marginally of some use in, for example, the determination of equitable geographical representation in the organs of the International Seabed Authority. For such purposes, I see that "Western Europe and others" is defined quite blankly as a "geographical region." I expect that true geographers will continue to find such usage annoying. When I say that the *global solution* has prevailed, I do not mean that *internationalism* has prevailed. On the contrary, nationalism in terms of coastal state rights appears to have won the day in a campaign spearheaded by developing countries. Although it may appear paradoxical that developing countries should disapprove of international arrangements that they could now control by weight of numbers, this in fact reflects a realistic appraisal of actual power bases as well as some of the factors I mentioned earlier. Some elements associated with this were mentioned in earlier chapters.

To the uninitiated eye the ICNT might appear to be extremely cognizant of developing country interests: it seems sometimes that every second paragraph makes mention of them. This is a reflection, perhaps, of genuine sentiments, which are widely shared at the Conference, although it is certainly not safe to conclude merely from the number of references to concern for developing countries that their interests are duly taken into account.

The area where concern for developing countries and regionalism converge to the greatest degree is Part XIV of the text, dealing with the transfer of technology, particularly Section 3 of that part, which calls upon states to promote the establishment of regional marine scientific and technological research centers, and obligates all states in the region to cooperate with the centers. The provisions go further than transfer of technology in the strict sense and encompass technical cooperation and cooperation in marine research. There is much to be said for regionalizing the transfer of technology. The technology is more likely to be appropriate to the needs of individual states and more suitable for direct application.

The desirability of enhancing the research capabilities of developing countries is also emphasized in Part XIII, dealing with marine scientific research, although regional solutions are not there given pride of place. Reference at one point to the need to act in accordance with the principle of respect for sovereignty might be taken to indicate a preference for a national solution.

Part XII, on the protection and preservation of the marine environment, establishes the framework, at least, for regional cooperation. A number of references are made to regional organizations and to the need to harmonize national policies at the appropriate regional level. More important, provision is made that *characteristic regional features* should be taken into account in the formulation of standards.

On the question of enforcement, there does not appear to be much scope offered for regional cooperation. This is particularly surprising in light of the regional consultation contemplated in other conventions, such as the International Convention relating to Intervention on the High Seas in Cases of Oil Pollution Casualties. Such cooperation is particularly necessary for developing states that are not likely to have technological capability independently to respond to pollution incidents. Of course, the history of negotiations on vessel-source pollution shows the sensitivity of the issue, and clearly there is a fear in some quarters that states may be prompted to develop, on the regional level, measures more restrictive than the convention calls for, and thus hamper international navigation.

Once again in Part XII, there is recognition of the need to provide scientific and technical assistance to developing states *inter alia* through regional organizations.

I turn now to the subject that is of more immediate interest to most states and that is the scope of regional cooperation contemplated in resource exploitation. As I said before, the trend has clearly been toward coastal state sovereign rights: for instance, with respect to continental shelf resources, no rights at all are contemplated for other states. Given this emphasis the text nonetheless leaves open considerable possibilities for regional cooperation, quite remarkably under the circumstances, and in practice the extent of cooperation is likely to be even greater than envisioned in the Law of the Sea Convention.

In some cases this responds to biological facts that cannot be completely ignored, even by lawyers, and these include the fact that the same fish stock or associated stocks may be in two exclusive economic zones, or both in one such zone and in the high seas adjacent. In such cases, and also with respect to highly migratory species and anadromous stocks in general, the coastal state rights would nonetheless predominate. It is interesting to note that mention of "subregional and regional" is highlighted as opposed to international arrangements. Cooperation is called for in the determination of conservation measures and in the flow of information, including cooperation at the subregional and regional levels.

The analysis is, of course, most critical when it comes to the allocation of fishing rights to foreign states. In the general provision on the granting of access to the surplus of the allowable catch, the requirements of developing countries in the subregion or region in harvesting part of the surplus are mentioned among the relevant factors to be taken into account. This point was given some attention at the latest session of the Conference on the basis of an amendment proposed to refer to developing countries in general, not only those in the subregion or region, thus providing opportunities under this heading for states themselves situated in resource-poor regions. In the debate on the proposal many of the general points I mentioned earlier were brought out, such as the conflict between the desire to demonstrate solidarity with developing countries and the need to sell access on the best terms.

The question of regionalism has often come up in the context of the rights of the landlocked states to exploit living resources. The ICNT provides for a right to participate on an equitable basis in the exclusive economic zones of adjoining coastal states. A further provision implies that in certain regions coastal states may grant to landlocked states of the same region equal or preferential rights. This latter provision, while perhaps adding nothing from a legal point of view, was included to reflect the desire of certain coastal states to put on record the possibility of such greater rights.

Particular mention is also made of the right of developing coastal states particularly dependent on fishing in neighboring waters, and developing coastal states without exclusive economic zones, to participate on an equitable basis in fishing in the subregion or region.

Under these headings efforts have been made to extend the content of the rights granted and to expand the number of eligible states as well as the geographical scope of the areas where the rights can be exercised. In the latter connection it is pointed out that it is states located in resource-poor regions that most need to gain access to fishing in other regions. On this issue as the ICNT stands, coastal states are clearly unwilling to go beyond a *regional* outlook in fishery arrangements.

I should mention also that some cooperation is contemplated with respect to the conservation of the living resources of the high seas. In fact, specific mention is made of the appropriateness of establishing subregional or regional fishery organizations.

Regional cooperation is mentioned also in other contexts that might have some relevance to developing countries. Here one could mention regional search and rescue services, the possibility of giving effect to the freedom of transit of landlocked states to and from the sea though regional or subregional agreements, and the maintenance in archipelagic waters of existing rights of immediately adjacent neighboring states.

I turn now to the question of enclosed and semi-enclosed seas. A commentator writing recently on the apparent success of comprehensive marine arrangements in the Baltic and the Mediterranean thought it was ironical that one of the few changes found in the Revised Single Negotiating Text was to reduce the obligation to cooperate and coordinate activities in enclosed or semi-enclosed seas. Ironical it may be, but the changes were a response to fundamental concerns of delegations on the subject. On the one hand, there is the concern of states located in enclosed or semi-enclosed seas that cooperation not be forced upon them. On the other hand, there was the fear of states outside the region that restrictive regimes might be established in the sea, which would discriminate against outside states and affect the freedom of navigation. They fear, for instance, that states bordering straits might seek to restrict traffic of certain types of vessels to those belonging to states in the area. Some states, moreover, would seem to be using the concept of a special regime for enclosed or semi-enclosed seas to promote their position on the subject of delimitation, and this of course is resisted by states supporting opposing positions. In short, there appears to be significant resistance to the imposition of a mandatory regime that departs from the general rules established for other marine areas.

Finally, I would point out that the possibility of special regional procedures for the settlement of disputes is provided for in Part XV. The same fear of exclusionary regimes is reflected in the stipulation that in order to be eligible for the purpose of optional exemptions a regional procedure must be open to all parties to a dispute.

It might be noticed that I have refrained from discussing whether regionalism is a "good thing," for developing countries in particular. It depends, of course on one's overall point of view. If one places great value on the process in which the Law of the Sea Conference is engaged, that is, the process of striving for a broadly acceptable comprehensive treaty, then, clearly, attempts to achieve through regional arrangements a solution that is at odds with solutions reached at the Conference would not be a good thing.

I must admit that I began my examination of regionalism with a somewhat skeptical attitude, on the basis of my experience at the Conference and of my knowledge of existing regional organizations such as NEAFC and ICNAF. After analysis, however, I am more confident that regionalism does have a role to play in marine affairs, and that in fact the Informal Composite Negotiating Text allows for extensive utilization of regional arrangements, particularly for developing countries, for it is there that regionalism has its future. ICNAF and NEAFC should not be taken as proof that regional arrangements cannot work. They show, perhaps, that they are no substitutes for effective coastal state jurisdiction, but when adopting the correct perspective they can perform useful functions in facilitating conservation of resources and scientific research. I suspect that the type of arrangement being developed in the South Pacific may prove the most successful model, but it is to be feared that the search for the ideal may prevent the attainment of the possible. Nonetheless, I recognize that the future for regional arrangements is not yet clear. With respect to developing countries we have seen that some characteristics favor regional solutions while others tend to discourage them, and in the end the advantages and disadvantages probably cancel each other out.

There is clearly a need for cooperation among states in the management of marine affairs. If, on the one hand, large-scale international cooperation is unwieldy and unacceptable and, on the other hand, nationalist policies alone are unsatisfactory, regional arrangements may provide the correct framework for the cooperation necessary.

Chapter Nine

Regionalism and the Law of the Sea: New Aspects of Dominance and Dependency

Barbara Johnson
Victoria, B.C.

The most fascinating (and many would say troublesome) aspect of the law of the sea negotiations is their connection with the broad political relationship between the North and the South. The developed/developing "gap" is a multidimensional one, characterized by asymmetries in political, economic, and military power. Even after numerous sessions of UNCLOS III, it is difficult to guess what the long-term impact of the Conference will be on the nature of world politics, and particularly on international organizations. The range of possibilities is, to say the least, wide. In future, UNCLOS III may be viewed as the series of negotiations where the new international economic order (NIEO) took on substantive meaning, making possible accommodation between North and South in the future; or as the Conference that overtaxed the UN system and revealed its inadequacy to cope with current global problems. It is no less difficult to speculate on whether the present configuration of world political forces will permit UNCLOS III to succeed. The linkage of UNCLOS III politics to general North-South politics may cause the Conference to fail, because the linkage widened the cleavage between developed and developing states in Committee I or, alternatively, because the linkage prevented the recognition of the real problems and interests of the developing states.

Over the last two years, the multilateral negotiations on the law of the sea have increasingly been supplemented, and perhaps supplanted, by subglobal action—be it unilateral legislation, or bilateral and regional agreements. In fact, the institute's theme this year suggests that the law of the sea is in some way being "regionalized." One interpretation of this suggestion would be that regional regimes or even institutions are taking over the tasks that UNCLOS III has failed to carry out. Perhaps it would be more accurate to suggest that as the global law of the sea regime is transformed, complex patterns of international integration and disintegration are occurring. In law of the sea politics, as in current international politics generally, there are no longer distinct moves in one single direction toward integration, but a whole set of integrative and disintegrative trends, varying along several dimensions of integration and varying according to issue and region. For instance, traditional marine regional arrangements (part of the power structure of the old regime) are on the decline, yet there are prospects for new types of regional cooperation. And, while unilateral and bilateral negotiations have upstaged the global negotiations, UNCLOS III has far from failed in its efforts at universal rule-making.

Besides general international trends and the nature of the emerging law of the sea regime, regional political factors will determine where there is cooperation and where there is conflict in the oceans. The new regime for the economic zone may affect the regional balance of power in some parts of the world, a possibility that will critically affect future regional developments. All these factors considered, the prospects for regional collaboration appear to be limited, and shaped in part by international and regional relations of dominance and dependency.

GENERAL TRENDS IN INTERNATIONAL POLITICS

The existence of an asymmetric distribution of power in the international system results from differences in capabilities among nation-states. Regardless of whether economic, military, or political indicators of capability and influence are used, the globe is currently marked by enormous disparities between the strongest and the weakest nation-states. The concept of asymmetry, which refers to a condition where a resource is not evenly distributed, has a long history of association with theories of conflict. While the underlying notion is that uneven distribution is directly or indirectly destabilizing, the connection is often vaguely made, with the range and shape of the asymmetry being either unspecified or difficult to establish. The most critical asymmetries are of course between the North and South, leading to a dominance-dependency relationship between them.

There are any number of suggestions, generalizations, partial hypotheses and partial theories accounting for the gap between developed and developing states, ranging from the subject of small states to economic development studies. At one extreme the literature views developing states as simply one type of weak or small state; at the other extreme (and coming closest to a fully developed theory) is Galtung's structural theory of imperialism.[1] In this view, imperialism is simply one form of dominance, but its practice is not restricted to capitalist states. Defining the developed states (both East and West) as the "center" and the developing states as the "periphery," he argues that the center maintains control by establishing a common interest between the center of the developed nation and one sector (the center) of the periphery nation, thus effectively penetrating it. Very high degrees of inequality within periphery nations allow for this separation of interests of the governing and business elite and the mass of the population. In terms of the structure of global relations, there is more interaction between the developed center and the periphery nations, and none among the periphery nations themselves. This feudal system of interaction allows for the maintenance of imperialism in economic, military, political, and cultural affairs, and in the field of communications. Politically, center nations are able to use international organizations to perpetuate dominance, whether in the United Nations, the specialized agencies, functional or regional international organizations. Economically, the theory is more solidly grounded, since in 1974 only six percent of international trade was among the developing countries.

In contrast to the imperialist theory, rather scattered and incomplete efforts to conceptualize the relationship between developed and developing states have been made by traditional military-political analysts examining relations between militarily weak and powerful states, and by analysts studying political regions dominated by one state. In a comparison of Latin American-U.S. politics and COMECON politics, one analyst argued that small states have considerable freedom to maneuver in hierarchial regional systems and that such efforts will intensify in future, since the international system is no longer strictly bipolar. Smaller states will thus seek to make more permeable the boundary between the regional system and the larger international system.[2] An even larger body of literature (area studies) examines power relationships in the context of each political region. However, given the importance of the economic dimension in contemporary world politics, it is inappropriate to examine North-South relations as an aspect of the small state problem, or to focus on the unique problems of each developing-country region.

Several other approaches occupy the middle ground in terms of theoretical level, but offer some possible directions for future law of the sea politics. One such view argues that power is not congruent across issues, but that patterns of power differ from issue to issue, and that different structures of international organization do affect outcomes. In this view "international power derives from patterns of asymmetrical interdependency between actors in issue areas in which they are involved with one another, and . . . states suffering from asymmetries in one issue area will seek to link that area to another in which they hold a preponderance of usable power."[3] While the notion of usable power is a valid one for UNCLOS III conference diplomacy, the overall dominance of the North over the South is still so strong that it seems unrealistic to argue that because of the OPEC example each issue has its own unique power structure. Another approach concedes the importance of the overall asymmetry between North and South, but argues that internal differences and the competition for regional hierarchy in the developing world will destroy Southern cohesion.[4]

Which trends, then, dominate the global political system? A continuance of the North-South split seems likely to prevail, in spite of the fragility of the accord,[5] and many forces tending to break Southern unity, such as the *embourgeoisiement* of OPEC countries, which Hansen has predicted. Several of the forces weakening Southern unity may have particular relevance for the law of the sea. First, while the political cohesion of the South may be maintained in certain multilateral settings, Northern economic penetration of Southern nations is likely to continue in new guises, often as transnational relationships. In particular, if economic conditions worsen again, and further disintegration of the international economic system continues (such as a breakup of GATT), then current efforts by developed states to seek long-term supply agreements and broad-ranging bilateral economic arrangements with developing states would intensify. In this situation, current political and economic asymmetries would be retained in practice, since the developing states would be weakened through isolation. Only those Southern states that had followed the Chinese example and dissociated themselves from the international political and economic system, or those strongly supported by OPEC states, could survive such pressures.

Second, problems of regional competition for dominance among both developed and developing states will also affect the future law of the sea relations of Southern countries. Hansen has perhaps overstated the problem of regionalism for Southern unity, since it may be questioned whether Southern cohesion is really impeded by differences among its members on local issues. Could not, for instance, problems of regional hierarchy and political distrust among neighboring states continue at one level and a cohesive front against developed states still be maintained on global issues? While the answer would appear to be yes, it is undoubtedly true that such problems would harm the chances for regional cooperation among developing states on the law of the sea.

The next question is how such trends will affect regional collaboration, given the shift to unilateralism and bilateralism on economic zone questions. Power disparities are most acute in regional politics, one state often emerging as the regional "hegemon." Because of this aspect of regional politics, it is usually argued that the global negotiating forum (with its open procedures and voting rules) improves the position of weak states. Since many developing states are weak, it is extrapolated that the position of the South is strongest in the context of multilateral negotiations. The hierarchy and isolation that characterize bilateral and regional relations between North and South are avoided in the UN forum. Assuming this is true, a shift away from multilateralism weakens the position of the developing states. In certain regions, developed states would then be able to intensify their control over ocean politics.

In a number of developing-country regions, one or two developed states interact with many developing states, and in all regions and subregions developing states compete with each other for regional dominance. In the past, developed states took a direct military role in such regions, but given the declining legitimacy of overt military force by developed against developing states, that role is now largely economic. This trend has been reinforced by the declining military-political hegemony of the United States and by the coastal states' increased abilities to prevent certain actions by the major powers.

In Oceania, Australia and New Zealand seek regional leadership over the South Pacific states. While they have sought to exclude some major powers, they are linked to the United States through ANZUS, and to Japan through informal economic ties. The acceptance of a Japanese economic role in the region follows from Australia's calculation that it is dependent on Japanese economic dominance in the western Pacific.

In the South China Sea, almost all the states concerned are developing ones, although Hong Kong and Singapore should be viewed as developed city-states. As the conflicts over the Paracels and Spratleys reveal, both China and Vietnam seek dominance. However, both states are supported by extraregional developed states, so that the region's shifting power alignments might eventually lead to a Soviet-Vietnamese coalition against Chinese and Japanese support for the ASEAN group. Farther north, in the Yellow Sea and East China Sea, developed and developing states are more evenly mixed, with the chief extraregional actor being the United States through its support for South Korea and Taiwan. Over time the Chinese position, now second to Japan's, seems certain to be strengthened.

In the Indian Ocean, the superpowers and South Africa exert influence over a much larger number of developing states. While the superpowers' naval interests range throughout the region, they are concentrated in the Horn of Africa. Among the developing states, Iran's position relative to India's has clearly strengthened since 1973.

In West Africa and the Gulf of Guinea, all the states of the region are developing, but France maintains continued influence through its economic role in ex-French West Africa. Nigeria clearly has no major challengers to its regional leadership. Of the eighteen states bordering the Mediterranean, half are developed and half developing, not including the superpowers. In the Caribbean, the United States is obviously dominant, with Mexico, Venezuela, and to a much lesser extent Jamaica asserting themselves as regional powers. Of the external developed states, the Soviet interest has been confined to Cuba, and British and French interest to economic aspects of their colonial possessions. In Latin America as a whole, taking the OAS as a region, the United States has also retained its dominant position, with Brazil, Venezuela, and Argentina competing for second place.

THE EMERGING LAW OF THE SEA REGIME

Besides broad developments in world politics, the emerging law of the sea regime will itself affect prospects for regional collaboration. UNCLOS III resulted from the politicization of ocean questions, particularly that of ownership of the deep seabed. "Politicization" is the heightening of general interest in an issue, and its linkage to other salient issues. Such linkage is both a characteristic of UNCLOS III, and a cause of the transfer of political activity from the transgovernmental system to UNCLOS III. Politicization is closely tied to the notion of regime change or the perception that a change in regime is necessary, and the concept emphasizes the competitive relationship between the transgovernmental law of the sea system (the power structure of the old regime) and the international rule-making one of UNCLOS III.

Among other (perhaps less flattering) descriptions, the UNCLOS III process is one of "regime construction"—the development of a new set of global rules and standards of behavior to guide the use of the oceans. The values to be promoted are fairly sweeping: the containment of conflict, equity, economic and social well-being, and environmental betterment. From the standpoint of international politics, it is not essential that binding and formal legal obligations be accepted by all participants. The extent to which such legal rules are laid down *may* be an indicator of the extent to which accommodation has been reached among conflicting interests. However, legal rules are not critical for the emergence of a successful global regime. Regimes can be complete or partial, depending on how stable they are and how well the rules are observed. While some stability and compliance are obviously desirable, it is questionable if it is desirable to seek maximum stability and compliance. For instance, legally binding rules in all spheres of fishery allocation and management might impede the development of a satisfactory regime and prevent conflict resolution. For example, if the principles of equity and nondiscrimination were fully built into a convention, then attempts by coastal states to make their interests symmetrical with particular distant-water states would be prevented.

At what point are informal rules so fragmented, and compliance with them so limited, that a global regime ceases to exist? It can be argued that there is always some regime—the minimum one being that every actor agrees the others can do exactly what they want.[6] However, while it is true that complete anarchy rarely exists, there ought to be patterns of discernible order for a regime to be said to exist. In judging what kind of regime is emerging from UNCLOS III, it is necessary to distinguish between a situation close to complete breakup of the Conference, following which a series of dissimilar extensions occur; and a more coordinated and sensitive set of responses. The difference between the two is that in the first case disputes would be settled through conflict or through negotiation without reference to rules suggested in the UNCLOS III texts. In the second case, which still appears to correspond to the present situation, states would make some effort to apply UNCLOS III rules.

The emerging global regime will affect regional developments, particularly when developed and developing states are involved in the same region. It is evident that a very weak global regime would allow dominance to be perpetuated in its most blunt form, since most developing states would be unable to invest a great deal in rule enforcement. A very strong global regime would leave no opportunity for regional institutions and regimes, particularly those connected with rule making. In certain cases, such as ship-generated pollution, there is a direct conflict between the existence of a regional and a global regime. The emerging regime does not prescribe regional ocean management; it prescribes national and international management. There are provisions for regional activity, but to a certain extent such articles concern issues where global agreement has been impossible to reach, so the prospects for regional collaboration may not be good. There are a number of areas where regional arrangements are either prescribed or seem to be unavoidable, such as:

1. Rights within the economic zone for the landlocked and geographically disadvantaged (LLGD) states, accommodation being made in the context of bilateral, regional, or subregional agreements;
2. Regional coordination for shared and adjacent coastal stocks, anadromous stocks, and highly migratory stocks;
3. Regional approaches for the problems of enclosed and semi-enclosed seas;
4. Regional approaches to control air- and land-generated ocean pollution, and designation of "critical areas" by coastal states and IMCO for control of ship-generated marine pollution;
5. Regional centers for marine scientific research; and
6. Boundary delimitation, since two and often more states of a region will be involved and since the principle of equity allows for the introduction of regional political considerations.

While the texts make limited and scattered requirements for regional collaboration, their attack on aspects of dominance and dependency is far more ambitious. The effort to reduce asymmetries in scientific and technological skills is particularly strong, as is shown in the marine scientific research and transfer of technology provisions. These provisions apply to the economic zone as well as to the exploitation of the deep seabed. Attempts to reduce dominance in economic capabilities are generally confined to the distribution of wealth from the seabed area and from revenue sharing, and of less significance than the effort to "equalize" scientific and technological skills. Before examining the implications of these provisions for regional marine integration, patterns of international integration and disintegration of ocean activities should be sketched.

Patterns of International Integration and Disintegration

The oceans involve a very large area of economic and political activity, some aspects of which are integrating and other parts disintegrating. Some of this integration and disintegration results from the overturning of the structures of the old law of the sea regime, but much other movement is impelled by forces outside UNCLOS III. Disintegration prevails, but there are some specific issues moving toward greater integration (e.g., the deep seabed, IMCO, dispute settlement). It must also be admitted that for centuries the oceans have been informally regulated by their users, so that there has been no centralized authority making and implementing rules for the oceans, although sporadic efforts at rule-making occurred in 1930, 1958, and 1960. While there is a great strengthening of national sovereignty over ocean resources, this phase can hardly be called decentralization since it replaces a system of minimal international regulation and even less rule adjudication.

While maritime commercial and naval movement has been unquestionably global in scope, there has also been a very strong regional tradition in efforts to regulate the uses of the seas. So while the organization of private and state enterprise with respect to shipping and fishing was global, governments often sought to control these operations regionally. The family of two dozen fishery commissions, more than any other sector, was guided by the regional tradition. But there have been regional regimes, for instance the six-mile territorial sea in the Mediterranean, and pollution control arrangements have been successfully made in the Baltic and Mediterranean. More recently, efforts at shipping control in congested waters have led to regional collaboration. Politically, too, there have been intensive regional campaigns—for the Latin American 200-mile territorial sea, for nuclear-free zones, and zones of peace in the Indian Ocean.

The trend to extended national jurisdiction is but one aspect of the long-term drive by developing countries to assume control over natural resources. Several factors suggest there will be further disintegration of international economic activities in the oceans, a principal one being the nature of the economic zone itself. While it is risky to guess how each national bureaucracy will adhere to or modify the EEZ provisions, it is probable that there will be a strong trend toward national autarky in the zones. How effective such efforts will be depends on whether transnational forces and bilateralism make autarky unworkable, as well as on internal conditions in the developing states. If the full national autarky route is followed, then the economic zone would be developed with minimal foreign involvement. Such developments would lead to further controls over the offshore operations of the oil companies, and nationalization in both the fishing and shipping spheres. In the case of fisheries, it would appear that more fish would be used for domestic consumption, so that eventually declines in the international fishery trade could be expected. Even with less ambitious steps, international fishing operations seem certain to become regionally based, as extraregional fishing fleets are forced out of the various ocean regions. Similarly, international shipping may eventually become regionalized, due to the desire of developing countries to control their own merchant marines and to other economic and technical developments forcing world shipping into a regional economic framework.[7] UNCLOS III, then is the most important but not the only force breaking up previously international patterns of activity.

PROSPECTS FOR REGIONAL COLLABORATION AND CONFLICT ON LAW OF THE SEA

In the present climate of world politics, and of law of the sea politics in particular, what are the prospects for regional ocean collaboration among developing countries? To answer this, I have examined the forces that appear to encourage regional cooperation, forces constraining that cooperation, and forces promoting active conflict within regions.

Forces Promoting Regional Cooperation:

1. Past interest in regional integration among developing countries.

The development of the EEC was watched with great interest by those in developing countries and even now some two dozen regional economic arrangements still exist among the developing countries. It might be expected that successful regional cooperation in one ocean region could lead to its imitation, or "echoing" elsewhere, just as the EEC example had a worldwide impact. Yet, while imitation certainly does occur, the first success story still has to take place, and that story has to be seen as having a moral elsewhere. There are no ocean regions that are immediate candidates for a strong regional movement, and it may be that policymakers view the world as being too complex and rapidly changing for a single form of regional cooperation to be acceptable in the way that the EEC model was twenty years ago.

There are two reasons for looking at studies on regional integration when evaluating the future of regional marine arrangements. First, attempts at building regional economic communities have failed for the most part, particularly those among developing countries. Since such efforts were based on the logic that cooperation in technical and economic matters could lead to successful political integration, their failure has implications for the growth of regional institutions based on technical and economic cooperation on marine issues. However, some of the findings from these studies do bear on the problems that may afflict regional ocean cooperation.

The study of regional integration mushroomed *after* the early European attempts at community building in the 1950s, the most ambitious of these studies being Ernst Haas's *The Uniting of Europe.* As attempts to imitate the European experience spread in the 1960's to East Africa, Latin America, and the Caribbean, political scientists also sought *ex post facto* explanations there. However, as the pace of European integration faltered, and the efforts in the developing world collapsed, academic interest in integration declined. Even by 1969, one observer noted that the achievements of over a decade of research were very much in doubt.[8]

European integration had been analyzed from the perspective of community building, and of neofunctionalism. The former approach stressed the importance of building common perceptions and shared values among the peoples of different countries in promoting integration. Transactional flows—the movement of people and goods—and the flow of communications across borders were used to measure the degree of integration. The second approach was a radical revision—and perhaps even a transformation of functionalist theories originated by Mitrany. In the immediate postwar years, the functionalists argued that a stable international community could be built if cooperative arrangements were introduced in specific, technical, and nonpolitical issue areas. A web of overlapping interests would be created when enough such international functional agencies were established, imposing a complex set of restraints on the formerly direct clash of national interests.

The neofunctionalists, on the other hand, argued that a regional community could be built if economic cooperation were undertaken, since such cooperation would automatically "spill over" into other, more contentious spheres. Senior bureaucrats and other elites with technical skills were the key element in this process, since they would undertake the cooperative measures that would eventually transform an economic community into a political one.

Three sets of variables within a region were identified as essential for integration to occur: certain background factors (such as elite complementarity, relative size and power of the national units involved); variables at the moment of union; and process variables (such as decision-making style). Turning to the case of developing countries, the neofunctionalists sought to modify their approach. This was a Herculean task, since the approach was predicated on the assumption that a highly industrialized society was undergoing transformation. It was suggested that while the Latin American Free Trade Associations (LAFTA) countries were not highly developed economically, a functional equivalent might exist in the form of an international factor, such as the climate of international trade.[9]

As the pace of integration slackened, the criticism of those who had tried to explain integration increased. The transactionalists were charged with having described conditions associated with integration, but having failed to explain anything at all. The neofunctionalists received even heavier criticism, starting with the argument that economic and political integration did not lie on a continuum.[10] Instead, processes and events were sharply discrete, and a distinction had to be made between "high" politics (defense/security questions) and "low" (welfare) politics, the latter being noncontroversial. Another valid criticism was that the theory was constructed only as a response to immediate events, without any sense of how such efforts were related to changes in the international system. Another enduring problem lay in the expectation of some mysterious "automaticity" by which technocrats were able to move from handling noncontroversial questions to political ones. As critics pointed out, why should one assume technocrats would be allowed to get away with such an assumption of power? As time showed, they were not allowed to get away with it, and in the years since the question of disintegration—be it of nation-states or of regional economic and political communities—has become as important a process as integration.

For the developing countries in particular, the notion of an automatic move from economic to political integration was untenable. In the first place, there were few nonpolitical questions in these countries, owing to the scarcity of political resources, the importance of personal leadership, and low levels of political legitimacy.[11] Since the problem in some developing countries was too much politicization of all issues, it made little sense to talk about the shift from nonpolitical to political issues.

While much of this criticism reads like a cautionary tale, there are still many experiments at regional integration among the developing countries, particularly ASEAN, the Central American Common Market, and the Andean Common Market (before Chile's withdrawal). Their progress is worth watching, since ocean collaboration may occur in the framework of such arrangements, and because asymmetrical relations have destroyed their chances of significant growth. For the developing countries, regional attempts to build economic communities resulted in rich members getting richer and the poor poorer. This result was particularly noted in the case of customs-union arrangements, such as existed in the early years of the East African Community. Kenya benefited much more than did Tanzania and Uganda, and although the arrangement was modified at the insistence of the latter two, it eventually collapsed. The fear of regional hierarchy being intensified was also a factor in the West Indies case, where the other islands feared Jamaican dominance. Although it was never conclusively shown that the countries integrating had to be of roughly equal size and power to succeed, it is certain that there must not be clear-cut winners and losers among states considering regional collaboration.

Besides shifts in the distribution of wealth and power, the regional communities may also have faltered because the spread of the multinational corporations made it possible to form a closed economic system. The desire to control transnational business operations partly explains the present shift to regional development banks, and regional efforts to develop common investment policies to deal with foreign interests. Some of the current efforts at regional ocean collaboration reflect similar concerns. The emerging trend may be away from purely functional arrangements just concerned with ocean issues, and equally away from attempts to build economic communities on the EEC model.

2. Developing countries' interest in regional self-reliance.

The concept of regional self-help or self-development may provide new impetus towards regional cooperation among developing (and in some cases developed) states. Such regional self-reliance implies a certain amount of economic dissociation from the prevailing international economic and political system. The impetus for such dissociation stems from the relative success of the

Chinese model of development.[12] However, while countries such as Algeria may be large enough to adopt a national self-reliance policy, for many of the smaller developing countries, regional efforts at self-reliance offer a more feasible alternative.

Self-reliance, as practiced nationally by the Chinese, offers a critical alternate life-style for many developing countries. While it can be loosely compared with autarky, self-reliance differs both from self-sufficiency and autarky in that it does not prevent exchanges of products or resources. Instead, "self-reliance means that given the need for a certain product, you should not enter into exchange to get the product before you have used up all possibility of producing it yourself."[13] So the economic concept of self-sufficiency in production is combined with the political requirement of a fully mobilized society to utilize national capacities. Certainly, in the case of offshore oil technology, China has not refused Western technology, but has imported what it needed to ensure technology was transferred as fully and as quickly as possible.

Regional efforts at self-reliance may stimulate future ocean collaboration. For instance, ASEAN and, in particular, its fisheries sector appear to be expanding. In the future, the role played by FAO-sponsored fishery organizations may be taken over by this regional group. While it might appear that economic forces alone prompt regional self-help efforts such as ASEAN, it is also true that developing states may seek regional economic collaboration in situations where they fear dominance by another state in the region, but where a defensive alliance is not possible. So, for instance, the strengthening of ASEAN also serves to provide some security against Vietnamese dominance of Southeast Asia. Concepts of regional self-reliance may never be practically implemented, since national attitudes and UN policy statements are often a poor indicator of future behavior. In at least some countries, the existence of corruption either among the political leadership or bureaucracy could prevent the adoption of self-reliance policies in ocean development, since foreign bidding for offshore resource rights can so easily involve rewards.

3. The developing states' need to collaborate in meeting penetration by developed states and multinational corporations under the new regime.

The emerging law of the sea regime seeks to use the economic zone to close off or separate coastal state resources from exploitation by the international community. However, as developing country representatives are well aware, attempts to permeate these new boundaries will be made. This external factor will provide a strong motive for regional cooperation among developing states, in contrast with the kind of internal, regional considerations that were assumed to motivate regional integrative efforts in the past. Regional policy harmonization (as in the case of foreign investment) should continue, since such efforts would be in accordance with general developments in regional collaboration, and also because harmonization provides a means of coping with the new kinds of transnational penetration produced in response to the new law of the sea regime. Developing countries have generally recognized that they would not have an effective bargaining position unless criteria and policies were unified against the industrialized centers of both East and West. For instance, the new twelve-member South Pacific Regional Fisheries Agency that has been proposed for South Pacific Forum member states is the first regional institution developed specifically in response to the problems (as much as to the potential benefits) raised by the new regime. The underlying purpose of the agreement is to coordinate policies on foreign fishing, so that distant-water states are not able to play off one developing state against another in maintaining access to the skipjack tuna fishery. Such exploitation is a real possibility, since Japan, South Korea, Taiwan, and the Soviet Union all have fleets in the South Pacific, and presently harvest 90 percent of the tuna catch.[14]

4. Major resource conflicts have now been settled conclusively, so regional arrangements can now be made.

As long as the nature and scope of coastal state authority was uncertain, coastal states naturally refused to make any regional commitments that might weaken their position. Now that most of the resource issues have been settled, it can be anticipated that some regional developments will proceed. For instance, in the case of the developed countries, a broad scientific research organization for the North Pacific is now informally endorsed by some American and Canadian officials, whereas several years ago both were adamant against becoming involved in such a scheme. Similarly, certain accommodations appear to have been made by Indonesia with respect to Malaysian distant-water fishing now that the exact rights of non-coastal states are clear.

5. Some efficiency criteria can be met regionally that cannot be met nationally.

This argument is the basic one made to support many types of regional economic integration, the criteria sought being the achievement of economies of scale, or cost sharing of certain goods and services. Given the limited size and resources of many developing states, a strong practical case can be made for regional ocean management. The costs of administering economic zones will be substantial, particularly if countries lack the existing infrastructure of scientific and technological personnel to carry out basic operations such as hydrographic surveys. The creation of joint enterprises is also likely to be seen as desirable, and in the case of both oil and fisheries, multilateral joint enterprises rather than just bilateral ones may be a possibility. Such enterprises might be incorporated within existing regional economic arrangements, so that new transgovernmental and transnational structures may emerge. In the case of fisheries, past regional cooperation has just dealt with harvesting, but in the future may equally stress the processing and marketing sectors. There may be potential for developing country fishery trade to increase, since it is very low now. For instance, intraregional trade in the Caribbean might increase in future, since states like Jamaica will lose part of their present regional catch.

However, the fact that rational economic reasons exist for some integration is a necessary but not a sufficient cause for collaboration in one issue area. Such integration would probably not even be extended into other ocean areas. Given past experience, it appears spillover would not occur, since economic and political integration do not lie on a continuum in the case of developing countries, and economic questions are also "high" politics. The experience in providing joint services among developing countries is mixed: while such efforts have not always failed, they have had a troubled history, and have generally not expanded beyond their initial mandate.

6. Collective situations will require regional collaboration.

Some of the problems that the UNCLOS III texts imply require a regional response have been suggested previously. In some instances, the problems that prevented global rule-making seem just as likely to impede regional rule-making. Still, some of these problems have a collective character that may compel a regional response. Unlike private economic goods, collective goods are a special kind that, when produced, provide equal benefit or harm to all, and from which none can be excluded. With growing interdependence, these situations (of which pollution is the commonest example) have become common internationally, and may provide opportunities for an important type of regional international collaboration in future. One observer has suggested that collective goods vary according to whether or not they can be divided, and according to whether or not they can be appropriated (i.e., the free rider problem), with four general situations being possible.[15] In a "normal" situation, a good or service (such as the continental margin resources) can be divided and appropriated, so the only reason for a regional or international organization to form would be to enhance or facilitate national action. In abnormal situations—those of a collective nature—national costs will not be fairly distributed without regional or international collaboration.

Situations of "joint supply and appropriability" may be common in the economic zones of developing countries. That is, once one state has produced a marine-related good or service, the opportunity cost of extending it to others is almost negligible. For instance, in regions such as the Gulf of Guinea, naval or aerial surveillance and enforcement for ship-generated pollution control and fisheries patrol may be as cheaply done for a group of states as for one. Similarly, in the areas of pollution monitoring and resource surveys a country could make its own efforts, and exclude others, but to no purpose since its costs would be the same. Another instance might be the regulation of shipping through straits by one of the concerned straits states. The Malacca Straits Council, for instance, initially involved just Japan and Singapore. However, as costs went up, other states could legitimately be required to collaborate, and Indonesia later participated.

In cases of "divisibility and nonappropriability," goods and services are at least theoretically divisible, but other countries cannot be excluded from benefit or harm. Boundary delimitation between adjacent or opposing states of the seabed or water column is entirely possible, but it may often not be done because the political costs will be too high. Joint management regimes may then have to be established to prevent one country from draining a common oil pool or common fishery at the expense of its neighbor(s). Salmon resources have traditionally had these characteristics, since the stocks could be divided but other states could not be excluded. The salmon states managed to alter this situation at UNCLOS III by "correcting" the nonappropriable character of the resource with a legal ban on new entrants.

In instances of "joint supply and nonappropriability," the good is produced at no extra cost at all to outsiders, and they can in no way be excluded, either for good or ill. Climate modification is the classic example, but although there are many examples for the oceans, what is in joint supply usually seems to be something undesirable. In enclosed and semi-enclosed seas, dumping and air- and land-generated ocean pollution afflict all the states of the region. Since they are all equally vulnerable, there is some likelihood they will collaborate successfully to set standards, arrange emergency procedures, and so on. In the case of highly migratory fish, conservation services (e.g., controls on spawning areas by coastal states where tuna spawned) would benefit all those fishing tuna equally, and none could be excluded from benefit. One "solution" then is that no measures are taken at all. Alternatively, the states most concerned with tuna fishing work out their own allocative arrangement and compensation plan for those countries who have provided management services.

7. Elite accommodation provides the basis for regional cooperation.

Hopefully, the UNCLOS III negotiations have indirectly promoted the cause of regional cooperation. National policymakers who have been active in the negotiations should have a higher interest in and commitment to a stable regime than those that have not received this unusual and protracted form of torture. Ten years of meeting should have built up extensive personal contacts among policymakers so that in future the regional channels of communication established at UNCLOS III remain open. Since law of the sea delegates have a common language and common understanding of at least parts of the new regime, conflicts arising from misperceptions and misinformation should be minimized. At times, this kind of elite accommodation may be more essential to stability than the existence of general rules. For instance, in the period of floating exchange rates following the breaking down of the Bretton Woods system, the ability of key financiers and bankers to communicate with each other on an international basis created some stability even in the absence of rules.

Forces Constraining Regional Cooperation or Promoting Conflict.

While there are good reasons to expect some degree of regional collaboration on ocean matters among the developing countries, such efforts will be sharply constrained by a number of international and regional political factors.

1. The evolution of law of the sea politics from "low" to "high" politics.

Whatever else UNCLOS III has done, it has successfully politicized both the question of deep seabed resources and of resources within the zone. The issues have become visible and emotive and now must be dealt with by political leaders rather than be technocrats. As with European integration, there has been a point after which management by technocrats becomes unacceptable. In the past it was assumed that the point was when defence and foreign policy questions became involved. Now, however, it is evident that the definition of what constitutes high and low politics has changed. Energy problems have destroyed the notion that military and defence questions are any more politically crucial than economic ones, and no one would suggest that the European Community's common fisheries policy was noncontroversial. Ocean issues should remain high politics, whether they are globally or regionally negotiated, because issues tend to be more politicized in developing countries and because of the linkage of ocean politics to the NIEO and resource shortages. UNCLOS III has had positive results in that political leaders in the developing world may now pay more attention to such mundane questions as fisheries and merchant marines, but the price of this new recognition is that technocrats will not control future developments.

2. The obsolescence of existing regional ocean arrangements.

Some of the existing regional regimes or institutions, such as those for nuclear-free zones or for pollution control are compatible with the emerging regime. Such regimes or institutions will survive, even though there may be little growth in areas such as ship-generated pollution (except in designated critical areas). Many of the regional fishery arrangements, however, are part of the power structure of the old regime and seem likely to disappear. Their problem is one of a low level of legitimacy as much as their redundancy. In the Indian and Pacific Oceans there has been a feeling that FAO and its regional councils did not give enough support to coastal state interests, and a suspicion that the Japanese did not wish FAO to take a strong role in the Pacific. On the other hand, some organizations may survive through adaptation, and because the problems involved in drawing up a new convention may appear to be insurmountable.

3. Lack of agreement among developing states at UNCLOS III.

While the African and Latin American groups sought to maintain a common law of the sea position, such unity has not even been attempted seriously among Asian states. For the most part, the LLGD question has split efforts to form regional positions, even though such positions were attempted as early as 1968. In particular, the concept of regional economic zones has received no support outside the LLGD group. The reason for this, from the standpoint of regional integration, is evident: winners and losers would be clearly identifiable. Adding on 200-mile economic zones and chunks of living and nonliving resources add visibly and quantifiably to a country's capabilities. Regional economic zones would require coastal states to give up visible resources to LLGD states for benefits which were weak and intangible.

4. The overwhelming impact of the international system on the developing world.

Even given further deterioration of UNCLOS III, it is difficult to imagine where successful regional regimes or institutions could be set up, since global issues would impinge. For instance, if the United States began deep seabed mining in earnest and attempted to negotiate bilateral agreements with concerned countries, some of the Pacific countries might be expected to develop in response a regional regime, since most of the operations would be in one sector of the Pacific. But given the collective character of the deep seabed question (as a divisible but nonappropriable resource) there is no way the problem could be successfully "encapsulated" within one region. Still, sudden political events such as unilateral deep seabed mining may yet be the external catalyst that prompts regional or international collaboration on the deep seabed issue. In the past, such external noncontinuous factors have provided motives for integration or regime formation more often than have long-term internal forces, (e.g., the role of the *Torrey Canyon* in changing the regime for ship-generated pollution).

5. The intensifying of regional conflict as a result of contiguity.

High levels of tension exist between many neighboring states, and states within a region, in the developing world. These may be aggravated both by new contiguities resulting from UNCLOS III and changes in the regional balance of power resulting from shifts in ocean resources. The idea that the seas serve as a buffer between warring states is an ancient one, in some respects outmoded by the communications revolution and the relative decline in the importance of naval power. And, as the governments of coastal states have found, the seas are more likely to given naval powers access to their shores than to protect them. Nevertheless, extended territorial seas and economic zones may promote regional conflict. An extensive group of studies suggest that geographic proximity may increase a country's involvement in foreign conflict.[16] So quite apart from the separate problem of marine boundary delimitation, the fact of increased worldwide contiguity will of its own increase conflict. This contiguity will have its most serious repercussions in the enclosed and semi-enclosed seas, where the 200-mile plus margin formula gives states many new neighbors as opposing states. For developing states, these problems will be most acute in the Aegean, Mediterranean, East China Sea, South China Sea, and possibly the Caribbean.

There are several aspects to the problem of geographic contiguity and conflict, the most general conclusion being that countries surrounded by many others get involved in more violent foreign conflict than geographically isolated states. While states have tended to become involved in wars in proportion to the number of states with which they share common frontiers, the actual increase in war has been less than expected, given the proportionate increase in air and sea power. On the whole, states with differences appear to be better off if they are geographically separated—only one study being unable to establish a correlation between number of borders with other countries and foreign conflict behavior. In addition, the likelihood of war increases when a single nation's territory is not contiguous, since strategic vulnerability is increased and intervention by other states becomes more likely. Whether the problem of contiguity is as severe in the case of sea boundaries as in land boundaries has not been explored. It might be assumed that sea boundaries do not have quite the emotive power of land boundaries (particularly when it is an economic zone rather than a territorial sea), but at the same time uncertainty about the precise location of a marine boundary may aggravate conflict.

The new regime, then, may generate disputes of varying severity. Many disputes associated with overlapping boundary claims for the territorial sea, economic zone, and continental shelf will be relatively minor. Such disputes will be widespread, however, and ambiguities in the convention over the importance of equitable principles versus equidistance will add to the difficulties. The end result may be that many boundaries will not be drawn, creating the opportunity for producing joint goods and services bilaterally or multilaterally.

More serious conflict is likely to arise when countries with political differerences become contiguous. While Greece and Turkey constitute the most serious problem, UNCLOS III may aggravate existing difficulties in other developing country areas.[17] In the case of Africa, it has been suggested that there is less hesitation to raise boundary questions now that the danger of intervention by ex-colonial powers is clearly past.[18] Another area of serious potential conflict concerns states with noncontiguous regions or territories, particularly offshore islands in another state's territorial sea or economic zone. The importance of islands in serving as basepoints makes it likely isolated islands will be pursued, not for themselves, but for the strength they give to national boundary claims. The rather vague distinction between rocks and islands in the texts may not prevent rocks being used for this purpose. The developing countries (and developed ones as well) that are troubled by the problem of offshore islands on the natural extension of the continental shelf of another state are widespread, with bilateral disputes between Greece and Turkey; Yemen (Aden) and Somalia; Italy and Tunisia; Cameroun and Equatorial Guinea and Spain and Morocco.[19]

6. The intensifying of regional asymmetries.

When several developed states are found in a developing country region, regional asymmetries are certain to exist. Even in regions that are solely populated by developing countries, oil politics and the economic development process have created uneven regional development.[20] In addition to these sources of tension, the shifts in natural resource wealth brought about by 200-mile economic zones may itself affect the power balance within regions, and in some instances regional hierarchy will be intensified. It is well known that the new regime will increase regional differentiation through increasing the capabilities of coastal states relative to their landlocked and disadvantaged neighbors. Besides changes in objective capabilities, the sense of relative deprivation that the LLGD states clearly have is also important in assessing potential for conflict. However, changes in power rank among coastal states as a result of UNCLOS III may ultimately produce more regional conflict. Many of the LLGD states are too weak to do anything about their situation, and are not involved in the game of seeking regional leadership.

SOME REGIONAL ASPECTS OF DOMINANCE AND DEPENDENCY

Some aspects of regional ocean collaboration among developing countries have been suggested, but these aspects must be viewed in context of the general relationship of dominance-dependency between the developed and the developing states. Major efforts at regional economic integration on the EEC model are not likely to be attempted in the future among the developing countries. The role of political communities such as the OAU is more viable, and the many existing weak regional and subregional arrangements will probably continue. Those arrangements that try to cope on several fronts with the problem of dominance and penetration—as the Andean Common Market and ASEAN have tried—may have the brightest futures. Another reason for the current lack of enthusiasm for full-fledged regional integration among political leaders is a simple and straightforward one—the potential effect of integration on the regional balance of power.

Regional collaboration is likely to develop with respect to a variety of ocean activities (particularly those of a collective nature), but there are strong constraints on the broad integration of marine activities. The principal difficulty is the extent to which resources and their development have become globally politicized. UNCLOS III has focused attention on questions of ocean use for the active public in many developing countries, so that these issues are now more visible—and therefore contentious—than in the past. UNCLOS III has resolved conflicts through the establishment of global values and the establishment of specific rules in many areas. But in creating pressure for boundary delimitation and in bringing sometimes hostile states into direct contact with each other it has laid the basis for regional conflict as well as collaboration. High interstate tension in some developing country regions as well as the lack of support for regional approaches at UNCLOS III suggest that ocean collaboration may be limited.

Asymmetrical relations will continue between developed and developing states, although the developing states on the whole lessen their dependency through extending resource control. The extent to which asymmetries will be perpetuated depends both on integrative and disintegrative trends in the law of the sea, and on such trends in the international economic sphere. Further, international economic disintegration would weaken the position of Southern states in two respects. Their general economic position would be weakened, and the developed states would increasingly emphasize bilateralism in their relations with developing states. Such an emphasis would further strengthen the present bilateral trend in the law of the sea, made necessary by the spate of unilateral legislation, and by the nature of the new ocean regime itself. So in future broad economic and political agreements may be negotiated bilaterally, in which ocean issues are just one of several bargaining chips. The major package agreement that two developed states—Australia and Japan—have sought may become a model for future agreements between developed and developing states.

Such changes would tend to accentuate the dependency condition, since vulnerability to bilateral pressures are both a cause and an indicator of dependency. Vulnerability can be demonstrated by the extend of trade with one developed state, or by measures of commodity concentration. It is worth examining some of the regions in which developing and developed states are found to get a sense of how regional power relations are affected by economic zone resources and dependency conditions.

In Oceania, the joint zones of the states and dependencies comprise six million square miles, one-fourth of the total world economic zone area. The regional states thus acquire resources that should allow them to substantially reduce their dependency on the ex-colonial powers and Japan. Within the region, however, Australia and New Zealand consolidate their dominant positions. New Zealand's GNP is about 30 times that of Fiji's, and Australia's is 150 times as great. While the developing island states acquire very large zones compared to most states, the total area is still smaller than the 3.4 million square miles acquired by Australia and New Zealand. Australia's strong interest in promoting and organizing the South Pacific Regional Fisheries Agency would suggest the developed states (including the ex-colonial powers) hope to strongly influence regional ocean policy.

Trends in other regions where developed and developing states interact can be indicated by comparing the states of the region in terms of their current power (as measured by absolute GNP), the area they gain with 200-mile economic zones, and their dependency (as measured by commodity concentration of exports).[21] As a glance at the Caribbean-Gulf of Mexico region shows (Table 9-1), the interplay of present power rank and changes in ocean capabilities shows how the regional balance of forces may be affected. High commodity concentrations, however, indicate both the individual vulnerability of each state and the vulnerability of the region as a whole to economic pressure from a developed state or states.

United States' gains with the economic zone allow it to maintain its dominant position in the region. Mexico strengthens its position as the second power in the region, while Columbia adds to its capabilities relative to Venezuela. Among the Central American states, Panama, which ranks below Guatemela as a subregional power, gains much more than its neighbors. In the case of Jamaica

Table 9–1. Trends in the Caribbean

	Current Power (GNP/10⁶)	*EEZ Area (naut. mi²)*	*Commodity Concentration (1968–73)*
United States	974,126	2,222,000	–
Mexico	43,070	831,500	13
Venezuela	10,607	106,100	104
Colombia	9,925	175,900	80
Cuba	4,406	–	93
Guatemala	1,942	28,900	47
Panama	1,340	89,400	86
Jamaica	1,098	86,800	37
Costa Rica	918	75,500	64
Nicaragua	813	46,600	49
Honduras	800	58,600	69
Trinidad and Tobago	747	22,400	92
Haiti	487	46,800	62
Barbados	118	48,800	48

Note: Besides the independent states, the Bahamas EZ area is 221,400 square miles; that of Martinique and Gyadeloupe 38,200 square miles.

and Barbados, their apparent gains are somewhat misleading, given the relative poverty of their waters. The developing states of the Caribbean are exceptionally vulnerable with respect to the United States and other developed states. The median for the region is 62, well above the average for the developing countries. Colombia, Panama, and Trinidad and Tobago are particularly dependent, and in the case of the first two the new bargaining chips they possess in ocean resources should reduce their vulnerability.

Japan maintains its dominant position in the South China Sea region, since its EEZ will be the second largest (Table 9–2). Whether or not Japan can use its

Table 9–2. Trends in the South China Sea

	*Current Power (GNP/10⁶)**	*EEZ Area (naut. mi.²)*	*Commodity Concentration (1968–73)*
Japan	413,070	1,126,000	–
China	n.a.	281,000	–
Indonesia	15,370	1,577,300	78
Philippines	10,330	551,400	50
Taiwan	10,226	114,400	5
Vietnam	n.a.	n.a.	n.a.
Thailand	9,180	94,700	43
Malaysia	6,565	138,700	65
Singapore	4,283	100	21
Cambodia	627	n.a.	[illegible]4
Laos	320	n.a.	[illegible]1

*GNP figures from World Almanac, 1977, compiled from AID figures.

power to guide ocean developments in the region is less certain. While Japan will maintain very strong influence on ASEAN, China and Vietnam will also become increasingly active in the South China Sea. Economic zone resources strengthen the Vietnamese position, since South Vietnam's zone alone had been 188,400 square miles. Similarly, Indonesia consolidates its position as third-ranking power. On the whole, the region seems capable of avoiding developed country dominance. Japan is the single major developed state in the region, and the region's median dependency figure is 46, much lower than for the Caribbean. Malaysia, Cambodia, and Indonesia are the most vulnerable to bilateral economic pressure. In future, Indonesia's expanded marine resource capability will strengthen its bargaining position.

France's economic leadership in the Mediterranean region is sustained, although Spain and Italy both make larger gains than France in their economic zones. In the Aegean, Greece's gains would narrow the power gap between itself and Turkey. Among the Saharan states, Morocco gains twice the amount Algeria does. Changes in power rank among middle-power, coastal states may be a destablizing factor in this region. If political relations are already bad, the state whose relative power position is declining seems most prone to initiate conflict. The region's developing states are less dependent here than in any other region (the median being 23), so that developed states within the region and external to the region should have limited influence on their ocean policies.

Finally, the South African region has not been included here since commodity concentrations are not a good indication of the dependency structure. The landlocked status of Botswana, Lesotho, and Swaziland is what must constrain

Table 9-3. Trends in the Mediterranean

	Current Power (GNP/10⁶)	*EEZ Area (naut. mi.²)*	*Commodity Concentration (1968–73)*
France	145,724	99,500	–
Italy	93,381	161,000	–
Spain	28,962	355,600	–
Yugoslavia	17,653	15,300	8
Turkey	13,036	69,000	40
Greece	8,358	147,300	22
Egypt	5,333	50,600	59
Israel	5,258	6,800	2
Morocco	3,100	81,100	24
Algeria	3,080	40,000	72
Libya	2,907	98,600	110
Lebanon	1,260	6,600	4
Tunisia	1,027	25,000	34
Albania	867	3,600	n.a.
Cyprus	506	29,000	15
Malta	189	19,300	1

their policy toward South Africa. Generally, however, the South African region is like the others described in that the developed dominant state makes the largest economic zone gains.

An essential aspect of dependency is not shown in trade data. New forms of transnational relations may emerge that will make it impossible for the new regime to work in the way it is legally supposed to. For instance, efforts to reduce asymmetries in scientific and technolgical skills are attempted in the general and specific provisions for the sharing of research and the transfer of technology. Direct exploitation may be lessened and regional centers for marine scientific research may help correct developed country biases on scientific research, which in the past led to such mistakes as the failure to develop general models suitable for the multispecies fisheries of tropical waters. But in most respects transfer of technology provisions will not be rigidly implemented because developing states will still be competing with each other for foreign investment. And while direct exploitation may be reduced, the more subtle forms in which it reappears—for example, more direct foreign investment, joint ventures, more manipulation of international markets—may be more difficult to control.

Finally, the prospects for changes in dominance-dependency structures have been examined with the assumption that there was a relatively moderate amount of disintegration on law of the sea rule-making. If the disintegration became more serious, particularly on the deep seabed question, dominance-dependency structures might be strengthened. Even if ISRA were established along the lines now proposed, elements of dominance must remain, since international organizations reflect the realities of power in the nation-state system. While it can even be argued that international organizations accentuate dominance, it seems more reasonable to note that the more recent international structures such as UNCTAD have mitigated the hierarchy and isolation that characterize bilateral relations between developed and developing states, ISRA, then, is more likely to modify dominance-dependency structures than bilateral arrangements are. One caveat is that the developed and developing states hold totally different images of what the fundamental nature of ISRA is. Thus, an apparent consensus would allow an organization to be established that would be revealed to be quite unworkable. A second caveat is that bilateralism might *not* be the mainstream response to unilateral action on deep seabed mining. While both bilateral agreements and the successful new forms of transnational cooperation that have emerged in this sphere do threaten Southern unity, the chance still remains that it might be maintained. In this event, unilateral action would be the catalyst that prompted the establishment of alternate international structures that, if adequately backed by OPEC states, might fundamentally challenge Northern dominance.

The law of the sea is neither being regionalized nor globalized. To argue so would be to suggest that global changes were as simple as the ebb and flow of the tide on an open beach. Since in reality present world conditions more closely resemble the currents found in a narrows, both integration and disintegration are occurring. In each aspect of law of the sea, the costs of interdependence and the collective nature of the situation differ, so that many specific regimes will emerge, and patterns of regional collaboration will vary. This complexity is revealed by the dispute settlement provisions, which rather than providing for generalized rule-adjudication, provide for many specific regimes, some of which are strong and some very weak. Within this context, the dominance and dependency that characterize relations between developed and developing states will be perpetuated but modified. Asymmetries may be most marked in regional politics, in part due to LLGD weakness, but mostly because several developed states strengthen their position in developing-country regions under the emerging regime for the law of the sea.

NOTES

1. J. Galtung, "A Structural Theory of Imperialism," *Journal of Peace* 8 (1971):81–117. Another study attempted to test the theory using foreign travel and trade data and found the economic patterns Galtung predicts but not the political ones. See J. Christopherson, "Structural Analysis of Transaction Systems: Vertical Fusion or Network Complexity," *Journal of Conflict Resolution* 20 (1976):637–62.

2. W. Zimmerman, "Hierarchial Regional Systems and the Politics of System Boundaries," *International Organization* 26:1 (1972):18–36.

3. R. Keohane and J. Nye, "World Politics and the International Economic System," in C.F. Bergsten (ed.), *The Future of the International Economic Order: An Agenda for Research* (Lexington, Mass.: D. C. Heath, 1973). Cited in R.D. Hansen, "The North-South Split and the Law of the Sea Debate," *Perspectives on Ocean Policy,* Ocean Policy Project, NSF, 1975, p. 114.

4. R.D. Hansen, *op. cit.,* pp. 109–33.

5. D. Smyth, "The Global Economy and the Third World in the U.N.," *World Politics* 29 (1977):594. This study of the sixth and seventh Special Sessions of the UN concluded that the West was more unified than the Third World on all substantive questions except resources. Socialist bloc countries were at least as unified as the Third World except for multinational corporations, monetary reform, and agriculture.

6. Oran Young, unpublished manuscript on Beringia (1976).

7. B.J. Abrahamsson "The Marine Environment and Ocean Shipping: Some Implications for a New Law of the Sea," *International Organization* 31, 2 (1977): 291–313.

8. R.D. Hansen, "Regional Integration: Reflections on a Decade of Theoretical Efforts," *World Politics* 21 (1969): 242–71.

9. E. Haas and P. Schmitter, "Economics and Differential Patterns of Political Integration: Projections about Unity in Latin America," *International Organization*, 28.

10. J.S. Nye, "Patterns and Catalysts in Regional Integration," in J.S. Nye (ed.), *International Regionalism: Readings* (Boston: Little, Brown and Co., 1968), pp. 333–49.

11. Ibid.

12. D. Smyth, in "The Global Economy," noted in his content analysis of UN debates the high incidence of references to the Chinese "self-help" model.

13. A. Lovbraek "The Chinese Model of Development," *Journal of Peace Research* 13 (1976):207–26.

14. *Far Eastern Economic Review* 97, 37 (Sept. 16, 1977): 62–63.

15. J. Ruggie, "Collective Goods and Future International Collaboration," *American Political Science Review* 66 (1972): 874–93.

16. The following findings are summarized in P.G. McGowan and H.B. Shapiro, *The Comparative Study of Foreign Policy: A Survey of Scientific Findings* (Beverly Hills: Sage Publications, 1973), p. 163.

17. Other areas include: " . . . India and Pakistan, and possibly also India and Bangladesh; the South China Sea (Vietnam, China, the Phillipines); the Sea of Japan (Japan, The U.S.S.R. and the two Koreas); Yugoslavia and Albania, and the eastern Mediterranean (Syria, Lebanon, Israel, Egypt)." Barry Buzan, *Sources of Dispute and Prospects for Conflict in the New Ocean Regime,* August 1, 1977 draft for a forthcoming Adelphi Paper.

18. Hansen, *supra* note 3.

19. Buzan, *op. cit.,* p. 15.

20. Hansen, *supra* note 3, p. 130.

21. There are obvious difficulties in using a single indicator of power, and GNP figures must themselves be viewed cautiously. Figures are taken from J.K. Gamble, *Global Marine Attributes* (Cambridge: Ballinger, Publishing Company, 1973), and *World Almanac.* 1977. The EZ area figures ignore variations in the resource potential of the zones. Commodity concentrations are calculated by the percentage share of a country's export market that the top three exports hold, weighted by the value of total merchandise. One hundred and thirteen developing states are then ranked from one (most independent) to 113 most dependent). Figures are from World Bank, *World Tables 1976* (Baltimore: Johns Hopkins Press, 1976), pp. 496–502.

Commentary

David Larson
University of New Hampshire

Rather than comment on Chapters Eight and Nine, I would like to look briefly at the work of the Indian Ocean Fishery Commission, since the emphasis of Article 70 of the ICNT seems to be on this kind of regional management.

The Indian Ocean falls into all three types of marine regions outlined by Lewis Alexander: (1) a physical region; (2) a management region; and, (3) an operational region. Physically, the Indian Ocean basin is bounded in the west by Africa and the Arabian peninsula, in the north by the South Asian subcontinent, in the east by the Southern Asian archipelago and Australia, and in the south by Antarctica. There is an important navigational opening around the Cape of South Africa to the west, which is the major east-west route of the supertankers from the Arabian/Persian Gulf, as well as the Suez Canal. In the east there are important international straits through the Indonesian archipelago at Malacca, Lombok, and Ombai. In the south there are important east-west routes for navigation to and from Australia to Western Europe. The Southwest Monsoon Current flows in a clockwise direction, and is largely bounded by the Horn of Africa, the Arabian peninsula, and the western side of the Indian subcontinent. The South Equatorial current is largely contained in the southern half of the Indian Ocean, and the Agulhas Current squeezes between Madagascar and Mozambique.

As a management region the Indian Ocean has made some progress but is still far from the levels of management achieved by the International Commission for the Northwest Atlantic Fisheries, for example. The initial movement toward some kind of regional ocean management came in 1968 under the auspices of the United Nations Food and Agriculture Organization (FAO) as part of a regional fisheries project sponsored by the United Nations Development Program. As such, the initial impetus for the Indian Ocean Fisheries Commission (IOFC) was largely developmental as a means of identifying and exploiting new sources of fish protein for the peoples surrounding the Indian Ocean Basin. It was recognized that development and management were two sides of the same coin, but the FAO philosophy was to emphasize development over management. The United States initially tended to support this developmental approach, partially because it felt that FAO had become politicized, and should essentially remain a technical body in an advisory capacity to the IOFC. As a result, the first meeting of the Indian Ocean Fishery Commission was not held until 1972, and there have been four such annual conferences since, the fifth session held in Cochin, India, in October 1977.

The first phase of the Indian Ocean as an operational region was for exploitation: Where were the resources, and what could be done to develop the fisheries? The second phase emphasized utilization: How could the fishery resources be processed, distributed, and marketed to the peoples of coastal states surrounding the Indian Ocean? The third phase was management of the resources: What could be done to achieve an optimum sustainable yield of both developed species (tuna and shrimp) and underdeveloped species (demersal). All three phases are now proceeding apace, since it has gradually come to be realized that they are interdependent, but the management phase has assumed the greatest role in the IOFC, largely due to the general consensus that there will be 200-mile "exclusive economic zones" coming to the region as a result of UNCLOS III. Interestingly, this has pushed the United States to the forefront, because of its vaunted management skills and the demand of the IOFC coastal states for technical assistance in managing the EEZ.

This rapid growth and development of the IOFC has caused some unresolved strains between its main objective of greater autonomy and the FAO/UNDP objective of retaining some central control. This tension is aggravated by the fact that most of the present and foreseeable funding of the IOFC ($2.5 million for the next three years) comes from outside the region, that is from FAO/UNDP, Sweden, Norway, and Canada. If the headquarters does move from Rome to the field, it will probably be established at Nairobi, but nobody knows where the funding for such a regional headquarters would come from. Also, it is feared that moving to the field might weaken the technical and research capabilities available through FAO headquarters in Rome. At the present time, the major actors in the IOFC are Kenya, India, Thailand, Bahrain, and Indonesia, with the United States and other advanced fishery countries supplying more in the way of economic and technical assistance.

The United States' policy seems to be one of sincerely trying to assist in the economic development of the Indian Ocean for the economic betterment of the region through rational ocean management. However, the credibility of the United States' position is somewhat eroded by the development of Diego Garcia as a naval base, and its reluctance to go along with United Nations

General Assembly Resolution 2832 (XXVI) of December 1971 on the "Declaration of the Indian Ocean as a Zone of Peace." There have been several resolutions since then, culminating in UNGA Resolution 31/88 (XXXI) of December 1976, calling for the "Implementation of the Declaration of the Indian Ocean as a Zone of Peace." However, there were recent reports in the *Christian Science Monitor* (e.g., November 10, 1977) that the third part of the new SALT II package may contain a superpower agreement to withdraw naval forces from the Indian Ocean. If so, this would be a significant step toward the demilitarization and regionalization of the Indian Ocean.

The future of the IOFC is rather ambiguous at this time. The Indian Ocean is a broad geographic region, with one of the heaviest coastal populations in the world, with potentially great fishery resources to help feed the region, but with enormous economic, technical, cultural, and management problems to overcome. If this experiment in regional ocean management is to succeed, it will require continued technical and research assistance from FAO; continued financial assistance from UNCP, Canada, Norway, Sweden, Australia, and the United States; as well as increasing regional cooperation among the coastal states. In addition, there are still significant problems of pollution, navigation and superpower involvement that have to be contended with.

Furthermore, migratory species, such as tuna, do not confine themselves to one region of the world ocean, thereby necessitating interregional cooperation particularly between the IOFC and the Indo-Pacific Fisheries Council (IPFC). Fortunately, there is a close interlocking directorate of the two bodies, so there seems to be progress in this area as well. Nonetheless, the fisheries outside national jurisdiction, except for the migratory species, are rather limited in view of the almost universal extension of 200-mile exclusive economic zones by most coastal states, which are estimated to encompass as much as 90 percent of the coastal or nonmigratory species. So in addition to the problems of vertical regional and interregional integration there are the problems of horizontal national fragmentation!

Therefore, I tend to conclude that, without an UNCLOS III convention with strong provisions for regional cooperation, the prospects for the IOFC seem rather dim, and the trend toward unilateral, national action by coastal states will probably accelerate.

Discussion and Questions

John Gamble: I have been asked by Dr. Pisarev if he might make a brief comment before I open general discussion and questioning from the audience.

Vladimir Pisarev: Recent developments in the legal regime of the oceans demonstrate that, along with negotiations on the comprehensive law of the sea treaty within the framework of the United Nations, attempts are being made by some countries to abandon the objective of securing the universal agreement and make the system of international ocean relations subject to arbitrary actions of some states or groups of states.

The U.S. unilateral legislation on the 200-mile fishing zone could be cited as an example of such approach, which has already complicated the work of the UNCLOS III. A dangerous trend toward separate solution of international ocean issues is reflected in U.S. attempts to secure access to the deep seabed for its companies on the ground of unilateral domestic legislation.

Professor G. Knight thinks that the United States could take the lead in developing the international law of the sea and that its legislation on marine matters could serve as a model for other nations. Soviet scientists consider such an approach unacceptable. U.S. attempts to impose its rules on other states and the international community might only lead to the impairment of generally recognized principles of international law. That point of view, by the way, is shared by many scientists and statemen in the United States, for instance, by former Secretary of State Kissinger in his address at Montreal in 1975.

Along with actions directed against international cooperation in the elaboration of the law of the sea, other alternatives to the comprehensive treaty approach are being developed under the pretext of possible failure by the UN conference to produce universal convention on the law of the sea. These alternatives range from the orthodox and unorthodox alternative approaches, developed by Professord D. Johnston at the Ninth LSI Annual Conference, to acquiescence in other nations' acts and even the use of force.

Among such alternatives there are some that provide for the making of a "package deal" and the conclusion of multiple limited treaties, as well as those that envisage the development by separate groups of nations of treaties or agreements, each reflecting a particular predisposition on the issues, without obtaining broad acceptance outside the group. I share Professor Knight's opinion that such an approach could produce a situation prone to conflict, since there would be differing legal theories operative in the same areas and with respect to the same resources of the sea.

I think that regionalization of the law of the sea, conceived as one such modification, would mean that all problems discussed now at the UN Law of the Sea Conference would be dealt with by groups of states (not necessarily belonging to the same region) on an arbitrary basis. This kind of regional diversification would lead toward a pluralistic regime for the world ocean, characterized by different levels of rights, obligations, and responsibilities for the states involved in ocean development. The pluralistic nature of such a development would create new difficulties among states in the distribution of rights to ocean wealth: difficulties between states belonging to a given regional agreement and nonmembers within the same area; between regional groups or states and amalgamations of countries based on common economic or political interests; and between different groups of states operating in marine areas beyond the limits of national jurisdiction.

As for the EEZ areas referred to in the ICNT, regionalization would lead to the establishment of a great diversity of national laws and would undoubtedly impede the rational exploitation of these marine regions for both coastal states and distant-water nations.

In such a situation the developing countries—those that have claimed sovereign rights over the living and mineral resources of vast offshore areas and those that are geographically disadvantaged or landlocked—would enter into a very complicated system of arrangements among themselves, as well as with the developed countries, outside the comprehensive, balanced, and generally recognized framework now being negotiated for the international law of the sea. Legal uncertainty of this kind would also reduce the developing countries' prospects of gaining technology, financial assistance, and managerial skills for mastering the offshore areas and the resources they need.

Thus, the regionalization of the law of the sea conceived as an alternative to the global approach within the scope of the comprehensive treaty does not help to achieve the major objectives: reduction of tensions, minimization of potential conflict, and the promotion of international cooperation in the peaceful uses of the world ocean for the benefit of all countries.

On the other hand, if the regionalization of the law of the sea is seen as a practical realization of the universal treaty and applied to specific situations, areas, and participants in the global ocean regime, it could be considered justified as an approach to some of the current problems of international economic relations. The basis for legitimate regionalization is to be found in the basic norms and principles of the UN Charter, and in the understanding that all states entering into regional agreements would be subject in international law to the obligations imposed by the comprehensive law of the sea treaty, whatever their geographic position, the composition of regional groups, and the terms in which such agreements are drawn up.

John Gamble: I would like to make a brief comment, and then take questions from the floor for the remainder of the session. It seems to me there has not been very close agreement today on the general usefulness of the regionalism concept of the Third World. I think that it has been presumed in some quarters that there is some positive good in regionalism, and I am not sure that what we have heard today would necessarily support this. It seems the term has been used in so many different ways that it has lost some of the meaning it might have for our understanding of the current situation of the developing countries. Any concept like this has utility only when it bears directly on the real world situation, and I think we have been using this term in ways so different from one another that we perhaps do not have a very common understanding of it. So perhaps one of the best things we could produce from a session like this would be a better term than regionalism. If we are not comfortable with it, then one of the more positive things we could do would be to suggest some alternative that perhaps fits the real world better.

Kazuo Sumi: Perhaps it would be better to introduce the ICES system into the Pacific Ocean. Despite the obvious need for international regional cooperation in the field of scientific research, the conservation of living resources, and the protection of the marine environment, nothing but confusion in the conservation and management of living resources is likely to arise out of the "ownership" provisions of the ICNT, especially from the language of Article 56, which recognizes the coastal state's "sovereign rights" to the resources of the exclusive economic zone. This kind of language allows little hope for the creation of a new international economic order. According to the ICNT, it would depend essentially upon the discretion of the coastal state whether landlocked and geographically disadvantaged states may be admitted to participate in the exploitation of the resources within the economic zone of the neighboring coastal state. On present evidence, most of the developed coastal states are likely to establish 200-mile zones. For example, I suppose that Dr. Johnson's country, Canada, has no intention of sharing its resources within the 200-mile zone with landlocked states. Since there is no such category on the North American continent, a country like Canada is free to monopolize its resources completely. As to the conservation and management of living resources, it is easier to achieve cooperation with the United States, but at present this kind of cooperation seems to depend on the resolution of ownership and delimitation issues in Georges Bank and other boundary areas.

Without solving the problem of distribution of resources, I think it will be very difficult to achieve international or regional cooperation.

Barbara Johnson: It seems to me you are saying that unless the allocation question is tied, for instance, to the question of scientific research, you won't have successful regional collaboration. In my opinion, the only hope now for regional organizations, particularly in scientific research, is for them to separate themselves from the allocation function. I think it is significant the ICES is surviving today, whereas those other organizations that have become heavily involved in questions of allocation are in the process of collapsing. What may happen is that the scientists who have lost their "purity" in the battle over allocation in the last ten years will be able to go back into forming international organizations designed only to deal with scientific questions. The allocation side of management will stay with the national government; the scientists will lose whatever power they had, but will regain their purity.

Chennat Gopalakrishnan: I would like first to make a comment on the presentation of Dr. Barbara Johnson. She hypothesized that in regions consisting of economically disparate countries attempts at integration would necessarily lead to destabilization or some other kind of disruption. We have just concluded a study of India focusing on different states of India with widely divergent per capita incomes over a ten-year period. As a result of the green revolution, the disparity in income among the different states has decreased substantially with no destabilizing effects. If the analogy is extended to a region consisting of a group of states, it would seem that perhaps it is premature to conclude that economic integration policy would necessarily lead to disruption and destabilization. It could very well lead to greater harmony, if one were to look at the Indian experience.

Along the same lines, Professor Alexander pointed out that approximately 42 percent of the potential economic zone would accrue to fifteen coastal states. What is intriguing is the fact that of these fifteen coastal states about six are major maritime powers and the rest "less developed" coastal states. So in any scenario of regional integration it is entirely conceivable that there will be at least one major maritime power and a cluster of less developed coastal states, which suddenly find themselves in possession of an enormous ocean frontier waiting to be exploited. It seems to me that some kind of positive collaborative arrangement is bound to emerge.

I would also like to comment on the potential role of transnational corporations. One of the major problems, as I see it, is the lack of a global code of conduct with respect to the operations of transnational corporations. In view of the fact that in any regional configuration there would be a major maritime, perhaps it would be a lot easier to develop a code of corporate conduct within the framework of the region. Enforcing such a code of conduct would also be easier within the regional context, because the collective influence of the other countries would have some kind of enduring impact. Perhaps Dr. Johnson would like to comment on this.

Barbara Johnson: With regard to the first point about the success in reducing disparities among the states of India without causing political tensions, I think the key has always been in having an appropriate regional economic integration scheme. The solution is to anticipate the changes in power and economic strength and introduce compensation at the beginning. That is precisely what can never be done at the international level. The political leaders are simply not able to accept the implications of that and take the compensatory measures at the beginning. It may be, however, that within certain regional settings, this is not impossible.

As to the potential role of the transnational corporations, I think you are quite right that the problem of a code of corporate conduct does touch on the future of ocean development. It may be more important to accomplish indirectly rather than directly: in the area of joint ventures, foreign investment, and marketing, rather than through control over the harvesting sector. These indirect forms of control by developed states are actually harder to control than direct exploitation. I do not see any future for a code of corporate conduct at a regional level. It is a problem of global reach, and the only way it can be tackled is globally.

Odidi Okidi: It is just a point of information that I am seeking. Were you suggesting that FAO would divorce IOFC from its own structure, if IFOC should go regional within the Indian Ocean area? Is there any reason why FAO should not have a field regional office in the form of IOFC, but financed directly by FAO, just as most other specialized agencies have their own regional offices within specific areas?

David Larson: The question whether the IOFC should be under more centralized FAO control or decentralized IOFC control has not been resolved. There is still a tension here. Part of the problem is due to the lack of field research facilities and personnel, compared with what is available at Rome. Now, it may be that the only way that you are going to develop research facilities and capable personnel is to decentralize and go to the field. I am not saying that is the way to go; the trade-offs involved have not really been made clear. But at this particular point in time, FAO and UNDP in combination are underwriting the IOFC for the next three years. There is a feeling that this kind of relationship may not be continued if the IOFC goes ahead with decentralization, and that the organization would have to come up with its own budget, perhaps in the vicinity of $2½ million. This is not an impossible task.

Odidi Okidi: What I do not understand is why it would be seen as necessary for FAO and UNDP to divest in the event of decentralization.

David Larson: I do not think the IOFC can have it both ways: you can not have the advantages of centralization, with research capability and financing, as well as those of decentralization, meaning local autonomy. I certainly sympathize with that, but I think there is a feeling that if they do go regional, FAO might feel it would be better advised to utilize its resources and personnel in other areas to get them started. Somebody in the audience may know more about this than I do.

John Marr: Mr. Chairman, there seems to be some confusion between the Indian Ocean Fishery Commission and the Indian Ocean Program. The Commission is a group of nations that is organized into a commission under the FAO Charter. The Indian Ocean Program is an FAO/UNDP Program financed by UNDP. First, FAO could not use the money for anything else, even if it wanted; and second, the Program tends to be a creature of the Commission, and I am sure if the Commission members decided to locate it in Nairobi, or any place else in the region, it would be located there.

David Larson: If I may go back to the previous question, Dr. Nyhart at MIT has come up with some preliminary figures that I think are interesting. Something like 90 percent of the nonmigratory species of fish will be within 200 miles and a very substantial amount of the oil resources will also be within 200 miles. What he is trying to establish is whether there is really a significant amount of resources left over, outside 200-mile limits, other than on the deep ocean floor.

Part IV

Marine Resource Management in the North Pacific Rim

Chairman
H. Gary Knight
Louisiana State University

The subject for this part is "Marine Resource Management in the North Pacific Rim." By "marine resources" we include the entire spectrum of uses of ocean space: minerals, living resources, transportation, environmental protection, and so forth. Naturally it is very difficult, even for all speakers combined, to cover all these issues, and all the national and regional interests involved, but I hope that none of you will be dissuaded from raising questions on matters that may not be directly addressed in the papers. The region encompasses the countries of the North Pacific Rim: the two Chinas, the two Koreas, Japan, the Soviet Union, the United States, and Canada.

To open the session this morning we have Dr. Choon-ho Park, who has already been introduced to you this week, so that I hesitate to go through another litany of his accomplishments, but perhaps I can merely note that he obtained his doctorate in public international law from Edinburgh University and he is now senior research fellow at Harvard Law School. As you heard last night, he was elected to membership on the Executive Board of the Law of the Sea Institute on Sunday. Dr. Park will be followed by Professor Hideo Takabayashi. Dr. Talabayashi, who is professor of international law at Ryukoku University, received his legal education, including a doctorate, at Kyoto University. In recent years he has been a fellow at the Woodrow Wilson International Center for Scholars in Washington, D.C., and has been dean of his law school in Japan. On Sunday he too was elected to the Executive Board of the Law of the Sea Institute.

Chapter Ten

Recent Developments in Marine Resource Diplomacy in the North Pacific Region

Choon-ho Park
Harvard University

INTRODUCTION

In the North Pacific Ocean, 200-mile fishery jurisdiction has come into force in a most dramatic fashion in 1977, for the problems of fishing rights still remain the major source of controversy over marine resource development in this region. Among the coastal states, Canada was the first to adopt a 200-mile fishing zone. This action, which took effect in January 1977, was not unexpected. However, the same kind of decision by the United States, announced in April 1976 to take effect in March 1977, gave a decisive impetus to the trend toward extended coastal state jurisdiction in the North Pacific. Surprised by what seemed like a second round of the Truman Proclamations, Japan was still hesitating to accept the United States' claim when the Soviet Union provided a further shock by not only recognizing the United States zone in November 1976, but also deciding to claim a 200-mile fishing zone of its own the following month. To regulate foreign fishing within its own offshore water, Japan itself was now forced to adopt precisely the same kind of unilateral measure that it had previously been so active in opposing. In July 1977 the limit of Japanese territorial waters was extended from three to twelve miles, and at the same time a 200-mile fishing zone around the Japanese coast was proclaimed. North Korea emerged as the fifth 200-miler in the region in August 1977, when it announced its own claim to a 200-mile economic zone. The North Korean jurisdiction was reinforced with what it calls an exclusive military boundary zone, which extends roughly fifty miles, on the average, from the shoreline.

These developments have left China and South Korea out of fashion. Reportedly, they too are cautiously moving for a 200-mile extension of jurisdiction, if for no other reason than to save face. Geographically, a 200-mile zone is not necessarily beneficial to them because, in the enclosed seas of Northeast Asia, the coastal states are all situated within 400 miles of one another, which means that whenever a coastal state extends its jurisdiction up to 200 miles problems are certain to arise between adjacent and opposite neighbors.

If South Korea happens to adopt a 200-mile zone before China—and this is a possibility—China would find itself in a rather awkward position. As a self-styled standard-bearer of the Third World, China has most enthusiastically campaigned in support of the regime of a 200-mile economic zone, but in its own region it may turn out to be the last to adopt it. Furthermore, to the extent that a 200-mile zone of jurisdiction proves to be more beneficial to the major maritime powers—the two superpowers in particular—than to the majority of the Third World countries, it would appear that China has in fact campaigned in the interest of the superpowers, whose maritime policy it has persistently sought to denounce.

The controversy over mineral resource development in the region concerns so far only three of the coastal states: namely, China, Japan, and South Korea. In the Yellow Sea and the East China Sea, the unilateral claims of these states considerably overlap, because each of them insists on a method of boundary delimitation that is not acceptable to the others. China relies on the natural-prolongation principle; Japan on the median-line principle; and South Korea on the median-line principle vis-à-vis China in the Yellow Sea, and on the natural-prolongation principle vis-à-vis Japan in the East China Sea. In the present political circumstances, no multilateral boundary agreement is possible. When five parties (including North Korea and Taiwan) argue over what would under normal circumstances require only three, even to bring all of them together for negotiations becomes nearly impossible.

Without a domestic supply of oil, Japan and South Korea have become so impatient at China's patience that they have made a bilateral arrangement to develop oil from what in their view lies far beyond Chinese jurisdiction in the East China Sea. Although the joint development pact has been ratified by both parties, significant obstacles remain to be overcome before Japan and South Korea can develop oil from the troubled waters of Northeast Asia.

On the nonresource side of maritime jurisdiction in this region, problems of navigation and protection of the marine environment may also be noted. For the United States and the Soviet Union, the importance of North Pacific sea-lane communications for their national security and economic interests does not require elaboration. Japan's viability as one of the world's largest economies depends predominantly on the safety of maritime transportation in the North Pacific, because it has to import over 600 million tons of raw materials, and export over 60 million tons of commodities every year, With appropriate allowance for the difference in scale, what can be said of Japan applies equally to South Korea. Because of its burgeoning foreign trade, China's dependence on sea transport is also increasing at a rapid pace. Furthermore, for domestic economic reasons, China must also rely more heavily on coastal shipping than other major powers in the region.

The problems of passage through straits used for international navigation are likely to be a potential source of controversey among the coastal states of the North Pacific region. Japan alone has as many as seventy two straits that are narrower than twenty four miles, and five of them are used as major routes by foreign merchant and military vessels. In fact, due to the importance of these five straits, Japan has, as a provisional measure, had to exempt them from the application of its claim to a twelve-mile territorial sea. One of the major reasons for this reservation may be noted with interest. The Japanese people are so sensitive to nuclear weapons that even the passage through Japanese territorial waters of foreign military vessels with nuclear weapons would constitute violation of what is called the "three nonnuclear principles" whereby Japan is not to make, hold, or allow nuclear weapons in Japanese territory.

Without a specific limit to its territorial sea, South Korea has been an odd man out in Northeast Asia, if not in the world. As in the case of Japan, one of the major reasons for its reluctance to declare what it is reported to have prepared, namely, a twelve-mile limit to its territorial sea, is the difficulty of handling the problems of straits. South Korea is aware of the gravity of security problems arising from the passage of Chinese, North Korean, and Soviet vessels through its straits.

With respect to the protection of the North Pacific marine environment, virtually no arrangements have been made at the regional level. In this region, there has been no serious accident of international marine pollution to date, and hence no real need for such arrangements has been felt. The coastal community consists of developed and developing economies, each of which entertains a different level of pollution consciousness. Even in the enclosed seas of Northeast Asia, which are more vulnerable to pollution than the rest of the water space in the region, no multilateral efforts have been made to regulate pollution hazards from different sources. This is in contrast to what is being done in other enclosed seas, such as the Baltic Sea, the North Sea, and the Mediterranean Sea.

With the density of sea traffic and the increase in seabed activities expected in the future, circumstances will not tolerate such regional inaction indefinitely. For instance, the Japan-South Korea agreement on joint development of the continental shelf requires the parties to regulate marine pollution in the area together. This would require South Korea to institute a marine pollution prevention law, as Japan did in 1970. Since the bilateral agreement could not enter into force without the enactment of domestic legislation by each party, preparations are reportedly under way in South Korea for such a law.

As noted earlier, the political climate among the five governments of the three Northeast Asian states is not conducive to regional cooperation for marine pollution control. On the other hand, it has to be pointed out that pollution problems are ideologically neutral in nature and therefore require to be treated likewise. A patch of spilled oil floating around in the middle of an enclosed sea would not wait for the coastal states to enter into political or ideological ping-pong games. The refusal of a coastal state to join multilateral arrangements for political reasons may simply deprive it of whatever benefit such arrangements may have to offer.

Now I would like to look at some specific developments that have taken place since 1976.

FISHERY RELATIONS BETWEEN JAPAN AND OTHER COASTAL STATES

Japan and the United States

Controversy over North Pacific fishing rights between Japan and the United States dates from the late 1930s, but with the establishment of the United States 200-mile fishing zone in March 1977, Japanese fishing within 200 miles of the United States has been placed at the discretion of the United States. Since no United States fishermen operate within 200 miles of Japan, there can be no reciprocal arrangements between the two states, insofar as their fishermen's North Pacific operations are concerned. Although the three-party convention of 1952 between Canada, Japan, and the United States is due to be abrogated in February 1978, Japanese fishing for salmon outside the United States zone will be regulated by new arrangements that are being negotiated.

Japan's determination not to abandon salmon fishing in the North Pacific may be seen from what the Japanese government has planned to do. In the face of the so-called species approach of the United States, a five-year plan has been made to promote Japan's own version of the species approach. Beginning in 1977, salmon would be hatched in much greater quantities for release into the North Pacific. This would simply mean the use of the high seas as a common pond in which to farm a particular species. The "national lake" would then become the "international lake," but the decade-old controversy over the migratory range of salmon originating in Japanese and North American rivers is not likely to fade away.

Japan and the Soviet Union

Japan's fishery diplomacy with the Soviet Union has been put to a strenuous test in 1977, and perhaps the worst is yet to come. On a number of points, Japan erred on the side of optimism, to say the least. First, in 1976 Japan erroneously thought that, since the Soviet Union was another major fishing state within 200 miles of the United States, the Soviet Union would not readily recognize the United States 200-mile fishing zone. From the standpoint of the Soviet Union, however, part of what it would have to give up within the United

States zone and elsewhere could be made up for by reducing Japanese catch within its own zone. Second, when negotiations for Japanese fishing within the Soviet zone deadlocked in April 1977, Japan intended to enhance its bargaining position by regulating Soviet fishing within its own zone, and consequently extended its territorial sea from three to twelve miles, and also proclaimed a 200-mile fishing zone in July 1977. Since Japan catches much more within the Soviet zone than the Soviet Union catches within the Japanese zone, the two measures that Japan took as a leverage on the Soviet Union not only proved to be less effective than Japan had anticipated, but also complicated the territorial issue over the so-called four Northern Islands. Third, the Soviet Union was further irritated when, while the fishery negotiations were under way in Moscow, an important Japanese trade mission visited Peking in late March 1977 to negotiate for long-term Sino-Japanese trade relations. Fourth, the Japanese government also had internal problems arising from the interdepartmental disagreement between the Ministries of Agriculture and Foreign Affairs.

Because of the territorial issue, negotiations in Moscow for an arrangement to regulate Japanese fishing within the Soviet fishing zone dragged on for roughly three months (beginning in early March 1977) and resulted in the signing of a provisional agreement only in late May. In the meantime, more than 7,000 Japanese fishing vessels—the usual number operating within 200 miles of the Soviet Union—were kept waiting impatiently into the season. Since Japanese and Soviet fishing zones would overlap around the four islands currently under Soviet control, it was literally a national concern in Japan to ensure, even at the expense of the catches in the Soviet zone, that nothing in the fishery agreement would affect Japanese claims to the islands. Consequently, it was provided in the agreement that nothing in it would change the position of either party with respect to these problems pending between them. But this provision was merely a crystal ball designed to reveal exactly what each party wanted to see. In reality, the islands are under Soviet control, and Japanese fishermen would have to obtain Soviet permission to operate in the offshore waters of what Japan regards as its own territory.

The Japan-USSR agreement of May 1977 was matched *mutatis mutandis* with the reciprocal USSR-Japan agreement of August 1977, signed in Tokyo, to regulate Soviet fishing within 200 miles of Japan. In October 1977, Japan and the Soviet Union agreed to extend until the end of 1978 these two provisional agreements, which would otherwise expire at the end of 1977. In the meantime, the two states have agreed to negotiate for a long-term fishery agreement—an arrangement they would need in any event, because the Northwest Pacific Fisheries Convention they signed in 1956 is to be abrogated in April 1978. On balance, Japan is no doubt right in thinking that, after four months of negotiations under excruciating circumstances, nothing has been settled. The two states will simply continue to conduct fishery negotiations every spring, a cumbersome process that they have been following for the past two decades.

Japan and North Korea

When the 200-mile economic zone of North Korea came into force on August 1, 1977, a military boundary zone was also proclaimed in order "to reliably safeguard the economic sea zone and firmly defend the national interests and sovereignty of the country." The military zone would extend to fifty miles in the Sea of Japan, and in the Yellow Sea to the outer limit of the North Korean economic zone, which ends at the median line with China. From the fact that the North Korean military zone is similar and adjacent to what China has maintained in the name of a military warning zone since 1950, and that the Soviet Union enclosed the Peter the Great Bay in 1957 with a 108-mile straight baseline, North Korea would appear to have relied on Chinese practice in the Yellow Sea and on Soviet practice in the Sea of Japan. In fact, the line that North Korea is reported to have drawn in the Sea of Japan is also roughly 100 miles out, though the waters enclosed would hardly meet even the most elastic definition of a bay.

Japan was so concerned about the future of its fishing within the North Korean economic and military zones that a private delegation which included ten members of the Diet, visited North Korea to negotiate fishery problems. As a result, a provisional agreement was signed in early September 1977, whereby (pending conclusion of a nongovernmental agreement–the two parties have no diplomatic relations) Japanese fishing vessels would continue to operate within the North Korean economic zone but outside its military zone.

With respect to the exclusivity of the North Korean military zone, it may be noted with interest that the proclamation excludes foreign fishing vessels from the category of shipping to be regulated within the zone. At first, this was misinterpreted by Japanese negotiators, who were stunned to learn from the North Koreans that foreign fishing in a military zone was out of the question from the beginning.

Now North Korea is pressing the Japanese government to endorse this private fishery arrangement, and South Korea is watching the development closely. By virtue of the Japan-South Korea fishery agreement of 1965, which allows Japanese fishing outside the twelve-mile fishing zone of South Korea, Japan catches twice as much in the South Korea zone as in the North Korean zone. Should Japan accept the North Korean request, South Korea would retaliate by abrogating the outdated fishery agreement of 1965 and declaring a 200-mile fishing zone. It should also be noted that for these reasons Japan has not applied its 200-mile fishing zone legislation to China and South Korea, in the hope of delaying the inevitable: the establishment of 200-mile fishing zones by its two important fishing neighbors.

CONTINENTAL SHELF ISSUES IN NORTHEAST ASIA

Japan and South Korea have been frustrated by the difficulty of reaching agreement on the continental shelf boundaries between themselves as well as with China. Out of impatience, Japan and South Korea signed a joint development pact in January 1974 whereby the surface boundary issue would be put aside so that they would proceed to develop the mineral resources from the seabed together.

South Korea ratified the agreement in December 1974, and has been pressing Japan to do the same. Japan was concerned not only about Chinese objections but also about the fact that the agreed area is situated entirely on its side of the median line. Obviously, in the course of the negotiations that began in late 1972 Japan was rather reluctant to yield to the prospect of an emerging 200-mile regime. It was not until June 1977 that the Japanese Diet ratified the pact, but by means of a procedural manipulation. Under Japanese parliamentary procedures, Lower House approval is sufficient for the ratification of a treaty, provided that the Diet remains in session for a minimum of thirty days beyond such approval. In May 1977, the Diet had to extend its session in any event to ratify the Japan-USSR fishery agreement, and the extension automatically effected the ratification of the Japan-South Korea shelf pact.

However, the instrument of ratification has not yet been exchanged because of a procedural obstacle. Japan has no seabed mining law, without which mining rights specified in the joint development pact cannot be granted, and opponents of the pact would seek to delay passage of the ad hoc measures drafted by the government.

Aside from these procedural obstacles, an important point should be noted with respect to the Japanese position. Since Japan has agreed with South Korea to develop jointly what is situated on the Japanese side of the median line, it will be difficult for Japan to press on China the median-line principle in the same area of the sea.

Commentary

Regional Cooperation in Marine Resource Management in the North Pacific

Hideo Takabayashi
Ryukoku University

The year 1977 marks a historic turning point in the management of marine resources. In the North Pacific region, a sudden change has occurred since the beginning of this year. Canada, the United States, the Soviet Union, and Japan, all countries facing the North Pacific rim, extended their fishery jurisdiction out to 200 miles from the shore. This new framework of coastal fishery management immediately replaced the traditional fishery regimes administered by international organizations.

In order to discuss the present situation of the North Pacific, we should look at each of the national enactments and the treaties relating to the fisheries, but since the Canadian, American and Russian legislation is familiar to the participants at this conference, I shall confine myself to speaking briefly about the recent Japanese legislation.

The Japanese law establishing the 200-mile fishing zone is essentially a provisional measure pending the outcome of the Law of the Sea Conference. Japan claims jurisdiction over fishing activities within the 200-mile zone. This law specifically stipulates in Article 2(3) that in exercising its jurisdiction "Japan shall respect the recommendations relating to the conservation and management of fishery resources of international organizations of which Japan is a member." Foreigners are required to obtain permission from the Japanese Minister of Agriculture and Forestry to take any fish in the zone, except for those fish that belong to the category of highly migratory species. In granting permission, the minister must be satisfied that the proposed activity will conform with "an international agreement or other arrangements," with prescribed catch limits, and with "other criteria prescribed by Cabinet Order" (Article 7(1). Catch limits shall be decided not only on the basis of Japanese and foreign fishing activity within the Japanese zone but also with respect to Japanese fishing activity in waters adjacent to foreign countries. Similarly, the minister may reduce or remit fishing fees charged to a foreigner applying to fish in the Japanese zone in circumstances where his own state has agreed to reduce or remit fees charged to a Japanese applying to fish in the zone of that foreign state. A person who has contravened the law is punishable by a fine not to exceed ten million yen (equivalent to $37,000 to $40,000 depending upon the fluctuation of foreign exchange rates), and any catch, vessel, and fishing gear used by the offender may be confiscated, but no imprisonment shall be imposed.

At present, Japan has not established the 200-mile zone along her northwestern coasts to the west of the line of meridian 135°E. longitude, where the coasts border the Sea of Japan and the East China Sea. The reason is that the Republic of Korea and the People's Republic of China have not yet established 200-mile zones, and the high seas fishery agreements with them are operating satisfactorily. In addition, both the Koreans and the Chinese are able to continue their fishing within the Japanese zone, as Japan declared by a Cabinet Order based on Article 14 that the fishermen of both countries are exempted from Articles 5 to 11 of the law.

Japan is so anxious to secure contractual settlements of fishery matters with other states that Article 16 expressly stipulates the supremacy of fishery treaty provisions over the provisions of this law. With respect to the management of highly migratory and anadromous species, this law anticipates fishery regulation through appropriate international organizations. Therefore, if an agreement establishing a regional management system for such species should be negotiated, Japan would be able to join and implement the system without amending this law.

A major portion of the North Pacific, one of the most productive fishing ground of the world, has now been divided into four zones of national jurisdiction as a consequence of the legislation of Japan, Canada, the United States, and the Soviet Union. In addition, for the regulation of the fishing activities of these four nations in these national zones, a network of bilateral fishery agreements between them has been concluded. But it should be noted that the scope of management authority exercised by these four states, as expressed in these enactments and agreements, is not identical.

All four states claim fishery management authority over: all coastal species within the 200-mile zone, all anadromous species that spawn in their fresh water, and all sedentary species on their continental shelves. But with respect to highly migratory species within the 200-mile zone, while some states expressly exclude them from their competence, others seem to include them in the category of coastal species. Especially in circumstances where the coastal species in one state's zone migrate to the neighboring zones, the cooperation of the adjoining states for the effective conservation of such species would be necessary, as provided for in the U.S.-Canadian agreement.

Under the traditional regime, an international fishery commission established by treaty was entrusted with two important functions: scientific research and the formulation of fishery regulations. The measures so adopted were generally enforced by the contracting parties against their own nationals. Now, under the new regime, circumstances have completely changed. Each coastal state will exercise exclusive jurisdiction over all fishing in the offshore waters, determining unilaterally the allowable catch, the capacity to harvest, and the allocation of surplus to foreigners. Thus, the coastal state has an exclusive competence to manage and enforce conservation measures formulated by itself, and if the available scientific evidence is inaccurate, then overfishing or underexploitation of resources might occur, which would adversely affect the resource management of neighboring states.

It is important in this regard that both the U.S.-Soviet and the U.S.-Japanese agreements provide for international cooperation in the conduct of scientific research and in the collection of fishery data on a continuous basis. I think this kind of cooperation should be extended to cover the whole migratory range of certain species and involve all states concerned within that range. Despite the coastal state's sovereign rights to the resources in the zone, a regional body of a scientific character could be established, provided its function is limited to the scientific assessment of the status of stocks and the recommendation of the allowable catch. It may also be desirable to assign to such a body the function of conciliation between member states.

I agree with Dr. Park that no multilateral agreement on fishing in the Yellow Sea and East China Sea is foreseeable in the near future. But despite continuing tension in the region, it may not be impossible to establish some kind of technical, nonpolitical cooperation among the littoral states—Japan, China, Taiwan, South Korea, and North Korea—in an effort to secure some degree of rational management of the fishery resources. Normal diplomatic relations do exist, after all, between some of these states: between China and Japan, Japan and South Korea, South Korea and Taiwan, and North Korea and China. If similar management arrangements could be negotiated within these four bilateral relationships, it is not impossible that they could have multiple effects similar to those that might be desired under a multilateral agreement on the same subject.

In conclusion, I should like to emphasize my belief that the management of fishery resources should be based on objective criteria, impartially applied, in order to secure a sufficient supply of protein from the sea for the ever-increasing world population, and that regional cooperation for the optimum utilization of these resources should be promoted in the interests of mankind as a whole.

Discussion and Questions

Gary Knight: Thank you, Dr. Park and Professor Takabayashi, for your stimulating presentations. We are well placed to have a general exchange of views and questions directed at the panelists. Perhaps Dr. Kolodkin would speak first.

Anatoly Kolodkin: I have a question for Dr. Takabayashi. What is your personal approach to the right-of-transit passage through the straits that are used now for international navigation? I mean not all coastal straits close to the Japanese coast, but only the four or five main straits. Do you recognize that the provisions of the future convention, for example Articles 37 and 38 of the ICNT, will also cover this situation, so that "all ships and aircraft enjoy the right-of-transit passage, which shall not be impeded," on the assumption that transit passage means the exercise of the freedom of navigation and overflight "solely for the purpose of continuous and expeditious transit of the strait?"

Hideo Takabayashi: Japan's recent law on the territorial sea provides that the provision of Article 1 (the extension of the breadth of the territorial sea to twelve miles) shall not apply to the Soya Strait, the Tsugaru Strait, the eastern channel of the Tsushima Strait, the western channel of the Tsushima Strait, and the Osumi Strait. This provision means that Japan has extended her territorial sea to twelve miles, but that exceptions are made in the case of international straits that are very important for international shipping. These five straits, each of them connecting high seas to high seas, are in areas where the breadth of the territorial sea is still limited to three miles. Therefore, these straits still keep their legal status as high sea routes, because Japan is very anxious about the right of passage through straits. Japanese law reflects this position for the time being, until the conclusion of UNCLOS III.

Choung-il Chee: I would like to make a couple of reflections on the remark made by the gentlemen from the Soviet Union. I am inclined to subscribe to his view, stated earlier, that there is no really substantive law concerning the EEZ and the fishery zone. (This is my personal opinion based on the 1974 Fisheries Case and others.) Such zones are not really legally valid yet, whatever measures the coastal state may undertake, because the issue is not yet settled, but the impact of unilateral action is harmful to other states. This provisional measure taken by the Soviet Union is a case in point.

One finds that South Korea has been fishing in high seas areas in the Okhotsk Sea to the point that the pollack catch almost exceeded 400,000 tons. Yet since this 1976 decree we have been thrown out of that area. Now, the South Korean government apparently tried to negotiate with the Soviet Union and was refused. So the Korean fishing fleet turned to the American side of the North Pacific, where a 200-mile zone has also come into effect. The U.S. government has allocated to the South Korean government a quota of only 85,000 tons. The result is that this 200-mile zone has done very grave damage to the deep-sea fishing interests of Korea. Because of its high nutritional value, South Korea relies heavily on the supply of fish. Of the entire supply of protein for South Koreans, 79 percent consists of fish protein. The yearly fish consumption of pollack alone is 200,000 tons. So with the 85,000 tons allocated to us by the United States, we are still short by 115,000 tons. It is not the selling of fish we are concerned with, but the eating. With the emergence of the 200-mile zone, our fishermen are being chased out of areas that they have been fishing in for ten years or more. Until these new concepts become established in international law, these actions are just political actions that violate the rights of other states. The ICNT contains provisions concerning the rights of noncoastal states that have been fishing in certain coastal areas, but at the moment these provisions are generally being ignored, and serious damage to these interests is being done.

Odidi Okidi: In response to the comment about the usefulness of the 200-mile economic zone, I just wanted to say that the concept originated, I believe, in the 1971 Colombo session of the Asian-African Legal Consultative Committee, and was meant by the developing countries to be one way of safeguarding their coastal interests in marine resources, just in case the impending Law of the Sea Conference failed to establish an international regime that would provide for the special interests of the developing countries. Now, Koreans, Russians, Japanese, and Taiwanese have been fishing in the Indian Ocean since the late 1940s, but more so in the early 1950s. Is this practice supposed to give them a "historic right" to the fishery resources off the coast of East Africa? How long can that be allowed to go on in the interest of protecting the economic interests of these distant fishing countries? I personally think that in the absence of an international regime that would regulate and exploit the resources to the advantage of the countries that do not have the capability to do so themselves, the coastal states (and I am referring particularly to the developing countries) should have the right to regulate the resources, so that the fisheries are not depleted before those states become capable of exploiting the resources themselves. There is one hitch: they may be incapable of enforcing the regulations. But although that problem remains, surely we have gone beyond the point of arguing that long-distance fishermen have established certain historical rights in international law that cannot be abrogated by new rules, such as those embodied in the EEZ. I think that it would be wrong for us to leave this session with a view that the EEZ is a misfit in the development of contemporary international law.

Kazuo Sumi: I would like to put two questions to Dr. Kolodkin. I completely agree with him that, at the present time, there is no international law of the economic zone. There is only a political practice, especially by developed coastal states in the North Pacific Ocean (the United States, Canada, Soviet Union, and Japan), and I deplore the establishment of 200-mile fishery zones without waiting for the final outcome of the Law of the Sea Conference. I appreciate the six Socialist countries' proposal submitted at the Caracas session, because it laid down that the determination of allowable catch or harvesting capacity by the coastal states must be reviewed by a regional fishery commision. Does the Soviet Union still maintain such a position? What do you think of the position of the landlocked and geographically disadvantaged states with respect to the economic zone, since they do not admit the exclusive rights of the coastal states and are now proposing a regional economic zone?

Anatoly Kolodkin: With respect to the first question: if I am not mistaken, we are in agreement with all the provisions of the ICNT, including its provisions on the economic zone and fishery matters. We are in favor of the provision that when the coastal state is unable to catch all the fish in its zone, the traditional fishing countries retain the right to continue the fishing in the zone. It seems to me that this approach is quite satisfactory, at least for my country, although I do not know about the other Socialist countries. On the second question, the provisions of this text on the regional economic zone are also satisfactory for us.

Barbara Johnson: I was wondering if Dr. Park thought that Japan was seriously altering its policy on international fishing and building its own fisheries on a basis of national self-sufficiency and through aquaculture, and whether these two trends are going to be equally important? Is there a real move away from international fishing, replacing it with simply a national fishery?

Choon-ho Park: This five-year plan set up by the Minister of Agriculture is, as I understand, still in the making. Professor Takabayashi tells me that it is still in a preliminary stage. From the standpoint of the law of the sea, the hatching of salmon in mass quantities to be released in the Pacific would not really settle the problem. The use of the high seas as an international pond for salmon farming would raise much the same problem in the new law of the sea as were raised before by international fishing in the high seas under the old law of the sea.

Gary Knight: The second panel this morning moves further east, to the Northeast Pacific region, and especially to the waters lying off the western coast of North America. Of the two papers we shall hear, one is by an American and the other by a Canadian. The first deals with fishery matters, and the second with problems of environmental protection.

As many of you know, Ambassador McKernan held the top fishery position in the U.S. State Department for many years and was a key negotiator at UNCLOS III as well as in a number of bilateral and regional forums. He is now director of the Institute of Marine Studies at the University of Washington, and in the last year he has been closely associated with the Northwest Regional Fishery Council.

The second paper is by Dr. James Kingham, director of the Environmental Emergencies Branch of the Environmental Protection Service in the Canadian federal Department of Fisheries and Environment in Ottawa. Previously he served in the International Ocean Affairs Division of that agency and played an important role in the development of Canadian ocean dumping control policy and legislation. In the last four years he has been a senior marine science adviser to the Canadian delegation at UNCLOS III.

Our first speaker would have been Ambassador McKernan, but unfortunately he has been unavoidably detained at the final hour. Professor William T. Burke, also of the University of Washington, has very kindly offered to read his colleague's paper. Professor Burke has been a prominent and distinguished participant in the affairs of this institute since its inception, and is a member of its executive board. A prolific and insightful writer, he is probably, if not certainly, the foremost legal authority on the law of the sea in the United States.

Chapter Eleven

Foreign Fisheries in the United States Zone, with Special Reference to the Northeastern Pacific Ocean

Donald L. McKernan
University of Washington
(presented by **William T. Burke**)

In 1945 foreign fishermen caught almost nothing off the coast of the United States; by 1973 their catch was about 3.5 million metric tons. Conservation action taken through various international conventions and bilateral agreements, plus some smaller catches from overfished stocks, reduced the foreign catch by about half a million tons during the next three years (1974–1976). Then, in 1977, the first year of implementation of the Fishery Conversation and Management Act, the foreign allocation under the act was set at 2.1 million metric tons. The biggest reductions were aimed at species under increasing demand by the United States fishermen (that is, black cod and tanner crab on the Pacific coast and off Alaska, and Atlantic squids and herring on the Atlantic coast), or at species that were considered overfished, or both. Examples of this latter category are Alaskan pollack in the Bering Sea, Pacific Ocean perch in the Gulf of Alaska, and the Atlantic herring of Mid-Atlantic and New England.

Within the United States several authorities viewed the passage of the Fishery Conservation and Management Act as an important and potentially favorable step toward improved management of fisheries of our coast, and as an equally favorable move toward developing a larger American fishing industry. But others in this country are not at all certain that the new national fishery management regime is in the broad public interest. Professor Giulio Pontecorvo believes that the inclusion of fishermen or their representatives on the regional fishery councils, with the responsibility to prepare fishery management plans, is tantamount to putting the fox in charge of the chicken coop, and, in this instance, with the consumer, rather than the farmer, poorer as a result.

While the total fish catch of some twenty to twenty-five nations fishing off the United States coast has declined from a high annual catch of about 3.5 million metric tons to about 2.1 million in 1977, the catch of several species of fish and shellfish of prime importance to the United States has dropped even more, probably exceeding 50 percent. A significant part of the decline in foreign allocation of catch came about because the biological assessment of the status of many of the stocks showed the stocks to be overfished. Overfishing in this sense means fishing at such a level of effort as to reduce the size of the stock below the level of abundance where it will, on the average, produce the maximum sustainable biological yield. The law requires the achievement, also, of an optimum yield from the fisheries. This has, thus far, resulted in a reduction of the total allowable annual catch (TAC) and the foreign allocation, especially in those cases where the United States fishermen shared the catch with foreign fishermen. For example, the foreign catch of Alaskan pollack in the Bering Sea has been about 1.5 million metric tons. United States scientists believe the stock can on the average sustain a production of about 1.1 million metric tons. On the other hand, there is some evidence that the current equilibrium yield is about a million metric tons, meaning that the stock is slightly overfished. The North Pacific Regional Fishery Council has recommended a foreign allocation of 950,000 metric tons. In this instance, the expected U.S. catch is expected to be zero.

The North Pacific Council has also recommended the total exclusion of the Japanese from the stocks of the largest of the two species of tanner crab fished by the United States and Japanese fishermen in the Bering Sea. It is confidently expected that the expanding U.S. fishery in 1978 will take all of the optimum yield set for the stock. The optimum yield is set quite conservatively; that is, it permits practically all the male crabs (only male crabs are harvested) to mate at least one season, and thus the optimum yield (set at about 50,000 tons for this species) may be only one-half to two-thirds of a safe, maximum biological yield.

In the first case cited, that of the Bering Sea pollack stock, foreign scientists would claim that the stock is capable of yielding 1.5 million metric tons. With respect to the tanner crab, the Japanese claim that there is no justification for setting the optimum yield so low, and that they should be permitted to continue to fish at their traditional level of about 10,000 to 12,000 tons along with the increased United States fleet.

I would like now to speak about some emerging problems for foreign fishing under the Fishery Conservation and Management Act (FCMA). Foreign fishermen have complained about the sharp reductions in total allowable catch of some species of fish. Two factors have affected those reductions. First, the FCMA requires that the basis for determining the surplus of stock available for allocation to foreign vessels will be that part of the optimum yield not harvested by United States fishing vessels. In the past the basis for allocation of catch among nations fishing common stocks of fish in shared waters, such as the ICNAF area, was most often the so-called maximum sustainable yield. Even in these instances the total allowable catches allocated among the nations often exceeded the annual biological surplus because of the nature of the bargaining process. Now, it must come as a shock to many distant water fishing nations that a single authority, the United States, requires under national law the achievement of fish stock levels somewhat above those that will produce the average maximum biological yield applying the "optimum yield" concept. Thus, a different, much more stringent, and even subjective standard is being applied for conservation purposes. Optimum yield may be defined as the amount of fish that will provide the greatest overall benefit to the nation (the United States), with particular reference to food production and recreational opportunities, and that is prescribed as such on the basis of maximum sustainable yield from such a fishery as modified by any relevant economic, social, or ecological factors.

Second, the law provides that the foreign allocation is that portion of the catch that will not be harvested by U.S. fishing vessels; but the regional fishery management coucils' views of the growth of the U.S. fisheries have so far not always been realistic, and when the domestic allowable catch is set beyond the likely domestic catch, the foreign catch is further reduced. Some council members have advocated further reductions in the foreign allocations, especially where U.S. fishing capacity is very large. They reason that with reduced foreign catches markets will be available for greater United States catches. That may or may not be the case. In the first place, the United States fleet may not be able to catch the fish and market it at the same price as the foreign competition, and the market may not be able to absorb higher prices. Furthermore, the market may be uniquely developed by a foreign nation or company, and they may not be willing or able to substitute U.S.-caught fish in that market. Beyond that, it is difficult to interpret the FCMA as permitting the U.S. government to withhold foreign allocation on the speculation that such action will increase the U.S. catch during the next year. Foreign fishermen have been having difficulty understanding the U.S. fishing regulations. The regulations are complicated and include procedures quite unique and cumbersome. Procedures for reporting and handling incidental catch and prohibited species are all giving the foreign fleets difficulty.

The recent arrest of a Polish vessel off New England is a case in point. The vessel had caught prohibited species and a few of the allowed species over a period supposedly prolonged in time by gear and power difficulties. Several of the federal agencies felt that the vessel should have been seized. The State Department and White House ordered it released on the basis of extenuating circumstances. The New England Council considered the government's action quite contrary to the law and said so in a letter from the executive director of the council to the secretary of state. The captain of the vessel was cited, and civil penalties are being assessed by the United States government.

On the other hand, foreign fishermen have complained that excessive fines of up to $250,000 have been assessed them for possession of fifteen or twenty prohibited species of fish or shellfish aboard the fishing vessel. It would appear that there have been excesses on both sides. On the whole, however, enforcement of the 200-mile fishery zone has been excellent and foreign fishermen are for the most part complying with U.S. laws and regulations. Most certainly, enforcement of the new fishery law has resulted in better control, more knowledge about the foreign catch of fish off the United States coast, including a more precise breakdown by species of the catch than has ever occurred before, even though the national management system has not yet been in operation a year. There is no question that control of fishing and compliance with fishing regulations are vastly improved. The transition to the 200-mile zone thus appears to be well understood and accepted by foreign fishing fleets, with relatively few cases of failure to comply with procedures.

Some new and unique business arrangements have been developed as a result of the new law. Foreign fishing enterprises have entered into joint ventures with American companies. These take many forms,–but the new type that has caused the most concern is one suggested for the North Pacific, which proposes to license or permit foreign processing vessels within the fishing zone, but outside the three-mile territorial sea, where fish would be purchased from American fishermen. Two such ventures are under consideration on the Pacific coast off the coast of Alaska. One such venture is between an American company located at Bellingham, Washington, and a Soviet government fishing enterprise. The other is between a Republic of Korea fishing company and an American firm located in Anchorage, Alaska. The U.S.-USSR joint venture would purchase Pacific hake from U.S. fishermen and process the hake on the Soviet processing vessel into frozen blocks; other products might also be produced. According to company officials, the frozen hake would most likely be transported to a Soviet port or to another foreign port in Canada or Mexico, and transshipped to the United States. It would also involve supplying the Soviet fishing fleet with fuel and supplies from Pacific Northwest ports. The U.S.-Korean joint venture would involve a Korean factory ship operating in the Gulf of Alaska, purchasing Alaskan pollack and other groundfish from U.S. fishermen. Frozen pollack blocks and frozen gutted pollack would be the chief products. The frozen gutted pollack would be sold on the Korean market and the blocks would be shipped from Korea to U.S. markets.

Objections have been raised to both of these enterprises. On the one hand, land-based fish processors claim the floating processors have an unfair economic advantage, and will diminish the opportunity for the development of the shore-based U.S. groundfish processing industry by unfairly competing for the catch of the limited number of domestic fishing vessels. This is particularly important in Alaska, where there are few vessels economically capable of trawling for pollack. Some fishermen also object to the joint venture concept. They would prefer to see the development of shore-based processing and, furthermore, object to the importation of the product into the United States after processing. They believe that a more stable, permanent market for their catch will grow out of the development of land-based processors. Other fishermen, looking closely at the economics of fishing certain species of groundfish (especially Alaska pollack in the Gulf of Alaska), have concluded that it would be uneconomical for American fishermen to fish low-valued species such as pollack unless there is a floating processing plant, either foreign or domestic, located virtually on the fishing grounds. Many of these fishermen, moreoever, are not confident that it would be profitable for the U.S. shore-based processing plants to handle Alaskan pollack or Pacific hake. They believe some of the opposition of the U.S. processors is designed to prevent competition for their fish and will result in lower fish prices being paid to them for their catch. Because of the large, but not unanimous, opposition from the producing and processing sectors of the local industry, both the Northwest and the North Pacific Regional Fisheries Councils have thus far recommended against issuing permits during 1977 and 1978 for such joint ventures. Both Councils indicate they intend to review conditions during the 1978 fishing season. Until either shore-based plants or American-owned and -operated floating processing plants are developed to provide a market for hake and Alaskan pollack from American fishermen, it appears unlikely that joint venture operations of these kinds with foreign companies will be looked at more favorably.

Now, some comments about the 1977 fishing season. If the foreign fisheries off Alaska are any indication, foreign fishing efforts off the U.S. coast through the first eight months of 1977 have declined. Off Alaska there was a drop of more than 25 percent. The sighting of Japanese fishing boats declined by only 7 percent, but Soviet sightings declined by 62 percent. Both Korean and Taiwanese vessels dropped by some 80 percent. As to the catches by foreign vessels off Alaska during this same period, only 37 percent of the foreign allocation of 1.6 million tons has been taken in the first eight months, leaving 63 percent to be caught in the remaining four months. Obviously, some reorganization was necessary within the foreign fleet; but the large drops in the sizes of the Soviet, Korean, and Taiwanese foreign fleets and their relatively low catches during the first eight months of the year lead one to wonder why there was such a delayed start. It does not seem reasonable to assume the fishing season is normally skewed to the later months of the year. It seems more likely the slow start under the 200-mile rule is occasioned by a purposeful reexamination of fishing strategy to be carried out in the face of the extended fishery jurisdiction.

Where do we stand now? Even though foreign fishermen were permitted to take about 2.1 million metric tons of fish within the U.S. fishing conservation zone, of which about 70 percent was from the North Pacific Ocean, there was considerable dissatisfaction by foreign governments over the initial unilateral action by the United States in extending its fishing limits to 200 miles, and also over the implementation of control by the United States. The major complaint appeared to be that the U.S. assertion of jurisdiction over a 200-mile fishery zone was premature, and a violation of international law. The reaction of distant-water fishing states was typified in the statement by the Consul-General Sono Uchida of the Japanese Consul-General's Office in Seattle in January 1977, just prior to the implementation of foreign fishing regulations on March 1, 1977: "The Japanese government still does not admit the legality of the 200-mile fishery zones. However, after the enactment of that law by the U.S., many other important countries followed suit. It may not be too far away that the 200-mile fishery zone will be admitted as part of international law, but until then Japan cannot help opposing such unilateral action which would hurt Japan very much." His prediction was correct. During 1976 and 1977 many nations extended their fishing limits, including Canada, the USSR, countries of the European Economic Community, as well as Mexico, and even Japan. Japan's move was clearly a necessary counter to the extension of jurisdiction by the USSR. The Soviet fishing fleet has since claimed very large traditional catches of fish in excess of 500,000 metric tons within the Japanese 200-mile zone and the two nations have been negotiating fishing rights within each other's fishing zone during most of 1977.

The problems are just beginning. What happens to the International North Pacific Convention or the Northwest Pacific Fishery Convention between the U.S.S.R. and Japan? In light of provisions of the new U.S. law, and the obvious moves of the USSR to curtail Japanese fishing of Asian stocks of salmon, the Japanese high-seas salmon fishery is in jeopardy. If the Japanese are to be permitted to continue to fish for salmon, even salmon of Asian origin, within the U.S. 200-mile zone, the Fishery Conservation and Management Act of the United States will require amendment, or a new convention will be necessary. This is but one example of foreseeable problems. New institutions in the North Pacific Ocean are necessary to take the place of the old. These will be different in nature from existing international fishing institutions. Past conventions had an overriding, stated objective of conservation, even though in some cases participants had less obvious goals. The new arrangements will stress coordination of statistics and cooperation in research activities as the coastal states assert tighter control over the regulation of the fisheries. With respect to the Northeastern Pacific Ocean in the fishing zone off the United States, foreign fishing will continue for the foreseeable future. It is inconceivable that the U.S. fisheries in that area and markets for many groundfish species will expand at a rate that will fully utilize such resources as Alaskan pollack and the several species of flounders. On the other hand, foreign fishing for salmon of North American origin, the incidental catch of halibut, and the catch of species such as black cod, Pacific Ocean perch, true cod, and at least the larger of the two species of tanner crabs, will be reduced to virtually nothing within a very few years. The future of U.S. fisheries for Pacific hake, some flounders, and the smaller and very abundant species of tanner crab found in the northern Bering Sea is admittedly somewhat less certain.

We are witnessing a historic and important transition in world fishery management. In the North Pacific Basin, there are definite winners and losers. The United States is a very big winner, gaining the exclusive authority over one of the very rich areas of the world ocean. Canada and the USSR may be net winners, but both will suffer some losses in their fisheries off the coast of the United States. The USSR will recover much of that loss by reduction in foreign fishing off the Pacific coast of the USSR. Japan, Korea, and Taiwan are major losers with severe curtailment of their fisheries off the coast of the USSR, the United States, and Canada. How they will accommodate these losses is as yet unclear. Obviously it is in the long-range interest of all North Pacific fishing countries to work together to mitigate as much as possible the problems of the losers and to think more clearly than has been the case so far about long-range fishery arrangements between the Pacific Rim countries. These new arrangements will have as their goals the improvement of our knowledge of the fishery resources, and must also insure the full use of the fishery resources of the region.

Chapter Twelve

Marine Resource Management in the North Pacific Rim and Problems of Environmental Protection

D. James Kingham
Fisheries and Environment
Canada

The problem of environmental protection in the Northeast Pacific was not nearly so serious a few years ago as it is now. Difficulties in oil supply from the Middle East combined with the discovery of profitable reserves in Prudhoe Bay, Alaska, have put unprecedented pressure on the west coast marine environment. At this moment on the west coast of Canada there is a public inquiry on the need for, and siting of, an oil port or terminal in British Columbia. Public sensitivity is great on the west coast, not only to protect the fisheries but also to protect the shoreline, and yet at this point the Canadian situation is one in which no general environmental protection law exists. Instead, we use the Fisheries Act in most instances, along with the Canada Shipping Act, to prevent operational vessel discharges, and the Ocean Dumping Control Act to regulate dumping activities at sea. Now, with the memory of oil spills on the east coast still fresh in our minds, the threat of serious pollution on the west coast of North America seems larger than ever.

I remember so vividly the debate of a few years back in the Marine Environment Protection Committee on proposals for retrofitting segregated ballast tanks (SBT) on existing oil tankers. The idea was dismissed by many delegations as too expensive and cumbersome, and it was supported by few. But now, partly because of the rash of accidents on the East Coast, some very powerful delegations are pushing the SBT concept at IMCO. What if they fail?

According to the ICNT, coastal states may only take steps in design, construction, equipment, and manning that conform to generally accepted international standards. But what if Canada and the United States agree to decide what types of tankers can bring oil from Alaska to the "Lower 48"? Does that make it a "generally accepted international standard"? Could we enforce it? I do not offer answers to these questions, but I think these are questions that have to be asked and answered.

I am not one of the "patchwork quilt" advocates, who argue that granting coastal states the power to set such regulations will result in such a maze of regulations that it will make ship operations impossible. I disagree with that argument for two reasons: first, a lot of the pollution prevention equipment is of an "add-on" nature; and second, our Canada-U.S. experience with sewage regulations on ships in the Great Lakes has not to our knowledge had any deleterious effect on shipping in that area. In practice, the shipbuilder would simply design his vessel to meet the most stringent standards of the areas for which it is intended. Let's face it, Pacific Rim countries, which depend so heavily on shipping, are not going to set regulations that will prevent ships from continuing to trade with them. The need for the most stringent regulations possible on oil tankers is obvious, when one observes that the number of oil spills increased alarmingly over the past few years. If the projections are valid, we can expect to see more than three quarters of a million tons of oil spilled into coastal waters by 1984.

When we turn to the environmental effects of resource exploitation, there are two activities likely to be of particular importance in the Northeast Pacific: oil exploitation and manganese nodule exploitation. We have seen examples of the damage that can result from offshore oil exploitation. A recent example is the Ekofisk blowout in the North Sea. Of greater importance, in the context of this Conference, is the Santa Barbara spill of a few years ago. We have been through many "crises" in water pollution in the last decade—mercury, phosphate, cadmium, DDT, PCB, and so on. In most cases, our awareness that a problem existed depended on our ability to measure extremely low concentrations of pollutants. By the time we could detect mercury at the parts-per-billion level, it was fairly widely spread through the water environment. Now, without wanting to sound apocalyptic about it, I think we should have great concern about the release of crude oil into the marine environment. Crude oil is made up of thousands of components. Many of these seem to disappear—but how can they really disappear in a relatively closed biosphere? Until we know what the persistent components are, where they go, and what effect they have on biosphere, we cannot adopt a complacent attitude toward them.

The ICNT says that states, in cooperation with competent international organizations, or acting through a diplomatic conference, shall develop rules and regulations to prevent pollution resulting from the exploitation of seabed resources. I suggest that this task is one that need not, and should not, await the final outcome of UNCLOS III. It is a task that should begin right now and could be developed on a regional basis in both the Northeast and Northwest Pacific regions. I understand that UNEP has already begun to look at the problem.

Similarly, the exploitation of manganese nodules poses certain threats to the marine environment because of the risk of spreading very fine sediment particles throughout the water column, increasing turbidity, decreasing photosynthetic activity, and affecting the gills of fish. Although this is not a Northeast Pacific problem, it is certainly a North Pacific problem, and one that would benefit from regional, if not global, norms and standards *before* mining begins.

The use of the oceans as dumping grounds for wastes is another activity that seems to call for regional cooperation in the Northeast Pacific. This activity is covered by the London Dumping Convention in 1972, to which both the United States and Canada are parties. Although the areas to which the convention applies were not spelled out in that text, it is obvious from the ICNT that the consensus view at UNCLOS III is that coastal states shall regulate dumping in their territorial sea, economic zone, or out to the edge of the continental shelf or margin. Because pollution is even more wide ranging than fish migration, the desirability of regional cooperation in this area is quite obvious. The powers of dispersion in the biosphere are so great that with each breath you take, you probably breathe in at least one molecule of air breathed by Aristotle. Similarly, improper dumping of wastes into the waters off one Pacific Rim country will have an effect on the waters of other Pacific Rim countries.

One area not specifically addressed in the ICNT, but highly amenable to regional cooperation, is that of marine environmental emergency clean-up. For the Northeast Pacific, Canada and the United States have signed a joint contingency plan to provide for the most effective response possible to a pollution incident, using the resources of both countries.

Finally, there must be regional cooperation with respect to marine scientific research. This is called for in the ICNT, and it already exists in the Northeast Pacific. Indeed, it exists right across the Pacific as well.

In the cases I have cited, regionalism is not intended to take the place of a global convention, but rather to supplement it. In my view, we would be wise to think of those regional steps that can and should be taken now in support of the provisions of the ICNT that deal with the preservation of the marine environment.

Discussion and Questions

Ross Thornwood: In talking about the preservation of the marine environment, I think we have a great deal to learn from the overexploitation and imminent extinction of the whales. As recently as three years ago, there were thought to be 800 orca whales from Alaska to Northern California. Now there are only 200 at most, consisting of eight or nine families. Washington, British Columbia, Alaska, and the United States have now made the taking of orcas illegal, because they are getting very close to species extinction. The International Whaling Commission, which is even older than the Law of the Sea Conference–something like 35 years now–was supposed to manage the whale so it could become a permanent resource for generations to come. What the IWC actually did was just the opposite: it "managed" the exploitation to the point of extinction, species after species, so that now all the great whales are very near extinction. For instance, the blue whale was nearly extinct some fifteen years before the IWC decided to do anything about it. Maybe the whale is gone now; we do not know. That is why we would like to stop the killing of these whales for at least ten years. But if the whale is gone, we have to try to apply this tragic lesson to all living things in the ocean. We must change some of our old ideas, because they are not working in the New World anymore. Let us learn from that and have some international cooperation to preserve these species.

Lee Alverson: I am sympathetic with some of the things said by the previous speaker, but we have to make decisions on fact and not on fantasy. If the facts on the status of the orca are as bad as he alleges, then I am surprised. The studies that were made in the Northeastern Pacific dealt with the stocks of whales that were essentially confined to the area from the Strait of Georgia to Southeastern

Alaska. There is no evidence that that particular stock is anywhere near extinction. In fact, it is in a very healthy state, but the surplus provided by that stock is much less than some people have perceived. In addition, orca is in worldwide distribution and has been almost unexploited on a global basis, except for its exploitation by the Norwegians and Japanese (at a very low rate). There are much better examples of overexploitation of whales.

I wish that Professor McKernan were here, because he has fallen into the usual mistake that most people make in talking about surpluses—a mistake that is causing many problems in the international arena. This mistake is in thinking that when the equilibrium yield of a stock has fallen below the maximum sustainable yield of the population, then in essence the stock has been overfished. In essense, the equilibrium yield of stock is always below maximum sustainable yield, whether it is underfished or overfished. It is just a matter of understanding the models. Unless you are looking at a substantial base of additional data, it has nothing to do with overfishing. The problem is that people are talking about reducing the yield to the lower levels because the equilibrium yield has fallen below the maximum sustainable yield. If a stock is properly managed, it should always be in consonance with what is happening in nature. The yield may be somewhat above or somewhat below the maximum sustainable yield, but many other factors have to be taken into account in the strategy of management. "Mismanagement" would be a better description for what is going on at the regional council levels in the United States at the present time.

Kazuo Sumi: I would like to ask Dr. Kingham a question. The first management system in the North Pacific Ocean was characterized by a complex network of ad hoc bilateral or trilateral agreements covering certain species over certain areas. I think a new philosophy must be introduced in order to achieve the purpose of conservation of living resources and the protection of the marine environment. First, all parts within the marine ecosystem interact with each other. Since all life is interdependent, any change that seriously interferes with any living system can have a major impact on life as a whole. Second, from now on large-scale economic projects—such as the extraction of oil and natural gas and the exploitation of the manganese nodules—will be introduced into the oceans and multiple uses of ocean space in the North Pacific Ocean will be intensified. So we must assess the impact of multiple uses on the productivity of the fishery resources. I think that in order to maintain the health of the ocean we must adopt some kind of mechanism, such as the environmental impact assessment techniques. I agree with Dr. Kingham in calling for the adoption of a comprehensive and integrated approach, but what kind of institutional framework in the North Pacific Ocean is he thinking of?

James Kingham: I recognize the interdependence in the ecosystem and the deleterious effect that could arise from large-scale economic projects. Not only in the ocean environment, but in our land environment as well, we have this kind of environmental impact assessment process in both Canada and the United States. Although it is in very different forms in the two countries, the objective is the same: to find out the effect. As far as the Northeastern Pacific is concerned—for both coasts of North America for that matter—whenever a project is proposed in one country that could have a serious effect on the environment (and therefore fisheries) of the other country, there are extensive bilateral consultations and negotiations. There is no advance, established, formal framework: it arises on a case-by-case basis. For example, recently there was a proposal for exploratory drilling in the Davis Strait between Greenland and Baffin Island on the northeastern coast and we had extensive negotiations with the Danes on safety procedures, on responsibility and liability provisions, and on baseline environmental studies. I do not think the problem needs comprehensive procedures to be established in advance. I think we have to deal with it on an issue-by-issue basis.

Francis Christy: Having been out of the country, I would like to get some information of a factual nature, or some opinions, on what is taking place in the United States, and I will ask these of Professor Burke. First, what is the current view in the United States with regard to the definition of "historic rights"? I understand the European Commission has not accepted such rights as a valid principle, and Australia and New Zealand consider them to be anything over 100 years. What is the U.S. position at the moment? Second, is there any chance of amendment to the FCMA with regard to sovereignty or control over tuna resources? Third, has there been any litigation brought by some other foreign countries with regard to the implementation of the FCMA?

William Burke: I am not aware of any pending amendment at this stage. I do not believe there has been any litigation brought by any foreign government or company over the implementation of the act. There has been litigation about foreign fishing under the FCMA, but the litigant in this case was a state of the United States, which complained that the optimum yield figure for herring in the Georges Bank was set too high and that the quota that was permitted for foreign fishing was excessive. That challenge eventually lost.

Gary Knight: On the tuna exception question and the possibility of eliminating it, I can add that the Gulf of Mexico Regional Fisheries Council has strongly recommended its deletion. We have a particular problem down there that involves the long-line tuna fishing fleet of Japan and their incidental catch of billfish, which has caused considerable concern among the recreational fishery in the Gulf. It has been temporarily resolved by an informal accommodation between the Council and the group representing the distant water commercial fishing industry of Japan, whereby they have agreed to certain procedures with respect to billfish that would enable them to survive. For that reason, there is a great deal of sentiment for eliminating the tuna exception.

Michael Hardy: Since the question of historic rights has come up several times, I think it would be helpful to set out the matter in the context in which we now find ourselves. The doctrine of historic rights was developed when fishing limits were relatively restricted, normally three to twelve miles. The present limits are now 200 miles and it is of the essence of the change that has occurred that the coastal state has sovereign or exclusive rights over the living resources within those limits. This approach, which has been accepted in state practice, is incompatible with the maintenance of historic rights as such by other states. I do not know of any country that has extended its limits subject to the historic rights of other states, apart from cases where particular treaty regimes, normally relating to local fishing near the frontier, have been kept in place. Thus the criterion of historic rights no longer applies, or is no longer accepted, as a title of right, but is merely a ground on which the other state may seek to persuade the coastal state to allow it to continue fishing. To put the matter round the other way, the factor of traditional fishing patterns is an element that the coastal state may itself take into consideration—and indeed, in order to maintain good relations with the states concerned, is quite likely to do so—but without normally being under an obligation in this respect. That is one of the consequences of the changes that have taken place in the nature of fishing arrangements, and I think it largely answers the issue raised by Francis Christy.

Carl Christol: I would like to get clarification from Mr. Kingham on the process of arriving at decisions. I may have misunderstood the gist of his remarks, but I gather that with respect to his example of cleanup plans for spills in the Northeast Atlantic, this would be appropriately resolved by bilateral arrangements between the United States and Canada, i.e., that insofar as tanker standards were concerned between the two countries, this would be suitable for bilateral arrangements, although reference was made to IMCO with the expectation that bilateral arrangements would be at a higher level of performance than the IMCO standards. With respect to the mining of manganese nodules and the environmental consequences, the suggestion was made that possibly a regional entity would be the proper authority to effect decisions. But then when reference was made to the control over the conservation of the fisheries off the west coast of the United States and Canada, the response was that this might be resolved unilaterally. I wonder what the rationale is for the different types of approaches to these problems.

James Kingham: I am not sure that I stated how the question of the conservation of fisheries management would be resolved, because that would be the area in which I possess the least expertise. We have a group of fishery experts here with sound scientific credentials and past experience in developing the management scheme in much the same way the United States has.

Albert Koers: I have a factual question. I am aware that at this moment renegotiations are taking place over the Inter-American Tropical Tuna Commission, but I would like to know if there are any other renegotiations of multilateral fishery conventions going on right now? One reason I have for asking this question is that I think that even within the 200-mile zone there is a need to continue scientific cooperation, and, in the North Atlantic at least, we have managed to maintain that cooperation both in the new ICNAF as well as the new NEAFC negotiations, but what of the situation in the North Pacific?

William T. Burke: The INPFC is now being renegotiated, and the United States and Canada are discussing their bilateral problems with respect to the Pacific coast salmon fisheries.

Lee Alverson: All three of the commissions in the North Pacific are reevaluating the situation in the aftermath of the 200-mile legislation.

Part V

Problems of Ocean Management in Southeast Asia

Chairman
John E. Bardach
University of Hawaii

Southeast Asia is recognized by geographers, even by writers of geography books, as a legitimate region. In fact, it is such a large region that for the purpose of our discussion on regionalism and regional arrangements in the oceans it is probably too large. It extends in an east-west direction from Burma to Papau New Guinea and in a north-south direction from Vietnam to the southern coasts of the Indonesian islands. Its geographic extent and heterogeneity make it unlikely to give rise to regional arrangements as a whole. Nevertheless, there are several areas and several problems in the realms of marine affairs and ocean law in Southeast Asia that could well be, or should be, considered on a regional basis. In fact, there are more of them than we can consider today. We shall deal only with two of those, either nascent or potential, regional problems. The first concerns environmental issues and ocean transportation: in essence, with the Straits of Malacca and Singapore (which is the second busiest ocean route in the world). The second will deal with fisheries in Southeast Asia where, perhaps more than in most other parts of the world, fish are the main protein staple.

Let me now introduce to you the participants in the first part of this afternoon's program. First is our principal speaker, Professor Danusaputro from the University of Padjadjarian in Bandung, who will talk about environmental issues and ocean transportation in Southeast Asia, with particular reference to the Straits of Malacca. This paper is co-authored by Dr. Mochtar Kusumaatmadja, who regrets not being able to be here, but has recently been appointed Acting Foreign Minister of Indonesia. The first commentator will be Dr. Julian Gresser of the University of Hawaii Law School, an expert in environmental law and Japanese law, who is adviser to various national and international agencies on environmental affairs. He will be followed by Mr. Shelley Mark, who is well known to most of us in Hawaii, a place he left not so long ago to go to larger playing fields. Mr. Mark is with the Environmental Protection Agency in Washington, D.C. The fourth speaker will be Professor Paul Alexander of the Department of Anthropology at the University of Sidney, who is a long-time specialist in local community issues in Southeast Asia. The final commentator will be Dr. Guy Pauker of the Rand Corporation, an Asian expert of long standing. He also worked for some years at the Environmental Laboratory of Cal Tech, so he not only has socio-political but also factual expertise in the area.

Chapter Thirteen

Elements of an Environmental Policy and Navigational Scheme for Southeast Asia, with Special Reference to the Straits of Malacca

Munadjat Danusaputro
Padjadjaran University
Indor

INTRODUCTION

The Eleventh Annual Conference of the Law of the Sea Institute has taken as the basis for its discussions the assumption that "however successful the currently convened Third UN Conference on the Law of the Sea may be in producing a Law of the Sea treaty for eventual ratification, it is probable that many—perhaps most—nations are now ready to consider alternative patterns of agreement which might produce results at once more immediate and more particularized than those expected from UNCLOS III." Further, these discussions should be "devoted to exploring the current viability of regionalization with respect to the most pressing legal and marine issues, and the extent to which regional agreement might complement and enhance the prospects for broad international agreement through UNCLOS."[1]

It is within the context of this search for a regional approach to specific problems that the main thrust of this paper is directed. It is a well-established recognition of the environmental approach that, because of the "oneness" of the human environment, even the most local environmental problem must be seen both globally and from the point of view of its long-term consequences.

On the other hand it is also a recognized fact that the world is heterogeneous, both in its natural environmental features and its patterns of man-made environmental development. Because of this heterogeneity, very few environmental problems can have uniform "global solutions." The existence of dissimilarity in both the natural and human environments requires us to search for a differentiated approach to the emerging problems.

Even those environmental problems that may have "global solutions," like those of pollution and its effects on climate, while they need to be recognized "internationally," can only be solved effectively by action at the national or regional level.[2]

Natural environmental systems are not perfect, and neither are human organizations in encountering environmental problems. At most, the environmental sciences can attempt to state what can and cannot be done, and to predict the outcome of alternative human actions. But in the end, only political will can ensure that any one particular human action will be implemented.

It is, therefore, the fundamental aim of every environmental policy to develop such a political will, both at the national and international level. In the present international system, in which the nation-state still constitutes the principal actor, it is always very difficult to get the political will mobilized unless it has been developed nationally and possibly through cooperation at the regional level.[3]

The satisfaction of man's basic needs, and the development of communities to satisfy social aspirations, will demand a growing amount of energy and natural resources. This demand will depend not only on "population growth" but also on the "mode of life," and on the "style and pattern of development" adopted, which vary substantially from country to country and from region to region. In tackling the problem of management of the environment in a given region (such as Southeast Asia), the first need is to assess the present state of the environmental conditions and to evaluate the alternative patterns of management: what each would cost in terms of capital and human effort, and how far each alternative would provide the optimum benefit.[4]

Methods of environmental survey and evaluation, leading to predictive models, may be provided by the results of the programs conducted by international organizations, such as Man and Biosphere (MAB) of UNESCO, IOC, FAO, UNEP, IMCO, and UNCLOS III. Part of this work may lead to the development of simple, comparable, and widely useful indicators, but because the world is heterogeneous, a degree of specialization and particularization is inevitable. This evidence again emphasizes the paramount importance of national and regional approaches in dealing with management problems of the environment, as illustrated in Southeast Asia.

THE SOUTHEAST ASIA REGION

Geographical Position and Significance

It has been observed by Lewis M. Alexander that there are no such things as "natural" or self-determined regions. Rather, a region is "an intellectual concept, an entity for the purposes of thought, created by the selection of certain features that are relevant to an areal interest or problem and by the disregard for all features that are considered to be irrelevant."[5]

These observations are fully applicable to the Southeast Asia region. The term "Southeast Asia" came into general usage only during the last two years of World

War II. The name was probably influenced by the creation of the "South East Asia Command" (SEAC) under Lord Louis Mountbatten in response to the Japanese strategic concept of "Greater East Asia War."[6] After the war Southeast Asia became a geographical concept of a more general character, adapting itself to the political development of the regions as it emerged as an area chiefly inhabited by newly independent states.

Southeast Asia today is the generally accepted designation for the area south of the Eastern Himalayan ranges, stretching from the Bay of Bengal and the Indian Ocean in the west and in the south to the Pacific Ocean in the east and southeast. It lies south of the Tropic of Cancer, while its archipelagoes spread eastwards from the Asiatic continent as far as the island of Irian (New Guinea). The archipelagoes "melt away" eastwards into the island groups of the West-central Pacific. The northern limit of Southeast Asia extends beyond the Tropic of Cancer to the southern political boundaries of China, and farther east its southeastern limit is formed by the political boundaries of Papua, New Guinea, and Australia, while its western limit extends along the political boundaries of Sri Lanka, India, and Bangladesh.

By this definition, Southeast Asia, with its off-lying archipelago, sprawls asymmetrically across the Equator, like a sword pointed toward the south. It covers an area just short of 1,500 miles in radius from a point off the mouth of the Mekong River, a region comparable to the whole area of the European region with its seas north of the African coast.

Southeast Asia's geographical significance lies in the fact that it consists of two different components, the western part of which is characterized predominantly by its land element, while in its eastern part the water (sea) element largely prevails. Its total water area is about three times its land area, thereby characterizing the unique contour and content of its natural environment.[7]

With almost 70 percent of its space consisting of marine areas, the Southeast Asia region is politically divided into ten developing countries: Burma, Thailand, Laos, Kampuchea (Khmer), Vietnam, Malaysia, Singapore, Indonesia, Brunei, and the Philippines. All capital cities of these ten Southeast Asian countries are near the sea, except Kuala Lumpur (Malaysia) and Vientiane (Laos). Two big archipelagic states accentuate the most prominent feature of the Southeast Asia region: Indonesia, consisting of 13,667 islands and islets, and the Philippines, comprising 8,730 islands.

The Southeast Asian Marine Environment

The geographical situation of Southeast Asia gives the region a geo-strategical importance. It lies between two continents (Asia and Australia) and between two oceans (the Indian and the Pacific). Accordingly the Southeast Asian marine environment, in particular, occupies a "crossroads" position of global significance. Moreover, the socio-political sensitivity of the region is heightened by the existence of different races, cultures, religions, outlooks, and usages.[8]

Three physical features, the Sunda Platform, the Sahul Shelf, and an upcropping of young mountain arcs fringing and lying between the platform and the shelf, constitute the chief physical characteristics of the Southeast Asian marine environment. Accordingly, the latter can be subdivided, according to depth, into these three areas: the shallow seas of the Sunda Shelf; the shallow seas of the Sahul Shelf; and the Austro-asiatic "mediterranean" basins between the Sunda Platform and the Sahul Shelf, which is subdivided by islands.

The festoons of mountains that enfold the Sunda chains and the Sahul shelves provide much scope for theories about mountain-building processes in which these mountains in many cases rise steeply from the flood of the Indian and Pacific Oceans to a height at some points of over 15,000 feet above sea level. In other localities the greater part of the mountain system is below sea level and only its topmost points emerge as strings of islands, complicating the passage throughout the Southeast Asian seas.[9]

Notwithstanding the many crucial dangers of passage through its seas, the seaways of Southeast Asia provide the shortest link between the two world oceans. The safety and continuity of Southeast Asian marine communications affect the interests of international navigation, both in peace and in war. The area is strategically significant because the seaways of Southeast Asia constitute a natural passage for navies seeking access from the Pacific to the Indian Oceans and back, particularly through the Straits of Malacca and Singapore.[10]

The South China Sea is similar to the Mediterranean in dimension and strategic position. The length of the Mediterranean is 2,300 miles, while the distance from Jakarta to Hong Kong in the South China Sea is some 2,100 miles. The Straits of Gibralter and the southern end of the Straits of Malacca are each eight miles wide. By contrast, the southeast entrance to the South China Sea is by the Bashi Channel and Luzon Straits, measuring 220 miles between Luzon and Taiwan.

Within the South China Sea, channels of navigation are clear; but the shallowness of its waters in the Straits of Malacca and Singapore and the Java Sea make navigation difficult for very large crude carriers (VLCCs) that are now being used in the area.

The Southeast Asian seas not only serve as a vital instrument to international navigation, they also constitute the greatest environmental resource and economic asset of Southeast Asia, which must increasingly consider environmental protection together with the development of its trade within and outside the region. Many ships bring cargoes from other countries, and export the products of Southeast Asia to any country that has a port. The ships that call are not only those that have business in either of the great oceans. It is in this fact that Singapore's importance lies, as it develops industries related to the sea: shipbuilding, ship repairing, ship servicing and handling, and the exploitation of submarine oil and minerals. The largest tanker afloat has berthed in her waters; her port is being provided with dock facilities for containerized ships; today docks for ships up to 400,000 tons are under consideration; and within the last two years Singapore's own shipping line has bought its first ten oceangoing ships.[11]

Of more immediate and direct interest to the great maritime powers is the importance of the Southeast Asia seas as a channel of transit. About 90 percent of Japan's oil comes from the Persian Gulf through the Indian Ocean, the Straits of Malacca and Singapore, the South China Sea, and the East Asian waters. The USSR's ships pass through these waters in transit from the Black Sea to Vladivostok. As the USSR and the Eastern European countries build up their merchant fleets, they are increasingly involved in Southeast Asia. Early in 1969, Bulgaria announced the opening of a sea service from Varna to Singapore. Almost 200 major shipping lines from fifty-three countries call at the port of Singapore, which has become the greatest tanker port and oil transshipment center in Asia.

U.S. merchant fleet and naval power have been developed in line with the American interest in the Asia and Pacific area. After 1945, access by sea temporarily revived the colonial link, but the ability to bring men and materials by sea did not help the old empires regain their former colonies. At present, the significance of Southeast Asia for the United States lies in the importance of this region and its seas as an area of transit connecting the Indian and Pacific Oceans.

The coexistence of political and economic interests of the great powers with the common interests of the peoples of Southeast Asia in the peace and environmental protection of the region is a measure of the centrality, complexity, and community of the environmental problems of the region, which necessarily require balanced arrangement and regulation.

These factors make the task of "marine environmental protection" more difficult for the countries of Southeast Asia, because an acceptable environmental protection policy and definition of "environmental protection purposes" would have to be created within the framework of a viable economy adjusted to the new opportunities and requirements of a technological world. The arrangement must also be mindful of the revolution of rising expectations, particularly for a harmony of classes and communalities and a creative climate of cooperation. This requires a maximum degree of involvement of the members of each nation in Southeast Asia, placing communication and mobilization of goodwill and understanding at a premium, as they affect the basic stuff of human needs.

These are the complicated environmental problems of the Southeast Asian marine environment created by geography and history. The problems are currently compounded by the increasing density of marine traffic through the vital Straits of Malacca and Singapore, particularly after the reopening of the Suez Canal and the emergence of mammoth tankers.

The Straits of Malacca and Singapore Environment

Multi-straits structure.[12] The Straits of Malacca and Singapore stretch between the Indonesian island of Sumatra and West Malaysia to the east and between the Riouw archipelago and Singapore to the south. The straits separate the Malay Peninsula and the Indonesian island of Sumatra, and connect the Indian Ocean to the South China Sea. They are the sea link between latitudes 6°N and 1°N from the Indian Ocean to Singapore Straits and the South China Sea.

The Malacca Straits are a funnel-shaped waterway. Its width varies from three miles at its narrowest passage near Singapore island to 300 miles at its widest, near the northwestern entrance between Sabang and the Kra isthmus. The southern portion of the straits is quite narrow. The channel is only twenty-one miles wide between Aruah Island and the coast of Sumatra and has a length of about twenty miles. Southward of the adjacent islands of Medang and Rupat, the straits have an average width of thirty miles, but northward of them the breadth is about forty miles from shore to shore. The narrow part of the area between Medang and the Malayan shore varies from twenty to twenty-five miles in width over a distance of about fourteen miles. Between Tanjong Tohor on the Malayan Coast, and the Tanjong Parit, the northern extremity of Bengkalis island off Sumatra coast, the fairway narrows to a width of less than twenty-six miles over a distance of about eleven miles. The width is only 8.4 miles between Karimun island and Pulau Kukub at the southwestern tip of Malaysia. The straits at their narrowest passage, near Singapore island, are only three miles wide.

The Malacca Straits include a tremendous sea area from the northwestern-most entrance between Pulau Perak (Perak Island) and Diamond Point to the southeasternmost entrance between Tahan Datok (Mount Datok) and Tanjong Pergam (Pergam Coast). In this zone there are at least three strait groups traditionally used for navigation by the coastal states. Accordingly, "Malacca Straits" is a collective term for many straits or strait groups, among which the Singapore Straits hold the key to the whole straits area.

Narrowness and Shallowness of the Straits. Among the strait groups in this area, nearly all key straits are of marginal breadth. The maximal breadth of the strait zone is 126 miles, while the minimal breadth is only 3.2 miles. Many of the straits are narrower than twenty-four miles, a distance narrower than the combined breadth of the territorial seas of the territorial states: Indonesia and Malaysia.

At different places the Malacca Straits are quite shallow. A hydrographic survey conducted jointly by Japan, Indonesia, Malaysia, and Singapore in 1970 noted that in the "330 sq. km" of the Philip Channel surveyed, thirty-seven points were found to be less than twenty-three meters deep. The Straits are up to twenty-four fathoms deep westward of the Aruah Islands, but only between three and seven fathoms deep southward of these islands. Within about thirteen miles of the Aruah Island, the fairway has depths of sixteen to twenty fathoms. Near the Aruah Island and the southern end of North Sands, there is a place called: "One Fathom Bank." Southward, there is a dangerous three and three-fourths fathom patch. The width of the navigable channel here is about four miles.

The straits vary from nine and one-half fathoms to over thirty between Medang Islands and Cape Rachado. There is, however, a dangerous shoal with two and one-half fathoms of water over it near the middle. Between Tanjong Tohor on the Malaysian coast, and Tanjong Parit, the northeastern extreme of Bengkalis (Indonesia), the depth varies from thirteen to twenty-six fathoms. Near the middle of the channel is Long Bank, which is only three fathoms deep. There are similar banks, some even shallower, between Long Bank and the islands close to Sumatra.

Tide and Currents.[13] The tides of the Malacca Straits are modified seasonally by winds that practically reverse through the year. The tides from the Indian Ocean progress eastward along the Malacca Straits. The straits are full of rocks, dangerous reefs and crosscurrents. The waters of the straits are calm, equatorially warm, and placid as they flow. These are the natural physical characteristics of the straits of Malacca and Singapore which constitute the sea link between the Indian Ocean, South China Sea, and the Pacific Ocean. With the opening of the Suez Canal in 1869, the dominant trade route from Europe to the Far East shifted from the "Cape Town/Sunda Straits" route to the "Suez/Malacca Straits" route. As trade and navigation between Asian countries and Africa, or between the Far East and the Western world grow, the importance of the Straits of Malacca and Singapore will increase day by day, and with it the position and role of Southeast Asia will also develop.

THE PRINCIPLES OF ENVIRONMENTAL POLICY IN THE STRAITS OF MALACCA AND SINGAPORE

Environmental Protection

The traditional formulation of the international law of the sea is derived from a world that has passed: the time of empires. In that world power was based upon ships of war and ships of commerce, and their freedom to sail the oceans. The axion of empire was the right to trade, the right of access to raw materials and to the markets on which the power and wealth of the industrialized countries were based; and this implied the right of access by sea. Free trade meant "unencumbered trade"; freedom of the seas was intended to secure "uninterrupted sea routes." Each was complementary to the other.[14] These principles reflected the interests shared by the great powers rather than those of the subordinate nations, and the interests or needs of the great powers were defined in legal rights. The major difficulties arising from these principles tended to focus not on the high seas but on the narrow and most convenient passageways between oceans, such as the Straits of Gibraltar and the Dardanelles, leading into the Mediterranean, the Suez Canal between the Atlantic and Indian Oceans, the Caribbean and the Panama Canal between the Atlantic and Pacific Oceans, and the Straits of Malacca and Singapore between the Pacific and Indian Oceans.

The old order of the seas assumed that the dominant role of the oceans was a "channel of communications." But the oceans are also a source of wealth in food and raw materials found in the sea, on the seabed, and in the subsoil. The concept of the sea as a source of wealth suggests that the sea is a source of national wealth similar to the land. New nations that are comparatively deprived of land-based resources are naturally induced to seek to redress the balance in seabed resources and at the same time to prevent a widening of the gap in wealth that would result from further harvesting of the fruits of the sea by the great powers, if unchecked by national boundaries. For coastal (nonmaritime) states, the right of transit is neither absolute nor dominant, but conditional and relative to other maritime interests of higher importance, specifically that of protection of the marine environment against damage caused by pollution in order to preserve it for succeeding generations.

The right of transit by traditional methods of navigation was presumed to be harmless. It was, therefore, guaranteed on the high seas, and in territorial waters it was secured by the doctrine of innocent passage. The freedom of navigation evolved as one of the most important freedoms of the seas as a result of the competing claims in the seventeenth century between the Dutch and English, on the one hand, and the Portuguese and Spanish, on the other. At that time freedom of navigation presented no danger to the marine environment because of the small number of vessels, the limited tonnage involved, and the use of wind as the sole source of power. The picture has increasingly changed over the years by the introduction of new means of propulsion: first the steam turbine, and later oil-burning engines. The tremendous increase in the number and size of vessels since the end of the Second World War has brought into question the acceptability of the traditional, unrestricted, freedom of navigation. Recently, this traditional freedom has incurred serious objections, particularly because of the increasing visibility and rising incidence of oil spillages inflicting serious damage on the marine environment and its resources. This problem has even caused some today to challenge the established doctrine of innocent passage.

Vessel pollution arises in various ways, accidental and deliberation. Among the latter type, the most common sources are the discharge of ballast and the washing of tanks by oil tankers. One estimate suggests that about 40 percent of the total amount (approximately 2,500,000 tons) of oil discharged into the ocean each year comes from these sources. The demand for strict controls over deliberate discharge and for improvement in construction standards, as well as requirements for modern equipment and fittings, can be expected to grow in the future.

As long as normal vessel operation was considered harmless, the coastal states were always required to have specific reasons to suspend innocent passage. Yet neither the historical development of this tradition nor its incorporation in the 1958 Convention on the Territorial Sea and Continguous Zone has led to an acceptable definition of innocent passage. As long as the passage did not threaten the peace, order, and safety of the coastal state, it was normally considered to be innocent. But now, with the increasing danger of sea pollution, it does seem apparent that the classical concept of innocent passage is no longer acceptable. This particular freedom of the seas is now subject to reexamination in the general effort to control pollution within a new system of order designed to stabilize the ocean environment and preserve its resources for the whole of mankind. The developed maritime nations do not object to the efforts and measures to assure protection of the marine environment, but they do have reservations concerning implementation methods that could frustrate the right of navigation under the pretext of pollution control regulations. For instance, they would prefer tanker construction to be undertaken according to uniform international standards, to avoid the possibility that one country could unilaterally draw up certain ships. Virtually all maritime nations have agreed to this concept.

However, while construction standards would be uniform throughout the world, environmental standards governing the discharge of effluents into the sea might vary according to geographical location, especially if sensitive marine ecosystems would become susceptible to damage. It is generally accepted that the establishment of variable environmental standards is of paramount importance for the well-being of coastal states and their resources. Such a special geographical location, with sensitive ecosystems, is to be found in the Straits of Malacca and Singapore. Together with the Strait of Dover, the Straits of Malacca and Singapore are regarded as the busiest sea lanes in the world. With the coming of the steamships, and after the opening of the Suez Canal in 1869, the Straits of Malacca and Singapore have provided the "grand trunk road" of sea communication from Europe to the Far East. The shipment of passengers and cargoes has grown formidably with the growth of Japanese and Chinese trade, and as the Southeast Asian countries began to produce tin and rubber. Each day more than 100 ships (each year more than 37,000 ships) navigate the Straits of Malacca and Singapore, and this number continues to grow with the development of European-Asian trade and navigation.[15] This trend has become more threatening with the appearance of supertankers about the middle of the 1960s. According to a report by Captain Yoshio Saito, secretary general of Japan's Malacca Straits Council, in the month of May 1972 alone fifteen supertankers of over 200,000 dwt passed through the Straits of Malacca and Singapore.[16] The danger of pollution by these vessels is enhanced by the special physical conditions of the straits, particularly by the shallowness of the straits at several places. Even within the 300 sq. km. of the Philip Channel off Singapore, for instance, there are thirty-seven points less than twenty-three meters in depth, the minimum draught for a 250,000 dwt tanker.

Most of these supertankers are destined for Japan, whose oil consumption is growing almost 20 percent annually. Japan's crude oil imports will increase to the staggering amount of 600 million tons a year by 1980. The great bulk of this will pass through the Straits of Malacca and Singapore, which therefore will face a tremendous increase in the burden of risk to their marine environment.[17] Being one of the leading maritime powers, Japan has a predominantly commercial interest in the Straits of Malacca and Singapore. The Japanese economy is sustained by a continuous flow of overseas raw materials and fuel supplies, which make up 80 percent of her requirements. Of these raw material imports, no less than 40 percent comes via the Indian Ocean and through the Straits of Malacca and Singapore.[18] It has been reported that 85 to 90 percent of Japanese requirements for oil must be imported from the Middle East and transported via the Indian Ocean and through the Straits of Malacca and Singapore. In addition to oil, Japan has to import nickel, timber, tin, bauxite, manganese, and copper chrome, much of which has also to be transported through the same sea route. Moreover, as Japan's imports have increased rapidly, so have her exports.

In the last decade Japan has made several efforts to diversify the sources of her supply, but it is not likely that the pattern will change significantly over the next ten to fifteen years. For at least the next two decades Japan will continue to be overwhelmingly dependent on her import of raw materials along the same lines as in the recent past, particularly in the case of oil, which must be imported from the Middle East. In the past few years, Japan has indeed started to turn to Southeast Asia for an increasing percentage of her oil needs. Indonesia has supplied 15 percent or more of Japan's requirements for crude oil. This means that Japan imports about 70 percent of Indonesia's petroleum export, or 50 percent of its total production. Indonesian oil is still in great demand by Japanese industry because of its low sulfur content. In May 1969, Japanese oil companies concluded an agreement for joint exploration of oil resources off the coast of West Malaysia and Sabah, while other companies have been involved in three exploration projects in the Gulf of Thailand, and in another offshore exploration with Burma in the Gulf of Martaban.[19]

When the Middle East conflict broke out in October 1973, followed by the "world energy crisis," Japan was hit hardest among the industrial countries and was forced to look for oil in China and the USSR. A series of agreements were concluded in 1973-73, which over time would reduce Japan's present overwhelming dependence on Middle East oil. However, Japan's spiralling need for oil will certainly continue to make that country the world's largest single importer of Middle East petroleum for a long time, and will thus heighten rather than reduce the importance of the Straits of Malacca and Singapore for Japanese navigation in transporting crude oil. In this context, it is easy to recognize how important the Straits of Malacca and Singapore are to Japan. In 1968 the Japanese Ministry of Transport set up the Malacca Straits Council as well as a Malacca Navigation Facilities Improvement Board, together with private oil and shipping companies. It was primarily for these reasons that Japan has demonstrated great interest in and concern over the initiative taken by Indonesia, Malaysia, and Singapore to combat the danger of pollution in the Straits of Malacca and Singapore.

The Marine Pollution Problems in the Straits of Malacca and Singapore

The crucial question is whether and to what extent the environmental, economic, security, and political requirements of the littoral states are compatible or at variance with the interests of the user states. Only if these interests converge can the Straits of Malacca and Singapore remain an environmentally protected area and at the same time a globally important and peaceful sea-lane of commerce. If, on the other hand, these interests are in conflict, then the straits are likely to become a bone of contention among the competing powers.

The attitude of each of the powers toward the Straits of Malacca and Singapore reflects its own perception of the coming order in the straits. This is evident in the positions adopted by the littoral states on the one hand, and by the user states on the other. The principal arguments of the coastal states against the use of the straits by supertankers are based mostly on the fear of massive pollution. In May 1972, Indonesia reiterated her stand taken since 1970:

> Every nation has the right to protect its territorial waters from use by other countries which could endanger the interest of its people, as by causing water pollution and damaging off-shore exploration and fishing industries. This will surely happen if heavy ships above 200,000 tons pass through the waterway which is shallow in several parts. (Statement of Chief of Staff of the Navy)

Similar sentiments were expressed by the Malaysian prime minister at the opening of the twenty-third UNCO (government party) Conference in 1972:

> Indonesia and Malaysia have the right to control the Straits of Malacca so that it will not be polluted by oil spills from tankers which can and will destroy the fish and the shores of both countries. If this happens, the means of livelihood of thousands of Malaysian and Indonesian fishermen will be jeopardized.[20]

By raising the problem of pollution, Indonesia and Malaysia have been able to highlight a major issue relating not only to the environmental protection of the Straits of Malacca and Singapore, but also to several other sea-lanes and the Southeast Asian waters in general.

Pollutants belong to several categories: domestic waste; industrial and agricultural effluents; waste discharged from ships; exploration of the mineral resources of the seabed; radioactive waste; waste from thermal power plants; and military pollution through dumping of poisonous gases and explosions. On the high seas, pollution occurs mainly through transportation of oil (accidental spills or deballasting operations); from the dumping of radioactive waste; and as a result of the mineral exploration and exploitation of the seabed and ocean floor.

In recent years several accidents at sea have posed serious hazards to the coastal population, for example, the well-known disaster of March 1967 in which the *Torrey Canyon,* a Liberian tanker of 118,285 tons, carrying a cargo of 119,328 dwt of crude oil, ran aground on the "Seven Stones Reefs," eight miles off Lands End in Britain, and spilled 30,000 tons into the sea and on the adjacent coastline of England and France to the detriment of fishing and tourist interests. Therefore, when in 1967 the *Tokyo Maru* of 151,288 dwt scraped its bottom while passing through the Straits of Malacca and Singapore, the shadow of *Torrey Canyon* loomed large.[21] In January 1968, another supertanker, this one of 200,000 dwt, was grounded just outside Singapore harbor.

To avoid the risk of grounding in the narrow waters of the straits, two other supertankers of a Japanese oil company, the *Niiseki Maru* and the *Kinki Maru,* carrying crude oil from the Persian Gulf, were ordered by their firm to make a detour by sailing through the Straits of Lombok and Makassar (as recommended by the Indonesian government) in order to guarantee safety of navigation, particularly for supertankers of over 200,000 dwt. Although this alternative sea route through the Straits of Lombok and Makassar has been recommended for their own safety of transit, many supertankers still prefer to sail through the Straits of Malacca and Singapore, ignoring the dangers of shallowness and narrowness of the waters there. This danger was proved once more by the dramatic grounding incident of the supertanker *Showa Maru* on January 6, 1975 just three miles from Singapore harbor. A supertanker of 237,698 dwt, owned by Thaiheiyo Kaiun Co. Ltd. Tokyo, the *Showa Maru* was carrying crude oil from the Persian Gulf to Japan under the command of Captain Soichi Mikami, one of the most experienced Japanese sailors to traverse the Straits of Malacca and Singapore.[22] The significance of the *Showa Maru* grounding incident went far beyond the facts of the spill: three leaking tanks and a 10 km long oil slick of 7,300 tons that threatened the island of Singapore, the west coast of Malaysia and the fishing grounds of the Riauw Islands chain in Indonesia. The incident created a rush of consultations among the three coastal states of the straits, which promised a new solidarity that neither UNCLOS III nor the recent passage of the U.S. warship *Enterprise* had been able to achieve. In the face of this new consensus and solidarity, the main user of the Straits of Malacca and Singapore, the Japanese, seemed eager to make concessions, particularly with regard to the need to divert the passage of supertankers of over 200,000 dwt through the Straits of Lombok and Makassar.

Since the grounding of the supertanker *Myrtea* in 1971, near the island of Bukom in the Straits of Singapore, the Indonesian government has been urging a 200,000 ton limit on tankers passing through the Straits of Malacca and Singapore. The *Showa Maru* incident was therefore seen in Jakarta as confirming the government's worst fears. Indonesia had long been insistent that the only safe route for very large crude carriers (VLCCs) of 200,000 tons and over heading for

Japan was through the Straits of Lombok and Makassar. Since October 1971, when the Japanese VLCC *Niiseki Maru* of 372,000 dwt became the first tanker to make its journey through these straits, others have followed. Tanker owners, however, object to diverting their tankers through the Lombok Straits. Their main consideration is that the detour costs more time and money. The route from the Persian Gulf to Japan through the Straits of Malacca and Singapore is 6,606 miles long, while through the Straits of Lombok and Makassar it is 7,605 miles, a difference of 999 miles. The time needed for the navigation of the route through the Straits of Malacca and Singapore is normally 17.4 days, while the route through the Straits of Lombok and Makassar would need 20.1 days, a time difference of 2.7 days sailing time. This time difference would increase the cost of each tanker sailing by an extra 10 million yen, causing an increase in the price of each kiloliter of oil in Japan on the order of 30 yen. Against this it may be said that the route through the Straits of Lombok and Makassar provides the possibility of increasing the tonnage of each tanker, thereby reducing the transportation cost considerably.

The Japanese shipping companies, however, seem not to be interested in countering the arguments set out above, and it is therefore unlikely that they will be easily persuaded to use the route through the Straits of Lombok and Makassar just in order to reduce the pollution hazards of the Straits of Malacca and Singapore.[24] This reluctance of the Japanese shipping world has pressed the three coastal states of Indonesia, Malaysia, and Singapore into a joint initiative to look for other arrangements to enhance existing efforts to protect the marine environment of the Straits of Malacca and Singapore against the growing threats and dangers of oil pollution. The first initiative consisted of a tripartite agreement to conduct several hydrographic surveys of the straits. The initial survey was carried out by the littoral states with the assistance of Japan, early in 1969, and another, completed late in 1970, identified thirty-seven shallow spots that could be dangerous for large tankers, such as the Japanese VLCCs.

Meanwhile, in January 1970, the chief of the administrative bureau of the Malacca Joint Council of Japan, Yoshio Saito, led a group of Japanese to negotiate with the coastal nations of the straits. The purpose was to expedite the signing of a memorandum on a "Four Power Survey Project." The mission reportedly tried to establish Japan as an equal partner with the three littoral states, particularly with regard to the right of exercising control over the Straits of Malacca and Singapore. It proposed separate treaties with each of the littoral states to undertake a proper hydrographic survey and dredging operations in the shallows.[25]

This approach of the Japanese mission produced a negative effect. The three littoral states approved the continuation of hydrographic surveys, but on their own terms, and a six-point agreement was signed to confirm their position on the

Straits of Malacca and Singapore:

(1) The Three Governments agree that the safety of navigation in the Straits of Malacca and Singapore is the sole responsibility of the coastal states concerned.
(2) The Three Governments agree on the need of tri-partite co-operation for the safety of navigation in the two Straits.
(3) The Three Governments agree on the formation as soon as possible of a body for co-operation of endeavours for the safety of navigation in the Straits of Malacca and Singapore.
(4) The Three Governments agree that the question of the safety of navigation and the problem of internationalization are two separate problems.
(5) The Governments of the Republic of Indonesia and Malaysia agree that the Straits of Malacca and Singapore are not international straits, though fully admitting the use of those straits for international shipping in conformity with the principle of innocent passage. The Government of Singapore duly takes note of the position of the Governments of the Republic of Indonesia and Malaysia on this matter.
(6) On basis of the understanding mentioned above, the Three Governments agree on the continuation of hydrographic survey.[26]

In the beginning there were still some differences among the three parties to this agreement, but eventually they were resolved. The three littoral states were able to develop a real consensus on the urgent need to protect the straits environmentally. Although it will take a long time to create a pollution-free environment in the straits, all three governments acknowledge the urgent need for systematically coordinated joint efforts to protect the marine environment of the Straits of Malacca and Singapore against the growing danger of oil pollution. More specifically, as a result of the findings of the joint hydrographic survey conducted since 1969 in the straits, the conviction has grown that one of the most effective measures to prevent the danger of oil pollution is the application of a *Traffic Separation Scheme* (TSS) designed to steer vessels clear of the shallow points in the straits.

In addition, an understanding has been developed on the need to limit the tonnage of tankers traversing the shallow Straits of Malacca and Singapore in order to minimize the risk of grounding. VLCCs of 200,000 dwt and over are now advised to use the Straits of Lombok and Makassar to avoid the danger of accidents in the Straits of Malacca and Singapore. Meanwhile, the three littoral states continue their hydrographic surveys to update all data and information on the physical condition of the Straits. Efforts are also made to improve navigational aids, particularly in the critical areas. All these efforts are conducted jointly, but for some specific projects foreign assistance has also been sought, particularly from the user states.

The dramatic grounding of the Japanese supertanker *Showa Maru* in January 1975 spurred the three littoral states to expedite their efforts to develop the necessary regulations and measures to prevent such a recurrence. In an eight-point statement issued on January 18, 1975, the Indonesian government again called for a limit of 200,000 dwt for tankers passing through the straits, since the physical evidence proved clearly that the Straits of Malacca and Singapore were not able to be traversed by bigger ships. The final paragraph of the statement reads: "This very damaging experience forces Indonesia once again to invite the other coastal nations, either trilaterally, or, if necessary, bilaterally, to regulate jointly the Straits of Malacca and Singapore for the welfare of the people of the coastal States along the Straits."[27]

As the foreign ministers of the three coastal states gathered for their meeting in Singapore in February 1975, it was announced that they would confine themselves to the immediate issues of *safety of navigation and compensation*. In their Joint Statement of February 19, 1975, it was pointed out, *inter alia,* that:

(1) In order to protect the coastal states from damages resulting from oil pollution, all Three Delegations were agreed on the need to maximize the safety of navigation in the Straits of Malacca and Singapore.

(2) A traffic separation scheme (TSS) should be established and immediate steps should be taken in this direction.

(3) Due to shallowness and narrowness of the Straits, the density of traffic, the limited maneuverability of the VLCCs and other factors, the VLCCs passing through the Straits should be limited, on conditions which would be discussed further by experts.

(4) A group of experts should be appointed to study the extent of the limitations and other related measures to enhance the safety of navigation.

(5) Advanced navigation aids and the possibility of improving navigation in the Straits should be further studied.

(6) A group of experts should be appointed from the Three Countries to work out measures to achieve close consultation, co-ordination and co-operation on anti-pollution policy and measures.

(7) There should be consultation and co-operation with regard to compensation for damage caused by oil pollution.

(8) The question of improving the various present schemes for compensation for damage arising out of oil pollution should be studied and steps should be taken to assure proper restitution.

(9) A body to be named "Council for the Safety of Navigation and the Control of Marine Pollution in the Straits of Malacca and Singapore" should be established at Ministerial level. There should be a committee, consisting of senior officials, to assist the Ministers in the discharge of their function.

(10) The Council of Ministers will meet once a year and the Senior Officials Committee will meet half yearly or at a higher frequency of meetings

> if necessary. The Council should establish the necessary expert groups to implement the various measures that have been agreed upon by the Three Governments.

Since the adoption of the Tripartite Agreement, annual ministerial meetings of the three states have been held, preceded by semi-annual meetings of senior officials, on the basis of the results of the meetings of the various groups of experts and of their recommendations.

Moreover, after four years of continuous joint hydrographic surveys in the straits, the Technical Working Group has formulated the Indonesia-Malaysia-Singapore Traffic Separation Scheme, Rules, and Recommendations. Aided by the results of other technical expert groups that worked on the basis of the provisions of the Tripartite Agreement, the senior officials meeting in December 1976 in Jakarta was able to present its recommendations on measures to enhance the safety of navigation and to promote close cooperation and coordination on antipollution policy and measures in the Straits of Malacca and Singapore. These recommendations were adopted at the Manila session of ministers on the occasion of the ASEAN foreign ministers meeting in February 1977, and constituted the content of the Tripartite Agreement on the Safety of Navigation in the Straits of Malacca and Singapore of February 24, 1977. The Tripartite Ministerial Meeting also set guidelines for the senior officials and technical expert groups to be worked out at their following meetings.

The Tripartite Agreement of February 24, 1977 has once again demonstrated the political will and concrete action of the three states bordering the Straits of Malacca and Singapore in dealing with their common concern with the protection of the marine environment of the straits in the face of the growing density of traffic, particularly of supertankers, and with the ever-mounting danger of oil pollution. The extent of their agreement was indicated by the terms of the Joint Statement that was issued along with the Tripartite Agreement:

(1) Vessels shall maintain a single under keel clearance (UKC) of at least 3.5 meters at all times during the entire passage through the Straits of Malacca and Singapore. They also shall take all necessary safety precautions especially when navigating through the critical areas.

(2) The delineation of the TSS in three specified critical areas of the Straits of Malacca and Singapore, namely in the One Fathom Bank area, the Main Strait & Philip Channel, and off Horsburg Lighthouse shall be defined.

(3) Deep draught vessels, namely vessels having draughts of 15 meters and above, are required to pass through the designated "Deep Water Route" (DWR) in the Straits of Singapore up to Buffalo Rock and are recommended to navigate in the specified route from Buffalo Rock

up to Batu Berhanti area. Other vessels are recommended not to enter the DWR except in an emergency.

(4) Navigational aids and facilities shall be improved for the effective and efficient implementation of the TSS.

(5) The existing voluntary reporting procedure and mechanism for large vessels shall be maintained.

(6) The principle of voluntary pilotage through critical areas in the Straits of Singapore shall be applied.

(7) VLCC's and deep draught vessels are advised to navigate at a speed of not more than 12 knots during their passage through critical areas, and that no overtaking shall be allowed in the DWR.

(8) Charts and current and tidal data shall be improved.

(9) Rule 10 of the International Regulation for Preventing Collisions At Sea, 1972, shall be applied as far as practicable within the TSS.

(10) The implementation of the TSS should not pose a financial burden on the Coastal States and the necessary funds shall be obtained from the users.

(11) A joint policy to deal with marine pollution shall be formulated.

(12) All tankers and large vessels navigating through the Straits of Malacca and Singapore shall be adequately covered by insurance and compensation schemes.

If this communique is compared with the statement of February 19, 1975, a great difference will be observed, which illustrates the progress made by the Tripartite Ministerial Meeting in the past few years. The three littoral states fully acknowledge that they still have their differences of interest and national policy, yet in dealing with the problem of protecting the Straits of Malacca and Singapore against further deterioration and damage caused by pollution from ships, they have already found common ground, and their policy is a remarkable achievement in implementing the spirit of regional cooperation.

Following the Tripartite Agreement of February 24, 1977 at Manila, the tripartite senior officials meeting was convened at Penang (Malaysia) in August 1977 to consider the implementation and enforcement of the joint traffic separation scheme (IMS-TSS), according to the instructions of the Tripartite Ministerial Meeting. This meeting decided to make a joint presentation of the IMS-TSS to the IMCO Meeting of September-November 1977 in London to secure its general adoption by the international shipping community.

With the implementation and enforcement of the IMS-TSS in the Straits of Malacca and Singapore, there will be a newly formulated navigation scheme for the Straits of Malacca and Singapore, which will contribute substantially to the safety of navigation in Southeast Asia, not only for the sake of the ship, shippers, and shipowners, but also for the safety of the marine environment and the well-being of the peoples along the coast of the Straits.

NAVIGATION SCHEME IN THE STRAITS OF MALACCA AND SINGAPORE

In conclusion, presenting the main objects, scope and principles of a navigation scheme regulating maritime traffic in the Straits of Malacca and Singapore the authors have thought it best to present *in toto* the report of the senior officials meeting held in Penang as presented to the Maritime Safety Committee of IMCO in November 1977.*

1. THE IMPLEMENTATION AND ENFORCEMENT OF THE TSS

Pursuant to the signing of the "Tripartite Agreement" of 24 February 1977 on the "Safety of Navigation on the Straits of Malacca and Singapore", the Meeting of Senior Officials of the "Three Coastal States" at Penang on 18–20 August 1977 has considered the implementation and enforcement of the "Indonesia-Malaysia-Singapore (IMS) Traffic Separation Scheme (TSS)" (IMS-TSS). Some basic considerations of the Meeting may be cited to illustrate the progress made by the "Tripartite co-operation" in establishing a "Navigation Scheme in the Straits of Malacca and Singapore."

It has once again been emphasized that the Straits of Malacca and Singapore may be regarded as one of the busiest waterway of its kind. Ships of many types and from numerous countries regularly pass through the Straits carrying cargo of different kinds. The "Three Coastal States" bordering the Straits do not begrudge the passage of these vessels. On the contrary, they welcome them, for it is their intention and aim to develop themselves into major maritime nations.

It is, however, important to bear in mind that the Straits of Malacca and Singapore constitute a vital life-line for the peoples of the "Three Coastal States." It is, therefore, imperative that the Straits should be kept safe for navigation and other activities, such as fishing, which plays an important role in the economy and in the life of many people who owe their living to this industry.

It is of paramount importance that international navigation which makes use of the Straits should take every precaution in order not to endanger the marine environment of the Straits. The majority of the users of the Straits have indeed a high sense of responsibility and have been scrupulous in their passage through the Straits. But at the same time, there are irrresponsible individuals who choose to clean out their tanks while passing through the Straits. Such practices may not be continued and appropriate measures against offending vessels must be taken.

One means of guarding against the incidence of pollution is to *ensure the safety of navigation by having a proper Traffic Separation Scheme* (TSS). Such a TSS has been endorsed by the Governments of the "Three Coastal States" and

*Since they consist of an official document, the following pages have been left unedited. *Editor.*

it remains to have the TSS formally adopted by the appropriate international maritime agency. The Penang-Tripartite Senior Officials Meeting, therefore, has concentrated its attention to the preparation of the coming consultation with the IMCO concerning the implementation and enforcement of the IMS-TSS. It is considered to be very important that the TSS be adopted at the earliest possible date. The earlier the TSS is adopted, the sooner the ships of the different maritime nations which pass through the Straits of Malacca and Singapore would be obliged to comply with the TSS. This would then reduce the chances of collision or vessels running aground, causing spillage which would pose serious threats to the marine environment of the Straits and consequently endanger the livelihood of many of the peoples of the "Three Coastal States."

The IMS-TSS which has been drawn up for the Straits of Malacca and Singapore is rather unique in that it corporates a minimum "Under Keel Clearance" (UKC) for vessels in their passage through the Straits. This provision is considered the minimum margin for vessels to safely navigate through the Straits, and it is obviously in the interests of shippers to comply with this minimum requirement.

Complementary to the implementation and enforecement of the IMS-TSS, the necessary provisions and regulations concerning the prevention and control of marine pollution must be issued. In the formulation of a "joint policy," considerations have been taken on the much wider aspects of the efforts of the "Association of the South East Asian Nations" (ASEAN) in combatting marine pollution, in particular the progress made by ASEAN Expert Group on Marine Pollution under the ASEAN Committee on Transportation and Communications.

In this context, the Penang-Tripartite SOM has also considered the need and possibility of creating a "Revolving Fund" for anti-pollution activities which could be used as an immediate source of funds to combat oil spills.

With regard to compensation for any damage caused by oil pollution, informal consultations have been conducted with TOVALOP and CRISTAL to devise ways for expediting adequate compensations either through TOVALOP and CRISTAL arrangements or through other insurance and compensation schemes.

An additional important programme was reported being in execution by the Technical Experts Group concerning the "Common Datum Charts" and "Currents and Tides" observation.

A "Joint Project" to produce "Common Datum Charts" of the Straits of Malacca and Singapore has been implemented by the "Three Coastal States" -Hydrographers of which the source materials have been completed Assisted by the Japanese Hydrographers, the "Three Coastal States"-Hydrographers have made their preparation to commence production of the "Common Datum Charts" in October 1977. After completion of this project, the shipping world will be provided with a newly up-to-date "Common Datum Charts" of the Straits of Malacca and Singapore, which will be instrumental for enhancing the safety of navigation through the Straits.

Another important "Joint Project" is the "Joint Tidal and Currents Studies in the Straits of Malacca and Singapore" which has been implemented through reconnaisance surveys carried out by using the Indonesia-Survey-Vessel KRI-Jalanidhi and Singapore-Survey-Vessel MV. -Mata-Ikan during the months July-August 1977. With the purpose of establishing "Tide Gauge Stations", the next stage of the studies have been performed with discussions on detailed items during the month of September 1977.

By implementing the two "Joint Projects," the "Three Coastal States" of the Straits of Malacca and Singapore have proved their seriousness in fulfilling their task and obligation to provide the necessary means for enhancing the safety of navigation in the Straits. From the sides of the user-Nations, there have been offered many assistances which illustrated the good understanding between the "Three Coastal States" and the Users of the Straits in succeeding the "sub-regional co-operation and co-ordination of efforts" for enhancing the safety of navigation in the Straits of Malacca and Singapore. In this respect, the assistances offered by Japan, farmost the principal user of the Straits, may be mentioned with particular attention.

It may be observed that after the "Tripartite Agreement" signed by the three Foreign Ministers of the "Three Coastal States" at Manila on 24 February 1977, a really big progress has been achieved in providing the appropriate NAVIGATION SCHEME for the transit through the Straits of Malacca and Singapore which will facilitate both the passing vessels and the peoples along the coast of the Straits to prevent accidents and to avoid the occurrence of threats of pollution of the marine environment. This NAVIGATION SCHEME has been established after 4 years long of Hydrographic surveys conducted jointly by the "Three Coastal States", assisted by Japan. And the surveys will be continued to monitor changes in the conditions of the Straits in order to be able to revise the scheme from time to time for the sake of the exactness of the data and informations.

2. THE INDONESIA-MALAYSIA-SINGAPORE (IMS)-TSS:

The Straits of Malacca and Singapore are long, bending, crowded, and in some parts are very shallow and narrow. Various accidents have occurred in the Straits, either collisions or groundings, or both, bringing about the necessity and needs to regulate traffic in the Straits, inter alia, by establishing a TRAFFIC SEPARATION SCHEME of which some fundamental provisions may be cited to illustrate its concept.

(a) Purpose:

The purpose of the establishment of a "Traffic Separation Scheme" (TSS) is to enhance safety of navigation. For this purpose, the Scheme should be revised, resurveyed and adjusted from time to time, so as to maintain their effectiveness and compatibility with marine resources exploitations, increasing traffic, and other developments.

(b) Navigational Aids:

In connection with the purpose set out above, Navigational Aids should be adjusted accordingly. The latest list of Navigational Warnings should be checked from time to time by the passing ships to ensure that any hazard has been properly charted and defective or missing Navigational Aids should be noted and reported.

(c) Delineation of the TSS:

The present delineation of the TSS is based on the results of about four years of Hydrographic Surveys conducted in the Straits jointly by the Coastal States, assisted by Japan.

The delineation of the TSS in three specified critical areas of the Straits of Malacca and Singapore, namely: (1) in the One Fathom Bank area; (2) the Main Strait & Philip-Cannel; and (3) off Horsburg Lighthouse, are shown in the illustrative map (Annex A). The coordinates of the TSS and the positions of the projected Navigational Aids are published in separate Annexes.

(d) Pre-planned transit:

A pre-planned transit through the Straits of Malacca and Singapore should be made in advance enabling vessels to navigate various shallow and narrow waters in critical areas in safety.

In this connection, the latest informations should be used and up-to-date Navigational Warnings should be taken into consideration.

(e) Shipboard guidelines:

To enhance the safety of navigation, shipboard guidelines should be provided, which include:

(1) Double checking of the pre-planned transit by a second officer;
(2) Double checking of the vessel's position at regular intervals during the voyage by experienced officers;
(3) Navigation Watch Keeping Procedures should be adjusted according to different navigational circumstances (congested waters vs. open seas; poor vs. good visibility, etc);
(4) Pilot services should be used through critical areas using the services of pilotage of the respective countries.

(f) Equipments on board vessels:

Vessels, particularly those with a draught of 15 meters or more should be equiped with:

(1) SSB radio installation, fitted with appropriate frequencies;
(2) Suitable electronic position fixing equipments which will provide sufficient fixing accuracy for navigating in the area.

Ships should be aware that anchoring may be necessary owing to the weather and sea conditions in relations to the size and draught of the ship and to the sea level, and in this respect take special account of the informations available from the pilot and from radio navigation information service in the area.

(g) Under Keel Clearance (UKC):

Vessels shall maintain a sigle UKC of at least 3.5 meters at all time during the entire passage throughout the Straits of Malacca and Singapore and that they shall also take all necessary safety precautions, especially when navigating through shallow and narrow waters and in critical areas.

(h) Rules of the TSS:

Rules 10 of the Collisions Regulations, 1972, shall be applied as far as applicable within the TSS in the Straits of Malacca and Singapore.

(i) Speed and Squat:

The relationship between Speed and Squat appears in Annex B. In this connection, it is recommended that deep draught vessels should reduce their speed, especially when navigating through shallow and narrow waters and in critical areas, to a maximum of 12 knots, compatible with the principles of safety of navigation.

No overtaking is allowed in critical areas, including in the Deep Water Routes (DWR).

Where necessary, transit speed should be decreased or increased in order to obtain the highest margin of safety.

(j) Report on actual transit:

The main objective of the reporting scheme is to improve safety of navigation, particularly of deep draught vessels transiting the Straits of Malacca and Singapore.

Those vessels, before entering, are required to report to the Director of Marine, Singapore, giving their Name; Speed; Deadweight; Draught; Load; Tonnage Time of passing certain point in the Straits; and anticipated routes. They should also report any faulty, defective or out of position of Navigation Aids, which may be observed during their transit of the Straits.

The Director of Marine, Singapore, will in turn broadcast these information to all ships at regular intervals via Singapore Radio. Ships should check that the operating frequencies and times of transmission conform with the latest informations.

The Director of Marine, Singapore, will broadcast messages concerning the passage of loaded deep draught vessels in the form of Navigational Warnings, at least four times during the anticipated period of transit. Messages concerning light laden large vessels will be broadcast at least twice during the transit.

(k) Deep draught vessels:

Vessels having a draught of 15 meters and above are considered draught vessels. Such vessels are required to pass through designated routes in the Straits of Singapore up to Buffalo Rock and are recommended to navigate in the specified route from Buffalo Rock to Batu Berhanti area. Other vessels are recommended not to enter DWR except in emergency. The illustrative map of the DWR is in Annex C.

Deep draught vessels are recommended to pass through critical areas by daylight.

(l) Recommended tracks for deep draught vessels:

The recommended tracks for Deep draught vessels in areas between One Fathom Bank area and the Entrance to Singapore Straits are indicated on the illustrative map in Annex D.

(m) Insurance

All ships navigating through the Straits of Malacca and Singapore, especially within the TSS, are required to carry a proper and sufficient insurance for accidents as well as for damage to marine environment and coastal population to such accidents.

(n) Enforcement:

This TSS shall be enforced by the States in whose waterways the TSS lies. There shall be co-operation and co-ordination among the Three Coastal States to guarantee proper enforcement of the TSS and all its regulations in the Straits of Malacca and Singapore.

3. ANTI-POLLUTION POLICY AND MEASURES:

(Some basic considerations on common regional policy and measures to prevent and combat marine pollution in the Straits of Malacca and Singapore):

A. BASIC CONSIDERATIONS:

(a) Oil Spills Caused By Marine Casualties

(1) Pollution of the sea by oil is one of the formal causes of damage to the marine environment which may cause permanent deterioration of the marine environment if no immediate measures are taken to correct the situation.

(2) Measures to be taken may be (i) *remedial*–i.e. those taken after the occurence of marine casualty and (ii) *preventive*–i.e. those taken to prevent marine casualties from occuring.

(3) The limitation of tonnage of supertankers using the straits is proposed in the framework of preventive measures to protect the marine environment.

(4) Although pollution of the sea may be caused by causes other than marine casualties of supertankers as e.q. (i) release of waste and oil and ballast or (ii) dumping of dangerous substances, damage of the marine environment caused by marine casualties involving super-tankers is our most immediate concern because of the magnitude of the (immediate) damage caused.

(b) Types of Damage

Damage caused by oil spills may effect:

(1) the deterioration of the site (recreations, sports, tourism);

(2) fisheries & living resources of the sea;

(3) damage and (permanent) deterioration of the environment.

(c) Cost and Assessment of Damages (Civil)

Damage to be claimed by victims of oil pollution damage include:

(1) costs of cleaning up the (immediate) environment: harbours, beaches, fishing ground;

(2) immediate damage or loss of source of living (of fishermen dependent on fishing and extraction of other living resources of the sea);
(3) permanent damage or deterioration caused to the marine environment as a whole (source and habitat of fish and other living resources).

While damage falling under category (1) and (2) are not difficult to assess, those under (3) are more difficult to assess because of the factors of regeneration and rehabilitation which may in turn depend on various factors depending on location, currents, climatic conditions, etc. etc.

An assessment of damage most likely to succeed or acceptable to the liable party therefore are: (1) and (2). Longterm damage to the environment (e.g. ecological damage) may be added as a secondary element in damage assessment or compensation.

(d) Penalties

Penalties also called punitive damage are those damages claimed in *addition* to civil damages arising out of civil liability.

These are, however, difficult to claim unless expressly provided by law (nationally enacted legislation or agreed by convention).

(e) Grounds for Liability and Cause for Action

Because of the special nature of punitive damages and their stringent legal requirements, this section will treat those damages that can be classified as civil damages and hence are actionable.

Legally speaking the party causing oil pollution damage may be liable on the following grounds:

(1) on the basis of national legislation previously enacted by the coastal or riparian state;
(2) on the basis of a convention to which both the ship-owner and riparian nations are party;
(3) on the basis of insurance liability voluntarily assumed by the party causing pollution (Tovalop, Cristal, 2 P & 1 insurance).

B. COMMON POLICIES:

(f) Coordination of Policies and Measures to Prevent/ Fight Pollution

(1) Pollution of the marine environment of the Straits being the main concern of the three riparian states (Indonesia, Malaysia and Singapore) it would be useful to compare the relative importance of a possible oil spill as a cause of damage to the riparian state's interests.
(2) Damage (and costs) caused by oil spills may be categorized as follows:
    (i) damages resulting from expenditures made in cleaning up the environment (harbour, beaches and the marine environment);
    (ii) consequential damages caused by the oil spill to tourism (recreation area, hotels), fishing (as a source of living) etc.

(iii) ecological damage, damage to the marine environment of a more permanent nature.

(3) The relative interest of the riparian states, (Indonesia, Malaysia and Singapore) differ in that Indonesia and Malaysia may be affected on all three counts whereas Singapore is only affected by and may be interested only in category (1). Singapore actually may benefit from a marine casualty. As an advanced port (harbour) she is able and willing to provide the services needed e.g. oil spill cleaning up (detergents), Salvage, repair (dock yard).

(4) There is, however, sufficient basis for a common policy on measures to prevent pollution and to cope with its consequences once the oil spill occurs. This guideline *will not deal* with preventive measures aimed at the crude oil carriers and their navigation through the Malacca and Singapore Straits as the ultimate cause and source of (possible) marine casualties and oil spills, as that is dealt with separately in other guideline dealing with safety of navigation and traffic separation schemes. This guidline proposes to deal with the oil pollution problems faced by the riparian states as potential victims.

(5) The protection of a state's interest in the preservation of its marine environment can be achieved through:
(i) national legislation;
(ii) participation in international conventions; and
(iii) through tripartite measures.

(6) The riparian states as sovereign entities are free to protect their interests through national legislation and participation in international conventions dealing with oil pollution (London 1954) and oil pollution damage caused by marine casualties (Brussels, 1969).
Unilateral action may from each state's point of view be the most satisfactory as by doing so each riparian state retains full control of the situation and may extract the greatest possible benefit for herself. Such a course of action, however, has its drawbacks. As it is unlikely that the effects of an oil spill-will be restricted exclusively to one of the three riparian states waters without affecting the others, unilateral action would result in competing claims (of jurisdiction) and may lead to chaos. From the point of view of the shipowners the result would be a much too enormous burden to bear. They may have difficulties in finding the necessary insurance premium which would become unduly high (prohibitive).

(7) There seems therefore to be no alternative for the three riparian states while retaining their sovereign right to take unilateral action to coordinate their policies and measures with respect to pollution control.

(8) *Coordination of the policies and measures with respect to pollution control:*
Tripartite cooperation in this field may take various forms e.g.
(i) consultation;
(ii) coordination;
(iii) cooperation.

Each respectively involving varying degrees of relinquishment of unilateral action.

Whatever form tripartite cooperation may take, certain basic principles should be borne in mind, the most important of which are:

(i) The interests to preserve the marine environment of the three riparian states, though showing common basic features on general principle, differ in detail. Singapore should be aware of and sensitive to the greater concern of Indonesia and Malaysia with the problem and that they have more at stake.

(ii) The measures taken should not amount to (a unduly) burdensome conditions for passage through the straits, hence should be selective e.g. applicable only to crude oil carriers.

(iii) Pending coordinated action regarding preventions of pollution from oil spills the three governments should agree on certain interim measures or action. (These may lie in another field e.g. in the regulation of passage through the straits). The *limitation of tonnage* and/or draught is an excellent interim measure, pending both the coordination of pollution policies and measures and regulation of passage (Traffic separation scheme: TSS).

The above paragraphs have dealt with principles underlying policies and measures to prevent pollution e.g. preventive action (through legislation) by governments.

(9) As a practical mater one should also consider and possibly agree upon *operational principles to deal with oil pollution damage and its consequences* (assessment of damages and compensation and further steps be taken) in the absence of accepted or stated common policies or courses of action.

(i) *Pro-ration of damages and compensation:*
It would be useful and conducive to further tripartite cooperation in this field to agree on a formula according to which damages and compensation payable by the ship-owner (and/or cargo-owner as the case may be) can be prorated amongst Indonesia, Malaysia and Singapore.

Note: Agreement amongst the three claiments is important as absence of agreement may impede the satisfaction of claims for damages).

(ii) Further steps to be taken:
According to the present state of the law especially liability for oil pollution damage, *the amounts recoverable* (in the absence of national legislation and rules of international convention determining otherwise) may be limited and *inadequate* to cover the damages sustained or to be sustained over and above the direct cleaning up costs covered by insurance voluntarily assumed by Tanker-owners and Cargo owners (TOVALOP and CRISTAL). The three governments should agree what steps they should take to safeguard the

recovery of damages not covered 1. *consequential damages:* e.g., to fishing as a source of living (direct and real and easy to assess or 2. *ecological damage:* which is more remote and more difficult to assess.

As *TOVALOP* and *CRISTAL* coverage aggregate to no more than US $ 30.000.000 (Thirty million US dollars) this means that steps may have to be taken other than civil-suit damages

(10) These are some basic considerations and ideas concerning the need to formulate "joint policies and measures" to prevent and combat the marine pollution in the Straits of Malacca and Singapore. In view of the gravity of the problem and because of the number of people and interests involved, it has been recommended that the "Three Coastal States" may define a common stand on the policies and measures to be taken for the prevention and control of oil pollution of the marine environment of the Straits of Malacca and Singapore.

NOTES

1. Quoted from the notice advertising the "Eleventh Annual Conference of the Law of the Sea Institute," Honolulu, Hawaii, November 14–17, 1977.

2. UNEP *Annual Review* 1975, p. 8.

3. R. St.J. Macdonald, Gerald L. Morris, and Douglas M. Johnston, "International Law and Society in the Year 2000," *Canadian Bar Review* (1973), p. 316.

4. UNEP *Annual Review* 1975, pp. 8–10

5. Lewis M. Alexander, *Regional Arrangements in Ocean Affairs* (May 1977), p. 11.

6. St. Munadjat Danusaputro, "South East Asia at the Crossroads of the World," (A synopsis of "Astra Jaya," Lemhannas, Jakarta, 1972), p. 5.

7. Cf. Y.R.E. Waddell, *An Introduction to South East Asian Politics* (1972), pp. 16–17.

8. Danusaputro, *op. cit.*, pp. 65–134.

9. E.G.H. Dolby, *Southeast Asia* (London, 3rd ed., 1954), pp. 8–10.

10. G.G. Thomson "South East Asia," in K.E. Shaw and G.G. Thomson, *The Straits of Malacca in Relation to the Problems of the Indian & Pacific Oceans* (Singapore, 1973), p. 106.

11. Ibid., p. 144.

12. *The Malacca Straits Pilot* (1975). See also, *Joint Hydrographic Survey of the Straits of Malacca and Singapore* (Straits of Malacca Council Publication, 1975). See also St. Munadjat Danusaputro, *Tata lautan Nusantara* (BPHN, Jakarta 1976) pp. 27–45. For a description of a more general character, see Shaw and Thomson, *op. cit.*, pp. 85–95.

13. See, generally, references in note 12.

14. G.G. Thomson, "The Malacca Straits: Who Has the Last Word?" *Pacific Community* 3, 4 (July 1972): 682–83; but c.f. C.P. Jessup, *The Law of Territorial Waters and Maritime Jurisdiction* (1927), pp. 120–122.

15. Bhabani Sen Gupta, T.T. Poulose, and Hemlata Bhatia, *The Malacca Straits and the Indian Ocean: A study of the Strategic and Legal Aspects of a Controversial Sea Lane* (1974), p. 37.

16. According to the report of *Asia Research Bulletin* 2, 3 (August 1972): 1080 B, 200 supertankers passed through the Straits of Malacca and Singapore in 1971.

17. According to Koji Nakamura in "Japan's Ace is Productivity," *Far Eastern Economic Review* 79, 8 (February 1972): p. 10, of the total world production of tankers in 1972 (26,534,000 dwt), Japan could claim 12,835,000 dwt. In the field of bulk carriers, Japanese shipyards produced 5,042,000 dwt of the 1971 world total output of 8,526,000 dwt.

18. *Far Eastern Review* 80, 13 (April 1973): 23.

19. *Far Eastern Economic Review* 78, 51 (December 1972): 21, cited by Sen Gupta et al., *Malacca Straits,* p. 60.

20. *Asia Research Bulletin* 2, 2 (June 1972): 1004 B.

21. Thomson, *supra* note 14, pp. 682–83.

22. Indonesian Petroleum Institute's official report, "Oil Pollution by the Supertanker Showa Maru."

23. Koji Nakamura, *Far Eastern Economic Review* 79, 8 (February 1973): 14.

24. Cf. "Showa Maru Afterspill," *Petroleum News, Southeast Asia* 5, 12 (March 1975).

25. Harish Chandola, "Casting Bread on Malacca Waters," *Economic and Political Weekly* (Bombay) VII, 17 (April 1972) 832.

26. Quoted in the daily *Sinar Harapan,* January 12, 1971.

27. "Showa Maru Afterspill," *supra* note 24.

Commentary

Julian Gresser
University of Hawaii

Increasingly the nations in Northeast and Southeast Asia will have to seek accommodations in the environmental field. The present tripartite arrangement stands as an isolated example. Indeed, the process of regionalization will most probably continue slowly, despite the fact that the problems themselves will become more severe. We are all aware that tanker traffic in this area increases, and that exploitation, particularly of oil and natural gas reserves, will intensify. As Japan, the principal industrialized country, and those other countries in the process of industrialization continue to develop, increasing pressures in the form of pollution will be placed on the marine areas of the region. The need for some sort of regional accommodation will surely be felt more and more as these pressures mount. Now if you examine the tripartite arrangement that has been effected, it grows out of recognition by the littoral states of a need not only to protect the area there for their own interest, but also the fact that they need to effect some sort of control on third party countries that are transiting this area, although not directly continguous to it.

This kind of motivation can be seen in other arrangements that are beginning to develop in this part of the world. The example that comes most clearly to mind is the recent drafting by the government of South Korea of a marine pollution control law modeled fairly closely on Japanese legislation and developed in consultation with the Japanese. Japan was concerned that increasing exploitation of mineral resources within Korean territorial jurisdiction, as well as tanker traffic going through Korean water, would produce pollution that would wash on to Japanese shores. This Korean legislation is being presented to the current session of the National Assembly. If approved, it might provide a basis for complementarity of national legislation in the region.

Another process that is afoot in marine protection is increasing cooperation among these countries in the general field of environmenal protection. For example, a number of countries in Southeast Asia have worked with the Japanese environmental agency in examining various aspects of Japan's laws. This is particularly interesting, because in a recent report presented by the government, Japan noted that all its achievements in the area of pollution control, which are considerable, have been made at virtually no economic cost—have had virtually no detrimental effect on the trajectory of economic growth. Indeed, the report notes that some of the most severely or stringently regulated industries have actually benefited from pollution control policies. Now, that is very attractive to these industrialized countries in the area, because it suggests that a model of economic growth is possible that could at the same time result in environmental protection. Recently the government of South Korea has tried to put together a package of general environmental legislation modeled in part on Japanese law but also drawing on experience elsewhere including the United States, where the emphasis is not only on pollution control but also on environmental management. Given this trend toward coordinated environmental management at the national level, not merely regulation, it may not be too long before such policy making will have derivative effects on the protection of these common areas in the marine environment *shared* by these countries. As you develop more comprehensive coastal zone or environmental planning, you necessarily control the principal source of marine pollution, which is land-based pollution. To this modest extent, then, it might be said that the nations of the region are developing a common vocabulary, a common jurisprudence that sensitizes all the nations of the region to begin to think collectively about some sort of cooperative arrangement for land-based sources of pollution and the like.

The third idea I would like to leave you with is that it seems to me that there is a critical opportunity now for international organizations to foster what I see as a process of accommodation. One specific example is a conference that ESCAP (Economic-Social Affairs Commission of the UN) is sponsoring in Thailand in December [1977]. This will be an introductory experts' meeting, where a whole range of countries, including Australia, Bangladesh, Cook Islands, Fiji, India, Indonesia, Pakistan, Papua New Guinea, Philippines, Singapore and Sri Lanka—to name only a few—have answered an official inquiry set up by the Commission on the extent of development of their environmental laws. Some of these countries have already managed to produce some impressive legislation. In cooperation with UNEP, ESCAP seems to me to be performing an absolutely critical role in catalyzing and coordinating this sort of particularistic development in these countries.

Another international organization which I think can have an increasingly profound impact is the World Bank. The World Bank is engaged in financing heavy industrial development projects in a number of these countries and has concerned itself recently with the environmental ramifications. The Bank has an environmental office and it sends out advisers to prospective countries that are trying to develop environmental management concepts. Indeed, it can be argued that the Bank has an affirmative obligation to see that one country does not obtain an economic competitive advantage by not regulating, and therefore, it has virtually an international mandate to coordinate its lending policies with respect to all the countries in the region in a manner that is conducive to regional development of environmental policies.

Finally, UNEP, as I understand, maintains or has extended its global-watch monitoring system to the area, and WHO has recently established a data exchange information office in Kuala Lumpur. Now, what this suggests is that at the international level, if these various international organizations recognize the opportunity that is presented to them, and coordinate their activities more closely, the chance to spark some sort of regional accommodation is very good. Although one hesitates to speculate on the particular form or design of this regional accommodation, I think what we really must recognize is that we are now viewing a process, an exciting growth process, but one which of course will be piecemeal, just like the development of environmental management systems at the domestic level. This piecemeal process will grow. Some solutions will be inadequate while others will be innovative, and as the whole region becomes more sophisticated and sensitive to the problem, the theory or solutions will be abandoned and a gradual movement to a more rational and fair institutional development seems likely.

Discussion and Questions

Shelley Mark (U.S. Environmental Protection Agency): I wonder what I am doing at a conference on the law of the sea. I am certainly neither a lawyer nor a seaman, and I have only been to Southeast Asia once. I appreciated Professor Danusaputro's paper and was impressed by its depth and coverage. Dr. Craven suggested that I should perhaps comment from an environmental policy perspective, and I will try to do this.

The *Argo Merchant* incident off Nantucket on the eastern coast of the United States, when seven and one-half million gallons of scarce and valuable oil was spilled, has certainly highlighted the issue of tanker traffic and oil spills in the popular mind. However, I think it is also agreed that oil spills are not by themselves the major source of pollution. The National Academy of Science study has indicated that only one-third of the oil pollution of the sea comes from ships; that perhaps 40 percent, roughly, comes from what they call "runoff" (in other words, from inland rivers, coastal industries, municipal waste disposal, and urban rural activities of all kinds); and that the remaining quarter or so comes from such activities as offshore oil exploration, onshore refining, and other miscellaneous activities. So oil spills are just one of several major sources for the ocean pollution problem.

The question is: What can a conference such as the Law of the Sea Conference do about all these problems? One can easily conclude from the statistics, and some additional evidence, that very little can be done. First, we all recognize the difficulty, the extreme difficulty, of arriving at international agreement. Where there has been agreement for joint action, the regulations have usually been quite lax, and the enforcement has been weak or nonexistent. Some international organizations that have been set up to try to deal with some of these issues for example, IMCO, have displayed the usual weakness of such organizations. But we cannot afford to do nothing. It has been long established and widely accepted by both developed and developing countries that the environmental problem is a global one and is becoming progressively worse, and that mankind is depleting irreplaceable resources and introducing pollutants into the air, into the water, and into the land at incredible and unacceptable rates. These actions and their consequences have proved to be interdependent and cumulative. For example, radioactive wastes and toxic substances have been detected in life forms and substances everywhere. The cumulative impact of other chemicals released into the atmosphere, it has been predicted, will drastically change weather patterns in the future, and the ultimate disaster could very well be an adverse effect upon the ozone layer, and therefore, a weakening of the protection of life itself from the millennium of effective and enforceable international agreements. What this suggests is that somehow we must focus on what we already have, what there has been some agreement on, and what might be improved upon. We should focus, therefore, on continued unilateral action by the major countries—who in this case, happily or unhappily, are also the major international polluters—and on some experiments in multilateral action by regional groupings with common awareness and common concern, as perhaps exemplified by some of the countries respresented at this meeting.

One might consider some of the laws that have been passed in the United States and see how they might be extended, or how they might be used, to meet some of these basic pollution problems. There has been some discussion on the potential for the extension of the National Environmental Protection Act, which is really the first of the environmental laws in this country. This statute has, of course, been famous, or notorious, for the requirement of environmental impact statements for a variety of purposes. The prospect is that perhaps the procedures that have been established in examining domestic environmental impacts might be applicable to international situations. Finally, I might say that the United States has already an arsenal of environmental legislation. All the necessary legislation has been passed on clean air, clean water, clean land, and toxic substances. So the authority exists to deal with these runoff problems that have contributed so much to the problems of ocean pollution. Perhaps by looking further into the possible modes of affecting international environmental assessment, in terms of defense, foreign aid, shipping, and other policies of the United States, and of requiring a more vigorous enforcement, we may discover at least one useful approach to this very broad global issue.

Paul Alexander (University of Sydney): I am not quite sure whether I want to make three points or to make one point three different ways, but what my comment stems from is a point made in Professor Danusaputro's paper where he draws a distinction between use-centered environmental policies and resource-centered environmental policies. He described use-centered environmental policies as those that embodied a techno-economic approach, designed to exploit the resources so as to extract the greatest amount in the shortest possible time. This was contrasted with a resource-oriented policy in which a crucial variable is the conservation of the resource for the use by future generations.

I would like to extend this notion of a resource-centered policy to a further and perhaps even slightly metaphorical sense, because in my view developing countries should place a very high value on the skills, the experiences, and the abilities of the traditional coastal communities, and should regard these communities as among the very important resources that any environmental policy ought to be designed to conserve. Notice I said "conserve," not "preserve from change," because what I am saying is not an anthropoligist's or antiquarian's plea for the preservation of a traditional culture, as if it were a living museum. Rather, it is an assertion of the rights of local communities to receive some consideration in the formulation of the law of the sea. Now, in part at least, the claim is a moral one, because these communities are often severely disadvantaged sectors of nations that are themselves severely disadvantaged in international terms. But if you prefer, the claim can be formulated in terms of strict efficiency. Because I think that given the socio-political conditions in many developing countries, especially in Southeast Asia, the customary practices and the customary systems of tenure in conjunction with appropriate modern technology often provide the most satisfactory basis for the development of modern coastal zone management and conservation practices.

It has become customary, in some circles at least, to look at environmental problems on a global basis, and I think there is much to be said for this, inasmuch as it gets away from earlier narrow nationalist interests. But I think it should also be recognized that while the global approach opens up some viewpoints, it also closes off some others. The discussion I have been listening to over the last couple of days has involved many value judgements about the rights, or non-rights, of local communities. In the discussion on the passage of oil tankers through narrow coastal waters, for example, it is worth bearing in mind that the people who would be most damaged by an oil slick are the fishermen who might be deprived of their livelihood for many months.

It is true that one can compensate for an oil slick, I suppose, by some sort of monetary award. But even assuming that the money ever reaches the fishermen, it is doubtful that it will ever repay their debts. Similarly, I think the cost of allowing an industrialized nation to fish within the coastal waters of a less developed country is not really the loss of fish that might be taken by the foreign vessels. The cost might rather be described in terms of inappropriate technolgoy introduced by the foreign fleet that serves as a false model: inappropriate, that is, for the development of the underprivileged nations that wish to run their own fishing industries. The type of fishing technology that you need if you are fishing 1,000 miles away from home and the type you need if you are fishing thirty miles offshore are not necessarily the same. But it is a point that always seems to be missed when countries are drawing up national plans.

I suppose it is inevitable for an anthropologist listening to the discussions of the past few days to attempt to work out the consequences of various policies in terms of the types of societies with which he is familiar, but it seems to me that the proposals for regionalization have a lot to offer developing countries in South or Southeast Asia. In part, this optimistic view is based on the belief that nothing can be much worse than the present picture. Thirty years of techno-economically oriented development within the coastal zones of developing countries, mainly in the fields of fishing, tourism, and transport, have certainly led to increases in the gross national product, but they have also had severe social costs. Employment opportunities have diminished, social inequalities are being exacerbated, and peasant fishing households are being further impoverished. The end result of economic development in the traditional fishing communities in South and Southeast Asia is that the peasant communities have consistently received the short end of the stick, a gift that they themselves are apt to describe in more colorful terms.

There are, however, several more positive reasons for optimism, some of which were crystalized for me by Dr. Johnson's paper, because she emphasized that while the UNCLOS III text made only limited and scattered provision for regional collaboration, its impact on the pattern of dominance and dependency may be long lasting. She later went on to point out that the concept of regional self-reliance, which was important for regional collaboration, presupposes a certain degree of economic dissociation from the prevailing economic and political system. I think these ideas can be taken further. In many developing countries the intent of dissociation is not merely economic, but rather cultural, intellectual, and perhaps scientific as well. It is a short step from the realization that the history of present, highly developed industrial nations is not an adequate model for the development of other countries to the appreciation that the cultural ideas associated with development in the past need not be associated with development in the future.

The very term "transfer of technology," which is widely used in these circles, reflects a prevailing (and I think mistaken) view that technology is socially and politically neutral: that whether in the form of a fish processing plant or a set of model bylaws for a cooperative, "technology" can be developed in one country and then transferred without effect to another irrespective of the cultural context. The results of this notion can be summed up in two images. The first is of a large Norwegian-designed fishing trawler going down the Sri Lankan coast taking the catch that would previously be taken by the traditional fisherman and costing so much to operate that the only market for the fish is the expatriate community. (The expatriate community is Kuala Lumpur, I might add.) The second image is of a coastal villager in New Guinea explaining that when the price of papaya was increased he brought himself an outboard motor and a fiber glass boat. He then allowed his traditional crop to rot. Now that the corporate price has gone down and oil prices have gone up, he has absolutely no way to get himself from the village to the nearby town.

Guy Pauker (Rand Corporation): Since I claim no special knowledge of the ICNT, I will not attempt to discuss Professor Danusaputro's paper in any detail. Instead I shall try to make some brief comments from the point of view of global management interests, which have occupied me for a number of years and have led me to increasingly pessimistic conclusions. I am in the position of believing that the international community is incapable at this time of creating the institutional mechanisms necessary to cope with the problems created by modern science and technology, and the economic and social demands derived therefrom. I do not think, despite earlier pleas we have heard for maintaining the concept of the open sea, that seventeenth-century concepts can do justice to all the problems that are created when supertankers, for instance, are permitted to transit freely through a complex body of water such as that represented by the Straits of Malacca and Singapore. After all, it is a matter that does not require any great imagination to know that even if most of the operators of such tankers would be highly responsible, it is the one reckless operator registered under the who-knows-which flag, carrying the who-knows-what kind of insurance, having who-knows-what kind of crew and skipper, that would do enough damage to affect very drastically those communities living along the coast that Professor Alexander referred to. In the light of this, I think the UN General Assembly made at least a step in the right direction after the 1972 Stockholm Conference when it approved the principle that international responsibility might arise through harming other nations by environmental degradation generated elsewhere. Yet I wonder whether anything else but a regional solution has any practical meaning in a place like the Straits of Malacca today. In reading the Mochtar-Danusaputro paper, I am struck not by the boldness but rather the timidity of the proposals put forward. The authors do not go beyond the hope that voluntary compliance will be feasible and that some reasonable rules will be accepted in negotiations with IMCO. But I would like to raise the question, both from the point of view of the global community, which is not yet set to handle these things directly, and from that of the specific interest, going all the way down to the local communities of Malay fishermen, whether one cannot begin to think more boldly and say what are the implications after Indonesia, Malaysia, and Singapore have reconciled all their own differences. Once these conflicts of interest are reconciled—and I think they will be—could not the three littoral states create a special trilateral authority for the Straits of Malacca, making it mandatory, not voluntary, to use pilots for the ships that go through these straits; making it mandatory, not voluntary, to enforce standards in the construction of tankers, if they want to go through these straits rather than through other waters; making it possible perhaps to collect a certain fee, not for the enrichment of the general treasury of any of the littoral states, but as a contingency fund to cover the costs of clean-up after a spill?

John Bardach: Thank you, panelists. I would now like to open general discussion. First, perhaps Professor Danusaputro should have an opportunity to answer Dr. Pauker's question, and then the audience can have its say.

Munadjat Danusaputro: I was asked about implementation procedures for the current proposals and the purpose of consultation with IMCO. Some of these regulations that are now recommended are not intended to be purely voluntary. For example, the underkeel clearance provision is obligatory, but the pilotage provision, on the other hand, depends on the cooperation of the country concerned. Where the country in question has provided pilotage service, it is mandatory for the ship to use it. In order to help establish "revolving funds," we have obtained an offer of $1.3 million from the Tankers Association of Japan. This example might be followed by other user states.

Kazuo Sumi: I understand Dr. Danusaputro's apprehension of tanker accidents in the Malacca Straits. As he said, we must have an approach not only from the aspect of control but also more systematically from that of the protection of the marine environment. In my view, it is useful to distinguish three kinds of approaches: pollution control, environmental modification, and preservation of the natural state. With regard to control, many speakers have referred to the different sources of marine pollution: first, land based; second, pollution from seabed activities; third, pollution arising from dumping at sea; fourth, vessel-source pollution; and fifth, pollution from the atmosphere. I think the suggested traffic separation scheme is going to be very useful, but at the same time we must pay attention to the need for an environmental modification program. For instance, at the present time some kind of scheme is being considered to establish a new canal, the Kra Canal, in Thailand, and a new waterway in that area would produce an impact on the Bay of Thailand and the Sea of Andaman. Also, many people are considering the exploitation of oil and natural gas in the South China Sea. If an accident should occur there, it would extend to the offshore of Japan, Korea, and China. With these projects in mind, we should adopt a prior environmental impact assessment system. Last year I proposed the establishment of a new organization, a "Southeast Asian Environmental Organization," at a symposium held in Tokyo. What do you think of the conclusion of an environmental treaty in Southeast Asia? And what do you think of the idea of establishing a new environmental organization in the region?

John Bardach: Thank you very much for your comment and suggestion, which is obviously the subject for another panel discussion of at least equal or greater length. We have had a suggestion for the establishment of a "Southeast

Asian Environmental Protection Organization." Professor Sumi did not indicate whether it should be private, or what organizations should adhere to it, or whether it should come through the national governments. Would anyone care to make a comment?

Munadjat Danusaputro: When we speak of Southeast Asia, we have to think of the region as a whole. Perhaps there are three possible levels of action: first, tripartite agreement among the three littoral states; second, ASEAN; and third, wider forms of regional organization. If I have mentioned only the tripartite agreement, that is because it seems to me to be the first step. Further steps will follow, and I hope soon.

Anatoly Kolodkin: It seems to me that some of the ICNT provisions, such as those on liability, would be applicable to the Malacca Straits situation. There are different methods in international law for establishing state responsibility. One is the general principle, which is included in Article 236, that states "shall ensure that recourse is available in accordance with their legal systems for prompt and adequate compensation or other relief in respect of damage caused by pollution to the marine environment by persons, natural or juridical, under their jurisdiction"; and that states "are responsible for the fulfillment of their international obligations concerning the protection and preservation of the marine environment." I would like to stress the need to elaborate the second method as it applies to straits. Article 42.5, for example, says that "the flag state of a ship or aircraft entitled to sovereign immunity which acts in a manner contrary to such laws and regulations or other provisions of this Pact shall bear international responsibility for any loss or damage that results to States bordering straits." In this case, we are talking not about the obligation of states to take measures to ensure liability or responsibility, but about the direct international responsibility of a flag state of a ship or aircraft entitled to sovereign immunity.

My second point is that we have also a very difficult problem in ensuring compliance with international rules in territorial waters and in straits, and it seems to me that it is very important to involve the competent international organizations, in particular IMCO. So I would like to draw your attention to Article 41 on the obligation and the right of bordering states to designate sea-lanes and prescribe traffic separation schemes for navigation in straits. At the same time, it is prescribed that such sea-lanes and traffic separation schemes shall conform to generally accepted international regulations. This article also contains the very important provision that states contemplating such measures shall refer them to the competent international organization and, on the other hand, that the organization may adopt only such sea-lanes and traffic separation schemes as may be agreed with the states bordering the straits. It seems to me that in this case UNCLOS III has elaborated a very important compromise, a very important balance between the interests of coastal states of the region and the international community.

My last point is that in the case of archipelagic states, there is a very significant provision about sea-lanes and the regime of navigation. I do not want to repeat all these provisions because they have a great resemblance to those applicable to straits; but I would like to stress my opinion that in archipelagic straits and waters the regime of passage should be at the same level established for international straits.

Munadjat Danusaputro: The three points submitted are in line with my own thinking. As to the obligation to consult with the competent international organization, we are now in the process of doing just that with IMCO. As to the status of archipelagic water and related matters, perhaps I might wait until my colleague Dr. Djalal has spoken tomorrow on this subject.

Hasjim Djalal: Very briefly, I have a comment on Mr. Pauker's reference to the possibility of collecting tolls. I think this is an idea people have been toying with for many years, but actually it is a most unpopular idea among the highly developed, maritime countries. We see that it is very unpopular, and for that reason we have been trying to work out some arrangement for consultations. For example, if we see the need for the establishment of navigational aids we are ready to undertake some consultations with the users—either the states or the shipping communities—to determine whether they would be in a position to help establish some of those aids. Since this is for their own use, we thought it would be a better and more profitable arrangement, rather than charging a toll.

Second, I think Professor Sumi referred to the possibility of Southeast Asia establishing an environmental organization. Technically speaking, this should present no difficulty, but one should be realistic in terms of the political situation in Southeast Asia. If we talk about Southeast Asia consisting of nine countries—the ASEAN five, three in Indochina, plus Burma—caution and delicacy are needed in any regional initiative.

Third, Dr. Kolodkin is certainly right that there is a discussion of the responsibility and liability of states in Article 236, but I think the situation would be somewhat different if the ship did not belong to a state enterprise or to the state itself. If the ship belonged to a state enterprise, then the principle of state liability would apply, we all agree. But our experience indicates that when we are dealing with a foreign tanker that is not owned by a state enterprise, they tell us, "Well this is a matter of civil affairs or private affairs; the government has nothing to do with this." One of the provisions we are trying to work out through IMCO is that all tankers navigating through the Straits of Malacca and Singapore should be covered by insurance and by a compensation scheme for oil pollution damage. Whether that would be a rule or a recommendation is subject to further discussion with IMCO. What I would like to impress upon Professor Kolodkin is that basically the spirit is there, but the modalities are still in negotiation.

Mike Trens: I am a merchant marine officer, licensed by my government to operate tankers. I might say, Dr. Danusaputro, that I am delighted that somebody–it doesn't matter who–has come up with a navigation scheme for the Straits of Malacca. As an operator, I know that the schemes presently in effect in the Mediterranean and the Straits of Gibraltar are very good, very effective. Before we had them we used to have chaos, so to that extent I am delighted. If Dr. Danusaputro has brought a copy of the proposed navigation scheme, perhaps I could look at it. I may be there within the next two months as a navigator of a tanker. In my view tankers going through the Straits should have insurance, liability coverage. Moreover, governments should ensure that tankers have competent licensed merchant marine or commercial operators aboard. In my country it is tough getting a license. Like so many others, I have sat in the examination room in San Francisco, for example, for three weeks, writing eight hours a day, forty-two very intensive subjects, to pass my license. I would recommend that standards throughout the world be established, so that everybody who runs these tremendous tankers is a properly licensed officer. Wait until you see these big LNG tankers. If you think that oil tankers are hazards, wait till you see an LNG on the line. There had better be competent, trained, experienced officers and men running these ships.

John Bardach: As indicated eralier, fish are very important in Southeast Asia. In fact, if you believe one of the world's leading fish experts, Dr. John Gulland, there may be in Southeast Asian archipelagic waters as much as fourteen million metric tons of unexploited fishery resources. Yet, at the same time, it appears that coastal fishermen are not doing so well, and that there are problems and complications that could be amenable to bi-, tri-, and quadrilateral–in short, regional–resolution. It may be a reflection on the state of regionalism, and the incentive to have regional arrangements, that the three panel members this afternoon are functionally related. You may wonder what an ICLARM is. Francis Christy, whom I have known long ago in more diffident days, says an ICLARM is a little animal. Well, ICLARM is an organization that deals with little and big animals, among other things. It is the International Center for Living Aquatic Resources Management. It is international in scope but has perched in Manila, and it deals to a large extent with problems of Southeast Asian fisheries. Dr. John Marr, who has a long career of experience with Pacific and Asian fisheries ever since he was director of the then National Marine Fisheries Lab in Honolulu, is now the director of ICLARM. Francis Christy, long immersed in fishery economics and this institute, is "on loan" to ICLARM from Resources for the Future in Washington, D.C. Dr. Helfrich was associated with ICLARM in its early formative days, and is now associate dean of research at the University of Hawaii. Dr. Marr will set the stage; Dr. Christy will talk about conflicts, problems, and the like; and Dr. Helfrich will comment on what the other two have been telling you.

Chapter Fourteen

Fishery Management Problems in Southeast Asia[1]

John C. Marr
International Center for Living Aquatic Resources Management

Fishery management problems in Southeast Asia are considered to be the problems of marine fisheries in the South China Sea. These involve primarily the countries bordering the South China Sea and, to a lesser extent, the non-South China Sea countries (Japan and Korea) fishing in the South China Sea. The South China Sea countries contain more than 25 percent of the world population. Fisheries are of importance to almost all of these countries as a source of protein, employment, contribution to GDP, and, in some cases, foreign exchange earnings. In rank of total annual production, including freshwater, four of the South China Sea countries rank among the first fifteen in the world and five produce in excess of one million metric tons. The present annual catch of marine fishes in the South China Sea is in the order of five million metric tons. Estimates of additional potential production have ranged as high as fourteen million metric tons.[2] Although most of the South China Sea countries are coastal states only, two of them, Thailand and Taiwan, are also distant-water states as well. The extension of zones of economic jurisdiction in the South China Sea to 200 miles will completely "close" the South China Sea: there will remain no high seas area within it. With the extension of jurisdiction, property rights will be established and the stage will be set, at least theoretically, for management.

In this context, then, I will describe (1) boundary/jurisdiction problems, (2) resource problems, and (3) development and management problems in the South China Sea. Finally, I will speculate upon ways of dealing with the development and management problems. Boundary/jurisdiction problems include both those associated with offshore islands and those associated with the offshore extension of terrestrial boundaries. Resource problems, or, more precisely, resource characteristics giving rise to problems in the development and management of fisheries, include the multiplicity of species and species distribution across political boundaries. Development and management problems include those associated with the resource characteristics just mentioned, the operations of distant-water fleets, and national and regional institutional arrangements or lack thereof. Future lines of action in dealing with these problems may include bi- and multilateral arrangements, joint or cooperative ventures, common access à la the EEC, and national and regional management mechanisms.

Generally speaking, boundary/jurisdictional disputes in the South China Sea area do not have their roots in fishery matters, and it is to be hoped that some mechanism may be found for minimizing their effects on the solution of fishery management problems. The main problems include: (1) Possible *mare nostrum* or even *mare clausum* claims on the part of the People's Republic of China. While such claims might constitute useful initial bargaining positions, they would be difficult to support and for present purposes such possibilities may be left aside. (2) Conflicting ownership claims exist in the case of the Paracel Islands and Spratly Islands (in the group of islands known collectively as the Dangerous Ground), which are claimed by two or more countries. (3) The location of the offshore extension in the Gulf of Thailand of the terrestrial boundary between Vietnam and Kampuchea is also disputed.

Unlike the higher latitude fish assemblages characterized by large numbers of individuals of a small number of species, fish assemblages in the South China Sea are characterized by relatively smaller numbers of individuals of a vastly larger number of species. The Indo-Malay fish fauna is made up of some 2,500 species. Thus, while the catches in some pelagic fisheries may be relatively pure, single-species catches, it is not uncommon in the demersal fisheries for a single trawl haul to take as many as 200 species. Furthermore, most of these species are widely distributed across one or more political boundaries.

A major development and management problem arising from fisheries based on large numbers of species is the lack of adequate stock assessment methodology. Furthermore, the species composition of the assemblage varies with fishing intensity. Thus, it is difficult to impossible to estimate the biological and economic yields requisite to rational management decisions. With respect to the rather wide species distributions across political boundaries, evidence from tagging experiments, or more sophisticated genetic studies, on the actual movements is largely lacking and is not likely to become available for more than a handful of species in the foreseeable future. In the absence of such information, it must initially be assumed for management purposes that such resources are in fact common to two or more countries according to their distribution.

In addition to the wide distribution of species, there is also the wide distribution of the distant-water fleets of Taiwan and Thailand. The activities of these fleets have already resulted in a number of intrusions into territorial waters and vessel seizures by the offended parties. Closure of the South China Sea will create still further problems.

The Thai distant-water trawl fleet is particularly interesting. Trawling in the Gulf of Thailand started in the early 1960s. The fishery was very profitable, grew rapidly and soon traced the classical course of fishery development, ending in overcapitalization at the producer's level and biological overfishing. Falling profits soon forced the larger boats out of the Gulf of Thailand to fish on the Sunda Shelf, in the Java Sea, and, eventually, as far away as the east coast of India. Soon vessels were being built for distant-water fishing only. This distant-water fleet now produces about 660,000 metric tons from non-Thai waters.[3] Thus, although Thailand is an economically developing country, its trawl fishery has the characteristics of the developed fisheries of economically developed countries: i.e., (1) the "local" fishing grounds are overexploited so that the catch rates are greatly reduced; (2) the fishery is overcapitalized at the producer's level; (3) there is a distant-water fleet, and (4) the distant-water fleet is characterized by modern, sophisticated vessels and gear. At the time of the uncontrolled growth of the Thai trawling fleet, it appeared that it came about because of the inability of the government, which was well informed about the status of the fishery and the resource, to manage the fishery. In retrospect, however, it is tempting to speculate that this apparent inaction was in fact part of a deliberate policy on the part of the government to encourage the development of a distant-water fleet.

The relative importance of the operations of these distant-water fleets in the South China Sea appears to be generally unappreciated. For example, it has recently been concluded, on the basis of a recent trawl survey of the Java Sea, that the fishery potential there was only about half that earlier estimated on the basis of extrapolations from the Gulf of Thailand.[4] However, if the catches of the distant-water fleets from Taiwan and Thailand are taken into account[5] as well as the coastal catches by Indonesian fishermen, the earlier projections appear reasonable. It would appear that about half the potential is already being harvested, rather than that the earlier estimates were too high.

In any case, the lack of access by these distant-water fleets to their traditional fishing grounds that will result from the impending extensions of jurisdiction will create a number of problems including loss of production, loss of employment, loss of return on investment, and secondary effects in ancillary industries and activities. In the case of Thailand, at least, the existence or potential existence of these problems will have a strong influence on foreign policy.

The institutional arrangements necessary to handle the fishery management problems include strong national fishery organizations and an appropriate regional organization. The latter does not exist in the South China Sea area and, while the South China Sea countries all have, or have had, fishery departments of varying levels of sophistication, it is doubtful that they will find it any easier—or any more difficult for that matter—to shoulder the problems associated with extended jurisdiction than do the fishery departments of developed countries.

Turning now to possible future courses of events in dealing with these regional problems, it has already been indicated that the potential mechanisms may include bilateral arrangements, joint or cooperative ventures, common access and regional management mechanism. Whatever mechanism or mechanisms are eventually involved, each concerned country must also have a strong national fishery department or agency. The exact nature of these will naturally vary from country to country, but they all must have two characteristics: (1) they must be able to provide the biological and socioeconomic information requisite to decision taking and (2) they must be able to effectively enforce whatever management decisions are taken.

At least one bilateral arrangement already exists in the area. It is between Thailand and Malaysia and was developed primarily as a result of the intrusion of the fishing vessels of one country into the territorial waters of the other. The mechanism established takes the form of a Ministerial Committee with subcommittees on fishing problems and on technical cooperation. In addition to the intrusion problem, the committee has also dealt with such matters as joint research efforts and lowering of import duties on fishery products. Additional bilateral arrangements may be made in the South China Sea area, but the general solution of fishery management problems, or at least the ability to deal with them, is not likely through a series of ad hoc arrangements.

Joint ventures or cooperative ventures (a cooperative venture is a joint venture in which the participants are from two or more economically developing countries) already exist and undoubtedly more will be formed. Joint ventures in shrimp and tuna fishing/processing already exist between Indonesia and Japan. Thailand is either already involved in, or is actively pursuing the establishment of, cooperative ventures in Malaysia, Burma, Bangladesh, and Indonesia. Through the control of effort, such joint ventures can also function as a management mechanism. They are, however, obviously short- to medium-term mechanisms that will become wholly national as technology transfer is completed.

A fishing industry association in the Philippines has recently proposed that "... The governments of each of the ASEAN group should permit or allow the citizens and domestic enterprises of the member countries to fish in any area within the region." This EEC-type proposal would be subject to the following conditions:

1. The member country within whose territorial limits a catch is made should be advised of any catch made.
2. If any catch is to be brought out of the country, the duties and taxes due on this shall accrue to and be collected by the country from whose waters the catch comes.
3. The fish exported from one ASEAN country to another shall be levied reduced duties and taxes, if not totally exempted from these.

This proposal will, it may be expected, be supported or opposed depending upon the presence or absence of distant-water fishing capability. The presence of distant-water fishing capability is the exception rather than the rule and the acceptance of this proposal therefore appears unlikely.

There are no existing multilateral bodies in the area acceptable in their present form or able to undertake the necessary management activities.[6] In fact, the only regional fishery management mechanism that would appear to be both adequate and feasible is a specially and carefully designed multilateral arrangement involving all South China Sea countries, and even this is fraught with obvious political difficulties. But there is urgent need for such a management body, a South China Sea commission. ASEAN, which has been showing increasing interest in fishery matters, could help bring such a commission into existence. While ASEAN membership does not presently include even a majority of South China Sea countries, the advantages of a South China Sea commission being brought into existence under the aegis of ASEAN probably outweigh the disadvantages.

In any case, strong national fishery organizations and an appropriate regional organization, all working together, would appear to be the most likely route to reduced conflict and confrontation and increased effective use of fishery resources in the South China Sea.

NOTES

1. Contribution No. 1, International Center for Living Aquatic Resources Management, Manila, Philippines, 1977.

2. J.A. Gulland, *The Fish Resources of the Ocean* (1971).

3. J.C. Marr, G. Campleman, and W.R. Murdoch, *Thailand: Fishery Development and Management Policies, Programmes and Institutional Arrangements* (Report to the Government of Thailand, 1975).

4. J. Saeger, P. Martosubroto, and D. Pavly, *First Report of the Indonesian-German Demersal Fisheries Project* (1976).

5. J.C. Marr, *Segara Anakan: Fishery Resources Aspect* (Report to the Government of Indonesia, 1976).

6. J.C. Marr, *Fishery and Resource Management in Southeast Asia* (Resources for the Future Program of International Studies of Fishery Arrangements, Paper No. 7, 1976).

Chapter Fifteen

Fishery Problems in Southeast Asia

Francis T. Christy, Jr.

INTRODUCTION

I intend to focus on the problems affecting the distribution and management of fishery resources in Southeast Asia, but before doing so I would like to make four points. First, not all of the problems that I will discuss are directly related to the changes taking place in the law of the sea. Many of them are primarily the consequence of increased values in fishery resources and would be present even if the UN Conference on the Law of the Sea were not being held and unilateral actions were not being taken. Second, the problems are not considerably different in nature from those that exist elsewhere in the world. While some of them may be a little more severe, others will be less. Third, the emphasis given to problems and difficulties should not be interpreted entirely as pessimism. As the saying goes, "to be forewarned is to forearmed." And fourth, these remarks are based on a study for ICLARM that is not yet completed and they should, therefore, be considered as tentative and preliminary thoughts.

The problems discussed are essentially of two kinds. One set relates to conflicts over the distribution of fishery wealth, and the other to the potential violations of agreements and regulations and the necessity for effective enforcement measures to achieve the efficient production of net benefits. These, of course, are not the only problems that need to be solved, but it is safe to say that unless they are solved, the best scientific research and the best management proposals and plans will be of little value.

I will begin by identifying and describing briefly some of the conflict situations and enforcement problems that are present or will be emerging in Southeast Asia. Some of the impediments to their resolution will be discussed, and finally, with some temerity, a few approaches that might be followed will be suggested.

KINDS OF PROBLEMS

First, with regard to the indentification of the problems, these are divided between those relating to the distribution of fishery wealth and those relating to the management of fishery resources. Although the distinction between these sets of problems is not very precise, it is desirable to attempt it, since the former are properly the subject of negotiations by representatives of the interested states rather than the subject of economic analysis, while the latter–the problems of management–can be measured against relatively objective criteria and evaluated in economic terms. Wealth distribution problems do, however, have significant implications for fishery management and, therefore, need to be described.

Distribution Problems. Perhaps the most important of these problems in the Southeast Asia region is the conflict over the ownership of the Paracel and Spratly Islands. The Paracels, lying in the northern part of the South China Sea, are claimed by the People's Republic of China, Taiwan, and Vietnam; and the Spratly Islands, to the south, are claimed by the PRC, Vietnam, and the Philippines. Because of the islands' strategic locations, the successful claimants will acquire jurisdiction over vast areas. The areas in dispute, however, may not be particularly rich in fishery resources, although it must be admitted that information is scanty. At the moment, the dispute appears to be focused more on strategic gains and the possibility of oil resources than on fisheries.

There is, however, one important implication for fisheries. This is that the possible creation of a regional fishery management agency that might cover, at least in part, the disputed areas, is likely to be delayed until the disputes are settled–and, as we heard from Dr. Choon-ho Park, this might take some time. Neither the PRC nor the Republic of the Philippines appears to be ready, as yet, to force the issue of ownership; and, as Dr. Park noted, the PRC is particularly unwilling to open the issue, since it would mean dealing with all the other territorial disputes it has with other countries. Since the attempt to create a regional fishery management agency could be construed as forcing the issue, such attempts are not likely to be made. In this regard, it might be noted that the PRC has reportedly warned SEAFDEC (the South East Asia Fisheries Development Center) against experimental fishing around the Spratly Islands.

A second important border dispute is in the Gulf of Thailand and affects the states of Thailand, Cambodia, and Vietnam. The dispute concerns not only the ownership of islands but also the boundaries used for the determination of median lines. This is currently having a direct effect on fisheries in that the disputed areas have been fished for centuries. Thai fishermen are being arrested, and their vessels are being confiscated, by Cambodian and Vietnamese patrol vessels. It is reported that many of the Thai fishermen purchase arms (at about US$25 for an automatic rifle) to protect them from the patrols. Here again, any attempt to manage the fishery resources is likely to fail as long as the dispute continues.

A second form of distributional conflict can be found in situations where a specific stock of fish swims through the waters of two or more coastal states. Management requires that the stock be treated as a unit wherever it swims, and this in turn requires the sharing states to adopt common measures and agree on who is to get what share.

One example of this may be skipjack tuna that are caught in the waters of both Indonesia and the Philippines. While knowledge is extremely imprecise on the movement of the skipjack, there is reason to believe that this stock is common not only to both these countries but also the countries of the Western Central and South Pacific. Most observers feel that there are opportunities for increasing the catch of skipjack. But it can also be noted that most of the countries in the region are planning to do just that—and that the aggregate expectations may be greater than the maximum sustainable yield. At some point, management will be required and, with it, decisions on the allocation of yields or benefits from the skipjack resource. Since the skipjack apparently migrate along the west coast of the Philippines—in the South China Sea— the possibility of membership by the Philippines in a South Pacific Fisheries Agency may raise the question of the Spratly Islands and the Paracels.

Another instance of possible sharing of stocks may be that of the chub mackerel that appear to migrate along the Vietnamese coast, in the Gulf of Thailand, and down to the Indonesian waters in the South China Sea. These are pelagic stocks that may offer some opportunities for increased catches, though here again there is very little information. It is clear, however, that Thailand, Malaysia, and Indonesia—all of which have overfished their in-shore demersal stocks—are planning to increase their catches of chub mackerel. It is likely that the Vietnamese have similar intentions. If the mackerel is a single stock, there is again a potential for conflict over distribution of fisheries wealth.

Management Problems. The problems of management in the region relate in part to the difficulties of controlling access or transit by foreign fishermen and in part to gear conflicts among fishermen of the same country. These problems largely involve the enforcement of agreements and regulations. Several states outside the region have a present or potential interest in the waters of Southeast Asia. The Japanese currently fish for shrimp in the Arafura Sea and for skipjack in the Banda Sea—both of which lie within the archipelagic waters of Indonesia. Fishermen from Taiwan and the Republic of Korea have fished off the coasts of the People's Republic of China and Vietnam in the past, and Taiwan has been attempting to work out an agreement with Indonesia for access to Indonesian waters.

In addition, in the past decade, as noted by Dr. John C. Marr, there has been a very rapid increase in distant-water fishing by Thailand, with the result that something like 660,000 tons (or about half) of the marine catch of Thailand comes from waters within 200 miles of foreign countries. There is, in particular, a large Thai trawler fleet operating off the Bay of Kuching along the northern coast of Sarawak. Because of this distant-water effort, Thailand has sought, without success, to join the group of Geographically Disadvantaged States at the UN Conference on the Law of the Sea.

Indonesia and, to a lesser extent, Malaysia, are the chief targets for the distant-water fishermen. Within Indonesia it is primarily the eastern areas of the Banda and Arafura Seas that are not as fully developed as the Java and other seas. These are large areas surrounded by small islands and extremely difficult, therefore, to patrol. There appears to be a fairly large degree of illegal fishing by some of the distant-water fishermen as well as some extortion by and bribery of local patrol forces. Piracy is also present in the region. A recent article in the *New Straits Times* of Malaysia (Kuala Lumpur, October 8, 1977) reported that Malaysian fishermen operating out of a port in the northeast coast of Sabah have been issued shotguns for protection against pirates.

In addition to problems of access there are also problems of transit. For example, when Indonesia extends its jurisdiction, it will separate the waters of Peninsula Malaysia from the waters of Eastern Malaysia, which may create difficulties for the transit of not only Malaysian fishing vessels but also Malaysian patrol vessels.

Another transit difficulty already apparent is that of the passage of Taiwanese vessels through Indonesian waters on their way to the waters off the west coast of Australia. This involves about 100 pair trawlers, each of which must obtain a "sailing instruction sheet" from the Indonesian Chamber of Commerce office in Taipei. The "sailing instruction sheet" requires the trawler to navigate a specific course through Indonesian waters and to carry a large sign identifying it as having acquired such a sheet. This is designed to facilitate surveillance of Taiwanese vessels by Indonesian patrols. No payment of fees is legally required for the "sailing instruction sheets," but it was reported to me that such payments are generally made by the Taiwanese fishermen.

As jurisdiction is extended, the problem of transit will become increasingly severe. The coastal state will want to be assured that the distant water vessel is not fishing illegally, and the distant-water vessel will want to be assured that it can pass through as expeditiously as possible.

Finally, one more problem might be mentioned. This is the conflict between fishermen in the same countries using different gears. While this problem is purely intranational and not affected by the law of the sea, it provides an indication of the difficulties of enforcement.

In each of the countries of Thailand, Malaysia, Indonesia, and the Philippines, the development of small trawlers ten or fifteen years ago has led to severe conflicts with the local small-scale fishermen fishing primarily for their own subsistence, using hand lines, gill nets, beach seines, and other small gear. There are some indications that this development has led to a decline in the proportion of high valued species in the catch and to a decline in the size of fish being caught. There are also some instances of local gear being damaged by the trawlers and a good deal of feeling that the trawlers are damaging the bottom.

In an attempt to deal with the conflicts, the countries have prohibited trawling in the in-shore waters. However, there appear to be widespread violations of these prohibitions in all of the countries, largely because the highly valued shrimp generally occur close to shore. Patrol vessels are few and far between. Patrol officers are susceptible to bribery. The courts are apparently quite lenient in imposing penalties. Licensing systems tend to be ineffective and in one instance reported to me the trawler fishermen used a boycott to achieve the release of one of their group who had been arrested. In short, as noted by several of the fishery administrators, control over the fishermen and fishing industry is extremely weak and ineffective. The inability of governments to implement effective controls over their fishermen is a fundamental problem, and unless this problem is solved, there is little chance of preventing a continued dissipation of the benefits that could be achieved from the use of fishery resources.

IMPEDIMENTS TO SOLUTIONS

The list of problems is not exhaustive, but it does serve to identify and illustrate the nature of the problems and of the impediments to the achievement of more rational fishery management. While there are various ways of classifying the impediments, one approach is to distinguish among those that are political, institutional, and economic in nature.

Among the political impediments, the most obvious with regard to regional approaches to management is the split between the Communist and non-Communist nations. The two multinational fishery agencies in the region—the UNDP/FAO South China Sea Program and the South East Asian Fisheries Development Center (SEAFDEC)— have membership from both Communist and non-Communist nations, but currently the Communist countries are not participating in the organizations. The Association of South East Asian Nations (ASEAN) is made up only of the five non-Communist countries. Thus, there is no forum, at present, in which the problems of common interest to all countries surrounding the South China Sea can be discussed, much less resolved.

Another set of political difficulties relates to the relationship of the Southeast Asian countries with the extra-regional countries that fish, or wish to fish, within the region. There is some antipathy towards the Japanese. Not all of the countries have diplomatic relations with the Republic of Korea, and Taiwan is virtually a nongovernment. These difficulties serve to diminish the net benefits that the regional coastal states might achieve from foreign access to their zones.

The most important of the institutional impediments—and I use the term "institution" in a broad sense to include social and cultural traditions—is the inability of the states to implement effective controls over their own and foreign fishermen. Bribery and piracy are pervasive throughout the region, and generally serve to defeat the purposes of resource management or reduce the net benefits to society that come from access agreements.

It might be noted, however, that in theoretical terms the effect of bribery and piracy may be beneficial with regard to improving economic efficiency in the industry. That is, bribery constitutes a form of tax, and piracy adds to fishing costs by increasing the risks. Such increased costs tend to reduce entry into the fisheries and thereby reduce the overcapitalization that is the general state of common property fisheries. Thus, if bribery and piracy were removed, this would lead to an increase in the amount of fishing effort but probably no increase in the amount of catch. It might mean more employment opportunities for fishermen, though no increase in the incomes of fishermen or in the contribution of fisheries to the economy of the countries.

The major disbenefits from bribery and piracy occur in a distributional sense rather than with regard to efficiency. It means that the economic rents are being captured by those who have the power to collect the bribes or engage in piracy. While neither piracy nor bribery should be condoned, it may be possible to subvert the institution of bribery in such a way as to achieve a more equitable distribution of the economic rents that are captured, while maintaining the beneficial tax aspects.

The third set of impediments in the implementation of effective management relates to the economic costs of enforcement; in particular, to the costs of surveillance and arrest. The water area of the South China Sea and the other seas of Southeast Asia is considerably larger than the aggregate land area of the surrounding countries, excluding China. Most of the fishing takes place from isolated villages, and communication is extremely difficult. In addition to this, there is some reluctance on the part of fishery administrators to invest in enforcement measures. As administrators, their rewards tend to be measured more in positive steps, such as a number of vessels built, fishermen trained, cooperatives established, than in such negative steps as a number of patrol craft, patrol officers, or arrests made. It is conceivable that enforcement costs together with the difficulties of overcoming administrative reluctance and of imposing effective measures may be greater than the benefits that can be obtained. This, of course, is somewhat of an academic question, not only because it depends upon what costs and benefits are included and how they are evaluated, but also because some attempts at enforcement will be made whether or not they are socially justifiable.

APPROACHES TO RESOLUTION

These political, institutional, and economic ingredients make it difficult to conceive of approaches to improved management that have a chance of being successful. The most that I can suggest, at this stage of my study, are a couple of general principles that may be helpful in identifying useful approaches. One principle is that of working, wherever possible, within the political, economic, and institutional constraints that exist in the region. More particularly, I feel that proposals for regional authorities or agencies may be valuable in setting targets toward which we should aim, but that they are not very useful in decisions on next steps. The decisions on next steps, for example, should recognize the existence of bribery. Thus, regulations that increase the opportunities for bribery, or that permit bribery to subvert the objectives of the regulations, should be avoided. Or, as indicated earlier, it may be possible to manipulate bribery systems so that the economic rents are distributed in more socially valuable ways than at present. At the moment, I have no clear idea how this can be done, but I am convinced that institutions such as bribery cannot be ignored.

The second principle is that of producing systems that create or stimulate the incentive for self-enforcement. In other words, the management measures and allocation agreements should be designed so that the fishermen themselves have an interest in maintaining the measures and agreements. Here, the institution of property rights can be used. For example, there are instances in the region where historically the fishermen of a particular community have been able to maintain a de facto, if not de jure, exclusive right over the resources in the waters off their coasts. With such a right, they have a greater interest than they would otherwise in ensuring that the resource will provide future returns. The establishment of such rights for all communities could be helpful, in some regards at least, in the enforcement of desirable regulations. I say "some regards," because I do not feel that it is desirable to provide the fishermen with shotguns and rifles to protect their rights. This approach is likely to have serious repercussions in the future, since there is no guarantee that the arms will be used only for the purpose of protecting legitimate rights. However, the communities can fulfill the function of surveillance and help to police, through peer pressure, their own fishermen. Again, I am not clear how property rights systems could be extended to cover migrating stocks or foreign fishermen; but unless there is some incentive for self-enforcement, the costs of enforcement may become greater than the benefits that can be achieved.

These general principles do not take us very far along the road to improved management and distribution arrangements, but they are the best that I can come up with at the present time.

Commentary

Philip Helfrich
University of Hawaii

I would like to dwell briefly on one aspect of the management of marine fisheries in Southeast Asia in the context of an extended economic zone of jurisdiction.

In the discussions that have preceded this paper there have been analyses of the merits and consequences of regionalism in the management of marine resources as well as a review of existing and contemplated national and regional mechanisms for management. For various reasons already elucidated, regionalism in the management of resources has come under active consideration in many parts of the world, including Southeast Asia.

Fishery development in the context of extended jurisdiction and management on a regional or subregional basis seems a likely eventuality in Southeast Asia, although the time scale and mechanisms for implementing a regional approach are far from being decided. Whether under regional, subregional, national, or some other combination of participants, it can be expected that a significant segment of the fishery will continue to involve large-scale exploitation by industrial fisheries. These may be locally owned enterprises, or more probably a bilateral or multilateral arrangement with distant-water fleets of a developed fishing nation, such as Japan. Operating under a regional plan with proper agreements, it is theoretically possible to exercise coordinated control of the conservation and management of fish stocks in the region. Such management is greatly enhanced, if a coordinated regional scientific research program exists to provide data for a better understanding of the stocks. Although a regional management plan might be well suited to the large industrial fisheries with a high level of national and/or regional institutional controls, regional bodies are not appropriate to manage the small-scale traditional fisheries that are prevalent in the Southeast Asian region.

Traditional fishermen in Southeast Asia vary throughout the region in terms of their customs, mode of operation, and degree of sophistication, but the fishermen involved can be generally characterized by their independence, resourcefulness, and lack of enthusiasm for fishery management plans and government controls. Most fishermen in Southeast Asia, being in the lower economic strata and having suffered the vicissitudes and adversities associated with their occupation, are as a group difficult to organize and place under a fishery management structure. At best, this can be done at a national level, and the success varies with various districts or coastal regions where ethnic, religious, socioeconomic, and political factors may result in a greater or lesser degree of cooperation with a government bureaucracy attempting to manage a fishery. Therefore, two different approaches may have to be employed to manage the sometimes contiguous stocks of fish exploited by traditional and industrial fisheries. Assuming a regional management approach is employed for the large-scale industrial fisheries, and some type of national regulation for small-scale traditional fisheries, then one is faced with the problem of how these two management systems are coordinated and integrated. This problem of dual control may be complicated and accentuated by the antagonism that frequently develops between local traditional fisheries and large-scale industrial fisheries, particularly if the latter includes distant-water vessels of a country from outside the region. The dispute between the near-shore traditional fishermen and the larger off-shore commercial vessels on the west coast of peninsular Malaysia is but one example of such a conflict. There are many others in the region.

This problem of coordination is further complicated by the fact that these two modes of fisheries, which in fact are not always clearly separated often exploit the same stocks at different stages of their life cycle or migration patterns. Accordingly, an additional dimension is added to the array of problems one faces in contemplating management of a fishery on a regional basis.

How does one effect coordination between fishermen controlled by a regional organization and those operating under a national or district regime? It is suggested that neither the national regime nor a regional body with extra-national participants may be well suited for the task. Rather a neutral, apolitical, international entity would be best suited for such a coordinating role. A UN agency might be the appropriate mechanism, except such agencies are not always apolitical.

This is but one of a series of problems that must be addressed if a regional approach to fishery management and conversation is adopted in Southeast Asia.

Discussion and Questions

Gordon Munro: I have one question, but I think I will do the unusual and share it between Dr. Marr and Dr. Bardach. I also have one comment directed toward Dr. Christy. There is some question about the potential in the South China Sea area, drawing upon the John Gulland figures. The top figure suggested was fourteen million tons per year, but in the discussion of the biological data base I got the very strong impression that the data base was almost nonexistent. So what confidence can we have in estimates of the magnitude of the potential? Surely, the fact that the estimate comes from the FAO is not sufficient to give us strong confidence.

John Marr: I certainly agree with your last statement, but I think the fact that it comes from John Gulland would give us a little more confidence. Comprehensive surveys have been made only in the Gulf of Thailand, and the larger estimates are based on extrapolations elsewhere in the shelf area. Probably the estimates for dermersal resources are pretty good, but when we get into the estimates for pelagic resources, I think the standard errors are much wider.

John Bardach: Perhaps I might amplify a little on this. The fact that some of the pelagic stocks are migratory and are exploited sequentially by a number of nations in different fisheries may have led to an overestimation of pelagic stocks. You will note from Dr. Marr's quotation that the figure of fourteen million metric tons is an upper limit, and I think it is probably a rather generous limit. No distinction was made between pelagic and demersal species. I do agree that at least in the waters of Indonesia, and I think probably also off the coastal areas of Vietnam, the estimates of dermersal stocks are pretty good. But given the insufficiencies of data, the figure may be somewhere between six and eight, and at the very most fourteen, million metric tons.

Gordon Munro: The comment I had for Dr. Christy is on his very interesting thesis that bribery can be beneficial with regard to the problem of enforcement within the area of gear conflict, such as that between trawls and in-shore fisheries. If I understood it correctly, the reason he gave for believing that the conflict cannot be removed is that the enforcement agency tends to be rather inefficient and corrupt. Is that fair? A few years ago I was involved in a rather intensive study on just such a conflict on the west coast of Malaysia, and what I would suggest is that the regulations broke down because these were unenforceable right from the beginning, because of the distribution of stocks and the market conditions that operated. In Malaysia the fishermen proved to be somewhat smarter than the administrators, which is a rather universal phenomenon.

John Bardach: I would like to add to this that our management paradigms, which we have easily transferred from the days of colonial administration, are derived from population dynamics, and our knowledge thereof in temperate zone waters is quite inadequate. It is very likely that we shall have to go back to square one for management paradigms for multispecies tropical fisheries.

Dolliver Nelson: I would just like to make a comment and ask for a further clarification from Dr. Christy on another point. If you accept bribery in one area of law enforcement procedure, for fishery management purposes, you may be in danger of accepting it throughout the whole procedure, and I think that is not something that should be undertaken lightly. You must look at the law as a whole: you cannot say, we accept bribery for fishery purposes but we won't tolerate it elsewhere within the legal system. It cannot be done; it is not divisible. The second point I would like to raise arises from this idea of distant-water fleets transiting through the economic zones of other states. I would just like Dr. Christy to elaborate on the procedure adopted, and to say whether he thinks it can be of general application.

Francis Christy: I do not think that I really meant that bribery should be accepted. I believe that bribery exists on a widespread basis and that somehow or other it might be possible to subvert it to a more beneficial system of distribution, but, as I said, I am really not at all clear how this can be done. In struggling with the problem of bribery, it occurred to me that one might be able to manipulate it in some way, so that it is not really bribery in the wholly negative sense but rather a tax mechanism that could be made to have beneficial aspects. With regard to transit, I do not think that I am really qualified to deal with that in general terms. I simply reported that there is the requirement for sailing instruction sheets to be issued to the Taiwanese fishermen on their way through the waters of Indonesia. Perhaps Dr. Djalal would be able to deal with the broader implications of this procedure.

Hasjim Djalal: Thank you very much. I actually do not want to make a comment, but simply put some questions. First, to Dr. Marr and to Dr. Christy. It is interesting for me to hear, if I understand it correctly from Dr. Marr, that the Philippines has proposed that the member ASEAN countries should permit one another's nationals to fish freely in their respective waters. I am not aware of that proposal, so I would like to know more about this: has that proposal been officially submitted, or is it simply an idea or opinion? It is very interesting, because I am not aware of any other ASEAN countries fishing in the Philippine waters. Maybe there is something more to it that we need to know about.

Second, with regard to this fee for transit, I think Dr. Christy was right in saying that there is no rule in Indonesia for paying for transit, but the way I look at it is that it can be regarded as something like a hunting fee charged for fishing in Indonesian waters. Such an arrangement already exists with certain Japanese fishing boats that come to Indonesia to fish. Some Taiwanese also fish in Indonesian waters, and, as you know, Indonesia does not have any diplomatic relations with Taiwan, although we do maintain a liason office in Taipei. Some of the Taiwan fishermen who fish in the Indonesian waters ask for the protection of a license and they may have to pay for it. Maybe later they don't fish there but decide instead to transit to Australia, but that is another matter. I agree with Dr. Christy that there is no rule in Indonesia that when you transit Indonesian waters you have to pay. The only rule is that transiting fishing boats are required to pass through certain sea-lanes. There is a rule saying that. The whole idea is to prevent them from using the transit right to fish while transiting, so we do require them to pass through specified lanes.

The proposal by Dr. Christy to stimulate self-enforcement on the part of the fishermen by allocating them certain resources sounds like a very interesting proposal, but it raises two questions. One, would it exclude other fishermen, probably local fishermen, from fishing the same stocks? If so, would it not deprive them of what is basically their basic need to fish these particular stocks, if they are allocated to somebody else? Moreover, even if they are given a certain stock to fish, what would prevent them from fishing on other stock if the first stock was already exhausted by them? I definitely agree with Dr. Christy that the basic problem is not so much allocation of the stocks as the need to improve enforcement agencies at sea. I certainly see this as one of the basic difficulties that we have in Indonesia, but of course if you look at it within the context of national development strategy, it is only one of many that the states will have to give priority to.

John Marr: I am sorry I do not have complete details on the proposal I mentioned. I believe it was made just before I left Manila to come to this meeting by a trade association associated with ASEAN. The proposal itself was made by a fishing industry association in the Philippines, not by the Philippine government. This association is made up of entrepreneurs who have tuna boats, or who buy tuna from the subsistence fishermen and resell it elsewhere.

Francis Christy: I appreciate very much Dr. Djalal's comments on this With regard to the transit issue, it is my understanding that the Taiwanese fishermen do receive sailing instruction sheets to go through certain specific lanes and I can understand the rationale for this. I understand that they do pay something for the sailing instruction sheets, which is not necessarily a legitimate payment but probably one that is made anyway. The property rights question you have asked—What would happen to those fishermen who did not have access to the waters claimed by the community or acquired by a community?—is already being raised to a large extent. There are limits to the resources in the shore areas—fairly severe limits. The problem of allocation is being dealt with at present in favor of those who are able to get the most fish under this kind of arrangement. So the fish goes to the small trawlers primarily. There has to be a limit, and someone has to bear the burden of reduced access to stocks, or some other kind of control. Now, how you do this is essentially a distributional question that does raise real problems. I would suggest that you provide some kind of exclusive right to a particular community in a particular area, as is done in Japan, I understand, and under this kind of system, you do have an incentive to control the fishery. This does not mean necessarily that the fishermen outside the community's area would be excluded. It may be decided that the community would let the others come in, provided they pay something for the privilege, but it does put the resource under someone's control, which is desirable.

William Burke: I have an awful temptation to speculate on how one institutionalizes violence for the purpose of improving fishery management. They have used every other tool; why not this? But I really want to comment on Mr. Nelson's question about transit. There is a very substantial amount of experience with this kind of clearance procedure, and perhaps it is an apt experience because most of it was during wartime, and I guess we are on the verge of "economic warfare" now. In those days use was made of a procedure called "clear search," and it was a very common practice. In fact, I think it has been used even during peacetime. The Cuban missile crisis comes to mind as an example. This transit problem is a fairly substantial one, particularly in the South Pacific, and, as I say, there is a large body of literature dealing with clearance certificates.

Kazuo Sumi: I would like to ask Dr. Christy one question about the relationship between fishery and environmental institutions, because tanker accidents and operational discharges have an impact on the productivity of fishery resources. What is the relationship between fishery and environmental management?

Francis Christy: I think this is a persistent and pervasive problem for all countries. The effects of pollution on fisheries can be severe, and it seems to me a matter for national governments to work out the arrangements to prevent these kinds of things from occurring, or at least to ensure that the cost either of the controls or the consequences are not too damaging to society. Now, which country wants to do that is largely a national rather than an international question, except possibly in regard to the issue of transit which has already been discussed in the context of tanker pollution problems in the Malacca Straits.

John Bardach: I would add that there is a certain danger in generalizing about the effects of organic additions in tropical waters. Various kinds of tropical waters react quite differently to these changes, and I am not aware of any exact, or close-to-exact, assessment of such pollution damage under clearly specified conditions.

Part VI

Regional Ocean Management: Problems of Methodology and Comparative Analysis

Chairman
Edward Miles
University of Washington

The first panel will attempt to focus on the methodological problems associated with the concept of regional ocean management.

After the initial presentations by Professor Munro and myself, we shall have some general discussion and questions from the floor. Later, we shall have an opportunity to draw upon the experience and perceptions of a number of panelists from different regions in a final discussion on specific policy problems in the context of what might be termed "economic zone management."

First, I would like to introduce our first speaker, a respected fishery economist from the University of British Columbia, with whom I have had the pleasure of working closely in recent years. Professor Gordon Munro has written widely on fishery management problems, not only those in Canada but also those arising in other regions.

Chapter Sixteen

Extended Fisheries Jurisdiction in a Regional Setting: Problems of Conflicting Goals and Interests

Gordon R. Munro
University of British Columbia

It is now readily apparent that, regardless of the final outcome of the Third Law of the Sea Conference, the international community has come to accept and will continue to accept the widespread implementation of exclusive economic zones. The prime advantage, we are told, of the EEZ regime is that marine resources, heretofore subject to nonexistent or weak international management, will become subject to effective management by individual coastal states. If marine resources are transboundary in nature, then hopefully pairs or groups of coastal states within regions will come together to impose effective management.

I have been asked to address myself as an economist to what I deem to be some of the primary issues pertaining to coastal state management of EEZs and to do so in a regional setting. Obviously this is an enormously broad topic. I propose to narrow it in two ways. First, I shall confine myself to fisheries. While I can lay some claim to expertise in this area, I can lay little claim to expertise in the areas of seabed mining, off-shore petroleum, marine transportation or marine pollution. Be that as it may, it is my hope that what I shall have to say pertaining to fisheries will be relevant to these other areas.

Second, I intend to confine my discussion to a consideration of what economists can say (if anything) about the difficult, if not intractable, issue of coping with an apparent multitude of conflicting goals and interests. If we are confused as to whose benefits we are attempting to enhance by managing the resources, then any discussion of optimal management programs becomes meaningless.

The research for this paper has been funded by the Donner Canadian Foundation and is part of a project in "Canada and the International Management of the Oceans" sponsored by the Institute of International Relations, University of British Columbia, Canada.

These problems are scarcely new. We have been worrying about them for many years. However, with the advent of the Third Law of the Sea Conference and the spread of the EEZs, the problems take on a new urgency. We would be foolhardy if we did not assume that the opportunity for a major reformation of the management of the world's ocean resources provided by the Third Law of the Sea Conference is an unique one.

It is all too easy to construct scenarios in which individual coastal states and groups of coastal states within regions throw away the unique opportunities for rational management of fishery stocks provided by extended fishery jurisdiction because of a failure to resolve goal conflicts. Moreover, some of the initial developments in response to expanded jurisdiction are not at all encouraging. The American system of dividing the management authority among eight regional councils and the federal government I find, as a Canadian, to be mildly terrifying. Indeed there is already evidence that this division has exacerbated fishery negotiations between the United States and Canada. In the case of my own country, the fisheries are under single control. Moreover, the Canadian government's central policy document on fishery management appears to have a clear overall goal.[1] However, when one reads further, the discovery is made that this overall goal is in fact broken down into ten subgoals. The nature of the trade-offs among them is left to the reader's imagination.

In this paper I wish to address myself to three areas of goal and interest conflict. The first relates to the conflict between economic and so-called noneconomic goals. The second area relates to what I like to term intertemporal interest clashes. These arise from the fact that major reformulations of fishery management policies promising substantial benefits in the distant future may call for heavy sacrifices in the present and near future.

These two conflict areas I discuss in the context of individual coastal states. If these conflicts within individual coastal states are not resolved, then cooperative management between or among coastal states in a region becomes hopeless. Moreover, if the other papers in this volume provide correct assessments of prospects for regional cooperation, our management concerns may in fact be largely focused upon individual states.

Having discussed these areas, I then wish to go on and discuss the problem of reconciliation of interests between or among states within a region, when these states are confronted with transboundary stocks demanding joint management.

The first area of conflict, the one involving economic and noneconomic, is one, I unhesitatingly admit, that economists have discussed at considerable length in the past. Nevertheless, I feel that a review is warranted. My own work on fishery management problems over the past few years has convinced me that we economists have not been particularly effective in putting across our point of view. The image we hold among our noneconomist colleagues, such as biologists, ecologists, political scientists, and lawyers, continues to be unfortunate—to say the least—with obvious consequences for our influence. We are seen as rather soulless individuals with an irrational and almost brutal passion for economic "efficiency" and profits, who are apparently oblivious to the fact that there are other goals that society considers worthy of attention. Indeed, it must be admitted that we now even have economists in the field of fishery economics attacking their fellow practitioners for their excessive attention to efficiency.[2]

With respect to the other two areas of goal and interest conflict, intertemporal and interstate, I see no need to justify discussing them. While economists may have worried about them, they have really had rather little to say about them up until the last few years. The intertemporal question, it is true, was recognized at the birth of fishery economics.[3] It would not be unfair to say, however, that there was a tendency from that time up until a few years ago to push the issue firmly into the background.

Our first step in dealing with the question of whose benefits are to be maximized in managing the EEZs is to ask whether the coastal states will be managing their EEZs on their own behalf, on behalf of the region as a whole, or on behalf of the entire international community. The coastal states will, in my view, almost certainly manage the EEZs with the sole object of maximizing their own benefits, in spite of public protestations to the contrary. Some may call this view cynical; I call it realistic. Moreover, this apparent selfishness on the part of coastal states may not necessarily be a bad thing. Although it is possible to attempt to specify a globally optimum management policy for fisheries, in practice it seems almost impossible to do so where the number of participants is at all large. This became abundantly apparent in ICNAF and was certainly one important reason why there was so much pressure on the U.S. and Canadian governments from their respective Atlantic coast regions to move towards an extension of fishery jurisdiction. With goals for the managers being simpler and more clearly defined under these new conditions, the likelihood of there being at least some positive net benefits generated by the fisheries is so much greater.

All of this may seem to be cold comfort to the distant-water nations. Yet even they may benefit. If fisheries hitherto pushed to the point of bioeconomic equilibrium are now subject to effective management and if, as part of this effective management program, distant-water nations are "hired" to harvest part of the resource or have part of the resource rented to them, then they can expect to enjoy some of the fruits of effective management.[4]

There is, of course, no guarantee that the coastal states will effectively manage the resources coming under their control through extended fishery jurisdiction. With this in mind, let me turn then to the question of conflict between economic and noneconomic goals and the economist's view of this conflict. This leads us to consider the question of the economist's passion for "efficiency."

First, let me attempt, as so many other economists have attempted (and failed), to correct a misconception about the economist's use of the concept of efficiency, a misconception that is at once both tenacious and pernicious. This is the belief that economists are concerned solely about the monetary returns from fisheries. The economist is really concerned about maximizing the net benefits to society from the resource. As such, he is well aware that monetary measures, such as prices of fish and fishing effort costs, may provide an inaccurate description of the social benefits and social costs associated with a given fishery. Therefore, when economists talk about maximizing rent from fisheries in their efficiency arguments, they should—if they are not doing so already—be talking about "social rent." The point was made well over a decade ago by Christy and Scott:

> In principle at least, it is possible also to take into account non-commercial or intangible benefits and costs in arriving at the best use of the region. . . . Rent can be a social concept, and the instruction to "maximize rent" can be a route to an ethically defensible optimum.[5]

As we shall see, this statement by Christy and Scott will have to be subjected to substantial qualification, but their point that the economist's perspective is a broad one will remain valid.

Having said this, we still have to ask why the economist gives so much attention to efficiency. There are, I think, two reasons for this. The first goes back to the bedrock proposition in economics that productive resources are scarce in relation to society's material wants. Consequently, when economists complain about inefficiencies in fisheries in terms of rent dissipation, what they are really complaining about is that, at the margin, productive resources are being employed in the fishery that would produce more for society elsewhere in the economy. This leads the economist in turn to ask two closely interrelated questions when confronted with the demand to consider goals in apparent conflict with the goal of "efficiency." First, are there not less costly means of achieving the desired "other " goal than by reducing efficiency within the fishery? If the answer to the first question is "no," then a second question must be asked. Has society, or whoever decides on society's behalf, really asked itself whether the benefits promised by achieving this "other" goal are going to be sufficient to offset the loss implied by reduced efficiency?

For example, suppose that achieving full efficiency in a particular fishery will produce a change in income distribution that society deems to be unacceptable. One cannot just accept inefficient management of the fishery without first asking whether less costly means cannot be found of dealing with the maldistribution of income. To take another example, suppose that we are confronted with the argument to the effect that a fishery should be expanded beyond its 'efficient" level in order that exports can be increased to alleviate a balance of payments deficit. The first question must be asked and can be answered in a straightforward manner. Economic theory since the early 1950s has shown that this sort of piecemeal, and inefficiency-inducing, approach to balance of payments problems is woefully inadequate and is, moreover, quite likely to produce negative results.

The second reason that economists emphasize efficiency first is because, as Giulio Pontecorvo has argued,[6] they are by training inclined to think in terms of the general welfare as opposed to the welfare of specific groups. Consequently when confronting "other" goals they tend to become suspicious that these may really represent claims being made by specific groups at the expense of the general public. For example, one of the ten goals for Canadian fishery management is protection of national security and sovereignty, i.e. enhancement of national defense.[7] Suppose then, in this context, that it is maintained that all vessels harvesting in the coastal state's EEZ should be domestic, because foreign trawlers and other fishing vessels constitute a national security threat. National defense is an important noneconomic goal and economists have long been prepared to admit that meeting this goal may well be worth the loss of substantial efficiency. Consequently, if in fact foreign vessels do constitute a significant security threat, the argument has to be accepted. On the other hand, the economist may wonder whether the real aim is not to protect the domestic fishing fleet and perhaps domestic boat building industry at the expense of the public. The fact that most economists have seen the national defense argument abused over and over again by industries asking for protection against foreign competition will do nothing to still their suspicions.

As a digression, this example brings us back to the position of the distant-water nations. The extent to which the distant-water nations enjoy benefits from the EEZs may well be dependent upon the extent to which the efficiency criteria are accepted within individual coastal states. It will almost certainly be true that, for many coastal states, efficiency criteria will dictate that the coastal state permit distant water fleets to harvest certain of their fisheries, albeit at a price. Working against these efficiency criteria, however, will be a powerful desire on the part of interests within each coastal state to protect and enhance the domestic fishing industry. Strengthening this desire, I suspect, will be a belief that national honor demands ultimate exclusive exploitation by domestic fleets of fishery resources within the coastal state's EEZ.

The position, then, of most economists with respect to the problem of conflicts between economic and noneconomic goals is that the best approach is to commence with the efficiency goal cast in terms of social net benefits. They would argue that this goal at least provides us with an important first approximation of the goal of maximizing society's net benefit from the resource.[8] Then, as a next step, one should weigh other goals that cannot be encompassed by the economist's efficiency goal, such as national security, by seeking answers to one or both of the questions I have raised.

The objection to this approach, of course, is that it appears to ignore basic political "realities." There is a great danger, however, that in surrendering without a struggle to political "realities," the analyst pushes efficiency into the background and thereby has no real basis for assessing the competing goals. The danger was expressed rather well by the Yale economist, Richard Cooper:

> . . . I have seen too many cases where policy-makers feel obliged to agree to sub-optimal [i.e., economically inefficient] policies because of so-called political constraints. Their advisors in turn confine themselves to trying to understand and reconcile the various expressed interests treating policy formation as a quasi-adversary process among those who show an interest and in the end recommending least-common-denominator compromises among conflicting objectives, with little or no consistency in approach, nothing to build on in the future, and neglect of considerations and relevant parties (such as consumers) which failed to make it into the arena where compromise was hammered out.[9]

In their discussion of the goal of rent maximization or efficiency, Christy and Scott qualify their enthusiasm for it by raising an important difficulty that can arise in moving towards fulfillment of the goal.[10] This is the fact that, in order to achieve the goal, heavy, albeit transitory, sacrifices may have to be endured. Thus, if efficiency demands that a particular fishery stock be built up, catches will have to be temporarily reduced and in addition a substantial and permanent reduction in fishing effort may be called for. If the vessels and fishermen lack alternative means of employment, the required fleet adjustment can prove to be very painful. The problem is one whose importance it is difficult to overstress, when we look at the future under extended fishery jurisdiction. As stocks, heretofore subject to international overexploitation, come under coastal state management, we can look forward to lengthy adjustment periods of stock rebuilding and "rationalization" of fishing industries.

To any competent student of economics, the problem of rebuilding a fishery is immediately recognizable as a problem in investment. The fishery resource can be viewed as a stock of capital. If we choose to build up the stock, this constitutes an act of investment. Hence what economists really require in attempting to analyse this problem is a capital theoretic approach that provides us with some basis for balancing off future gains against present investment costs: that is, of determining to what extent it makes sense to reduce present fishing activity in the hope of future benefits perhaps five or ten years hence. The capital theoretic approach is also required to examine a second and equally important problem. Suppose that the decision is taken to rebuild certain stocks. What is the "least cost" path of adjustment? Should the stocks be rebuilt as quickly as possible by introducing severe cutbacks in current total allowable catches (TACs), even at the threat of severe disruption of the present industry? Or, on the other hand, should the TAC cutbacks be made less draconian, even though society will thereby be forced to wait longer for the promised benefits of a rebuilt fishery?

The need for such a capital theoretic approach was recognized over twenty years ago in a classic article by Anthony Scott.[11] However, capital theory, which by its very nature is dynamic in the sense that time enters explicitly into the analysis, has always been regarded as one of the more difficult areas of economics. Moreover, as we recognize today, the mathematical techniques required for effective application of capital theory to fishery problems were not available twenty years ago. Consequently, economists tended to content themselves, until a few years ago, with a static or timeless analysis.

The static theory was and is useful in pointing out the consequences of allowing a common property resource, such as a fishery, to be subject to unregulated exploitation and in pointing to the inadequacies of the biologists' maximum sustainable yield (MSY) criterion for fishery management. As we shall note, however, the theory did tend to overestimate the extent to which overexploited fishery stocks should be rebuilt and, more important, revealed itself to be impotent in dealing with adjustment problems created by the "investment" program.

Over the past few years, economists have been able to develop an effective (and operational) dynamic theory of fishing. In part, this was the result of new mathematical techniques becoming available. In any event, while I do not claim that we can offer precise prescriptions for the resolution of intertemporal conflicts, we are in a far better position to analyse the problem than we were before.

The nature of the dynamic approach can perhaps be seen most clearly by contrasting it with the more standard static analysis. The static approach commences with the almost universally accepted proposition that an open access fishery will, if left unregulated, become economically "inefficient" in the sense that excessive fishing effort will be employed in harvesting the resource. The cause, of course, is the common property nature of the resource. The theory then goes on to deal with the question of the appropriate or "efficient" level of effort with respect to a given fishery. The answer is that the level of fishing effort that maximizes the sustainable "rent" from the resource is the efficient or optimal level.

The dynamic approach, while being concerned with the optimal allocation of fishing effort to given fisheries, perceives the basic problem of fishery management as an asset management problem. A fishery biomass is a capital asset that, similar to man-made capital assets, is capable of generating a return to society through time. If society, as owner of the resource, chooses to invest in, that is, build up the fishery resource, then society, like every other investor, will be asking whether the game is worth the candle. We attempt to do this by relating expected yield or return at the margin on the resource asset to something that we call the social rate of discount.

In part, the social rate of discount (interest rate) can be seen as reflecting society's rate of time preference, its tendency, for good or for ill, to give preference to the present over the future—but only in part.[12] For even if society is prepared to give equal weight to the distant future and the present, the social rate of discount for a given fishery should not be set equal to zero. The decision to reduce harvesting for a specified period of time implies not only forgone present consumption opportunities, but forgone investment opportunities as well. Capital in the form of fish can be transmuted via the market system into physical capital. Hence the social rate of discount must also reflect the yield on other forgone investment opportunities, or, as the economist would say, the opportunity cost of capital.

Thus the economist, by incorporating an interest rate or social rate of discount into the analysis, is not callously disregarding the future, but is taking into account that investment in fisheries, or other marine resources, constitutes but one (or a few) of the many investment opportunities open to society. This point has been made very effectively by Scott, when he was dealing with conservation of natural resources in general, but what he says can be applied without modification to fishery resources.

> Conservation of [natural] resources is not only analytically analogous to investment in capital goods; it is also in each planning period, an actual alternative to investment in . . . . available goods. . . . Society must constantly choose how it will allocate resources among competing uses and among periods of future time. Conservation of [natural] resources is only one of many possible choices; one that implies sacrificing present consumption and *investment in produced means of production* in favour of increased future supplies of a group of "natural" resources. . . . . It is ridiculous, then, to say that conservation is a movement which has the welfare of the future particularly in mind; conservation will not necessarily increase in the future's inheritance but merely change its composition from "capital goods" to natural products.[13]

The dynamic theory tells us that the optimal biomass level, the long-run biomass target, is that level at which the yield offered by the resource at the margin, the "own rate of interest" of the resource (to use the economist's jargon) is equal to the social rate of discount. The corresponding optimal level of fishing effort prescribed by the theory is simply the minimum required to harvest the sustained yield associated with the optimal biomass level.

The undesirable consequences of an open access common property fishery, by the way, are now seen as arising mainly as a consequence of excess disinvestment of the resource. With no one owning the resource, the resource or asset is subject to no management. Re-expressing this proposition, we can say that the fishermen act as if the appropriate rate of discount were equal to infinity. Determining the appropriate social discount rate is, of course, difficult, but scarcely impossible. The authorities confront this problem all the time in dealing with public works and development projects.

The opposing static model, it can be shown,[14] is like the dynamic model with the discount rate set equal to zero. There are two drawbacks to this. First, this will very likely lead to an overinvestment in the fishery resource. Even if one is prepared to argue that future generations are as important as the present one, we are not justified in setting the discount rate applicable to fisheries equal to zero percent. We come back to the point made by Scott that it is illegitimate to ignore the opportunity cost of capital.[15] Hence to use a very low rate of discount may in fact harm rather than assist future generations. This is particularly true for developing countries, for whom the opportunity cost of capital may be rather high.

Second, if one uses a zero discount rate, the model seems (at first glance) to imply that the pain and difficulties of the adjustment phase can be ignored because they are temporary. The result, if we are not careful, is that we take what appears to be an uncompromisingly ruthless approach to investment in the resource.[16] It scarcely enhances our ability to persuade fishing industries to accept rational management programs.

It would, however, be grossly unfair for me to imply that all, or even many, of the economists using the static model ignored the difficulties of the adjustment phase. I have already referred to Christy and Scott. I should also refer to extensive discussions of this problem by J. Crutchfield and others.[17] They were all compelled, however, to adopt a rather ad hoc approach to the question. They argued that if labor and capital cannot be moved easily out of a fishery then the losers ought to be compensated. If this is not possible politically or otherwise, then for "practical reasons" the reduction of the fleet should be a gradual one. However, this does not really offer us an analysis of the best adjustment path, but rather is presented as a set of concessions that must be made in order to effect the desired fleet reduction.

With the use of dynamic models, we can do much better than this and can analyze various adjustment paths in terms of their optimality. To return to the case in which vessels, as well as fishermen, cannot be readily shifted out of the industry, it turns out that the optimal biomass level and corresponding harvest rate are, at any point in time, not independent of the stocks (numbers) of nonshiftable harvesting inputs. Thus the appropriate adjustment policy becomes complex.

Clark, Clarke, and Munro demonstrate with regard to an overexploited fishery that, if the vessels employed in the fishery have little value outside the fishery, then the optimal policy is one of building up the resource slowly (except in extreme circumstances).[18] It may possibly be desirable to utilize the existing fleet "flat out" during the adjustment phase, while at the same time not replacing vessels as they come to the end of their economic life. This policy would remain in force until the long-run biomass target was achieved. Thus a gradual reduction of the fleet is not merely a concession to practical reality, but is in fact an optimal policy and would be so even if the authorities could pay vessel owners to leave the industry through a buy-back scheme or similar device. While the authors deal only with the case in which physical capital is difficult to relocate, it takes little imagination to extend the analysis to include nonshiftable labor.

To repeat, then, while we as economists cannot claim to have resolved all intertemporal conflicts, our ability to analyze the problems has been greatly enhanced over the past few years.

We come finally to consider the problem of conflict among states in a region attempting to manage transboundary stocks. Let it be supposed, for the sake of simplicity, that the relevant states are uniform to the extent that for each the goal of economic efficiency is paramount. There will, nonetheless, be no reason to suppose that the states will be uniform with respect to perceived optimal biomass levels, harvest rate, and so forth, with respect to any transboundary stock. Differences in effort costs, markets, and perceived discount rates can lead to a wide range of perceived biomass optima.

This problem was certainly considered in the past. Indeed Christy and Scott devoted two chapters to the topic,[19] but were forced to restrict themselves to generalities. Thus they argued that participating states should at least strive to arrive at agreements in which each of the states is seen to be better off than it would be without an agreement.

They were, however, attempting to consider arrangements, such as ICNAF, in which between ten and twenty states were involved—a daunting assignment. With the coming of UNCLOS III, in which effective control of most of the stocks is given to the coastal states, the problem within any given region is surely much simplified. To take one example, hake stocks migrate along the Pacific coast of North America from California to British Columbia. Up until 1977, they had been subject to little effective management. Before extended fishery jurisdiction any truly effective management scheme would, at the very least, have had to take into account the desires of the United States, Canada, the USSR, Poland, and Japan. In time, one could expect that the aspirations of Taiwan and South Korea would also have to be considered. Now, with extended fishery jurisdiction in place, effective property rights over the stock reside with the United States and Canada. Hence, the management problem is much eased.

Can economists say anything about this somewhat simpler problem of goal conflict among joint owners of a fishery resource? Some progress has been made. Lee Anderson has done some work on this problem, using a static model.[20] I have also made an attempt.[21] Both Anderson's work and my own are theoretical exercises and hence must not be regarded as providing precise formulae for settling conflicts between joint owners of a fishery resource. Rather the theory should be seen as a framework within which we can order our thoughts and examine the problems in a rational manner. The establishment of the framework is an essential first step.

In this work I have found it most useful to combine the dynamic analysis used for fisheries confined to the waters of a single state with the theory of games. The latter body of theory has been used widely by economists, political scientists, and others in analysing problems of conflict resolution. The segment of game theory that I employ is referred to as the theory of cooperative (as opposed to competitive) games. The participants or "players" are competitors in that they will be striving to have their own objectives met. At the same time, however, they have an incentive to cooperate, as all parties recognize that each stands to lose if cooperation is not forthcoming.

My work has so far been confined to negotiations between two partners. This may appear somewhat restrictive, but I argue that it is a useful beginning, because with the advent of extended fishery jurisdiction there are bound to be several cases of two-country negotiations over the management of transboundary stocks. In any event, if we are incapable of dealing with a two-entity case, we shall certainly be in no position to go on to more difficult cases involving three or more parties. Fortunately, I can report that the results I have obtained are satisfying in that they make good economic sense. I report some of the details of the model in an appendix.

The theory of cooperative games makes a very useful and clear-cut distinction between "games" or arrangements in which it is possible for one partner to make transfer payments to the other and those in which it is not possible for such payments to take place. An example of the former would be the North Pacific Fur Seal Convention, in which Canada and Japan agreed to refrain entirely from sealing and to leave the harvesting of the seals to the United States and Russia. In return, however, the United States and Russia agreed to turn over a certain percentage of the harvest to Canada and Japan. An example of agreements without such "side" payments would be agreements arrived at under the pre-1977 ICNAF.

What the analysis immediately reveals is that life is much easier in terms of conflict resolution if it is politically possible for side payments to be made. Then it becomes quite probable that the problem of there being a nonunique biomass optimum will disappear. The appropriate policy then becomes that of aiming for the policy that will maximize the global return from the resource. Bargaining between the two partners in turn determines how the proceeds will be divided.

To return to the example of the fur seals, the Americans and Russians harvested seals on land, while the Canadians and Japanese harvested them at sea. There is clear evidence that the land harvest was a lower cost operation than the pelagic one.[22] Thus with side payments possible, the optimal policy would obviously be for the low-cost partners to do all of the harvesting and then pension off their high-cost partners. This, of course, is precisely what happened.

To take another example, let it be supposed that the two partners are uniform with respect to fishing effort costs but hold divergent views as to the appropriate rate of discount to apply in managing the resource in question. One country might, for example, push for a discount rate close to zero, while the other country, having a high opportunity cost of capital, might press for a rate of say 15 percent. The analysis suggests that the global return from the fishery will be maximized if the fishery is managed as if it were owned outright by the low-discount-rate country. The reason is simply that the low-discount-rate partner, by definition, places a higher value upon the resource. Since it places a higher value on the resource, it will be able to make transfer payments to its partner and thereby "bribe" its partner into accepting its management plan.

If it is not possible to make transfer payments between the two partners, then the situation becomes substantially more difficult, for there will indeed be a multiplicity of biomass optima unless the two partners are identical in terms of effort costs and in their positions vis-à-vis the demand functions for the harvest, and agree on the appropriate discount factor. However, all is not lost. The analysis does suggest that a unique outcome can be established. The first problem that must be settled is that of distributional shares. What I view as the most realistic outcome is one in which the prospective partners agree to fix harvest shares or proceed shares (which usually will amount to the same thing) before proceeding to the management plan. One obvious way of determining the shares would be to base them on the historical catch records of the two countries. We can, in the analysis, allow for the possibility that the harvest shares are permitted to vary through time. However, I regard this as rather unrealistic.

Once the harvest shares are determined, there will still be differences over the appropriate management policy. Let me take two examples. Suppose, first, that the two states insist upon using domestic—as opposed to third country—fleets exclusively, and suppose further that fishing effort costs differ between the two countries. If, in addition, the costs of harvesting the fish are sensitive to the stock size, as seems to be true for most fisheries, then the high-cost country will, *ceteris paribus,* press for a larger biomass than its partner. Or let it be supposed that while effort costs are identical, the two countries differ with respect to their perception of the appropriate discount rate. The low-discount-rate partner, with its relatively conservationist bent, will press for a larger biomass than its high-discount-rate partner.

The analysis suggests that compromise solutions can be reached. In the case of cost differences, we in effect take a weighted average of the harvesting costs of the two partners. The weights reflect the relative bargaining strengths of the partners. The outcome in the case of differing discount rates is somewhat more complex. It might be expected that we would move toward a weighted average of the two discount rates. Essentially this is correct, but the weighted average is not constant through time. Rather it will vary over time with the influence of the high-discount-rate partner becoming steadily weaker. Yet this surely makes good sense, as by definition the interest of the high-discount-rate partner in the future is less than that of its low-discount-rate partner. The derivation of this outcome is discussed in detail in the appendix.

Thus it is not impossible to subject the problem of managing transboundary stocks to rigorous analysis. The analysis is, however, confined to two-country situations. It should be possible to extend it to three or more countries, but there is a quantum increase in the level of difficulty. Not surprisingly, the larger the number of countries, the greater is the degree of difficulty.

The difficulty in extending this form of analysis to many-country situations may give us some insight into why international arrangements such as ICNAF proved to be so unwieldy, in contrast to several agreements involving two or a few countries such as the International Pacific Halibut Commission or the North Pacific Fur Seal Convention. It may also lend some credence to the claim of the supporters of extended fishery jurisdiction that coastal state management will lead to improved management regimes.

CONCLUSIONS

The coming of extended fishery jurisdiction brings with it the promise of improved management of fishery resources within regions and hopefully throughout the world. Many obstacles will have to be surmounted, however, before this promise is realized. One important set of obstacles appears in the form of conflicting goals and interests with respect to management of the resources. A failure to reconcile these conflicts will certainly place the realization of the promise of improved management in serious jeopardy. There will first be conflicts within individual coastal states between economic and apparent noneconomic goals. Within these states there will also arise the potential for what we might call intertemporal conflict. Restoration of fisheries and rationalization of fishing industries can be expected to be lengthy and painful processes. Hence, the interests of the present will have to be balanced against those of the future. Moreover, care will have to be taken to minimize these conflicts by searching for the minimum-cost-adjustment paths. Finally, within the regions we must anticipate that there will be conflicts among different states exploiting the same common resources, such as transboundary stocks.

This paper attempts to present the economist's perspective on these conflicts. With respect to the first set of conflicts we restate the economist's plea to use the goal of economic efficiency as the starting point, in spite of the criticism that such an approach lacks political "realism." Intertemporal conflicts present a greater problem because by definition dynamic analysis is required. We argued that the absence of key mathematical techniques made it very difficult for the fishery economist to address himself effectively to this problem until a few years ago. Over the past few years, however, substantial progress has been made. The nature of the progress and its implications for policy are described. The last set of conflicts are the hardest of all to deal with, as the economist has to combine dynamic analysis with bargaining theory. However, within the recent past, economists have been able to make significant progress in creating an analytical framework for the reconciliation of interstate conflicts.

These problems of conflict resolution have been with us for a long time in fisheries, particularly in regional settings. With the coming of extended fishery jurisdiction, however, they take on a new urgency. If we prove ineffective in addressing these problems, it could well be that the jurisdictional expansion, one of the few major achievements of UNCLOS III, will come to nothing.

Appendix: The Optimal Management of a Transboundary Fishery Resource: Selected Examples

In this appendix we shall set up a model that will permit us to analyse the optimal management policy of a transboundary fishery stock.

Let us by way of introduction consider the optimal management policy through time for a stock confined to the waters of a single state.

We assume that the stock can be modeled effectively with the standard Schaefer model.[23] Let $x(t)$ denote the biomass at time (t). The natural growth or production function is given by:

$$\dot{x} = F(x). \tag{1}$$

Upon introducing a harvest rate $h(t)$, Equation (1) is modified to:

$$\dot{x} = F(x) - h(t), \tag{2}$$

where in the Schaefer model we assume that

$$h(t) = q\,E\,x \tag{3}$$

where E denotes a fishing effort and q, a constant, the catchability coefficient.

Assume that the price of fish provides an adequate measure of marginal social benefit (gross) of harvested fish, and that marginal effort cost is an accurate measure of marginal social effort cost. If we assume further that the demand for fish and the supply of effort inputs are infinitely elastic, the optimization model can be formulated as follows:

maximize

$$\int_0^\infty e^{-\delta t}[p - c(x)]\,h(t)\,dt \tag{4}$$

subject to

$$x = f(x) - h(t) \tag{5}$$

$$0 \leqslant h(t) \leqslant h_{max} \tag{6}$$

$$0 \leqslant x(t), \tag{7}$$

where

δ = instantaneous social rate of discount

p = price of fish

$c(x)$ = unit cost of harvesting

h_{max} = maximum feasible harvest rate

We now have a linear optimal control problem, where the problem is to determine the optimal control $h(t) = h^*(t)$, $t \geqslant 0$ and the corresponding optimal biomass $x(t) = x^*(t)$, $t \geqslant 0$.

The corresponding Hamiltonian of the problem is:

$$H = e^{-\delta t}\left\{[p - c(x)]h(t)\right\} + \lambda(F(x) - h(t)), \tag{8}$$

where λ is the adjoint variable. Through a straightforward application of the maximum principle,[24] it is possible to determine the optimal equilibrium biomass and thus the optimal equilibrium harvest policy. The optimal equilibrium biomass, x^*, is given by:

$$F'(x^*) - \frac{c'(x^*)F(x^*)}{p - c(x^*)} = -\frac{d(e^{-\delta t})/dt}{e^{-\delta t}}, \tag{9}$$

which reduces to

$$F'(x^*) - \frac{c'(x^*)F(x^*)}{p - c(x^*)} = \delta\ . \tag{10}$$

The L.H.S. is the "own rate of interest" of the biomass.

The optimal harvest rate is given by

$$h^*(t) = F(x^*) \tag{11}$$

Now let us suppose that the fishery is exploited by two neighboring countries that are prepared to contemplate establishing a binding agreement for the management of the fishery. We assume that both countries sell the fish in the world market and face a perfectly elastic demand function for the fish. We assume further that the two countries are identical in every respect except that their perceptions of the appropriate discount rates differ. Denote the two discount rates by δ_1 and δ_2 and assume that $\delta_1 < \delta_2$.

Finally we assume for the time being that the two countries agree upon a division of the harvest, whatever that harvest might be, and that these shares are fixed indefinitely. Denote the harvest shares by α and $1 - \alpha$ where $0 \leqslant \alpha \leqslant 1$. The objective functionals of the two partners can be expressed as:

$$\text{P.V.}_1 = \int_0^\infty e^{-\delta_1 t}\,\alpha[p - c(x)]\,h\,dt \tag{12}$$

$$\text{P.V.}_2 = \int_0^\infty e^{-\delta_2 t}\,(1 - \alpha)[p - c(x)]\,h\,dt. \tag{13}$$

The desired management policies of the two countries will differ. If we let $x_1^*(t)$ and $x_2^*(t)$ denote the optimal biomass levels, as perceived by countries 1 and 2 respectively, it is easy to demonstrate that $x_1^* > x_2^*$. In other words country 1 will opt for a more conservationist policy than its partner.

We turn for a solution to the bargaining problem to J.F. Nash's theory of two-person cooperative games,[25] dealing with the case where no side payments are possible. While each partner will compete with the other, they will both have an incentive to cooperate by recognition of the fact that each stands to gain through cooperation.

We introduce the term "payoff." A "payoff" is an expected return to a player that we shall define as the present value of expected returns from the fishery for a given partner or player. The first set of payoffs we consider are those the two players would enjoy if there were no cooperation. These two payoffs which we shall denote as π^0 and θ^0 respectively constitute the "threat point." We might determine the threat point by applying competitive game theory. Clark[26] shows that if J.F. Nash's theory of competitive games[27] is employed, the threat point payoff will be associated with the fishery moving to and remaining at bionomic equilibrium.

Nash is able to prove in his theory of two-person cooperative games that a unique solution to the "game" can be determined if six straightforward, and not unduly restrictive, assumptions are realized. One general assumption that we should mention is that the two partners can in fact make a binding agreement through time.

The six assumptions are first that the solution is contained within the feasible set of solutions. The second assumption is one of rationality in that the solution payoffs are not less than their corresponding threatpoint payoffs. Clearly no agreement (solution) can be achieved if one player is worse off than he would be with no agreement. The third assumption is that of Pareto optimality, in that once the solution outcome is reached no one player's position can be improved except at the expense of the other. The remaining three assumptions are: (a) symmetry–numbering of the players is irrelevant; (b) independence of linear transformations–the solution is unaffected by monotonic linear transformations of the payoffs; (c) independence of irrelevant alternatives.

To determine the set of "efficient" or Pareto optimal outcomes we characterize each such outcome as an objective functional to be maximized where the objective functional consists of a weighted average of the objective functional of the two players. The weights we denote as β and $1 - \beta$, where $0 \leqslant \beta \leqslant 1$. Thus we have a combined objective functional:

$$\text{P.V.}^* = \beta\, \text{PV}_1 + (1 - \beta)\text{PV}_2, \tag{14}$$

which upon writing out becomes:

$$\text{P.V.}^* = \int_0^\infty \left\{\beta\, \alpha\, e^{-\delta_1 t} + (1 - \beta)(1 - \alpha)e^{-\delta_2 t}\right\}[p - c(x)]\,h\,dt. \tag{15}$$

The Hamiltonian of this problem is:

$$H = (\beta\, \alpha\, e^{-\delta_1 t} + (1 - \beta)(1 - \alpha)e^{-\delta_2 t})\left\{[p - c(x)]\,h(t)\right\} + \lambda(F(x) - h(t)). \tag{16}$$

For any given β, we can, through application of the maximum principle, determine the optimal biomass. This is given by the equilibrium equation:

$$F'(x) - \frac{c'(x^*)F(x^*)}{p - c(x^*)} = \frac{\delta_1 \beta\, \alpha\, e^{-\delta_1 t} + \delta_2(1 - \beta)(1 - \alpha)e^{-\delta_2 t}}{\beta\, \alpha\, e^{-\delta_1 t} + (1 - \beta)(1 - \alpha)e^{-\delta_2 t}}. \tag{17}$$

Equation (17) should be compared with Equation (9).

The determination of β is given to us by the application of Nash's theory of cooperative games. Given that the aforementioned six assumptions hold, Nash is able to prove the existence of an unique solution, and hence an unique β given by the maximization of the following:

$$\text{maximize } (\pi^* - \pi^0)(\theta^* - \theta^0)\,, \tag{18}$$

where π^* and θ^* are the solution payoffs.

If the unique β^* is equal to 1, the R.H.S. of Equation (17) reduces to δ_1. Similarly if the unique β^* is equal to 0, the R.H.S. of Equation (17) reduces to δ_2. If, as is much more likely, $0 < \beta^* < 1$, we have on the R.H.S. of Equation (17) a complex weighted average of δ_1 and δ_2, which we shall denote as $\delta_3(t)$. What it is important to observe is that $\delta_3(t)$ is time variant. Indeed it can be stated that

$$\lim_{t\to\infty} \delta_3(t) = \delta_1\,. \tag{19}$$

From this it follows that the optimal biomass level $x^*(t)$ is also a function of time and will approach through time the optimal biomass level desired by country 1.

If side payments are possible, then our problem becomes somewhat simpler. We seek out that policy that will produce the largest global return. We set up a combined objective functional as before, but now weight $\text{P.V.}_{\cdot 1}$ and $\text{P.V.}_{\cdot 2}$ equally. There is no point in providing differential weights with side payments possible. Second, since we are seeking to maximize the global return we no longer constrain ourselves by fixing α through time, but rather permit α to be time variant and thus to become a control variable.

One of the conditions of the maximum principle is that the Hamiltonian H be maximized with respect to each control variable at all time t, $t \geqslant 0$. The Hamiltonian is linear in α (as well as h), thus the aforementioned requirement calls for us to set α equal to 1 or to 0, depending upon whether $\partial H/\partial\alpha > 0$ or $\partial H/\partial\alpha < 0$.

Upon the differentiation of Equation (16) with respect to α we have:

$$\frac{\partial H}{\partial \alpha} = \left\{\beta e^{-\delta_1 t} + (\beta - 1)e^{-\delta_2 t}\right\} [p - c(x)]\, h(t)\,. \tag{20}$$

Since the appropriate β is $\beta = 0.50$, it must be true that $\partial H/\partial\alpha > 0$ because $e^{-\delta_1 t} > e^{-\delta_2 t}$. Hence it is appropriate to set $\alpha = 1$ for all time.

The unsurprising consequence of $\alpha = 1$ can be seen by returning to Equation (17). The equilibrium equation now becomes:

$$F'(x^*) - \frac{c'(x^*)F(x^*)}{p - c(x^*)} = \delta_1\,. \tag{21}$$

The preferences of country 1 should be followed throughout.

The proper interpretation of these results is not that country 2 should necessarily give up all harvesting activities. Actually it is a matter of indifference as to how the harvesting activities are divided since the harvesting costs are identical. Rather one should interpret the results as saying that since country 1 places a higher value on the resource asset than country 2, the policy preferences of country 1 should be followed throughout. Country 2 would then be compensated for following a more conservationist policy than it would otherwise tolerate by receiving a side payment(s) from country 1.

How would the total returns be divided? This can be determined by an application once more of Nash's theory of cooperative games. Let the threat point payoffs be π^0 and θ^0 as before and the payoffs resulting from the bargaining be $\pi^\dagger$ and $\theta^\dagger$. Let the maximum total return from the fishery be γ.

Once again a Nash solution will be achieved by maximizing the expression:

$$\text{maximize } (\pi^\dagger - \theta^0)(\theta^\dagger - \theta^0)\,, \tag{22}$$

which we can rewrite as:

$$\text{maximize } (\pi^\dagger - \pi^0)(\gamma - \pi^\dagger - \theta^0)\,. \tag{22a}$$

Since

$$\pi^\dagger + \theta^\dagger = \gamma\,, \tag{23}$$

Maximizing Equation (22a) with respect to $\pi^\dagger$ we have

$$\pi^\dagger = (\gamma - \theta^0 + \pi^0)/2$$

and

$$\theta^\dagger = (\gamma - \pi^0 + \theta^0)/2\,. \tag{24}$$

Each partner receives an average of the return it could expect without cooperation and the marginal contribution it makes by accepting an agreement with side payments.

NOTES

1. Canada, Environment Canada, *Policy for Canada's Commercial Fisheries* (1976).

2. David W. Bromley and Richard C. Bishop, "From Economic Theory to Fisheries Policy: Conceptual Problems and Management Prescriptions," in Lee

G. Anderson (ed.), *Economic Impacts of Extended Fisheries Jurisdiction* (1977), pp. 281–302.

3. Anthony Scott, "The Fishery: The Objectives of Sole Ownership," *J. Pol. Econ.* 63, 116 (1955).

4. See Gordon R. Munro, "Canada and Fisheries Management with Extended Jurisdiction: A Preliminary View," in Anderson, *op. cit.,* pp. 29–50.

5. Francis T. Christy, Jr., and Anthony Scott, *The Common Wealth in Ocean Fisheries* (1965), p. 222.

6. Giùlio Pontecorvo, letter of May 5, 1976 to Richard C. Hennemuth, Deputy Center Director, Northeast Fisheries Center, Woods Hole, Massachusetts, circulated to participants of the University of Delaware Conference on "Economic Impacts of Extended Fisheries Jurisdiction."

7. Canada, *Policy for Canada's Commercial Fisheries, op. cit.*

8. Lee G. Anderson, "Optimum Yield: The Law, Economic Theory and Practical Application," unpublished paper, Dept. of Economics, University of Delaware (1977).

9. Richard N. Cooper, "An Economist's View of the Oceans," *J. World Trade Law* 9, 357 (1975), p. 358.

10. Christy and Scott, *op. cit.,* p. 222.

11. Scott, *supra* note 3.

12. To the extent that the social discount rate is a reflection of time preference, the approach that we are taking can be seen as the classic utilitarian one. To those who object that the more fashionable Rawlsian approach be taken, I would point out that our time horizon is infinite and quote Kenneth Arrow: "Under altruism toward future generations forever, the difference between the maximim (Rawlsian) criterion and the utilitarian disappears." Kenneth Arrow, "Rawls' Principle of Just Saving," *Swedish J. Econs.* 75, 323 (1973), p. 333.

13. Anthony Scott, *Natural Resources: The Economics of Conservation* (1973), pp. vii–viii.

14. Colin W. Clark and Gordon R. Munro, "The Economics of Fishing and Modern Capitol Theory: A Simplified Approach," *J. Envir. Econs. and Man.* 2, 92 (1975).

15. Scott, *supra* note 13.

16. This is certainly not to suggest that if one uses a zero discount rate, one invariably ignores the question of the optimal adjustment path. If one uses an explicitly dynamic model, no problem should arise. See F.P. Ramsey, "Mathematical Theory of Saving," *Econ. J.* 38, 543 (1928). If a static model is used, one can much more easily fall into the trap of sliding over the problems of adjustment.

17. See for example, FAO, *Economic Effects of Fishery Regulation* (1962).

18. Colin W. Clark, Frank H. Clarke, and Gordon R. Munro, "The Optimal Exploitation of Renewable Resource Stocks: Problems of Irreversible Investment," Dept. of Economics Resources Paper No. 8, University of British Columbia (1977).

19. Christy and Scott, *supra* note 5.

20. Lee G. Anderson, "Optimum Economic Yield of an Internationally Utilized Common Property Resource," *Fishery Bull.* 73, 51 (1975).

21. Gordon R. Munro, "Canada and Extended Fisheries Jurisdiction in the Northeast Pacific: Some Issues in Optimal Resource Management," paper presented to Fifth Pacific Regional Science Conference, Vancouver, 1977.

22. D.G. Paterson and J. Wilen, "Depletion and Diplomacy: The North Pacific Seal Hunt, 1896–1910," unpublished paper, Dept. of Economics, University of British Columbia, 1976.

23. M.B. Schaefer, "Some Considerations of Population Dynamics and Economics in Relation to the Management of Marine Fisheries," *J. Fish. Res. Bd. Can.* 14, 669 (1975).

24. Clark, Clark, and Munro, *supra* note 18.

25. J.F. Nash, "Two-Person Cooperative Games," *Econometrica* 21, 128 (1953).

26. Colin D. Clark, "Mathematical Models in the Economics of Renewable Resources," Technical Report No. 77–4, Institute of Applied Mathematics and Statistics, University of British Columbia (1977).

27. J.F. Nash, "Non-cooperative Games," *Annals of Maths.* 54, 286 (1951).

Chapter Seventeen

On the Utility of Regional Arrangements in the New Ocean Regime

Edward L. Miles
University of Washington

THE PROBLEM

Since the Caracas session of the Third United Nations Conference on the Law of the Sea (UNCLOS III) in 1974, there has been interest in "regional arrangements" as a mechanism for resolving certain problems generated by the approach adopted to defining the exclusive economic zone. The emphasis in this approach has been on spatial characteristics rather than on the relative concentration/dispersal of the various activities to be regulated. It is widely apparent that the definitions contained in the Single Negotiating Text (SNT), the Revised Single Negotiation Text (RSNT), and the Informal Composite Negotiating Text (ICNT) cannot automatically be applied to all coastal areas of the world, because their relevant spatial characteristics differ considerably. The approach adopted, therefore, will give rise to a series of negotiations between neighbors, on the one hand, and between neighboring coastal states and noncoastal states wishing to utilize the area affected, on the other.

In addition to this concern, major regional issues have surfaced in the actual negotiations in four major contexts:

First, in Caracas these issues arose as a result of proposals by eight members (excluding the United Kingdom) of the European Economic Community (EEC), which had as their objective the placing of severe limits on individual coastal state authority over living resources in the economic zone.[1] Opponents of this proposal found it ironic that such a wide scope of authority currently being proposed for regional fisheries commissions now appeared desirable to the same

The author is grateful to Messrs. Stephen Gibbs, Michael Hardy, and James Kingham for detailed comments on an earlier draft.

people who had historically been among its strongest opponents. This led to a heated debate with members of the Latin American and African groups in which one of the very influential African delegates characterized regional fisheries commissions as "clubs for plunder."[2]

Second, the question of "regional arrangements" has been raised repeatedly in Caracas, Geneva (1975), and New York (1976–77) by the Landlocked and Geographically-Disadvantaged Group (LL & GDS). The effect of this would be to leave for later negotiation in a much smaller forum the details of access to resources. However, none of the coastal states is willing to provide guarantees of access to mineral resources of the continental shelf or margin for the LL & GDS group. The situation is more complex concerning living resources. The Africans are willing to share with neighboring LL & GDS within the zone and to use the Organization of African Unity (OAU) as the mechanism for doing so. The Latin Americans and Asians are less willing to share. The Latin Americans since 1975 profess to be willing to allow access to the excess (i.e., after the coastal state has helped itself), if any is left. Most coastal states involved insist that such sharing be subject to Articles 61 and 62 of the ICNT.[3] These rights are nonreviewable in the dispute settlement procedure proposed.

The third context reflects a *sui generis* situation within the EEC, since a wide range of issues being negotiated within UNCLOS III has greatly influenced the bargaining between EEC member states, on the one hand, and between the commission and member states, on the other. The latter dimension is particularly interesting because the Commission seeks consciously to substantiate the extent to which there has been a transfer of powers from the member states to the Community and is aided in doing so by its independent position under the EEC Treaty and the common policies that have been adopted. The most important common policy that has been affected by UNCLOS III developments is, of course, the common fisheries policy. This has led the Commission to propose and the Council to accept: (1) that there be an EEC-wide exclusive fisheries zone of 200 miles; (2) that negotiations be held *on a Community basis* as regards access by Community fishermen to the resources of third states; and (3) that the EEC become a party in its own right to any treaty which might emerge from the Conference.

The fourth context is represented by the extensive debate on the issue of "Enclosed and Semi-Enclosed Seas." However, this question is analyzed in detail by Dolliver Nelson in a paper in this volume.

If one looks at the references to "regional arrangements" that appeared in the RSNT, as catalogued by the Portuguese delegation,[4] it is clear that the primary implicit or explicit models of such arrangements are, first, organizations and, second, either regional fishery management commissions or the FAO-sponsored regional fishery nonmanagement commissions. There is therefore a wide range of possible types of arrangements that are not considered and about which there is considerable ignorance prevailing.

My objective in this paper is to evaluate, on the basis of information presently available, the utility of this range of possible types of arrangements. Such an evaluation should prove useful in adapting to the modifications required by the new ocean regime, whether or not a generally acceptable treaty is produced by UNCLOS III. In doing so, I shall have recourse to a considerable body of work on approaches to regional integration in Western Europe, Latin America, and Africa. This literature yields valuable insights on what one should and should not expect from such research. In applying a body of mainly theoretical literature to the concerns of decisionmakers dealing with particular marine policy problems, I shall assume only that decisionmakers wish to cope with a variety of perceived problems relative to the utilization of the marine environment, and not that they necessarily wish or ought to wish to pursue conscious strategies of regional integration.

THE PROBLEM REFORMULATED

Let us begin by putting aside the specific issues as they arose in the context of actual negotiations and ask instead what generalized objectives decisionmakers are likely to pursue across a variety of specific situations. These may be characterized in terms of gaining or safeguarding access to wealth (redistributing the flow of income), access to knowledge (enlightenment), increasing one's own capabilities (skill), denying access to real or potential competitors, facilitating regional stability and conflict resolution, marine-oriented agreements as side payments for nonocean issues, resource conservation, management of conflict within and across various ocean uses, and the like. However, almost as important as *what* objectives actors pursue is *how* they think about the multiple trade-offs required on the values identified. These strategic questions have very cogently been spelled out by Ernst Haas:

> Do the government people you have in mind think in terms of systematic trade-offs among multiple *uses* of ocean space (i.e. fisheries v. mining v. transport, etc.)? Do they think of trade-offs in terms of differential *benefits* derivable from one use as opposed to another? How do they figure the benefits (i.e. in terms of trade, employment, aggregate income, disaggregated income, etc.)? Do they subordinate all this to some undifferentiated notion of national welfare? Conversely, do they self-consciously figure in terms of multi-use, multi-actor and multi-benefit terms (i.e. some inchoate sense of some 'public good out there')? If all or none of the foregoing, what links do *they* see with regional arrangements? Are there implicit in *their* thinking some explicit analogies with common markets, collaborative R & D agreements, regional environmental protection arrangements? Are these analogies implicit rather than explicit? How extensively are these people aware of experiences in UNEP and the UN specialized agencies? Is the model the variety of regional fisheries agreements?[5]

These questions constitute the crux of the problem. Let me summarize some answers based on personal observations of the conference process since 1973 and multiple interviews with a large number of delegates. Perceptions of the problems identified held by delegates at UNCLOS III run the gamut and are quite inchoate. There are at least two reasons for this. One is that from the point of view of policies implied, the notion of the exclusive economic zone is revolutionary and subversive of the traditional structure of many ocean management decision-systems. The second reason is that, for most countries, the people who negotiate jurisdiction are not the same people who manage marine uses on a day-to-day basis, and therefore the operational consequences of jurisdictional decisions are often not immediately apparent to them.

One finds more often, therefore, evidence of only nascent awareness of the need to define a shifting pecking order of priorities relative to the multiple uses of ocean space. One finds less often any awareness of the trade-offs between benefits derivable from one use as opposed to another, and there is almost no perception of the need to operationalize concepts of net benefits derivable from ocean use in general.

With respect to the questions concerning links and implicit or explicit analogies to common markets and other models, one finds that most actors regard regional fisheries commissions as the basic model. They are, of course, aware of the UN specialized agencies and UNEP but, in the main, both representatives of advanced industrial countries and the Group of 77 find these to be of declining, if any, utility.

On the other hand, there is increasing interest in experimenting with various forms of regional and quasi-regional arrangements for a variety of reasons. Some of these reasons are complementary, as for example the interest of distant-water fishing countries like Japan and the USSR in securing access to fisheries resources in foreign economic zones and the interests of developing countries with resources to increase fish production for protein or foreign exchange and to expand fishing and fish processing capabilities. This kind of arrangement is also growing between *developed* countries (e.g., United States-USSR) as well as between *developing* countries. For instance, there is an emerging arrangement between Trinidad-Tobago and Brazil in which Brazil provides Trinidad with continued access to shrimp resources, but on a joint venture basis which helps Brazil to expand its processing capacity, and in addition Brazil seeks to garner a larger share of Trinidad's petroleum exports.[6]

In addition to countries seeking access to resources, others seek access to knowledge. In the United States, for example, both sets of interests are present. The United States is attempting to accommodate the interests of domestic tuna fishermen, as previous arrangements (the Inter-American Tropical Tuna Commission) have been seriously impaired by extensions in coastal state jurisdiction in the Eastern Tropical Pacific. At the same time, U.S. distant-water academic and governmental oceanographers are finding themselves in increasingly difficult situations. For the major oceanographic research institutes with large distant-water operating capacity, an average of 35–45 percent of annual ship time has historically been spent within the economic zones of other countries and denials of access are getting more and more frequent. This is occurring simultaneously with a decline in real federal research support. The latter is barely staying abreast of inflation, in particular with increases in the cost of food, fuel, and labor.

There is consequently growing interest in devising regional collaborative arrangements in areas of particular interest to U.S. scientists in which technical assistance of some kind is exchanged for access in such a way that the transfer is useful to the coastal states involved, as defined by their own priorities, and each individual U.S. unit avoids having to pay on a per vessel per trip basis.

Within the FAO-sponsored regional fishery commissions, significant changes are also slowly taking place.[7] Several of these commissions have now been assigned management responsibilities. There is particular concern for creating mechanisms that facilitate better collection and exchange of data on the status of the stocks than has so far been possible. There is increasing concern for the need to devise adequate arrangements to handle the problem of sharing stocks that migrate across particular jurisdictions. This is especially a problem in regions like the Gulf of Guinea and the South China Sea.

Given these problems, what varieties of responses are possible and how should the analysis be approached? It is clear that the EEC situation is *sui generis,* though parts of that experience may be transferable. In answering the question posed, the focus will be on the appropriateness of some regional formulae for managing ocean resources and ocean uses on a decentralized basis.

REGIONAL ARRANGEMENTS DEFINED[8]

There are essentially two choices in defining a region. The first is to use location/contiguity as the determining criterion and infer that there is a direct causal relationship between this characteristic and the pattern of activities and policy problems dealt with. This turns out to be an excessively limiting approach, since countries are often more tightly connected in terms of their transactions with countries outside the "region" than within. The second alternative is to treat location as being secondary and focus instead on the pattern of activities and perceived policy problems that should be at least analytically separable from the rest of the world. A policy problem is defined as the perception by some actor of the need to choose between different objectives or courses of action. The notion of choice reflects concern with both the processes of decision and of implementation. The second alternative is the approach taken here.

Marine regional arrangements represent attempts by *two or more* countries to respond to some perceived set of policy problems related to ocean use in a specified portion of the world ocean.[9] If the countries involved are all situated around the locus of the perceived problems, we call the arrangements fully regional. If countries from other parts of the world are also involved, we call the arrangements quasi-regional.

The arrangements differ in their degree of centralization of decision making and their scope of decision-making capacity (i.e., number and type of issues). For illustrative purposes, arrangements can be arrayed in relation to the diagonal in a matrix defined by the two dimensions of high to low centralization and restricted to wide scope. Specific examples would therefore range from loose arrangements to share information to relatively highly centralized arrangements of significantly wide scope restricting the freedom of maneuver of individual state members.

ONE ANALYTICAL APPROACH

I have argued elsewhere that the observable variations in global ocean politics is reducible to five sets of dynamics.[10] These are

1. differences in capabilities of ocean use and therefore in the distribution of income and other values generated by such use.
2. Differences in biogeophysical conditions of states.
3. Differences in national objectives vis-à-vis ocean use.
4. The extent to which the substantive issues are 'pure', i.e., pertain only to the activities of ocean use, or 'contaminated', i.e., penetrated by external, non-ocean-related issues.
5. The organizational demands of conducting negotiations in institutionalized settings at the global level (i.e., group structure, issues, coalitions and rules of procedure).

The first four of these are generally applicable to regional ocean politics as well. The fifth is applicable whenever a definite regional or quasi-regional organization is involved. As people's expectations about ocean exploitation change, this affects the first three factors significantly. This process has been observed for the concept of the exclusive economic zone and some of these reverberations are now spilling over into the area of regional arrangements.

Given the multifarious alternative possibilities available from very loose to very tightly centralized and given the desire of decisionmakers to be able to cope with a variety of marine policy problems generated by the process of ocean use, it seems to me most useful to begin by asking the following set of questions relative to specific arrangements proposed or reevaluating existing ones:

1. What values are at stake? Or what objectives are sought?
2. Who are the relevant actors?
3. How important are the values perceived to be?

4. What capabilities relative to the activities in question exist and how are they distributed?
5. What skew in the distribution of benefits is perceived by whom?
6. What are the existing patterns of control and how are the relevant decision processes organized?
7. What are the specific issues?
8. What coalitions exist or are likely?
9. What are the likely outcomes?
10. What are the likely long-run effects of specific outcomes?

Now, governments do not commit themselves to new arrangements generally unless the same objectives cannot be obtained elsewhere at less cost.[11] Costs may be monetary or political. Therefore, some criteria must be specified by which composite judgments of relative utility will be made. I recommend the following nonexhaustive list in no order of priority:

1. Economic efficiency.
2. Equity.
3. Flexibility, i.e., adaptability in the face of dynamic phenomena.
4. Comprehensiveness and timeliness in information gathering and analysis of trends.
5. Effectiveness with respect to stated and unstated goals.
6. Responsiveness to constituencies.
7. Conflict resolution potential.

We already know which variables constitute critical constraints and supports for effective task performance. The most crucial questions are: what are perceived by the actors to be the benefits to be derived from participation and how are they to be distributed? This leads to a further set of questions: Are the benefits to be derived indivisible and of high value, so that their attainment would be impossible without effective collaboration (e.g., longer and more accurate weather forecasts)? If the benefits are divisible, is the result still greater than the perceived sum of the separate contributions (e.g., nuclear research in the Centre European pour la Recherche Nucléaire)? If the benefits are divisible, how are costs to be apportioned? If costs are borne solely by participants, then perceptions of the ratio of benefits to individual costs will set real limits to collaboration, where benefits are divisible and side payments not utilized (e.g., EURATOM). If the costs are borne primarily by some *deus ex machine* (e.g., private foundations), then the question of the ratio can be deferred. (e.g., International Rice Research Institute).

The expectations participants have about the nature of the benefits is positively related to the degree of national commitment to the activity. However, an additional critical though independent variable is the quality of national and regional leadership available. The tasks for the leadership are to convey some vision of the future to various participants, to pay attention to the bargaining process characterizing the relationship, to secure adequate resources for task performance, to be responsive to, and therefore be able to mobilize, constituencies, and to seek to multiply the values to be traded off so that participants are not forced into making deals only on a single dimension.

A second group of important variables for effective regional collaboration would include: the size and quality of the pool of technical experts that can be pressed into service, the density and variety of transaction patterns already existing between the relevant participants, the nature of the institutional arrangements and the degree of coordination between them across different activities, and the degree of externalization (i.e., the ratio of pure to contaminated issues and the roles of external actors).

All this we already know and should keep in mind as we proceed to devise regional responses to the new ocean regime. There are already many existing examples of regional arrangements which are empty vessels, to put it bluntly, and we should guard against their multiplication.

SOME ADDITIONAL LESSONS TO BE LEARNED FROM ATTEMPTS AT REGIONAL INTEGRATION

These experiences are relevant for our purposes *if states wish to consider arrangements that approach higher degrees of centralization.* Professor Joseph Nye, for instance, defines a regional organization as one that is based on formal agreement among governments, in which membership is restricted on the basis of geography, and in which there is created a diplomatic forum assisted by an international bureaucracy.[12] The scope of the arrangements can differ with respect to the number and type of tasks to be assigned and the relative distance between the constituent units. The latter is important because it relates to intensity of interactions, the effects of size on cohesiveness, and the problems of enforcement.

For our purposes, two dimensions of the regional integration phenomenon that Nye analyzes are relevant. The first is the degree of preexisting economic integration defined in terms of (1) trade interdependence (i.e., the proportion of intraregional exports to total exports); (2) whether or not there are common external tariffs; (3) the degree of factor mobility; (4) the extent to which there is harmonization of fiscal and monetary policies; and (5) the scope of shared services (i.e., total annual expenditures by jointly administered services as percentage of GNP).[13] These phenomena constitute an infrastructure and a body of common experiences that can facilitate the emergence of new joint enterprises among regional actors. They are a necessary but not a sufficient condition for effective collaboration of the more highly centralized type.

The second dimension relates to possibilities of political integration defined in terms of: (1) the salience of joint activities to governments; (2) the extent of national commitment; (3) the degree of policy coordination (budgets and staff) on particular issues; (4) the nature of constituencies; and (5) the distribution of gains and losses.[14]

Nye hypothesizes that if, over time, higher levels of integration are achieved, the process becomes more politicized (i.e., controversial) as a result of increasing salience to governments and constituencies. This increased politicization tends to affect decision-making style substantially, making the process more difficult by involving more players and issues. While this increased politicization is not necessarily bad for continued integration, it does incur higher costs.[15]

> Whether or not politicization acts as a brake on further integrative responses depends on the configuration of political interests in the member countries, and this pattern in turn may depend to a large extent on timing. The important question is whether the support of groups benefitted and of mass opinion grows quickly enough to overcome the opposition of other groups and the likely proclivities of many political decision-makers toward inertia or hostility as their sense of sovereign control is increasingly lessened. The problem facing further integration is not politicization but *premature* politicization before supportive attitudes have become intense and structured. This is particularly a problem in many less developed countries.[16]

Ernst Haas has provided a convenient inventory of propositions derived from the literature on regional integration.[17] His definition of this phenomenon is: "The study of regional integration is concerned with explaining how and why states cease to be wholly sovereign, how and why they voluntarily mingle, merge, and mix with their neighbors so as to lose the factual attributes of sovereignty while acquiring new techniques for resolving conflict between themselves."[18] Some of the findings that have relevance for the creation of marine regional arrangements are as follows:

Empirical Generalizations: Global[19]

1. Members of regional groupings perceive themselves as being increasingly inter-dependent as the volume and rate of transactions between them rises as compared to third countries.

2a. Actors will evaluate interdependence as negative if they feel their regional partners profit more than they; negative evaluations can be predicted in common markets and free trade areas of less developed countries.

b. Actors will evaluate interdependence as positive if they feel they benefit equally with their partners in *some* issue area though not necessarily in all simultaneously; such a pattern can be predicted in economic arrangements between industrialized countries.

3. The proliferation of organizational channels in a region (both governmental and private) stimulates interdependence among the members

as they increasingly resort to these channels for the resolution of conflicts. However, a positive evaluation of such interdependence on the part of the actors cannot be predicted . . . .

4. A critical mass composed of integrative activities in a number of issue areas likely to result in a culmination of de facto or de jure political union is difficult to identify and hazardous to predict. Many fields of potentially integrative activity, after successful accomplishments, result in 'self-encapsulation' organizationally and attitudinally and therefore may not contribute to the evolution of new demands by actors. Other areas of perceived interdependence result in the creation of rival organizations whose activities may nor may not contribute to overall integration.
5. Of all issues and policy areas the commitment to create a common market is the most conducive to rapid regional integration and the maximization of a spill-over. Military alliances, even if equipped with far-ranging competences and standing organs, have triggered very little permanent integrative consequences. Arrangements limited to the setting up of common technical and scientific services tend toward self-encapsulation.[20]

THE EXCLUSIVE ECONOMIC ZONE AND EXPECTATIONS ABOUT FUTURE MARINE REGIONAL ARRANGEMENTS

Professor Lewis Alexander has recently produced a comprehensive descriptive catalog of existing marine regional arrangements, thereby relieving me of the necessity of describing trends.[21] In this section, I shall, therefore, try to answer one question: What can we expect of regional arrangements in the new ocean regime?

Existing regional arrangements are restricted to marine science, pollution control, fisheries, and shipping. They tend to be dominated by national governments in their decision-making except in the case of liner conferences[22] and, with few exceptions, they tend to be isolated from each other. Most of these arrangements are either independent organizations or programs of organizations of varying degrees of complexity and centralization. Some are agreements that define the rules of the game for periodic meetings of states. Very few organizations have their own independent scientific staffs.

In terms of performance, those dominated by governments tend to be either inflexible or flexible within a very narrow range and tied to conditions characteristic of the time at which they were created. Consequently, they cannot respond effectively and rapidly to major changes in external conditions. All, including the liner conferences (which are oligopolistic), tend to be neglectful of economic efficiency as a value. In part because they are quite responsive to national constituencies, it is extremely difficult to get comprehensive, effective organizational programs out of them. Their performance as conflict resolvers is mixed and, in fact, inflexibility generates additional conflict when serious inequities are perceived by participants. What therefore can we expect of them in the new regime?

Fisheries

It seems to me that we can expect that existing management commissions based on an open-access regime either will pass out of existence or be significantly renegotiated to conform to the new conditions. Indeed this is already taking place and should be concluded in the next year or two at most. In their places we can expect to see several different kinds of arrangements. Where stocks fall within the 200-mile zones of coastal states, there are likely to be four types of quasi-regional arrangements emerging. These are: (a) arrangements to divide the surplus, as in the case of Canada and the Northwest Atlantic; (b) arrangements to provide access to foreigners on some favored basis as a result of joint ventures or other forms of payment; (c) arrangements for more detailed and comprehensive collection of data on catch levels and catch per unit effort (CPUE) by the foreigners and even joint research operations oriented both to monitoring the status of stocks and discovering new ones; and (d) arrangements that require drastically reduced levels of fishing by foreigners.

Situations in which stocks are shared either within 200-miles or between the economic zone and the area adjacent to it present the greatest complexities and therefore the greatest difficulties. This is particularly true for the Northeast Atlantic, the Gulf of Guinea and the Southeast Atlantic, and the West Central Pacific. To a lesser extent, it is true of the Northeast Pacific and the East Central Pacific.

In the case of the Northeast Atlantic, there are thirteen states and two competing jurisdictions (i.e., Northeast Atlantic Fisheries Commission [NEAFC] and the EEC). Not all members of NEAFC are members of the EEC and there are significant internal strains in each unit. Most of the stocks, however, are already overexploited and the recent declaration of an EEC-wide 200-mile fisheries zone does not solve the problem of allocation of quotas among the membership and the unwillingness of the states in question to impose significant effort controls on the reduction fisheries. In addition, the extremely difficult job of managing extensive multiple species fisheries remains.

The problems of the countries on the Gulf of Guinea relate both to the issue of sharing and to the lack of an adequate scientific and information base. As a management capacity emerges in the Committee for the East Central Atlantic Fisheries (CECAF), an FAO-sponsored body, it is proving to be difficult to extend CECAF's boundaries southward to cover the resources off the coast of Angola. Angola was not included originally in CECAF as a result of the internal war with Portugal. Instead, it was included in the independent, treaty-based International Commission for the Southeast Atlantic Fisheries (ICSEAF). The reason for the current difficulties is that the socialist countries, particularly the

USSR, are opposed to Angola being merged into CECAF because they have an effective voice in the management decisions of ICSEAF and they would lose it under CECAF. Presumably, as part of the price of continued Soviet support of the South West Africa People's Organization (SWAPO) for the independence of Namibia, the SWAPO delegates are also stoutly resisting the extension of CECAF's boundaries.

In both the CECAF region and the South China Sea, problems of sharing are accentuated by uneven development of fishing capacity in the coastal states and the fact that developing states with a distant-water capacity are unable to pay as much as developed states can for access. The lack of an adequate science/information base also plagues the coastal states of the South China Sea.

In these three regions, we can therefore expect the initial focus to be on devising arrangements for sharing the resources among the coastal states. This would be complicated in the Gulf of Guinea and the South China Sea by simultaneous pursuit of access by nonlocal distant-water states in the form of joint ventures and the like. In both of these areas, we can expect continuing attempts to increase the stock assessment capacity by FAO. Coastal states may also wish to include assistance on research as part of the price for access for nonlocal distant-water fishing countries.

The question of management on a regional basis goes hand in hand with the question of sharing among coastal states. Gunnar Saetersdal has dealt with this important problem in a recent concise FAO paper.[23] Saetersdal points out that there are some serious difficulties affecting any attempts to negotiate national quotas for coastal states once the total allowable catch (TAC) per stock is annually determined. The simplest criterion for sharing has been the pattern of historical fishing defined either as a proportion of current yields in the zones or the means of recent periods.

> This would, however, (he says), give a reasonable allocation only for stocks which have been exploited at approximately the same rate in each of the zones. But for many stocks the fishery has for various reasons been concentrated in particular parts of the distributional area of the fish. Furthermore, considerable fluctuations often occur in the distribution on many of these fish stocks, both seasonally, or over a shorter or longer period of years and this will evidently complicate a simple 'historical' allocation. The question of what historical period to take as a base is often disputed in principle since the fishery policy of some countries may have been more dynamic and changeable than that of others . . . .
>
> The harvestable part of a fishery resource is only one component of a resource complex which consists, in addition, of a reproductive phase and a recruiting and growth phase. Further, the whole resource complex is of course dependent on the productivity of lower trophic levels in the sea. The geographic distribution of these various phases and of the system of primary production in the sea does not necessarily coincide with that of the fishable part of the population. For example, the main areas of the

> juvenile pre-recruit fish may be located in the zone quite separate from that in which the main fishery occurs. . . .[24]

Saetersdal then suggests the application of five major criteria which should guide negotiations for long-term proportional allocation of the TAC. These are:

1. The occurrence and migrations of the fishable part of the stock.
2. The occurrence of juvenile and pre-recruit fish.
3. The spawning area and the distribution of egg and larvae.
4. The history of the fishery including the distribution of catch rate of exploitation and fishery regulations.
5. The state of exploitation of the stock.

One possible drawback of Saetersdal's approach is that it restricts negotiators to bargaining only on one dimension, the fishery, albeit a broadened definition of that. This carries with it severe restrictions on the flexibility of negotiators especially where, as he points out, significant variations in the geographic distribution of fishing operations exist. It seems unlikely to me that in those three difficult regional situations acceptable solutions can be found to quota allocation problems among the coastal states without extensive resort to side payments and the flexibility that comes with simultaneous negotiation on more than one dimension. It is simply unlikely that costs and gains can be equitably distributed solely on the basis of the fishery, especially taking into account the complexities that Saetersdal so clearly summarizes.

To be sure, it is more difficult to manage negotiations on several dimensions simultaneously and, in cases where fishing capacity is highly developed, tradeoffs will imply trading off fishermen and this may entail political consequences unacceptable to a national government. Conversely, even where such vested interests do not exist, as in the case of some developing coastal states, there may be few, if any, items that will be regarded by the parties as desirable side payments. These, however, are the extremes and most situations will fall somewhere in between.

With respect to situations in which stocks are shared within and outside of 200-mile economic zones, the problems may be a little easier to deal with than in the former case. For example, the salmon problem of the North Pacific is a complicated, multidimensional problem that involves the United States and Canada, the United States and Canada, and Japan, Japan and the USSR, and Japan/USSR in relation to United States/Canada/Japan. The United States/Canadian problem is itself multidimensional in that it involves three sets of distributional questions in addition to being linked to boundary negotiations on the East and West coasts and, by implication, the sharing of other significant fisheries and potentially significant petroleum deposits.

Even in the face of these difficulties, significant progress has recently been made toward a comprehensive, highly innovative solution to the entire range of problems, once a decision to move in this direction was made by the two heads of state for reasons that in part transcended the merits of the issues in question. With respect to the Japan/United States/Canada arrangements, specifically the International North Pacific Fisheries Commission (INPFC), it is likely that these arrangements will be substantially changed in the near future. However, given the recent (May 1977) drastic curtailment of Japanese fishing in the Soviet zone, the Japanese appear to be dragging their feet on the renegotiation of INPFC until a more definite *modus vivendi* is worked out with the USSR. This does not appear to signal any greater difficulties on the issue of Japanese high seas salmon fishing for the United States since the United States continues to hold a very significant trump card in the Japanese allocations of Alaskan pollock quotas for the Northeast Pacific. Indeed, the value of this card has appreciated considerably as a result of the heavy-handed treatment of the Japanese by the Soviets.

The situation concerning the distribution of tuna stocks (primarily yellowfin and, to a lesser extent, skipjack) in the Eastern Tropical Pacific is also difficult but not inherently unresolvable. This is especially so given the shift in fishing patterns for yellowfin and the success achieved by the U.S. fleet in increasing the quantity of fish taken outside 200-mile zones. For instance, between 1964 and 1971 an average of 62.43 percent of the total yellowfin catch in the Eastern Tropical Pacific was taken from within 200 miles of twelve coastal states. However, 76.1 percent of the total Commission Yellowfin Regulatory Area (CYRA) catch was taken from within 200 miles. The figures for skipjack are 92.33 percent and 95.33 percent respectively.[25]

Contrasted with this, the figures for the period 1970–1974 show a marked shift. During that time an average of 57 percent of yellowfin from the Eastern Tropical Pacific were taken from within 200 miles. The same figure applies to the catch from the CYRA, which means that fishing was increasingly concentrated outside of 200 miles (though primarily still within the CYRA).[26] The figures for skipjack in this period are 86 percent.

The major issue within the IATTC has been the U.S. share of the catch, which has declined from 82.4 percent for yellowfin and 70.8 percent for skipjack in 1970 to 68.0 percent and 60.3 percent in 1974 respectively.[27] While negotiations in the Law of the Sea Conference (UNCLOS III) have resulted in the fragmentation of management authority over tuna resources, the coastal states of the Eastern Tropical Pacific would now appear to have a significantly increased incentive for renegotiating regional arrangements rather than just letting the IATTC dissolve. The reasons for this are primarily the successful shift in fishing patterns as regards yellowfin and the fact that such regional arrangements would give the coastal states a voice in management decisions affecting operations *outside* of 200 miles. In addition to this, regional arrangements would provide the coastal states with significant assistance in monitoring, information gathering, and the results of scientific research that may not otherwise be available.

New arrangements are also emerging in the Western Central Pacific and the Southwest Pacific, which also affect tuna primarily, though it is at the moment unclear what substantive changes will be imposed in the short run. The reference here is to the adoption of management responsibilities by the Indo-Pacific Fisheries Commission and the creation of the South Pacific Forum and the South Pacific Fisheries Agency.

Marine Science

There are currently three types of regional and quasi-regional activities concerning marine science. These are: (1) programs of the International Oceanographic Commission (IOC); (2) programs of regional scientific organizations such as the International Council for the Exploration of the Sea (ICES), the International Council for the Scientific Exploration of the Mediterranean (ICSEM), and the Cooperative Investigations of the Mediterranean (CIM); and (3) ad hoc multilateral problem-oriented investigations of general theoretical interest like Project FAMOUS, the Mid-Ocean Dynamics Experiment (MODE), the Barbados Oceanographic and Meteorological Experiment (BOMEX), and the Joint Oceanographic Institutions for Deep Earth Sampling (JOIDES).

Activities in the first category represent pooling of national resources with respect to descriptive oceanographic surveys. There is little integrated scientific planning and coordination and the quality of the output varies considerably. The variables that appear to affect performance are the nature of the scientific problem and the degree of interest it generates together with the extent of national commitment to the effort and a willingness to commit the necessary resources in money, shiptime, equipment, and manpower. Where there is high interest in and national commitment to a set of carefully formulated scientific questions, these programs tend to be effective. Where there is low interest in the project as a whole or in parts of it, performance tends to be low or variable.

Of the second category, only ICES is an effectively functioning entity. The other two are very weak in substantive programs and performance. ICES has historically been dominated by countries of the Northeast Atlantic since its founding in 1902, encompasses membership of high capability and produces generally effective scientific programs. Indeed, several of these programs relating to fisheries and marine pollution are tightly integrated investigations and go considerably beyond the mere pooling of national efforts.

The third category includes some of the most advanced work being done in oceanography today. The players are all major maritime countries, the projects are large-scale, problem-oriented theoretical investigations, and considerably more centralized and substantively integrated than IOC programs.

The new ocean regime is likely to affect category one activities primarily and could, to a lesser extent, affect new forms of category three activities depending on the location of the investigations. Category two activities (e.g., ICES) are substantially insulated from these perturbations.

Even during the deliberations of the Seabed Committee, the work of the IOC appeared to be very sensitive to impending changes in the law of the sea. The Latin American countries, in particular Brazil and Argentina, mobilized the Group of 77 within the IOC on issues of coastal state control of marine scientific research in the economic zone and on the relative priority to be accorded scientific investigations of pollution in the marine environment versus technical assistance. This conflict spilled over into the Seabed Committee and the Law of the Sea Conference, where developing countries privately expressed considerable hostility to the IOC as a rich nations' club.

The increasing politicization of all issues within the IOC, combined with the natural progression of oceanographic research away from descriptive surveys to problem-oriented theoretical investigations, had an increasingly adverse effect on IOC programs and resulted in a decrease in real resources available for mobilization by the leadership. the increase of the salience of the marine scientific research issue in context of the new regime has also resulted in an expansion of IOC's membership at a time when there is great concern about the decreasing effectiveness of the organization.

Since developing countries now make up the largest constituency, the leadership has attempted to shift priorities to regional programs which meet the perceived needs of developing and developed coastal states and to technical assistance. This shift can be seen in the emergence of IOCARIBE as the successor organization to the Cooperative Investigations of the Caribbean (CICAR), the cooperative investigation of the El Niño phenomenon off Peru, and the cooperative investigation of the Western and Central Indian Ocean. However, there is considerable opposition among the advanced maritime countries within the IOC to such a shift for several reasons.

In the first place, these delegations argue that there is a real need to produce a comprehensive evaluation of all cooperative investigations and the conditions under which they ought to exist; that the current rules are seriously outmoded, having been written in the early 1960s, and have therefore not kept pace with either advances in marine science or advances in marine scientific planning; and that they do not agree with priorities established in several of these programs. A further difficulty is generated by the attempt to tie regionalization of IOC programs to questions of access. The implications of this can be observed in the reactions to proposals by the secretary in 1974–75 to create regional instrumentation centers.

For advanced maritime countries, it appeared unwise to proceed with regionalization of IOC's programs before the marine scientific research negotiations were concluded in UNCLOS III. In addition, even if these countries acceded to coastal state control of marine scientific research, a preferred mechanism of exchange appeared to be arrangements directly constructed between the advanced country and developing coastal states in whatever location was given priority. From this point of view, therefore, IOC technical assistance programs were competitive with direct national links and the effectiveness of the IOC was regarded as being low; consequently, there was not much incentive to be involved as a general rule.

For other developed countries, especially the USSR, there was sustained opposition to regionalization precisely because they first wished to make a definite link between technical assistance and access via the mechanism of organizational programs. On the other hand, countries like Canada were for regionalization as a means of facilitating research through competent international organizations.

The most important dimension to bargaining within the IOC and outside on issues of marine scientific research in the immediate future will be the conditions under which technical assistance will be exchanged for access. The politicization of the IOC has not abated since 1972; it has increased and it is unlikely to decrease in the short run, whatever the outcome of UNCLOS III, because the locational and programmatic details of the transition to a new regime must still be negotiated. IOC regional programs may, in particular cases, be the chosen instruments, but they will have to compete with an increasing number of special arrangements to be concluded between a few advanced maritime countries and developing coastal states in regions defined as being of high priority by the advanced countries.

Marine Pollution Control

Attempts to negotiate regional arrangements to respond to perceived problems in different parts of the world will continue, but they will not be affected very much by the new ocean regime as defined in the ICNT. These articles, except in the case of flag state/coastal state jurisdiction in respect to ship-generated pollution, are excessively general and empty of specific, immediate effect. The dynamics to which programs of marine pollution control will continue to respond are: considerable differences of view in the formulation of scientific plans, the localized nature of many problems and the subsequent variation in national priorities, differences in capabilities among countries, scarcity of funds, and interagency jurisdictional conflict over program and resources.

With respect to ship-generated pollution, the situation is a little unclear in the long run. If a treaty is signed, the new regime will strengthen flag state controls via the global mechanism (IMCO) at the expense of coastal states. Certain coastal states, for example the United States and Canada, will find that global standards are weaker than existing domestic legislation in many instances. If polluting incidents involving tankers increase, these will generate more insistent demands for more stringent controls among various domestic constituencies. The same will be true for coastal states that are not significant port states but that still sustain the effects of oil spills, tank washings, bilge cleanings, and the like.

Given these pressures, if UNCLOS III produces no treaty that is generally acceptable, it is unclear how stable the enforcement provisions relating to ship-generated pollution in the ICNT will be. Considerable variety may emerge in national legislation, though their application may be restrained by effective performance in IMCO and subsequent ratification by coastal states. If a variety of national regulations begins to be applied, then the attractiveness of regional alternatives will increase, at least for the flag states.

Shipping

The new ocean regime will have no impact on the organization of liner conferences and therefore on the commercial regulation of the world shipping industry. On the other hand, if the UNCTAD Code of Conduct for Liner Conferences[28] ever comes into force, liner conferences could be seriously affected by a trend towards increasing bilateral regulation of shipping services. This is at the moment unlikely in the short-run, but somewhat unclear in the long-run.

POSSIBLE LONG-TERM MULTIPURPOSE MARINE REGIONAL ARRANGEMENTS

It is possible to foresee that in the long run a variety of marine regional arrangements will be required in order to deal with the juxtaposition of jurisdictional changes and the effects of advancing technology. The economic zone is a multipurpose zone for which coastal state decisionmakers will be called upon to make coordinated policy cutting across a variety of activities that are now only haphazardly connected. Simultaneously with this, rapid advances in marine technology are producing greatly intensified and diversified activities within the neritic zones of the world ocean. In the future, coastal states will be called upon to manage multiple uses and use conflicts of the near coastal environment to a degree never before experienced. When this occurs in regions like the North Pacific, the Northeast Atlantic, the Mediterranean, the West Central Pacific, and the West Central Atlantic, there will be an increasing incentive to create a wide variety of multipurpose regional collaborative arrangements ranging from the exchange of information to substantive, joint regulation of particular activities.

A similar situation is even now affecting one special regional arrangement concerning the Antarctic and the disposition of the resources of the Southern Ocean and its continental margins. Several very difficult questions arise here. First, the Antarctic Treaty of 1959, based on the assumption that there was no urgency for dealing with distributional questions concerning resources of the area, achieved a suspension of claims to sovereignty over territory by the seven claimant states: Argentina, Australia, Chile, France, New Zealand, Norway, and the United Kingdom. A restricted arrangement for twelve signatories was therefore possible, the other interested parties being Belgium, Japan, the USSR, South Africa, and the United States. The arrangements were to remain in force for thirty years after entry into force, and the latter occurred in 1961. Since 1961, six additional states have acceded to the treaty. They are: the Netherlands, Poland, Czechoslovakia, Denmark, Romania, and Brazil.

Since the early 1970s, issues of possible living and nonliving resource exploitation have put the stability of the present regime into serious question since they aggravate existing, and sometimes competing, jurisdictional problems especially of the claimant states. Article IV of the treaty declares that the Antarctic landmass is not subject to the sovereignty of any state and, by inference, this would extend to the adjacent ocean areas as well. Similarly, Article VI applies to the area of the ocean south of 60°S latitude in which (undefined) high seas rights are protected. But as possibilities of exploiting mineral (especially hydrocarbon) resources of the continental shelf and krill, demersal and other marine mammal resources besides whales either emerge or loom nearer than previously thought, jurisdictional claims merge with changes in the ocean regime and new questions arise.

For instance, will the claimant states assert 200-mile economic zones around territory adjacent to the continent? Will an United Kingdom zone extend around the South Sandwich Islands, south of the Falklands? If so, this economic zone will extend south of 60°S. The same would be true for Australia and McDonald and Heard Islands.

The exploitability of resources raises questions not only about distribution but about conservation and environmental protection. All of these issues occur simultaneously, though the package may be decomposed and approached sequentially. For instance, there seems to be greater urgency relating to conservation and management of the krill resource for which large-scale exploitation is imminent. However, the countries with the greatest interest in krill are precisely those whose vessels are now being excluded from zones around the world. These countries are also ones with the greatest amount of information about the population dynamics of krill; this is particularly true of the USSR and Japan. What is the incentive for these countries to provide the necessary information and submit to some regulatory regime?

One reply that is sometimes made is that both these countries and the claimant states see some utility in settling the issues in a limited forum, thereby preserving the treaty, before they spill over into a global forum like the United Nations. Perhaps so, but what guarantees are there that the forum will indeed be limited? The Group of 77 has already declared its interests in this issue and the point was addressed in some detail by the delegation of Sri Lanka at the meeting of the Heads of State of Non-aligned Countries in Colombo in August 1976. The position is that the resources of Antarctica, like the resources of the seabed beyond national jurisdiction, are the "common heritage of mankind" and not subject to national appropriation. It is unlikely, therefore, given the intensity of the present North/South confrontation and the imminent failure of UNCLOS III precisely on the seabed question, that the Group of 77 would be disposed to leave the field to the twelve signatories, the six acceding states, and a few other interested parties.

In the abstract, it would be possible to conceive of alternative arrangements that may avert the rush to a territorial solution, but existing constraints on the negotiations imposed by the seven claimant states make this very difficult indeed. Trying to predict likely new arrangements for Antarctica is therefore a very hazardous activity, made more so by the heavy cloud of secrecy surrounding the official negotiations.

CONCLUSIONS

On the basis of the perspective developed in this paper, the utility of marine regional arrangements in the new ocean regime will be quite different from the expectations in evidence at UNCLOS III. There will be a profusion of regional and quasi-regional arrangements limited in scope and of very low centralization. Most will not be organizations and those that are will be quite different from preexisting fisheries management commissions. The greatest effect in the short run will be felt in the areas of fisheries and marine science. Fewer significant changes are foreseen in the short run for ship-generated pollution control and commercial shipping activities.

Most future arrangements will be based on "goods" to be exchanged. Only a few will be based on "goods" to be produced. Significant changes are predicted for the long run in the latter connection for multipurpose marine regional arrangements. When there are both "goods" to be produced and organizations to be created, experiences of regional integration attempts in Western Europe, Africa, and Latin America have useful lessons to teach, particularly with respect to mistakes to be avoided. In this connection, the total context within which the new organization is to fit is crucial, and adequate care should be taken in the preliminary analysis and design to fit the organization to the context. Strategies are also of great importance and the ways in which benefits are to be produced and divided will determine much of the future of the organization. Moreover, benefits should be defined in multidimensional fashion so that gains of some players need not always incur losses of others in all areas.

NOTES

1. See Doc. A/CONF. 62/C.2/L.40
2. See the whole debate on the economic zone and preferential rights in the Summary Records, Docs. A/CONF. 62/C.2/SR. 21–31.
3. Article 61 (1): "The coastal state shall determine the allowable catch of the living resources in its exclusive economic zone." Article 62 (2): "The coastal state shall determine its capacity to harvest the living resources of the exclusive economic zone . . . ."
4. "Annotated Table on References to Institutional Mechanism Contained in the Revised Single Negotiating Text," prepared by the delegation of Portugal to the Third United Nations Conference on the Law of the Sea (fifth session), New York, Rev. 1, August 24, 1976.
5. Private communications, March 11, 1977.

6. *The Trinidad Guardian,* October 5, 1977, p. 1.

7. See FAO, Dept. of Fisheries, *Report on FAO Committee on Fisheries and International and Regional Fishery Bodies,* Doc. #FID/C/331, Rome, 1975; and Edward Miles, *An Assessment of Proposed Changes in the Law of the Sea on Regional Fishery Commissions, on FAO Technical Assistance Programmes in Fisheries and on the FAO Committee on Fisheries and Department of Fisheries,* Doc. #COFI: C.4/76/ Inf. 3, February 1976.

8. An alternative approach can be found in Lewis Alexander, *Regional Arrangements in Ocean Affairs,* Final Report under Contract N0014–75–C–1165, Fleet Analysis and Support Division, Office of Naval Research, May 1977, Chapters 1 and 2.

9. No distinction is seen to be necessary between "bilateral" and "regional."

10. Edward Miles, "The Dynamics of Global Ocean Politics," in Douglas M. Johnston (ed.) *Marine Policy and the Coastal Community* (1976), p. 151.

11. John Gerard Ruggie, "Collective Goods and Future International Collaboration," *American Political Science Review* 66 (1972): 874.

12. Joseph S. Nye, *Peace in Parts* (1971), pp. 5–8.

13. Ibid., Chapter 2.

14. Ibid.

15. Ibid., pp. 88–89

16. Ibid., p. 89

17. Ernst Haas, "The Study of Regional Integration: Reflections on the Joy and Anguish of Pre-theorizing," *International Organization* 24 (1970): 607.

18. Ibid., p. 610.

19. Ibid., pp. 614–616.

20. With respect to marine regional arrangements, I am of the opinion that this is a good and not a bad since the objective is merely to respond adequately to a set of commonly perceived policy problems and not necessarily to trigger higher levels of integration.

21. Alexander, *supra* note 8.

22. These are not included in Alexander's catalog.

23. Gunner Saetersdal, "Problems of Managing and Sharing the Fishery Resources under the New Ocean Regime," FAO, COFI/77/Inf. 11, April 1977.

24. Ibid., pp. 3–4.

25. Data fron National Marine Fisheries Service, Southwest Fisheries Research Center.

26. James Joseph and Joseph W. Greenough, *Alternatives for International Management of Tuna Resources,* (In press, 1977), Table 2, p. 30.

27. FAO, Dept. of Fisheries, "Information Note on the Fisheries Situation in the Eastern Pacific," March 1976, Annex F, Table 2, p. 19.

28. See UNCTAD, United Nations Conference of Plenipotentiaries on a Code of Conduct for Liner Conferences: Vol. I *Reports and Other Documents,* 1975; Vol. II *Final Act (Including the Convention and resolutions) and Tonnage Requirements,* 1975. See also: Bernhard J. Abrahamsson, "The Marine Environment and Ocean Shipping: Some Implications of a New Law of the Sea," *International Organization* 31, 2 (Spring 1977): 291–312.

Discussion and Questions

Lewis Alexander: After these three and a half days of discussion the question must come up, what have we got out of all this? Is there anything that one can say about regionalism in ocean management? First, I think we have something here that, for want of a better term, we might call regional management theory or marine regional theory. For the first time a group of people are focusing on marine regional arrangements of various types and trying to come up with some sort of a codified or unified body of knowledge to look at these developments. I think we have two ways of doing this: either by an empirical, case-by-case approach to the study of various marine regional arrangements that exist, or could exist, in order to discover what might be common or transferable, or else through theoretical models such as those discussed by Professor Miles, in the hope of discovering in what conditions these models might be applicable to real life situations. Obviously we are just at the beginning of what could be a very interesting subject of inquiry. Because the matter is so elusive, I thought it might be useful to make four points. The first is that regionalism is a process and regardless of whether it is likely to be particularly effective, there are not too many alternatives. Either ocean management is conducted unilaterally, globally, or regionally. So whether it works or not is an alternative with which we have to live. A second point—and I think Dr. Christy pointed this out very well—is that there are many problems that regionalism cannot solve. So the question is what can it not do, or not do effectively, as well as what might it be able to do effectively. Third, one of the more important questions is what the future functions and powers of these arrangements are likely to be. Are they really set up to decide? As has been pointed out during this conference, they exist for different reasons, and so the amount of authority given to them differs considerably. Finally, I believe that if we look at conceptual models and try to base them on past experience, we are in a fair amount of trouble, as Professor Miles has pointed out, given the important changes now taking place in the law of the sea. But I do think there is a common body of knowledge, whatever name it may have, and that this conference has helped at least to identify the most important questions to be addressed.

David Austen: I am a little perplexed. Both presentations this morning were extremely interesting, but they struck me as being somewhat detached from the real world, in the sense that developing countries such as those in the Indian Ocean do not perceive rational ocean management or cost/benefit analysis as being the first priority or prime concern. They are concerned primarily with maximizing available resources: call it development and utilization of resources for their own national benefit. This notion of rational ocean management is very much a developed world perspective, which the developing countries I am familiar with find somewhat irrelevant in the short term. Dr. Abbadi, who is quite familiar with the Indian Ocean, might disagree with me, but at least that is my perception. I would like to ask both panelists how they would treat this problem of perception or priorities.

Gordon Munro: Let me try and respond to this. I am not familiar with the countries in the Indian Ocean, but the comment that these countries were attempting in some sense to maximize their resources, to develop what they have, is essentially an economic problem. If these countries ignore efficiency criteria, which is what I was talking about, there is no question that this will inhibit their growth. I have had some experience in developing countries. For example, I spent two and a half years in Malaysia, and when I went out there, I must confess that I did go out with the view that probably a lot of the economics that I had grown up with in a developed country, such as the concern with efficiency, probably wouldn't apply. But after two and a half years the conclusion I came to was that these countries simply cannot afford the luxury of ignoring efficiency criteria. I might add that this view is now becoming quite prevalent among development economists, including the development economists coming from developing countries. In the case of fisheries, these countries are faced with the problems of scarce resources and indeed these problems are more acute than what we face in the developed world. If they mismanage or overexploit their fisheries, then it will be at a cost to the rest of the economy: a developmental cost. I suppose a lot of this does sound very theoretical. Perhaps I should have started out this morning by saying how ivory is my tower. But no, I think the purpose of theory, whether economic or political theory, is simply to provide a framework to think rationally and intelligently about these problems, and I would certainly argue that the type of problem that I am looking at does have relevance to these areas.

Edward Miles: I too think your characterization of the situation is incorrect.

I do not see it in terms of developed versus developing. I think it is quite incorrect to say that developing countries in the Indian Ocean or elsewhere are not interested in the rational management of marine resources. For the last five or six years I have had extensive conversations with representatives of developing countries from the Indian Ocean and elsewhere about this very problem, and I find quite great concern about the management process and how one ought to approach it, and about the difficulties they face in trying to do what I am suggesting they should do. On the other hand, I have some involvement also in the United States, which has certain pretentions to be a developed country, and one cannot find any better performance here in terms of rational ocean management. In fact, one would have to say that our national ocean policy is a disaster area, given the dissipation of benefits. The Japanese do much better than the United States in data collection and the evaluation of priorities with respect to navigation, coastal fisheries, hydrocarbon development, and so forth. One finds in Japan much more detailed thinking about systematic trade-offs than in the United States. The experience in Western Europe is varied: for instance, in the United Kingdom and the Netherlands it is quite sophisticated, in other places not so sophisticated.

So I think that we countries in the world who use the ocean face a new set of utilization problems. Historically, we have done certain things, either deliberately, because they have been politically acceptable, or without much thought. Now we are on the threshold of a much changed set of conditions that come from the juxtaposition of two elements: the jurisdictional revolution and the technological revolution. There is considerable interest around the world in trying to find ways of doing things better, managing whatever marine resources one has more rationally. In short, I agree with Professor Munro on the utility of theory in this context, to provide alternatives to people who make decisions about the ways in which problems ought to be conceptualized and the choices that ought to be made. We cannot make the decisions for them, though I am inclined to think that one ought to do that as well, but that may be just personal excess.

Barbara Johnson: I was interested in Dr. Miles' recommendation of a multiple use approach instead of a sectoral one to enable governments to arrive at an accurate calculation of what their overall interest is. In the development of the North Sea, I wonder if he thinks things would have been different if the governments of that region had indulged in this kind of calculation first. I assume they did not, and that it was a kind of sectoral development. Would it have looked all that different, if this multiple use approach had been taken?

Edward Miles: I do not know enough about the North Sea to answer the question in detail. I know a little bit more about the North Pacific, and it is quite clear to me that we shall soon be at the point of making certain choices, and that there are a whole variety of consequences that flow from going down one route rather than another: whether you allow hydrocarbon exploitation in certain areas at the expense of salmon fisheries, for instance, or what you do with respect to coastal fisheries (in Japan, say) versus hydrocarbon exploitation or increased volume of tanker traffic in certain areas, and what social discount rate you will adopt with respect to the set of consequences that flow from the choices made. If the people who are dislocated are primarily the coastal fishermen who operate on the basis of hereditary fishery rights and therefore must be compensated, what do you do about the long-term social problem involved in shifting activities as well as occupations? I suspect there would be a major problem in determining social discount rates that make sense, and in fact we have been advised by all of our economist friends that we ought not to try, because the conceptual difficulties are horrendous. But whatever the "number crunching" difficulties inherent in the construction of a multidimensional matrix, we ought at least do better than what is now being done in the approach to systematic choice.

Abdelkader Abbadi: I suppose that if an ivory tower were constructed here, we would all be interested in visiting it: economists, politicians, political scientists, and everyone else. I would certainly be among the first to visit. I think it is to the credit of Dr. Alexander that he has underlined the fact that regionalism—or perhaps regionalization—is a process, a new concept that might possibly take various forms and shapes. I think that most of the difficulties come from the fact that we are at the beginning of the process of regionalization, and that we have not yet seen the definitive shapes that it might take in the future. Professor Miles is not sure either what kind of forms it will take, but he suggests that there are regional arrangements that I can trade off. I would have liked to have heard an analysis resting more squarely on the concept of national interest. We have not heard much about this here, yet it tends to be predominant in any kind of regional cooperation. As pointed out by Professor Larsen, we are beginning to see regional cooperation in the Indian Ocean, but as you know this is a type of regional cooperation that is based on political and security matters. Those are the features that are at this stage prevalent. We have established at the United Nations, as you all know, the Indian Ocean Committee. We have not seen yet groups or committees established from the Pacific or Atlantic, or the Mediterranean, but I think this underlies the importance that certain nations are attaching to security matters in that particular region. Perhaps we might in the future concentrate on some of these other aspects.

Part VII

Specific Policy Problems in Economic Zone Management

Chairman
Edward Miles
University of Washington

This is the second half of the morning program, and the concluding panel of the conference. In preparation for this discussion, several questions were sent to the panelists:

1. What changes in policy are required and/or implied for their countries by the establishment of exclusive economic zones?
2. How are existing arrangements affected by this trend, and how is the transition being managed?
3. What problems have been solved by the extension of coastal state jurisdiction?
4. What problems have been created and/or remain unsolved?
5. What new regional arrangements appear to be required?

Since several of the panelists are government officials, it should be remembered that the rules under which they appear here are that they do so in their personal capacities, and that nothing that they say is to be taken as representing the views of their governments. Our first panelist is Dr. Hajim Djalal of Indonesia. Dr. Djalal has been involved in law of the sea negotiations from the Seabed Committee through to the present time, and is involved primarily with Committee Two matters. He is, therefore, extremely knowledgeable about the problems not only at UNCLOS III but the problems of Indonesia generated by changes in the law of the sea. Dr. Djalal will be followed by commentaries from the three other members of the panel: Dr. Alverson, Dr. Szekely, and Mr. Nakanchi. My colleague Dr. Alverson is director of the Northwestern and Alaskan Fisheries Research Center in Seattle, which is part of the National Marine Fisheries Service of the United States. He is also a member of the faculty of the Institute for Marine Studies at the University of Washington. He will be followed by Dr. Alberto

Szekely, who is professor of international law at the Institute of Legal Research at the University of Mexico and a member of the Mexican delegation at UNCLOS III. The final commentator will be Mr. Kiyofumi Nakauchi of the Japan International Cooperation Agency, who has kindly agreed to take the place of Mr. T. Saito of the Japanese Ministry of Foreign Affairs.

Chapter Eighteen

Indonesia and the New Extensions of Coastal State Sovereignty and Jurisdiction at Sea

Hasjim Djalal
Department of Foreign Affairs

The recent extensions of coastal state sovereignty and jurisdiction under the international law of the sea include the application of the archipelagic state regime, the twelve-mile territorial sea, the twenty-four-mile contiguous zone, the 200-mile exclusive economic zone, the continental shelf up to the "outer edge of the continental margin," and the various other jurisdictions with regard to the preservation of the marine environment and scientific research. I will, however, limit my observation to the application of the archipelagic state regime, the continental shelf, and, eventually, the exclusive economic zone, as they relate to Indonesia.

ARCHIPELAGIC STATE REGIME

It is clear that Indonesia's attention to the law of the sea during the last twenty years has centered on the implementation and enforcement of the archipelagic state regime as an important unifying factor for an archipelagic country like Indonesia. It is therefore worthwhile to have a quick look at the application of the archipelagic regime to Indonesia and how it affects Indonesian policies with regard to fisheries, transportation and navigation, and the protection of the marine environment.

Fisheries

Since Indonesia declared its archipelagic state regime in 1957, great attention has been given to the development of fisheries. Internally, provincial governments have been given certain rights to regulate and protect coastal fishermen, in some

The opinion expressed in this paper is totally personal and does not necessarily reflect the position of the Indonesian government.

cases up to six miles from the coasts. In these coastal areas, the use of modern equipment and trawlers has often been prohibited, so as to protect the small, economically weak, coastal population. To help them, the government has also encouraged the establishment of cooperatives, and a special bank has also been devoting its attention to helping these small fishermen, who number about one million. Most of these fishermen operate in the Straits of Malacca, the Java Sea, and along the coasts of Flores Sea and the Straits of Makassar.

The central government regulates the fisheries in the rest of the archipelagic waters. This is the area for the operation of a substantial fishing industry. The government makes arrangements with far distant fishing nations, especially Japan, to catch tuna in the Banda Sea under payment of certain fees. In some cases, the government also enters into joint venture arrangements with various foreign companies to exploit the resources of the archipelagic waters. All this has helped Indonesian national income substantially.

Traditional fishing rights and other legitimate activities of the immediately adjacent neighboring countries in certain areas of the archipelagic waters are recognized. Studies are now being undertaken to determine the elements of "traditional fishing rights," the "legitimate activities" involved, and the "area" to which the rights and activities are applied.

As generally understood now, the notion of "traditional fishing rights" refers to the *fishermen* themselves, their *equipment,* their *catch,* and the *area* of their fishing activities. According to this definition: (1) The fishermen in order to be protected under this category must have been fishing for a sufficient length of time in the area; thus, newcomers could not be regarded to have "traditional fishing rights". (2) Their equipment must be sufficiently "traditional"; thus, fishermen using modern technology could not be regarded as falling under the definition of "traditional fishing rights"; otherwise, local and poor fishermen using traditional equipment would be placed at a tremendous disadvantage. (3) Since the catch of "traditional fishing" is normally not very substantial, the notion of "traditional fishing rights" excludes the possibility of a sharp increase in the catch by using modern equipment and methods or by establishing large-scale joint ventures with "nontraditional" fishermen. (4) The area or the fishing ground of traditional fishing rights must have been frequented for a sufficient length of time; the area, therefore, should be relatively easy to determine by observing the actual practice. As far as Indonesian archipelagic waters are concerned, the area of traditional fishing rights should be limited to, or be located along, the perimeter or border region of the archipelagic waters.

It should also be very clear that "traditional fishing rights" should be distinguished from the traditional right to fish. While it can be argued that under the defunct international law every state has "traditional right" to fish on the "high seas," which may or may not become part of the regime of archipelagic waters or of the exclusive economic zone, regardless of whether such right has been actually exercised or not, under the notion of "traditional fishing rights" such right would only be recognized if it has been *actually traditionally exercised* for a sufficient length of time.

Transportation and Navigation

Under Indonesian law, innocent passage for foreign vessels is recognized in the archipelagic waters. Thus, commercial transportation and navigation have not been affected at all under this regime. In fact, Indonesia, being archipelagic, is predominantly dependent on shipping and navigation, not only for its interinsular communication but also for its international trade and transportation. There is simply no other link between the archipelagic state of Indonesia and its major trading partners, including its immediate neighbors; since air transportation is often too expensive. Thus, it is one of the basic interests of Indonesia to promote international trade and navigation, through or within the archipelagic waters.

Admittedly, there is the problem of noncommercial vessels. For this purpose, a special regime of sealane passage has been designed through the archipelagic waters, which are important for transit navigation between the Indian and the Pacific Oceans. Under this regime, the right of foreign vessels to transit through such sealanes is recognized; yet such transit should be carried out in accordance with certain rules and regulations that are now being finalized at UNCLOS III. The sovereignty of the archipelagic state in archipelagic waters, including designated sealanes, is not however, questioned or affected, as reflected in Article 49 (4) of the Informal Composite Negotiating Text (ICNT). The whole purpose of establishing the archipelagic sealane passage regime is simply to facilitate international transit through the archipelagic waters. That is why the sealanes have been defined in the ICNT in terms of "axis": vessels are allowed to navigate through the sealanes following the axis, and are allowed to deviate from the axis only to a distance of not more than twenty-five miles from either side, provided further that they shall not approach the coasts closer than 10 percent of the distance of the waterways in narrow channels. The implementation of sealane transit principles through the archipelagic waters has yet to be worked out and regulated. Up to now, Indonesia has only established one sealane for fishing vessels through Makassar and Lombok Straits. The Indonesian government is now studying the possible location for other sealanes in the archipelagic waters.

Environmental Protection

For a long time Indonesia has thought of the archipelagic waters as an entire ecosystem. It would be extremely difficult, if not impossible, to protect the environment of the archipelagic waters by protecting only the coastline. The configuration of the waters and their characteristics are such as to require a single, unified approach. By acceptance of the archipelagic regime, it is now possible for the government to devise a unified policy, and national legislation is being worked out to that effect. Various local and provincial legislations throughout the archipelago are now being collected, sorted out, and analyzed, with a view to formulating new national legislation that will guarantee environmental protection for the archipelagic ecosystem as a whole.

The application of archipelagic principles also enables the government to exclude the use of archipelagic waters for dumping oil and other wastes, and enables the archipelagic state to take the necessary steps to protect the environment from such harms.

Problems

Although much has been done by way of implementing the archipelagic principles, many problems remain to be solved or worked out in detail. Some of the most important among them are:

a. In the field of administration and jurisdiction, the archipelagic waters have yet to be allocated to the various local provinces, especially in the Java, Banda and Flores Seas. This allocation is important in view of the need to exercise local governmental control, district court jurisdiction on civil or criminal matters, and enforcement of customs and immigration regulations.

b. In the field of national defence and security, much has also been done to protect the safety, stability, and unity of the country. Yet, much more has to be done, especially in strengthening law enforcement, which cannot be easily or quickly accomplished because of the emphasis given in national development planning to agriculture. Moreover, the problem of securing cooperation and effective coordination between the various enforcement agencies at sea requires constant attention. This problem will become much more complicated if the regime of the exclusive economic zone is to be added to those of the continental shelf and archipelagic waters.

CONTINENTAL SHELF

Since the notion of continental shelf refers to the seabed area beyond the territorial sea, it should be clearly kept in mind that, for Indonesia, its continental shelf lies well offshore, outside both the territorial sea and archipelagic waters. Therefore, although *geologically* speaking some of the seabed under Indonesian archipelagic waters or territorial sea may fall within the meaning of continental shelf, *legally* speaking Indonesia does not consider it as part of the regime of continental shelf but as part of the regime of archipelagic waters or territorial sea, according to which Indonesia has *full territorial sovereignty* over the area instead of merely *sovereign rights* to the exploration and exploitation of resources.

Based on the Geneva Continental Shelf Convention of 1958, Indonesia made a declaration on its continental shelf in February 1969, later enacted into Law No. 1, 1973. On the basis of these instruments, Indonesia has since successfully negotiated various boundary agreements with its neighbors; and most of them are now in force. Practically all Indonesian continental shelves in the Andaman Sea, the South China Sea, the Arafura Sea, and the Timor Sea have been delimited with India, Thailand, Malaysia, Papua New Guinea, and Australia. There are some unresolved issues, however; primarily the delimitation issues with Vietnam in the South China Sea, with Malaysia and the Philippines in the Celebes Sea, and with Australia in some parts of the Timor Sea. Indonesia is looking forward to the successful negotiation of those issues in the near future. Moreover, some tripartite arrangements would still have to be negotiated to tie up loose ends after boundary delimitation.

The recent trend at UNCLOS III seems to suggest that the outer limit of the continental shelf will be the "outer edge of the continental margin," however that phrase may be defined. If such trend prevails, Indonesia would have to define the outer edge of its continental margin in the Indian and Pacific Oceans in accordance with the text of the convention. Luckily, this problem would not require bilateral negotiations with neighboring countries, since there is no neighbor closer than 400 miles in the Indian and the Pacific Oceans and there is no neighbor having a mutual margin other than those stated above.

EXCLUSIVE ECONOMIC ZONE

Fisheries

It should be noted that Indonesia is one of the few countries in the Pacific and Indian Ocean regions that until now has not declared or established its own EEZ. This does not mean, however, that Indonesia will not have its EEZ in the near future. It should be reemphasized that, as far as Indonesia is concerned, its EEZ would be an area *outside* both its archipelagic waters and its territorial sea, and that the regime would be the same or as close as possible to the text of the ICNT.

Since Indonesia has not yet established an EEZ, the policy changes that may take place are hypothetical. Domestically, national legislation would have to be drafted that would give power to the central government to control and manage fisheries along the coasts, leaving the provincial governments to manage the coastal fisheries. New development programs would also have to be reoriented to the 200-mile EEZ, when and as far as necessary.

When Indonesia establishes its own EEZ outside its territorial sea around the Indonesian archipelago, the management of its EEZ and marine environment will have to be coordinated with the management of the archipelagic waters, since the two areas are interrelated and in physical fact would form an integrated ecosystem, although the legal regimes of the two areas are different.

Regionally speaking, arrangements with the neighboring landlocked and geographically disadvantaged states countries would have to be worked out, either through joint ventures or other means established by the coastal state. In fact, some joint venture arrangements have already been made with foreign companies for fishing in the Arafura Sea, which under the new law of the sea would fall under the EEZ of Indonesia.

Navigation

Since the freedom of navigation and overflight are recognized in the EEZ, there seems to be no need to make new arrangements. The only things that may be necessary here are perhaps: (1) The need to protect exploration and exploitation efforts in the EEZ and to see to it that such protection measures would not unduly cause problems to navigation and overflight; and (2) The need to ensure that navigation and overflight in the EEZ would be closely related to routes customarily used for international navigation in the EEZ or to transit through the archipelagic waters, especially through archipelagic sealanes. Presumably there would be no need for a vessel or an aircraft to be found in the Indonesian EEZ, unless it is in transit or on its way to transit the archipelagic waters. The freedom of navigation and overflight in the EEZ, therefore, would also have to be interpreted under the circumstances of an approach to the entry or exit points of the archipelagic sealanes.

There are, also, the problems of laying, repairing, and maintaining undersea cables and pipelines belonging to other states, but these problems, I believe, could be solved on the basis of the text of the new convention.

The conduct of other freedoms of the sea in the EEZ would depend very much on the provisions finally agreed to at UNCLOS III. As we all know, this is one of the remaining major issues in the current negotiations. From the coastal states, point of view, it would be only proper for them to make laws and regulations in the EEZ that would protect their sovereign rights and facilitate their efforts to make use of the natural resources under their jurisdiction. It would seem that this right would have to take precedence over other undetermined or undefined "freedoms" of the high seas.

Environmental Protection

In conformity with prevailing international law, such as the Brussels Intervention Convention of 1969 with regard to oil pollution caused by ships, and the trend at UNCLOS III, national legislation would have to be contemplated for the protection of the marine environment in the EEZ. National legislation would equally have to be formulated for the conduct of scientific research in the EEZ and over the continental shelf.

Like fisheries in the EEZ, the protection of the marine environment and the conduct of scientific research in the EEZ and on the continental shelf would have to be coordinated with the protection of the marine environment and the conduct of scientific research in the archipelagic waters and the territorial sea around them, although the legal regime of the archipelagic waters, the territorial sea, the EEZ, and the continental shelf are different. Both the protection of the marine environment and scientific research in the EEZ and on continental shelf, on the one hand, and those in the archipelagic waters and territorial sea, on the other, are closely interrelated, and therefore need to be under the control of the coastal or archipelagic state concerned.

Two forms of regional cooperation are worth mentioning in this context: *first,* the joint efforts of the littoral states of the Straits of Malacca and Singapore, namely Indonesia, Malaysia, and Singapore; and *second,* the efforts of ASEAN, consisting of Indonesia, Malaysia, the Philippines, Singapore, and Thailand, through its Working Group on the Protection of the Marine Environment to protect the environment of the Southeast Asian waters.

With regard to the Straits of Malacca and Singapore, the three coastal states have agreed since their Joint Statement on November 16, 1971 that the safety of navigation in the Straits of Malacca and Singapore is the responsibility of the three coastal states and that they will cooperate toward this end, thus advancing the cause of protecting the marine environment through measures to enhance safety of navigation. One measure is the introduction of the traffic separation scheme (TSS) in the straits together with all its rules and regulations, including the requirement of a minimum under keel clearance (UKC) of 3.5 meters for all vessels navigating the straits. It is hoped that such measures will soon be endorsed by IMCO. The three coastal states have also established a Council of Ministers to handle the problems of safety of navigation and coordinate measures for protecting the marine environment in the Straits.

With regard to the ASEAN Working Group, the five member countries have been giving serious attention to the protection of the marine environment in Southeast Asia, especially in the ASEAN waters. They have also been obtaining cooperation on this matter from relevant international organizations such as UNEP and other agencies.

PROBLEMS

Delimitation

The establishment of the EEZ in Southeast Asia would definitely create problems of delimitation between opposite and adjacent states. It is interesting to note that the ICNT has formulated separate articles for the delimitation of EEZ, (Article 74) and continental shelf (Article 83) boundaries, although the principles adopted in both cases are very similar, if not the same. This raises a question whether the existing continental shelf boundaries could be taken as the boundaries for the EEZ as well, or whether a totally new set of boundary agreements for the EEZ would have to be negotiated. It would seem to me that the boundary of the EEZ between adjacent and opposite states would not necessarily be identical with those of the continental shelf, and therefore should be negotiated together. There are many reasons for this, such as:

1. The outer limit of the continental shelf ("200 miles or the outer edge of the continental margin") is not the same as the outer limit of the EEZ (200

miles). Since the two concepts are different and their outer limits are also different, the actual lines of delimitation between opposite and adjacent states could also be different.

2. The delimitation of the continental shelf boundaries could be very much influenced by various factors, such as the geomorphological and other seabed topography and configuration, while the delimitation of the EEZ, which is essentially for the water column area, would not be influenced by those seabed characteristics, at least not to the degree they influence the delimitation of the continental shelf. Therefore, while the boundary of continental shelf often deviates from the normal median line for various reasons, the reasons to deviate from the median line would be much less for the delimitation of the EEZ.

3. As I have stated above, the ICNT itself is devising two separate articles to deal with the issues, one for the EEZ and another for the continental shelf, thus implying the possibility of different delimitation of boundary lines of the EEZ and the continental shelf.

If the above situation is correct, in the sense that the boundary line of the continental shelf does not necessarily constitute the boundary line for the EEZ, then Indonesia, after establishing its own EEZ, would have to start a new round of negotiations with all its neighbors to determine the boundary of their respective EEZ.

Rights of Landlocked and Geographically Disadvantaged States

Although the principles for the arrangement of the rights and interests of this category of states have been stipulated in the ICNT, and therefore hopefully in the next convention, the actual implementation of those rights and interests would still have to be worked out in detail through bilateral agreements between the states concerned. As far as Indonesia is concerned, no attempt has been made at this stage, simply because Indonesia has not yet established its EEZ.

Applicable Seabed and Subsoil Regime

It is interesting to note that the EEZ regime would include also the seabed and subsoil beyond the twelve-mile territorial sea up to the distance of 200 miles from the baselines. At the same time, the continental shelf regime also includes the same seabed and subsoil beyond the twelve-mile territorial sea up to the distance of 200 miles from the baselines or up to the outer edge of the continental margin. What regime, then, is to be applied to the seabed and subsoil beyond twelve miles: the regime of EEZ or the regime of continental shelf? The answer to this question seems to be important, because the two regimes are different, especially in treating the rights and interests of the landlocked and geographically disadvantaged states and in the protection of the marine environment and scientific research.

In the absence of any rules to this effect, it would seem to me that an *optional* principle would be applied, in the sense that coastal states would have the liberty to choose which regime they wish to apply to such seabed and subsoil areas, depending on the interests they wish to protect.

REGIONAL ARRANGEMENTS

It is noted that the South Pacific Forum has decided to establish "a South Pacific Regional Fisheries Agency" that will be opened to all members of the forum as well as to all coastal countries in the South Pacific who support the sovereign rights of the coastal state to conserve and manage living resources, including highly migratory species, within the 200 mile zone. It is not clear whether Indonesia is considered by the Forum states to be one of the countries in the area that could join the Agency.

The problem in Southeast Asia could be different from the problem in the South Pacific. In view of the geographical proximity of the countries in Southeast Asia, where practically all the waters of the region outside the archipelagic waters and the territorial seas would be covered by the EEZ, it is not yet clear whether a new regional arrangement would be required or whether the arrangement through the regime of EEZ and semi-enclosed seas as now being developed in the ICNT would be sufficient. In any case, the member countries of ASEAN, namely, Indonesia, Malaysia, the Philippines, Singapore, and Thailand, have already established a special working group for environmental protection. They have also cooperated within the context of the CCOP to deal with the survey of petroleum resources in the region; and together with some other countries in the region, some of them have also cooperated under the Indo-Pacific Fisheries Council (IPFC), South East Asian Hydrographic Organization, and other bodies.

It is interesting also to note that of all the coastal countries in the Pacific and Indian Ocean regions, only the member countries of ASEAN have not yet taken any definite step toward the establishment of an EEZ or exclusive fishing zone. This is perhaps due to several considerations:

1. The preference to wait for the conclusion of UNCLOS III, so that the result of the conference would not be prejudiced by unilateral actions;
2. The geographical discrepancy among the ASEAN member countries, thus creating differences in attitude toward the new law of the sea, although the different views do not necessarily lead to confrontation or opposition. The desire to maintain harmony may have created the need for caution among the ASEAN countries; and
3. The desire to maintain and promote regional harmony and good-neighborly relations, thus the desire not to force things that are coming anyway.

I, for one, believe that the EEZ is being born normally, naturally and healthily, and therefore there is no reason to conduct a "caesarean operation" to force the birth through unilateral actions.

CONCLUSION

Within the last twenty years, Indonesia has been devoting its attention to implementing and enforcing the archipelagic state regime and the twelve-mile territorial sea. Much has been done in the fields of fisheries, navigation and environmental protection, as well as in the field of maintaining and promoting national unity, security, and stability. Yet much more has to be done in strengthening various national enforcement agencies at sea as well as in promoting effective coordination among the various national enforcement agencies.

Within the last ten years, Indonesia has also been devoting increasing attention to the development of its continental shelf resources outside its archipelagic waters and territorial sea. Significant and important progress has been achieved in negotiation with neighboring countries to delimit the continental shelf of the respective countries in the Andaman, South China, Arafura, and Timor Seas. Some boundary delimitations would still have to be negotiated, however, with Vietnam in the South China Sea, with Malaysia and the Philippines in the Celebes Sea, and with Australia in some parts of the Timor Sea. Given the spirit of good-neighborliness and the desire of the countries concerned to avoid the situation in which their respective positions might become intractable, I see no reason why delimitation negotiations could not be held in the near future, thus completing these continental shelf boundary lines. In addition, some tripartite points would still have to be negotiated in order to tie up the loose ends of the bilateral continental shelf boundary negotiations. Moreover, the "outer edge of the continental margin" of Indonesia in the Indian and the Pacific Oceans would still have to be studied, defined, and delimited in the near future.

Indonesia and other ASEAN member countries are among the few states in the Indian and Pacific regions that, for various reasons, have not yet established their own respective EEZ or exclusive fishing zone. When the proper time comes, Indonesia will almost certainly establish also its own EEZ. At that moment:

1. Negotiations would have to be undertaken again with the neighboring countries to delimit the respective EEZ boundaries.
2. Negotiations would seem to be appropriate with the adjacent neighboring landlocked and geographically disadvantaged to determine and regulate their participation in the exploitation of the living resources of the EEZ in accordance with the text of the convention or at least with the ICNT.
3. National development programs would, whenever necessary, be adjusted to the 200-mile EEZ, and the various national enforcement agencies at sea would have to be substantially strengthened and more efficiently coordinated.

There has been effective cooperation between the littoral states of the Straits of Malacca and Singapore to promote the safety of navigation in the straits, thus promoting the efforts to protect the marine environment. Equally, there has been cooperation among the ASEAN member countries against pollution in the Southeast Asian waters. It is, however, still uncertain, whether regional cooperation in other fields would be required in the near future, in view of the fact that most, if not all, of the waterways in Southeast Asia would fall under the sovereignty or sovereign rights of the coastal states.

It is possible that this situation, for nationalistic and other political reasons, may reduce rather than increase the possibility for regional cooperation on matters that would fall under national sovereignty, sovereignty rights or jurisdiction. But it is equally possible that, given the diversity of the states in Southeast Asia, either in size, level of economic development, or natural resources, regional cooperation based on the principles of state sovereignty and sovereignty rights would be possible and even perhaps necessary. Indonesia, for one, has already been cooperating with its ASEAN partners in the field of petroleum; and Singapore, as a trading center and a base for exploration and exploitation, has already taken some benefit from the oil exploration and exploitation in Southeast Asian offshore areas. If cooperation is possible for oil, other or similar cooperation, based on the principles of state sovereignty and sovereign rights mentioned above, could also be possible in the EEZ in Southeast Asia as a whole.

Commentary

Lee Alverson
National Marine Fisheries Service

Professor McKernan has covered much of what I intended to say, and Professor Takabayashi also made a number of comments that were relevant to what I had in mind. But perhaps I might make some rather short comments and answer some of the questions raised by Professor Miles.

I see some disadvantages in being the last on the agenda. Much of what has been said is being recycled at this point. Having some training in population dynamics, I have made some notes and observations. It appears to me that the population of a conference is maximized at the outset. Almost immediately there is a decline in the stock caused by the departure of some exotic species, that I presume are press, politicians, and those who feel that everything that is worth being said was said in the opening address. Then I have observed a short period of stability in the numbers with, however, a slow but perceptible decline in numbers. I suspect this may be a density-dependent feature, but I think it is more likely to be density independent. After a couple of days I have noted some changes appear in the structure and morphology in the appearance of the people at this conference; the addition of some adipose tissue suggesting a very good supply in the local area and a reddening of the epidermis that has some peculiar relationship to this particular environment. This leaves us at this point with a very small residual population. What are the advantages of this? Well, I have been told that the residual population is a tenacious group of intellectual people, who are the bright ones and really want to know. There has been one other interpretation that they are the dull ones, who have not found out that the external environment has more to offer than oratory at this conference. Now, you can take your choice.

Let me move on and examine some of the questions that have been raised in the North Pacific context. Perhaps I can be excused for being very parochial about this, looking at it from the vantage point of the Fishery Conservation and Management Act (FCMA) of the United States, since I have been preoccupied recently with its technical implementation and with providing the technical and scientific input into the decision making of two of the eight Councils that have been established in the United States under the new statute. In any event, after eight years of association with UNCLOS III I have really lost my capacity to understand the significance of what is going on at the global level. At the regional level—particularly between Canada, the United States, and the distant-water countries operating in the Northeast Pacific—what has been happening?

First, the scientific institutions associated with these appear to have had a major breakdown in that part of the world. The International North Pacific Fisheries Commission, a technical-scientific forum, to a large extent no longer exists as a source of technical input into decision making or the development of management plans. Somehow or other, the international community operating in the Northeastern Pacific has not yet identified its appropriate roles in supplying an information input into the new Regional Council of the United States. Instead there is a tendency to deal at a national, political, government-to-government level in trying to influence decisions rather than providing input at the appropriate technical level.

This may be corrected when there is a better understanding of the new law, but at present there is a major void, a total lack of provision for exchange of technical, statistical, and biological information in the Northeastern Pacific as a result of the U.S. act. This suggests that we need some sort of new scientific forum, as Barbara Johnson mentioned the other day, a body that would be somewhat released from the concepts of administrative responsibility and more closely associated with the problems of environmental and resource management. We are now looking at that possibility in the Institute essentially to resolve this particular issue. We need a peer group review of scientific activity in the North Pacific, something that no longer exists. If this does not happen, I am rather convinced we will end with nationalized sciences; and far be it from me to suggest that scientists will be willing to conform to the political and economic pressures on them to come to some decisions that support the parochial interest. But that may be what will happen if we do not reestablish a more effective international peer group review in this particular area.

I think it is also important to eliminate redundancies in scientific effort that have arisen in the past through a variety of bilateral and multilateral arrangements. What we need is a single forum where all the parties can get together and have an appropriate dialogue that relates to technical assessment of the stocks in the Northeast Pacific. I think there is a hesitancy on the part of certain people to give up the old forums; if we had a single forum such as ICES in the North Atlantic, it would cut down substantially on the traveling, and this might not be acceptable to some globe-trotters.

As to the other issues, I do see the problems of allocation of surplus. They have been dealt with by Professors McKernan and Munro. There is the problem of ability to establish what the total allowable catch is, and then identify the surplus that should be available to foreign nationals. There is the problem of identifying "national capacity." It is not quite clear in some minds what is intended under the legislation to constitute an "excess." The transboundary stock issue has already been discussed by a number of speakers. I will only suggest that at times this problem is overstated. In reality the managerial problems associated with transboundary stocks relate not merely to fish with tails that move across certain boundaries but to the vast proportion of the biomass that is transboundary in character. For a great number of species, for example, between Canada and the United States, and also between Mexico and the United States on the west coast, the transboundary issue is not of major importance and is not a problem that is insurmountable, either for purposes of "biological management" or from the viewpoint of particular national (social or economic) objectives. Nor do I think that the much-discussed problem of highly mobile species is insurmountable. In a recent critical FAO paper written by Gunar Saderstall, some guidelines on how we might address this problem are put forward. There are certainly a number of alternative approaches.

One thing our act does not provide is some amplification of the different concepts of science policy underlying the FCMA and other national legislation, such as the Marine Mammals Act, the Coastal Zone Management Act, and others. They are incompatable at a national level, and perhaps also as perceived by other countries who would operate in the U.S. economic zone. From a practitioner's standpoint I think one of the major problems I perceive in this age of multiple legislative approaches to ocean management is that of the details that this kind of legislation seems to require at the national level. In the United States it is rather formidable. That is, the documentation process, the research underpinning that is supposed to be mandated by the act, requires a rather meticulous procedure in following through to the conclusion of a management decision. In many respects the juridical concepts or implications are not yet understood, and I guess they have to be ferreted out over the next several years.

I do want to make a comment on environment in response to a comment made over the last few days. I think the environmental issue is important, but I am a little bit concerned about the types of expressions used. The terms "tragedy" and "catastrophe" are terms that convey different meanings to different people and establish a certain fear syndrome in the public mind. I would much rather that the individual tempted to use these terms talk about these dangers in a more quantitative sense. What is the "tragedy" of an oil spill or blowout in relation to fish destroyed at a time when we need urgently to produce energy? Is it a fact that the oil in a given situation has generated some biological "catastrophe"? The annual fish mortality caused by direct exploitation in the Bering Sea alone exceeds every one of the major oil spills that have occurred across the world over the last ten years. All these things have to be put in the proper perspective. "Catastrophe" is not a very meaningful thing as far as I am concerned, and it may divert our energies. I still think that at the present time the greatest threat to the resources in the ocean are those associated with direct exploitation activities. In the long term, resource mismanagement may be the most serious source of environmental degradation at sea. I do not like to see the two divorced, because I do not think they are mutually exclusive. In making an examination of living resource management, one needs to have a total understanding of the acts or mortalities that are being imposed, and I do not really see how you can examine so-called environmental protection unless you understand clearly what is it you are trying to protect and from what.

Finally, what about the new U.S. fishery legislation? Is it achieving its goals? It think it is a little early to pass judgment on the decisions that have been made under the act, and I am going to be a little caustic to Professor Munro, in response to one of his comments: the implication that the dismissal of joint venture activities in the North Pacific was due to U.S. fear of competition with low-paid foreigners in the off-shore. I think this comment shows only a preliminary understanding of why that decision was made. I quite understand that that was the industry's concern, but let me point out that in the Korean venture, which would have reallocated 130,000 tons away from the Japanese, the Korean applicants had not demonstrated that they had been unable to line up one U.S. vessel for the exploitation purpose. In fact, there had been no technical exploration of whether this type of venture could be successful at all, no evidence of a harvest capacity to supply that particular venture, which would have meant that we would have disinvested the Japanese exploitation of that particular resource for an unknown, unidentified U.S. interest. There was no fleet capacity to be involved or identified, no technical evidence that it could go forward. I think the essential reaction was that it not be permitted till such time that some evidence has been demonstrated, that the applicants had lined up the appropriate harvesting capability in the U.S. fleet, before we disinvested a major Japanese fishery. As far as the Soviet-U.S. venture is concerned the same can be said. That case was not as difficult, because we did not have to disinvest another country involved, but even in that venture there was not one U.S. vessel that had signed to fish with that venture, so that it is questionable whether there was a legitimate right to go ahead and authorize the venture. It is, however, true that strictly from an industry point of view there was the fear that the low labor costs of foreign fishermen were going to put the domestic processor out of business. But, as I say, I think we should be careful in making judgments about what is going on within the Council itself.

From my perspective, one of the major objectives of the act is the conservation of the resources, and I suspect for the first time in twenty-five years in the Northeastern Pacific the stocks are now under fairly rigid control, and do have an opportunity of rebuilding.

Commentary

Alberto Szekely
Institute of Legal Research
University of Mexico

I should like to speak briefly about the exclusive economic zone established by Mexico. First of all, why was the Mexican exclusive economic zone adopted, and why was it adopted when it was adopted? Mexico felt that by 1976 a legal justification had arisen for establishing an exclusive economic zone: namely, that a consensus was developing at UNCLOS III to justify such an action. The reason why it was adopted when it was adopted can be seen in two ways. First, the decision to establish the zone was based on the fact that its establishment could help to consolidate that consensus. Mexico proceeded to the adoption of its exclusive economic zone on the basis of the Revised Single Negotiating Text of 1976. As a matter of fact, the Mexican law is a copy of the relevant articles of the RSNT. Second, however, there was another reason for establishing the zone in 1976 instead of waiting for the conference to end, as in the case of Indonesia, which we have just heard about—namely, a domestic political reason. With a change of administration coming at the end of 1976, the president of Mexico at the time, who had advocated originally the patrimonial sea idea and later supported the exclusive economic zone concept by giving very specific instructions to the Mexican delegation, felt that it was necessary for history to record the establishment of the zone within his administration. Other than that there were no other reasons for establishing the zone, such as the need to protect our natural resources. The best proof of this fact is Mexico's traditional negligence regarding its marine resources, despite the fact that it is a large coastal state.

I should also like to refer to Mexico's unique marine position. Mexico is one of the twelve countries that would benefit the most, in terms of area, by establishment of an economic zone. The only other developing country on the list is Indonesia. Mexico is a very large coastal state with 10,000 kilometers of coastline, and it could be said that it is a very rich marine state. Very recently an inventory of Third World marine resources was prepared, and what comes clear out of this work is that very few developing countries benefit from the establishment of an exclusive economic zone of 200 miles as much as Mexico does. The abundance of living resources and its peculiar geographic position in regard to undersea minerals makes Mexico a country greatly benefited by the establishment of the EEZ. Before we established our economic zone, Mexico had a twelve-mile territory sea and no national development plan for the exploitation of the living resources within our territorial sea. As a matter of fact, our fishing activity was very limited. Our national fishery institute estimates that there are about 500 species of potential commercial value within our 200-mile zone, of which we presently exploit twenty, only five of which are of high commercial value besides the tuna of the Eastern Pacific. It is also estimated that the potential harvest within Mexico's exclusive economic zone is between half a million and three quarters of a million tons a year, without taking into account the sardines of the Gulf of California, which are estimated to have an abundance of about half a million tons.

The very fact that we have such a large coast line opens up great possibilities in coastal management. We have large oil deposits under our continental shelf within the Gulf of Mexico, especially in the southern sector. The most interesting aspect, I believe, and one that has received very little attention within the country, is the existence of manganese nodules within the Mexican exclusive economic zone. Studies of the geographical distribution of nodules have produced varying estimates of the concentration and quality of manganese nodules within the Mexico zone. For instance, there is a map being circulated here that shows that Mexico is the only country with significant concentrations of manganese nodules within its economic zone. Mexico also has an international interest in nodules, because of its relative proximity to the large mineral deposits within the Clipperton Islands area, which is supposed to be the richest nodule field of all. Mexico will undoubtedly have an interest in processing plants both for its own manganese nodules, whenever it acquires the capability to exploit them, and also for the manganese nodules of the international seabed area.

Now, in response to the questions that have been put to me, I am going to be very brief. As regards changes in policy since the establishment of our exclusive economic zone, I believe that Mexico has not yet acquired a really developed national consciousness of the importance of its marine resources for the future of the national economy. There are very few agencies, governmental or private, interested in acquiring as much knowledge as possible on the potential of these resources. Unfortunately, I do not see any major effort aimed at taking full advantage of the benefits that could be gained from the establishment of the exclusive economic zone. Unfortunately also, the problem of our national fishing industry, which is plagued with corruption problems, leads us to expect that the traditional problems that Mexico has had with its exploitation of land resources—

not only mining but also agriculture—which have kept our country in constant social turmoil, will probably be transplanted to the management of our ocean resources. The establishment of the economic zone has not really led to a change in policy toward the exploitation of marine resources.

There is some evidence of a tendency of the new government to enter into several joint ventures, but of a very limited nature and without the framework of a national development plan. As to the impact on existing arrangements, Mexico was not committed really to any conventional arrangements for the exploitation of these marine resources before the establishment of the exclusive economic zone, other than the Inter-American Tropical Tuna Commission for the yellowfin tuna of the Eastern Pacific. In the exercise of its right to choose with whom to enter into arrangements for the exploitation of surpluses, Mexico has recently concluded agreements with the United States and Cuba for the surpluses of some of those five species that I have mentioned.

Have there been any problems solved by the establishment of the Mexican exclusive economic zone? Frankly, I think not. This may be the natural result of the political nature of the establishment of the zone. Other than the regulation of foreign fishing within our 200 miles, the problems that could be solved through the establishment of the zone are really more of a national character. For instance, the establishment of a zone could obviously help to increase the food supply for the fastest increasing population in the world, which is Mexico's. It could also help solve the problem of unemployment, but, as I said, in the absence of a development plan for marine resources, these problems do not seem to be in the process of solution.

Which problems have been created, or remain unsolved, besides the previously mentioned ones, because of the creation of the zone? First of all, problems of enforcement could not be regarded as peculiar to Mexico. The problem of enforcement is common to all countries that are establishing 200-mile zones. Our main problem that remains to be solved is the problem of evaluation of resources. We lack a national inventory of resources. We do not have a precise idea of the abundance of species and other resources. We have very little knowledge even of our own harvesting capacity, and therefore it will be difficult to estimate the total allowable catch of specific species if Mexico does undertake a major fishing effort within a development plan. Therefore, the greatest challenge to Mexico now is to know what our resources are, before we can prepare a plan of development. There are other problems that remain to be solved, such as that of boundary delimitation. We have delimited sea boundaries with the United States and Cuba within the Gulf of Mexico, and with the United States in the Pacific, but not for the seabed with the United States. We are going to have a difficult problem with delimitation of our marine boundaries with Guatemala, because we have a traditional conflict there over what criterion should be followed to divide our waters, and, of course, we have the very difficult problem of delimitation with British Honduras—a problem Mexico has left pending until the problem of the legal status of that territory is resolved. As you know, Mexico has defended the position that the people of British Honduras should exercise their right of self-determination.

As to regional arrangements, if we adopt Professor Miles' definition of regional arrangement, then we could include the bilateral agreements that we have concluded with the United States and Cuba within the Gulf, which deal mostly with delimitation problems and living resources. But as pointed out earlier this week, Mexico should take the initiative for regional cooperation in environmental management of the Gulf and Caribbean, because of the possible detrimental effects of oil exploitation both on Mexico's and the United States' continental shelf. Finally, Mexico has found that the establishment of an exclusive economic zone, and the very existence of the new institution of the EEZ within the new law of the sea, makes the present arrangements under the Inter-American Tropical Tuna Commission completely incompatible with coastal state authority, and it will be necessary to adjust that regime to the new realities in the law of the sea. For this reason, Mexico together with Costa Rica convened a conference of plenipotentaries in September of this year in San José, Costa Rica, for the adoption of a new regional arrangement for the exploitation of the highly migratory species of the Eastern Pacific. At this conference we have aimed at implementing the two objectives of conservation and optimum utilization through regional arrangements. In Mexico's view, these objectives can be attained through a system by which a global maximum quota is adopted annually, one which will be respected by all the countries that are members of today's IATTC, through nationally allocated quotas calculated on the basis of resource adjacency.

In conclusion, I would submit that Mexico's establishment of an economic zone is really just a gesture so far. It will not make us any richer, as long as the country does not have the national will to rationally exploit the resources of our zone.

Commentary

Kiyofumi Nakauchi
Japan International Cooperation Agency

At an earlier session, Professor Takabayashi, Dr. Park, and others explained in detail how Japan and its neighboring coastal states have been involved in the establishment of the 200-mile limit. Nevertheless, let me make some additional comments on the situation in the Northwest Pacific region, and then respond to the five questions presented by Professor Miles.

Following the United States and the Soviet Union, the Japanese national Diet passed the "Law on Provisional Measures Relating to the Fishing Zone" in May 1977 for the purpose of securing something like an equivalent position in negotiating with the Soviet Union new provisional arrangements for reciprocal fishing within their respective 200-mile zones. This 200-mile fishing zone legislation has some features worth noting. First, the Japanese fishing zone is limited to certain designated areas: in some areas in the Japan Sea and along the coast in the East China Sea, twelve miles was prescribed as the outer limit of the fishing zone. Also, the Japanese 200-mile limit is not applied in areas adjacent to China and South Korea, so that Chinese and South Korean fishermen are presently permitted to fish even within the designated fishing zone boundary.

There are two major reasons for these provisional measures. First, Japan wished to avoid involvement in the territorial conflicts with South Korea over claims to Takeshima Island in the Japan Sea, and also with Taiwan and China, which are claiming the Senkaku Islands in the East China Sea. Second, Japan does not wish to provoke China and South Korea, whose fishery relations with Japan are still delicate, though restabilized. The new balance depends upon two recent treaties: an official Japanese-Chinese fishery agreement, replacing a nongovernmental arrangement which lasted over twenty years, and the 1965 Japanese-South Korean fishery agreement. As a result, Japanese fishing has been allowed to increase somewhat to higher catch levels in the Sea of Japan and the East China Sea.

After Japan's unilateral action in July 1977, North Korea declared the establishment of a 200-mile economic zone, and in September 1977 the second commission of the Japanese-North Korean Friendship Promotion Association visited North Korea, partly in order to sound out the possibility of concluding a nongovernmental fishery agreement. After these negotiations the North Korean authorities announced that: (1) Japanese fishermen would be allowed to fish within the Korean 200-mile limit without any entry fee or license; and (2) these tentative measures would be implemented from October 1977 to June 1978.

North Korea also announced the establishment of a so-called military warning zone, designed to preserve the 200-mile economic zone and to protect it from military threats. This special zone is fifty nautical miles wide in the Japan Sea, but it overlaps with the economic zone in the Yellow Sea. In this military zone, all military aircraft and warships are prohibited. Civil vessels and aircraft, on the other hand, are permitted to navigate in and over that special zone with advance consent of the North Korean authorities. It is emphasized that civil vessels or aircraft having military purposes or trespassing economic interests are prohibited from passing through the military zone. Without special agreement, it would be impossible for Japanese fishermen to engage safely in fishing in the Korean military zone. The North Koreans have suggested that the Japanese government secure a temporary nongovernmental agreement between the Association and North Korea, but the Japanese government has not yet responded positively, since the two governments have no diplomatic relations and the Japanese government maintains the policy of strengthening political and economic ties with South Korea. Moreover, it is Japan's contention that such a military zone violates generally accepted international rules. Regardless of such arguments, it seems that continuous and safe fishing operation within the North Korean 200-mile zone would depend chiefly on preserving a balance between Japan's political and economic relations with North Korea and those with South Korea.

South Korea has hinted that the establishment of its own 200-mile economic zone is now under consideration. This has been delayed partly because of the territorial issues in the general region. South Korea as well as Japan has been inhibited from taking unilateral initiatives because of the sensitivity of these issues. Perhaps the most serious of these is that of delimiting the continental shelf in the East China Sea. This area is clearly vital to the coastal nations, since the substrata, particularly around the Senkaku Islands over which Taiwan, Japan, and China have made conflicting claims, may include large amounts of petroleum, as suggested in the ECAFE report. It seems that the islands may have extremely valuable oil reserves offshore, and it does not seem fair and equitable, to me at least, that the Senkaku Islands should have too decisive a bearing on the question of title to these reserves.

As for Japanese and South Korean agreements on the delimitation on the continental shelf, within a joint development area Japan and South Korea will jointly exploit submarine resources, especially petroleum and natural gas, for more than fifty years and share benefits as well as costs for exploration and exploitation on an equal basis. In Japan special laws and regulations are now being prepared for implementing the finally ratified delimitation agreement between South Korea and Japan. This joint development zone in the East China Sea exists, as a matter of fact, on the Japanese side of the supposed median line between Japan, China and South Korea.

In 1973 when the delimitation agreement between South Korea and Japan was signed, the Chinese authorities strongly protested, insisting that both governments should take full responsibility for any consequences that might ensue from the implementation of the bilateral agreements. The Chinese position is, I think, that delimitation should be made in consultation with all the parties concerned, and that in the event of nonagreement there cannot be any mechanical application of the median line principle. Presently, China shows no sign of intending to set up its 200-mile limit along the coast in the East China Sea. It appears that China has very little necessity to begin exploring and exploiting submarine petroleum in the sea, although it has been eager to develop off shore oil in the Pohai Bay, an area of internal waters whose average depth is less than fifty meters. China continues to develop new oil deposits on land more vigorously than ever, and is self-sufficient with domestic production on land and probably in the Pohai Bay.

With regard to boundaries in the Japan and East China Seas, my personal preference would be draw median lines and disregard Senkaku and Takeshima Islands. The existence of economically and politically differentiated states and of some serious territorial issues in the Northwest Pacific region should not be allowed to discourage regional cooperative arrangements for effective fishery management as well as environmental protection. Regional arrangements will no doubt be required in the future in order to effectively manage living and nonliving resources, and to prevent environmental contamination which may be caused by off-shore petroleum exploitation in the East China and Japan Seas, and within the Soviet 200-mile limit, for instance, in some areas close to the Sakhalin Islands.

Some brief comments on Japanese fishery policy problems. The new economic zone regime has considerably affected the Japanese fishing industry. Yet despite the nation's heavy dependence on fisheries, its development of a large-scale fishing industry, and the unique fish-eating habits of the Japanese people, I do not notice the government of Japan has changed its fundamental policies and ultimate goals. It is now a matter of national priority for the government to manage the living resources much more effectively within the new 200-mile limit, to maintain annual fish production levels as much as possible, and not to reduce the degree of national self-sufficiency in fish supply. However, the method of realizing these goals must be changed. For example, the Japanese government should strengthen its diplomatic efforts in negotiations with other coastal states over the calculation of total allowable catch and available surpluses of less utilized living resources, on the basis of existing scientific, economic and social considerations. On the other hand, the new ocean regime opens Japan's eyes to the need for more effective and fuller utilization of living resources within its 200-mile fishing zone and beyond. For that purpose Japan is beginning a number of new, large- and small-scale, fishery redevelopment plans. Here I can indicate only a few examples: the development of artificial fishing grounds, more efforts for increasing breeding and hatching capability, exploitation of unutilized species such as deep-sea bottom fish, and in particular the exploitation of krill in the Antarctic Ocean and other species outside national jurisdiction.

Finally, I would like to comment on the future of regional fishery arrangements. Existing fishery arrangements in the subregion of Northwest Pacific are separated from each other and based on bilateral agreements, due to political and economic complexity and uncertainty. Unless such conditions are improved and territorial issues are also finally settled, it is difficult to expect a significant improvement in subregional fishery cooperation in the Northwest Pacific. However, I think it is quite desirable to consider the possibility of setting up a regional fishery commission for the entire North Pacific sphere, whose membership would be open to all coastal and geographically disadvantaged states in the North Pacific Rim region. The commission's major task would be to collect information and scientific data and to carry out scientific research with independent scientists and survey vessels. Hopefully, the commission could eventually be converted into a fishery management body authorized to decide MSY and total allowable catch of major important species of fish and to devise proper systems for fish allocation and revenue sharing among member states and other newcomers.

Discussion

Perhaps we should ask two of our panelists to respond to comments addressed to them: first, Professor Munro, about whom certain nasty things were said, and to whom a specific question was addressed; and then Mr. Rozental.

Gordon Munro: First, let me deal with the nasty remark. I must confess that until yesterday the example of protectionism I was planning to use was that of the bill on offshore oil transshipments to the United States, but I decided I might get keel hauled by some of the audience. So I thought I would play it safe and take an example from Professor McKernan's paper. I am quite prepared to admit that there might be all sorts of other reasons why the joint venture schemes in Alaska and off the coast of Washington were put to one side; but, to the extent that the complaints from the industry about low-cost foreign competition played a major factor in that decision, then my point still holds, and certainly the impression given in the McKernan paper was that this was a major factor. With regard to the question, the biological model that we were using is one that we, in Canada at least, still use extensively for management purposes. Clearly, in cases where the Schaefer model is inapplicable, my comments may be inapplicable.

Andres Rozental: I will be very brief. Alberto Szekely painted a rather bleak picture of Mexico and its exclusive economic zone. In the two years since the adoption of the Mexican exclusive economic zone began being planned in 1975, some encouraging things have also occurred in Mexico. We have upgraded the government department that used to handle fishing matters to a cabinet-level department of fisheries with a very much larger staff; we have concluded bilateral agreements with the United States and Cuba, which among other things will give Mexico over two million dollars a year of additional income in the form of fees and license income from surplus; we have concluded, at a much higher level, scientific research agreements with the United States and Cuba to improve our understanding of the existence of living resources within our economic zone in the Gulf; we have undertaken a campaign to increase domestic consumption of fish in Mexico, which, unfortunately, traditionally has been very low, one of the lowest per capita for a coastal, resource-rich country; we have undertaken joint ventures with some countries that have lost (in some sense) by the establishment of economic zones (countries such as Spain, whose fleets were almost totally idled because of the loss of their traditional fishing grounds) in order to use their technology and their harvesting capacity within our economic zone; we have adopted a national fishery plan for the first time in Mexican history, which foresees within the next six years of this administration a 380 percent increase in catch; we have undertaken the renegotiation of the Atlantic Tuna agreement, whereby Mexico is demanding a 40 percent increase in catch quota allocations this year; and we are making changes in our national legislation to eliminate a stumbling block to fishery development in Mexico, whereby fishing cooperatives were given the exclusive right to harvest certain species in Mexico, specifically shrimp. This, unfortunately, has not worked as well as it was supposed to. It was a social experiment more than anything else and probably will be changed in the near future.

Regarding mineral resources in the economic zone, Mexico has about twenty billion barrels of proven reserves on its land territory and within its territorial sea and about 100 billion barrels of probable reserves, and that does not count what exists beyond twelve miles up to 200 miles in the Gulf and in the Pacific, especially off the coast of Baja, California. So I believe that Dr. Szekely's picture is bleaker than it should be. We have a lot of problems in Mexico, and, as he has said, we have not been able to fully utilize and maximize the benefits. But as he also said, Mexico is probably one of the developing countries most benefited by the economic zone; and, being a developing country, we have all sorts of problems that slowly will make the maximization of our economic zone resources a medium- to long-term effort.

Special Caucus: The South Pacific and the Law of the Sea

Chairman
John Craven
Law of the Sea Institute

John Craven: First, I want to explain why we are having this caucus, and why I think it is a significant addition to the conference agenda. Since we started preparing this program a dynamic movement for regionalization has been taking place here in the Pacific on the part of the South Pacific Forum nations. Already they have come to a tentative regional agreement with respect to their fishing zones, and indeed these same nations will be meeting again this week in Suva to continue these discussions seeking a more permanent regional solution for their fishery problems. We felt this conference would be seriously deficient if we did not have some discussion of the issues arising and of the precedents that might be set as a result of these actions by the South Pacific nations. To that end we decided to set up a caucus—and very much a caucus in which you all are participants.

In seeking a caucus leader we exchanged correspondence with Prime Minister Ratu Mara of Fiji, who, as you know, has long been a leader in law of the sea diplomacy. Prime Minister Ratu Mara suggested to us that the most able caucus leader we could find was Joji Kotobalavu, his foreign minister, and we prevailed upon him at short notice, to accept an arduous flight schedule to come to our conference. With him is Mr. Donald McLoughlin, who is the Fiji delegate at UNCLOS III, and together they represent the distilled essence of Fijian wisdom in the law of the sea.

I would like to complete my introduction by quoting a reply I just heard our distinguished speaker give to the question of what time it was in Fiji: two hours behind, but a day ahead! With that progressive thought in mind, I have pleasure in turning the forum over to a "day-ahead" leader of regionalism in the South Pacific. Secretary Kotobalavu.

The South Pacific and the Law of the Sea

Joji Kotobalavu
Foreign Minister of Fiji

INTRODUCTION

I should like first of all to express my warm thanks to the Law of the Sea Institute for the honor of being invited to take part in the proceedings of your eleventh conference. We have been greatly encouraged by your interest in recent developments in the South Pacific on law of the sea matters. I personally have found my attendance here quite rewarding and useful. As some of you may know, countries in the South Pacific, including countries with interests in our region, will be meeting in Fiji this Friday to work out details of a South Pacific Regional Fisheries Agency.

We in Fiji and the other island countries of the South Pacific have followed with close and keen interest the progress of UNCLOS III. I say progress because we do share the hope that there will eventually be a satisfactory accommodation of the diverse interests represented at the conference. In fact we regard the successful conclusion of a global law of the sea treaty as essential to our future economic well-being, and principally for three reasons.

First, we are all, with the exceptions of New Zealand, Papua New Guinea, and Australia, small island countries with relatively limited land resources. For us, the only way we can hope to expand our economy is in the exploitation of the resources of the ocean around us. Therefore, the consensus or near-consensus at the United Nations Law of the Sea Conference on the right of coastal states to establish exclusive economic zones is a development that will have a direct positive impact on our efforts to develop a viable economy and to expand employment opportunities for our people.

Second, there are states, like Fiji, that are not just island states, but states composed of hundreds of islands often separated by pockets of high seas within their island group. Yet for us, the sea has always been regarded not just as the link among our component islands but as the element that gives our country its unity. We have, therefore, greatly welcomed the consensus at UNCLOS III in favor of a separate regime for mid-ocean archipelagic states like Fiji. We view this as an acceptance by the international community of the essential unity of land territory and archipelagic waters of an island state like Fiji, while, of course, recognizing the right of overflight and sea passage.

Third, as small countries, we do not have the necessary means and facilities to enforce recognition of our exclusive economic zones. It is, therefore, to a global law of the sea treaty that we shall have to look for the recognition and protection of our exclusive rights to manage the resources of our economic zone for the benefit of our people.

With the progress so far achieved at UNCLOS III, countries in the South Pacific have taken actions at two levels.

At the *national* level, countries have adopted, or are in the process of adopting, legislation that will enable them to declare 200-mile exclusive economic zones. New Zealand has actually established its economic zone. Australia, Papua New Guinea, and Western Samoa have already passed legislation under which they will be able to declare their economic zones. In Fiji's case, our Parliament will at its session commencing later this month be looking at draft legislation that will enable us to establish an archipelagic state regime and declare a 200-mile exclusive economic zone, although we have yet to decide when exactly we shall declare baselines and zone. However, at its meeting in Papua New Guinea in August of this year, the South Pacific Forum, which comprises the eleven independent states and self-governing countries in the South Pacific, decided that member countries should endeavor to complete by the end of March of next year all the necessary legislative and administrative procedures to establish their individual exclusive economic zones.

At the *regional* level, the South Pacific Forum has decided that a South Pacific Regional Fisheries Agency should be established. While the countries will be establishing national economic zones, they see merit in regional cooperative and collaborative arrangements, basically for two reasons:

First, because almost all of these countries will have common boundaries, because of the limited technology they have at this stage to take the allowable catch, and because of their limited capability to enforce recognition and acceptance of their exclusive rights, it makes sense that they should pool their *economic zone* resources and coordinate actions to ensure that in their exploitation the maximum possible benefit will accrue to them.

Second, there is an acceptance of the need to enter into regional arrangements to ensure that the *high seas* resources of the region are exploited not to the disadvantage of the South Pacific nations and to ensure that in the management of these resources there is recognition of the very heavy dependence of these countries on the resources of the sea for their economic future.

The decision to set up the South Pacific Fisheries Agency is *not* a reaction against the rather slow progress at the United Nations Law of the Sea Conference. This initiative has been taken within the context of the recognition by UNCLOS III of the desirability for regional cooperative and collaborative arrangements. In fact, the Forum countries have interpreted this recognition as the necessary mandate for them to act. Entering into regional arrangements on matters of common interest and concern to them is not something new: we already have existing regional arrangements to pool resources in education and training, and to promote cooperation in shipping, civil aviation, trade, and telecommunications.

However, while a decision has been made to set up a South Pacific Regional Fisheries Agency, detailed aspects of this organization have yet to be worked out. At its meeting in Port Moresby in August 1977 only two guidelines were set by the Forum: first, the Agency should be basically an *advisory* body (i.e., the authority to determine the allowable catch and to allocate surplus economic zone resources will remain vested in each coastal state): and second, the Agency would be open to all Forum countries and all countries in the region with coastal states interests who support the sovereign rights of the coastal state to conserve and manage living resources, including highly migratory species, in its 200-mile economic zone.

There are, then several questions that remain to be answered. For instance, what should be the exact nature and objectives of the Agency? Does it apply only to the living resources of the economic zone, or will it also embrace the living resources of the high seas in the region? Will it cover only certain specific fish species in the economic zone? Will it cover certain specified fish species both in the economic zone and in the high seas? Will it cover conservation as well as management of resources or species? Will it also include research, marine environmental protection, and transfer of technology? These are some of the basic issues which hopefully will be clarified at the next meeting to be held in Fiji.

Personally, I am optimistic that a satisfactory regional arrangement will be agreed upon. There are already a number of working regional arrangements in other fields. It should have been agreed that the most practical approach is not to seek the ideal at this stage, but to begin with what is possible now. I would also like to stress again that our success in a regional arrangement will depend very much on the successful conclusion of a comprehensive treaty at UNCLOS III, for we see our regional arrangement not as an alternative to the global approach but as a necessary initiative to complement it.

That is all that I would like to say at this stage, but, as I said at the beginning, we shall be happy to answer any questions that you may like to put forth.

Questions

Question: You spoke of a possible intergovernmental regime or policy relating to fish on the high seas beyond the 200-mile zones. I looked at a map of the region recently and found there would be little left under the high seas regime. I would like your reaction to this—how much of the high seas would be left?

Joji Kotobalavu: These national zones will cover a geographical area stretching from Malaysia in the west to French Polynesia in the east; from the Gilbert Islands in the north, to New Zealand in the south—that covers a very wide area. It will be up to the Forum, or the countries of the Pacific, to decide whether in fact the Agency's scope should be limited mostly to the resources of their respective national economic zones. Our main concern is this: fish do not recognize national boundaries, either those between two national economic zones or between a coastal state and high seas. So, while we are talking about maximizing returns to us from the exploitation of marine resources, we may find ourselves in a situation where resources are taken away from us before they enter our economic zone, either from the economic zone of another country or from the high seas. It is for this practical reason that we in Fiji are very keen on entering into regional arrangements.

Donald McLoughlin: With regard to pockets of the high seas off to the northwest of Fiji there is a pocket of high seas that is directly in the migratory path of algae-eating tuna. The whole concept of management for such a species is that high seas pockets between national zones should be brought under overall regional control, so that the same protective measures can be applied to the stocks as they pass from zone to zone. Without such an extension of regional authority, it is difficult to see how highly migratory species could be managed.

Question: I have a number of questions. First, will the scope of the Agency's membership be determined? Second, what will be the relationship between the new Agency and the existing regional commission, the Tuna Commission? Third, will the membership rely on the enforcement capability of one, two, or possibly three members, or will each have to rely on its own? Fourth, since fishery research and management have been consistently underfunded, not only in the Pacific but throughout the world, and since the financial picture of the members of the new Agency is not too great, on what sort of research and management base will the Agency arise?

Joji Kotobalavu: First, the question of scope of membership will not be finally resolved until the nature of the functions of the organization is clarified. The initial guidelines are mostly geographical in nature. All I can say at this time is that the Forum countries themselves have not restricted membership of the Agency to the Forum membership. They have said they will welcome other countries to enter as members. The final position of the scope of membership will depend on agreement on objectives and functions of the agency, for which the meeting in Fiji is being held. Chile, for example, has already expressed active interest in taking part, and they will be attending this meeting in Suva. I think the difficult aspect of this question will be more of one between the countries in the area and the distant water fishing countries.

We are very concerned about the relationship between the Agency and the other organizations. The Fiji delegation will want this meeting in Fiji to clarify this relationship. I was very interested to see the long list of regional organizations circulated by Professor Alexander the other day. What will be the relationship, for example, between this Agency and FAO, which does a lot of work in the region? Or with ICLARM? Or with the University of the South Pacific itself, which has set up a center to undertake research in marine resources? Obviously, because of our limited resources we do not want to set up organizations with parallel functions.

The question of enforcement has been looked at more in terms of national action. Internationally, we look to countries helping one another through the exchange of information, but we have no intention of setting up a supranational organization that would undertake this task of enforcement, policing the boundaries of the economic zones.

On the question of scientific research and management, there has been a suggestion that the Agency's research center might be set up in Sydney. The question of how the Agency will be financed has not been resolved and, again, this will only be decided finally when there is agreement on the question of functions, membership, and objectives. At the moment there has been a draft proposal circulated to the countries suggesting financial contributions from the Forum countries, but there has been no agreement on this.

Question: Mr. Kotobalavu, I am interested in your statement that you can only be successful if there is a global law of the sea treaty. Why is the success of your agency dependent on a successful outcome at UNCLOS III?

Joji Kotobalavu: I was speaking of recognition of whatever action we take, by countries outside the region. It is all very well for us to set up an agency to coordinate the conservation and management of tuna in the economic zone. What if some of the distant water fishing countries simply ignore it? If we have a global treaty that provides for our right of control, our exclusive right of control, over the tuna resources within our economic zones, we see this as helping us in getting the other countries to respect this right.

Donald McLoughlin: We intend to "hinge" the Agency on the law of the sea treaty. The treaty would be the legal background to the formation of the Agency, and what the Agency would attempt to achieve would be the aims and objectives set up already in the ICNT: those underlying the concept of the regional cooperation in the ICNT.

Question: You spoke of retaining control over the adjacent resources. What about pooling the control over the surplus stocks?

Joji Kotobalavu: This is something the countries will have to consult and agree upon. I think the feeling at the moment is that New Zealand at least will certainly wish to retain the right to allocate and issue licences on surplus stocks. I do not see the countries in the region surrendering to a regional agency their rights to issue licences on surplus resources.

Comment: There are intermediate options between total control and total surrender.

Joji Kotobalavu: It is for the countries to look at specific issues like that of access to surplus resources or to particular species such as tuna. I am afraid the final answers to some questions will very much depend on the outcome of future discussions, especially on the issue of whether the Agency's mandate will be extended to all living resources of the economic zones or limited to a selected number of species.

Question: Would you have any indication what policies the states' members of the new Agency are likely to adopt with regard to scientific research by foreign nations in the EEZ?

Joji Kotobalavu: Not at this stage. This is something that will have to be looked at by the member countries.

Question: The ICNT excludes from the proposed dispute settlement system any matters that relate to the exercise of the coastal state's exclusive jurisdiction within the economic zone. Now, in the South Pacific how would you see fishery disputes handled in the region after the establishment of the Agency: first, in the event of disputes between a member of the Agency and an outsider; and second, in the event of disputes between members?

Joji Kotobalavu: This too will have to be looked at in detail. But we have great faith in our Pacific way of settling disagreements between us. Whatever procedures we set up they will not be inconsistent with the provisions of the global law of the sea treaty. I stress this, because it is very important.

Donald McLoughlin: The draft that has been circulated definitely contemplates dispute settlement procedures as between members, but we have not yet come to the problem of working out dispute settlement procedures as between members and nonmembers.

Question: On more than one occasion today we heard of the difficulty in obtaining international funding for scientific research in support of regional fishery bodies. In fact, much of the funding available comes from the United Nations Development Program, and the UNDP allocates these funds by reference to priorities set by national planning bodies. What is the priority that your own country sets on your marine development?

Joji Kotobalavu: A very high priority, and this is reflected on a regional basis by the decision of the countries that are members of the University of the Pacific to set up a marine resources center with Canadian assistance. There is also agreement among the South Pacific countries that exploitation of marine resources should be given very high priority in programs both at the national and regional levels.

Question: When you weigh this against development of civil aviation, agriculture, and public health, where does this stand in relative priority?

Joji Kotobalavu: Even higher priority, because how do we pay for our social services, and public health? It will have to be from the development of natural resources. But we are faced with two difficulties: first, the escalating cost of fertilizer imports, and second, the difficulty of getting access into the markets in developed countries. We therefore see our economic future not just in terms of the development of agriculture, but also of our marine resources. There can be no question of the South Pacific Island countries, either at the national level or the regional level, not according very high priority to marine resource exploitation, ocean research, and related areas. But, of course, they devote equal priority to education. The importance they attach to education is reflected in their decision to set up the University of the South Pacific. At its meeting in Port Moresby the Forum decided that a telecommunications training center in Fiji should be used to provide training for the region as a whole.

Question: Would you be willing to comment on the current sources of energy of your country?

Joji Kotobalavu: The escalation of prices has severely affected our economy. The immediate effect was a $10 million increase in our annual fuel import bill. In Fiji, we are certainly giving very high priority to the development of our own energy resources, like hydroelectricity and local energy resources in the rural areas. This is reflected at the regional level by the decision of the countries that participate in the University of the South Pacific to set up a Center for Applied Studies. One of the areas the center will be looking into is the utilization of local energy resources and transfer of technology: simple technology for our use.

Question: What kind of relationship do you expect to emerge between the Agency and the South Pacific Forum?

Joji Kotobalavu: When the Forum considered this issue in August, there was no undertaking that the Agency would be a part of the Forum. What the Forum stressed was that whatever organizational arrangement was finally arrived at, it should be an arrangement that will insure there is maximum benefit to the countries in the exploitation of the resources of their economic zones and the pockets of high seas in our region. Whether this would take the form of a new agency, or different organizational arrangements within an existing agency is a matter that will be discussed at this meeting in Fiji. Again, it relates to the question of the functions and objectives of the Agency. Once you have reached agreement on that, then the questions of membership and decision-making arrangements will fall into place. I think the difficulty at this stage is if the countries were to try to look at all these issues together; they will have to separate them and consider them one by one. My personal view is that we should begin by looking at the objectives and functions.

Question: I was wondering if you could outline the elements of the status of Minerva Reef.

Joji Kotobalavu: That, of course, is a matter that will have to be resolved by

Fiji and Tonga. New Zealand also has an interest in this. If it is accepted that Minerva Reef can generate its own economic zone, that will have some effect on the manner in which the economic zones of Fiji and New Zealand are drawn. This situation has not yet been resolved, but, again, we hope it will be settled in a Pacific way. Under the ICNT, as you know, a drying reef (that is, a low-tide elevation) cannot generate a territorial sea or an EEZ, if it is wholly situated more distant than the breadth of the territorial sea from the adjoining or adjacent territory. But there is the other question of the historical claim of Tonga, which we shall have to take into account in negotiations. Since Tonga is not recognized as an archipelagic state, the delimitation issue is essentially an EEZ delimitation issue.

Question: It occurs to me that since so little is known about the South Pacific Islands, their problems, their future, and so forth, there might be an opportunity sometime in the not-too-distant future for a professional group, such as this one represented here, to visit some of the South Pacific Islands and to exchange ideas on these problems. Perhaps the Law of the Sea Institute itself might have a role. How would you view such a proposal?

Joji Kotobalavu: The U.S. government has shown a lot of interest in this kind of suggestion. You are always welcome to hold one of the Law of the Sea Institute meetings in Fiji or one of the other territories. I see a lot of merit, for example, in the idea of your Institute working together with the University of the South Pacific, with the Marine Resource Center which is being established here.

Question: According to Article 296 in the ICNT, no fishery dispute can be submitted to third party adjudication if it involves the calling into question of the exercise of coastal state discretion under Articles 61 and 62: in such matters as the determination of total allowable catch and the allocation of surplus stocks. How would the Agency get around this barrier, if one member country objected to a decision of this kind?

Joji Kotobalavu: The Agency would not be determining the allowable catch. We are working within the framework of the ICNT. The coastal state in each case would determine the allowable catch and the allocation of surplus. So, we do not see any conflict arising from this.

Question: In light of these difficulties in the area of dispute settlement, would it not be essential to have a clear understanding where national discretion ends and regional management authority begins?

Joji Kotobalavu: Well, we do not know at this stage even if the Agency will be engaged in scientific research, whether its authority will cover pollution control or be confined to conservation. I do not see the coastal states in the region delegating to a regional body the right of control over the economic zone resources.

Donald McLoughlin: What is contemplated is that the Agency should make recommendations to the individual coastal states but that the coastal state itself ought to make the decisions. In the event of such a decision being unreasonable or a manifest abuse of power, then it may be necessary to consider what kind of dispute settlement or appeal procedure should be adopted.

Question: The projected regional agency seems determined to secure control over highly migratory species such as tuna in a manner that seems contrary to Article 64, as interpreted by the United States. How would you like to see this difference settled?

Joji Kotobalavu: Well, if you disagree with a friend, there are two things you can do. First, you can invite him into the fold, and hope that by being aware of your position, he will accept a moral obligation to respect your position. The second alternative is to keep your friend out of the fold. This is a choice that I can happily say the South Pacific Conference has not yet had to make, but much will depend on the functions and objectives of the Agency. In our own case, we see merit in arrangements that would include not only the coastal states of the South Pacific region, but also countries from outside the region, particularly if the Agency's functions include the management of tuna in the high seas of the South Pacific. We do not want to end up in a situation where the fishing fleets of country X come and anchor immediately outside our economic zone and take all the tuna before they enter our waters. This would make nonsense of the concept of an economic zone.

Question: Does the Forum concede that distant water fishermen are likely to continue to predominate in the Pacific waters, or would it insist on a mix between the distant fishermen and the local industry? In one or two of the coastal states the local fishing industry is becoming stronger each year. Has there been any intent on the part of the other smaller coastal nations to increase their capacity to fish?

Joji Kotobalavu: I did mention that whatever arrangements we arrived at for the resources within the economic zones of the countries of the area or resources in the high seas in the South Pacific, we would like to see an arrangement that recognizes the heavy dependence of the South Pacific countries on fishery resources, including the need of countries like Fiji to have wider access to some resources to support its own fishing industry. So we certainly have an interest in seeing that, whatever international arrangement we arrive at, there is some degree of preference given to countries within the area.

Question: In what you said about the control over migratory species, do you speak for Fiji or for the South Pacific Forum as a whole?

Joji Kotobalavu: I speak for Fiji, though this is also the view of almost all the South Pacific Forum countries. If you read the text of the Forum's declaration, there is a reference to this. In fact, their statement on membership flowed from their position on highly migratory species in the economic zones. There must be recognition of the right of coastal states to the resources, including highly migratory species, of the economic zone. So, one can actually say that all the Forum countries take this view.

Question: Could you give some information about the size and capability of the South Pacific fishing industry?

Donald McLoughlin: Of last year's regional total production Fiji's catch was 15,000 tons. In Fiji we have thirty-five vessels engaged in fishing. About thirty are longliners and five are engaged in pole fishing. All pole fishing boats are interested in skipjack tuna, yellow fin, and albacore. As evidenced by the tonnage, there is obviously a much larger fleet under charter.

Joji Kotobalavu: The biggest fishing fleet is in American Samoa.

Question: What protection do you have with the Coast Guard?

Joji Kotobalavu: Well, with the help of the U.S. Navy we have two protection vessels. The countries that are going to have a lot of difficulties in policing their economic zones are countries to the north of Fiji, like the Solomon Islands and the Gilbert Islands. This is where the long distance fishing fleets will enter the South Pacific. Once they have entered the economic zones of these countries, we should be able to know where they are at any stage thereafter. It is part of the understanding that countries will inform one another of movements of foreign fleets in the economic zones. While there will be no regional enforcement agency, there will be cooperation in the exchange of information, and help in surveillance and policing of territory. This is partly why the Forum decided to have the permanent Agency established in the Solomon Islands.

Question: Excuse my ignorance, but in the Forum area are there any problems involving whaling?

Donald McLoughlin: None. The whales are further south, off New Zealand. There is no whaling taking place in the Forum area.

Question: Historically, there has been major whaling activity in the South

Pacific. I have read somewhere that there is still a little bit going on in Tonga. Is this not so?

Joji Kotobalavu: I do not think they have been exploited on a commercial basis.

Donald McLoughlin: We did have a rather substantial whaling activity once in the South Pacific, around Fiji waters, but this has not existed in the last fifteen years. There may be a limited volume of subsistence whaling in Tonga, but there is no organized whaling. They may use small boats to harpoon whales for their own use.

Joji Kotobalavu: It is historical in the sense that our first contact with the West was through whalers and sandlewood traders.

Question: There was some discussion about having next week's conference limited to the Pacific islands and possibly Australia and New Zealand. Was the decision final?

Joji Kotobalavu: No. There was actually an agreement by the Forum that there should be very wide participation, since the problem is really a technical one. I think the facilities at the headquarters of the South Pacific Bureau are rather limited, and they would like to keep numbers down. We certainly would like to see as many countries and organizations as possible attending. If in the end there is agreement that the function of the Agency is to be focused exclusively on highly migratory species in the high seas, I know that Fiji will certainly support an agency with very wide membership.

Question: This is probably an embarrassing question for the United States in Hawaii. Do you see any way in which the state of Hawaii, the territory of Guam, and the U.S. Trust Territory, can somehow affiliate with the South Pacific Forum and somehow separate ourselves from the policy of our own country, which is somewhat Atlantic-oriented?

Joji Kotobalavu: This is a legal problem, but one, again, that can be resolved in a Pacific way. The Forum comprises independent states and self-governing countries. The South Pacific Commission membership is limited to independent states, but the SPC agreement allows for self-governing countries to accede with the consent of the metropolitan government. Assuming the U.S. government agrees that the U.S. Trust Territory can enter into an international agreement on its own, we still have to ask whether France would agree. This is an issue that has to be resolved. How can territories in the South Pacific that are not members of the Forum be brought into full participation in the proposed Agency? We have countries like Tuvalu and Gilbert Islands, which are self-governing countries, but which have been allowed to accede to the SPC agreement. I am sure we can find a way to allow the American territories to take part in this Agency while recognizing the stand of the U.S. administration on highly migratory resources within the national economic zones.

The difficulty is not with the U.S. government and its territories, but more with the French territories because of their view of the relationship between their territories in the Pacific and metropolitan France. It is complicated by the fact that we are associated with the EEC through the Lomé Convention. Fiji, Papua New Guinea, Tonga, and Western Samoa. But at the same time the French territories benefit from the EEC arrangement by virtue of fact they are territories of France. The benefits we get from the EEC through the Lomé Convention apply only to our relations with France; they do not apply to our relations with the French territories in the Pacific.

Donald McLoughlin: It is France that has to resolve its position with its own territories. France always argues that its territories in the South Pacific are an integral part of its land territory in metropolitan France. So there is an anomaly to be dealt with, but it is something for France to settle with its territories, not the EEC as a whole, although we would have an interest in the EEC by virtue of our membership in the Lomé Convention.

Question: What is the view of the states of the South Pacific Forum as to the applicability of the continental shelf theory of "natural prolongation of the land mass"?

Donald McLoughlin: Australia and New Zealand are the only two Forum members that are affected, and we have in the past maintained that we respect their position.

Joji Kotobalavu: Mention was made this morning of the problems that arise in regional groupings that include both developed and developing countries, depending on the degree of economic development and degree of political influence. We hope that these arrangements that we are trying to promote will work. They will only work if there is mutual recognition of special needs: there has to be a give-and-take basis for compromise. That was a very good point mentioned this morning. It is not easy to arrive at a workable regional arrangement without problems. There will always be problems because of the differences in economic status. The poorer countries will tend to see the benefits of regional cooperation accruing to the more developed of the members, even if this is not so. But this is how countries may see things. Whatever arrangements are finally agreed to, we will want to insure that the decision-making process will have regard for insuring that the maximum benefit of exploitation of marine resources should flow to the countries within the region. We have had experience with other organizations in which there are big and small countries, developed and developing countries. Our experience is that juridical equality does not necessarily guarantee your interest.

Luncheon Meeting

Chairman
Richard Young

Good afternoon, ladies and gentlemen. Our feature attraction today is Professor Kazuomi Ouchi, who is professor of law at Seinan Gakuin University Law School in Kyushu, Japan. But his educational training took him further afield from Japan than that. He actually got to New Haven, to the Yale Law School, and while, as a Harvard man, I deplore this, I recognize that there is such an institution and that its quality has been improved in recent years by the students it has had from overseas! He tells me that back in 1967 and 1968 he was an Adlai Stevenson Fellow at the United Nations, where he heard the delegate of Malta make a certain speech, which many of you will recall, on the subject of the law of the sea, and this inspired him to become a scholar in that area. That, as we know, is practically ten years ago, and you have now had ten years of ripe experience, sir, in this field. He is going to talk to us this afternoon on "Japan and the Law of the Sea," and I take great pleasure in introducing to you Professor Ouchi.

Japan and the Law of the Sea

Kazuomi Ouchi
Seinan Gakuin University

Japan has depended for her survival and prosperity upon the full utilization of the oceans. Certainly the current radical reconstruction of the regimes of the ocean does not seem to help her in any sense, and therefore it is only natural that Japanese efforts throughout UNCLOS III have been focused on the maximum defense of traditional rights and of the status quo of the ocean regimes.

A close comparison of Japan's claims with the relevant ICNT provisions exposes the rather sad state of Japanese conference diplomacy. One cannot but wonder how a nation could lose so much and gain so little in diplomatic negotiations. Our diplomatic corps has been accused by the Japanese public of being a total loser in the crude grabbing game of ocean resources.

The cruelest consequence of UNCLOS III Japan has had to suffer is, of course, the emergence of the 200-mile fishery management or economic zone. It appears a matter of time before Japan will be totally excluded from foreign 200-mile zones, judging from the current trends based on the alleged consensus among nations participating at the conference. Theoretically, this is possible, but reality should be quite different. I submit that the total exclusion of the Japanese fishermen from the Northeast Pacific Zones of both Canada and the United States, for example, is quite unlikely in normal and peaceful circumstances, unless the Americans start eating fish at least every other day.

I think there is a myth that the Japanese are interminable fish-eaters. In fact, we often prefer steaks to "sliced raw fish." Last year I was fortunate enough to live in Texas for a year. Even there I would choose beef rather than fish, if I had a choice. For only $3.25 I could buy a steak as large as a Japanese rubber sandal, and only slightly less tender than Kobe beef. My little body could hardly consume it. When I wanted fish, I kept saying to myself, "Wait till you get home.

Over there, fish are still cheaper than here." In other words, the Japanese are eating fish because it is cheaper than beef or pork. If the United States or Canada charge too high a fee for fishing within their 200-mile zones, we would rather go to Australia to import beef.

The eating habits of the peoples in the world are not going to change suddenly, but in Japan at least changes in *cooking* habits are taking place. Young Japanese wives invariably dislike having to cook fish, because the whole kitchen smells for days. This is one of the reasons why Japanese do not eat nutritious species such as sardines and mackerel. Thus, it is not entirely unrealistic to anticipate that in the future the bargaining power will incline toward the buyer rather than the seller. Japan is the first fish-producing nation, and the second fish-buying nation—second only to the United States. If our fishermen were to be excluded from other coastal states' off-shore zones, Japan might well be the *first* fish-importing country.

In a longer perspective, however, the 200-mile economic zone—the only ultimately dependable arena for Japanese fishing industries—may actually benefit Japan in several respects. With the highly advanced techniques and knowledge expected to be available by 1985, Japan within her own 200-mile zone will take nearly ten million tons of the approximately eleven million tons of fish that the entire population will demand. This at least is the prediction of the fishing industry's special research group. Such a fish-farming project would not be feasible in the absence of an exclusive 200-mile zone, if foreign distant-water fishing activities continue to increase within our own areas.

Japan decided to extend her territorial waters to a twelve-mile limit mainly because of the urgent pressures from coastal fishermen, whose fishing grounds were being increasingly invaded by foreigners. When the fishing technologies of many countries are rapidly improving, no state can continue, under the present ocean regime, to permit the virtual domination of its own off shore or coastal resource areas. In the long run, it is better to protect and secure the entire stock within coastal waters than to depend precariously on the yield from distant-water fishing. Nevertheless, there is no reason why Japan should not continue to rely on the regional arrangements offered by such friendly nations as the United States, Canada, and the USSR, inasmuch as such arrangements are beneficial to all the countries involved.

In the design of regional arrangements, I suggest two things are vital:

1. Japan should be brought into the regional decision-making process in some capacity, particularly in the gathering of relevant data and the effort to achieve scientific objectivity;

2. Japan as a grantee of the fishing right should not be subjected to abrupt policy changes by the coastal states, which might cause economic dislocation.

In fact, unilateral actions that have taken place recently may be criticized not so much for their substantive objectives as for the abrupt manner in which they were initiated. By being allowed to participate in the regional decision-making process, Japan can maintain the stability of her expectations for the shared resources of the foreign fishery zones.

Another myth that has often been repeated is the so-called consensus among nations. Mr. Elliot Richardson has repeatedly emphasized the existence of consensus among states on a 200-mile fishery zone. But we should never ignore the fact that this consensus did not include Japan, one of the major marine nations in the world. Japan's opposition to a 200-mile zone was apparently irrelevant to the alleged consensus on that regime, whereas U.S. opposition could alone negate any existence of consensus on the seabed regime.

In July 1977 Japan proclaimed her own 200-mile fishery zone, but it was a reluctant, passive action, simply to reciprocate USSR and U.S. unilateral actions. It seems consensus can hardly be separated from power politics.

The influence of power politics in establishing new ocean regimes is reflected not so much in the declared goals as in the way we go about realizing them. Sensitivity to the emotions, expectations, and anticipations of other nations must be felt in the ways negotiations are conducted and pursued.

Recently Japan has been greatly dismayed by the lack of leadership within the United States on the part of the State Department, whose policies have been overruled by a group of congressmen and senators representing several coastal states. We have been told that the U.S. people have always rallied behind the State Department in foreign affairs, a fact that can be proved by many judicial and administrative decisions and legislative actions. But for some reason this does not seem to be the case with law of the sea diplomacy. It makes me feel that perhaps our Japanese diplomats will have to employ multiple strategies by penetrating the internal political arenas in Washington, D.C., and the capitals of certain states represented on regional fishery councils under the new U.S. legislation.

Similarly, our government really has not been able to locate consensus on many issues among political branches and private interest groups, and this has contributed to a rather tardy, weak Japanese diplomacy. When the State Department or the Ministry of Foreign Affairs loses credibility, the social and diplomatic processes of the world community should be considered to be in a state of chaos. Perhaps I should be kind to both governments and, rather than attack their inconsistencies and incompetences, stress the complexity of the problem of the law of the sea.

Luncheon Meeting

Chairman
John Craven

The strength of the Law of the Sea Institute and of its annual meeting is the fact that all of the speakers and all the participants are here because of their individual capabilities and interests and knowledge of the law of the sea. It is in that individual capacity that all the speakers have been invited. At the same time we recognize that every individual is associated with some institution—a university, a governmental agency, a delegation—that has a vital role in the development of the law of the sea. Therefore, it was quite understandable and appropriate that as we looked over this program we wished to include a speaker from the Congress of the United States, but one who could address us in an individual as well as a representative capacity. Our first thought was to look at the most influential committee: and one understands there is really only one significant committee in Congress, and that is the House of Appropriations Committee. All else is, as we say in Hawaii, shibai.

Congresswoman Burke has been a member of that committee, but, more than that, she has been very much interested, active, and influential in the affairs of the ocean. Therefore, I am particularly proud and pleased to introduce as our luncheon speaker Congresswoman Yvonne Braithwaite-Burke, who will present to us "A Congressional View of the Law of the Sea."

❋

A Congressional View of the Law of the Sea

Yvonne Braithwaite-Burke
US House of Representatives

It is indeed an honor for me to be here in Hawaii and to speak before what must be the first Law of the Sea Institute forum since the Institute moved to this beautiful paradise of the Pacific earlier this year. I want to congratulate Dr. John Craven and the other people who participated in the decision to bring this prestigious institute to Hawaii, where oceanic culture is everywhere in evidence. I can think of no place in the world that provides a more peaceful setting for discussions and deliberations about our ocean frontier. Certainly, there can be no more proper a place for those discussions and deliberations than Hawaii—our nation's only truly oceanic state.

The Hawaiian people have indelibly etched into the pages of history a culture that bespeaks the sea. Their life, their literature, their lore, all stem from the sea. The early Polynesian feats of seafaring stand second to none. They were the great navigators of all time. They knew the sea. And they still know how to use the sea.

My subject today is law of the sea, a subject of profound importance in this world of challenge that faces us today. I have been less than inspired by the results of the UNCLOS III negotiations to date. We have been participating in these negotiations for some ten years or more with little in the way of specific accomplishment. And, in spite of having produced an Informal Composite Negotiating Text in New York last July, the negotiators remain poles apart on the key issues involved in the development of an international ocean regime.

With all due respect to Ambassador Elliot L. Richardson and those who came before him, American leadership thus far in the sensitive negotiations has been lacking and Congress has made their job difficult. We have failed to bring vision to the conference tables, whether in Caracas, New York, Geneva, or elsewhere.

What has been lacking has been a clear vision of wherein the American national interest reposes in regard to the oceans.

Unfortunately, the United States has joined the maritime march to extend its boundaries and to husband what it considers its own coastal and fishery resources. Acting in an atmosphere of extreme pressure, with the passage of the Fishery Conservation and Management Act of 1976, the United States has followed a precedent established by the Latin American nations to unilaterally extend their jurisdiction to a 200-mile sovereign limit. When the United States took its action, many other nations followed in domino fashion. The establishment of these limits has not been without its problems. Both the struggles at UNCLOS III and the differences over the 200-mile limit underline the problem of achieving satisfactory jurisdiction over the seas and waterways.

My concern is that if we are to really have a world ocean, and if it is to be a future frontier, the people of the world are going to have to be united. And we cannot expect to have a future frontier without the freedom of the seas that nations traditionally have enjoyed throughout the years. Limited access or denial of access would destroy many opportunities that we now recognize the oceans offer: a wealth of minerals, hopes for medicine, and an abundance of food.

One of those very areas has been receiving considerable national and international attention recently. That area is one about which I have always been quite concerned: the Panama Canal. I have had the privilege of visiting Panama and the canal, and to talk to many of the people in and out of politics. As you know, we signed a treaty with Panama in September. Under the existing 1903 treaty, the United States pays $2.3 million annually. In the future, we will be paying $10 million.

It is not only money that is involved in Panama, however. We have come to recognize that the people of Panama are very sensitive to our presence in their country. In the name of defense, we have not only established bases and a military strength, but of perhaps greater symbolic significance, we have our own government, the Canal Company, operating in the midst of a foreign nation. Does it make economic sense to spend $22 million to maintain a governmental organization in the middle of another country? That amount represents what we appropriate after the deduction of revenues.

There are many who argue about the strategic military position of the Panama Canal. I believe we can maintain the military bases and negotiate them as we do every other base throughout the world. But most military people believe the canal itself is not defensible; its defense depends upon the attitudes of the people who live in Panama. It also depends upon the friendliness of our neighbors in Latin America and how they react to our presence in Panama. I believe we must retain our right to influence the operation of the canal, but I do not think we need to have schools, hospitals, stores, and the accoutrements of a government in order to operate it. As the matter now stands, in the eyes of the people of Panama and of Latin America, the specter of colonialism hangs over the shoulders of the United States. I think we must be sensitive to the Panamanian peoples' concern that their country has been divided. In their eyes, the United States is curtailing expansion of their cities and impeding their ability to control their own destiny.

These conflicts made negotiations quite delicate. It is my hope that the debate over the ratification of the treaty does not become so destructive of good will and of such an emotional nature that in the future we will not be able to have worldwide access to the canal. These canal negotiations, the treaty, and the circumstances surrounding its ratification will have worldwide impact. The commercial and strategic importance of the canal cannot be overlooked. We must be sure that this agreement guarantees free passage over this significant checkpoint for ships of *all* nations, and that it will be ratified in a way that we do not undermine the friendship of our Latin American neighbors.

Lack of a clear understanding of the oceans has been very much a problem in the canal negotiations, also. It is unfortunate, I think, that in a nation with such a rich maritime heritage, a majority of Americans still think of water principally as a means of quenching thirst; many more look upon the water only as a danger, a problem, often considered a forbidding and hostile world. Land is considered the prime source of life. It is where we live, where we farm, and where we mine. It is something we can own and improve.

We have become land-oriented creatures, though this has not always been true of America. It was not the original intent of the founders of communities around Massachusetts Bay to establish a predominantly maritime community. The first and foremost object of Winthrop and Dudley, Endicott and Saltonstall, was to found a church and a commonwealth in which Calvinists and Puritans might live and worship.

They intended the economic foundation of New England to be rooted in the land, but they failed. Out of stark necessity, New England was forced to turn to the sea. The civil war in England in 1641 cut short the flow of emigrants and foreign commodities, and the colonists turned to the oceans, bays, and rivers. The founders had resourcefully recruited artisans with diverse skills and secured a variety of useful tools. Out of these circumstances, the shipbuilding industry was launched.

Maritime trade flourished. American clippers were the most competitive trade carriers in the world. People read the signals from the ships and the signals from the sea. As the people's lives became intertwined with the sea, the youthful nation struggled for its place in the world. With much of the population concentrated along the seaboard, America sensed the pulse of the sea and derived vitality from it. Americans, however, began to turn their backs on the sea when they started to move westward in covered wagons to develop the land. Special schools, Land Grant Colleges, were created to help the people conquer the problems and harvest the fruits of the nation's fertile soil. The creative talents of the people were attracted inland.

It was not until 1941 that America became interested once again in the sea. We marshalled our forces and people to become the greatest maritime power of all time. Unfortunately, that position was short lived. Following the war, our interest in the sea diminished, and we have witnessed in the years since then a deterioration of our naval strength, the deplorable near destruction of our commercial maritime strength, and a regrettable lack of marine and oceanic research.

In my estimation, we have been shortsighted in failing to view the sea as essential to our quest for a better quality of life and as a crucial factor to our survival. The oceans are the last and greatest resource reserve on our planet. The oceans are vital to the maintenance of a healthy planet and the life form of that planet. They are a necessary medium for international trade and communication. To maintain our position in the world, we are going to have to return some of our attention to the waters that surround us.

As a member of congress, I am very pleased to report to you that our new Secretary of Commerce, Juanita Kreps, has indicated the administration is interested in working with the legislative branch to develop new initiatives to establish a policy for the oceans. President Carter has indicated to us that he wishes to work not only to reestablish our strength on the seas, but to resume a position of leadership in maritime commerce.

Hopefully, this future will bring some wisdom from the Law of the Sea Institute that will be hopeful to our negotiators. It was out of exasperation, I would assume, that Ambassador Richardson suggested following the 1977 sessions in New York that perhaps the United Nations was not the place for law of the sea discussions, if the interests of the United States and all nations were to be served. He might very well be right.

The Law of the Sea Institute might take the lead in this matter and revitalize our law of the sea perspective. We, the United States, cannot write a new constitution of the sea by ourselves. American leadership, if it is to be viable in a rapidly changing world, must of course be sensitive to international politics, but willing also to move toward the realization of the vast humanistic bounties offered by the oceans. To assist in the role of leadership, I urge that this Institute establish in cooperation with all seafaring nations of the world an oceanic confederation composed of representatives of all nations having an interest in the oceans.

As I visualize it, this oceanic confederation would not be a one-shot program of fact-finding, but a continuing, multicultural, interdisciplinary educational and oceanic research effort on a worldwide basis. It would, with its collection of scientists, educators, politicians, and others, take an in-depth look into some of the more profound oceanic problems, particularly some of those that are especially vulnerable to charges of "resource grabbing" by the strong and powerful. It would be designed operationally to do something now to develop and produce tangible results or products from the resources of the oceans. Here, at the crossroads of the Pacific, it would impart to the world the view that we are moving, and not just talking, that we are usefully engaged in developing the uses of the oceans.

I would strongly recommend, of course, that the United States take immediate action to develop a national ocean policy, and to pursue a course of action relative to the law of the sea that would be rational and lead to a more mature development of world oceanic leadership by the United States. Only through such action can we reaffirm that America remains the great oceanic power of modern times.

Even though it has been recognized that the Selden-Grotius controversy over freedom of the seas continued for nearly 200 years, the concept proposed by Grotius gradually won widespread acceptance as being in the common interest of all nations. There has been much conjecture during UNCLOS III that modern technology was forcing the maritime nations of the world to reorient themselves into the Selden concept of a closed sea.

The fact that the Law of the Sea Conference has been bogged down for ten years, to my mind, highlights the fact that the seas must remain open. This freedom of the seas doctrine is considered a milestone in the development of international oceanic law and has served mankind well for some 350 years. It has benefited the international community by stimulating trade, forging cultural links, and generally expanding mankind's horizons. I contend that this open seas policy serves both the security of the volatile world and the people who are a part of that world.

Buckminster Fuller has argued that the thinking that has come out of the sea has changed our world. Here in Hawaii, I contend that you can bring people together for the purposeful motivation of moving the world ahead on the seas. If you can do this, if you can generate the interest for the best oceanic minds in the world to take a prolonged look into the promises offered by the seas, you will have taken a giant step toward increased enlightenment of the oceans and the great potential benefit they hold for mankind.

Banquet Meeting

Chairman
Richard Young

We are highly honored this evening to have Governor Ariyoshi as our guest of honor and our speaker. He is a native of Honolulu, and a graduate both of Michigan State University and of the University of Michigan Law School. The governor went on to practise law in Honolulu, and even became president of the Bar Association of Hawaii some years ago. For some twenty years, I believe, he has been active in public and political affairs, going back to the old territorial days. I also understand that he has never lost an election, and thus fulfills Lloyd George's dictum that in order to be a statesman you have to keep office, otherwise you cannot be a statesman As governor of our only insular state–perhaps I should say "geographically insular," because we have some insular states on the mainland in another sense–he cannot help but be deeply immersed in ocean problems and ocean policies. It, therefore, seems particularly appropriate at this institute's inaugural conference at its new home in Hawaii, that he is here to address us.

Banquet Address

George Ariyoshi
Governor of Hawaii

I am especially pleased to address you this evening, since the subject of your conference is of major concern to me. The chief executive of an island state is aware, as few other executives are aware, of the importance of the law of the sea. He is particularly aware of the problems of regional laws and arrangements and the jurisdictional dilemmas that are created. I would therefore share with you this evening the concerns of the state of Hawaii, knowing that these concerns are the concerns of your conference.

The state of Hawaii is the only one of the fifty sovereign states that is completely oceanic. We are, in fact, an archipelago, extending more than fifteen hundred miles from the big island of Hawaii to the tiny island of Kure.

Most people think of our state in terms of the populated islands of Hawaii, Maui, Molokai, Lanai, Oahu, Kauaii, and Niihau. But the Leeward Islands provide the extension that allows the United States to exert jurisdiction over an ocean domain of more than 600,000 square miles.

The management of the resources and the protection of the environment of the archipelago are the prime responsibility of the people of Hawaii through the elected officials of the state of Hawaii.

But we are not alone. Federal jurisdiction and responsibility is also present. Within the Hawaii Archipelago, the strategically important island of Midway is a territory of the United States but is not a part of the state of Hawaii. To the south, the island of Palmyra is a territory of the United States but is not a part of the state of Hawaii—and with the passage of the 200-mile extended fishing-zone bill, Hawaii finds itself zone-locked by 600,000 square miles of territory under the management of the federal government.

An additional preemption by federal jurisdiction also exists in the Leeward Chain as a result of an executive order by President Theodore Roosevelt. This order sets aside nearly all of the islands of the Leeward Chain as a fish and wildlife preserve. Legislation currently before the Congress would convert these islands to a wilderness preserve.

Other sovereignties are close enough to interact with the economic and environmental life of the state of Hawaii. The Line Islands, which are the southern counterpart of the Leeward Chain, include a number of islands whose sovereignty is in dispute between the United States and the United Kingdom. One of these islands–Christmas Island–is of potential economic significance, and all of the islands form the basis for extended economic zones.

Thus there is a complexity and multiplicity of jurisdiction in our region of the Pacific, which is undoubtedly similar to the complexities of jurisdiction in the many other ocean regions with which you are concerned. In the past, this complexity has been unimportant. In the past, most of these islands were remote, were relatively uninhabited, and were not of economic significance. Because of remoteness, their environment was not threatened. Today and in the future, this is no longer true.

The economic potential of these remote islands is just at the threshold of development. Initial surveys show them to be rich in fishing resources: reef fish, lobster, shellfish, rock cod, and red snapper. (You will have to recognize these fish by their Hawaiian names–kumu, ula, opimi, mempachi, and opakapaka.) Another economic resource of increasing value is the precious coral of which jewelry unique to these islands is made.

In the future, we expect that the manganese nodules to the south of Hawaii will be mined for manganese, copper, and cobalt. The regime for management of these nodules is of major concern to your community, and–I believe–is now the largest stumbling block in negotiating a United Nations treaty on the law of the sea. As a potential site for processing, Hawaii has a vital economic stake in these deep seabed resources.

A necessary element of manganese nodule processing is energy. Once again, the state must rely on energy from the ocean and from the ocean environment. Our primary source of energy at present is oil, shipped by sea in tankers. Most recently, geothermal energy has been discovered on the Big Island of Hawaii, and a major federal grant has been approved to develop this resource. Large quantities of this superior form of energy should be available in the not-too-distant future for ocean industry and ocean mining. In the more distant future, energy will be extracted from the difference between the temperature of the deep ocean waters and the sea-surface. This "ocean thermal energy" has its greatest potential in tropical waters. If it is successful, we may expect to see large numbers of ocean thermal energy plants and related ocean industries located throughout the tropical waters of the Pacific.

A side benefit of this form of energy comes from the large amounts of deep ocean nutrients that will be brought to the surface. This artificial upwelling will provide the fertilizer for aquaculture of sea plants and fish. Thus, farming of the sea is almost certain to be added to fishing of the sea as a major economic resource.

These attractive economic benefits are not to be extracted without cost. The great ease with which immigration to these islands can now take place raises the specter of uncontrolled and unwise growth.

Such growth would be surely detrimental to Hawaii's unique environment. Quite obviously, one of the greatest resources of these islands is their rare and unique beauty. It is an environment in delicate balance. We have the responsibility to protect more endangered species than any other state of the Union. They are endangered only because they are unique to this tropical environment. Economic development must therefore be balanced against this equally compelling need to preserve and protect our environment.

Even those of you who are first-time visitors ought to realize the importance of careful and knowledgeable management of all the resources of the archipelago. The land and sea cannot be separated. They are both part of the same ecological system.

The daily management dilemmas that flow from the fundamental unity of land and sea have led me to a fundamental principle that should guide you in formulating the law of the sea. The jurisdiction for managing the ocean waters and seabed surrounding any island-state must vest with the peoples who inhabit that island-state. Due consideration must, of course, be given to traditional rights and duties, constitutional provisions, international law and treaties. But oceanic archipelagos are unique, separated as they are from other states and peoples by vast expanses of international waters.

Looking at this principle, you can understand my major concerns. The United Nations draft treaty quite properly recognizes archipelagos. It insures appropriate sovereignty and secures international rights. But in the current draft, archipelagic status is denied to oceanic archipelagos that are a part of continental states, even when these archipelagos are oceanic and remote. This is not a trivial omission. It could be destructive of the capability of this state to wisely manage the resources of this major region of the Pacific.

I am concerned that current texts for the regime of the deep seabeds do not accord adequate, assured access for enterprises that desire to base their operations in Hawaii. The world community will be ill-served if the exploitation of these valuable resources is not accomplished efficiently and with due concern for the environment. Delay and denial here are not appropriate responses to the issue.

Under current national and international law, I am concerned for the management of migratory species. The green sea-turtle unknowingly lays its eggs in a federal fish and wildlife preserve; its juveniles migrate into state waters on state reefs. They then proceed into the 200-mile zone, having passed through waters of uncertain jurisdiction. They then probably migrate into international waters beyond the protection of the Endangered Species Act, ending their journey in islands of disputed jurisdiction. The laws for protection and preservation change as the green sea-turtles cross the boundaries. (Indeed, the species may be endangered purely as a result of psychological shock.)

The green sea-turtle is only one of the migratory species of significance. The mahimani, ono, and aku (the dolphin-fish, wahoo, and aku) are also of concern. I am particularly concerned about the management of tuna. This commercially valuable species is excluded from the United States fisheries legislation. Other states and nations may not similarly refrain. This resource, which is abundant in the archipelago, may therefore be fished internationally without reciprocity for our tuna fishermen operating in other economic zones.

I am concerned about the ultimate resolution of sovereignties in the Line Islands and Phoenix Islands. Each of these islands has an economic zone with a potential for fishing and for mariculture. Each has a potential for ocean thermal energy development, and many have a long-range potential as a visitor destination. Should these islands be exploited without due regard for the environment, for conservation, or without appropriate economic and social constraints, then subsequent developments could pose a threat to the economy and environment of Hawaii.

I am concerned about limitation of access to the economic zone and the economic resources of the archipelago. This problem is similar to the problem the state faces with respect to immigration. Our state must find mechanisms within the framework of our constitution for limitation of the rate of immigration and the rate of exploitation of our economic resources.

I am concerned about freedom of scientific research. The oceanographic ships of our university spend a substantial portion of their time within 200 miles of other nations, gathering scientific information of value to all. Restrictions in their operations would seriously limit or delay our understanding of the ocean.

I am sure that these concerns of mine are shared by other oceanic communities. As you deliberate on the general principles of regional management, I hope you will consider the dilemmas of this archipelago, and I challenge you to develop fundamental principles for the management of ocean recources that can be applied equitably and fairly to each oceanic region regardless of the complexities of jurisdiction and sovereignty.

It is also my hope that you will have time for more than deliberations. Indeed, I do not believe that you can fully appreciate the need for ocean management unless and until you have explored these islands. One can not truly appreciate the potential of geothermal energy without standing at the brink of Kilauea's volcano. One can not truly appreciate the potential for solar energy and ocean thermal energy without a sojourn on the Kona Coast. One can best understand Hawaii's potential as an astronomical observatory by a visit to the crater of Haleakala on Maui. One can only feel the full force of the potential for wind energy by visiting the Pali on Oahu. One can more clearly understand the nature of Hawaiian archipelagic waters during an inter-island journey on the hydrofoil or a deep-sea fishing trip. The vastness of the Pacific comes true once again with the voyage of the Hokule'a. Yet the unity and closeness of the Pacific is evident to one who has shared ideas by satellite—or visited the island Pacific nations by jet—or experienced the oneness of the human aspirations of Pacific islanders.

But of greatest importance, one can not appreciate the importance of quality of life in these islands without feeling the *spirit of Aloha*—a spirit both unique and undefined. It is the spirit that leads us to recognize that the ocean is the common heritage of mankind; that regardless of who is the manager, the ocean must be managed for the benefit of all; that international and regional agreements can only be effective if motivated by this spirit of cooperation and compassion.

I would leave you this evening with that spirit and with my hope that you will not fail—that you will return to these conferences again and again, as you *confront* and *resolve* the critical issues of the law of the sea.

Appendix: List of Participants

A. Abbadi
Political Affairs Officer
Section for Sea and Ocean Affairs, UN

C. Paul Ake
Naval Legal Service Office
Pearl Harbor, HI

Leonard F. Alcantara
Office of the Chief Counsel
U.S. Coast Guard, DOT
Washington, DC

Lewis Alexander
Department of Geography
University of Rhode Island

Paul Alexander
Anthropology Department
University of Sydney, Australia

Dayton Alverson
National Marine Fisheries Service
Seattle, WA

Lawrence Ang
Attorney-General's Chambers
Singapore

Howard L. April
Office of International Affairs, NOAA
Washington, DC

Dennis W. Arrow
School of Law
Oklahoma City University

John Bardach
Resource Systems Institute
East-West Center
Honolulu, HI

Richard Bilder
Law School
University of Wisconsin

Mark Buflo
Honolulu, HI

William T. Burke
School of Law
University of Washington

Dexter Cate
Honolulu, HI

Robert W.B. Chang
Judge
Honolulu, HI

Choung-il Chee
Law School
Seoul National University, Korea

Francis T. Christy
ICLARM
Manila, Philippines

Bert Cole
Public Lands Commission
Olympia, WA

E.L. Cope
Office of Public and International Affairs, DOT
Washington, DC

Harland B. Cope, USN(Ret.)
Aiea, HI

William G. Court
Department of Geography
University of Hawaii

William A. Crane
U.S. Navy, JAGC
Pearl Harbor, HI

John P. Craven
Director, Law of the Sea Institute
Honolulu, HI

Carl Q. Cristol
International Law
University of Southern California

William Dalton, USN
Camp Smith, HI

S.M. Danusaputro
Faculty of Law
Padjadjaran University
Bandung, Indonesia

Christine Dawson
Institute for Marine Studies
University of Washington

Hasjim Djalal
Ministry of Foreign Affairs
Jakarta, Indonesia

John W. Drapeau
Office of Joint Chiefs of Staff, DOD
Washington, DC

William Erb
Office of Marine Science and Technology Affairs, State Department
Washington, DC

Gudmundur Eiriksson
Ministry of Foreign Affairs
Reykjavik, Iceland

Daniel Finn
Lawyer
Honolulu, HI

Masayoshi Fumoto
Eikikaku Company
Tokyo, Japan

Hiroaki Furuno
Kyodo News Service
(c/o "Hawaii Hochi")
Honolulu, HI

Tsutomu Fuse
Meisei University
Tokyo, Japan

John King Gamble, Jr.
Social and Behavioral Science
Pennsylvania State University
Erie, PA

Alan J. Goldman
Providence, RI

Chennat Gopalakrishnan
Agriculture and Resource Economics
University of Hawaii

Jeffrey B. Green
Honolulu, HI

Julian Gresser
Law School
University of Hawaii

James E. Grise, USN
Aiea, HI

Gina Gusmano
Honolulu, HI

Gardner Haight
CINCPAC (SJA)
Camp Smith, HI

Roland A. Hames
Honolulu, HI

Jaydee Hanson
Department of Geography
University of Hawaii

Michael Hardy
Commission of the European
Communities
Brussels, Belgium

Captain Harlow
Alexandria, VA

Robert L. Hartig
Anchorage, AK

Edward A. Hauck
U.S. Government
Herndon, VA

Phillips Hawkins
United States Steel Corporation
Pittsburgh, PA

Geoffrey Haynes
Assistant Attorney General
Juneau, AK

Robert Hazlehurst, Jr.
Marathon Oil Company
Findlay, OH

Susan Heftel
Honolulu, HI

Edward E. Henry, Jr.
Honolulu, HI

Richard Hildreth
School of Law
University of San Diego

Shurei Hirozawa
First Hawaiian Bank
Honolulu, HI

Ann Hollick
School of Advanced International Studies
Johns Hopkins University

Stanley Hong
Theo H. Davies & Co., Ltd.
Honolulu, HI

William J. Huckins
Bank of Hawaii
Honolulu, HI

William B. Hussey
Foreign Affairs Consultant
Beverly Hills, CA 90210

Boris Imerekov
Oceanographic Committee of the USSR
Moscow, USSR

Robert T.B. Iversen
National Marine Fisheries Service
Honolulu, HI

Michael Jacobs
U.S. Coast Guard Legal Office
Honolulu, HI

David L. James
Dillingham Corporation
Honolulu, HI

Howard F. Jeter
International Relations Officer
State Department
Washington, DC

Barbara Johnson
Victoria, BC, Canada

Douglas M. Johnston
Faculty of Law
Dalhousie University
Canada

Kent M. Keith
Lawyer
Honolulu, HI

George Kent
Department of Political Science
University of Hawaii

John C. Khil
Honolulu, HI

Judith T. Kildow
Scripps Institution of Oceanography
La Jolla, CA

James D. Kingham
Environment Canada
Hull, Quebec

Gary Knight
University Law Center
Louisiana State University

Albert W. Koers
Institute of International Law
University of Utrecht
The Netherlands

Anatoly L. Kolodkin
Scientific Research Institute of Maritime Transport of the USSR
Moscow, USSR

Joji Kotobalavu
Secretary for Foreign Affairs
Ministry of Justice
Suva, Fiji

David Larson
Law Department
University of New Hampshire

Marilyn P. Lee
Honolulu, HI

Reinier Lock
Lawyer
San Francisco, CA

Linda Luke
Lawyer
Honolulu, HI

Shelley Mark
Environmental Protection Agency
Washington, DC

John Marr
ICLARM
Manila, Philippines

Curtis Marshall
U.S. House of Representatives
Washington, DC

William H. Matthews
Director, Environment and Policy Institute
East-West Center
Honolulu, HI

Carol McCabe
UN Association of Southern California
Newport Beach, CA

David McLoughlin
Legal Consultant to Govt. of Fiji
Swanbourne, Western Australia

Edward Miles
Institute for Marine Studies
University of Washington

Patsy Mink
Asst. Secretary of State for Ocean & International Environmental and Scientific Affairs
Washington, DC

Yoshihiko Miwa
The Nihon Kogyo Shinbun
Tokyo, Japan

J.K. Meenan
School of Law
University of San Diego

James W. Moreau
Commander, 14th Coast Guard District
Honolulu, HI

James B. Morin, USN
Washington, DC

W. Patrick Morris
Chief Minority Counsel
Washington, DC

Robert W. Morse
Dean of Graduate Studies
Woods Hole Oceanographic Institution

Alfred G. Moss
Honolulu, HI

Gordon Munro
Department of Economics
University of British Columbia

Rodney Nakano
Department of Planning and Economic Development
Honolulu, HI

Dolliver Nelson
Sec. of Drafting Committee
UN Third LSI Conference

C. Odidi-Okidi
University of Nairobi, Kenya

John Olney
Action Resources Inc.
Honolulu, HI

Kazuomi Ouchi
Law School
Seinan Gakuin University
Fukuoka City, Japan

Arvid Pardo
Von Kleinsmid Center
University of Southern California

Choon-ho Park
Culture Learning Institute
East-West Center
Honolulu, HI

Walter B. Parker
Joint State/Federal Land Use Commission
Anchorage, AK

Guy Pauker
Rand Corporation
Santa Monica, CA

Vladimir Pisarev
Senior Research Fellow
Academy of Sciences of the USSR

Carla E. Pistor
Honolulu, HI

Renate Platzoder
Stiftung Wissenschaft und Politik
Haus Eggenberg, Germany F.R.

Giulio Pontecorvo
Graduate School of Business
Columbia University

Robert E. Rau
Lawyer
Honolulu, HI

Rod G. Reimer
Honolulu, HI

Roland Rieve
Bank of Hawaii
Honolulu, HI

Ralph Rodamaker
Kirkland WA

Claire Rodamaker
Kirkland, WA

Fred Rohlfing
Lawyer
Honolulu, HI

David A. Ross
Geology and Geophysics Department
Woods Hole Oceanographic Institution

Andres Rozental
Department of Foreign Relations
Government of Mexico

Alan F. Ryan
Office of Internat'l Marine Policy
NOAA
McLean, VA

Bryan E. St. John
Petro Canada
Environmental and Social Affairs
Ottawa, Canada

Sharon Saito
Kaneohe, HI

Branko N. Sambrailo
Yugoslavia Academy of Sciences & Arts
Zagreb

Yung Shang
University of Hawaii

Alan B. Sielen
Environmental Protection Agency
Oakton, VA

Kirk Sinclair
Bermuda Marine Group Ltd.
Hamilton, Bermuda

Robert A. Skillman
National Marine Fisheries Service
Honolulu, HI

Leah J. Smith
Woods Hole Oceanographic Institution

Robert Smith
Office of the Geographer
Department of State
Washington, DC

Robert M. Smith
Chaminade University of Honolulu

Manville F. Strong
Institute Development Research Center
Ottawa, Canada

Kazuo Sumi
Institute of International Environmental Law
Yokohama, Japan

Gerald Sumida
Lawyer
Honolulu, HI

Stanley Swerdloff
Office of the Marine Affairs Coordinator, State of Hawaii

Alberto Szekely
College of Law
Arizona State University, Tempe

Hideo Takabayashi
Faculty of Law
Ryukoku University
Kyoto, Japan

Rudolph L.S. Tamayo
Honolulu, HI

Ross Thornwood
Honolulu, HI

William J. Trainor
Department of State
Washington, DC

Mike J. Trens
Marine Consultant
Honolulu, HI

Shailendra K. Upadhyay
Nepal Mission to the UN

Mark Valencia
Environment and Policy Institute
East-West Center
Honolulu, HI

Joseph E. Vorbach
Special Assistant for Law of the Sea
U.S. Coast Guard, DOT
Washington, DC

Michael Wascom
Congressional Liaison, Sea Grant Office
Washington, DC

Lesley S. Williams
Lawyer
Pearl Harbor, HI

Allen Wooddell
Lawyer
Honolulu, HI

T.K. Woods
CINCPACFLT
Honolulu, HI

Richard Young
Counsellor-at-Law
Van Hornesville, NY

Handbuch für
Maschinenarbeiter

Von

Dr.-Ing. Siegfried Werth VDI

Mit 113 Abbildungen im Text

Berlin
Springer-Verlag
1942

ISBN-13: 978-3-642-94128-3 e-ISBN-13: 978-3-642-94528-1
DOI: 10.1007/978-3-642-94528-1

Softcover reprint of the hardcover 1st edition 1942

Vorwort.

Die Freude an der Arbeit
macht das Leben schön.

Diese Anleitung soll allen Maschinenarbeitern ein handliches, übersichtliches und nützliches Lehrbuch sein. Man kann sich aus ihm für alle täglich auftretenden Arbeitsfragen leicht Antwort holen. So wird bei eifriger Durcharbeit auch ein Umschüler, der aus einem fremden Beruf kommt, sich in Kürze über die wesentlichsten Dinge in der Metalltechnik gut unterrichten. Aber auch der gelernte Facharbeiter wird vieles finden, was vielleicht in Vergessenheit geriet oder inzwischen durch den Fortschritt der Technik neu hinzukam. Die Handlichkeit verlangt Beschränkung des Umfanges, und deshalb kann hier nicht von vollständiger Darstellung aller Fragen die Rede sein. Wer über diesen Rahmen hinaus weiter vordringen will, findet am Schluß Hinweise auf geeignetes Schrifttum.

Im ersten Teil „Allgemeine Betriebskunde" sind bis auf die Abschnitte 7 Kegelberechnungen und 8 Teilkopfberechnungen die technischen Grundlagen gebracht, die jeder Maschinenarbeiter als Gedankengut kennen und beherrschen soll. Im zweiten Teil „Besondere Betriebskunde" gehen die Abschnitte 9, 10, 11 und 12 ebenfalls jeden an. Die übrigen Abschnitte enthalten eingehend besondere Bearbeitungsgebiete. Von diesen muß man sich sein Gebiet aussuchen. Trotzdem ist manches aus den Nachbargebieten wichtig.

Befolgt man die Hinweise und Ratschläge, so wird die praktische Arbeit erfolgreich und gut ausfallen. Man bekommt den richtigen Blick für das Anfangen, und stellt sich mit der Zeit die Sicherheit ein, so läuft die Arbeit von der Hand, und das Gefühl der Beherrschung verschafft neue Arbeitsfreude. Arbeitsfreude aber ist die Grundlage für Zufriedenheit und bringt gleichmäßigen und gesicherten Verdienst. Sie macht das Leben schöner und dazu will dieses Handbuch helfen.

Berlin, im Oktober 1942.

S. Werth.

Inhaltsverzeichnis.

I. Allgemeine Betriebskunde.

Die allgemeine Betriebskunde umfaßt das theoretische Rüstzeug. Dieses ist Voraussetzung für das Verständnis und die gestellten Anforderungen an den Ausfall der Arbeit. Es handelt sich sozusagen um das ABC des Maschinenarbeiters. Nur wer gründlich Lesen und Schreiben gelernt hat, kann später fließend lesen. Gerade das Kennen und Beherrschen der theoretischen Grundlage ermöglicht schnelles Erfassen und damit hohe Leistung.

Abschnitt 1.
Allgemeines.

Zum Verständnis der in den folgenden Abschnitten angewandten Kurzzeichen ist ihre Bedeutung wichtig. Diese Kurzzeichen umfassen alle möglichen Begriffe und sind nicht willkürlich angenommen, sondern normalisiert und den Normen entnommen.

1. Was ist Norm?

Das Wort *Norm* kommt aus dem Lateinischen „vorschriftsmäßig". Normung bedeutet eine planmäßige Vereinheitlichung von Abmessungen und Eigenschaften von gewerblichen und Industrieerzeugnissen. Es tritt eine gewisse Ordnung und ein systematischer Zusammenhang ein. Die Vorteile liegen auf der Hand. Man hat für Teile desselben Verwendungszweckes jetzt noch eine Sorte oder eine Sortenreihe, während früher beliebig viel Formen angefertigt wurden. Es werden so unnötige Mehrarbeiten vermieden. Die Normung findet sich auf allen Gebieten menschlichen Gemeinschaftslebens. Man denke nur an die Vereinheitlichung von Sprache, Schrift, Zeit, Maßen, Gewichten, Geldmitteln, Gebräuchen usw. Von diesen interessiert uns hier besonders der Ausschnitt der technischen Normung.

2. DIN- und ISA-Normen.

Sämtliche Stellen, die sich mit technischer Normung in Deutschland befassen, sind im Deutschen Normenausschuß zusammengefaßt (DNA).

Dieser gibt Normenblätter als Ergebnis besonderer Erfahrungen unter Mitarbeit der Industrie heraus, die allgemein nützlich und notwendig sind. Diese Blätter heißen DIN-Blätter, die Abkürzung von ***Das ist Norm***. Ein weiterer Schritt zur Zusammenfassung mehrerer Länder, z. B. von Europa, zu einheitlichen Normen führte dann zur Gründung der ISA. „ISA" bedeutet „International Federation of the National Standardizing Associations", zu deutsch: „Internationaler Verband der Nationalen Normen-Vereinigungen". Im Wesentlichen von Deutschland stark beeinflußt, wurden zum großen Teil die deutschen Normen übernommen. Man hat damit eine Vereinheitlichung für alle Länder mit metrischem Maßsystem geschaffen.

3. Metrisches und Zoll-Maßsystem.

Überall da, wo das Meter als Längenmaß gilt, wie z. B. Deutschland, Dänemark, Schweden, Norwegen, Schweiz, Frankreich, Spanien, Italien, sind alle anderen Maße auf diesem Meter oder einem Teil davon aufgebaut. Man spricht vom metrischen Maßsystem.

In England und in den Vereinigten Staaten von Amerika als Hauptvertretern dagegen hat sich der Zoll als Längenmaß durchgesetzt, ein Zoll = 25,4 mm. Entsprechend hat man dort auch andere Gewichtseinheiten, die sich aber auf das metrische System umrechnen lassen. Zum Teil sind auch in den DIN- und ISA-Normen verschiedene Grundelemente, wie Schrauben, Muttern usw. übernommen, die aus dem Zollsystem stammen, und z. B. Zollsteigung haben. Man ist aber bestrebt, auch diese Abmessungen im Laufe der Zeit durch metrische zu ersetzen.

4. Allgemeine Grundnormen.

Die Grundnormen sind grundlegend für die gesamte Technik und Industrie und umfassen allgemeines, wie Einheiten, Formelzeichen, Benennungen, Formate. Das Wesentliche ist im folgenden herausgegriffen:

a) Längen: Die Kurzzeichen bedeuten jeweils

1 Kilometer	= km	= 1000 m
1 Meter	= m	= 100 cm = 1000 mm
1 Zentimeter	= cm	= 10 mm
1 Millimeter	= mm	= 1000 μ
1 Mikron oder My	= μ	= $^1/_{1000}$ mm = 0,001 mm
1 Zoll	= 1″	= 25,4 mm

$^1/_{100}$ mm	= 0,01 mm	(ist zwar in der Werkstätte ein übliches Maß, aber nicht genormt)

Der Zoll wird in Bruchteilen wie $^1/_{16}{}''$, $^3/_8{}''$ usw. unterteilt.

b) Flächen:

1 Quadratkilometer	= km^2	= 1000000 m^2
1 Quadratmeter	= m^2	= 10000 cm^2
1 Quadratzentimeter	= cm^2	= 100 mm^2
1 Quadratmillimeter	= mm^2	

Entsprechend lassen sich Quadratzoll in mm^2 umrechnen.

1 Quadratzoll hat 643 mm^2.

c) Räume:

1 Kubikmeter	= m^3	= 1000000 cm^3
1 Kubikzentimeter	= cm^3	= 1000 mm^3
1 Kubikmillimeter	= mm^3	
1 Liter	= 1000 cm^3	

d) Gewichte:

1 Tonne	= t	= 1000 kg
1 Kilogramm	= kg	= 1000 g
1 Gramm	= g	= 1000 mg
1 Milligramm	= mg	= 0,001 g

e) Verschiedenes:

1 Grad Celsius	= ^{0}C	= Maßstab für die Temperatur, Gefrierpunkt von Wasser = 0^0 C, Siedegrad des Wassers in Meereshöhe = 100^0 C.
1 Umdrehung	= U	= Umdrehung von Wellen oder Rädern.
Prozent	= %	= 1 Hundertstel oder eins von Hundert, z. B. 30% = $^{30}/_{100}$ = 0,3.
Bezogen auf	= /	= z. B. Vorschub in mm/U = Vorschub gerechnet in Millimeter je Umdrehung; oder v = m/min = Schnittgeschwindigkeit gerechnet in Meter je Minute. (Erklärung von Vorschub und Schnittgeschwindigkeit in Abschnitt 10.)

plus $= + =$ und
minus $= - =$ weniger
mal $= \cdot \times$ z. B. 3 mal 4 gleich 12 kann man auch schreiben: $3 \times 4 = 12$ oder
$3 \cdot 4 = 12$
geteilt durch $= : \;—\; /$ z. B. 12 geteilt durch 4 gleich 3 kann man auch schreiben:
$12 : 4 = 3$
$12 / 4 = 3$
$\frac{12}{4} = 3$

5. Technische Grundnormen.

a) Normaltemperatur. Bei verschiedenen Temperaturen hat dasselbe Stück verschiedene Längen. Bei Erhöhung der Temperatur dehnt es sich aus. Bei Temperaturabfall zieht es sich zusammen. Verschiedene Stoffe dehnen sich verschieden aus, z. B. Messing anders als Stahl und anders als der Werkstoff für die Meßlehren. Man muß also für die Feststellung von richtigen Maßen Werkstück und Meßlehre auf gleiche Temperatur bringen und dann messen, und zwar einheitlich bei allen Messungen. Die Normaltemperatur ist mit 20° C für das DIN- und ISA-System festgelegt. Nur bei dieser Temperatur haben Meßwerkzeuge ihre vorgeschriebenen Größen. Erwärmte Werkstücke müssen also, sobald sie Normaltemperatur angenommen haben, endgültig gemessen werden, wenn genaue Maße festzustellen sind.

b) Normdrehzahlen. Man braucht für verschiedene Zwecke kleinere und größere Drehzahlen an den Maschinen, die durch Schaltungen eingestellt werden. Zwecks Vereinheitlichung sind diese Drehzahlen genormt und in einer Reihe festgelegt. Manchmal sind dann an der Maschine einige Zwischendrehzahlen fortgelassen. Die vorhandenen passen jedoch immer wieder in die Normreihe.

c) Zeichnungsnormen. Von den genormten Abmessungen der Zeichnungen ist es manchmal wichtig, ihre Bezeichnung zu wissen, da nach diesen eine Einordnung in eine Kartei vorgenommen werden kann. Man

Tabelle 1. Zeichnungsabmessungen.

Bezeichnung	A 0	A 1	A 2	A 3	A 4	A 5	A 6
Abmessung in mm	841 × 1189	594 × 841	420 × 594	297 × 420	210 × 297	148 × 210	105 × 148

spricht z. B. von einem Zeichnungsblatt A 4 und meint dann die Größe, wie sie in Tab. 1 steht. Legt man zwei Blätter A 4 mit den längeren Seiten zusammen, so bilden sie gemeinsam das Format A 3, d. h. jeweils Formate mit den breiten Seiten aneinandergelegt, ergibt das nächstgrößere Format. Ein geteiltes Format ergibt entsprechend das nächstniedrigere Format.

Auf jeder Zeichnung Abb. 1 befindet sich unten rechts entweder das Schriftfeld mit Stückliste bei Zusammenstellungen oder das Schriftfeld allein bei Einzelteilzeichnungen. Dieses Schriftfeld enthält u. a. die Werkstoffangabe, die bei der Bearbeitung für die Wahl von Schnittgeschwindigkeit und Vorschub wichtig ist. Es kann auch sein, daß diese Werkstoffangabe aus der Stückliste oder Begleitkarte zum Werkstück entnommen werden muß. Das Kennzeichen der Zeichnung ist die Zeichnungsnummer, die gleichfalls auf dem Schriftfeld steht.

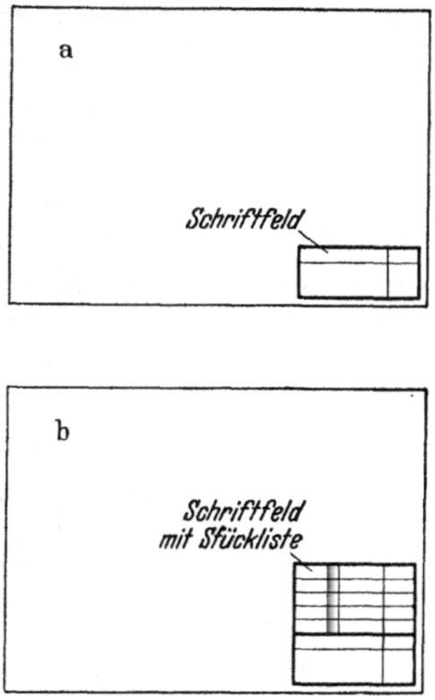

Abb. 1. Zeichnung mit Schriftfeld und Stückliste.

6. Benutzung der Normblätter.

Für die Bearbeitung werden öfter DIN-Normblätter gebraucht, sobald es sich darum handelt, z. B. Steigungen, Kerndurchmesser, Flankenwinkel von Gewinden festzustellen. Man muß sich dazu das angegebene DIN-Blatt anschaffen. Einfache Zeichnungen am Kopf dieser DIN-Blätter erleichtern das Finden der gesuchten Maße an den Werkstücken.

Abschnitt 2.
Rechnen und einfache Mathematik.

Rechnen ist eine ganz einfache Sache. Man braucht nur einige wenige Grundbegriffe aus der Schule zu können oder sie jetzt wieder im Gedächtnis aufzufrischen. Das Einmaleins und das Zusammenzählen von Zahlen werden hier vorausgesetzt.

1. Zehnersystem.

Eine geschriebene 1 bedeutet einen Einer (Abb. 2). Links daneben setzt man eine zweite 1; diese bedeutet einen Zehner. Sie ist 10 ×

so groß wie die Einer 1. Links neben die Zehner 1 setzt man eine dritte 1. Sie bedeutet 1 Hunderter. Sie ist 10 × so groß wie die zweite, die Zehner 1. Und weiter die vierte 1 ist 10 × so groß wie die dritte 1 usw. Daraus ergibt sich: Jede 1 nach links ist 10 × so groß wie die vorhergehende 1 nach rechts, oder: *Jede 1 nach rechts ist 10 × so klein wie die vorhergehende nach links.*

T H Z E z h t
1 1 1 1, 1 1 1

Abb. 2. Wertigkeiten der Stellen.

Setzt man nun rechts neben die Einer 1 noch eine 1, so muß nach dem vorhergehenden Satz diese 1 den 10. Teil der Einer 1 betragen, einen Bruchteil also, und zwar ein Zehntel. Zur Deutlichkeit schreibt man sie kleiner. Um es noch deutlicher zu machen, trennt man die Zehner 1 und die Zehntel 1 durch einen Strich oder durch ein Komma. Setzt man rechts neben die Zehntel 1 noch eine 1, so bedeutet diese, wieder nach unserem obigen Satz, den 10. Teil der Zehntel 1, also ein Hundertstel, die nächste 1 ein Tausendstel usf. Links vom Komma stehen die Ganzen, rechts die Brüche. Man nennt diese Wertschätzung der Stellen oder Zahlen das *Zehnersystem* oder *Dezimalsystem.*

2. Teilen oder Dividieren.

Welche Schreibweise gibt es?

$12 : 4 = 3$ heißt 12 geteilt durch 4 gleich 3

$\frac{12}{4} = 3$ heißt ebenfalls 12 geteilt durch 4 gleich 3

$12/4 = 3$ heißt auch 12 geteilt durch 4 gleich 3.

Wir haben also drei Schreibweisen für denselben Zweck. Diese sind nicht unnötig, sondern es ist manchmal praktischer, in dieser oder jener Form zu schreiben.

Es gibt gewöhnliche oder gemeine Brüche, z. B. $^1/_4$, $^1/_5$, $^6/_7$. Die Zahl über dem Bruchstrich ist der Zähler, die unter dem Bruchstrich der Nenner.

In der Technik werden aber meistens Dezimalbrüche, z. B. 0,1, 2,5, verwendet. Bei ihnen sieht man nur die Zähler. Der Nenner ergibt sich aus der Stelle hinter dem Komma. Er ist immer eine 1 mit so viel Nullen, als der Zähler Stellen hat, also $0{,}75 = \frac{75}{100}$ oder $1{,}75 = 1\frac{75}{100}$ oder $0{,}075 = \frac{75}{1000}$.

Wie macht man aus einem Gemeinbruch einen Dezimalbruch? Man teilt einfach den Zähler durch den Nenner.

1. Beispiel: $^1/_4 = ?$

$^1/_4 = 1 : 4 = 0{,}25.$

```
10
 8
――
20
20
――
 0
```

Ein Ganzes oder ein Einer läßt sich ohne Zerstückelung durch 4 nicht teilen, geht also 0 mal. Ich verwandle den Einer in Zehntel. Das geschieht einfach durch Anhängung einer Null. Da jetzt die Ganzen aufhören, setze ich hinter die Null ein Komma. 10 Zehntel durch 4 ist 2 Zehntel. Die 2 Zehntel stehen in der 1. Stelle hinter dem Komma. Die Abrechnung: $2 \times 4 = 8$, Rest 2. Die 2 Zehntel verwandle ich wieder durch Anhängung einer Null in Hundertstel. 20 Hundertstel durch $4 = 5$ Hundertstel. Die 5 kommt in die 2. Stelle der Hundertstel. Abrechnung: 5×4 Hundertstel = 20 Hundertstel, Rest 0.

Somit ist $^1/_4 = 0{,}25.$

2. Beispiel: $3^1/_4 = ?$

$3^1/_4 = \frac{13}{4} = 13 : 4 = 3{,}25.$

```
12
――
 10
  8
 ――
 20
 20
 ――
  0
```

13 Ganze durch 4 = 3 Ganze. 4×3 Ganze = 12 Ganze. Rest ein Ganzes, Komma setzen. Jetzt wie Beispiel 1.

3. Beispiel: $\frac{75}{1000} = ?$

$\frac{75}{1000} = 75 : 1000 = 0{,}075$

```
   0
 ――――
  750
    0
 ――――
 7500
 7000
 ――――
  5000
  5000
  ――――
     0
```

Wie muß man nun teilen, wenn das Ergebnis nicht aufgeht?

4. Beispiel: $30 : 11 = ?$

30 : 11 = 2,72~~727272~~ . . . = 2,73

```
22
――
 80
 77
 ――
  30
  22
  ――
   80
   77
   ――
```

Wenn eine Rechnung eine dauernde Wiederholung von gleichen Zahlen hinter dem Komma ergibt, wird man immer einen Rest behalten.

An sich kommt man desto genauer an das richtige Ergebnis heran, je mehr Stellen man hinter dem Komma ausrechnet. Wie genau man das Ergebnis braucht, entscheidet die Aufgabe. Jeder sieht ein, daß nach einer gewissen Stellenzahl jede weitere Zahl zwecklos ist, weil sie praktisch z. B. bei Längenmaßen nicht gemessen oder eingestellt werden kann. Deshalb ist nach einer bestimmten Stellenzahl abzubrechen.

Für das 4. Beispiel soll es genügen, das Ergebnis auf 2 Stellen hinter dem Komma zu haben. Um die zweite Stelle hinter dem Komma möglichst genau zu erhalten, stellt man noch die dritte Stelle fest. Liegt diese zwischen den Zahlen 5 und 9, so zählt man zu der zweiten Stelle 1 hinzu, man erhöht die zweite Stelle. Das Ergebnis ist dann 2,73.

5. Beispiel: 40 : 73 = ?

Nach demselben Verfahren, wie für das 4. Beispiel, ergibt sich folgende Rechnung:

	40 : 73 = 0,547 = 0,55
	400
(5 · 73 =)	365
	350
(4 · 73 =)	292
	580
(7 · 73 =)	511
Rest	69

3. Gradeinteilung.

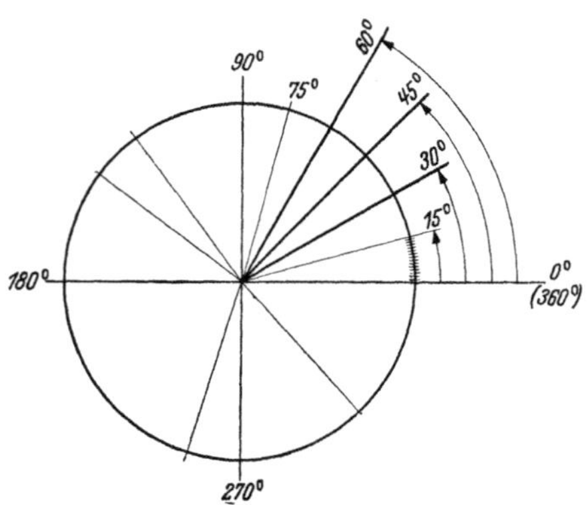

Abb. 3. Kreiseinteilung in Grade.

Der Kreisumfang wird in 360 gleiche Abschnitte eingeteilt. Zieht man jetzt vom Mittelpunkt strahlenförmige Linien durch die 360 Teilpunkte des Kreisumfanges Abb. 3, so verlaufen diese Linien zur Nulllinie unter verschiedenen Winkeln. Die Größe der Winkel wird durch die Zahl der Abschnitte angegeben, Grade genannt mit dem Kurzzeichen °. Bei 90° ist ein Viertel Kreisumfang erreicht, die beiden Schenkel des Winkels stehen dann senkrecht zueinander. Man spricht von einem rechten Winkel.

In Abb. 4 sind verschiedene Winkel herausgezeichnet; alle Winkel bis 90° heißen spitze Winkel, über 90° stumpfe Winkel.

Die Abweichungen zweier schräg zueinander liegender Geraden wird also durch den Winkel zwischen diesen genau festgelegt. Zur feineren

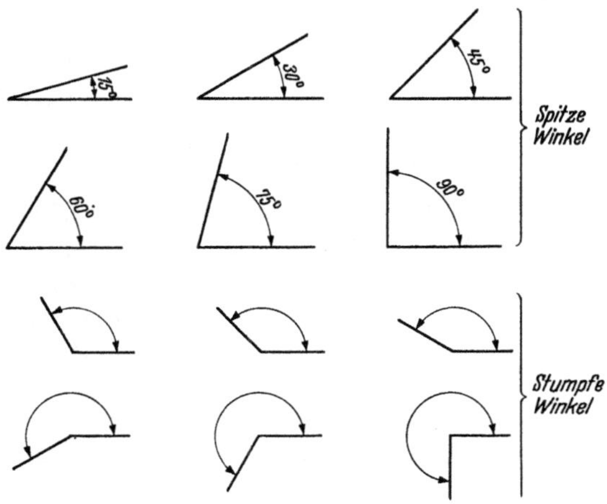

Abb. 4. Verschiedene spitze und stumpfe Winkel.

Unterteilung wird ein Grad (geschrieben 1°) in weitere 60 Minuten jede Minute in weitere 60 Sekunden eingeteilt. Es ist dann

der ganze Kreisumfang		= 360°
1/4	,,	= 90°
1 Grad	= 1°	= 60′
1 Minute	= 1′	= 60″
1 Sekunde	= 1″	= 1″

Man darf eine Sekunde nicht mit einem Zoll verwechseln, sie haben beide dieselbe Schreibweise 1″.

30 Minuten	= 30′	= 0,5°
36 ,,	= 36′	= 0,6°
42 Sekunden	= 42″	= 0,7′

Umrechnungsbeispiel:

$$27°\,42' = ?° \qquad \frac{42'}{60'} = 0{,}7° \qquad 27°\,42' = 27{,}7°.$$

4. Übliche Winkelbezeichnungen.

Ist ein Winkel mit einem Buchstaben bezeichnet, so ist dazu oft ein griechischer benutzt. Üblich sind:

α = Alpha	Hauptwinkelbezeichnungen	$\varkappa$ = Kappa
β = Beta		λ = Lambda
γ = Gamma		φ = Phi
δ = Delta		η = Eta

5. Winkelbeziehungen.

Bei einem Winkelmaß kommt es nicht auf die Länge der Schenkel an, sondern auf die Winkelweite zwischen den Schenkeln. So sind die Winkel in Abb. 5a gleich groß. In Abb. 5b sollen die Winkel α und β beide je 30° haben. Beiden Winkeln ist der Schenkel *1* gemeinsam. Wenn sie aber gleich groß sind, so müssen die Schenkel *2* und *3* parallel sein. Genau so kann man rückwärts schließen, daß die Winkel α und β gleich groß sind, wenn die Schenkel parallel sind.

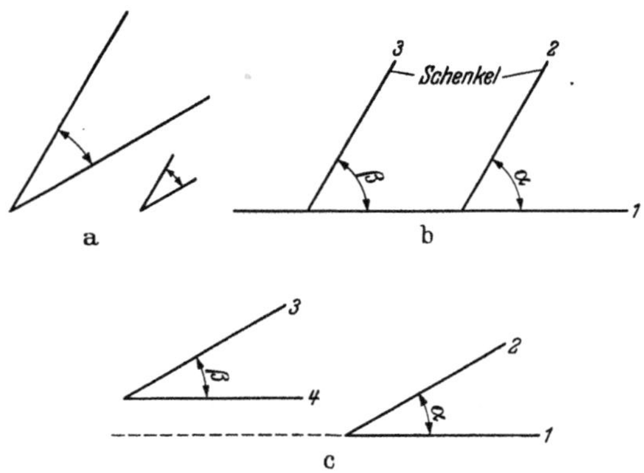

Abb. 5. Gleiche Winkel bei parallelen Schenkeln.

In Abb. 5c ist der Winkel β parallel nach oben verschoben. Die Schenkel *2* und *3* sind parallel geblieben. Ebenso die Schenkel *1* und *4*. Auch hier sind die Winkel α und β gleich groß. Desgleichen sind in Abb. 6a die Winkel α und β gleich, denn sie haben die Schenkel *1—1* und *2—2* gemeinsam. In Abb. 6b ist der Winkel β nach links verschoben, Schenkel *3* ist

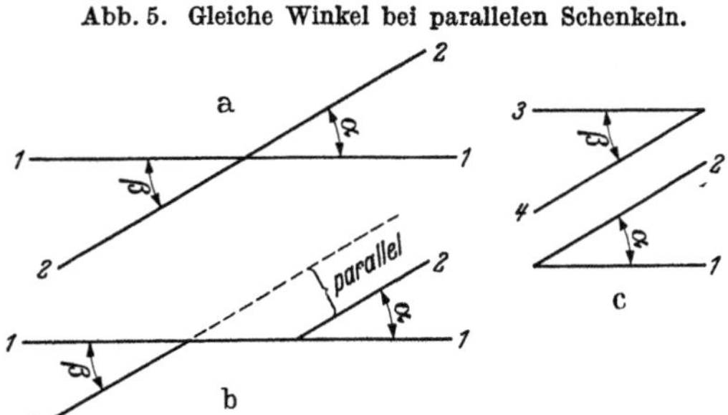

Abb. 6. Gleiche Winkel.

aber parallel zu 2 geblieben. Somit ist $\alpha = \beta$. Auch im Fall Abb. 6c sind die Schenkel *2* und *4* und *1* und *3* parallel und somit α und β gleich.

Allgemein ergibt sich also der Lehrsatz:

Zwei Winkel sind immer dann gleich, wenn ihre Schenkel parallel zueinander liegen.

Stehen zwei Schenkel senkrecht aufeinander, so bilden sie einen rechten Winkel und umschließen 90° (Abb. 7a). Verdreht man nun, wie in Abb. 7b, um den Punkt *0* den Schenkel *1* bis zur Stellung *2* und gleichzeitig den Schenkel *3* bis zur Stellung *4*, soll zwischen *2* und *4* der rechte Winkel erhalten bleiben. Dann muß aber auch der Winkel α gleich dem Winkel β sein; das besagt, daß *zwei Winkel auch dann gleich sind, wenn ihre Schenkel senkrecht aufeinander stehen*, wie in Abb. 7c.

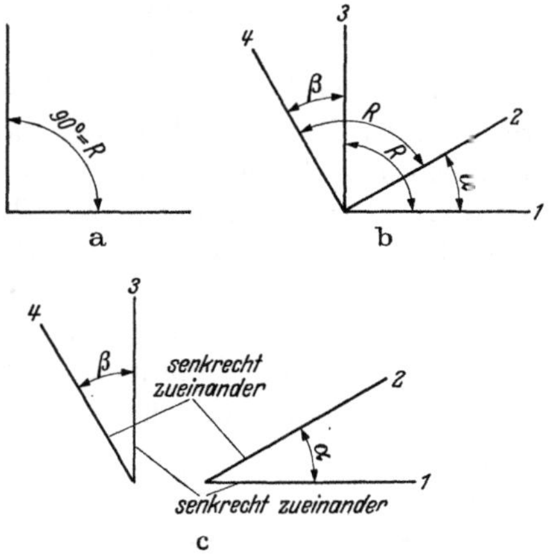

Abb. 7. Gleiche Winkel bei senkrecht zueinander stehenden Schenkeln.

In Abb. 8 haben die Winkel α und β die Schenkel *1* und *2* gemeinsam. Dabei ist *1* eine Gerade. Eine ganze Umdrehung um den Punkt *0* ist bekanntlich in 360° eingeteilt. α und β zusammen umfassen jedoch eine halbe Umdrehung. Somit sind α und β zusammen gleich 180°.

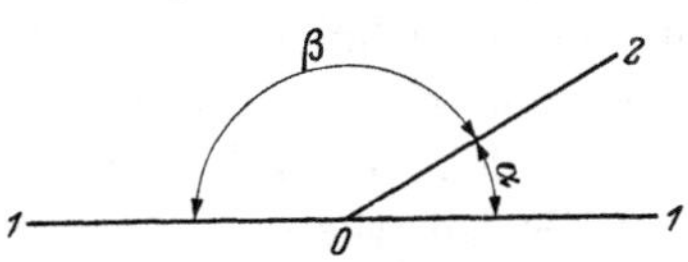

Abb. 8. Ergänzungswinkel β zum Winkel α.

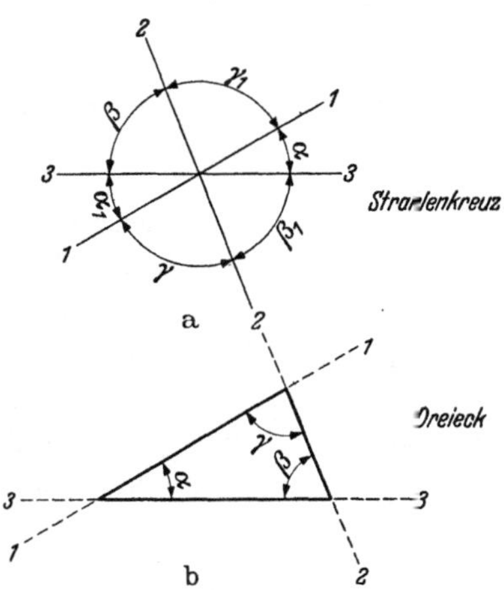

Abb. 9. Winkel im Dreieck und Strahlenkreuz.

Man kann also zum Winkel α stets den zugehörigen Ergänzungswinkel β ausrechnen. Bei Messungen kann man den Winkel β messen und den gewünschten Winkel α ausrechnen, was oft im praktischen Betrieb vorkommt. Ist z. B. $\alpha = 30^0$, so ist $\beta = 180 - 30 = 150^0$.

Im Strahlenkreuz Abb. 9a liegen die Winkel α, β und γ. Ihnen jeweils gegenüber liegen die gleich großen Winkel α_1, β_1 und γ_1. In Abb. 9b bilden die Geraden *1—1*, *2—2* und *3—3* ein Dreieck. Gleichzeitig liegen diese Geraden aber parallel zu den gleichen Geraden im Strahlenkreuz. Somit sind die Winkel α, β und γ im Dreieck gleich groß wie die im Strahlenkreuz. $\alpha + \beta + \gamma + \alpha_1 + \beta_1 + \gamma_1$ im Strahlenkreuz betragen zusammen 360^0, weil es sich um eine ganze Umdrehung um den Punkt *0* handelt. Da aber $\alpha = \alpha_1$, $\beta = \beta_1$ und $\gamma = \gamma_1$ sind, ist auch $\alpha + \beta + \gamma = \alpha_1 + \beta_1 + \gamma_1 = 180°$. Das besagt, daß die Winkel im Dreieck zusammen 180^0 betragen müssen.

Wenn nun einer von diesen Winkeln im Dreieck 90^0 beträgt, oder einem rechten Winkel gleich wird, wie in Abb. 10a···d, so spricht man von einem rechtwinkligen Dreieck. Dann haben die übrigen Winkel $\alpha + \beta$ zusammen immer 90^0. Wenn daher in einem rechtwinkligen Dreieck ein Winkel außer dem rechten bekannt ist, kann man den anderen ausrechnen. Ist z. B. $\alpha = 43°$, wird $\beta = 90 - 43 = 47°$.

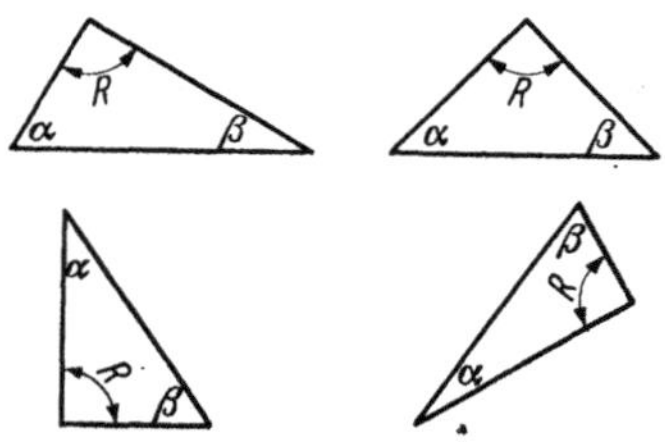

Abb. 10. Rechtwinklige Dreiecke.

Wie kann nun in einem rechtwinkligen Dreieck aus den Seitenlängen der Winkel α oder β ausgerechnet werden?

6. Winkelberechnung in einem rechtwinkligen Dreieck mit der Tangensbeziehung.

Im Dreieck Abb. 11 befindet sich der rechte Winkel oben. Die gegenüberliegende und längste Seite dieses Dreiecks heißt Hypotenuse. Die beiden Schenkel, die den rechten Winkel einschließen, heißen Katheten. Diese Ausdrücke entstammen aus der griechischen Sprache. Für den Winkel α unterscheidet man Gegenkathete a und Ankathete b, je nachdem, ob die Katheten am Winkel dran oder gegenüber liegen.

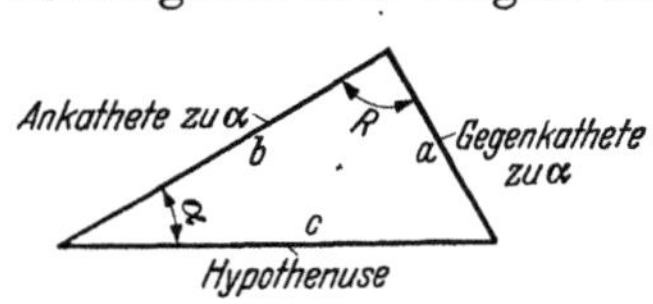

Abb. 11. Winkel und Seitenbenennung im rechtwinkligen Dreieck.

Uns interessiert jetzt die Größe vom Winkel α. Man kann den Winkel aus der Länge der Katheten ausrechnen. Zur Berechnung benutzt man die Tangensbeziehung, die in der Mathematik Tangensfunktion genannt wird. Tangens α oder geschrieben tg α ist das Verhältnis von Gegenkathete zu Ankathete. *Man präge sich folgenden Satz ein: tg α ist gleich Gegenkathete dividiert durch Ankathete.* Für die Berechnung nimmt man die Länge von a und teilt sie durch die Länge b, erhält eine Zahl; diese Zahl ist der Tangens α. Die Werte für tg α liegen genau fest und sind unabhängig von der Größe der Dreiecke. Sie gelten aber nur für rechtwinklige Dreiecke und sind in der Tabelle 2 enthalten.

1. Beispiel: Für die Abb. 12 soll der Winkel α ausgerechnet werden. Es ist die Gegenkathete $a = 40$ mm, die Ankathete $b = 90$ mm. Dann ist

$$\operatorname{tg}\alpha = \frac{a}{b} = \frac{40}{90} = \frac{4}{9} = 0{,}4444\ \ldots$$

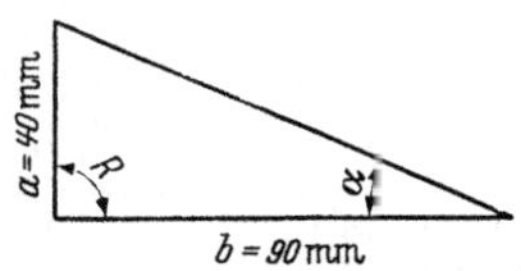

Abb. 12. Berechnungsbeispiel für α.

Jetzt muß aus Tabelle 2 der Wert für den Winkel α entnommen werden. Dort sind folgende nächstliegende Werte vorhanden:

$$\operatorname{tg} 23^0\,50' = 0{,}442$$
$$\operatorname{tg} 24^0 \quad = 0{,}445$$

Unser Wert von 0,444 liegt näher bei tg 24^0; findet man die Zahl nicht ganz genau in der Tabelle 1, so schätzt man die Minuten ab, indem man sich die Zahl zwischen die zwei nächstliegenden denkt. Der Winkel α ist also schätzungsweise $23^0\,57'$. In vielen Fällen wird diese Genauigkeit für die Einstellung der Maschine oder Messung ausreichen. Bei verschiedenen tg-Werten sind die Unterschiede verschieden, sie müssen jedesmal ausgerechnet werden.

2. Beispeil:

$\operatorname{tg}\beta = 2{,}00 \qquad \beta = ?$

$\operatorname{tg} 63^0\,20' = 1{,}99$

$\operatorname{tg} 63^0\,30 = 2{,}01$

Geschätzt ist $\beta = 63^0\,25'$.

Es gibt noch weitere Winkelberechnungen und Beziehungen, die hier fortgelassen sind, da man fast immer mit der Tangensberechnung auskommt. Man muß nur stets die Dreiecke genau ansehen, feststellen, wo der rechte Winkel liegt und welches Gegen- und Ankathete sind.

7. Berechnung des Kreisumfanges.

Der Umfang eines Kreises läßt sich mit Hilfe der Zahl Pi $= \pi$ (griechischer Buchstabe) ausrechnen. Es ist $\pi = 3{,}14$.

Der Kreisumfang ist $U = \pi \cdot \text{Durchmesser} = \pi \cdot D$. Ist z. B. $D = 100$ mm, so wird der Umfang $U = 3{,}14 \cdot 100 = 314$ mm.

Tabelle 2. Tangensfunktion.

Grad	Tangens (tg)						Grad	Tangens (tg)					
	0′	10′	20′	30′	40′	50′		0′	10′	20′	30′	40′	50′
0	0,000	0,003	0,006	0,009	0,012	0,015	45	1,00	1,01	1,01	1,02	1,02	1,03
1	0,017	0,020	0,023	0,026	0,029	0,032	46	1,04	1,04	1,05	1,05	1,06	1,07
2	0,035	0,038	0,041	0,044	0,047	0,049	47	1,07	1,08	1,08	1,09	1,10	1,10
3	0,052	0,055	0,058	0,061	0,064	0,067	48	1,11	1,12	1,12	1,13	1,14	1,14
4	0,070	0,073	0,076	0,079	0,082	0,085	49	1,15	1,16	1,16	1,17	1,18	1,18
5	0,087	0,090	0,093	0,096	0,099	0,102	50	1,19	1,20	1,21	1,21	1,22	1,23
6	0,105	0,108	0,111	0,114	0,117	0,120	51	1,24	1,24	1,25	1,26	1,26	1,27
7	0,123	0,126	0,129	0,132	0,135	0,138	52	1,28	1,29	1,30	1,30	1,31	1,32
8	0,141	0,144	0,146	0,149	0,152	0,155	53	1,33	1,34	1,34	1,35	1,36	1,37
9	0,158	0,161	0,164	0,167	0,170	0,173	54	1,38	1,38	1,39	1,40	1,41	1,42
10	0,176	0,179	0,182	0,185	0,188	0,191	55	1,43	1,44	1,45	1,46	1,46	1,47
11	0,194	0,197	0,200	0,203	0,206	0,210	56	1,48	1,49	1,50	1,51	1,52	1,53
12	0,213	0,216	0,219	0,222	0,225	0,228	57	1,54	1,55	1,56	1,57	1,58	1,59
13	0,231	0,234	0,237	0,240	0,243	0,246	58	1,60	1,61	1,62	1,63	1,64	1,65
14	0,249	0,252	0,256	0,259	0,262	0,265	59	1,66	1,68	1,69	1,70	1,71	1,72
15	0,268	0,271	0,274	0,277	0,280	0,284	60	1,73	1,74	1,76	1,77	1,78	1,79
16	0,287	0,290	0,293	0,296	0,299	0,303	61	1,80	1,82	1,83	1,84	1,85	1,87
17	0,306	0,309	0,312	0,315	0,319	0,322	62	1,88	1,89	1,91	1,92	1,93	1,95
18	0,325	0,328	0,331	0,335	0,338	0,341	63	1,96	1,98	1,99	2,01	2,02	2,04
19	0,344	0,348	0,351	0,354	0,357	0,361	64	2,05	2,07	2,08	2,10	2,11	2,13
20	0,364	0,367	0,371	0,374	0,377	0,381	65	2,14	2,16	2,18	2,19	2,21	2,23
21	0,384	0,387	0,391	0,394	0,397	0,401	66	2,25	2,26	2,28	2,30	2,32	2,34
22	0,404	0,407	0,411	0,414	0,418	0,421	67	2,36	2,38	2,39	2,41	2,43	2,45
23	0,424	0,428	0,431	0,435	0,438	0,442	68	2,48	2,50	2,52	2,54	2,56	2,58
24	0,445	0,449	0,452	0,456	0,459	0,463	69	2,61	2,63	2,65	2,67	2,70	2,72
25	0,466	0,470	0,473	0,477	0,481	0,484	70	2,75	2,77	2,80	2,82	2,85	2,88
26	0,488	0,491	0,495	0,499	0,502	0,506	71	2,90	2,93	2,96	2,99	3,02	3,05
27	0,510	0,513	0,517	0,521	0,524	0,528	72	3,08	3,11	3,14	3,17	3,20	3,24
28	0,532	0,535	0,539	0,543	0,547	0,551	73	3,27	3,31	3,34	3,38	3,41	3,45
29	0,554	0,558	0,562	0,566	0,570	0,573	74	3,49	3,53	3,57	3,61	3,65	3,69
30	0,577	0,581	0,585	0,589	0,593	0,597	75	3,73	3,76	3,82	3,87	3,91	3,96
31	0,601	0,605	0,609	0,613	0,617	0,621	76	4,01	4,06	4,11	4,17	4,22	4,27
32	0,625	0,629	0,633	0,637	0,641	0,645	77	4,33	4,39	4,45	4,51	4,57	4,64
33	0,649	0,654	0,658	0,662	0,666	0,670	78	4,70	4,77	4,84	4,92	4,99	5,07
34	0,675	0,679	0,683	0,687	0,692	0,696	79	5,14	5,23	5,31	5,40	5,48	5,58
35	0,700	0,705	0,709	0,713	0,718	0,722	80	5,67	5,77	5,87	5,98	6,08	6,20
36	0,727	0,731	0,735	0,740	0,744	0,749	81	6,31	6,43	6,56	6,69	6,83	6,97
37	0,754	0,758	0,763	0,767	0,772	0,777	82	7,12	7,27	7,43	7,60	7,77	7,95
38	0,781	0,786	0,791	0,795	0,800	0,805	83	8,14	8,34	8,56	8,78	9,01	9,26
39	0,810	0,815	0,819	0,834	0,829	0,834	84	9,51	9,79	10,08	10,4	10,71	11,06
40	0,839	0,844	0,849	0,854	0,859	0,864	85	11,4	11,83	12,25	12,7	13,20	13,73
41	0,869	0,874	0,880	0,855	0,890	0,895	86	14,3	14,92	15,60	16,3	17,17	18,07
42	0,900	0,906	0,911	0,916	0,922	0,927	87	19,1	20,21	21,47	22,9	24,54	26,43
43	0,933	0,938	0,943	0,949	0,955	0,960	88	28,6	31,24	34,37	38,2	42,96	49,10
44	0,966	0,971	0,977	0,983	0,988	0,994	89	57,3	68,75	85,94	114,5	171	343

Abschnitt 3.

Zeichnungskunde.

1. Allgemeines über Darstellungen.

Die Sprache der Technik und damit der Werkstatt ist die Zeichnung. Der Konstrukteur bringt seine Gedanken zu Papier und zeichnet Maschinen und Teile.

Die anschaulichste Form ist die perspektivische Darstellung, doch sind die Maße verzerrt, verkürzt. Für die Einzelfertigung ist eine wirklichkeitsgetreue Zeichnung vorteilhafter. Diese muß dann unmittelbare Ansichten enthalten. Da nun eine Ansicht oft nicht genügt, müssen mehrere Ansichten von verschiedenen Seiten gezeichnet werden. Wie diese anzuordnen sind, ist festgelegt. Bewährt hat sich die rechtwinklige Parallelprojektion als einfachste und wirtschaftlichste Form. Sie kommt für technische Zwecke allgemein zur Anwendung.

Die Werkstatt muß in der Lage sein, nach Zeichnung einen Körper mit den gleichen Abmessungen herzustellen. Außer der Form sind daher auch Maße und Schnitte für die Innenform in der Zeichnung enthalten. Ihre Güte ist wesentlich für eine einwandfreie Fertigung, und diese für ein richtiges Funktionieren des Werkstückes am zugedachten Verwendungszweck.

Wie entsteht eine rechtwinklige Parallelprojektion?

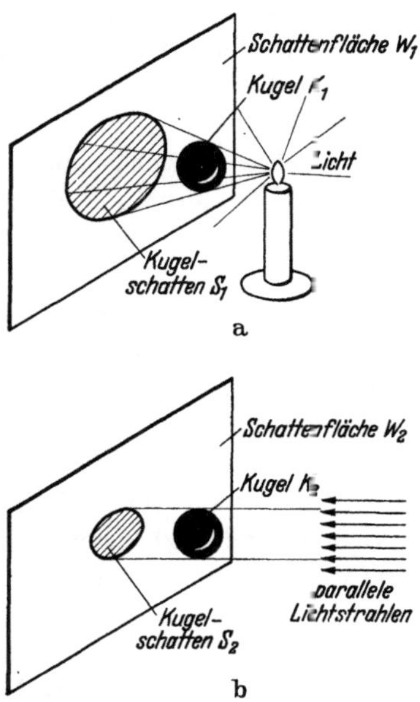

Abb. 13. Auswirkung von parallelen Lichtstrahlen.

2. Rechtwinklige Parallelprojektion.

(Grundlage für die technisch übliche Darstellungsart.)

Ein Licht wirft nach allen Seiten seine Lichtstrahlen. Eine Kugel K_1 (Abb. 13a) wirft auf eine Wand W_1 einen Schatten S, der je nach den Abständen von Licht zu Kugel und von Kugel zu Wand größer im Durchmesser wird als die Kugel selbst. Die äußersten Lichtstrahlen für den Schatten umschließen den Winkel α.

Stellt man sich jetzt vor, daß die Lichtquelle, z. B. die Sonne, sehr weit entfernt ist, so würde der Winkel zwischen den die Kugel einschließenden Lichtstrahlen so klein werden, daß er praktisch gleich Null wird, d. h., die Lichtstrahlen laufen parallel. Man spricht vom parallelen Licht, Abb. 13b

Bei parallelem Licht erfolgt keine Verzerrung des Schattens, wenn dieser auf eine zu diesen Lichtstrahlen rechtwinklig stehende Fläche W_2 fällt. Projeziert man die Umrisse eines Körpers durch parallele Strahlen auf eine rechtwinklig stehende Fläche, so spricht man von rechtwinkliger Parallelprojektion.

3. Grundsätzliche Darstellungsweise der technischen Zeichnung in drei Ansichten.

Für jede technische Zeichnung benutzt man nun die Parallelprojektion, aber gleichzeitig in mehreren Richtungen mit dem Vorteil, daß keine Verzerrungen der Abmessungen eintreten, so daß die senkrecht zur Blickebene liegenden Maße erhalten bleiben. Es gibt die drei Achsen $X\,Y\,Z$, von denen jede Achse zu jeder Achse senkrecht steht (Abb. 14).

Durch zwei sich schneidende Achsen wird immer eine Ebene festgelegt. Hier durch XY die Ebene I, durch YZ die Ebene II und durch Ebene ZX die Ebene III. Auch diese drei Ebenen stehen aufeinander senkrecht.

Senkrecht auf diese Ebenen soll paralleles Licht fallen, also in drei verschiedenen Richtungen und der Körper K wird durch diese parallelen Lichtstrahlen getroffen, die nun auf den Ebenen ein Schattenbild des Körpers erzeugen.

Jetzt denkt man sich nach Abb. 14b die Ebene I nach unten, die Ebene III nach rechts bis in die Richtung der Ebene II geklappt (gestrichelte Stellung). Damit sind jetzt alle drei Ansichten in einer Ebene, wie die Abb. 14c zeigt.

Läßt man nun die für die Anschauung nicht mehr notwendigen Achsen $X\,Y\,Z$ fort, so gibt sich die grundsätzliche Anordnung jeder technischen Zeichnung Abb. 14d. Es ist hierbei sehr wichtig, sich genau den Richtungssinn beim Klappen zu merken, da bei falschen Klappungen leicht Irrtümer und dabei Fehler auftreten können.

Um alle Darstellungsarten auf andere Weise zu erklären, ist in Abb. 15 gezeigt, wie man sich auch durch Umkanten eines herumgekippten

Werkstückes die normale Lage der Ansichten vorstellen kann. Gerade dieses Umkanten des wirklichen Stückes ermöglicht vielfach die genaue Bestimmung der dazugehörigen Maße in der Zeichnung. Es kann aber auch notwendig werden, daß man ein weiteres Umkanten nach links ausführen muß, das dann sinngemäß wie das Umkanten nach rechts erfolgt, wie später in Abb. 36 genauer gezeigt wird. Hierbei ist wichtig, daß bei einem Umkanten wohl eine Verschiebung des neuen Bildes in der Kantrichtung zulässig ist, das neue Bild jedoch normalerweise nicht gedreht oder schräg seitlich zur Klapprichtung verschoben ist.

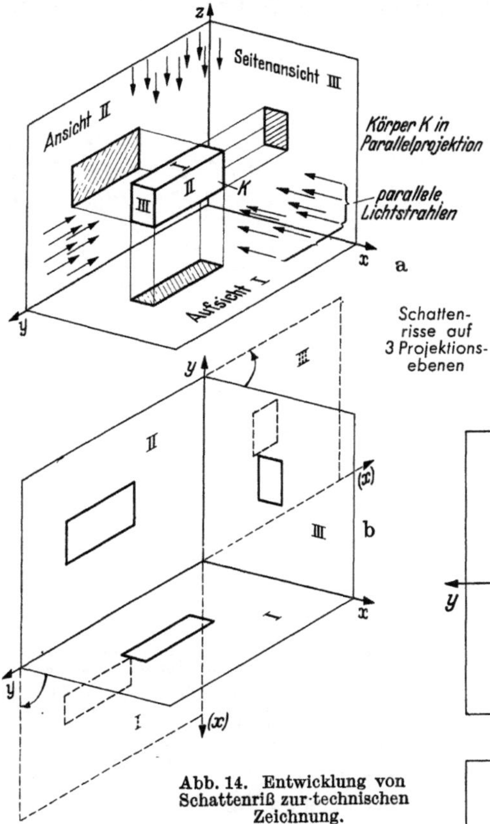

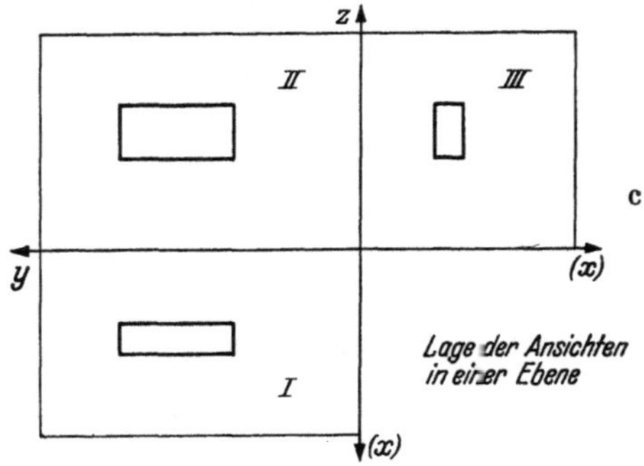

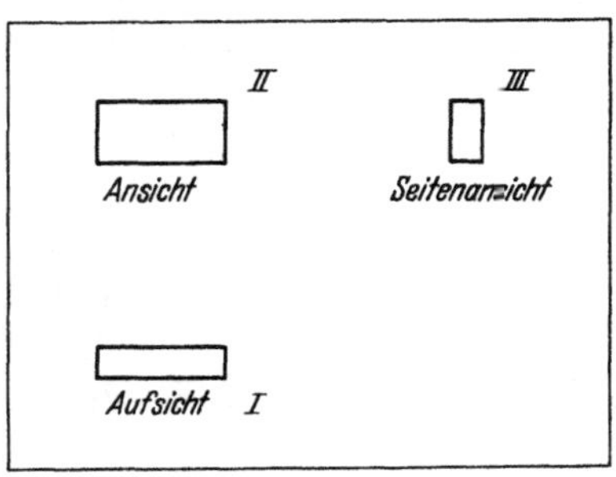

Abb. 14. Entwicklung von Schattenriß zur technischen Zeichnung.

4. Vereinfachte Ansichten durch Sinnbilder.

Um bei einfachen Teilen, wie einer Welle Abb. 16, nicht unnötige Ansichten zeichnen zu müssen, vereinfacht man die Darstellung nach folgender Überlegung.

Die rechtwinkligen Parallelprojektionen der Welle in Abb. 16a ergeben nach Abb. 16b drei Ansichten, von denen die Ansicht *3* gegenüber der Ansicht *1* nichts Neues bringt, da die Welle rund ist. Die An-

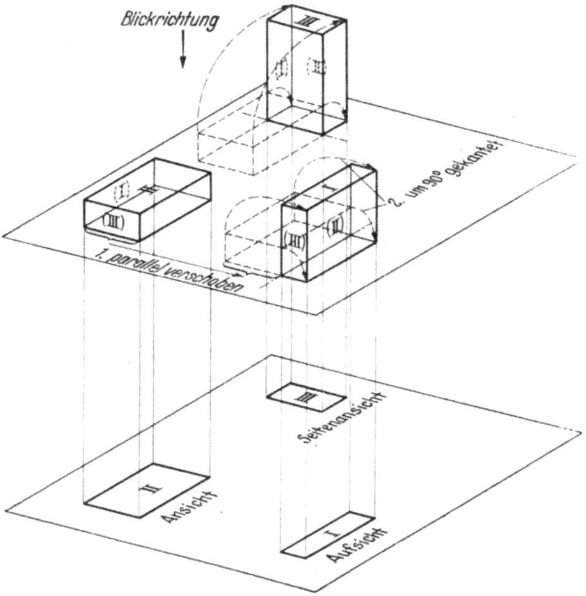

Abb. 15. Richtiges Klappen eines Körpers zur Darstellung in drei Ansichten.

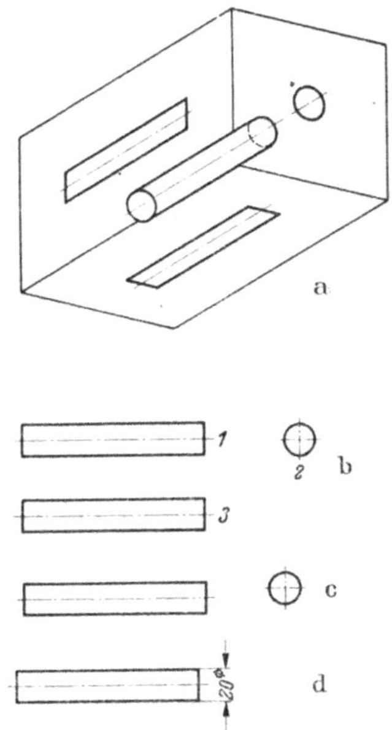

Abb. 16. Vereinfachte Wellenzeichnung durch Kurzzeichen.
a) Welle in Projektion; b) Welle in drei Ansichten; c) Welle in zwei Ansichten; d) Vereinfachte Zeichnung der Welle mit Kurzzeichen für Durchmesser.

sicht *3* kann also fortfallen, wie in Abb. 16c gezeigt. Da die Welle aber rund ist, kann man auch die Seitenansicht *2* fortlassen, wenn man durch ein Sinnbild, hier das Zeichen für Durchmesser (⌀), bereits in der Ansicht *1* angibt, daß es sich um einen Drehkörper handelt. Die endgültige und vereinfachte Zeichnung stellt Abb. 16d dar. Ein weiteres Sinnbild ist das Kurzzeichen für Vierkantprofile, das diese Form ▱ hinter dem Maß trägt (Abb. 17a···b).

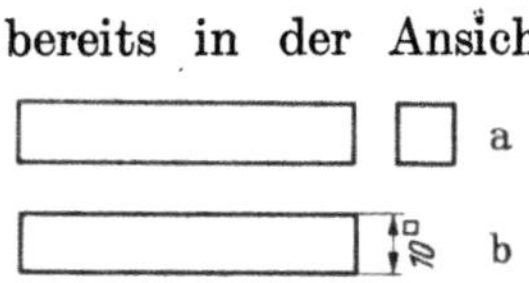

Abb. 17. Vereinfachte Darstellung durch Vierkantkurzzeichen.

5. Ausführung der Ansichten und Linienbedeutung.

In den Ansichten wird all das mit ausgezogenen Linien gezeichnet, was direkt gesehen wird. Erhöhte Punkte werden eingeebnet gedacht

(Abb. 18); verschiedene Strichstärken und unterbrochene Linien dienen zur Unterscheidung nach folgender Festlegung (Abb. 19):

1. Starke Vollinie: für sichtbare Kanten und Umrisse.

2. Strichlinie: für unsichtbare (verdeckte) Kanten und Umrisse, für Kernlinien bei Schrauben, Fußkreise bei Zahnrädern usw.

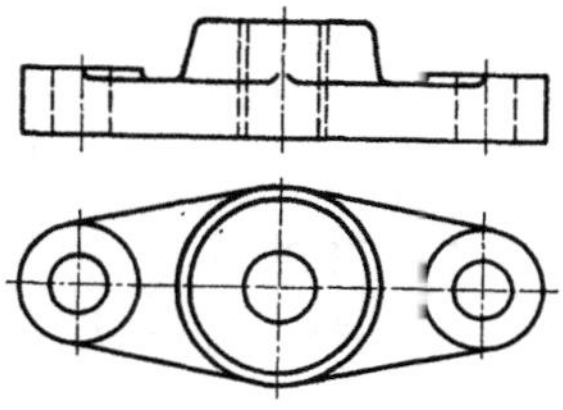

Abb. 18. Darstellung einer Traverse.

3. Feine Vollinie: als Maß- und Maßhilfslinie und zum Schraffieren von Schnittflächen; zum Andeuten einer scharfen Kante in der Grundform. Die Andeutung solcher Kanten (durch eine feine Vollinie) erleichtert das Lesen von Zeichnungen, wie Abb. 20 für eine geneigte Fläche zeigt.

4. Starke Strichpunktlinie: Zur Angabe von Schnittebenen (die Striche hier kürzer als bei den Mittellinien und stärker als bei den sichtbaren Kanten).

5. Feine Strichpunktlinie: für Mittellinien, Teilkreise bei Zahnrädern,

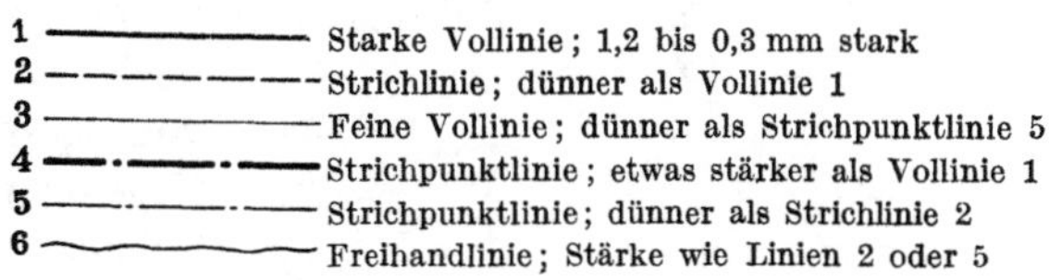

Abb. 19. Linienstärken.

Bearbeitungszugabe, z. B. bei Schmiedestücken; für Teile, die vor dem dargestellten Gegenstande liegen.

6. Freihandlinie: für Sprengfugen und Bruchkanten bei Metallen in der Stärke der Strichlinien, für Bruchkanten bei Holz (Zickzacklinien) in der Stärke der Strichpunktlinie unter 5.

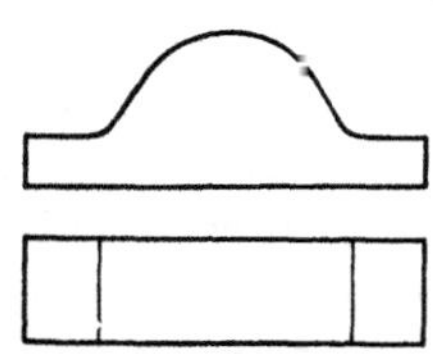

Abb. 20. Andeutung von Übergängen durch dünnere Linien.

Zu bemerken ist bei Abb. 18, daß bei den Übergängen des ovalen Flansches in die seitlichen Augen oder den mittleren erhöhten Nabenteil die Kanten leicht gekrümmt auslaufen. Für die gestrichelte Linie nimmt man an, daß ein Körper durchsichtig ist und diese Kantenschatten durchschimmern.

Zur Ersparnis von einfachen Ansichten oder auch Schnitten kann man leicht übersehbare Anlagen von Lochkreisen mit Locheinteilung,

Flanschformen, Querschnitte usw. in dünnen Linien senkrecht zur zeichnerischen Ebene, z. B. wie in Abb. 21a···b, einzeichnen.

Eine Vereinfachung ist bei der Darstellung von Gewinden getroffen. Es wird nicht jede einzelne Gewindezacke, wie sie durch einen Schnitt entsteht, und die dazugehörige Gangriefe gezeichnet, da dadurch das ganze Bild verwirrt würde. Man verwendet die in Abb. 22 gezeigten Kurzzeichen. Im *Gewindeloch* (Innengewinde) Abb. 22a wird der *Innendurchmesser des Gewindes voll*, der äußere gestrichelt gezeichnet. Bei einem *Bolzen* (Außengewinde) Abb. 22b wird der *Außendurchmesser voll*, der Innengewindedurchmesser gestrichelt gezeichnet. Kommt in einer Zusammenstellung 22c eine Schraube in einem Gewindeloch vor, so wird immer der volle Teil, also hier Schraube oder Bolzen, auch im Gewindeteil voll gezeichnet. Das Gegengewinde der Mutter liegt dann im Bolzengewinde eingeschlossen. Hört der Bolzen jedoch in der Gewindebohrung auf, so wird das Gewindeloch weiter, und zwar der Innengewindedurchmesser jetzt voll und der äußere gestrichelt gezeichnet. Das Ende des Loches hat fast immer die charakteristische Form, die von der Bohrerspitze herrührt. Man spricht von Sacklöchern und Gewindesacklöchern im Gegensatz zu Durchgangslöchern (Abb. 22a).

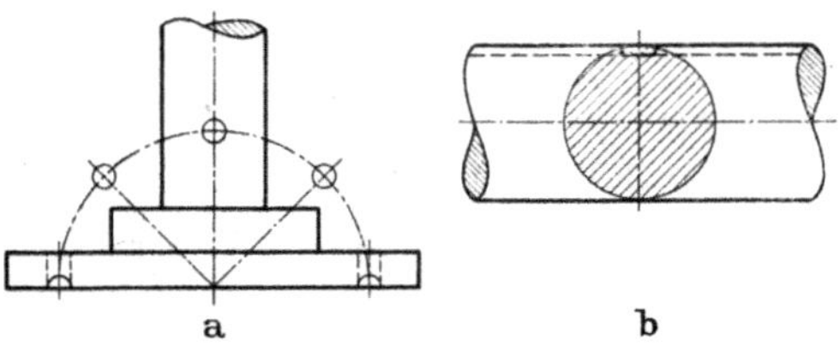

Abb. 21. Im Werkstück eingezeichnete Schnitte oder Ansichten.

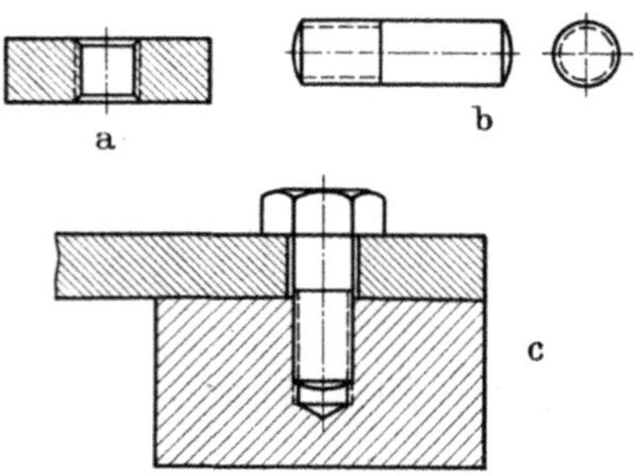

Abb. 22. Gewindedarstellung nicht geschnittener Bolzen.

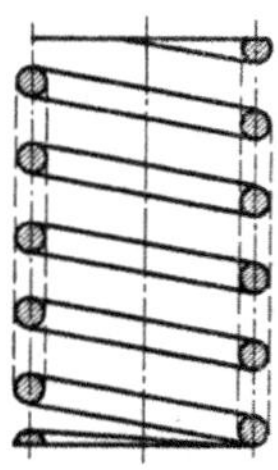
Abb. 23. Zeichnung einer Feder.

Federn sehen wie in Abb. 23 aus. Die einzelnen Windungen haben zwar scheinbar keinen Zusammenhang miteinander, doch verläuft der fortgeschrittene vordere Teil in der anderen Schräglage, wie bei einer Vorstellung der ganzen Feder leicht einleuchtet.

6. Schnitte.

Vielfach würde das Durchstricheln innen verlaufender Kanten oder Umrisse kein klares Bild der Form ergeben. Deshalb denkt man sich einen Teil oder den ganzen Körper durchgeschnitten. Normalerweise erfolgt der Schnitt durch die Mitte (Abb. 24a). Die Seitenansicht (Abb. 24b) ist an sich überflüssig, wenn die Vermaßung des Körpers in Abb. 24a die Durchmessersinnzeichen trägt, weil der Körper rund ist. Die bei diesem Schnitt abgetrennte Fläche ist schraffiert, und zwar gleichmäßig die beiden Seiten, weil es *ein* Teil ist.

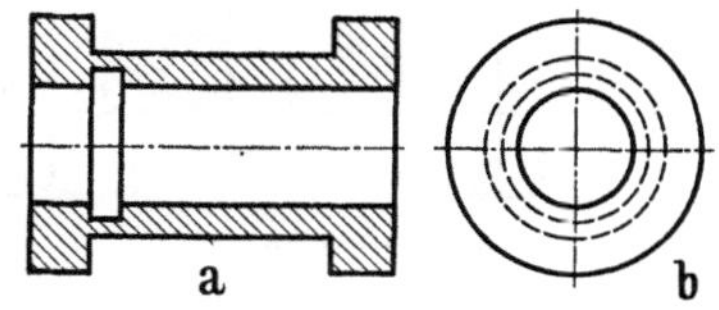

Abb. 24. Schnitt durch eine Buchse.

Wenn dagegen die Büchse geteilt ist (Abb. 25a···b), werden die zwei Hälften in verschiedener Richtung schraffiert, weil es *zwei* Teile sind.

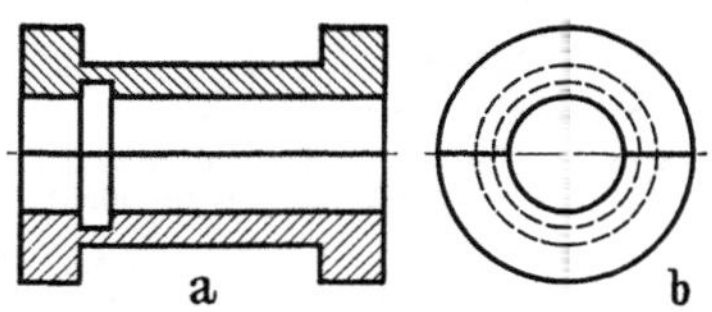

Abb. 25. Schnitt durch eine geteilte Buchse.

Führt man einen Schnitt durch ein Schwungrad, wie in Abb. 26a···b, der durch einen Arm geht, so wird der Schwungradkranz und die Nabe schraffiert, der Arm jedoch nicht, trotzdem der Schnitt hindurchläuft (Abb. 26a). Um aber die Form des Armquerschnittes anzugeben, kann nach Abb. 26b in den Arm ein Schnitt „c" gelegt werden. Man denkt sich den Arm bei „c" durchgeschnitten und den Schnitt an dieser Stelle um 90° gedreht hineingezeichnet.

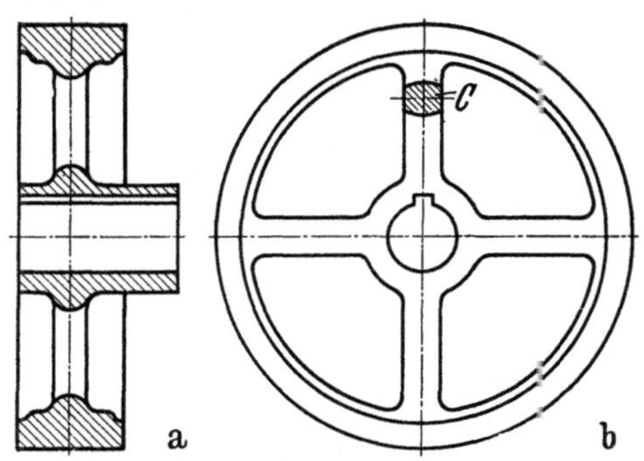

Abb. 26. Zeichnung eines Schwungrades.

Als Regel gilt: Alle vollen Teile, wie Schrauben (Abb. 27), Muttern, Nieten, Bolzen, Unterlegscheiben, Splinte, Keile, Stifte, Kugeln, Wellen, Zapfen, Rippen, Arme von Schwungrädern, Zahnräder und Riemenscheiben, Kettenglieder werden niemals im Längsschnitt, sondern stets in Ansicht gezeichnet. Wenn jedoch ein Querschnitt vorliegt, werden auch diese Teile geschnitten (Abb. 28c) (der durchgehende Bolzen).

In Abb. 28b sieht man nun, wie zur besseren Übersicht ein Stück des Bolzens herausgebrochen ist. Die Bruchfläche ist dann zur Hälfte etwa schraffiert. Die Rippen sind, wie in Abb. 28c, ebenfalls nicht geschnitten.

Abb. 29 zeigt den Unterschied der Bruchflächen zwischen Metall, einem Rohr und Holz.

Manchmal wird auch die eine Hälfte eines Körpers im Schnitt, die andere Hälfte in Ansicht gezeichnet (Abb. 30). Bei der Ansicht sind dann die Innenbohrungen durchgestrichelt. Durch Angabe der Durchmessersinnzeichen wird festgelegt, daß es sich um einen Drehkörper handelt.

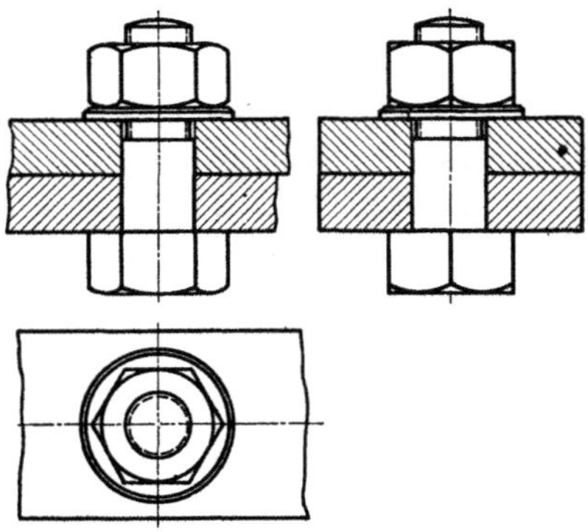

Abb. 27. Volle Teile in Ansicht gezeichnet, auch wenn ein Schnitt durchläuft.

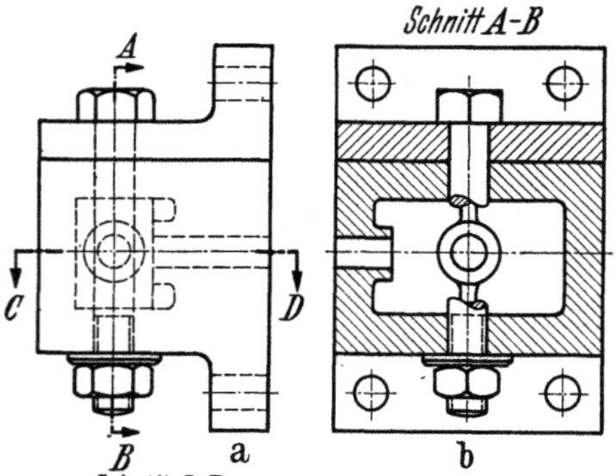

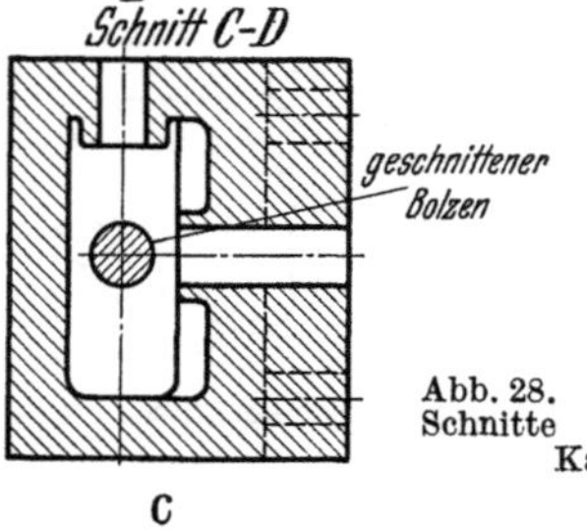

Abb. 28. Ansicht und Schnitte durch einen Kasten.

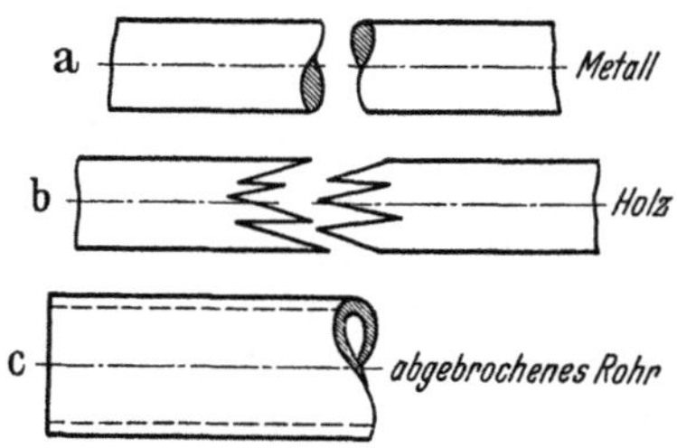

Abb. 29. Verschiedene Bruchflächen.

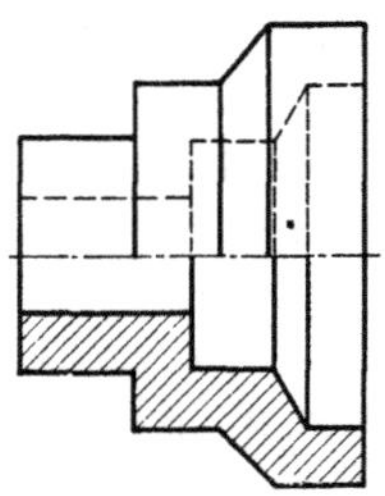

Abb. 30. Halbseitige Darstellung in Schnitt und Ansicht eines Körpers.

Wenn in einer Platte mehrere Bohrungen vorkommen (Abb. 31 a ··· b), die nicht in einer Achsrichtung liegen, die aber doch durch einen Schnitt dargestellt werden müssen, so kann ein abgesetzter Schnitt gezeichnet werden. Die Pfeile an den Enden der Schnittlinien geben die Blickrichtung an, mit der auf diesen Schnitt gesehen wird. Der Schnitt selbst wird nach Abb. 15 richtig nach rechts umgelegt. Die Pfeile sind hier z. B. nicht notwendig, da ein Irrtum ausgeschlossen ist, wie der Schnitt anzusehen ist. Bemerkenswert ist bei der Ansicht Abb. 31 a, daß die zwei kleinen Löcher beide von oben als gleiche Kreise gelten, im Schnitt aber die Form ganz verschieden ausfällt. Ebenso ist in der gestrichelten Linie des großen Loches nicht erkennbar, ob es sich um ein Gewinde oder um eine Eindrehung handelt. Erst der Schnitt gibt hierüber Aufschluß bzw. die Vermaßung.

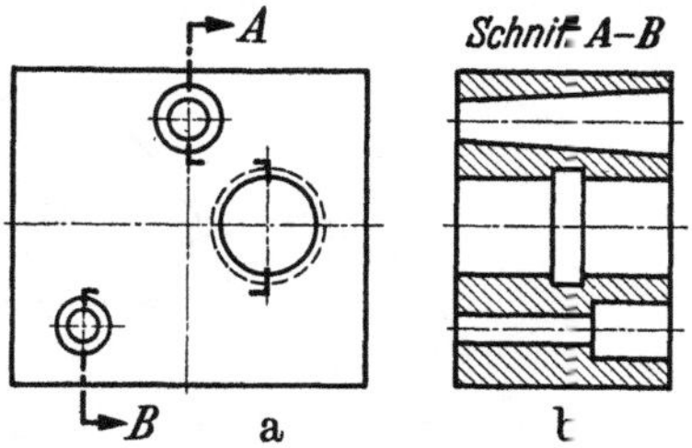

Abb. 31. Abgesetzter Schnitt.

Es kann auch vorkommen, daß der Schnittverlauf unter einem Winkel verdreht weiter verläuft (Abb. 32). Dann denkt man sich die Schnitthälfte *BO* um den Punkt *O* gedreht, wie in Pfeilrichtung (Abb. 32 a), bis dieser Teil in die Richtung *I—I* fällt. Nach rechts geklappt ergibt sich dann Abb. 32 b. Hier wird scheinbar von der Regel abgewichen, daß bei einem Schnitt alle zueinander gehörigen Linien in gleicher Höhe liegen müssen, weil die Bohrung „*z*" in Abb. 32 b tiefer liegt, als nach den durchpunktierten Linien angedeutet ist. Die Zeichnung ist aber trotzdem richtig, da ja der Schnitt *BO* in die Ebene *I—I* hineingefügt ist und dann erst nach rechts geklappt wurde. Dadurch liegt die Bohrung „*z*" auf dem Teilkreisdurchmesser „*d*"

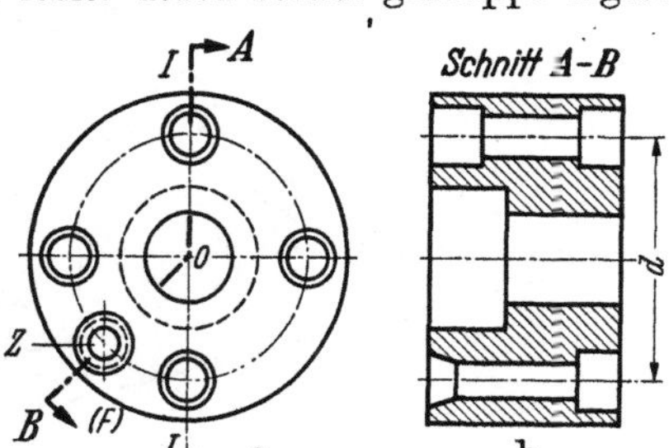

Abb. 32. Winkelschnitt.

7. Schräge Kantungen und Schnitte.

Wenn ein Werkstück eine schräge Fläche hat, auf der z. B. verschiedene Bohrungen mit Abständen im richtigen Verhältnis erkennbar sein müssen, so muß man zu schrägen Klappungen oder schrägen

Schnitten greifén. Das in Abb. 33 gezeichnete Beispiel ist zwecks Anschaulichkeit schräg umgelegt.

Das in Abb. 33 gezeigte Stück ist in Abb. 34b in Ansicht gezeichnet, wie es in Abschnitt 3 erklärt ist. Jetzt soll die schräge Fläche mit den Punkten *1, 2, 3, 4* in richtiger Ansicht dargestellt werden. Das Werkstück muß derart gekantet werden, daß diese schräge Fläche parallel zur Hauptfläche *I* zu liegen kommt.

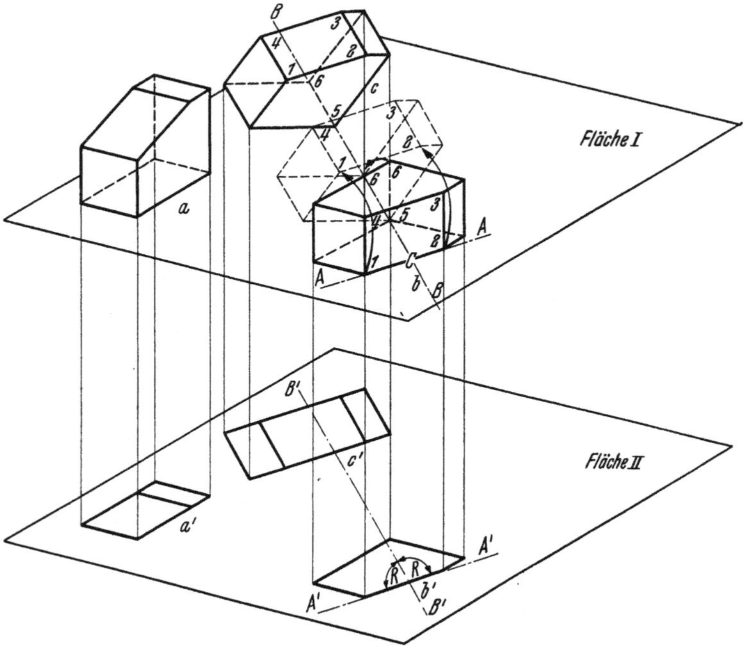

Abb. 33. Schräge Kantung.

Die Linie *B—B* soll senkrecht auf der Linie *A* stehen, also bei dem Punkt „*o*" jeweils einen rechten Winkel mit der Linie *A—A* bilden. Nun wird das Werkstück um den Punkt *5* hochgeklappt, so daß die Kanten *5—6* in die Linie *B—B* zu liegen kommt, ohne daß dabei das Werkstück nach rechts oder links umfällt. Die Kante *1—2* bleibt auch in der neuen Lage parallel zu *A—A*. Dadurch liegt jetzt die Fläche *1, 2, 3, 4* parallel zur Fläche *I*.

Man könnte die neue Ansicht direkt auf die Fläche *I* projezieren, tut das aber nicht, weil dann die Ansichten *b* und *c* dicht beieinander zu liegen kommen. Man verschiebt daher den geklappten Körper um ein an sich beliebiges Stück entlang der Linie *B—B*. Zeichnet man jetzt die Aufsicht der drei Stellungen des Körpers auf die Fläche *II*, so ergibt sich die Darstellung *a' b' c'*. Dasselbe Umkanten, jetzt nicht mehr perspektivisch dargestellt, sondern in technischer Form zeigt Abb. 34a···c. Hier haben wir nun die schräge Fläche in natürlicher Ansicht, auf der auch richtige Maße eingeschrieben werden können.

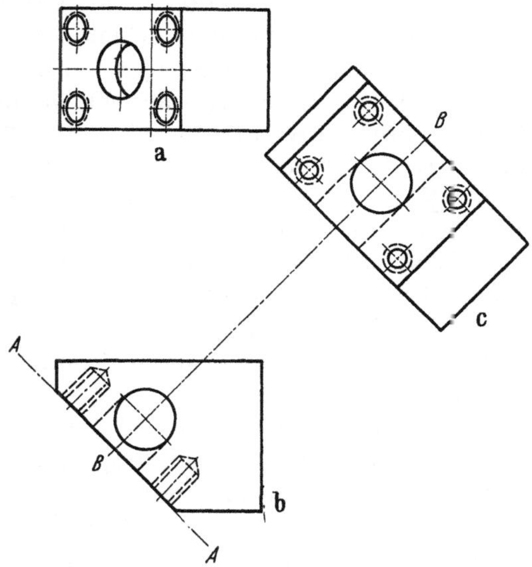

Abb. 34. Schräge Klappung eines Blockes mit ebener und unverzerrter Ansicht der schrägen Fläche.

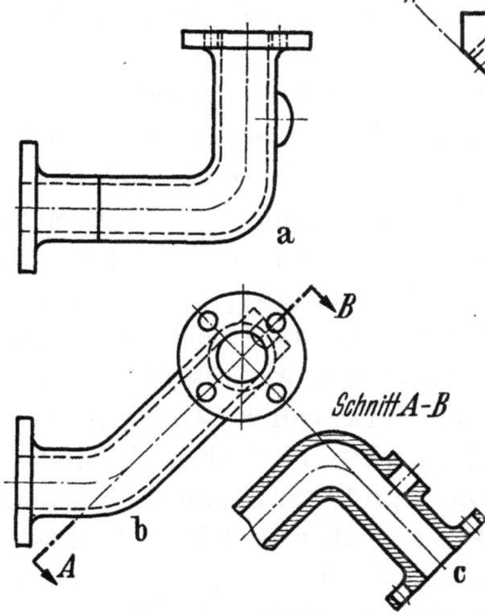

Abb. 35. Schräge Klappung mit Schnitt durch Rohrkrümmer.

Bei einem Rohrkrümmer Abb. 35a···c lassen sich durch die Ansicht *A—B* nicht genau die Maße der Warze mit Gewindeloch angeben. Auch hier wird durch einen Schnitt *A—B* senkrecht durch die Warze und durch Umlegen des Schnittes, wie in Abb. **33**, ein genaues Abbild wiedergegeben. Nur der gerade im Schnitt liegende und wesentliche Teil des Krümmers ist gezeichnet. Der Rest ist abgebrochen gedacht.

Allgemein kann man sich merken, daß jede Ansicht oder jeder Schnitt stets senkrecht zu der Ansicht oder Schnittebene liegt, auf die er bezogen ist; in dieser senkrechten Richtung kann er beliebig verschoben sein.

8. Verschiebungen von Ansicht und Schnitten.

Bei komplizierten Werkstücken ist es aus Platzmangel manchmal nicht möglich, Ansicht und Schnitte in der richtigen Klapplage zu zeichnen (Abb. 36). Vom gezeichneten Zylinderblock ist a) die Ansicht, b) die Aufsicht, c) die Seitenansicht von rechts. Diese drei Ansichten liegen richtig. Bereits die Schnitte *d—e* liegen nicht richtig, weil sie in der Aufsicht b eingezeichnet sind, aber von der Ansicht a her nach rechts geklappt wurden. Man hätte also richtiger die Schnittlinien in Abb. 36a eingetragen; jedoch ist die Eintragung in b viel besser, weil man sofort sieht, daß hier der Schnitt *A—B* durch die Zylindermitte geführt ist, während man bei einer Eintragung in a erst suchen müßte, wo der Schnitt verläuft. Es ist daher trotz der Eintragung des Schnittverlaufes *A—B* in Abb. 36b ein Schnitt durch *a* gedacht und dieser richtig nach rechts umgelegt.

Für den Schnitt *C—D* trifft in bezug auf die Lage dasselbe wie für *A—B* zu. Er ist auch in *b* eingetragen, jedoch in a geschnitten gedacht und richtig nach rechts umgelegt, aber nun ein Stück weiter nach rechts verschoben, da am eigentlichen Platz bereits der Schnitt *A—B* gezeichnet ist. Zu bemerken ist die Abknickung des Schnittes, die nicht in der Mitte erfolgte, wo die Rippe läuft, sondern darunter. Dadurch enthält *C—D* eigentlich zwei Schnitte. Der Schnitt *E—F* soll zeigen, wie die Form an der Stoßstelle des Zylinderblockes innen aussieht. Durch die Pfeilrichtung ist angegeben, daß der Blick von unten nach oben gedacht ist. Die richtige Lage des Schnittes wäre in „*f*" oben. Weil aber bei dieser Lage die Zeichnung unhandlich groß wird, und rechts und links neben dem Schnitt „*f*" freie Felder bleiben würden, ist dieser Schnitt parallel zu sich, d. h. ohne Drehung nach der Stelle „*f'*" verschoben worden. Ähnlich ist es mit dem abgesetzten Schnitt *GFIK*, der in richtiger Lage von *a* aus an der Stelle *b* liegen müßte. Hier ist aber schon *b* gezeichnet, so daß er weiter in der Klapprichtung nach unten verschoben nach „*g*" kommen mußte. In „*g*" würde er aber wieder ungünstige erhebliche Vergrößerung der Zeichnung hervorrufen, da rechts und links leere Felder bleiben würden.

Er wird also in sich parallel, d. h. ohne Verdrehung, an den freien Platz unter *d* und *e* nach „*g'*" verschoben, jetzt jedoch so, daß die

Hauptlinien mit der Aufsicht *b* in der Höhe übereinstimmen. Die Pfeilrichtung von Schnitt *GFIK* besagt, daß der Blick von oben herauf-

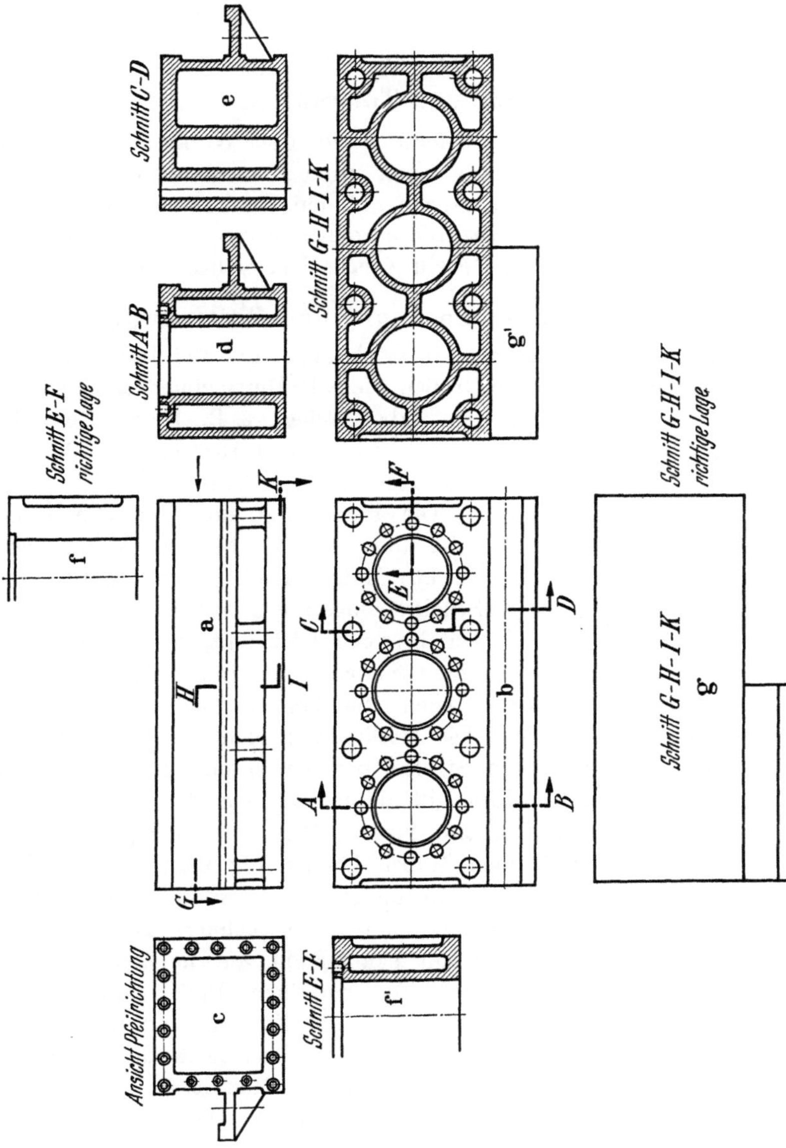

Abb. 36. Schnitt durch Zylinderblock.

fällt, daß also von der Aufsicht *b* ein oberer Teil abgeschnitten gedacht ist. Durch den abgeknickten Schnitt fallen auf der rechten Hälfte von Abb. 36*g'* die Linien für den Vorsprung fort.

Abschnitt 4.

Maße und Toleranzen.

Außer dem Bild, das die Zeichnung von dem Werkstück vermittelt, braucht man zur Herstellung auch seine Abmessungen. Zu diesem Zweck sind Maße und Toleranzen auf den Zeichnungen eingetragen. Diese werden nicht immer an die einzelnen Kanten herangeschrieben, sondern nach bestimmten Regeln zwecks Übersichtlichkeit abgerückt.

1. Maße, ihre Anordnung und Eintragung.

Sämtliche Maßeintragungen in Zeichnungen der Metalltechnik gelten in Millimetern. Sind andere Größen wie z. B. Meter eingetragen, so muß das dabei stehen, z. B. 15 m. Normalerweise schreibt man aber dafür 15000, das sind 15000 mm = 15 m.

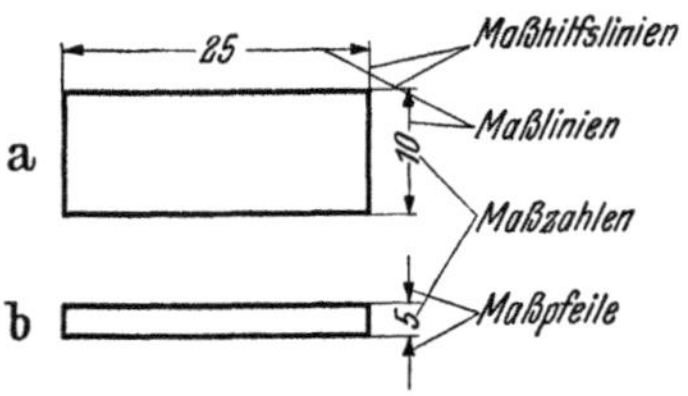

Abb. 37. Benennung der Linien für die Maßeintragung.

Die Benennung der einzelnen Linien geht aus Abb. 37 hervor. Wenn nicht direkte Maße zwischen den Kanten eines Stückes eingetragen werden können, oder zur besseren Übersicht, werden Maßhilfslinien verwendet, die in der Regel senkrecht zu den gemeinten Kanten stehen. Sie können auch schräg herausgezogen werden (Abb. 38). Die Maßlinien jedoch werden parallel zur gemeinten Strecke der Abmessung gezeichnet. Das Maß selbst gilt dann zwischen den Kanten bzw. Maßhilfslinien, bis zu denen die Pfeilspitzen gehen. Bei kleinen Maßen können die Maßpfeile auch von außen hinkommend gezeichnet werden (Abb. 37b).

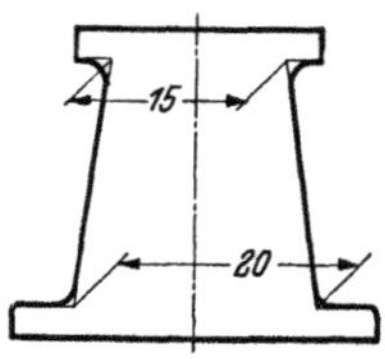

Abb. 38. Vermaßung unzugänglicher Stellen.

Der in Abb. 39a⋯b gezeichnete Bolzen ist ein Drehkörper mit 4kant-Kopf, wie die Zeichen ⌀ und ▱ angeben. Die einzelnen Maße gelten jeweils zwischen den Kanten oder Maßhilfslinien. Zu beachten ist, daß die ganze Länge größer als 90 mm wird, da dazu noch die Höhe „*h*" für die Kuppe mit 30 *r* (gemeint ist 30 mm Radius, da sonst immer ⌀-Eintragungen stattfinden) hinzuzurechnen ist. Das rohe Stück muß also länger sein. Ferner muß man beachten, daß beim Drehen des Ansatzes für den ▱ Kopf Abb. 39a, gekennzeichnet durch die gekreuzten Flächen, der Drehdurchmesser größer sein muß, wie Abb. 39b zeigt. Falls, wie in Abb. 39a, eine Abrundung der Ecken vorhanden sein soll, muß der Radius auf der Zeichnung angegeben sein. Das Durchmesserzeichen wird fortgelassen, wenn beide Maßpfeile in der Kreislinie erscheinen, das Stück ist dann nach Zeichnung rund.

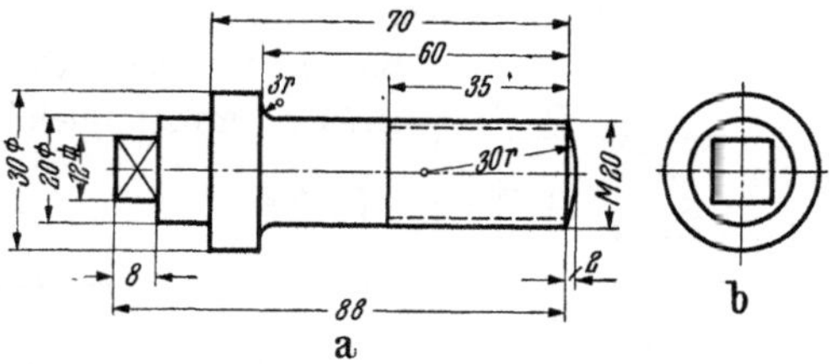

Abb. 39. Maßeintragungen.

Sind an einem Werkstück nach Abb. 40 viele Ansätze vorhanden, so daß auf jeder Seite sehr viele Durchmesserangaben und Maßlinien notwendig wären, so können zur Übersichtlichkeit nur die eine Hälfte der Maßlinien und Pfeile gezeichnet sein. Wenn dann das Maß mit dem Durchmesserzeichen eingeschrieben ist, gilt es bis zur entsprechenden Kante der anderen Hälfte. Ebenso können bei Durchmesserangaben (Abb. 41a) nur ein Teil der Maßlinien angegeben sein oder wie in Abb. 41b eine Abknickung der Maßlinien stattfinden, damit eine genaue Einzeichnung des Ausgangspunktes mit dem Abstand 10 mm vorgenommen werden kann, um nicht unnötig viel Zeichenpapier bei maßstäblicher Eintragung zu erhalten.

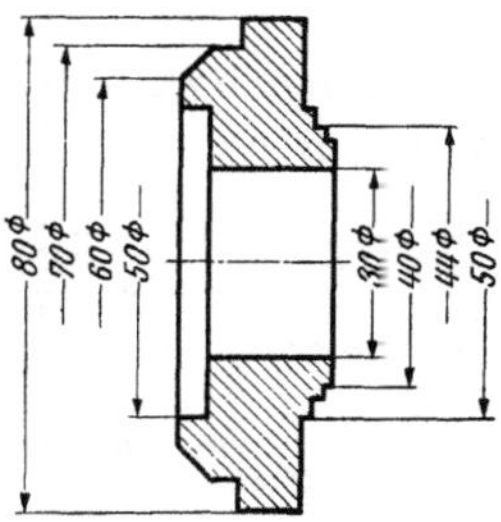

Abb. 40. Fortlassen einer Hälfte von Maßlinien zur besseren Übersichtlichkeit.

Ein Teil nach Abb. 42 enthält innen eine Kugelfläche, deutlich an der Angabe 20 Kugel erkenntlich. Hier muß besonders vorsichtig gearbeitet werden.

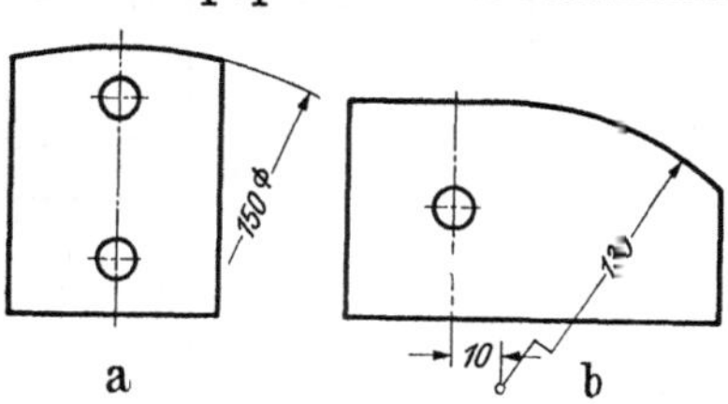

Abb. 41. Eintragungen von großen Radien und Vermaßung.

2. Gewinde.

Die Gewindevermaßung wird immer bis zum äußeren Gewindedurchmesser eingetragen (Abb. 43). Bei Außengewinden bis zu den vollen Gewindelinien, bei Innengewinden bis zur gestrichelten Außendurchmesserlinie (Abb. 43b). Die Art und Größe der Gewinde wird mit Kurzzeichen angegeben. Steht z. B. in der Zeichnung „M 25“, so bedeutet das ein metrisches Gewinde, dessen Abmessungen in einem Normblatt festgelegt sind. Bei metrischen Gewinden ist der Außendurchmesser immer gleich der Bezeichnung, hier also 25 mm. Bei der Angabe $^1/_2''$ (gesprochen ein halb Zoll) handelt es sich um Zollgewinde, dessen Hauptabmessungen aus Aushängen im Betrieb entnommen werden können.

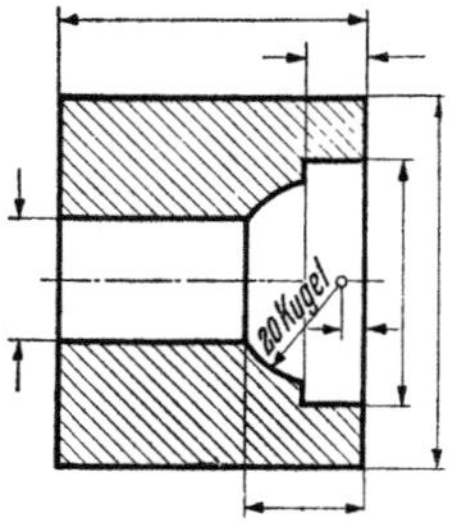

Abb. 42. Vermaßung einer Kugel.

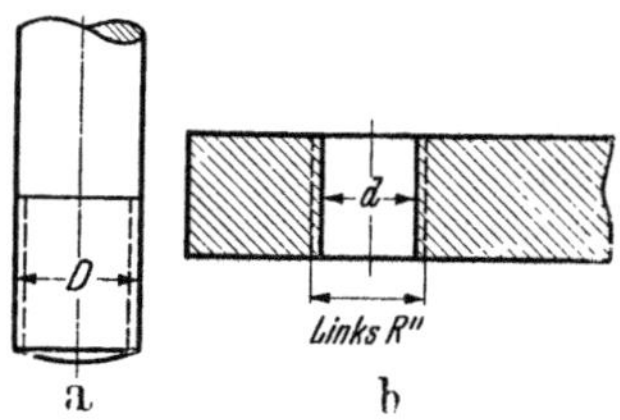

Abb. 43. Sinnbild für Gewinde.

Normalerweise haben alle Gewinde Rechtssteigung, wenn keine Bemerkung in der Zeichnung steht. Bei Linkssteigung wird wie in Abb. 43b „Links“ eingeschrieben. Die Größe des Kerndurchmessers zeigt Abb. 44.

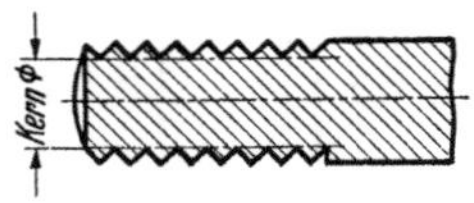

Abb. 44. Kerndurchmesser bei Gewinden.

3. Oberflächenzeichen.

Für die Oberflächengüte sind verschiedene Kurzzeichen auf den Kanten des Werkstückes oder den Maßhilfslinien eingetragen, und zwar immer auf der Seite, wo die Abnahme der Späne durch das Werkzeug erfolgen soll (Abb. 45). Wenn kein Bearbeitungszeichen vorhanden ist, findet auch keine Bearbeitung statt; diese Stelle bleibt roh. Das Zeichen ~ bedeutet eine ganz rohe Bearbeitung durch Schmirgeln oder Feilen, Verputzen von Nähten, die durch eine Maschinenbearbeitung selten vorgenommen wird.

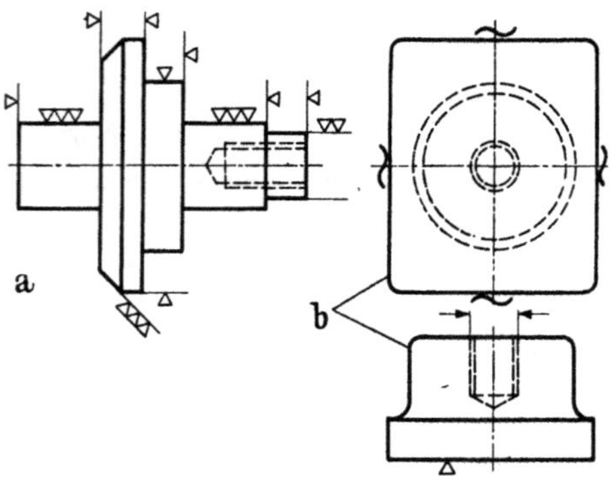

Abb. 45. Verschiedene Oberflächenzeichen.

Das Beispiel Abb. 45a wird bearbeitet:

1. Nach Abb. 46b die Seitenflächen des ▱ nicht, weil „∼“ vorhanden ist. In besonderen Fällen grob schruppen, Riefen dürfen deutlich sichtbar sein.

2. Nach Abb. 46a ▽. Riefen dürfen mit bloßem Auge noch sichtbar sein.

3. ▽▽ Riefen dürfen mit bloßem Auge nicht erkennbar sein.

4. ▽▽▽ Keine Riefen und glatte Oberfläche.

Wichtig ist, daß diese Oberflächengüten nichts besagen über die Genauigkeit der Abmessung, vergleiche folgenden Abschnitt. Ebenso nichts über die Herstellungsverfahren, also Drehen oder Schleifen usw. Die Bearbeitungsart ist allein durch die Arbeitsvorschrift festgelegt.

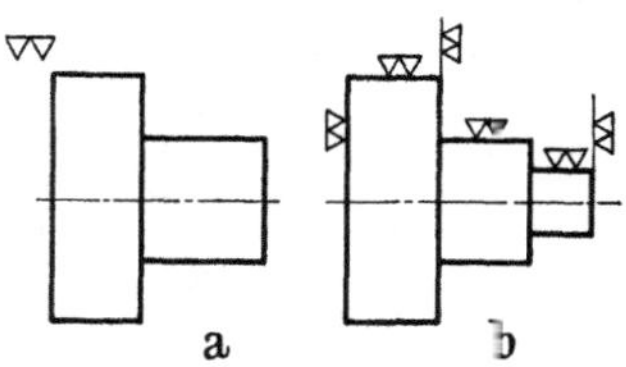

Abb. 46. Bearbeitungsoberzeichen.

Befindet sich am Werkstück kein Bearbeitungszeichen (Abb. 46a), auf der Zeichnung jedoch (meistens über dem Schriftfeld) das Bearbeitungszeichen ▽▽, so sind sämtliche Flächen nach ▽▽ zu bearbeiten, wie in Abb. 46b gezeichnet.

Trägt die Zeichnung außer dem Zeichen ▽▽ noch das andere Zeichen ▽▽▽ dahinter in Klammern, so sind alle Flächen nach ▽▽ zu bearbeiten, die mit ▽▽▽ versehenen Flächen dagegen feiner (Abb. 47).

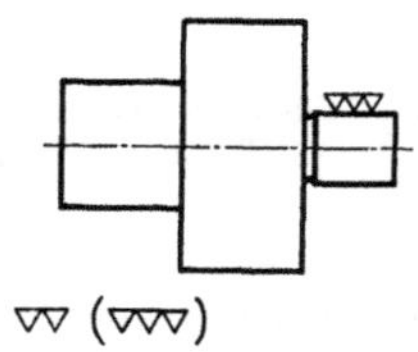

Abb. 47. Bearbeitungsoberzeichen.

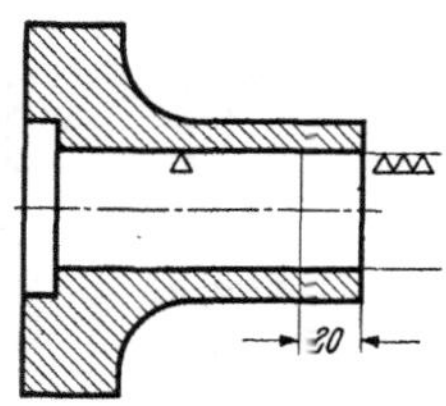

Abb. 48. Verschiedene Bearbeitung der gleichen Bohrung.

Wenn in einer Bohrung (Abb. 48) zwei Bearbeitungszeichen stehen, ▽ und ▽▽▽, so wird die Bohrung auf die hier angegebene Länge von 20 mm nach ▽▽▽ bearbeitet und der übrige Teil der Bohrung mit ▽.

Gewinde werden allgemein nicht mit Oberflächenzeichen versehen, müssen aber immer ▽▽▽ entsprechen.

4. Toleranzen und Passungssysteme.

Ein Maß genau einzuhalten ist praktisch überhaupt nicht möglich. Man muß stets eine Abweichung zulassen, auch wenn diese nur ein Bruchteil eines tausendstel Millimeters wäre. Je kleiner diese zulässige

Abweichung wird, um so länger wird die Arbeitszeit und um so teurer das Stück. Aus diesem Grunde versucht man durch eine geeignete Konstruktion möglichst große Abweichungen der Maße zulässig zu machen und nur einen geringen Teil der Maße mit kleinen Abweichungen festzulegen. Man spricht vom „Tolerieren“ der Maße. Gerade bei Serienfertigungen müssen aus der Zeichnung die Toleranzen erkennbar sein. Sache des Konstrukteurs ist es, die Teile so zu tolerieren, daß sie trotz der Abweichungen austauschbar bleiben.

5. Allgemeines über Toleranzen.

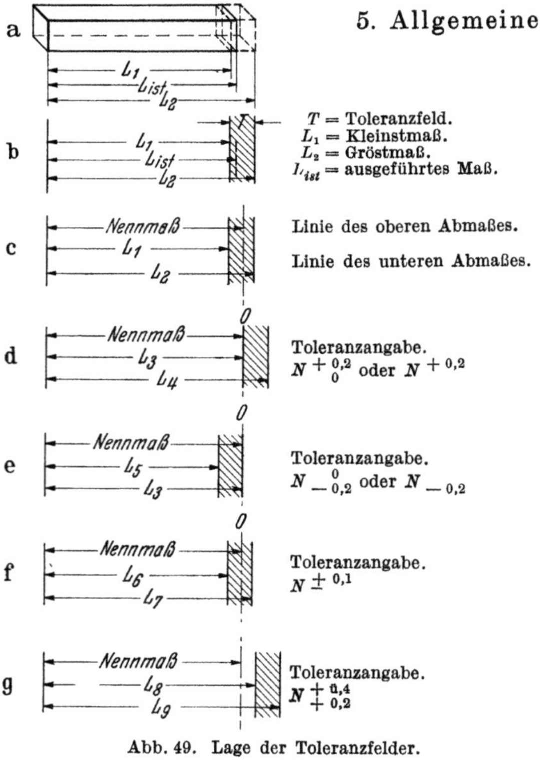

Abb. 49. Lage der Toleranzfelder.

Mehrere nach Zeichnung gleiche Werkstücke (Abb. 49a) werden daher mit verschiedenen Längen zwischen L_1 dem Kleinstmaß und L_2 dem Größtmaß bei der Fertigung ausfallen. Das in Abb. 49b schraffierte Bild zwischen dem oberen und unteren Maß heißt „Toleranzfeld“, die wirklich ausgefallene Länge „L_{ist}“ ist das „Istmaß“, die Breite des Toleranzfeldes = der Toleranz ist „T“. Das Nennmaß ist das auf der Zeichnung angegebene theoretisch genaue Maß und soll nach Abb. 49c hier innerhalb des Toleranzfeldes liegen. Die Linie des genauen Nennmaßes heißt „Null-Linie“. Die Begrenzungslinien des Toleranzfeldes werden mit oberem und unterem Abmaß bezeichnet. Von der Null-Linie aus betrachtet sagt man nun, daß die Toleranz über Null liegt (Abb. 49d), das untere Abmaß ist dann gleich Null, oder unter Null liegt (Abb. 49c), das obere Abmaß ≐ Null. In Abb. 49f liegt das obere Abmaß über Null und das untere Abmaß unter Null. Es handelt sich jetzt darum, die Größe der Abmaße anzugeben und in der Zeichnung festzulegen. Dabei wird das obere Abmaß immer hoch, das untere stets tief hinter das Maß gesetzt (Abb. 49g).

6. Einfache Toleranzangaben.

Eine einfache Eintragung der Toleranzen ist in Abb. 50 angegeben. Hier erscheinen:

80 ± 0,2	das Maß darf also	80,2	bis	79,8	betragen.
100 + 0,3	„ „ „ „	105,3	„	105,0	„
20 ⌀ + 0,2 − 0,1	„ „ „ „	20,2 ⌀	„	19,9 ⌀	„
35 ⌀ − 0,05	„ „ „ „	35,0 ⌀	„	34,95 ⌀	„
10 ⌀ + 0,02 − 0,03	„ „ „ „	10,02 ⌀	„	9,97 ⌀	„

Die Toleranz ist also immer vom genauen Nennmaß zuzuzählen oder abzuziehen, je nach dem Vorzeichen. Aufpassen muß man bei dem Abziehen von 0,01 mm, das sind hundertstel Millimeter, damit nicht versehentlich stattdessen $^1/_{10}$ mm gerechnet wird.

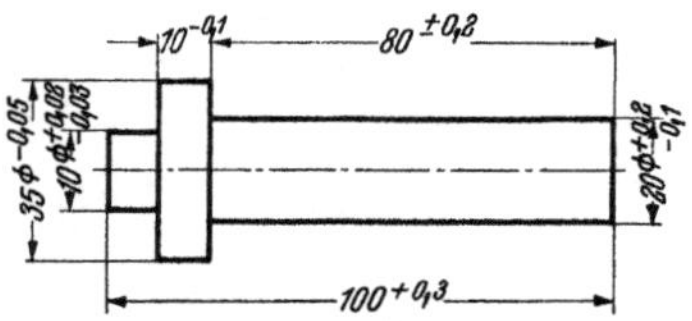

Abb. 50. Einfache Toleranzangaben

7. Toleranzen nach dem DIN-Passungssystem.

Man hat sich nun zwecks Übersichtlichkeit bei der Konstruktion überlegt, welche Toleranzen einheitlich z. B. für die zueinandergehörigen Wellen und Bohrungen gewählt werden müssen, um einen bestimmten Sitz für das Funktionieren der beiden Teile gegeneinander zu erhalten. Diese sind in einer Zahlentafel zusammengefaßt und erleichtern so dem Konstrukteur die Arbeit. Damit dieser nicht jedesmal die verschiedenen Toleranzen aus Zahlentafeln entnehmen und sie in die Zeichnung eintragen muß, werden für den gewünschten Sitz allgemeingültige Kurzzeichen verwendet.

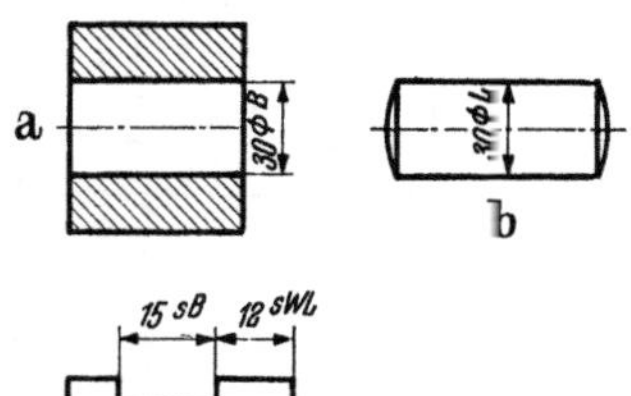

Abb. 51. Eintragungen von DIN-Passungen.

Die in Abb. 51a gezeichnete Buchse soll in der Bohrung mit der Toleranz B auf das Maß 30 mm ⌀ B gefertigt werden, die Welle in

Tabelle 3. Kleine Buchstaben.

Nennabmaße in $\mu = {}^1/_{1000}$ mm für Außenmaße.

Paßtoleranzfeld	Nennbereich in mm																					
	1 bis 3	3 bis 6	6 bis 10	10 bis 18	18 bis 30	30 bis 40	40 bis 50	50 bis 65	65 bis 80	80 bis 100	100 bis 120	120 bis 140	140 bis 160	160 bis 180	180 bis 200	200 bis 225	225 bis 250	250 bis 280	280 bis 315	315 bis 355	355 bis 400	400 bis 450	450 bis 500
a 11	-270 -330	-270 -345	-280 -370	-290 -400	-300 -430	-310 -470	-320 -480	-340 -530	-360 -550	-380 -600	-410 -630	-460 -710	-520 -770	-580 -830	-660 -950	-740 -1030	-820 -1110	-920 -1240	-1050 -1370	-1200 -1560	-1350 -1710	-1500 -1900	-1650 -2050
b 11	-140 -200	-140 -215	-150 -240	-150 -260	-160 -290	-170 -330	-180 -340	-190 -380	-200 -390	-220 -440	-240 -460	-260 -510	-280 -530	-310 -560	-340 -630	-380 -670	-420 -710	-480 -800	-540 -860	-600 -960	-680 -1040	-760 -1160	-840 -1240
c 11	-60 -120	-70 -145	-80 -170	-95 -205	-110 -240	-120 -280	-130 -290	-140 -330	-150 -340	-170 -390	-180 -400	-200 -450	-210 -460	-230 -480	-240 -530	-260 -550	-280 -570	-300 -620	-330 -650	-360 -720	-400 -760	-440 -840	-480 -880
d 9	-20 -45	-30 -60	-40 -76	-50 -93	-65 -117	-80 -142		-100 -174		-120 -207		-145 -245			-170 -285			-190 -320		-210 -350		-230 -385	
d 10	-20 -60	-30 -78	-40 -98	-50 -120	-65 -149	-80 -180		-100 -220		-120 -260		-145 -305			-170 -355			-190 -400		-210 -440		-230 -480	
d 11	-20 -80	-30 -105	-40 -130	-50 -160	-65 -195	-80 -240		-100 -290		-120 -340		-145 -395			-170 -460			-190 -510		-210 -570		-230 -630	
e 8	-14 -28	-20 -38	-25 -47	-32 -59	-40 -73	-50 -89		-60 -106		-72 -126		-85 -148			-100 -172			-110 -191		-125 -214		-135 -232	
e 9	-14 -39	-20 -50	-25 -61	-32 -75	-40 -92	-50 -112		-60 -134		-72 -159		-85 -185			-100 -215			-110 -240		-125 -265		-135 -290	
f 7	-7 -16	-10 -22	-13 -28	-16 -34	-20 -41	-25 -50		-30 -60		-36 -71		-43 -83			-50 -96			-56 -108		-62 -119		-68 -131	
f 8	-7 -21	-10 -28	-13 -35	-16 -43	-20 -53	-25 -64		-30 -76		-36 -90		-43 -106			-50 -122			-56 -137		-62 -151		-68 -115	
g 5	-3 -8	-4 -9	-5 -11	-6 -14	-7 -16	-9 -20		-10 -23		-12 -27		-14 -32			-15 -35			-17 -40		-18 -43		-20 -47	
g 6	-3 -10	-4 -12	-5 -14	-6 -17	-7 -20	-9 -25		-10 -29		-12 -34		-14 -39			-15 -44			-17 -49		-18 -54		-20 -60	

h 5	0 −5	0 −5	0 −6	0 −8	0 −9	0 −11	0 −13		0 −15		0 −18			0 −20			0 −23		0 −25		0 −27	
h 6	0 −7	0 −8	0 −9	0 −11	0 −13	0 −16	0 −19		0 −22		0 −25			0 −29			0 −32		0 −36		0 −40	
h 8	0 −14	0 −18	0 −22	0 −27	0 −33	0 −39	0 −46		0 −54		0 −63			0 −72			0 −81		0 −89		0 −97	
h 9	0 −25	0 −30	0 −36	0 −43	0 −52	0 −62	0 −74		0 −87		0 −100			0 −115			0 −130		0 −140		0 −155	
h 11	0 −60	0 −75	0 −90	0 −110	0 −130	0 −160	0 −190		0 −220		0 −250			0 −290			0 −320		0 −360		0 −400	
j 5	+4 −1	+4 −1	+4 −2	+5 −3	+5 −4	+6 −5	+6 −7		+6 −9		+7 −11			+7 −13			+7 −16		+7 −18		+7 −20	
j 6	+6 −1	+7 −1	+7 −2	+8 −3	+9 −4	+11 −5	+12 −7		+13 −9		+14 −11			+16 −13			+16 −16		+18 −18		+20 −20	
k 5	— —	— —	+7 +1	+9 +1	+11 +2	+13 +2	+15 +2		+18 +3		+21 +3			+24 +4			+27 +4		+29 +4		+32 +5	
k 6	— —	— —	+10 +1	+12 +1	+15 +2	+18 +2	+21 +2		+25 +3		+28 +3			+33 +4			+36 +4		+40 +4		+45 +5	
m 5	+7 +2	+9 +4	+12 +6	+15 +7	+17 +8	+20 +9	+24 +11		+28 +13		+33 +15			+37 +17			+43 +20		+46 +21		+50 +23	
m 6	+9 +2	+12 +4	+15 +6	+18 +7	+21 +8	+25 +9	+30 +11		+35 +13		+40 +15			+46 +17			+52 +20		+57 +21		+63 +23	
n 5	+11 +6	+13 +8	+16 +10	+20 +12	+24 +15	+28 +17	+33 +20		+28 +23		+45 +27			+51 +31			+57 +34		+62 +37		+67 +40	
n 6	+13 +6	+16 +8	+19 +10	+23 +12	+28 +15	+33 +17	+39 +20		+45 +23		+52 +27			+60 +31			+66 +34		+73 +37		+80 +40	
r 6	+19 +12	+23 +15	+28 +19	+34 +23	+41 +28	+50 +34	+60 +41	+62 +43	+73 +51	+76 +54	+88 +63	+90 +65	+93 +68	+100 +77	+109 +80	+110 +84	+120 +94	+100 +98	+144 +108	+150 +114	+166 +126	+170 +132
s 6	+22 +15	+27 +19	+32 +23	+39 +28	+48 +35	+59 +43	+72 +53	+78 +59	+93 +71	+101 +79	+117 +92	+125 +100	+133 +108	+151 +122	+159 +130	+169 +140	+190 +158	+202 +170	+226 +150	+244 +208	+272 +232	+292 +252

Tabelle 4. Große Buchstaben.

Nennabmaße in $\mu = {}^{1}/_{1000}$ mm für Innenmaße.

Paß-tole-ranz-feld	Nennbereich in mm																					
	1 bis 3	3 bis 6	6 bis 10	10 bis 18	18 bis 30	30 bis 40	40 bis 50	50 bis 65	65 bis 80	80 bis 100	100 bis 120	120 bis 140	140 bis 160	160 bis 180	180 bis 200	200 bis 225	225 bis 250	250 bis 280	280 bis 315	315 bis 355	355 bis 400	400 bis 450	450 bis 500
A 11	+330 +270	+345 +270	+370 +280	+400 +290	+430 +300	+470 +310	+480 +320	+530 +340	+550 +360	+600 +380	+630 +410	+710 +460	+770 +520	+830 +580	+950 +660	+1030 +740	+1110 +820	+1240 +920	+1370 +1050	+1560 +1200	+1710 +1350	+1900 +1500	+2050 +1650
B 11	+200 +140	+215 +140	+240 +150	+260 +150	+290 +160	+330 +170	+340 +180	+380 +190	+390 +200	+440 +220	+460 +240	+510 +260	+530 +280	+560 +310	+630 +340	+670 +380	+710 +420	+800 +480	+860 +540	+960 +600	+1040 +680	+1160 +760	+1240 +840
C 11	+120 +60	+145 +70	+170 +80	+205 +95	+240 +110	+280 +120	+290 +130	+330 +140	+340 +150	+310 +170	+400 +180	+450 +200	+460 +210	+480 +230	+530 +240	+550 +260	+570 +280	+620 +300	+650 +330	+720 +360	+760 +400	+840 +440	+880 +480
D 9	+45 +20	+60 +30	+76 +40	+93 +50	+117 +65	+142 +80		+174 +100		+207 +120		+245 +145			+285 +170			+320 +190		+350 +210		+385 +230	
D 10	+60 +20	+78 +30	+98 +40	+120 +50	+149 +65	+180 +80		+220 +100		+260 +120		+305 +145			+355 +170			+400 +190		+440 +210		+480 +230	
D 11	+80 +20	+105 +30	+130 +40	+160 +50	+195 +65	+240 +80		+290 +100		+340 +120		+395 +145			+460 +170			+510 +190		+570 +210		+630 +230	
E 8	+28 +14	+38 +20	+47 +25	+59 +32	+73 +40	+89 +50		+106 +60		+126 +72		+148 +85			+172 +100			+191 +110		+214 +125		+232 +135	
E 9	+39 +14	+50 +20	+61 +25	+75 +32	+92 +40	+112 +50		+134 +60		+159 +72		+185 +85			+215 +100			+240 +110		+265 +125		+290 +135	
F 7	+16 +7	+22 +10	+28 +13	+34 +16	+41 +20	+50 +25		+60 +30		+71 +36		+83 +43			+96 +50			+108 +56		+119 +62		+131 +68	
F 8	+21 +7	+28 +10	+35 +13	+43 +16	+53 +20	+64 +25		+76 +30		+90 +36		+106 +43			+122 +50			+137 +56		+151 +62		+165 +68	
G 6	+10 +3	+12 +4	+14 +5	+17 +6	+20 +7	+25 +9		+29 +10		+34 +12		+39 +14			+44 +15			+49 +17		+54 +18		+60 +20	
G 7	+12 +3	+16 +4	+20 +5	+24 +6	+28 +7	+34 +9		+40 +10		+47 +12		+54 +14			+61 +15			+69 +17		+75 +18		+83 +20	

6	+7 0	+8 0	+9 0	+11 0	+13 0	+16 0	+19 0		+22 0		+25 0			+29 0			+32 0		+36 0		+40 0	
7	+9 0	+12 0	+15 0	+18 0	+21 0	+25 0	+30 0		+35 0		+40 0			+46 0			+52 0		+57 0		+63 0	
8	+14 0	+18 0	+22 0	+27 0	+33 0	+39 0	+46 0		+54 0		+63 0			+72 0			+81 0		+89 0		+97 0	
11	+60 0	+75 0	+90 0	+110 0	+130 0	+160 0	+190 0		+220 0		+250 0			+290 0			+320 0		+360 0		+400 0	
6	+3 −4	+4 −4	+5 −4	+6 −5	+8 −5	+10 −6	+13 −6		+16 −6		+18 −7			+22 −7			+25 −7		+29 −7		+33 −7	
7	+3 −6	+5 −7	+8 −7	+10 −8	+12 −9	+14 −11	+18 −12		+22 −13		+26 −14			+30 −16			+36 −16		+39 −18		+43 −20	
6	— —	— —	+2 −7	+2 −9	+2 −11	+3 −13	+4 −15		+4 −18		+4 −21			+5 −24			+5 −27		+7 −29		+8 −32	
7	— —	— —	+5 −10	+6 −12	+6 −15	+7 −18	+9 −21		+10 −25		+12 −28			+13 −33			+16 −36		+17 −40		+18 −45	
6	0 −7	−1 −9	−3 −12	−4 −15	−4 −17	−4 −20	−5 −24		−6 −28		−8 −33			−8 −37			−9 −41		−10 −46		−10 −50	
7	0 −9	0 −12	0 −15	0 −18	0 −21	0 −25	0 −30		0 −35		0 −40			0 −46			0 −52		0 −57		0 −63	
6	−4 −11	−5 −13	−7 −16	−9 −20	−11 −24	−12 −28	−14 −33		−16 −38		−20 −45			−22 −51			−25 −57		−26 −62		−27 −67	
7	−4 −13	−4 −16	−4 −19	−5 −23	−7 −28	−8 −33	−9 −39		−10 −45		−12 −52			−14 −60			−14 −66		−16 −73		−17 −80	
7	10 −19	11 −23	13 −28	16 −34	20 −41	−25 −50	−30 −60	−32 −62	−38 −73	−41 −76	−48 −88	−50 −90	−53 −93	−60 −106	−63 −109	−67 −113	−74 −126	−78 −130	−87 −144	−93 −150	−103 −166	−109 −172
7	−13 −22	−15 −27	−17 −32	−21 −39	−27 −48	−34 −59	−42 −72	−48 −78	−58 −93	−66 −101	−77 −117	−85 −125	−93 −133	−105 −151	−113 −159	−123 −169	−138 −190	−150 −202	−169 −226	−187 −244	−209 −272	−229 −292

Abb. 51b auf das Maß 30 mm ⌀ L. Wie groß die Abmaße sind, kann aus DIN 7665 entnommen werden. Hier wird

30 B = 30,025 bis 30,000 mm ⌀
30 L = 30,060 bis 30,025 mm ⌀

Die Toleranzen sind für verschiedene Durchmesserbereiche abgestuft. Wenn das Maß gerade auf der Grenze eines Bereiches liegt, z. B. bei 30 mm, ist die Toleranz des höheren Bereiches als von 30···50 mm zu verwenden. Dieselben Toleranzen kommen auch bei Abstandsmaßen, z. B. Nuten oder Leisten (Abb. 51c) vor. Man unterscheidet bei der DIN-Passung vier Gütegrade und Sitze,

Edelpassung,
Feinpassung,
Schlichtpassung
Grobpassung,

von denen die Edelpassung die kleinsten Toleranzen hat, die bis zur Grobpassung immer größer werden, jeweils innerhalb eines Durchmesserbereiches.

8. Toleranzen nach dem ISA-Passungssystem.

Die DIN-Passungen sind seinerzeit für Deutschland ausgearbeitet worden und ihre Buchstabenbezeichnung lehnt sich mit ihren Abkürzungen an das deutsche Passungswort an, z. B. „eB" = Edelbohrung. Es bestand der Wunsch, ein einheitlich gültiges System für möglichst viele Länder einzuführen, damit auch im Ausland bei Reparaturen usw. das in der Zeichnung stehende Kurzzeichen verstanden wird und die dort vorhandenen Lehren und Meßwerkzeuge benutzt werden können. Ferner auch, damit einfach genormte Teile ohne weiteres in ausländische Maschinen oder Anlagen eingebaut werden können.

So entstanden die ISA-Toleranzen, an deren Entwicklung Deutschland hervorragend beteiligt war. Es besaß das gut durchgearbeitete DIN-System, das mit geringen Ausnahmen die Grundlage für die ISA-Norm abgab bzw. direkt übernommen wurde. Daher die häufige Übereinstimmung von ISA- und DIN-Lehren.

Statt vier Gütegrade bei der DIN-Passung haben wir bei der ISA-Passung 16 Qualitäten, von 1···16 immer gröber werdend abgestuft. Für die Fertigung sind die Qualitäten IT 5 bis IT 11 festgelegt.

Jedes ISA-Passungskurzzeichen setzt sich aus einem Buchstaben und einer Zahl, der Qualität, zusammen. Bohrungen haben alle große

Buchstaben, die Bohrung mit dem unteren Abmaß Null heißt „H“. Wellen haben alle kleine Buchstaben, die Welle mit dem oberen Abmaß Null heißt „h“.

Die verschiedenen Abmaße sind ebenfalls nach Durchmesserbereich abgestuft und sind auf den Tabellen 3 und 4 zu finden. Die Abmaße

sind in μ $1\,\mu = {}^1/_{1000}$ mm $= 0{,}001$ mm eingetragen.
Es sind $15\,\mu = 1{,}5$ hundertstel Millimeter.

Die Nabe in Abb. 52 hat folgende

Maße und Abmaße.

10 ⌀ H7 = 10,018 bis 10,000 mm ⌀
30 ⌀ e8 = 29,960 bis 29,911 mm ⌀
20 ⌀ h6 = 20,000 bis 19,987 mm ⌀

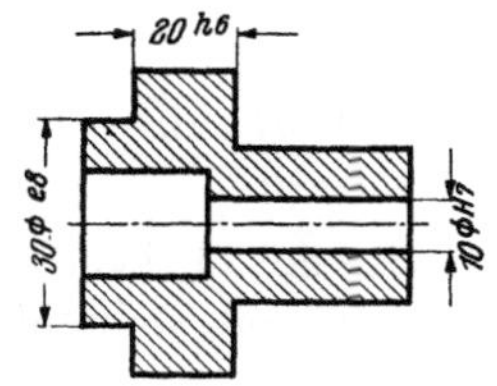

Abb. 52. Eintragung von ISA-Toleranzen.

9. Toleranzen für untolerierte Maße.

Wenn bei einer Reihe von Maßen auf den Zeichnungen keine Toleranzen stehen, so ist das kein Grund, entweder die Maße sehr fein oder ganz grob einzuhalten. Es muß vielmehr dazu eine Anweisung der Betriebsleitung vorliegen, welche Toleranzen als zulässig gegeben sind. Für viele Zwecke reichen die in Tabelle 5 aufgeführten Abmaße aus.

Tabelle 5. Toleranzen für untolerierte Maße nach HgN 11329.

Abmessung in mm	0 bis 10	10 bis 30	30 bis 80	80 bis 180	180 bis 360	360 bis 500	500 bis 750	750 bis 1000	1000 bis 1500	1500 bis 2500	2500 bis 4000	4000
Toleranz mm	±0,2	±0,3	±0,4	±0,5	±0,6	±0,7	±0,9	±1	±1,2	±1,4	±1,6	±2

Abschnitt 5.

Meßkunde.

Nachdem in den vorigen Abschnitten die Ausführung der Zeichnung, die Eintragung der Maße und die Kennzeichen der Toleranzen behandelt sind, wird im folgenden die Durchführung der Messungen erklärt. Als Grundsatz gilt, daß eine Toleranz nur mit *dem* Meßwerkzeug gemessen werden soll, dessen Genauigkeit *gerade* dazu ausreicht. Es leuchtet ein, daß man z. B. ein grob ausgebranntes Blech, das auf 1000 mm Länge eine Toleranz von ± 3 mm haben soll, nicht mit einem Meßinstrument mit einer Genauigkeit von 0,01 mm messen wird. Entsprechend wird man bei Toleranzen von 0,2 mm, z. B. mit einer Schublehre, auskommen. Jedenfalls ist es peinlich zu vermeiden, feinere Meßgeräte durch Benutzung für die Messung gröberer Toleranzen unnötig zu verwenden, abzunutzen und dadurch für die feinere Messung unbrauchbar zu machen.

Fast sämtliche Messungen werden als Längenmessungen ausgeführt, die mit normalen Werkzeugen vorgenommen werden können. Man kann dabei zwischen einfachen, verstellbaren und festen Meßwerkzeugen unterscheiden.

1. Einfache und verstellbare Meßwerkzeuge für direkte Messung.

In der Tabelle 6 sind die für die Fertigung gebräuchlichen, einfachen und verstellbaren Meßwerkzeuge aufgeführt. Außer der Spalte über die Genauigkeiten, die erreichbar sind, gibt die Spalte Anwendbarkeit an, von welchen kleinsten Toleranzabweichungen ab Messungen

Tabelle 6. Meßbereich von Meßwerkzeugen.

Bezeichnung des Meßwerkzeuges	Erreichbare gesamte Meßgenauigkeit in mm	Anwendbar bei einer Gesamttoleranz und größer von mm
Zollstock	0,5	1,0
Bandmaß	0,3	0,6
Stahllineal	0,25	0,5
Schublehre ohne Nonius .	0,2	0,4
„ mit $^1/_{10}$ Nonius	0,1	0,2
„ „ $^1/_{20}$ „	0,05	0,1
„ „ $^1/_{50}$ „	0,02	0,04
Mikrometerschrauben . . .	0,005	0,01

mit diesem Werkzeug durchzuführen sind. Wenn eine Schublehre auf 0,1 mm genau mißt, so heißt das, daß bei verschiedenen Messungen die gleiche Person oder verschiedene Personen an ein und demselben Werkstück, z. B. entweder 30,0 oder 30,1 herausmessen. Das Stück war immer dasselbe und hat das Maß 30,05 mm. Die Toleranz des Werkstückes soll jedoch mit 30 $\pm$ 0,2 mm angegeben sein. Es genügt also vollkommen, wenn man aus der Messung 30,0 oder 30,1 weiß, daß die Abmessung bestimmt innerhalb des zulässigen Toleranzfeldes von 29,8 bis 30,2 mm liegt. Es ist völlig unnötig, mit einer Mikrometerschraube das Werkstück nachzumessen und festzustellen, daß es 30,05 mm hat; die Messung mit dem teureren Meßwerkzeug dauert länger und verkürzt damit den Verdienst. Die angegebenen erreichbaren

Meßgenauigkeiten liegen nicht allein im Werkzeug, sondern das wesentlichste dabei ist das Meßgefühl, das jeder selbst durch Vergleich des Meßdruckes, das Anstellen des Meßwerkzeuges und die Ableseart praktisch erproben muß.

2. Einfache Maßstäbe.

Bei der einfachen Längenmessung eines Werkstückes Abb. 53 wird mit Hilfe eines Zollstockes, Bandmaßes oder Stahllineals der Nullpunkt des Maßstabes an der einen Meßkante genau angelegt. Der Maßstab selbst muß parallel zu der zu messenden Kante liegen. Eine Hilfsleiste erleichtert z. B. das Anlegen des Nullpunktes. Man kann auch das Werkstück auf eine genaue Tischfläche stellen und den Maßstab parallel heranhalten (Abb. 54).

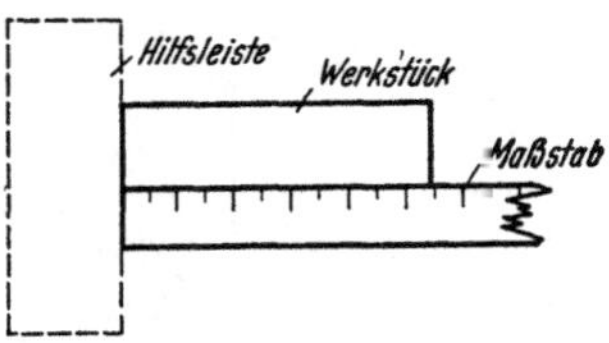

Abb. 53. Messung mit Zollstock.

Wenn der Maßstab schief gehalten wird, wird das Maß zu groß gemessen.

Auf der zweiten Meßkante muß jetzt das Maß abgelesen werden. In Abb. 55a ist die Meßstelle vergrößert dargestellt. Außerdem ist jetzt

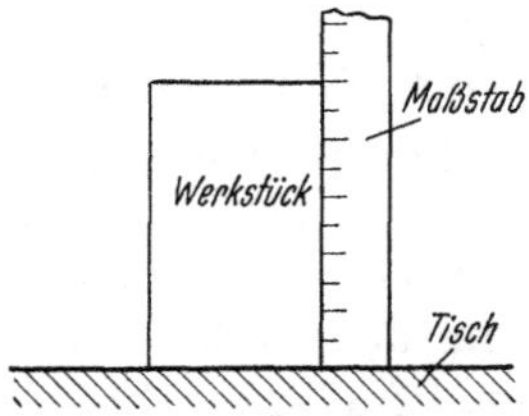

Abb. 54. Richtiges Anlegen von Maßstäben.

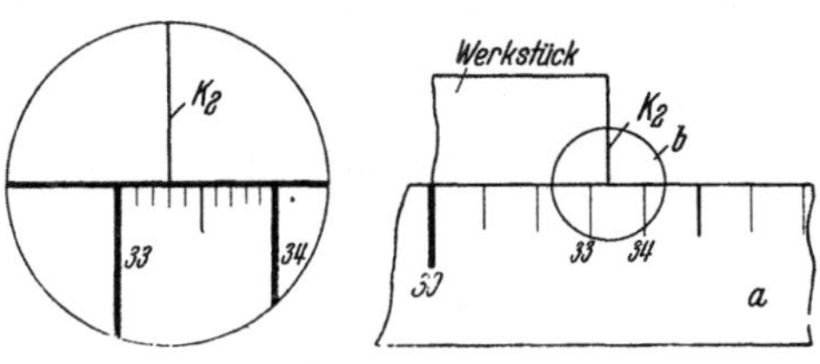

Abb. 55. Schätzen zwischen zwei Maßstrichen.

der Kreis Abb. 55b, in dessen Bereich das genaue Maß abgelesen werden muß, wiederum vergrößert in Abb. 55c gezeichnet. Auf dem Maßstab sind nur die Millimeterteilstriche, hier 33 und 34 zu sehen. Man denkt sich nun den Zwischenraum in weitere 10 Teile gleich je $^1/_{10}$ mm Zwischenraum eingeteilt, wie in Abb. 55c gestrichelt angedeutet. Man schätzt ab, welchen dünnen Strich die Meßkante K_2 etwa treffen würde; hier im Beispiel ist es der dritte Strich. Das Maß ist also 33 und $^3/_{10}$ $= 33{,}3$ mm. Die größten Fehler treten bei der Schätzung von 0,2 und 0,8 mm auf.

3. Schieblehren.

Mißt man mit einer Schieblehre (Abb. 56a), so müssen die Schenkel satt auf den Meßflächen liegen. Der bei der Fertigung entstehende leichte Grad an den Kanten des Werkstückes muß vorher mit einer Feile oder mit einem Schaber fortgenommen sein. Das Maß wird jetzt auf dem Schieber mit Hilfe des Nonius abgelesen. Die Maßstelle *b* ist in Abb. 56c stark vergrößert herausgezeichnet.

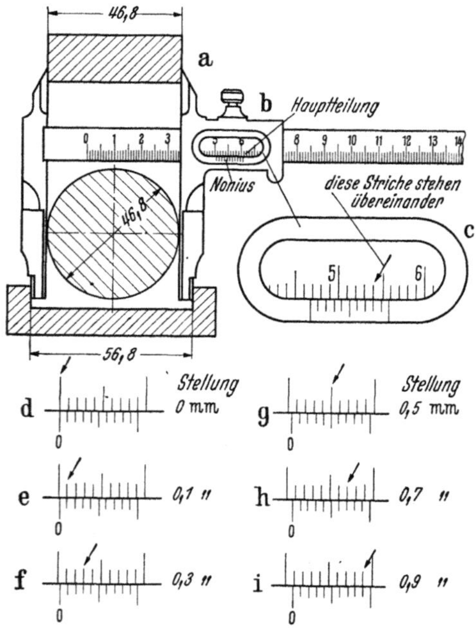

Abb. 56. Messen mit Schieblehre und Ablesung.

Warum kann man mit dem Nonius $^1/_{10}$ mm ablesen? 9 mm sind in 10 gleiche Teile, den Nonius, geteilt. Also ist ein Teil gleich $^9/_{10}$ mm. Wenn nun, wie in in Abb. 56e, auf dem Nonius der erste Teilstrich mit der Hauptteilung übereinstimmt, der Abstand bis zum Noniusnullstrich beträgt jedoch $^9/_{10}$ mm, dann steht der Noniusnullstrich zur Hauptteilung um $^1/_{10}$ mm verschoben nach rechts. Verschiedene Stellungen sind in den Abb. 56d···i gezeigt. Auf die Abb. 56c angewendet muß folgendermaßen abgelesen werden:

1. Die Nullstellung des Nonius liegt zwischen 46 und 47 mm, also auch das Maß dazwischen.

2. Der Noniusstrich mit 0,8 liegt genau unter einem Strich der Hauptteilung.

3. Danach ist das Maß $46 + 0{,}8 = 46{,}8$ mm.

Entsprechend erhält man bei feineren Noniusteilungen z. B. $^7/_{20} = 0{,}35$ mm oder $^{39}/_{50} = {}^{78}/_{100} = 0{,}78$ mm Zusatzlänge zu den ganzen Millimeterlängen.

4. Mikrometerschrauben.

Die Mikrometerschraube erlaubt deswegen eine genauere Messung, weil durch die Benutzung einer Schraube mit feiner Steigung und Anbringung an einem größeren Umfange die Zwischenräume zwischen den Teilstrichen vergrößert sind. In Abb. 57a ist eine Mikrometerschraube im ganzen und in Abb. 57b···e die Meßteilung im besonderen gezeichnet. Jede Umdrehung einer Schraube entspricht $^1/_2 =$ 0,5 mm. Der zugespitzte Rand der Meßschraubenhülse trägt eine Rundteilung mit 50 Teilstrichen. Jeder Zwischenraum zwischen zwei Teilstrichen entspricht $^1/_{100} = 0{,}01$ mm.

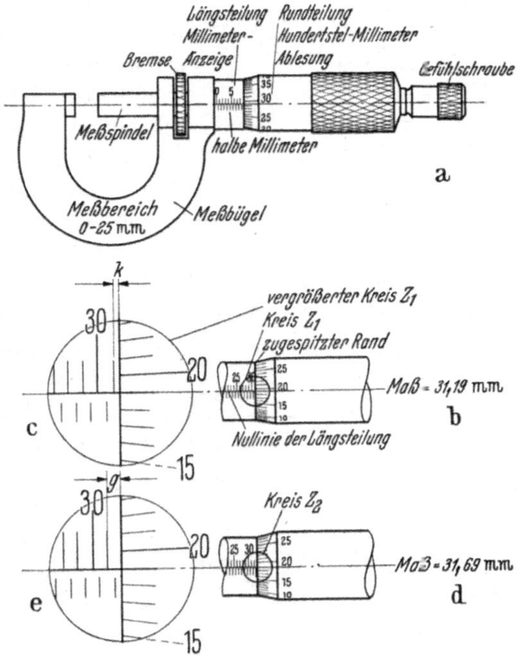

Abb. 57. Mikrometerschraube und Ablesung.

In der Zeichnung Abb. 57b···c steht der Rundteilstrich 19 auf der Nullinie der Längsteilung. Auf der Längsteilung kann man abzählen, daß der Längsteilstrich 31 gerade zu sehen ist. Der Abstand *k* ist kleiner als $^1/_2$ mm. Das eingestellte Maß ist dann $31 + 0{,}19 =$ 31,19 mm.

Wenn dagegen der Abstand „*g*“ (Abb. 57e) von der zugespitzten Kante der Meßschraubenhülle größer wird, als die Hälfte zwischen zwei Teilstrichen der Längsteilung, der Zwischenstrich der unteren Längsteilung wird sichtbar, dann ist die Meßschraube bereits einmal herumgedreht. Die Verschiebung beträgt bereits 0,5 mm und das zusätzliche Maß. Das jetzt eingestellte Maß ist dann 31 + 0,5 (für eine Umdrehung der Meßschraube) + 0,19 = 31,69 mm. Zwischen zwei Teilstrichen kann man auf etwa $^1/_2$ hundertstel = 5 tausendstel mm = 0,005 mm schätzen.

5. Fehlermöglichkeiten beim Messen.

Die Eigenfehler der Meßwerkzeuge sind durch den Messenden selbst nicht beeinflußbar. Es treten aber eine Reihe persönlicher Fehler auf, die teilweise vermieden werden können.

a) Meßdruck. Bei der Benutzung der Schieblehren und Mikrometerschraube ist es möglich, schon bei Anwendung kleinster Kräfte die Schenkel oder den Bügel aufzubiegen. Man muß durch praktische Vergleiche mit einer erfahrenen Person das Gefühl für den anzuwendenden Meßdruck erhalten. Mikrometerschrauben tragen deshalb zum Teil Schraubenköpfe mit Ratschen, die beim Erreichen eines bestimmten Meßdruckes nicht weiter zuspannen. Trotzdem sind auch mit solchen Ratschen Fehlmessungen möglich.

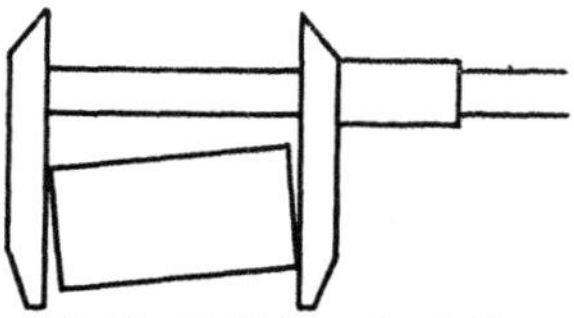

Abb. 58. Meßfehler durch Verkanten des Meßwerkzeuges.

b) Verkanten. Auch das Verkanten der Maßwerkzeuge gegenüber dem Meßwerkstück bringt persönliche Meßfehler (Abb. 58). Man muß z. B. bei Schieblehren möglichst den starren Schenkel fest an die eine Werkstückfläche herandrücken und dann den beweglichen Schenkel nachschieben, daraufhin die Klemmschraube auf den Reiter festziehen, die Schieblehre abnehmen, und das Maß ablesen. Schwieriger ist schon das Messen von Wellen mit Mikrometerschrauben (Abb. 59), da bei einem Verkanten der Mikrometerschraube aus der richtigen Maßebene ein zu großer Durchmesser gemessen wird. Man muß in zwei Richtungen schwenken. Bei der Längsschwenkung, also aus der Maßebene heraus, muß man die kleinste Stelle suchen, bei der Querschwenkung in der Maßebene den größten Durchmesser, wenn man von einer kleineren Einstellung der Schraube ausgeht. Hierbei muß bei richtiger Einstellung ein gefühlsmäßig zu erkennender Widerstand beim Gleiten der Maßflächen über das Werkstück zu verspüren sein. Die Mikrometerschrauben

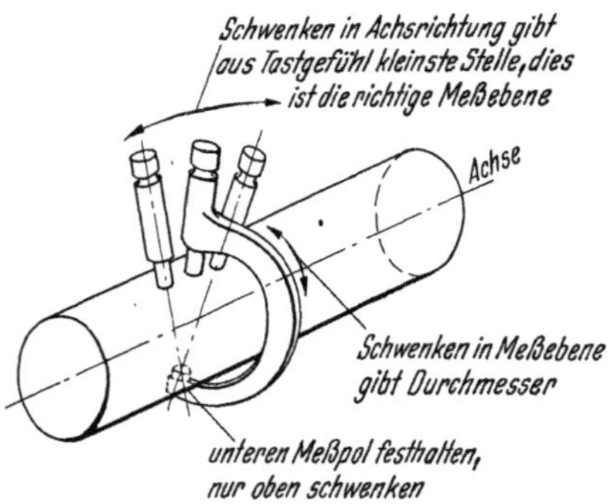

Abb. 59. Messen von Wellendurchmessern.

haben auch eine Feststelleinrichtung, so daß das selbständige Verstellen der Schraube unterbunden werden kann.

Bei Messungen an Wellen bzw. Bohrungen ist immer an mehreren Stellen des Umfanges zu messen, da entweder durch fehlerhaftes Arbeiten oder durch die Maschine unrunde Durchmesser entstehen können.

Noch schwieriger ist das richtige Messen einer Kugel (Abb. 60). Hier muß sowohl in der Richtung *I—I* wie auch *II—II* durch mehrmaliges Nachprüfen und Schwenken der richtige Durchmesser gefunden werden. Der Punkt „*U*" bleibt zweckmäßigerweise festgehalten, während der Punkt „*O*" der Suchpunkt ist.

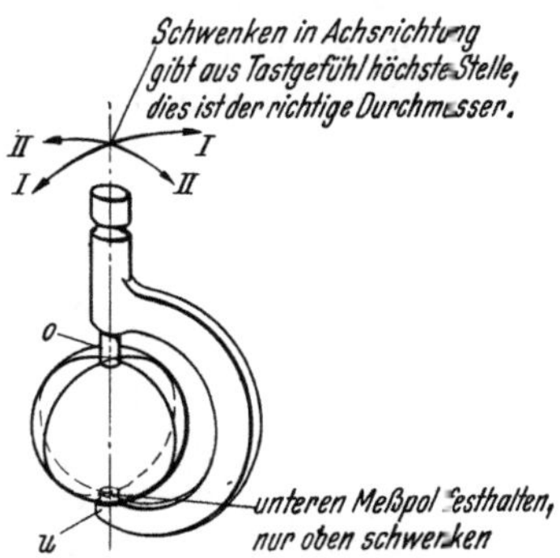

Abb. 60. Messen von Kugelflächen.

6. Temperatureinflüsse.

Wie bereits in Abschnitt 1 „Allgemeines" erklärt, findet bei Erwärmung von Metallen eine Längsausdehnung statt. Das besagt, daß z. B. ein Stichmaß bei Erwärmung länger wird, also ein größeres Maß messen würde. Einheitlich ist als Bezugstemperatur 20° C gewählt. Die Lehren stimmen also bei 20° genau. Demnach müssen auch die Werkstücke richtig genommen bei 20° C gemessen werden. Ist ein Werkstück infolge der Bearbeitung warm geworden, müssen genaue Maße in abgekühltem Zustand gemessen werden.

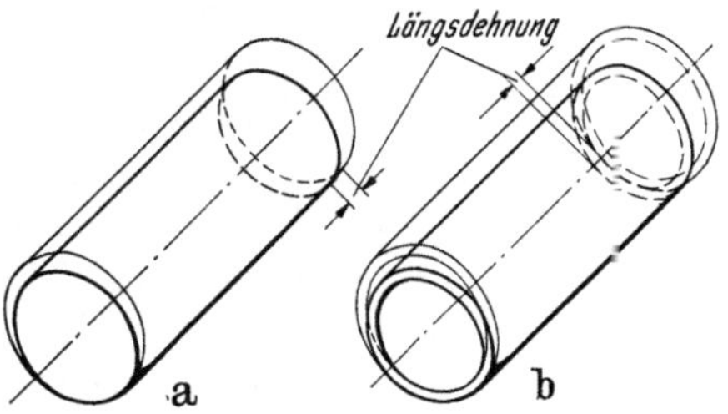

Abb. 61. Wachsen von Wellen oder dünnwandigen Büchsen bei plötzlicher Erwärmung. Wellen bei höherer Temperatur als Normalausdehnung.

Bei einer Erwärmung spricht man auch vom Wachsen der Stücke. Eine Welle (Abb. 61a) wird daher einen größeren Durchmesser bei höherer Temperatur als 20° haben. Eine dünnwandige Buchse (Abb. 61b) kann ebenfalls innen und außen größer im Durchmesser sein als bei Normaltemperatur. Anders verhalten sich Bohrungen, die im Verhältnis zur Wandstärke klein sind (Abb. 62). Bei der Bearbeitung werden die Randzonen um die Bohrung schneller warm als die von der Bohrung weiter fortliegenden Randschichten. Außen bleibt die Welle also kalt und innen wird sie warm. Da sich jedoch die innerste Ringzone durch die Erwärmung ausdehnen muß, nach außen kann sie es nicht, weil die starke äußere Ringzone nicht nachgibt, findet eine Ausdehnung nach Innen statt. Hier wird also die Bohrung durch starke Erwärmung kleiner. Das bedeutet, daß bei einer fertigen Bohrung, die im warmen Zustand und bei momentaner großer Wärmezufuhr gepaßt hat, im kalten Zustand bei 20^0 zu groß ist.

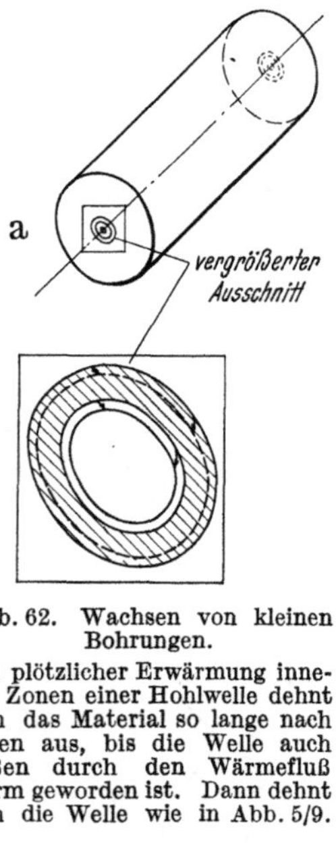

Abb. 62. Wachsen von kleinen Bohrungen.

Bei plötzlicher Erwärmung innerer Zonen einer Hohlwelle dehnt sich das Material so lange nach innen aus, bis die Welle auch außen durch den Wärmefluß warm geworden ist. Dann dehnt sich die Welle wie in Abb. 5/9.

Die Ausdehnung oder auch die Schrumpfung der innersten Ringzone erfolgt mit einer gewissen Zeitverzögerung, so daß es auch passieren kann, daß die einer Bohrung nachlaufenden Reibahlen nicht wieder zurückgenommen werden dürfen, weil die Bohrung durch das zugeführte Kühlmittel (Seifenwasser oder Rüböl) wieder erkaltet und somit enger wird, so daß sich das Werkzeug beim Zurückfahren klemmt und meistens zu Bruch geht.

Die Ausschußgefahr ist bei kleinen Bohrungen besonders groß. Mindestens wird es möglich sein, nach Gefühl bei großen Wandstärken die Bohrung kleiner als die Lehre zu halten. Bei Normaltemperatur geht sie dann auf. Umgekehrt ist es jedoch bei dünnwandigen Buchsen. Eine Berechnung der Kleinerhaltung ist sehr schwierig und praktisch nicht möglich, weil die Werkstückform und die Wärmeausbreitung eine Rolle spielen.

Ferner ist es wichtig, Meßwerkzeuge nicht zu lange in der Hand zu behalten, um sie nicht zu erwärmen und sie möglichst vorsichtig und an den Ecken zu berühren, wo kein direkter Einfluß auf die Meßweite stattfinden kann.

7. Sehfehler (Parallaxe).

Beim Ablesen von Maßen zwischen Werkstückkanten und Maßstab würde ein Beobachter bei genau senkrechtem Sehen auf den Maßstab

Abb. 63, Stellung *1*, das richtige Maß mit 45 ablesen. Wenn er dagegen schräg auf den Maßstab sieht, Stellung *2*, so erscheint ihm die Werkstückkante mit dem Maße 46 übereinzustimmen. Diesen Meßfehler bezeichnet man mit Parallaxenfehler. Es muß also stets genau senkrecht zur Teilung abgelesen werden. Dies ist wichtig für alle Abmessungen mit Zollstock, Schieblehre und Mikrometerschraube.

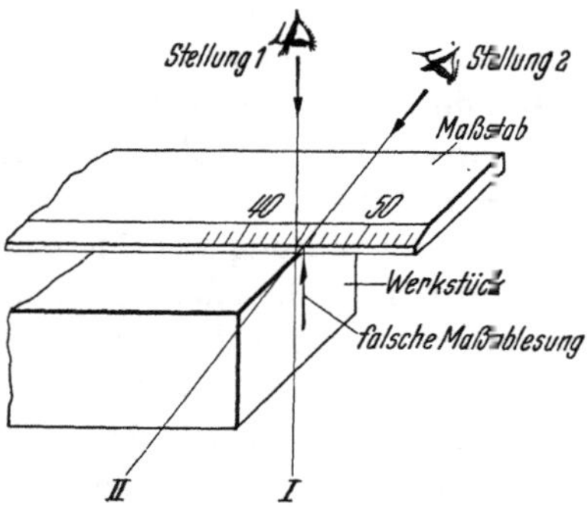

Abb. 63. Sehfehler bei Maßablesungen.

8. Anwendungsbereich der Meßwerkzeuge.

Toleranzen, die für Grobpassungen oder die Qualität IT 11 von 50 mm aufwärts passen, können mit der Schieblehre mit $^1/_{10}$ mm Noniusteilung gemessen werden, z. B. 50 H 11 und größer, jedoch nicht 50 H 7. Bei kleineren Durchmessern und sonst bei allen Durchmessern mit feineren Qualitäten oder Gütegraden sind Mikrometerschrauben zu verwenden.

9. Feste Meßwerkzeuge.

Kommt ein bestimmtes Maß öfter vor, sei es bei Massenherstellungen eines Werkstückes oder durch die oftmalige Anwendung infolge seiner günstigen Größe, so haben feste Meßwerkzeuge, oder Lehren genannt, bedeutende Vorteile gegenüber einstellbaren Meßwerkzeugen. Aus diesen Gründen entstanden Rachenlehren, Grenzlehrdorne und Stichmaße als typische Meßlehren.

Zur Erfassung der Toleranz vereinigt man übrigens bei Rachenlehren und Grenzlehrdornen die Maße für das zulässige Größtmaß und das zulässige Kleinstmaß in einem Stück.

10. Rachenlehren.

Es ist leicht einzusehen, daß bei Rachenlehren das Größtmaß, die „Gutseite", über das Werkstück herübergehen muß, während das Kleinstmaß, die „Ausschußseite", nicht mehr herübergleiten darf Das Messen muß mit Gefühl erfolgen. An sich ist das Maß des Werkstückes richtig, wenn die Gutseite durch das Eigengewicht der Lehre herübergleitet. Durch Anwendung von größeren Kräften ist es ein Leichtes, die dünnwandig und leicht gebaute Rachenlehre auch über ein größeres Maß, als sie selbst hat, herüberzudrücken. Der Bügel federt auf, verbiegt sich und die teure Lehre wird unbrauchbar. Natürlich ist dann auch das gemessene Maß am Werkstück größer als auf der Lehre angegeben, weil die Lehre aufgedrückt war. Das Werkstück entspricht dann doch nicht dem gewünschten Maß und muß nachgearbeitet werden. Das kostet unnötige Zeit und bringt Verdienstverlust. Man messe also gleich richtig.

Die Ausführung der Messung erfolgt gleichsinnig wie in Abb. 59. Die untere Fläche oder eine Fläche des Meßschenkels wird festgehalten und der andere Schenkel senkrecht zur Achse einer Welle hinübergeschwenkt. Dabei muß ein Verkanten der Lehre vermieden werden. Sobald das Werkstück dem Gewicht nach wesentlich leichter als die Lehre wird, kann man auch das Werkstück in die Lehre hineinführen.

11. Grenzlehrdorne.

Bei Grenzlehrdornen kommt es darauf an, den Dorn genau senkrecht zur Bohrung einzuführen. Rohe Gewalt hilft hier überhaupt nicht. Wenn der Dorn sich verklemmt, muß er herausgeholt und neu angesetzt werden. Hineinstauchen oder Schläge mit einem Hammer sind auf keinen Fall zulässig, da der Dorn bei dünnwandigen Werkstücken die Bohrungen aufweiten würde und außerdem durch Ansetzen von feinem Grad zu falschen Messungen führen muß. Auch hier muß die Gutseite in die Bohrung hineingehen, die Ausschußseite aber nicht.

12. Stichmaße.

Stichmaße werden meistens bei großen Durchmessern verwendet. Ihre Handhabung ist schon schwieriger, da das Ansetzen sinngemäß wie in Abb. 60 bei einer Mikrometerschraube für Außen- und Innenmessung erfolgen muß. Zu einem Maß gehören stets zwei Stichmaße, eines für die Gutseite und eines für die Ausschußseite.

Bei allen festen Meßlehren muß unbedingt ein zu langes In-der-Hand-Halten vermieden werden, weil sonst bei Temperaturanstieg eine Längenänderung eintritt, die zu Fehlmessungen führt.

13. Sonderlehren.

Für viele Zwecke sind Sonderlehren entwickelt worden, die der besonderen Messung Rechnung tragen. Ihre Benutzung und ihre Fehlerquellen entsprechen den festen Lehren, da sie ebenfalls feste Lehren sind. Man muß sich nur stets überlegen, in welchen Hauptrichtungen man das Größt- bzw. Kleinstmaß suchen, und wie man deshalb bei der Messung mit der Lehre pendeln muß. In schwierigen Fällen wird stets eine Anleitung für den Gebrauch gegeben.

14. Endmaße.

Eine besonders hohe Genauigkeit in der Herstellung tragen Endmaße, das sind feste Maße, die bis zu 0,001 mm, manchmal bis zu 0,0005 = $^1/_2$ Tausendstel mm abgestuft sind. Sie dienen zur Nachprüfung und Einstellung von Lehren und sind nicht für den allgemeinen Gebrauch in der Werkstatt bestimmt.

Für den Einstellzweck an der Maschine benutzt man Meßklötzchen, die im Äußeren fast gleich wie die Endmaße, doch mit gröberer Genauigkeit, ausreichend für ihren Verwendungszweck, hergestellt sind.

15. Vergleichsmeßwerkzeuge.

Mit die einfachste und ursprünglichste Meßmethode ist die mittels Vergleich mit einem Musterstück. Hierzu gehört auch der Anschlagwinkel.

a) Anschlagwinkel. Beide Schenkel bilden zusammen einen Winkel von 90°, stehen also senkrecht aufeinander. Durch Anlegen an ein Werkstück direkt oder Anlegen an ein Werkstück, wobei dieses und der Winkel auf einer genauen Fläche stehen, z. B. einer Anreißplatte oder Tuschierplatte, kann man mit dem Auge die Breite eines Lichtspaltes abschätzen. Zu diesem Zweck muß der Grat am Werkstück sorgfältig entfernt sein. Das Auge ist für Verbreiterung des Lichtspaltes, also auch Schiefstellung der Werkstückfläche gegenüber dem anliegenden Winkel äußerst empfindlich, so daß bereits bei einiger Übung schon Abweichungen von wenigen Hundertstel Millimeter erkennbar sind. Auch hier ist genaue senkrechte Anlage der Schenkel an die Meßlinie wichtig.

b) Haarlineal. Ein Haarlineal benutzt auch die gute Empfindlichkeit des Auges gegenüber einem Lichtspalt und ist ein an der Meßkante scharf zugespitztes Lineal mit genau gerader Meßkante. Es dient zur Nachprüfung von Kanten oder Flächen auf ihre Geradheit und ermöglicht die Feststellung von wenigen hundertstel Millimetern Abweichung. Die Meßkante muß sehr schonend behandelt werden, weil ihre Beschädigung jede weitere richtige Messung unmöglich macht.

c) Taster. Messungen mit einem Taster sind die schwierigsten überhaupt. Hier ist allein das Meßgefühl ausschlaggebend. Durch Zu- oder Aufklopfen eines Schenkels wird das Maß ermittelt, wobei die in Abb. 59 angeführten Schwenkrichtungen unter Festhalten eines Tastschenkels am Werkstück auszuführen sind. Nach Ermittlung des Maßes durch die Taststellung muß dieses wiederum an einem Maßstab, einer Schublehre oder Mikrometerschraube verglichen werden, so daß weitere Fehlermöglichkeiten durch falsches Einstellen des Meßwerkzeuges oder Zusammendrücken der Tastschenkel gegeben sind.

d) Meßuhr. Mit einer Meßuhr können Unterschiede von 0,01 mm, das ist die Zeigerablenkung zwischen zwei Teilstrichen bei der üblichen Bauart, abgelesen werden. Ein direktes Messen eines Maßes ist nicht möglich; für diesen Fall muß man von einem Musterstück, einem Kaliberdorn oder einem Endmaßsatz das Grundmaß der Meßuhr einstellen. Dies erfolgt durch Einstellen der Meßuhr auf Höhe und Verdrehen des Zeigerblattes genau auf Null oder ein anderes Grundmaß. Die Uhr muß dann an das zu messende Werkstück oder umgekehrt herangeführt werden. Die Abweichung des Zeigers gegenüber dem eingestellten Grundmaß ergibt dann den Maßunterschied des Werkstückes zum Musterstück. Es findet also ein Vergleich statt. Hierin liegen die verschiedenen Fehlerquellen, so daß eine einwandfreie Messung gewiß Übung voraussetzt. Wichtig ist, durch ganz leichtes Klopfen an der Uhr den toten Gang herauszubringen, ferner stets in gleicher Bewegungsrichtung des Taststiftes zu messen und nicht beim Einstellen einmal sich hineinbewegen, den Taststift beim Werkstückmessen aber sich herausbewegen zu lassen. Man überzeuge sich vor Gebrauch stets, ob die Uhr leicht spielt und ob nicht bei bestimmten Stellungen eine Klemmung eintritt. Diese Störungsstellen sind bei dem Messen durch anderes Einstellen der Uhr zu vermeiden. Bei starkem Klemmen des Tasters darf dieser auf keinen Fall geschmiert werden, da das Öl die Uhr verharzt und unbrauchbar macht. In einem solchen Fall ist sie sofort zur Reparatur abzugeben. Eine Umdrehung des großen Zeigers entspricht einem Hub des Taststiftes von 1 mm. Die Zahl der Millimeter zeigt ein kleiner Anzeiger innerhalb des Zifferblattes an. Wichtig ist, daß bei solchen Vergleichsmessungen der Taststift genau parallel zur Meßrichtung läuft, weil sonst falsche Messungen stattfinden.

Eine vielfache Anwendung findet die Meßuhr bei Schlagmessungen von Wellen oder zum Ausrichten von Werkstücken und Vorrichtungen.

Auch hier muß die Uhr vorher auf leichtes Spiel geprüft werden, weil bei schlechten Uhren durch toten Gang und Hängenbleiben 0,02 mm und mehr Falschmessungen entstehen können.

16. Feinere Instrumente.

Für die Messung von tausendstel Millimeter gibt es noch feinere Vergleichswerkzeuge, wie Minimeter, Optimeter, Orthotest usw., die große Ablesegenauigkeit haben, deren Meßbereich dafür aber eingeschränkt ist. Sie kommen für höchste Meßgenauigkeit in Frage. Bei allen Vergleichsmeßwerkzeugen sind ebenfalls Einflüsse durch Temperatur, Sehfehler usw. zu beachten, die sich auch hier in starkem Maße auswirken.

17. Behandlung der Meßwerkzeuge und Selbstkontrolle.

Es ist ganz klar, daß man nur mit sorgfältig behandelten und gepflegten Meßwerkzeugen richtig messen kann. Die Genauigkeit des Meßwerkzeuges ist mit ausschlaggebend für das Ausfallen des Werkstückes und jede noch so sorgfältige Arbeit kann zu Ausschuß werden, wenn das Meßwerkzeug nicht stimmt. Man muß deshalb darauf sehen, daß keine Beschädigungen auftreten, sei es durch Fallenlassen oder Anschlagen an harten Kanten oder Verunreinigung. Jede Gelegenheit zum Nachprüfen durch die Kontrolle oder den Betrieb nimmt man wahr, um sicher zu sein, daß die auch bei sorgfältiger Behandlung trotzdem eintretende Abnutzung die zulässigen Grenzen nicht überschreitet. Solche Abnutzungen werden beschleunigt, wenn Schublehren oder Rachenlehren z. B. über umlaufende Teile gepreßt werden. Durch die Reibung an den Meßflächen muß eine wenn auch im Einzelfalle geringe Abnutzung eintreten. Man mißt nur am ruhenden Werkstück. Eine Schieblehre halte man sich als Eigentum. Man wird dadurch mit ihr vertraut, kennt ihre vielleicht auftretenden kleinsten Abweichungen und kann durch leichte Korrektur genau mit ihr messen. Auch hier prüft man durch Selbstkontrolle des öfteren die Genauigkeit nach. Zum Beispiel kann man mit einem Grenzlehrdorn von genau 40,000 mm = 40 B Gutseite oder 40 H 7 Gutseite feststellen, ob die Schieblehre genau auf 40 mm anzeigt. Entsprechend prüft man Rachenlehren mit Grenzlehrdornen oder mit Endmaßen. Pflege vor allem dein Meßwerkzeug und du wirst auch mehr Geld verdienen!

Abschnitt 6.

Grundsätze beim Spannen von Werkstücken.

Keine Arbeit ist möglich, ohne die Werkstücke auszurichten und gegen den auftretenden Schnittdruck festzuhalten. Schnittdruck ist die vom Werkzeug bei der Spanabnahme ausgeübte Kraft auf das Werkstück. Ihre Größe und Richtung ist maßgebend für die Wahl der Spannwerkzeuge und die Art ihres Ansatzes.

Die Richtung des Schnittdruckes wird genauer unter Absatz 9 erklärt. Sie verläuft oft schräg zur Aufspannung: Der größte Teil dieses Schnittdruckes, den man sich für die Betrachtung nach den Hauptrichtungen der Maschine aufteilt, heißt Hauptschnittdruck. Dieser muß besonders genau erkannt werden, um ihn aufzufangen.

Hier werden nur die Kräfte auf das Werkstück besprochen. (Die gleichen Kräfte in genau entgegengesetzter Richtung wirken auf die Werkzeuge.)

1. Direktes Spannen.

Man wird stets versuchen, die Werkstücke auf eine Maschinenfläche zu spannen, die senkrecht zum Hauptschnittdruck liegt. Dann geht der Kraftfluß direkt in die Maschine und die Spannorgane haben nur gegen seitliche Verschiebung zu sichern. Das wäre dann direktes Spannen, wie es z. B. auf der Räummaschine oder Stoßmaschine normalerweise der Fall ist.

2. Indirektes Spannen.

Indirektes Spannen liegt dann vor, wenn die Kraft des Hauptschnittdruckes umgelenkt werden muß; z. B. ist auf einer Waagerechtfräsmaschine die Richtung des Hauptschnittdruckes waagerecht gerichtet. Parallel zum Aufspanntisch geht die Kraft ins Werkstück hinein. Das Werkstück muß nun senkrecht zur Kraftrichtung nach unten auf den Tisch gespannt werden. Durch die Zusammenpressung von Werkstückfläche und Tischfläche entsteht zwischen beiden Flächen Reibung. Diese Reibung muß jetzt größer als der Hauptschnittdruck sein. Es ist festgestellt, daß zur Erzielung dieser Reibkräfte etwa 5mal soviel senkrechte Spannkräfte notwendig sind. Das heißt, man muß Spanneisen usw. 5mal so kräftig drücken lassen, ehe man die notwendige Reibung gegenüber dem Hauptschnittdruck erreicht hat. Es besteht daher die Gefahr, leicht geformte Werkstücke zu verdrücken. Sie können

Ausschuß werden. Man versuche stets, direkt zu spannen. Der Ausfall der Arbeit, die Güte der gefertigten Teile und die Richtigkeit der Teile ist durch richtiges Spannen bedingt, so daß diesem größte Aufmerksamkeit geschenkt werden muß.

Zunächst muß jetzt die richtige Lage der Werkstücke auf der Maschine hergestellt werden.

3. Ausrichten der Werkstücke auf der Maschine.

Bei der Bearbeitung soll eine bestimmte Fläche am Werkstück erzielt werden. Die Bewegungsrichtung der Werkzeuge liegt durch die Maschine fest. Ein Walzenfräser erzeugt eine Fläche parallel zum Tisch, der den Vorschub ausführt. Die Begriffe Vorschub, Schnittiefe usw. sind in Abschnitt 10 eingehend erläutert. Auf einer Hobelmaschine werden Flächen parallel zum Aufspanntisch hergestellt. Beim Drehen werden Zylinderflächen oder Kegelflächen erzeugt, deren Achsen oder Symmetrielinien zwischen den Spitzen der Maschine oder in der verlängert gedachten Spindelachse der Maschine liegen. Diese Erkenntnis ist der *erste* Grundsatz für das Ausrichten der Werkstücke.

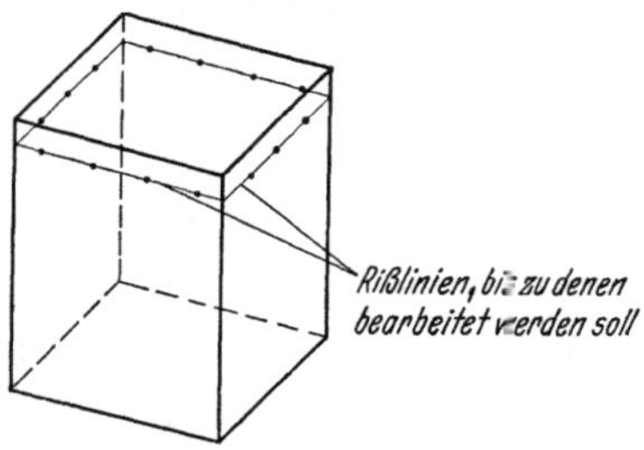

Abb. 64. Rißlinien.

Es müssen also jetzt die Werkstücke *so* aufgespannt werden, daß unter der Maschinenbearbeitung die gewollten oder angerissenen Flächen entstehen.

Eine ebene Fläche ist *nicht durch eine* Rißlinie, eine gerade Linie bestimmt, sondern nur *durch zwei aufeinander abgewinkelte* Rißlinien. Bei Vierkantstücken geht der Riß deshalb mindestens über zwei Flächen oder über alle vier (Abb. 64). Beim Ausrichten dieses Umfangrisses wird von der Aufspannfläche mit einem Höhenreißer der Riß ausgerichtet. Man fährt praktisch „herum“. Erst wenn die Höhe gleichmäßig eingestellt ist, kann mit der Bearbeitung begonnen werden. Die *ebene Fläche* muß somit *zweifach bestimmt* werden, nämlich in zwei aufeinander senkrechten Richtungen.

Eine zentrierte, rohe Welle wird zwischen Spitzen gespannt, dadurch liegt sie genau in der Spindelachse und ist zweifach bestimmt.

Muß ein vorgedrehtes Stück auf einer Planscheibe neu ausgerichtet werden, so wird mit Kreide oder einer Reißnadel oder genauer mit der

Meßuhr zunächst der Umfang zum genauen Laufen gebracht. Ist das Werkstück länger, so prüft man den Rundlauf einmal dicht an der Einspannstelle, ferner am freien Ende (Abb. 65). Dadurch erfolgt eine zweifache Bestimmung der Welle, sie liegt jetzt außen genau in der Spindelachsenrichtung. Kurze, runde Werkstücke werden außen auf Rundlauf ausgerichtet und als zweite Bestimmung an der Stirnfläche auf axialen

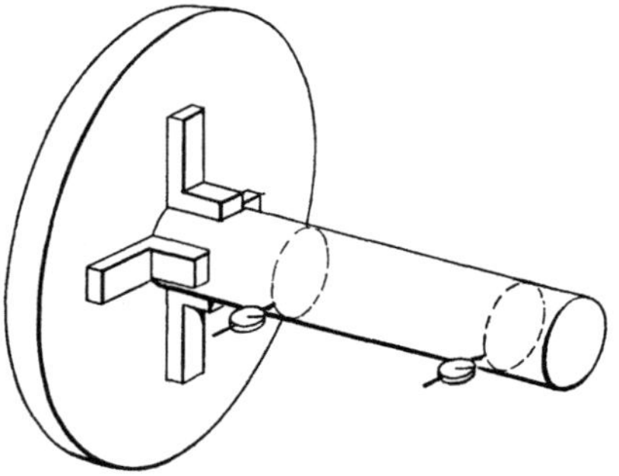

Abb. 65. Ausrichten einer Welle an zwei Meßstellen.

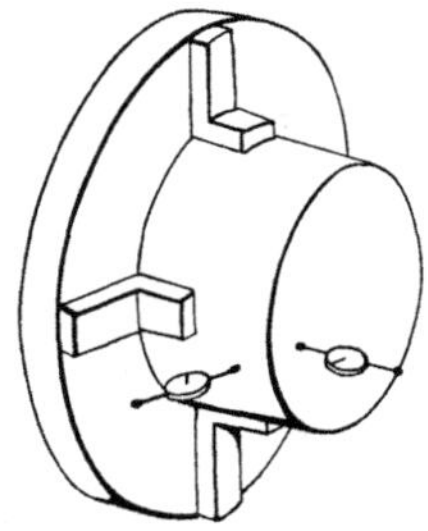

Abb. 66. Ausrichten eines Drehkörpers in zwei Richtungen.

Schlag nachgerichtet (Abb. 66). Genau so kann auch ein Ausrichten roher Stücke nach Anriß erfolgen. Es wird dann mit einer Reißnadel der Riß abgeglichen.

4. Vorrichtungen.

Vorrichtungen sind so gebaut, daß das einzelne Ausrichten der Werkstücke fortgelassen werden kann und das Spannen erleichtert wird. Sie sind ihrem Zweck entsprechend regelmäßig, d. h. Achse und Fläche für die Maschinenanlage oder Aufnahme von Werkstücken stehen senkrecht oder parallel oder im gewünschten Winkel zueinander. Man muß jetzt nur zu Anfang prüfen, ob die Vorrichtung richtig aufgespannt ist.

Bei rundlaufenden Vorrichtungen kann an zwei Durchmesserstellen, oder an einer Durchmesserstelle und einer Planfläche gemessen werden. Wichtig ist, daß die Aufspannstellen für die Werkstücke laufen, auch wenn die Vorrichtung selbst schlägt. Bei Flächenvorrichtungen, z. B. bei Fräsmaschinen oder Bohrmaschinen, müssen die Aufspannstellen für die Werkstücke parallel liegen und manchmal eine seitliche Anlage zwecks genauer Ausrichtung in Vorschubrichtung haben. Es muß stets überlegt werden, welchen Zweck in bezug auf die Richtigkeit des Werkstückes die Vorrichtung hat und welche Abweichungen in der Anlagefläche zu Fehlern führen. Diese Abweichungen sind zu prüfen.

5. Auflage der Werkstücke auf der Maschine.

Zur Bearbeitung müssen die Werkstücke fest und sicher aufgespannt sein. Rohe Flächen liegen nicht glatt an, sondern nur auf Oberflächenerhöhungen. Diese können sich unter dem Schnittdruck zusammendrücken und somit die Lage des Werkstückes verändern. Die bearbeitete Fläche wird dann nicht eben, sondern krumm. Es muß somit eine sehr feste Einspannung roher Werkstücke vorhanden sein.

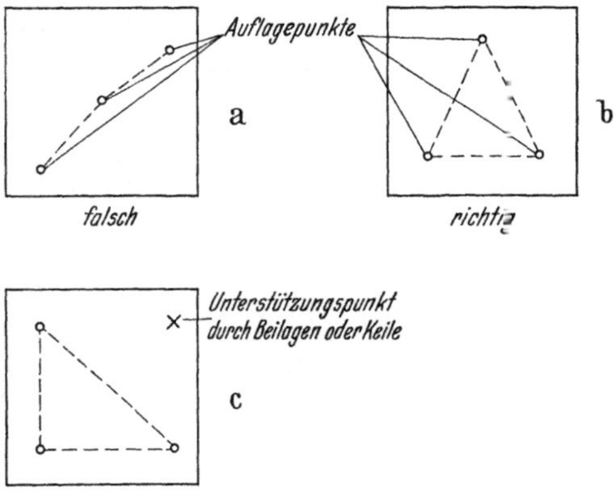

Abb. 67. Anordnung der Auflagepunkte.

Muß das rohe Werkstück auf eine Fläche gespannt werden, so ist eine eindeutige Lage erreicht, wenn dieses Stück auf drei Punkten aufliegt, die nicht in einer Flucht liegen, sondern möglichst gleiche Abstände voneinander haben, und zwar jeder Punkt von jedem anderen (Abb. 67). Wenn diese Auflage nicht erreichbar ist, muß ein vierter Unterstützungspunkt durch Beilagen oder Keile geschaffen werden (Abb. 67c). Dabei ist gefühlvoll so viel beizulegen, daß immer noch die anderen drei Auflagepunkte in Anlage bleiben. Bei zuviel oder zuwenig Beilagen wird das Werkstück unbestimmt gelagert und verzieht sich unter der Festspannung oder gibt beim Schnitt nach.

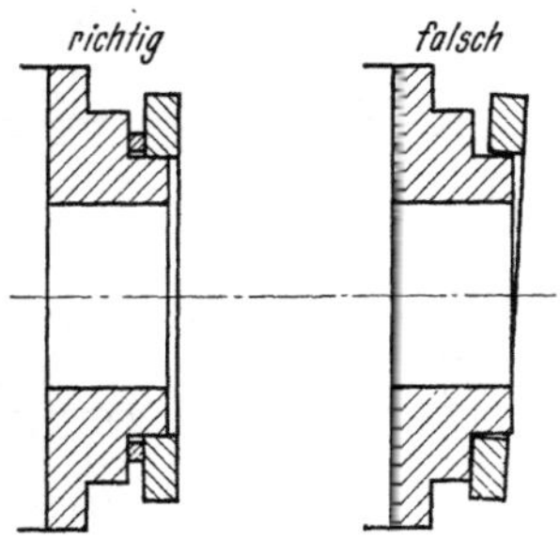

Abb. 68. Spannen schmaler Ringe im Dreibackenfutter.

Ist eine bearbeitete ebene Fläche vorhanden, so kann diese direkt auf den Tisch der Maschine gespannt werden. Um die Haftreibung zwischen zwei Metallflächen zu vergrößern, legt man dünnes Papier dazwischen. Beim Spannen von Teilen im Futter muß auf gute Anlage an den Backenflächen gesehen werden (Abb. 68).

Durch das Spannen soll erreicht werden:

a) Eine feste Lage des Werkstückes gegenüber dem Schnittdruck und gegen Verschieben.

b) Trotz fester Spannkräfte keine Verbiegung der Werkstücke, da diese nach dem Entspannen sich wieder frei geben und die Arbeitsflächen sonst krumm werden.

6. Spannelemente.

Zu diesen gehören Spanneisen, Spannschrauben, Parallelstücke, Vorstecker.

Die Spanneisen müssen richtig angesetzt werden, sonst ist ihre Kraftwirkung gering. In der Anordnung nach Abb. 69a sitzt die Spannschraube in der Mitte zwischen den Druckstellen des Spanneisens auf dem Werkstück und der Anlage. Die Kräfte A und B sind gleich groß. Die Abstände a und b sind gleich. Wenn dagegen, wie in Abb. 69b, die Spannschraube dicht am Werkstück sitzt, wird die Kraft B bedeutend größer als A. Wieviel größer der Abstand a gegenüber b ist, soviel größer wird auch die Kraft B am kürzeren Hebelarm. Der Zweck des Spanneisens ist aber der, das Werkstück gut festzuspannen und nicht die Auflage, also muß man stets die Spannschrauben so dicht wie möglich am Werkstück anordnen.

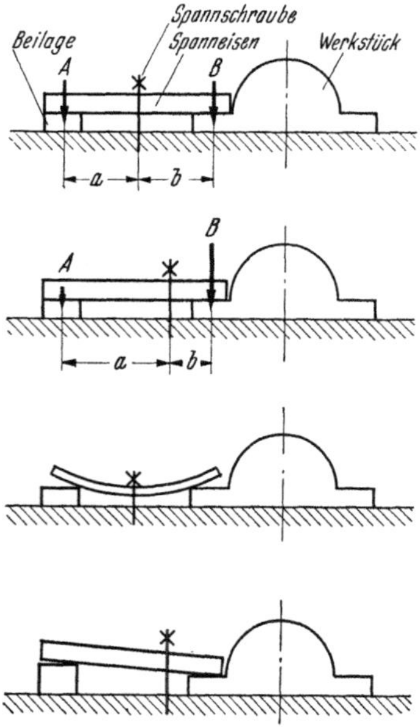

a Spannschraube schlecht angeordnet, zu kleine Spannkraft B auf Werkstück.

b Spannschraube richtig, dicht am Werkstück angeordnet.

c Spanneisen zu schwach, biegt sich durch und gibt nach.

d Beilage zu hoch, Spanneisen liegt nur mit Kante auf.

Abb. 69. Anordnung von Spanneisen.

Ein weiterer Fehler liegt vor, wenn das Spanneisen zu schwach ist und sich durchbiegt; es gibt nach und lockert sich unter dem Schnittdruck (Abb. 69c). Ungleiche Höhen zwischen Spannauflagen und Werkstück (Abb. 69d) haben zur Folge, daß das Spanneisen nur mit den Kanten aufliegt, nicht richtig drückt und sich beim Schnittdruck lösen kann.

7. Spannhilfswerkzeuge.

Spannhilfswerkzeuge sind Aufspannwinkel, Stützböcke, Treppenböcke, Spannkloben, verstellbare Stützböcke.

Aufspannwinkel dienen dazu, Werkstücke senkrecht zur Maschinenaufspannfläche aufzuspannen. Sie müssen selber genau winkelig sein und gut auf der Maschine festgespannt werden. Stützböcke werden vielfach bei rohen Werkstücken verwendet. Nimmt man zu einem festen Stützbock zwei verstellbare Böcke hinzu, kann jede Fläche nach Anriß genau ausgerichtet werden. Treppenböcke und Spannkloben sind besonders ausgebildete Hilfswerkzeuge, die eine vielseitige Anwendung gestatten.

8. Spannwerkzeuge.

Hierzu gehören Schraubstöcke, Stahlhalter, Zweibackenfutter, Dreibackenfutter, Planscheiben, Vorrichtungen.

Schraubstöcke sollen kräftig und zur Arbeit geeignet gewählt werden. Vorsicht bei Gußeisen, dieses platzt bei harten Schlägen mit Hammer oder Gegenständen. Werden rohe Werkstücke im Schraubstock gespannt, so legt man unter den Werkstücken Auflagen bei und klopft die Werkstücke kurz vor dem Festspannen mit einem Hammer nach unten, damit sie fest aufliegen.

Stahlhalter dienen zur Aufnahme der Werkzeuge und sind ebenfalls vorsichtig zu behandeln. Die Auflageflächen für die Werkzeuge müssen stets eben und sauber sein. Zwei- oder Dreibackenfutter sind Universalvorrichtungen. Rohe Teile soll man möglichst nicht im Futter spannen, sondern in der Planscheibe. Die Futter müssen für Fertigarbeiten geschont werden, damit sie ihre Genauigkeit behalten. Vorrichtungen sind Spannwerkzeuge für einen besonderen Fall.

9. Richtung der Schnittkräfte und ihre Auffangung.

Beim Außendrehen entstehen durch die Spanabnahme Kräfte am Umfang der Werkstücke, die diese zum Herumdrehen im Futter oder der Spannung veranlassen wollen. Für eine kräftige Mitnahme muß gesorgt werden, da die Verdrehungskräfte durch die Klemmkräfte im

Futter, in der Planscheibe oder durch das Drehherz aufgenommen werden. Beim Fräsen oder Hobeln (Abb. 70) wirken die Hauptkräfte des Schnittdruckes in der Vorschubrichtung. Auch hier werden Klemmkräfte durch die Spanneisen erzeugt.

In oben angeführten Fällen wirken die aufgebrachten Haltekräfte nicht gegen die Schnittrichtung, sondern senkrecht dazu. Durch Reibung der Werkstücke auf der Auflagefläche werden die Schnittkräfte abgefangen. Die Reibkräfte sind bedeutend kleiner als die senkrecht wirkenden Spannkräfte, und zwar kann man etwa rechnen, daß fünfmal zuviel Spannkräfte aufgewandt werden müssen, als Reibungskräfte zur Verfügung stehen.

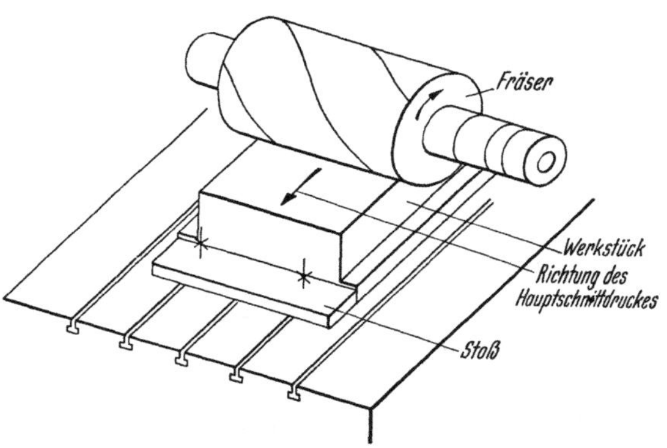

Abb. 70. Stoß zur Aufnahme des Hauptschnittdruckes.

Aus diesem Grunde werden, sofern nur möglich, Stöße zur Aufnahme des Hauptschnittdruckes angeordnet (Abb. 70). Diese Stöße dienen vor allem zur verstärkten Aufnahme des Schnittdruckes. Die Spanneisen werden davon entlastet und dienen besonders zum guten Festhalten des Werkstückes auf der Auflagefläche. Die Stöße müssen wiederum gleichfalls mit fünffacher Kraft angezogen werden, um den Schnittdruck aufzuhalten.

Die Richtung des Schnittdruckes geht in Richtung der Spanabnahme; der Schnittdruck drückt auf die Schneide und Spanfläche der Werkzeuge in der Richtung, wie die Späne abgenommen werden. Beim Hobeln liegt die Hauptkraft in Vorschubrichtung, daher der Gegenstoß vorn. Beim Fräsen mit geradverzahnten Fräsern liegt der Hauptschnittdruck ebenfalls in Vorschubrichtung. Beim Fräsen mit spiralverzahnten Fräsern kommt dazu noch eine seitliche Schubkraft senkrecht zu den Schneidzähnen. Hier muß gegen seitliches Verschieben ebenfalls möglichst ein Stoß vorgesehen werden. Beim normalen Drehen ist der Hauptschnittdruck auf das vorne eingespannte Werkzeug gerichtet. Der Drehstahl wird also nach unten gedrückt und muß daher gut festgespannt sein, sonst kommt er ins Schwingen und das Werkstück rattert.

Beim Einspannen in Schraubstöcke soll der Schnittdruck möglichst auf die festen Backen hin gerichtet sein. Geht er auf die verstellbaren Backen zu, so kann unter den Erschütterungen bei der Arbeit ein Lösen der Spindel vorkommen. Das Einspannen und Bearbeiten längs des Spannschlitzes im Schraubstock soll vermieden werden. Hier werden die Schnittkräfte nur durch Reibkräfte aufgenommen, d. h. eine fünffache Spannkraft ist notwendig. Dadurch kann es vorkommen, daß die Werkstücke verdrückt und bereits bearbeitete fertige Flächen beschädigt werden. Oder man ist gezwungen, mit kleineren Schnitten zu arbeiten, was mehr Zeit kostet.

10. Kraftfluß beim Spannen.

Grundsätzlich muß die Spannkraft immer über der Auflagestelle eingeleitet werden. Wenn wie in Abb. 71a das Spanneisen zu kurz angesetzt wird, muß die Kraft in der gewundenen Richtung zur Auflagefläche gelangen und verbiegt dabei das Werkstück. Dagegen findet nach Abb. 71b keine Verbiegung durch Spannkräfte statt.

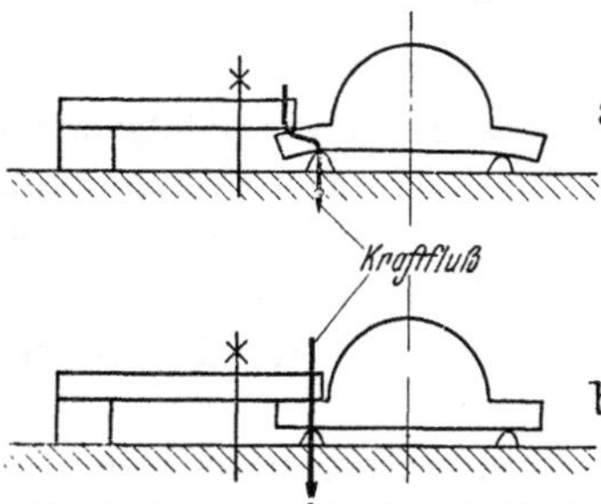

Abb. 71. Anordnung der Spannkräfte über den Auflagepunkten.

Genau so ist es falsch, einen U-förmigen Träger nach Abb. 72a zu spannen. Hier muß das Werkstück durchfedern. Es wird unter dem Spanndruck zusammengepreßt, bearbeitet und geht nach dem Entspannen wieder auf. Die Arbeitsfläche wird krumm. Hier muß, wie in Abb. 72b, für direkten Kraftfluß die linke Wand gespannt werden.

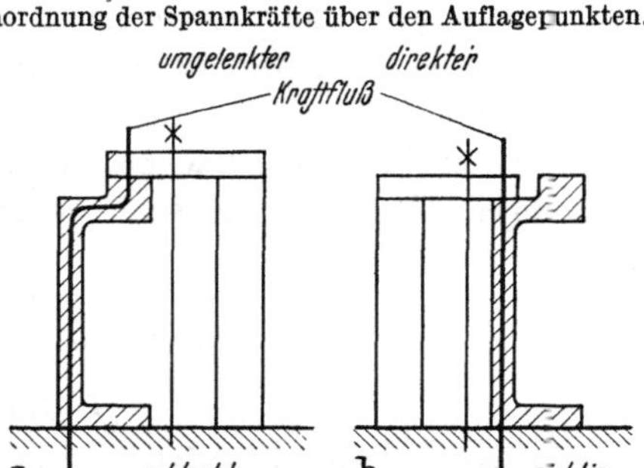

Abb. 72. Vermeidung des Verspannens dünner Werkstücke.

Beim Stoß in Abb. 73a ist die Kraft auf die dünne Stirnwand gerichtet. Diese biegt sich durch, da der Kraftfluß erst quer zu den Längs wänden und dann von diesen in der Hauptschnittrichtung laufen muß.

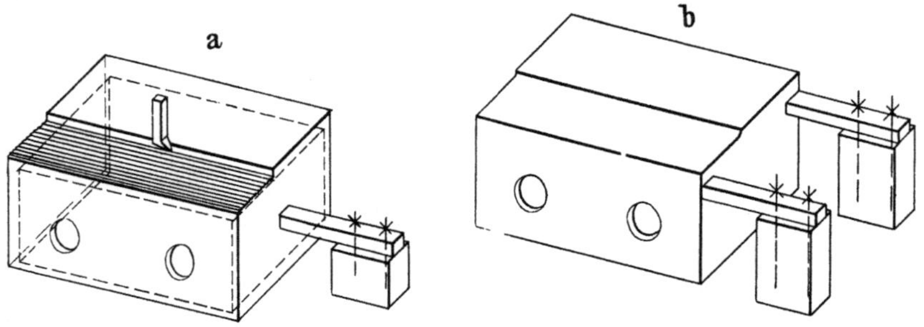

a) Falsch, Stoß geht auf schwache Stirnwand, die sich durchbiegt, umgelenkter Kraftfluß. b) Richtig, Stöße gehen auf Längswände, direkter Kraftfluß.

Abb. 73. Anordnung des Stoßes, um Verbiegungen des Werkstückes zu vermeiden.

In Abb. 73b dagegen bleibt die dünne Stirnwand unbelastet, da hier der Kraftfluß des Stoßes direkt auf die Längswände geht.

11. Fehlermöglichkeiten und Abhilfe.

Schlechter Arbeitsausfall kann folgende Ursachen haben:

1. Werkstück war nicht fest gespannt und hat sich bei der Arbeit verschoben. Fester spannen oder Stoß anbringen.

2. Arbeitsflächen krumm. Auflage nicht gerade, Werkstück verspannt durch umgelenkten Kraftfluß, Auflagefläche ungenügend, Spanneisen zu schwach.

3. Werkstücke werden herausgerissen. Spannanordnung nicht richtig, Haftreibung nicht ausreichend, weil zu schwach festgezogen, direkte Spannung versuchen oder Stoß anordnen, Papierauflagen vergrößern Haftreibung.

4. Unsaubere Oberflächen können auch vom schlechten Spannen herrühren. Mehr Spanneisen anordnen.

Abschnitt 7.

Kegelberechnungen.

1. Kegel.

Ein Kegel (Abb. 74a) ist ein runder Körper, dessen Grundfläche ein Kreis ist, der sich bis zu seiner Spitze gleichförmig verjüngt. Schneidet man ein Stück der Spitze ab, so entsteht ein Kegelstumpf (früher Konus genannt) (Abb. 74b).

Der Kegelstumpf wird durch zwei verschieden große Kreisflächen begrenzt. An einer Welle kann ein Teilabschnitt kegelig sein (Abb. 74c). Man unterscheidet schwache Kegel bis zu einem Kegelwinkel von 90° und steile Kegel mit höheren Winkeln.

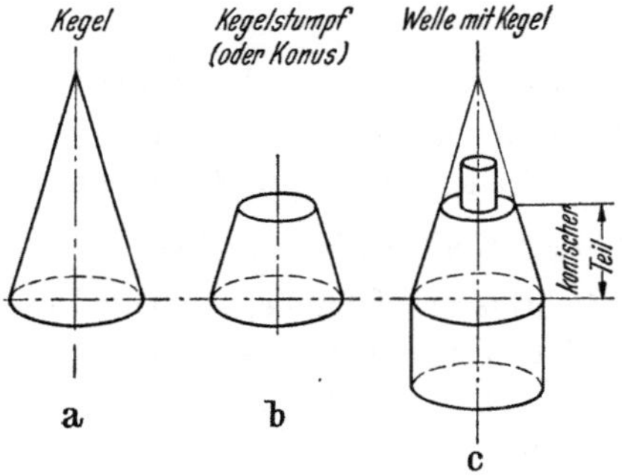

Abb. 74. Kegel und Konusse.

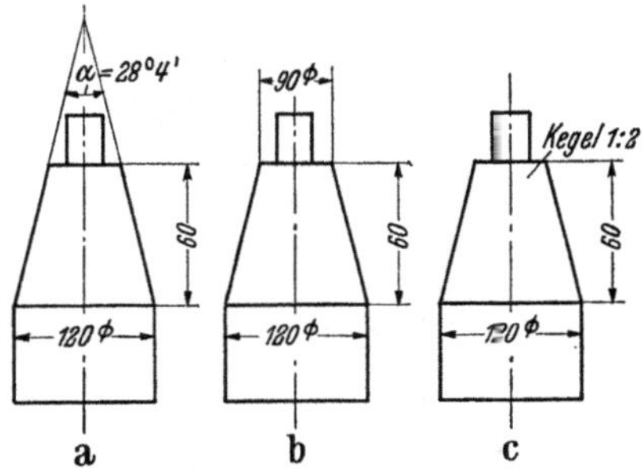

Abb. 75. Verschiedene Vermaßung eines Kegels.

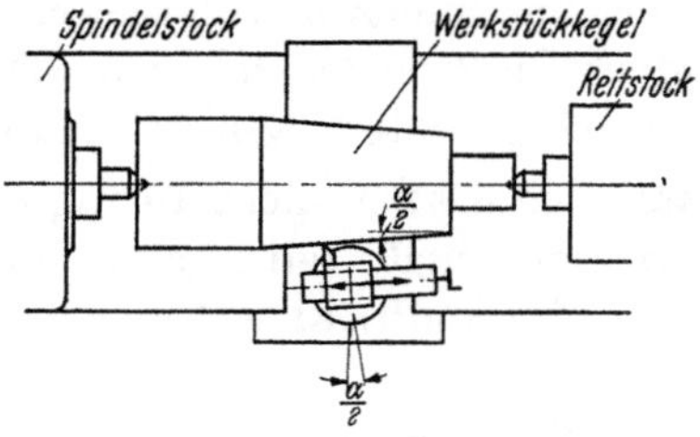

a Supportverstellung um den Winkel α.

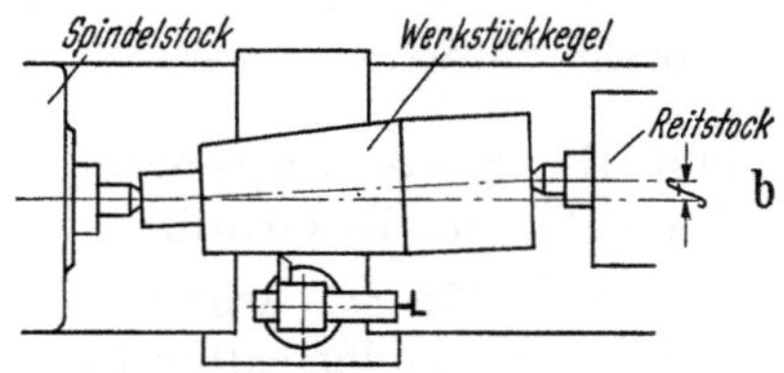

b Reitstockverstellung aus der Mitte.

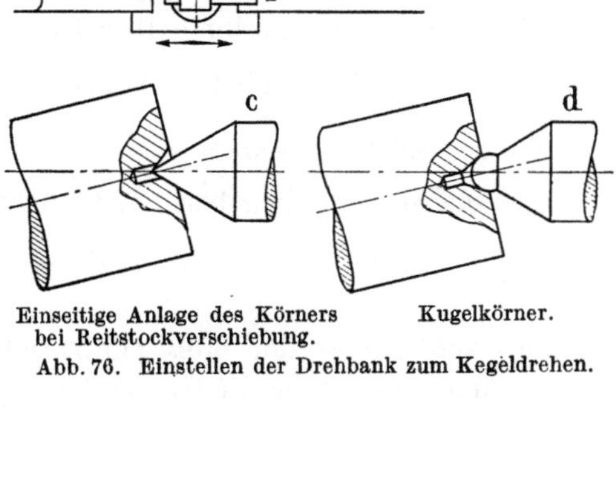

Einseitige Anlage des Körners bei Reitstockverschiebung. Kugelkörner.

Abb. 76. Einstellen der Drehbank zum Kegeldrehen.

2. Kegelvermaßung.

Der kegelische Abschnitt kann verschieden vermaßt sein. Er wird bestimmt nach Abb.75 außer der Angabe der Länge und dem größten Durchmesser durch weitere Angaben:

Fall a den ganzen Kegelwinkel α, z. B. 28° 4′,

Fall b den kleinsten Durchmesser,

Fall c die Kegelsteigung. Mit Kegelsteigung ist gemeint, wieviel der Durchmesser auf die Länge zunimmt. In Abb. 75b nimmt der Kegel auf der Länge 60 mm von 90 mm ⌀ auf 120 mm ⌀ zu. Der Unterschied ist also 120 — 90 = 30 mm. Die Steigung errechnet sich dann zu

$$\frac{30}{60} = \frac{3}{6} = \frac{1}{2} = 1:2.$$

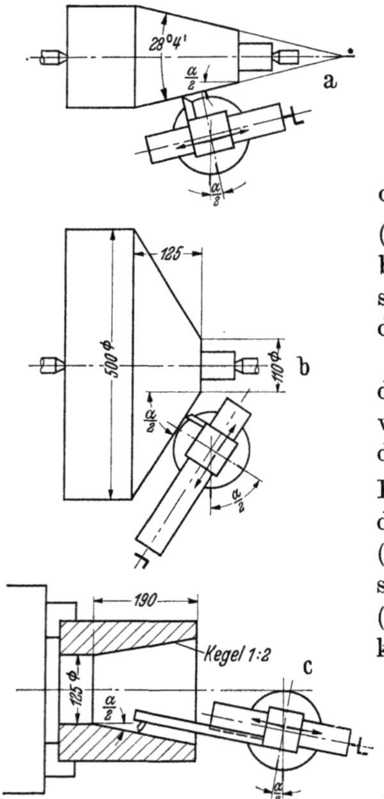

Abb. 77. Einstellungen des Supportflansches für verschiedene Kegelwinkel.

3. Einstellung der Drehbank.

Das Kegeligdrehen kann erfolgen durch

1. Verdrehen des Supportflansches um den halben Kegelwinkel $\frac{\alpha}{2}$ (Abb. 76 a). (Das Richtige und Übliche, wenn die Drehbank das Verdrehen des Supportflansches zuläßt. Innen- und Außenkegel drehen möglich.)

2. Verschieben des Reitstockes aus der Achse der Maschine Abb. 76b schlecht, weil Reitstock für Zylindrischdrehen wieder genau eingerichtet werden muß. Ferner läuft der Körner nicht richtig in der Zentrierung und reibt sich auf (Abb. 76c). Einwandfreies Arbeiten gestattet uns ein Körner mit Kugelspitze (Abb. 76d). Nur schlanke Außenkegel können gedreht werden.

4. Einstellung des Supportes, Umrechnung in Grade.

Wie die Abb. 77a···c zeigen, muß der Support jeweils um den halben Kegelwinkel $\frac{\alpha}{2}$ aus seiner Nullstellung verdreht werden. Dieser Winkel $\frac{\alpha}{2}$ muß somit ermittelt werden.

Fall a. Abb. 77a. Da hier der Kegelwinkel angegeben ist, braucht dieser nur halbiert zu werden, $\frac{28^0\,4'}{2} = 14^0\,2'$. Der Support muß also um $14^0\,2'$ verdreht werden.

In welcher Richtung der Support verdreht werden muß, ergibt sich aus der Lage des Werkstückes in der Maschine. Falls die Gradeinteilung auf dem Supportflansch nicht von Null aufwärts geht, sondern von 90° abwärts, muß der Unterschied $90^0 - \frac{\alpha}{2} = 90 - 14^0\,2' = 75^0\,58'$ ausgerechnet und eingestellt werden.

Man kann die Grade auch einzeln an der Teilung abzählen.

Fall b Abb. 77b. Gegeben sind die zwei Durchmesser und die Länge des Kegels. Der Winkel $\frac{\alpha}{2}$ ist der halbe Kegelwinkel. Nach Abb. 78a u. b berechnet man den Winkel $\frac{\alpha}{2}$ aus einem Hilfsdreieck. Dieses ist rechtwinklig und die Berechnung von $\frac{\alpha}{2}$ erfolgt nach Abschnitt 2, Gleichung 1 mit Hilfe des $\operatorname{tg}\frac{\alpha}{2}$. Gegenkathete $a = 195$ mm, Ankathete $b = 125$ mm.

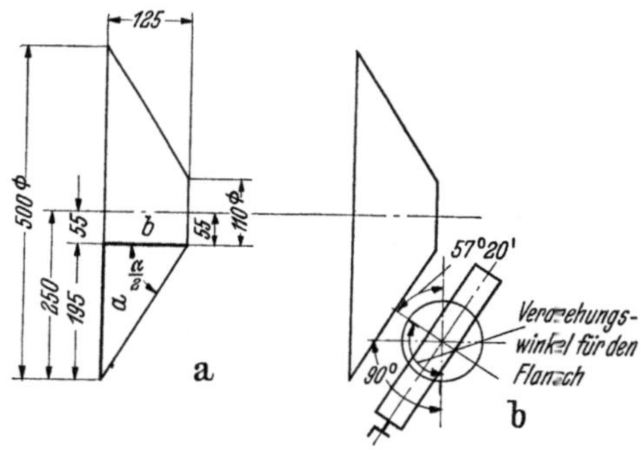

Abb. 78. Berechnung des Winkels $\frac{\alpha}{2}$ aus einem Hilfsdreieck.

$$\operatorname{tg}\frac{\alpha}{2} = \frac{a}{b} = \frac{195}{125} = 1{,}56\,.$$

$\frac{\alpha}{2}$ ist jetzt nach Tab. 2 auszurechnen und ist $57^0\,20'$.

Da man beim Drehen die Handkurbel fast immer vorn haben muß (Abb. 77b), liegt der Winkel $57^0\,20'$ von rückwärts gerechnet. Der Halbkreis hat 180^0. Also wird die Verdrehung des Supportes $180^0 - 57^0\,20'$ von der vorderen Nullstellung gerechnet. Beginnt die Teilung der Grade nicht vorne, kommen auch noch $90^0 - 57^0\,20'$ Einstellung in Frage. Tab. 7 enthält übliche Kegelwinkel.

Fall c Abb. 77c. Gegeben sind ein Durchmesser, die Länge des Kegels und die Steigung. Kegel 1 : 2 bedeutet, daß auf jeweils 2 mm Länge der Durchmesser um 1 mm größer wird. Den halben Kegelwinkel $\frac{\alpha}{2}$ kann man jetzt leicht nach folgender Regel berechnen:

Steigung ausrechnen $1 : 2 = 0{,}5$,

die Hälfte nehmen $\operatorname{tg}\frac{\alpha}{2} = 0{,}5 : 2 = 0{,}25$,

aus Tab. 2 den Winkel $\frac{\alpha}{2}$ ablesen mit $14^0\,2'$.

Tabelle 7. Kegelwinkel.

Kegel 1 : k	Kegelwinkel	Einstellwinkel an der Bearbeitungsmaschine $a/2$
1 : 0,289	120°	60°
1 : 0,350	110°	55°
1 : 0,500	90°	45°
1 : 0,652	75°	37° 30′
1 : 0,866	60°	30°
1 : 1,207	45°	22° 30′
1 : 1,50	36° 52′ 12″	18° 26′ 6″
1 : 1,866	30°	15°
1 : 3	18° 55′ 30″	9° 27′ 45″
1 : 3,429	16° 35′ 40″	8° 17′ 50″
1 : 4,072	14°	7°
1 : 5	11° 25′ 16″	5° 42′ 38″
1 : 6	9° 31′ 38″	4° 45′ 49″
1 : 10	5° 43′ 30″	2° 51′ 45″
1 : 12	4° 46′ 20″	2° 23′ 10″
1 : 15	4° 49′ 6″	1° 54′ 33″
1 : 16	3° 34′ 48″	1° 47′ 24″
1 : 20	2° 51′ 52″	1° 25′ 56″

Kegel 1 : k	Kegelwinkel	Einstellwinkel an der Bearbeitungsmaschine $a/2$
Morsekegel 0 1 : 19,212	2° 58′ 54″	1° 29′ 27″
Morsekegel 1 1 : 20,047	2° 51′ 18″	1° 25′ 39″
Morsekegel 2 1 : 20,020	2° 51′ 40″	1° 25′ 50″
Morsekegel 3 1 : 19,922	2° 52′ 34″	1° 26′ 17″
Morsekegel 4 1 : 19,254	2° 56′ 38″	1° 28′ 19″
Morsekegel 5 1 : 19,002	3° 0′ 6″	1° 30′ 3″
Morsekegel 6 1 : 19,180	2° 59′ 12″	1° 29′ 36″
1 : 30	1° 54′ 34″	57′ 17″
1 : 50	1° 8′ 46″	34′ 23″

5. Umrechnung der Einstellung des Supportes in Millimeterverdrehung, wenn keine Gradeinteilung am Flansch vorhanden.

Ist keine Teilung auf dem Flansch des Supportes mit dem Durchmesser „d“ vorhanden, kann man sich folgendermaßen helfen:

In der Nullstellung werden zwei Risse a und b (Abb. 79a) angebracht, die zunächst übereinander stehen.

Verdreht man den Support um den Betrag „f“, der der Steigung des Kegels entspricht, so kann mit dem Support konisch gedreht werden. Wie groß muß der Betrag „f“ sein?

Fall a. Ist der Kegelwinkel gegeben, so nimmt man für den halben Winkel $\frac{\alpha}{2}$ aus der Tabelle den Wert für $\operatorname{tg}\frac{\alpha}{2}$, z. B. $\operatorname{tg}\frac{\alpha}{2} = 0{,}25$, dann ist

$$f = \frac{d}{2} \cdot \operatorname{tg}\frac{\alpha}{2}.$$

Beispiel: Kegelwinkel α ist 60°, $d = 280$ mm Supportflansch Durchmesser.

$$\text{Winkel } \frac{\alpha}{2} = \frac{30}{2} = 15^0,$$

$$\operatorname{tg}\frac{\alpha}{2} = 0{,}268,$$

$$f = 140 \times 0{,}268 = 37{,}5 \text{ mm}.$$

Der Riß b muß also um 37,5 mm gegenüber a verdreht werden. Für steilere Kegel ist dieses Verfahren ungenau, die wirkliche Verdrehung wird etwas kleiner. Bis $\frac{\alpha}{2} = 15^0$ genügt aber dieses Verfahren.

Fall b. Ist der größte und kleinste Durchmesser des Kegels angegeben, wird $\operatorname{tg}\frac{\alpha}{2}$, wie in Absatz 4, Fall b, berechnet und daraus die Verdrehung „f“.

Beispiel: $D = 120$ mm ∅, $D_1 = 90$ mm ∅, $l = 60$ mm ∅,
$d = 280$ mm Supportflansch-∅.

$$\frac{a}{b} = \frac{15}{60} = 0{,}25 = \operatorname{tg}\frac{\alpha}{2}, \quad f = 140 \cdot 0{,}25 = 35 \text{ mm}.$$

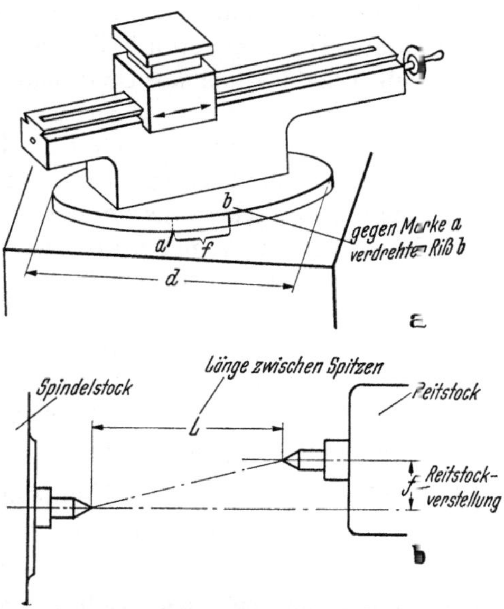

Abb. 79. Messung der Flanschverdrehung in mm und Berechnung der Reitstockverstellung.

Der Riß b muß also um 35 mm gegenüber a verdreht werden.

Fall c. Gegeben ist die Kegelsteigung mit 1 : 4. Maßgebend ist die halbe Steigung als $\operatorname{tg}\frac{\alpha}{2}$ mit $1 : 8 = 0{,}125$, $f = \frac{d}{2} \cdot \operatorname{tg}\frac{\alpha}{2}$.

Beispiel:
$d = 280$ mm Supportflansch-∅
$\operatorname{tg}\frac{\alpha}{2} = 0{,}125$
$f = 140 \cdot 0{,}125 = 17{,}5$ mm.

Der Riß b muß um 17,5 mm gegenüber a verdreht werden.

6. Berechnung der Verstellung des Reitstockes.

Nach Abb. 79b ist die Verstellung des Reitstockes „h“ zu berechnen. Zunächst muß die halbe Steigung des Kegels ermittelt werden, wie das in Abschnitt 4 erfolgt ist. Es ist dann

$$h = L \cdot \operatorname{tg}\frac{\alpha}{2}. \qquad \text{(Gl. 2)}$$

L ist Abstand zwischen den Spitzen, also gleich der Werkstücklänge.

Beispiel: Länge des Werkstückes 370 mm,
Halbe Steigung $\operatorname{tg}\frac{\alpha}{2} = 0{,}125$,
$L = 370 \cdot 0{,}125 = 46{,}3$ mm.

Der Reitstock muß also um 46,3 mm aus der Achse der Maschine nach hinten verschoben werden.

Beim Drehen eines Kegels mit Reitstock sollte man nicht zu weit hinausgehen, da man sonst das Zentrum zu arg ausweitet, also die Körnerspitze nicht mehr dem Zentrum entspricht und man somit nur ungenaue und unsaubere Arbeit erhält. Eine bessere Arbeit ermöglicht der Kugelkörner nach Abb. 76d.

Abschnitt 8.

Teilkopfberechnungen.

Bei vielen Arbeiten an der Fräsmaschine oder Stoßmaschine sind bestimmte Teilungen erforderlich, die auf den Zeichnungen in Grad angegeben sind und nun auf Umdrehungen der Teilscheiben umgerechnet werden müssen.

Im Teilgerät befindet sich eine Übersetzung mit Schnecke und Wechselrädern, die konstant bleibt. Man muß zunächst wissen, wie oft muß man die Teilscheibe herumdrehen, damit eine Umdrehung der Teilspindel erfolgt. Es kommen für Umdrehungszahlen 20, 30, 36, 40 vor. Diese Zahl ist auf den folgenden Berechnungen mit n bezeichnet. Ist also $n = 36$ U, so muß man die Teilscheibe 36mal herumdrehen und erhält eine Umdrehung der Teilspindel.

Die Gradeinteilung, siehe Abschnitt 2, hat 360^0 über den ganzen Umfang. Eine Viertelumdrehung ist gleich 90^0, also bei $^1/_4$mal 36 U $= 9$ U, dreht sich die Teilspindel um 90^0. 1^0 ist dann der 360. Teil von n. Bei $n = 36$ ist $1^0 = \frac{36}{360} = {}^1/_{10}$ Umdrehung der Teilscheibe. Damit man nun Brüche von $^1/_{10}$ Umdrehung auf der Teilscheibe ausführen kann, hat diese Lochkreise mit verschiedenen Lochzahlen. Bei $^1/_{10}$ Umdrehung z. B. könnte man bei einem Teilkreis von 10 Löchern bei dem Umfang um 1 Loch weiterdrehen, dann ist $^1/_{10}$ Umdrehung gemacht. Wenn aber kein Lochkreis mit 10 Löchern vorhanden ist, nimmt man den doppelten Lochzahlkreis. Bei 20 Löchern dreht man jetzt 2 Löcher weiter, dann sind ebenfalls $^1/_{10}$ Umdrehung ausgeführt. Wenn man einen Bruch oben und unten auf das Doppelte oder Dreifache oder Vierfache erhöht, bleibt das Verhältnis immer gleich, die Erhöhung ist so zulässig.

Sind jetzt Teilungen von 3^0 auszuführen, so muß die Teilscheibe $3 \cdot {}^1/_{10}$ Umdrehung $= {}^3/_{10}$ U gedreht werden. Die Teilscheibe muß also $^3/_{10}$ herumgedreht werden, beim Lochkreis $20 = 2 \cdot 3 = 6$ Löcher.

Allgemein wird die Drehzahl der Teilscheibe ausgerechnet nach

$$\text{Umdrehungen } U = \frac{n}{360} \cdot \text{Grad.} \qquad \text{(Gl. 3)}$$

Beispiele:

1. *Aufgabe:* $3^0\,30'$ sollen geteilt werden. $n = 36$.

Lösung: $3^0\,30' = 3^1/_2{}^0 = {}^7/_2{}^0$.

$$U = \frac{n}{360} \cdot 3^0\,30' = \frac{36}{360} \cdot {}^7/_2 = \frac{1}{10} \cdot \frac{7}{2} = \frac{7}{10 \cdot 2} = \frac{7}{20}.$$

Die Teilung erfolgt auf dem Lochkreis 20 und zwar um 7 Löcher weiter.

2. *Aufgabe:* $17^0\,45'$ sollen geteilt werden. $n = 36$

Lösung: $17^0\,45' = 17^3/_4{}^0 = 17 \cdot \frac{4}{4} + \frac{3}{4} = \frac{4 \cdot 17 + 3}{4} = \frac{71}{4}.$

$$U = \frac{36}{360} \cdot \frac{71}{4} = \frac{1}{10} \cdot \frac{71}{4} = \frac{71}{40} = \frac{40 + 31}{40} = 1 + \frac{31}{40} \text{ Umdrehungen.}$$

Die Teilscheibe muß also ein ganzes Mal und dazu $\frac{31}{40}$ weiter gedreht werden, d. h. auf dem Lochkreis 40 um weitere 31 Löcher.

3. *Aufgabe:* $68^0\,10'$ sollen geteilt werden. $n = 36$.

Lösung: $68^0\,10' = 68^{10}/_{60}{}^0 = 68^1/_6{}^0 = \frac{6 \cdot 68 + 1}{6} = \frac{409^0}{6}.$

$$U = \frac{n}{360} \cdot \text{Grad} = \frac{36}{360} \cdot \frac{409}{6} = \frac{1}{10} \cdot \frac{409}{6} = \frac{409}{60} = 6\,\frac{49}{60} \text{ Umdrehungen.}$$

Die Teilscheibe muß 6mal herum gedreht werden und dazu noch 49 Löcher auf dem Lochkreis 60.

Wie groß für jede Maschine n ist, muß aus der Maschinenbeschreibung entnommen oder ausprobiert werden. Mit dieser Grundzahl lassen sich leicht die notwendigen Lochzahlen ausrechnen, wie die obigen Beispiele zeigen.

Die Umrechnung von Minuten in Grad ist in Abschnitt 2 eingehend behandelt.

II. Besondere Betriebskunde.

In den ersten Abschnitten sind die allgemein notwendigen Kenntnisse geschildert, wie sie als grundlegendes Handwerkszeug für die Bearbeitung gebraucht werden. Im folgenden werden jetzt die besonderen Verfahren wie Drehen, Hobeln, Fräsen, Bohren, Reiben usw. behandelt. Hier werden zunächst die Werkzeuge, dann die zu wählenden Schnittgeschwindigkeiten, d. h. Umdrehungszahlen, Vorschübe und schließlich alle die besonderen Kleinigkeiten behandelt, die so leicht zu schlechtem Arbeitsausfall führen können, wenn man sie nicht beachtet. Vorausgeschickt werden diesen Betrachtungen die Erklärungen über die Werkstoffe und ihre Bezeichnungen sowie die Begriffe Schnittgeschwindigkeit, Vorschübe und Spantiefe.

Abschnitt 9.

Maschinenwartung, Einstellung und Vorrichtungsbehandlung.

Die Bezeichnung und das normale Aussehen der Maschinen, wie Drehbank, Revolverbank, Ständerbohrmaschine, Radialbohrmaschine, Waagrecht-Senkrecht-Fräsmaschinen, Bohrwerk, Hobelmaschine, Stoßmaschine usw. werden vorausgesetzt. Die Bedienung der Maschinen muß doch an Ort und Stelle erklärt werden und ist in kurzer Zeit leicht zu erlernen.

Es ist verständlich, daß eine abgenutzte Maschine nicht mehr so genau arbeiten wird wie eine neue. Man muß dann durch Anfügen eines zusätzlichen Arbeitsganges mit feinerer Spanabnahme die verlangte Genauigkeit des Werkstückes herstellen. Die Schnelligkeit der Abnutzung kann aber durch sachgemäße Behandlung der Maschinen weitgehend vermindert werden. Es ist erreichbar, daß Maschinen noch nach Jahren neuwertig sind, wenn bei der Bedienung folgende Gesichtspunkte peinlichst beachtet werden.

1. Zur Beachtung.

1. Überzeuge dich stets bei Arbeitsbeginn, ob sämtliche Schmierstellen reichlich Fett haben bzw. ob die Schmierpumpe läuft und richtig fördert. Prüfe die Lagerstellen während des ganzen Laufes der Maschine durch Handauflegen auf ihre Erwärmung.

2. Säubere alle Gleitbahnen für Supporte, Werkzeuge und fette sie ein, auch manchmal während der Arbeit, wenn Späne anfallen. Kleine Späne und Staub zwischen Führungsbahnen führen zum Fressen, vermindern die Genauigkeit von Maschine und Arbeit. Reparaturen halten dich auf.

3. Steige nicht auf Führungsbahnen, sondern lege ein Brett oder einen Schutz darüber. Beim Ein- und Ausspannen schwerer Stücke muß gleichfalls eine Unterlage auf der Maschine liegen, um Beschädigungen durch Schlag oder Anstoßen unmöglich zu machen.

Angeschlagene Stellen auf den Gleitbahnen treten hervor, lenken die Supporte ab und geben ungenaue Arbeiten. Alles, wie Hammer-schläge, Fallenlassen von Werkzeugen usw., trägt zur Beschädigung der Maschine und zur Wertverminderung bei.

4. Das Schalten der Maschine darf nie unter Last oder im vollen Lauf erfolgen, sondern soll bei Stillstand oder letztem Auslaufen ohne Gewaltanwendung stattfinden.

5. Bei Benutzung von Kühlmitteln für reichliche Kühlung sorgen. Kühlwasserpumpen sauber halten, Spanfangkasten von Zeit zu Zeit gründlich säubern, Spritzwasser darf nicht über die Maschine hinausgeschleudert werden, besonders nicht auf oder in Kabelkanäle, da Kurzschlußgefahr vorhanden.

6. Stets auf saubere Haltung der Aufnahmen für Werkzeuge, Konusse, Flächenanlagen usw. achten, da nur ein gut sitzendes und schlagfrei laufendes Werkzeug saubere Arbeit liefern kann.

7. Halte Ordnung im Werkzeugschrank! Schone die Werkzeuge, denn nur so kann schnell und verdienstreich gearbeitet werden.

8. Auch die Arbeitsstücke können mit gleicher Anstrengung gerade und übersichtlich geordnet werden. Das erleichtert die Kontrolle und zeugt von richtiger Einstellung zur Arbeit.

9. Halte deinen Arbeitsplatz von Schmutz und Spänen rein, denn dazu ist während des Maschinenlaufes meist reichlich Zeit vorhanden.

10. Alle diese Punkte sind wichtig, denn nur durch die Vermeidung aller möglichen, auch kleiner Fehler können Dauererfolge erzielt werden.

2. Beistellungen an Maschinen.

Sollen auf einer Drehbank von einer Welle 4 mm im Durchmesser heruntergedreht werden, so stellt man den Support mit dem Drehstahl soweit ein, bis das Werkzeug schabt. Diese Stellung merkt man sich an der Einstellskala oder verschiebt die Einstellskala auf Null Die Beistellung für die Spanabgabe muß jetzt gleich der halben Durchmesserverringerung also gleich 2 mm sein. Das trifft sowohl für Außen- als auch für Innendrehen zu. Dagegen muß beim Plandrehen die ganze Spanabnahme, also 4 mm, beigestellt werden.

Bei allen neuen Maschinen ist die Beistellung sinnfällig, d. h. bei Rechtsdrehung läuft der Support nach vorn in Spindelrichtung gesehen, die Skalen tragen jedoch verschiedene Einteilungen (Abb. 80). Man muß sich jeweils vorher überlegen, wieviel Beistellung einem Skalenstrich entspricht und wieviel das auf den Durchmesser ausmacht.

In Tab. 8 sind verschieden vorkommende Verhältnisse zusammengestellt. Es ist einzusehen, daß bei Fräs- und Schleifmaschinen unterschiedliche Teilungen vorkommen werden, weil ganz verschiedene Beistellungen entsprechend den Arbeitsverfahren notwendig sind.

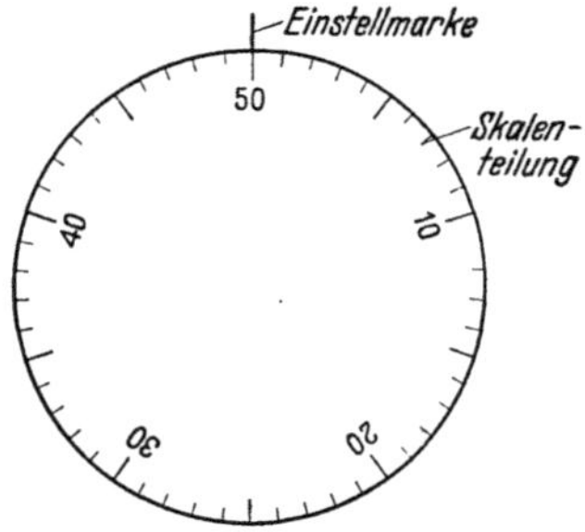

Abb. 80. Beispiel für Skalenteilung.

Das Anstellen eines Fräsers wird erleichtert, wenn man zwischen Werkstück und Fräser ein dünnes Stück Papier hält. Dieses wird abgeschnitten, sobald der Fräser die Werkstückoberfläche erreicht, also berührt.

Beim Bohren von Löchern mit genauer Tiefe ist darauf zu achten, daß die Bohrerspitze über diese Tiefe meist hinaus eindringt. Beim Einstellen von festen Anschlägen muß also erst das Loch so weit angebohrt werden, bis der ganze Bohrerdurchmesser anzuschneiden beginnt. Von hier ab kann die Tiefe eingestellt werden.

Tabelle 8. Beistellungswerte bei verschiedenen Skalenteilungen und Skalenwerten.

Zahl der Skalenteilstriche am Umfang	Maßänderung für 1 Skalenstrich in mm	Damit Beistellung für eine ganze Skalenumdrehung in mm	Durchmesseränderung in mm	
			für 1 Skalenstrich	für 1 Spindelumdrehung
50	0,01	0,5	0,02	1
50	0,02	1	0,04	2
50	0,025	1,25	0,05	2,5
50	0,05	2,5	0,1	5
50	0,1	5	0,2	10
100	0,01	1	0,02	2
100	0,02	2	0,04	4
100	0,025	2,5	0,05	5
100	0,05	5	0,1	10
100	0,1	10	0,2	20

3. Werkzeugbefestigung.

Bei Drehbänken wird der Drehstahl in den Stahlhalter eingespannt. Seine Auflagefläche muß eben und glatt sein, da das Vorbedingung für festen Sitz des Werkzeuges ist. Zum Ausgleich der Spitzenhöhe und zur Schonung werden Beilagen dazwischengelegt.

Bei Bohrern ist es wichtig, daß diese genau rund laufen und mittig geschliffen sind und genau in Bohrrichtung stehen. Bei konischen Auflagen muß der Konus satt anliegen. Keineswegs darf der Bohrerlappen zur Hauptmitnahme gegen Verdrehung dienen, da er bei normaler Beanspruchung abreißt. Ein guter Konussitz ist aber nur zu erreichen, wenn die konischen Flächen peinlich sauber und nicht verschlagen sind. Man muß also den Bohrer und die Aufnahmespindel bzw. die notwendigen Konushülsen sorgfältig gegen Schläge oder Verletzungen aller Art schützen. Vor allem dürfen nicht bei Verwendung von Hämmern beim Lösen des Konusses auf der tragenden Fläche Schlagspuren zurückbleiben. Durch Einbeulung werden die Rundpartien auf der Konusfläche herausgedrückt, stehen vor und machen einen satten Konussitz unmöglich. Das Werkzeug läuft dann nur mit Schlag und ohne Halt. Auch Bohrer mit zylindrischem Schaft und Beschädigungen dieses Schaftes müssen unweigerlich schief im Bohrfutter eingespannt werden. Man sorge deshalb dafür, jedes Werkstück fest und schlagfrei einzuspannen, denn ohne diese Vorbedingung kann keine gute Arbeit geleistet werden.

4. Allgemeine Werkzeugaufnahmen.

Wird ein Werkstück zwischen Spitzen gedreht, muß für eine richtige Ansenkung Sorge getragen sein. Wie in Abb. 81 gezeigt, muß das vorgebohrte Loch für die Körneransenkung so weit in das Werkstück hineingehen, daß die Körnerspitze frei wird, da sonst nur diese anliegen und in kurzer Zeit fressen würden. Reichliche Schmierung dieser Stelle ist vorzunehmen. Werden die Werkstücke mehrfach umgespannt, muß stets bei jedem Einsenken die Körneransenkung und die Körnerspitze sorgfältig gereinigt werden.

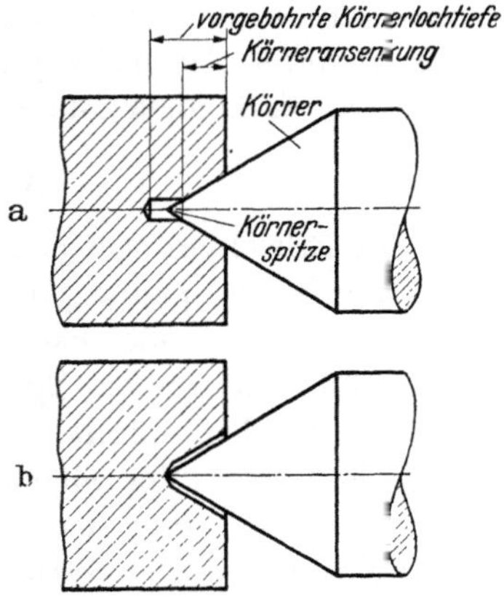

Abb. 81. Richtige und falsche Ausführung der Ankörnung
a) Richtig. Spitze läuft frei, Kegelflächen tragen.
b) Falsch. Spitze trägt allein, frißt und nutzt sich ab. Werkstück gibt nach.

Bei Drehherzen legt man gegen Beschädigung des Werkstückes ein Zwischenstück unter die Halteschraube. Patentfutter werden als Zwei- und Dreibackenfutter verwendet; sie sind nur für bereits vorgearbeitete Teile gedacht und sollen für Vorschrupparbeiten nicht verwendet werden, da sie dafür zu schwach sind und dann feinere Arbeiten mit ihnen nicht mehr ausgeführt werden können. Beim Spannen von Ringen, wobei die Backen über den Futterdurchmesser weit hinausgeschraubt werden müssen, können Späne in die jetzt hervortretenden Spiralzähne des Futters eindringen. Beim Zuspannen setzen sich diese dann innen fest. Das Futter klemmt und muß stets auseinandergenommen werden, was Zeitverlust bedeutet. Man deckt in solchen Fällen diese Spiralgänge mit Papier oder Putzwolle ab. Für grobe Arbeiten dienen Planscheiben als Spannorgane. Mit diesen können die kräftigsten Stücke sicher gespannt werden. Rohe Teile niemals in Dreibackenbutter spannen. Beim Aufschrauben von Planscheiben und Patentfutter auf den Spindelkopf der Maschinen müssen unbedingt die Gewinde beider Teile ganz sorgfältig gesäubert und eingefettet werden, weil sonst nach längerer Arbeitszeit ein Abnehmen unmöglich werden kann. Wenn dann infolge des festen Sitzes oder Fressens des Gewindes die Futter mit Gewalt heruntergeholt werden müssen, wird meist die Spindel verbogen, die Genauigkeit der Maschine ist bedeutend verringert und kann niemals wieder erreicht werden. Und das nur als Ursache von Unachtsamkeit. Weitere Spannorgane, z. B. für Bohrmaschinen, Fräsmaschinen, sind Schraubstöcke, bei denen man ebenfalls auf gute Instandhaltung der Führungsbahnen sehen muß. Das Zuspannen soll nur von Hand erfolgen. Die Spannhebel sind so lang, daß die Handkräfte ausreichen. Es ist grundsätzlich falsch, durch Anwendung von Verlängerungen übermäßige Kräfte anzusetzen, sie können zum Sprengen des Schraubstockes führen.

5. Vorrichtungen.

Zur Erleichterung vieler Arbeiten werden Vorrichtungen verwendet, das sind Sonderspannorgane. Auf Drehbänken ist es zweckmäßig, diese Vorrichtung jedesmal nach dem Aufspannen auf Rundlauf zu prüfen. Auch hier müssen die Spannstellen nach jedem Ausspannen gut gesäubert werden, damit die Werkstücke in die gewünschte richtige Lage kommen. Vor allem ist auf gute Anlage an den Spannflächen und spielfreien Sitz der Zentrierung zu achten. Sämtliche Teile an Vorrichtungen, wie Spannpratzen, Schrauben, Muttern, Unterlagscheiben, Einstellehren usw., müssen immer dabeibleiben, weil sonst bei wiederholter Benutzung bedeutend Mehrverlustzeiten durch Neubeschaffung entstehen, als der einmalige Vorteil des Entfernens eingebracht hat.

Die Genauigkeit der Vorrichtung ist sehr groß. Man soll sie deshalb vorsichtig behandeln, damit nicht durch Hinwerfen oder Schläge Abweichungen der Form auftreten. Beim Ausrichten auf Planscheiben oder Spannplatten kann man sich durch Beilagen von Papier helfen.

Drehdorne müssen vor dem Aufbringen des Werkstückes gut eingefettet sein. Man staucht die Werkstücke auf ein Stück Holz oder anderer weicher Unterlagen, niemals auf harten Unterlagen, da sonst ein Verschlagen der Dornstirnkanten eintritt.

6. Verschiedenes.

Beim Schruppen mit starker Spanabnahme tritt durch Erwärmung eine Verlängerung des Werkstückes ein. Durch die Spannung zwischen den Spitzen, also mit Reitstock, wird das Werkstück festgehalten und erhält eine erhöhte Längsspannung. Unter diesem Druck versucht die Welle auszuweichen und biegt sich durch. Es tritt unter der Wirkung der Spanabnahme ein Rattern auf. Man muß daher von Zeit zu Zeit nachprüfen, ob der Reitstock noch die richtige Spannung in der Körnerspitze hat und diese entsprechend nachrichten. Da diese Fehlermöglichkeiten bei jedem Arbeitsgang auftreten, sind sie stets neu zu beachten. Genaue und saubere Arbeiten sind nur bei restloser Vermeidung dieser Gefahrenquellen möglich.

Abschnitt 10.

Werkstoffkunde und Gliederung nach Zerspanbarkeit.

1. Allgemeines.

Das Eisen ist ein Element. Man muß es aus Eisenerzen gewinnen, da es im reinen Zustand in der Natur nicht vorkommt. Durch die Verhüttung, bei der die chemischen Verbindungen des Eisens mit Sauerstoff und anderen Grundstoffen gesprengt werden, wird das Eisen frei und geschmolzen. Dieser chemische Prozeß der Eisengewinnung wird im Hochofen durchgeführt, der etwa 20···30 m hoch und mit feuerfesten Steinen ausgemauert ist. Das Roheisen aus dem Hochofen wird entweder in einfachen Sandformen zu meterlangen Barren, zu „Masseln" vergossen oder in flüssigem Zustand zu Stahl weiterverarbeitet. Bei der Stahlherstellung werden die noch im Roheisen vorhandenen nicht erwünschten Beimischungen im flüssigen Zustand verbrannt. Dem fast reinen Eisen werden dann wieder die gewünschten Zusätze beigefügt.

Eine Verbindung von zwei oder mehreren Elementen gibt eine Legierung. Auch Stahl ist eine Legierung aus Eisen und Kohlenstoff bzw. noch weiteren Elementen. Eisen, Kupfer, Zink, Zinn, Aluminium, Nickel usw. sind Metalle und Elemente. Es gibt 92 Elemente, von denen nur ein Teil Metalle sind, nämlich die, die einen elektrischen Strom gut leiten, gutes Wärmeleitvermögen und einen besonders metallischen Glanz haben.

Legierungen sind Messing, Tombak, Bronze, Weißmetall, Rotguß, Aluminiumlegierungen. Durch die Art der Zusammensetzung einer Legierung erhält der Werkstoff ganz neue und verschiedene Eigenschaften, wie Festigkeit, Dehnbarkeit, Zähigkeit, Härte, Schmelztemperatur, magnetische Eigenschaften, elektrische Eigenschaften, Schweißbarkeit.

Aufgabe eines Konstrukteurs ist es, den für seine Konstruktion benötigten Werkstoff so auszuwählen, daß er in seinen mechanischen und sonstigen Eigenschaften entspricht, trotzdem aber im Preis wirtschaftlich bleibt. Anfangs stellten nun die einzelnen Werke Werkstoffe mit bestimmten Eigenschaften her, die Werksbezeichnungen erhielten. Der Zweck der Normung war der, aus dieser großen Zahl von vorhandenen Werkstoffmarken eine Auswahl zu treffen, wobei dennoch alle erforderlichen Sorten vorkamen. So entstanden die Werkstoffnormen mit bestimmten Kurzzeichen für die verschiedenen Werkstoffklassen.

2. Werkstoffnormen.

Folgende Begriffsbestimmungen sind festgelegt.

St = Stahl ist alles ohne Nachbehandlung schmiedbare Eisen. Es gibt Flußstahl und Schweißstahl.

Stg = Stahlguß ist in Formen vergossener Stahl, verschmiedbar, ist also elastisch.

Ge = Gußeisen ist Eisen, das aus Roheisen allein oder Brucheisen, Stahlabfällen usw. geschmolzen und in Formen vergossen ist. Es ist nicht schmiedbar und spröde.

Te = Temperguß aus Roheisen gegossen und durch Wärmebehandlung zäh, hämmerbar, leichter bearbeitbar und in kleinem Maß schmiedbar gemacht.

ECN = Einsatz-Chrom-Nickel-Stahl. Eine Legierung aus Eisen und weiteren Metallen, besonders Chrom und Nickel.

VCN = Vergütungs-Chrom-Nickel-Stahl. Legierung aus Eisen mit besonders Chrom und Nickel.

Ms = Messing ist eine Legierung aus Kupfer und Zink.

GBz = Gußbronze ist eine Legierung aus Kupfer und Zinn.

WBz = Walzbronze ist eine Legierung wie GBz, jedoch gewalzt.

Rg = Rotguß ist eine Legierung aus Kupfer, Zinn, Zink und Blei.

WM = Weißmetall ist eine Legierung aus Kupfer, Zinn, Antimon und Blei.

SnL = Lötzinn eine Legierung aus Zinn und Blei. Es kommen auch Legierungen aus Blei mit den Metallen Antimon, Quecksilber, Wismut usw. vor.

MsL = Schlaglot, eine Legierung aus Kupfer und Zink.

Sn = Zinn = Metall.

Aluminiumlegierungen.

Kenntlich an der Zusammensetzung der Kurzzeichen, als erstes „Al" als Abkürzung für Aluminium.

Al-Cu-Mg Al-Cu Al-Mg-Si	Hochwertige Legierung gewalzt oder geschmiedet, besser: geknetet aus Aluminium mit verschiedensten Metallen, Knetlegierungen genannt.
G-Al-Cu G-Al-Zn-Cu G-Al-Si	Aluminium-Gußlegierungen aus Aluminium mit verschiedenen Metallen, Gußlegierung genannt.

Für alle Legierungen sowie Stahl und Eisen sind durch weitere Zahlen hinter den Kurzzeichen besondere Zusammensetzungen oder Eigenschaften angegeben. Die Aufführung aller dieser Zahlen geht hier zu weit; sie sind aus den verschiedenen DIN-Blättern ersichtlich.

3. Eigenschaften der Werkstoffe in bezug auf die Zerspanbarkeit.

Die Herstellung der maßgerechten Werkstücke durch Spanabnahme ist außer vom Werkzeug auch abhängig vom Werkstoff, seiner Festigkeit und seiner Form. Danach richtet sich dann die Einstellung der Maschinen, wie schnell sie laufen (Schnittgeschwindigkeit, siehe Abschnitt 11), und welche Vorschübe gewählt werden können. Man spricht von der Zerspanbarkeit der Werkstoffe.

Es würde nun im Rahmen dieses Buches zu weit führen, alle Eigenschaften der Werkstoffe mit ihren Einflüssen anzugeben. Das Hauptmerkmal für uns ist hier die Festigkeit. Diese bestimmt zu 90 % die Zerspanbarkeit. Die Sondereigenschaften der einzelnen Legierungsbestandteile machen meist nur 5···10 % aus, in besonderen Fällen allerdings auch bis zu 30 %. Aber diese Fälle wird man dann durch Versuche bei der Fertigung selbst ausprobieren.

Die Festigkeit der Werkstoffe wird durch die Zerreißprobe oder die Härte bestimmt. Es gibt dafür die Brinellhärte, die Rockwell-Härte, die Vickers-Härte, die Ritzhärte, die nach bestimmten Verfahren festgestellt werden. Angegeben oder umgerechnet werden die Werte in kg/mm^2 Festigkeit.

Bei der Normung der Werkstoffe nach ihrer Zusammensetzung sind gleichzeitig verschiedene Festigkeitswerte mit festgelegt. Diese Werte haben auch eine Toleranz, z. B. hat St 50.11 von 50 bis 60 kg/mm^2 Festigkeit, d. h. man kann einen Stab mit 1 mm^2 Querschnitt mit 50 bis 60 kg belasten, dann reißt er. Wenn der Stab einen größeren Querschnitt hat, z. B. 1 $cm^2 = 100\ mm^2$, dann hält er $100 \cdot 50 = 5000$ und $100 \cdot 60 = 6000$ kg bis zum Zerreißen aus.

So kann es also vorkommen, daß zwei Werkstücke mit derselben Werkstoffangabe Unterschiede in der Festigkeit haben. Das bedeutet, daß sie eine verschiedene Zerspanbarkeit haben, und daß also verschiedene Schnittgeschwindigkeiten gewählt werden müssen. Diese weichen meist wenig voneinander ab.

In den Abbildungen der Abschnitte 13 und folgend sind die verschiedenen genormten Werkstoffe nach Festigkeitsbereichen zusammengestellt, wie sie für die Beurteilung der Zerspanbarkeit, d. h. Wahl der Schnittgeschwindigkeit und Vorschübe notwendig sind. Es kommt auch vor, daß manche Werkstoffe sich wohl gut drehen, aber schlecht fräsen lassen. In diesen Fällen sind die Werkstoffe am Kopf der Zahlentafeln für die Schnittgeschwindigkeiten oder Umdrehungszahlen in verschiedenen Bearbeitungsspalten aufgeführt, so daß dieses Verhalten berücksichtigt ist. Ebenso sind die schwerer zu bearbeitenden Werkstoffe anderen Bearbeitungsspalten zugeteilt. So ist z. B. Vergütungs-Chrom-Molydbän-Stahl = VCMo 125 in Spalte 23 bis 24 angegeben, obwohl seine Festigkeit $70 \cdots 80\ kg/mm^2$ ist und normale Stähle dieser Festigkeit in Spalte 19 bis 20 stehen. Man kann daher aus dieser Tafel nicht die Festigkeit ablesen, sondern nur die Zerspanbarkeit. Die verschiedenen Bearbeitungsspalten sind von 1 bis 24 laufend numeriert.

Abschnitt 11.

Schnittgeschwindigkeit, Vorschub und Spantiefe.

1. Was ist Schnittgeschwindigkeit bei geradliniger Bewegung?

Auf einer Langhobelmaschine ist ein Werkstück aufgespannt, das 12000 mm = 12 m lang ist und überhobelt werden soll. Die Maschine soll nun so eingestellt sein, daß genau in einer Minute das Werkstück mit seiner ganzen Länge an dem Hobelstahl vorbeiläuft. Da das Werkstück in einer Minute 12 m zurückgelegt hat, beträgt die Geschwindigkeit 12 m/min. Bei dieser Geschwindigkeit erfolgte die Spanabnahme oder der „Schnitt“. Deshalb bezeichnet man diese als Schnittgeschwindigkeit v, hier $v = 12$ m/min.

Schnittgeschwindigkeit ist immer die Geschwindigkeit, mit der sich Werkzeug und Werkstück gegeneinander bei der Spanabnahme bewegen. Bei dem Beispiel einer Langhobelmaschine steht das Werkzeug still und das Werkstück bewegt sich. Es kann aber auch umgekehrt sein. Bei einem Schnellhobler bewegt sich der Hobelstahl gegen das festgespannte Werkstück (Abb. 82). Bei der Spanabnahme hat der Stößel mit dem Stahlhalter eine bestimmte Geschwindigkeit. Hier rechnet man nun so, wieviel Hobellänge aneinandergereiht der Hobelstahl in einer Minute zurücklegen würde, wenn er ohne Unterbrechung schneiden könnte. Aus der gesamten Länge in einer Minute ergibt sich dann wieder die Schnittgeschwindigkeit v. Diese Schnittgeschwindigkeiten leuchten ein, weil sie geradlinig sind.

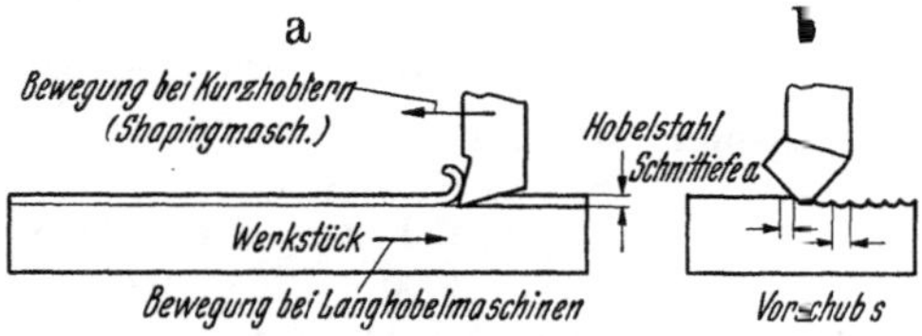

Abb. 82. Geradlinige Bewegungsrichtung an Hobelmaschinen.

Bei neueren Hobel- und Schnellhobelmaschinen (Shaper oder Shaping) und Stoßmaschinen ist für verschiedene Schaltungen direkt die Schnittgeschwindigkeit angegeben und kann eingestellt werden. Bei älteren Maschinen findet man oft nur die Zahl der Hübe je Minute. Es muß also jetzt diese Zahl in die gewünschte Schnittgeschwindigkeit umgerechnet werden, oder umgekehrt.

Bei Langhobelmaschinen mit langen Hüben und verhältnismäßig kurzer Umsteuerzeit kann man rechnen mit

$$v = \frac{2 \cdot H \cdot n}{1000} \qquad \text{(Gl. 4)}$$

$$\text{oder} \quad n = \frac{v \cdot 1000}{2H}. \qquad \text{(Gl. 5)}$$

Hierin bedeuten

v = Schnittgeschwindigkeit in m/min,
H = Tischhub in mm/min,
n = Zahl der Hübe/min.

Beispiel: $H = 2700$ mm,

$n = 7{,}4$ Hübe/min,

$$v = \frac{2 \cdot H \cdot n}{1000} = \frac{2 \cdot 2700 \cdot 7{,}4}{1000} = 40 \text{ m/min}.$$

Bei Kurzhobelmaschine wirkt sich die Umsteuerzeit stärker aus. Hier diene als Faustformel die Regel

$$v = \frac{\pi \cdot H \cdot n}{1000} \qquad \text{(Gl. 6)}$$

oder

$$n = \frac{v \cdot 1000}{\pi \cdot H}. \qquad \text{(Gl. 7)}$$

Beispiel: $H = 150$ mm Hub,

$n = 27$ Hübe-min,

$$v = \frac{\pi \cdot 150 \cdot 27}{1000} = \frac{3{,}14 \cdot 150 \cdot 27}{1000} = 12{,}7 \text{ min}.$$

Diese Schnittgeschwindigkeit bleibt nicht über den ganzen Hub gleichmäßig, sondern hat auf halbem Wege etwa die ausgerechnete Größe und ist zu Anfang und Ende des Hubes geringer. Die höchste Schnittgeschwindigkeit ist aber für die Leistungsfähigkeit des Werkzeuges maßgebend.

Für Stoßmaschinen rechnet man nach Gleichung 6 und 7.

2. Was ist Schnittgeschwindigkeit bei Drehbewegungen?

Viele Werkzeuge und Werkstücke haben rundlaufende Bewegungen. Es muß jetzt überlegt werden, wo bei diesen Drehbewegungen die Schnittgeschwindigkeiten auftreten.

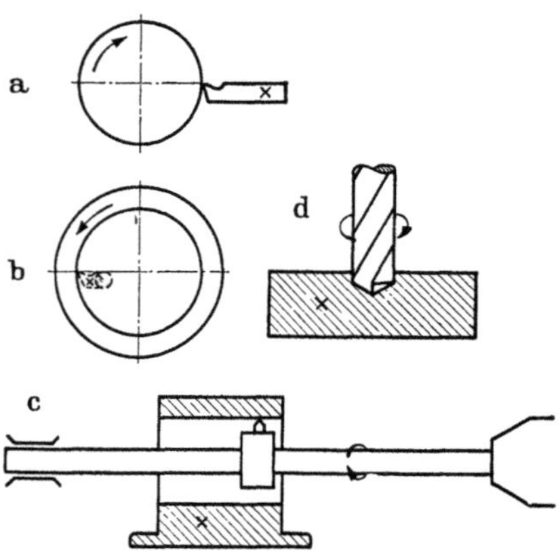

Abb. 83. Drehbewegungen.

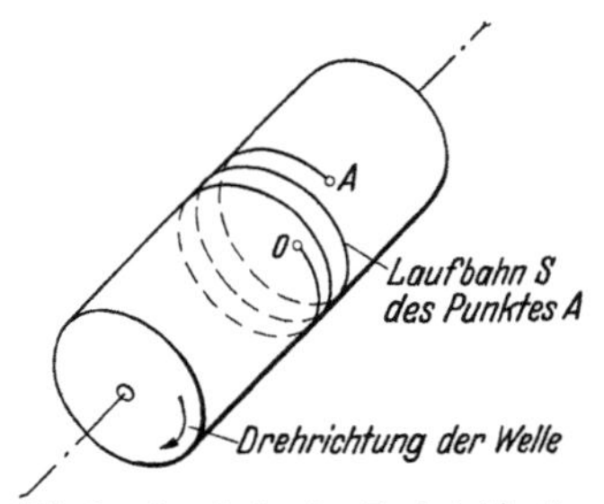

Abb. 84. Laufbahn der Drehstahlspitze auf einer Welle.

Beim Abdrehen einer Welle nach Abb. 83a steht der Drehstahl fest und das Werkstück, hier die Welle, dreht sich. Dieses Abdrehen ist nur möglich, wenn gleichzeitig bei der Drehbewegung der Welle ein gleichmäßiges Vorschieben des Drehstahles erfolgt.

Die genauere Erklärung des Vorschubes erfolgt weiter unten. Wir betrachten jetzt die Laufbahn des Punktes A auf der Welle (Abb. 84). Der Punkt A legt auf der Welle durch das Vorschieben des Drehstahles eine Schraublinie S zurück, die man sich auf die Welle aufgetragen denken kann. Die gesamte Länge der Schraubenlinie S in einer Minute soll von A—O gehen. Diese Länge wird gemessen oder ausgerechnet. Ist sie z. B. 13 m, dann hatte der Punkt A die Geschwindigkeit 13 m/min. Da aber bei dieser Geschwindigkeit der Schnitt erfolgt ist, ist dies auch die Schnittgeschwindigkeit $v = 13$ m/min.

3. Wie wird die Schnittgeschwindigkeit ausgerechnet?

Wenn man einen Kreisdurchmesser D mit der Zahl $\pi = 3{,}14$ mal nimmt, erhält man die Länge des Kreisumfanges. Zum Beispiel bei einem Durchmesser $D = 100$ mm, der Umfang $L = 100 \cdot 3{,}14 = 314$ mm. Wenn sich eine Welle mit diesem Durchmesser D einmal herumdreht, so legt ein Punkt A auf dem Umfang eine Strecke von $D \cdot \pi$ mm zurück. Dreht sich jetzt die Welle in einer Minute n mal herum, $n =$ Umdrehungszahl, so wird der Punkt A in der Minute eine Strecke von $\pi \cdot D \cdot n$ mm zurücklegen. Nimmt man $n = 43$/min. an, so beträgt dann die Geschwindigkeit 13500 mm/min = 13,5 m/min. Diese Umfangsgeschwindigkeit erhält man also bei einer Welle von 100 mm ⌀, wenn man an der Drehbank eine Umdrehungszahl von 43 U/min einstellt. Da beim Überdrehen der Welle der größte Durchmesser gleich dem Wellendurchmesser ist, hat man jetzt bei 43/min eine größte Schnittgeschwindigkeit von 13,5 m/min. Diese Umrechnung von Umdrehungszahl auf Schnittgeschwindigkeit kann man auch allgemein angeben. Es ist

$$\text{Schnittgeschwindigkeit } v = \frac{\pi \cdot \text{Durchmesser} \cdot \text{Umdrehungszahl}}{1000} \qquad \text{(Gl. 8)}$$

oder

$$v = \frac{\pi \cdot D \cdot n}{1000}.$$

Entsprechend ist

$$\text{Umdrehungszahl } n = \frac{\text{Schnittgeschwindigkeit } v \cdot 1000}{\pi \cdot \text{Durchmesser}} \qquad \text{(Gl. 9)}$$

oder

$$n = \frac{v \cdot 1000}{\pi \cdot D}.$$

1. Beispiel: $D = 250$ mm ⌀, $n = 25$ U/min, $v = ?$

$$v = \frac{\pi \cdot D \cdot n}{1000} = \frac{3{,}14 \cdot 250 \cdot 25}{1000} = 19{,}6 \text{ m/min}.$$

2. Beispiel: $v = 25$ m/min. $D = 150$ mm ⌀. $n = ?$

$$n = \frac{v \cdot 1000}{\pi \cdot D} = \frac{25 \cdot 1000}{3{,}14 \cdot 150} = 33 \text{ U/min}.$$

Man kann hiermit für jede Drehbewegung die Umfangsgeschwindigkeiten für verschiedene Durchmesser und für verschiedene Umdrehungszahlen ausrechnen.

Nachdem klar ist, welche Durchmesser beim Drehen genommen werden müssen, stets die größten an den Stellen, wo die Spanabnahme erfolgt, muß jetzt für die anderen Arbeitsverfahren die Kenntnis der richtigen Durchmesserwahl erreicht werden.

Beim Innendrehen (Abb. 83b) gibt der innere größte Durchmesser das Maß für die Umfangs- und somit Schnittgeschwindigkeit ab. Bei einem Bohrer steht das Werkstück still (auf einer Bohrmaschine) und der Bohrer dreht sich, oder der Bohrer steht still (Drehbank) und das Werkstück dreht sich. Die größte Umfangsgeschwindigkeit tritt immer am größten Bohrerdurchmesser auf, so daß dieser Durchmesser mit seiner Geschwindigkeit das Maß für die Schnittgeschwindigkeit angibt. Bei einem Fräser liegt das Werkstück auf einem Frästisch still und der Fräser dreht sich. Die größte Umfangsgeschwindigkeit und damit Schnittgeschwindigkeit tritt beim größten Fräserdurchmesser D auf. Auf einem Bohrwerk läuft eine Bohrstange mit einem Messer um (Abb. 83c), dessen äußerster Durchmesser die Schnittgeschwindigkeit bestimmt.

4. Was ist Vorschub?

Beim Hobeln wird bei jedem Hubende das Werkzeug ein Stück quer zur Hobelrichtung verschoben (Abb. 82b). Die Verschiebung s, die auch an den Hobelriefen erkennbar ist, ist der Vorschub, der hier in mm/Hub ausgedrückt wird.

Beim Überdrehen einer Welle (Abb. 85) wird der Support bei jeder Umdrehung der Welle ein bestimmtes Stück, nämlich den Vorschub s, weitergeschoben sein. Auch hier kann an der Breite der Drehriefen der Vorschub erkannt werden.

Entsprechend wird die Verschiebung eines Bohrers je Umdrehung in der Bohrrichtung mit Vorschub bezeichnet.

Das Fräsen macht eine Ausnahme. Hier wird der Vorschub nicht auf die Umdrehung des Fräsers bezogen, sondern man gibt den Vorschub des Frästisches in mm/min an.

Wie groß ist nun der Vorschub je Fräszahn? Das ist für die Wahl der Vorschubgeschwindigkeit von Wichtigkeit, weil die Belastung jedes Fräszahnes die Schnittgeschwindigkeit bestimmt.

Wenn sich ein Fräser z. B. einmal herumdreht und dabei der Frästisch um 4 mm vorgeschoben wird, so hat dieser Fräser einen Vorschub von 4 mm/Umdrehung erhalten. Hat nun der Fräser 8 Zähne, so bekommt jeder Zahn $^1/_8$ von diesem Vorschub = 0,5 mm/Zahn. Abb. 86. Bei n U/min kommen $8 \cdot n$ Zähne in der Minute in Eingriff auf dem Werkstück. Bei einem Vorschub des Frästisches von s mm/min wird damit der Vorschub je Zahn

$$s_z = \frac{s}{z \cdot n}, \qquad \text{(Gl. 10)}$$

wenn z die Zähnezahl ist.

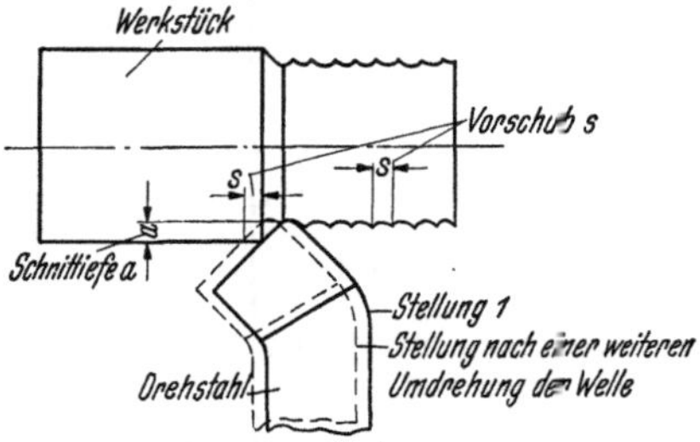

Abb. 85. Vorschub beim Drehen.

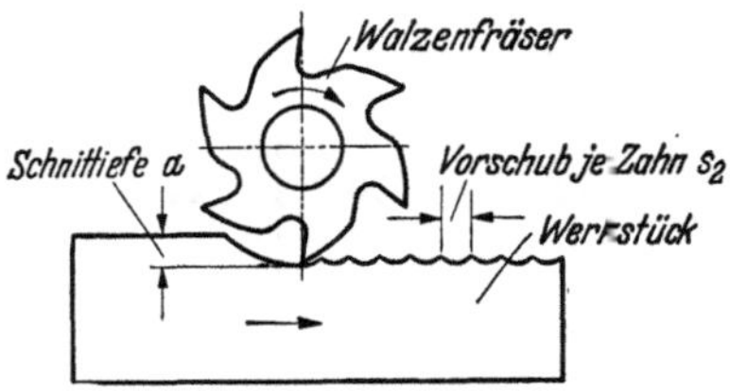

Abb. 86. Vorschub beim Fräsen.

Beispiel: $s = 60$ mm/min,

$z = 8$ Zähne, $n = 30$ U/min,

$$s_z = \frac{60}{8 \cdot 30} = \frac{60}{240} = 0{,}25 \text{ mm}.$$

Tabelle 9 enthält eine Zusammenstellung mit den Bezugsgrößen für die Vorschübe. Die Fläche aus Schnittiefe mal Vorschub nennt man Spanquerschnitt.

Tabelle 9. Abhängigkeit des Vorschubes von der Arbeitsart.

Arbeitsart	Drehen	Bohren	Hobeln Stoßen	Fräsen	
Vorschub in	mm/U	mm/U	mm/Hub	mm/min	mm/Zahn

5. Was ist Schnittiefe?

Die Schnittiefe ist, wie für Abb. 85 gezeigt, gleich dem halben Durchmesser Unterschied $D - d$ beim Überdrehen einer Welle. In den

Tabelle 10. Zulässi

Spanquerschnitt		Leichtmetall		Rotmetall			Gußeisen		
Schnittiefe	Vorschub		Al-Mg-Mn			Ms 58···63			
		Elektron	Al-Mg-Si		Rg 4 · Rg 8···10		Ge 18.91		Ge 30.91
		Al	Al-Cu-Mg	Cu	GBz 10 · GBz 14	GBz 17	Ge 12.91	Ge 22.9	
Festigkeit				12 15	20 30	50 75	12 18	25	30
a mm	*s* mm/U	1 2	3 4	5 6	7 8	9 10	11 12	13	14
							Zulässige Schnittgeschwindigkei		
▽▽▽									
0,3	2···5	1200	600	70	50	30	55	30	14
0,5	0,1			110	70	50	75	45	20
▽▽									
0,5	0,3			100	60	40	68	35	16
2	0,5	500	200	70	50	30	55	30	14
4	0,5			60	40	25	50	26	13
▽									
2	0,75			60	40	25	50	26	13
2	1	200	120	55	36	22	47	23	11
4	1			48	30	17	40	20	9,5
4	1,5						35	17,5	8
8	1,5						29	14	7
12	1						30	14,5	7,5
				Zulässige Schnittgeschwindigkeiten für Hartmeta					
▽▽▽									
0,3	2···5						80	50	25
0,5	0,1			700	500	300	130	90	50
▽▽									
0,5	0,2			600	450	300	110	80	45
2	0,3			400	350	300	100	65	30
4	0,3						90	55	25
▽									
2	0,4			400	350	300	90	55	25
4	0,4			350	300	250	80	50	22
8	0,5			300	250	200	70	45	18
12	0,8			250	200	150	60	35	10

Schnittgeschwindigkeiten für Drehen.

Stahl und Stahlguß											
						SoSt 3	SoSt 4	SoSt 100			
								NCT 3			
					EC 100 v	VMC 140 v		VCMo 240 v			
Stg 38.81	Stg 45.81	Stg 52.81	Stg 60.81			EC 80					
			VCN 25	VCN 25 v		ECMo 80					
	EN15		ECN 35								
St IV bis VII 23	StX 23		VCN 15	VCN 15 v		VCN 45	VCN 45 v				
	StC 25.61	StC 25.61 v	StC 45.61	StC 45.61 v			ECMo 100 v				
StC 10.61	StC 16.61	StC 35.61	StC 35.61 v	StC 60.61		StC 60.61 v		VM 125 v			
St 00.11	St 37.11 St 42.11	St 50.11	St 60.11	St 70.11				VCMo 125 v			
30	40	50	60	70	80	90	100	110	120	kg/mm²	
15	16	17	18	19	20	21	22	23	24	Lauf. Nr.	
										a	*s*
für mittleren Schnellstahl.										▽▽▽	
70		42		30		22		16		0,3	2···5
95		55		40		30		22		0,5	0,1
										▽▽	
85		50		36		27		19		0,5	0,3
70		42		30		22		16		2	0,5
65		39		28		20		14,5		4	0,5
										▽	
65		39		28		20		14,5		2	0,75
60		35		24		18,5		12		2	1
53		32		22		16		10,5		4	1
46		27,5		19		14		9		4	1,5
40		23		16		12,5		8		8	1,5
42		25		17		13		8,5		12	1
(nach Art Widia S 58 oder Titanit U 3 für Stahl).										▽▽▽	
120		70		55		43		27		0,3	2···5
200		100		80		68		50		0,5	0,1
										▽▽	
200		100		80		68		50		0,5	0,2
120		70		55		43		35		2	0,3
100		60		45		35		27		4	0,3
										▽	
100		60		45		35		27		2	0,4
90		55		42		32		25		4	0,4
70		45		35		25		20		8	0,5
55		36		28		20		16		12	0,8

Abb. 82 und 86 ist gleichfalls die Schnittiefe eingezeichnet. Beim Fräsen und Hobeln ist sie der Unterschied zwischen der vorhandenen Werkstückoberfläche und der neuerzeugten Oberfläche. Beim Bohren gibt es keine Schnittiefe, da dort der Vorschub maßgeblich ist.

Allgemein wird die Schnittiefe in Millimetern angegeben.

Abschnitt 12.

Bestimmende Einflüsse auf die Wahl der Schnittgeschwindigkeit.

Folgende Haupteinflüsse treten auf:

1. Zerspanbarkeit des Werkstoffes.
2. Form des Werkstückes.
3. Eignung der Werkzeugmaschine.
4. Leistungsfähigkeit des Werkzeuges.
5. Vorschub und Schnittiefe.
6. Art der Kühlmittel.

1. Zerspanbarkeit des Werkstoffes.

Die Zerspanbarkeit des Werkstoffes kann meistens mit seiner Festigkeit angegeben werden. Lediglich bei einigen besonderen Legierungen, wie ECN, Mg und Chromvanadiumstähle usw. verschiebt sich die Zerspanbarkeit gegenüber den Fällen gleicher Festigkeit. Die in Abschnitt „Werkstoffkunde“ zusammengestellten Werkstoffe sind nach gleichen Bearbeitungseigenschaften sortiert. Es können daher auch Werkstoffe mit höherer Festigkeit in einer anderen Bearbeitungsgruppe stehen.

Aus dem Schriftfeld oder der Stückliste entnimmt man die Werkstoffbezeichnung für das zu bearbeitende Werkstück und benutzt diese zur Ermittlung der Schnittgeschwindigkeit in der Tabelle 10 usw.

Handelt es sich um Fliegwerkstoff, der in Zahlen angegeben ist, so kann aus Tabelle 24 entnommen werden, in welche Bearbeitungsspalte dieser hineingehört.

Als **Beispiel:** StC 45.61 (ohne Vergütung) gehört zur Gruppe 18/19.
StC 45.61v (vergütet) gehört zur Gruppe 19/20.

2. Form des Werkstückes.

Es gibt schwere gedrungene, mittlere schlanke, leichte und sperrige Werkstücke ihrer Form nach. Eine dünnwandige Buchse mit einem großen Durchmesser würde sich bei einem großen Spanquerschnitt verbiegen. Man kann sie also nur mit leichteren Spänen bearbeiten. Welche Werkstücke nun kräftig, mittel oder leicht anzusprechen sind, muß von Fall zu Fall entschieden werden und wird nach einiger Übung leicht möglich sein. Eine zu große Beanspruchung des Werkstückes wird sich stets in schlechter Arbeit äußern, denn die gewünschte Form, ob rund oder kantig, wird nicht erreicht, weil die vorher bearbeiteten Flächen verdrückt, also krumm sind und ein Nachrichten die zuletzt erzielten, vielleicht geraden Flächen mitverdrücken würde. Eine Nacharbeit kostet dann nur wieder Zeit und Geld. Jeder muß hier selbst empfinden, wo die Grenze liegt.

3. Eignung der Werkzeugmaschine.

Allgemein wird von der Betriebsleitung die Arbeit an die geeignetste Maschine geleitet. Sollte jedoch aus irgendwelchen Gründen eine andere, weniger geeignete Maschine, z. B. zu kleine Maschine gewählt werden, so können dann nur kleinere Spanquerschnitte zulässig werden

4. Leistungsfähigkeit des Werkzeuges.

Ein gutes Werkzeug, seine richtige Anwendung, Wartung und Einstellung erleichtert ganz wesentlich die Arbeit; man kann fast sagen, ist die halbe Arbeit. Maßgebend ist die Zeit, in der ein Arbeitsgang durchgeführt werden kann. Abhängig ist die Schnelligkeit außer den genannten Einflüssen von der Leistungsfähigkeit des Werkzeuges. Diese setzt sich zusammen aus:

a) der Güte des Werkzeug-Werkstoffes,

b) der Form des Werkzeuges,

c) der anwendbaren Beanspruchung des Werkzeuges.

Die Auswahl der Güte des Werkzeug-Werkstoffes ist Sache des Betriebes. Die Form des Werkzeuges wird weitgehend durch Vorschriften in der Werkzeugmacherei festgelegt. Beim Selbstanschleifen jedoch und zur Kontrolle ist die Kenntnis wichtig und wird daher ausführlich in den Abschnitten 12 bis 18 behandelt.

Zu c. Die Beanspruchung des Werkzeuges ist ausschließlich vom Arbeiter abhängig und wird durch seine Einstellung der Maschine bedingt. Sie setzt sich zusammen aus gewählten Vorschüben und Schnittiefen und den dazu richtigen Schnittgeschwindigkeiten, die wieder vom Werkstoff und der Form des Werkstückes abhängen. Diese Zusammenhänge muß man kennen, um daraus die höchste Leistung erreichen zu können. Denn nur mit höchster Leistung ist höchster Lohn erreichbar und gerechtfertigt. Die einstellbare Schnittgeschwindigkeit wird nun bestimmt durch die Standzeit.

5. Was ist Standzeit?

Sie sei an folgendem Beispiel erklärt.

Eine Welle wird mit einer Schnittgeschwindigkeit von 20 m/min mit einem gleichbleibenden Spanquerschnitt geschruppt. Dieses Schruppen muß nach 20 Minuten unterbrochen werden, weil der Drehstahl plötzlich stumpf geworden ist. Man sagt nun, dieser Drehstahl hat auf diesem Werkstoff bei diesem Spanquerschnitt eine Standzeit von 20 Minuten gehabt. Er hat 20 Minuten Schnitt durchgestanden. Nach dem Neuanschliff wird jetzt dieselbe Welle mit demselben Spanquerschnitt aber mit 22 m/min überdreht. Der Stahl stumpft bereits nach 7 Minuten ab. Diesmal betrug seine Standzeit also 7 Minuten. Nach einem weiteren Anschleifen wird jetzt mit demselben Spanquerschnitt nur mit 18 m/min Schnittgeschwindigkeit weitergedreht. Der Drehstahl steht 150 Minuten. Bei 17,5 m/min Schnittgeschwindigkeit hat der Stahl eine noch bedeutend höhere Standzeit von 600 Minuten.

Der Unterschied von den Schnittgeschwindigkeiten für eine Standzeit von 60 Minuten und von 600 Minuten ist sehr gering. Nimmt man noch kleinere Schnittgeschwindigkeiten, dann steht das Werkzeug bedeutend länger und wird meist durch andere Beschädigungen zerstört. Nun wird man die Schnittgeschwindigkeit möglichst hoch wählen, um den Arbeitsgang schneller zu beendigen. Andererseits darf man nicht zu hoch gehen, weil sonst ein dauernder Drehstahlwechsel vorgenommen werden muß. Als geeignete Schnittgeschwindigkeit hat sich nun die erwiesen, bei der der Drehstahl etwa 60 Minuten reine Laufzeit steht, und man spricht daher immer von der Stundenschnittgeschwindigkeit „v_{60}“, das ist die, bei der das Werkzeug 60 Minuten Standzeit hat. Es kommt jetzt darauf an, aus der Festigkeit des Werkstoffes, der Form des Werkstückes und der Standzeit des Werkzeuges die richtige Stundenschnittgeschwindigkeit v_{60} im voraus zu bestimmen und einzustellen. Im folgenden wird einfach nur von Schnittgeschwindigkeit gesprochen, gemeint ist stets v_{60}.

6. Einfluß von Vorschub und Schnittiefe auf die Standzeit.

Der Spanquerschnitt ist die Fläche aus Vorschub mal Schnittiefe. Er wird in mm^2 angegeben. Es ist nun nicht so, daß z. B. bei 4 mm^2 Spanquerschnitt eine bestimmte Schnittgeschwindigkeit vorhanden ist, sondern diese hängt von der Zusammensetzung von Vorschub und Schnittiefe für sich ab. Nach Tabelle 10 beträgt z. B. für einen Werkstoff von 50 kg/mm² Festigkeit die Schnittgeschwindigkeit für 4 mm Schnittiefe und 1 mm Vorschub/Umdrehung bei einem guten Schnellstahl 40 m/min. Bei 2 mm Schnittiefe und 2 mm Vorschub/Umdrehung wird $v = 34$ m/min. Bei 8 mm Schnittiefe · 0,5 mm Vorschub/Umdrehung jedoch $v = 45$ m/min.

In allen Fällen ist der Spanquerschnitt $f = 4\ \text{mm}^2$. Man sieht also, daß die Zusammensetzung des Spanquerschnittes von wesentlicher Bedeutung ist. Ähnlich liegen die Verhältnisse beim Fräsen.

7. Kühlmittel.

Das Kühlen und Schmieren der Werkstoffe beeinflußt die Standzeit der Werkzeuge von 5 bis zu 30%; d. h. ohne Kühlmittel liegt die zu-

Tabelle 11. Kühlmittel für verschiedene Arbeitsarten.

Werkstoff	Drehen Hobeln Stoßen	Fräsen Sägen	Bohren Senken	Reiben	Gewindeschneiden	Schleifen
Stahl	BE Rüböl	BE Rübölersatz	BE Rübölersatz	Rübölersatz Talg	BE Rüböl dickeres Fett	BE Rübölersatz
Stahlguß Temperguß	BE	BE	BE	Rüböl trocken	BE Rüböl	BE
Gußeisen	trocken	trocken Preßluft Wasser + 5% Soda	trocken BE Petroleum	trocken Rüböl Maschinenöl	trocken BE	trocken BE Preßluft
Messing Bronze	trocken BE	BE	trocken BE	trocken Rüböl	trocken Rüböl	trocken BE
Kupfer	BE	trocken BE	BE Rüböl	BE	trocken Rüböl	BE
Aluminium u. Legierungen	trocken BE	trocken BE Rübölersatz	BE Rübölersatz Petroleum	Rüböl Terpentin Petroleum	BE Rüböl trocken	trocken Rüböl Petroleum
Silumin	trocken BE	BE Rüböl	BE	Petroleum Terpentin	BE Rüböl	BE Rüböl
Elektron	trocken oder 4% wässerige Natriumfluoridlösung niemals Wasser anwenden, da Explosionsgefahr					

BE = Bohröl-Emulsion

lässige Schnittgeschwindigkeit unter den Angaben auf den verschiedenen Abbildungen. Bei 5% Abzug ist die ermittelte Schnittgeschwindigkeit mit 0,95 malzunehmen, bei 30% Abzug mit 0,7. Zum Beispiel ist $v = 40$ m/min minus 5% $= 40 \cdot 0{,}95 = 38$ m/min oder bei $v = 50$ m/min minus 30% $= 50 \cdot 0{,}7 = 35$ m/min. Die Tabelle 11 enthält geeignete und notwendige Kühlmittel. Verwendet man beim Bohren und Reiben Terpentin, so fällt die Bohrung kleiner aus als bei Verwendung von Rüböl. Es kann dies manchmal zur Einhaltung von kleineren Toleranzen wichtig sein, vgl. auch Abschnitt 15.

Abschnitt 13.

Drehen, Hobeln, Stoßen.

Beim Drehen, Hobeln und Stoßen liegen im wesentlichen gleiche Verhältnisse vor. Daher sind die im folgenden ausführlich behandelten Darlegungen über das Drehen entsprechend auf das Hobeln und Stoßen zu übertragen.

1. Bedeutung des Spanquerschnittes auf die Dauer der Laufzeit.

An einem einfachen Beispiel (Abb. 87) soll grundsätzlich gezeigt werden, welchen großen Einfluß die richtige Wahl des Spanquerschnittes auf die Laufzeit hat. Laufzeit ist die gesamte Zeit, während der der Drehstahl im Schnitt ist. Eine Welle aus St 50.11 mit den rohen Maßen von 160 mm ⌀ und 720 mm Länge soll im Teil *a* auf 150 mm ⌀ und 600 mm Länge angedreht werden. Welche Spanquerschnitte und Schnittgeschwindigkeiten muß man wählen und wielange dauert die Laufzeit?

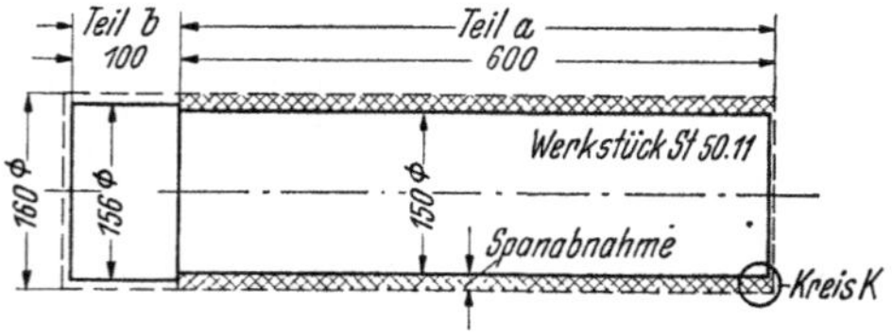

Abb. 87. Drehbeispiel.

In Abb. 88 sind drei Möglichkeiten zusammengestellt, wie man vorgehen kann. Insgesamt sind von 160 mm ⌀ auf 150 mm ⌀ 10 mm im Durchmesser oder eine Spantiefe von 5 mm abzuheben. Da zwei Bearbeitungszeichen die Oberfläche vorschreiben, muß man einen Schrupp- und einen Schlichtspan nehmen. Wie verteilt man nun diese beiden Späne?

Fall 1. Im Fall 1 wird bei 3 mm Schnittiefe mit 0,5 mm/U Vorschub geschruppt. Die Schnittgeschwindigkeit $v = 41$ m/min wird aus der Tabelle 10 entnommen, und zwar aus der Bearbeitungsspalte 18. St 50.11

Nr.	Vergrößerter Kreis K mit Spanbild	Arbeitsart	Spanquerschnitt Schnittiefe a mm	Vorsch. s mm/U	Schnittgeschwindigkeit v_{60} m/min	Drehzahl n U/min	Laufzeit min	Laufzeit Gesamt min
1	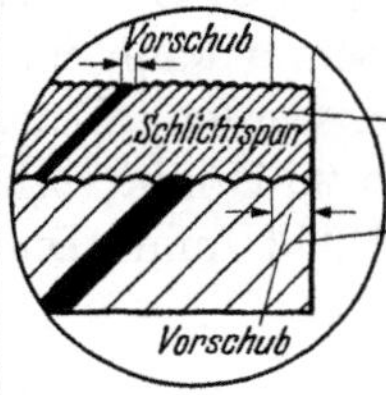	Schlichten	2	0,2	48	(99) 95	31,5	47,5
		Schruppen	3	0,5	41	(82) 95	16	
2	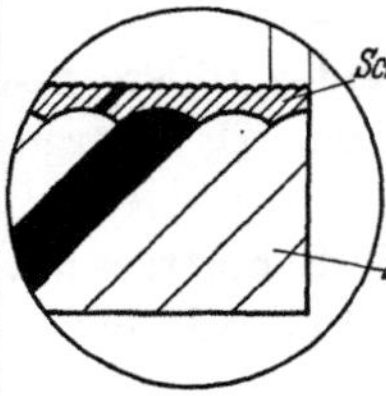	Schlichten	0,5	0,2	58	(122) 118	25,5	35,5
		Schruppen	4,5	1	31	(61,5) 60	10	
3	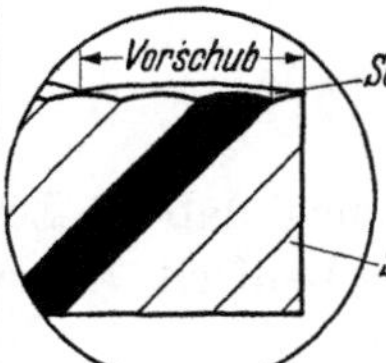	Schlichten	0,3	3	35	(74) 75	2,7	12,7
		Schruppen	4,7	1	31	(61,4) 60	10	

Abb. 88. Beispiel für Wahl des Spanquerschnittes.

steht im Kopf dieser Tabelle und überdeckt die Spalten 17 und 18. Mit dieser Schnittgeschwindigkeit ergibt sich nach der Gleichung 6 oder aus der Tabelle 13 für 160 mm ⌀ eine Umdrehungszahl von 82 U/min. Da diese Umdrehungszahl die Maschine nicht enthält, muß die nächsttiefere genommen werden, hier 75 U/min. Wie lange dauert die Laufzeit für den ersten Span? Der Vorschub beträgt 0,5 mm/U. In einer Minute macht die Spindel 75 U/min; infolgedessen wird der Support in einer Minute Umdrehungszahl mal Vorschub $= 75 \cdot 0{,}5 = 37{,}5$ mm weitergeschoben. Die Laufzeit T dauert jetzt so lange, bis der Support die ganzen 600 mm verschoben ist, also Lauflänge 600 mm geteilt durch 37,5 mm Vorschub/min = 16 min.

Die Laufzeit kann man auch direkt ausrechnen nach der Gleichung

$$\text{Laufzeit } T = \frac{\text{Lauflänge } L}{\text{Vorschub } s \cdot \text{Umdrehungszahl } n}. \qquad \text{(Gl. 11)}$$

Wie lange dauert jetzt der Schnitt des Schlichtspanes? Der Schlichtspan von 2 mm Schnittiefe und 0,2 mm/U Vorschub kann mit einer Schnittgeschwindigkeit von 48 m/min abgehoben werden. Dazu muß nach Tabelle 13 für 154 mm ⌀ eine Drehzahl von 99 U/min vorhanden sein. Die nächstliegende Drehzahl der Spindel ist 95 U/min. Die Laufzeit ist dann

$$T = \frac{600}{0{,}2 \cdot 95} = 31{,}5 \text{ min}.$$

Die gesamte Laufzeit beträgt 16 min + 31,5 min = 47,5 min.

Fall 2. Wählt man jetzt für das Schruppen eine größere Spantiefe von 4,5 mm und einen größeren Vorschub von 1 mm/U, so ergibt sich folgendes Bild:

Bei diesem größeren Spanquerschnitt sinkt die Schnittgeschwindigkeit auf 31 m/min gegen 41 m/min in Fall 1. Die Spindeldrehzahl muß kleiner eingeschaltet werden und beträgt jetzt 60 U/min. Da wir aber jetzt den Vorschub verdoppelt haben, ergibt sich als Laufzeit

$$T = \frac{600}{1 \cdot 60} = 10 \text{ min}.$$

Wir haben also das zunächst überraschende Ergebnis, daß die Schnittgeschwindigkeit gesunken ist und trotzdem die Laufzeit kürzer geworden ist. Der Grund liegt im Verhalten des Drehstahles. Bei doppelt so großen Spanquerschnitten sinkt die Schnittgeschwindigkeit nicht auf die Hälfte, sondern sie liegt höher als die Hälfte. Dadurch gewinnt man Zeit. Man merke sich deshalb als Grundsatz:

Schruppen immer mit großen Vorschüben und großen Schnittiefen, aber kleineren Schnittgeschwindigkeiten, um möglichst viel Werkstoff abzuheben.

Wie liegen nun die Verhältnisse bei dem übrigbleibenden Schlichtspan? Mit der Spantiefe von 0,5 mm und dem Vorschub von 0,2 mm/U ist jetzt durch den kleineren Spanquerschnitt eine höhere Schnittgeschwindigkeit von 58 m/min zulässig, d. h. 122 U/min oder 118 einstellbare Umdrehungen an der Maschine können genommen werden. Durch diese höhere Drehzahl bei gleichem Vorschub wie im Fall 1 beträgt jetzt die Laufzeit

$$T = \frac{600}{0{,}2 \cdot 118} = 25{,}5 \text{ min}.$$

Also auch hier ist die Laufzeit gesunken gegenüber Fall 1, weil zum Schlichten nur ein kleinerer Span übriggeblieben ist, der schneller abgehoben werden kann. Somit wird die gesamte Laufzeit

$$T = 10 \text{ min} + 25{,}5 \text{ min} = 35{,}5 \text{ min}.$$

Wir haben somit an demselben Werkstück durch bessere Wahl der Spanquerschnitte 12 min Laufzeit eingespart. Man merke sich:

Schlichten immer mit möglichst kleinen Spänen und hoher Schnittgeschwindigkeit, aber kleinen Vorschüben, um eine gute Oberfläche zu erzeugen.

Man muß stets bemüht sein, beim Schruppen viel Zeit herauszuholen, um das Schlichten oder Fertigmachen in Ruhe und gewissenhaft vornehmen zu können.

Fall 3. Wie wir bei Fall 1 und 2 beim Schruppen gesehen haben, bringen große Vorschübe stets Zeitgewinne ein. Kann man nicht auch beim Schlichten große Vorschübe wählen?

Für viele Arbeiten ist das möglich, so z. B. für Ge fast immer und für Stahl bei starren Werkstücken. Große Vorschübe sind bei Stahl dadurch begrenzt, daß Rattern auftritt. Dann müssen andere Spanwinkel, andere Schnittgeschwindigkeiten oder kleinere Vorschübe genommen werden. Bei unserer Welle ist bei richtiger Form und richtigem Anstellen des Drehstahles auch ein großer Vorschub von 3 mm/U möglich. Der Drehstahl muß dazu nachschneiden, d. h. er muß mit der ganzen Breite schneiden und dazu leicht ballig geschliffen werden (Abb. 89). Gelingt es, mit diesem Vorschub zu arbeiten und vermindert man die Spantiefe für dieses Schlichten auf 0,3 mm, so ergibt sich folgendes:

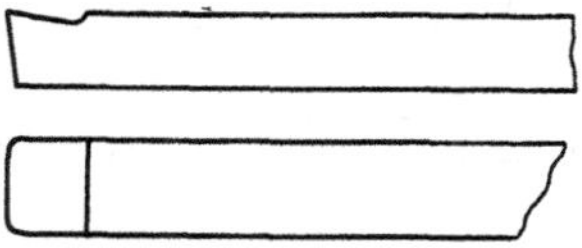

Abb. 89. Breitstahl zum Schlichten mit großen Vorschüben.

Beim Schruppen mit 4,7 mm Spantiefe und 1 mm/U Vorschub wird bei 60 Spindelumdrehungen/min die Laufzeit 10 Minuten wie in Fall 2. Beim Schlichten mit 0,3 mm Spantiefe und 3 mm/U Vorschub und einer Schnittgeschwindigkeit von 30 m/min erhält die Spindel 75 U/min und die Laufzeit sinkt auf

$$T = \frac{600}{3 \cdot 75} = 2{,}7 \text{ min}.$$

Die gesamte Laufzeit beträgt dann nur noch $10 + 2{,}7 = 12{,}7$ min. Statt 47,5 min in Fall 1 brauchen wir also hier nur 12,7 min, das ist rund $^1/_4$ Zeit gegenüber den ersten Spanquerschnittsverhältnissen. Man wird also danach trachten, auch beim Schlichten mit ganz großen Vorschüben zu arbeiten. Falls Rattern auftritt, kann die Drehzahl auf die Hälfte herabgesetzt werden, die Laufzeit wird dann zwar doppelt so lang, also 5,4 min, aber immer noch wesentlich viel kürzer als 25,5 min von Fall 2. Die Bemühungen um ruhigen Lauf bei großem Vorschub lohnen sich ganz bestimmt. Man merke sich:

Wenn möglich, schlichten mit Breitstahl und Vorschüben von 2 bis 5 mm/U.

Entsprechend gilt für Hobeln und Stoßen:

Große Spanquerschnitte beim Schruppen, Schlichten mit kleinen Spänen, möglichst mit Breitstahl und hohen Vorschüben.

Nachdem jetzt klar ist, wie die Spanquerschnitte für ein wirtschaftliches Arbeiten gewählt werden müssen, werden jetzt alle die vielen Voraussetzungen erörtert, die zur erfolgreichen Durchführung dieser Arbeiten notwendig sind.

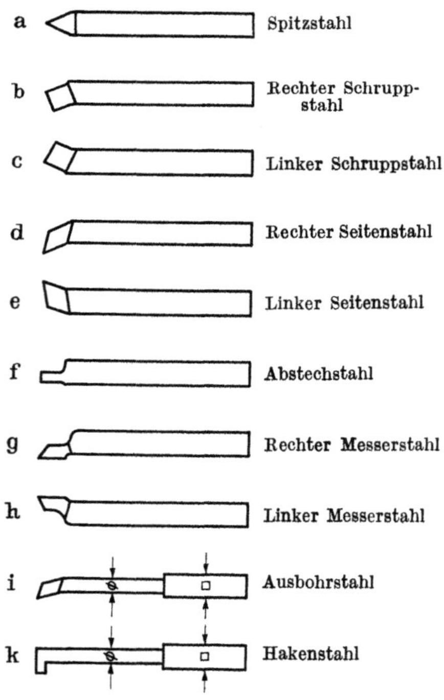

Abb. 90. Gebräuchliche normale Drehstahlformen.

2. Allgemeine Formen der Drehstähle.

Abb. 90 zeigt eine allgemeine Übersicht über die gebräuchlichen normalen Drehstähle, die richtiger Drehmeißel genannt werden, um das Wort Stahl für die Werkstoffbezeichnung allein zu verwenden. Wegen des eingebürgerten Werkstattgebrauches soll hier die Bezeichnung Drehstahl für das Werkzeug beibehalten bleiben. Beim Drehen werden folgende Hauptbegriffe für die Bearbeitungsarten unterschieden: Schruppen, Schlichten, Feinschlichten oder Feinen, Ausbohren, Hinterstechen. Welche Arbeitsweise anzuwenden ist, geht aus der Zeichnung durch die Bearbeitungszeichen hervor.

Oftmals ist es jedoch notwendig, vor dem Schlichten oder Feinen einen Schrupparbeitsgang vorauszuschicken, um den Hauptwerkstoff abzuheben. Hier kommt es darauf an, die Werkzeugform und ihre Anwendung zu erklären.

Da die Drehstähle teilweise selbst angeschliffen werden, ist in Abb. 91 die Beschreibung der Winkel erläutert. Hierin bedeuten als festgelegte Bezeichnungen

α = Freiwinkel (früher Rückenwinkel),
β = Meißelwinkel (früher Keilwinkel),
γ = Spanwinkel (früher Brustwinkel),
$\varkappa$ = Anstellwinkel (früher Einstellwinkel),
λ = Schneidensteigung,
ε = Spitzenwinkel.

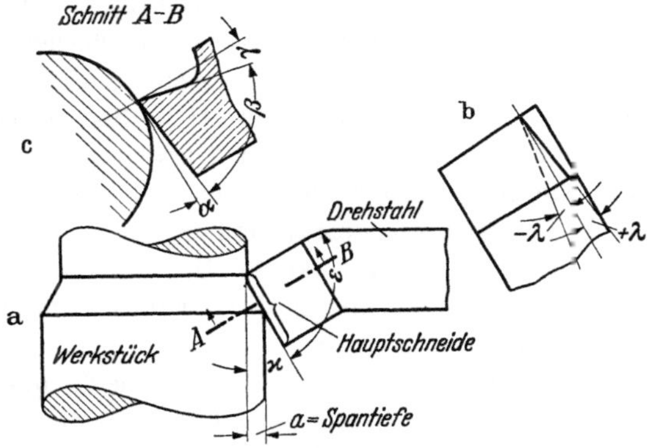

Abb. 91. Winkelbezeichnungen am Drehstahl.

Die drei Winkel α, β und γ betragen zusammen 90^0, d. h. wenn zwei Winkel, z. B. α und γ festgelegt sind, kann Winkel β ausgerechnet werden. Ist z. B. $\alpha = 5^0$ und $\gamma = 12^0$, so wird $\beta = 73^0$.

3. Wie entsteht die Abstumpfung des Drehstahles aus Schnellstahl?

Die gesamte Zerspanungsenergie wird in Verformungsarbeit (Späne) und in Wärme umgesetzt. Wir betrachten den Verbleib der Wärme genauer. Ein Teil der Wärme geht in das Werkstück, dieses wird warm; ein Teil geht in die Späne, sie werden ebenfalls warm. Ein Teil wird an die Luft abgestrahlt und vom Kühlwasser fortgeführt, dieses wird auch warm. Der Rest der Wärme geht in den Drehstahl, dieser Teil interessiert uns.

Die dem Drehstahl zugeführte Wärmemenge muß nun abgeführt werden, denn wenn die Wärmemenge weiter ohne Abfluß zugeführt wird, erhöht sich die Temperatur des Drehstahles immer mehr. Bei einer bestimmten Höhe der Temperatur wird das Material des Drehstahles weich. Dann sinkt seine Festigkeit, und es gibt bei dem vorhandenen Schnittdruck nach, Teilchen der Schneide lösen sich ab, der Stahl wird stumpf. Es kommt also darauf an, soviel Wärmemenge abzuführen, wie zugeführt wird. Wie wird nun die Wärmemenge am Drehstahl abgeführt und wie kann man dieses Abführen verbessern?

Wir betrachten jetzt nur den Teil der Zerspanungswärmemenge am Drehstahl. Diese Menge wird einmal durch Strahlung der Drehstahloberflächen an die Luft und besonders durch reichliche Kühlung abgeführt. Es ist deshalb besonders wichtig, daß der Kühlstrom reichlich und direkt auf die Schneide geleitet wird. Ferner fließt ein Teil der Wärmemenge durch den Drehstahlquerschnitt ab. Was kann man tun, damit ein möglichst großer Querschnitt vorhanden ist, weil dann die Wärmemenge besser abgeführt wird? Dazu müssen wir uns erst überlegen, wo und wie die Wärme in den Drehstahl kommt.

Die Zerspanungswärme entsteht

1. durch das Stauchen des Spanes, Stauchwärme,

2. durch die Reibung des Spanes beim Abfließen über den Drehstahl, Spanreibwärme,

3. durch Reibung der Hauptschneide und Spitze beim Abtrennen des Spanes vom Werkstück, Trennwärme.

Nach Abb. 92 wird jetzt die Stauchwärme und Spanreibwärme entsprechend der Fläche des Spanquerschnittes (auf der Abb. 92 schraffierte Fläche) dem Drehstahl zugeführt. Dazu kommt die Trennwärme durch das Abtrennen des Spanes, die direkt in die schmale Schneide des Drehstahles eintritt, und zwar so breit auf der Schneide, wie der Span breit ist. Somit wird die Schneide am höchsten mit Wärmezufuhr belastet, einmal durch die Stauchwärme, von der ihr ein Anteil zugeführt wird, und ferner durch die Trennwärme, die ihr ganz zugeführt wird. Beim Schnitt wird dauernd neue Wärmemenge zugeführt.

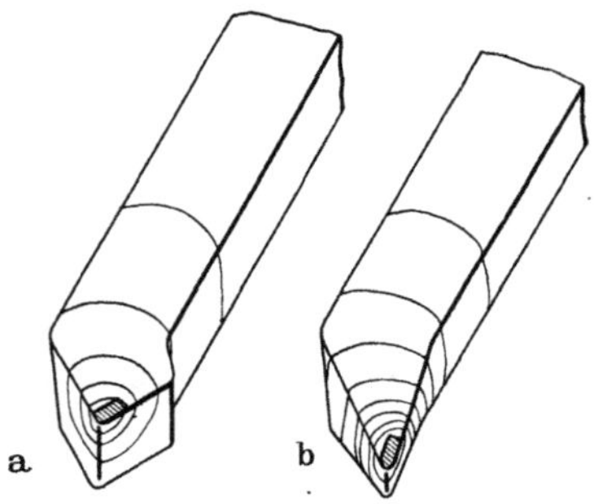

Abb. 92. Wärmestauung beim Seitenstahl (*b*) durch nicht ausreichenden Stahlquerschnitt für den Wärmeabfluß.

Wichtig für die Standzeit des Drehstahles ist allein die Wärmeabfuhr von der Schneide und insbesondere von der Spitze, die am schlechtesten die Wärme abführen kann. Die Abfuhr durch das Kühlmittel ist bereits besprochen. Jetzt ist die Abfuhr der Wärme durch den Querschnitt zu betrachten.

Die Wärme sucht sich auszugleichen und fließt durch den Drehstahl nach dem kühleren Schaft und den Stahlhalter hin ab. Die Schnelligkeit hängt vom Temperaturunterschied und dem Flußquerschnitt ab. Stellen wir uns einmal einen dünnen Draht vor, so leuchtet es ein, daß durch diesen eine große Wärmemenge viel langsamer abfließen kann, als wenn wir dazu einen dicken Stab nähmen. Genau so ist es hier. Bei einem Schruppstahl ist von der Schneide aus gesehen mehr Fleisch vorhanden als bei einem Spitzstahl. Der Spitzstahl eignet sich daher zum Schruppen weniger gut, weil er die großen Wärmemengen nicht abführen kann. Genau so kann man auch mit einem Einstechstahl nicht große Späne abheben, weil er einmal wohl die Kräfte nicht aushalten würde, dann aber auch auf keinen Fall große Wärmemengen abführen kann. Man braucht also zum Schruppen für große Späne, d. h. für große Wärmemengenabfuhr geeignete Drehstähle mit viel Fleisch an der Schneide, nämlich Schruppstähle, und zwar möglichst große Schruppstähle.

Der Vorgang beim Abstumpfen verläuft nun so, daß bei richtiger Schnittgeschwindigkeit gerade so viel Wärme zugeführt wird, wie abgeführt werden kann, so daß eine bestimmte Temperatur an der Schneide bleibt. Diese Temperatur liegt etwas unter derjenigen, bei der der Drehstahl beginnt weich zu werden. Wenn jetzt durch das Abtrennen des Spanes vom Werkstück allmählich die Schneide stumpfer wird, entsteht an der Freifläche, das ist die Fläche, wo der Freiwinkel α liegt, eine kleine Phase längs der Schneide. Diese Phase kommt zum Anliegen am Werkstück und reibt. Dadurch entsteht nun zusätzliche Reibungswärme. Diese erhöht die Wärmezufuhr über die Menge der Wärme, die abgeführt werden kann. Die Temperatur an der Schneide steigt, steigt schließlich so weit, daß der Drehstahl weich wird. Die Schneide wird so heiß, daß sich plötzlich Teilchen von ihr abtrennen und auf dem Werkstück manchmal kalt aufschweißen. Man sieht dann blanke Riefen. Wenn nicht sofort ausgeschaltet wird, und zwar der Vorschub zuerst, geht der Drehstahl völlig zu Bruch. Man muß beizeiten ausschalten, damit möglichst wenig nachgeschliffen werden muß. Diese blanken Stellen am Werkstück sind nun bedeutend härter als der Werkstückwerkstoff, da es sich meist um Schnellstahlteilchen handelt. Sie können mit Schnelldrehstählen abgedreht werden, aber nur mit einer Schnittgeschwindigkeit von 4···6 m/min. Erst wenn wieder reiner Werkstoff vorhanden ist, darf die normale Schnittgeschwindigkeit eingestellt werden. Es ist vorteilhaft, eine größere Abrundung der Spitzen vorzunehmen, weil dadurch die Wärmeabfuhr begünstigt wird und die Schnittgeschwindigkeit höher gewählt werden kann.

4. Wie entsteht die Abstumpfung des Drehstahles mit Hartmetallplättchen?

Die neuzeitlichen Hartmetalle sind gesinterte Legierungen. In Kugelmühlen werden Gemische aus harten Karbiden des Wolframs, Titans, Molybdäns, Tantals und einem Bindestoff (meist Kobalt oder Nickel) zu feinem Pulver gemahlen. Dieses wird dann in Stahlformen unter einem Druck von 1000 bis 2000 kg/cm² zu Stäben gepreßt. Jetzt erfolgt kein Gießen oder Schmelzen, sondern das Sintern, ein Brennen, ähnlich wie in der Keramik.

Durch eine Vorsinterung bei rund 1000° steigt die Festigkeit der Preßstäbe so weit, daß sie mit dünnen Schleifscheiben zu Plättchen geschnitten werden können. Diese werden dann auf ihre Form geschliffen. In besonderen Öfen werden diese Formstücke mehrere Stunden bei Temperaturen von 1400 bis 1500° fertiggesintert. Sie haben jetzt annähernd die fertige Form. Die Plättchen werden auf Schaftmaterial hart aufgelötet und bilden mit ihm zusammen den Hartmetalldrehstahl usw. Beim Schnitt kommt nur das Hartmetallplättchen zur Spanabnahme. Wie verhält sich dieses?

Es sind also harte Teilchen, die durch ein Bindemittel aneinandergekittet sind. Die Karbide sind hart und gestatten die hohen Schnittgeschwindigkeiten, durch das Zusammensintern wird aber das Hartmetall spröde. Es verträgt daher keine schlagartige Beanspruchung, darf nicht angestoßen werden oder beim Schneiden Erschütterungen ausgesetzt sein, weil diese sofort zur Lockerung des Gefüges und zum Ausspringen kleiner Teilchen an den Ecken und Kanten führen.

Die Abstumpfung kann auf zwei Arten herbeigeführt werden. Einmal wie bei Schnellstahl durch Entstehen einer Phase an der Freifläche, erhöhte Wärmezufuhr und Entstehung hoher Temperatur an Schneide und Spitze. Diese Temperaturen erzeugen Eigenspannungen im erhitzten Teil und sprengen kleine Teilchen ab. Die Schneide springt stellenweise aus. Sofort muß das Werkzeug ausgewechselt und nachgeschliffen werden, da beim Weiterdrehen kurz danach größere Teile herausplatzen.

Die zweite Möglichkeit entsteht durch Erschütterungen unter Schnitt. Dauernde Druckänderung beim Schnitt durch Schwingungen der Welle, starkes Rattern usw. lockern das Gefüge der Schneide und Spitze und führen zum Abspringen kleiner Schneidenteilchen. Also stets auf ruhigen Lauf der Maschine achten, sonst andere Schnittgeschwindigkeiten wählen oder Abhilfe schaffen, weil sonst die Standzeit des Hartmetalls sehr kurz ist.

5. Erkennen der Abstumpfung.

Bei einiger Übung ist es leicht, eine beginnende Abstumpfung der Drehstähle zu erkennen. Die Oberfläche des Werkstückes wird rauher, schließlich sehen die letzten Drehriefen sehr blank aus, was durch Aufschweißen von Schnellstahlteilchen auf das Werkstück entsteht, wie oben ausgeführt. Bei Hartmetall tritt auch das sogenannte „Rundfeuern" auf. Es laufen Funkenbündel um die Welle herum, ein Zeichen der starken Abnutzung. In diesen Fällen ist sofort das Werkzeug zu wechseln.

6. Welchen Einfluß haben die Winkel am Drehstahl auf die Schnittgeschwindigkeit?

Je kleiner wir die Winkel α und γ machen, desto mehr Fleisch bleibt unter der Schneide stehen. Für den Freiwinkel α hat sich gezeigt, daß 4 bis 6°, also etwa 5° die beste Größe ist. Der Drehstahl schneidet gerade noch frei, und die Schneide ist gut unterstützt. Machen wir diesen Winkel bedeutend größer, so wird die Schneidenunterstützung und die Wärmeabfuhr schlechter. Der Stahl muß also früher stumpf werden, es kann auch sein, daß seine Schnittgeschwindigkeit herabgesetzt werden muß.

Je kleiner wir den Spanwinkel γ machen, desto mehr Fleisch bleibt stehen und desto besser wird die Wärmeabfuhr. Es entsteht aber viel Staubwärme, weil wegen des ungünstig kleinen Spanwinkels der Werkstoff sich schlechter abheben läßt. Je größer wir den Spanwinkel γ machen, desto kleiner wird der Schnittdruck und desto kleiner wird die Stauchwärme. Der Span rollt auch besser ab. Aber die Wärmeabfuhr wird schlechter. Man sieht also, daß daher der Spanwinkel γ vermittelt werden muß. In Tabelle 12 sind nun für verschiedene Zerspanbarkeiten der Werkstoffe geeignete Winkel angegeben. Dabei können die Spanwinkel aus den geschilderten Gründen in einem größeren Bereich liegen, ohne daß eine wesentliche Beeinflussung der Schnittgeschwindigkeit auftritt. In dem unteren Teil der Tabelle 12 aufgeführte vereinfachte Mittelwerte für die Winkel können als Standardwerke angenommen werden. Diese Winkel sind den Schnittgeschwindigkeiten in der Tabelle 10 zugrunde gelegt. Wählt man andere Winkel, ändern

Tabelle 12. Geeignete Winkel am Drehstahl.

Winkel	Schnittwinkel in Grad für Schnellstahl							
Werkstoff	Leichtmetall	Rotmetall	Gußeisen		Stahl und Stahlguß			
Gruppe	1…4	5…10	11…12	13…14	15…18	19…20	21…22	23…24
α	5…7	5…7	4…6	4…6	3…5	3…5	3…5	3…5
γ	15…40	12…30	12…22	10…18	10…18	8…12	4…10	—3 bis +5
$\varkappa$	90…30	90…45	60…45	60…45	60…45	60…45	60…45	60…45
λ	—10 bis +5	—5 bis +5	—3 bis +5	0…5	—3 bis +5	0…+5	0…+5	0…+3
α	5	5	5	5	5	5	5	5
γ	30	25	18	12	18	12	8	3
$\varkappa$	60	60	45	45	45	45	45	45
λ	—7	0	+5	+5	+5	+5	+3	+3
Drehstahl Nr.	1	2	3	4	3	4	5	6

sich die Schnittgeschwindigkeiten, und zwar werden sie kleiner. Welchen Einfluß hat der Spitzenwinkel ε auf die Schnittgeschwindigkeit?

Der Spitzenwinkel ε soll möglichst groß sein, er kann am besten so groß sein, daß der Drehstahl gerade nicht mehr am Werkstück nachschneidet. Dann ist viel Fleisch für die Wärmeabfuhr und eine lange Standzeit vorhanden.

Welchen Einfluß hat der Einstellwinkel $\varkappa$ auf die Schnittgeschwindigkeit? Wie die Abb. 93a bis c zeigt, wird mit dem Einstellwinkel $\varkappa$ die Lage der Hauptschneide zum Werkstück angegeben. Bei einem Messerstahl ist $\varkappa = 90^0$ (Abb. 93a), bei einem Flachstahl wird $\varkappa = 0^0$. Die zulässigen Schnittgeschwindigkeiten gegenüber dem Normalstahl mit $\varkappa = 45^0$ lassen sich für

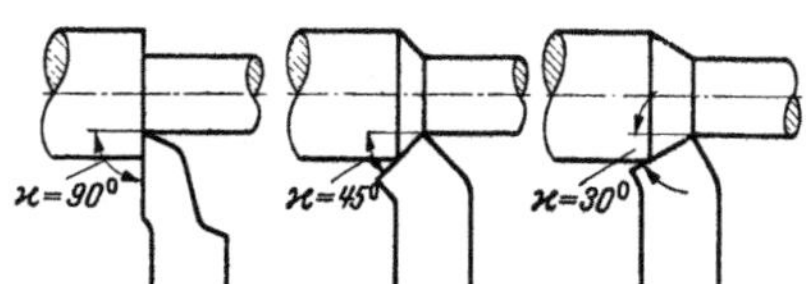

Abb. 93. Verschiedene Anstellwinkel $\varkappa$.

verschiedene Winkel $\varkappa$ umrechnen. Für die Schnittgeschwindigkeiten in Tabelle 10 ist allgemein $\varkappa = 45^0$ angenommen. Setzt man für diese Schnittgeschwindigkeit 100% an, so erhält man bei gleichen Span- und Freiwinkeln (es sind stets gleiche Schnittiefen und Vorschube angenommen) für $\varkappa = 30^0$ 125 % für die Schnittgeschwindigkeit, die also ein Viertel höher liegt. Ist z. B. $v\ (45^0) = 40$ m/min, dann ist $v\ (30^0) = 40 \cdot 1{,}25 = 50$ m/min. Bei $\varkappa = 60^0$ sinkt die zulässige Schnittgeschwindigkeit auf 80 %, bei $\varkappa = 90^0$ auf 66 %. Das würde also bedeuten, daß man möglichst flache Stähle verwenden soll, weil hierbei die Wärmeabfuhr am günstigsten ist. Die Grenze für kleine Winkel $\varkappa$ liegt darin, daß einmal die Werkstücke bei flachen Winkeln sehr leicht rattern und dann die Schnittgeschwindigkeiten nicht eingehalten werden können und ferner daran, daß man beim Schruppen nicht die Ecken ausfahren kann. Bei kurzen Längen ist das oft wichtiger. Am ruhigsten schneidet der Drehstahl mit $\varkappa = 90^0$, er hat aber nur eine Schnittgeschwindigkeit, die $^2/_3$ so groß ist wie bei $\varkappa = 45^0$. Dafür können aber die Ecken ohne Umspannen des Stahles ausgefahren werden. Man merke deshalb:

Bei großen Schruppmengen $\varkappa = 45^0$ wählen, bei starren Werkstücken auch $\varkappa = 30^0$ wählen, beim Auftreten von Rattern Spanwinkel γ ändern, Drehzahl ändern, Vorschub ändern oder $\varkappa$ größer wählen.

Welchen Einfluß hat die Schneidensteigung λ? Die hängende Schneide, wie in Abb. 91, gibt mehr Fleisch für die Wärmeabfuhr, jedoch werden die Späne auf die Welle geleitet und beschädigen die Oberfläche, beim Schlichten deshalb nicht günstig. Bei fallender Schneide zwar bessere Spanabfuhr, aber ab $\lambda = 3^0$ und größer können nur kleinere Schnittgeschwindigkeiten genommen werden. Die Messung der Winkel erfolgt mit festen oder einstellbaren Lehren. Senkrecht zur Schneide messen!

7. Hohlkehlen am Drehstahl.

Bei längeren Arbeiten entsteht durch den Spanabfluß auf der Spanfläche, das ist die Fläche, an der der Spanwinkel liegt, eine Auskolkung (Abb. 94). Diese ist hohlkehlenartig. Es ist klar, daß sich der Span die für ihn günstigste Form selbst erzeugt. Man kann diese Form durch Anschleifen von Hohlkehlen vorweg erzeugen, vergrößert dadurch jedoch nicht die Schnittgeschwindigkeit, sondern erzeugt nur ein besseres Abrollen des Spanes. Manchmal wird diese Hohlkehle notwendig sein, wenn längere Fließspäne entstehen, die Gefahren bedeuten, oder den Abtransport erschweren. Durch Hohlkehlen lassen sich kurze Bruch-

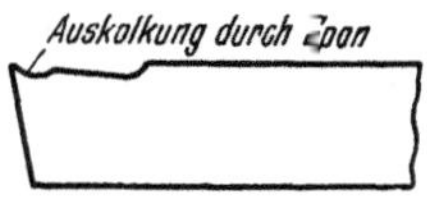

Abb. 94. Auskolkung auf der Spanfläche eines Drehstahles.

späne erzeugen. Die Form solcher Hohlkehlen ist aus Abb. 95 ersichtlich. Man merke sich:

Lieber zu kleine Hohlkehlen anschleifen, Span kolkt diese richtig aus.

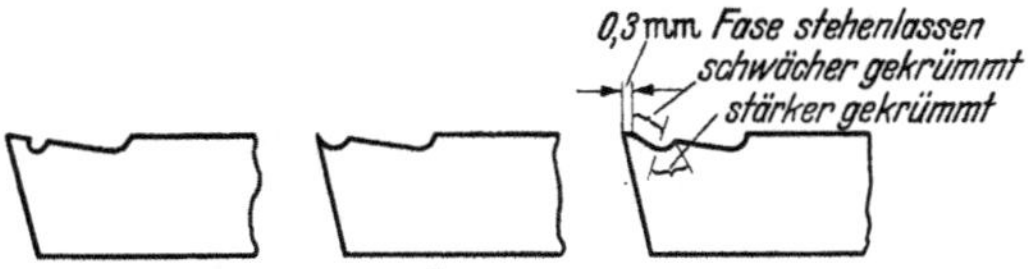

a	b	c
falsch Hohlkehle zu klein und zu tief, verschlechtert Spanfluß.	falsch Hohlkehle dicht an Schneide schwächt diese. Stahl stumpft sofort ab.	richtig Form der Hohlkehle und Lage ist entscheidend.

Abb. 95. Form und Lage einer Hohlkehle.

8. Einstellung der Drehstähle.

Es ist richtig, Schrupp- und Schlichtstähle rund 1 % des Drehdurchmessers über Spitzenhöhe auf dem Vordersupport oder entsprechend unter Spitzenhöhe auf dem Hintersupport einzustellen wie in Abb. 96a. Bei 100 mm ⌀, also 1 mm über Spitzenhöhe. Gewindestähle nach Abb. 96b müssen genau auf Spitzenhöhe stehen, da sonst eine Profilverzerrung des Gewindes eintritt. Abstechstähle nach Abb. 96c

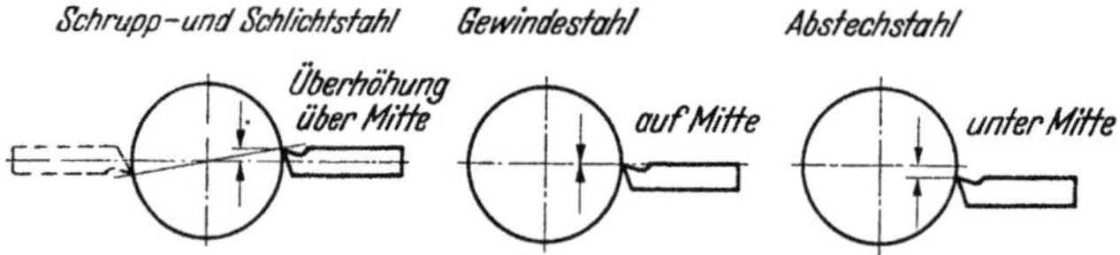

a b c

Abb. 96. Einstellung der Drehstähle.

müssen aber unter Spitzenhöhe stehen, weil sie sonst leicht in das Werkstück hineingezogen werden und durch die plötzliche Mehrbelastung abbrechen.

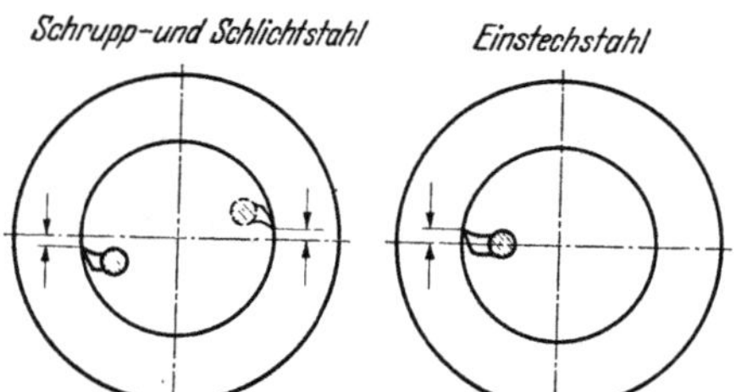

Abb. 97. Einstellung der Ausbohrstähle.

Beim Ausbohren von Bohrungen nach Abb. 97 liegen die Verhältnisse umgekehrt. Hier sollen die Schrupp- und Schlichtstähle unter Mitte liegen, die Einstechstähle über Mitte. Meistens müssen die Ausbohrstähle auch weiter hinterschliffen werden, damit sie an der Wandung nicht mit dem unteren Ende der Freifläche anstoßen. An der Hauptschneide hält man dann etwa 5° Freiwinkel ein, die tieferliegenden Teile der Freifläche schleift man weiter fort. Es ist nicht falsch, alle Stähle genau auf Mitte zu stellen.

Die Stähle sollen so kurz wie möglich und fest im Stahlhalter oder auf dem Support eingespannt werden, um ein Federn auf das Kleinstmaß zu beschränken. Die Ausladung „w" (Abb. 98) soll nicht größer als 1× der Stahlhöhe „h" sein. Durch Erschütterungen und Federn des Stahles sinkt die Schnittgeschwindigkeit und verschlechtert sich die Oberfläche des gedrehten Werkstückes. Blechbeilagen dienen zum Ausrichten bei der Höhe der Einstellung. Es muß auch unbedingt eine glatte und satte Auflage des Drehstahles vorhanden sein, wozu die Auflageflächen am Stahl vorbearbeitet sein sollten.

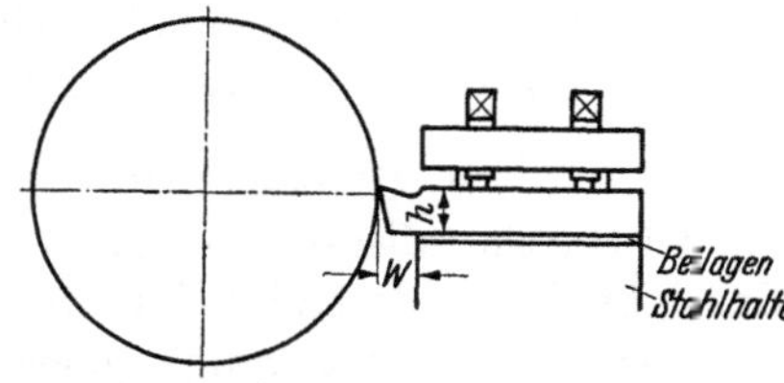

Abb. 98. Einspannung der Drehstähle.

9. Fehler beim Schleifen der Werkzeuge.

Im großen unterscheidet man Drehstähle aus Werkzeugstahl, Schnellstahl und Hartmetall. Drehstähle aus Werkzeugstahl sind durchgehendes Material. Schnellstahl und Hartmetallplättchen werden auf sogenanntes Schaftmaterial, das ist billigerer Werkstoff, aufgeschweißt oder aufgelötet. Beim Schleifen dieser Stähle können die normalen Schleifscheiben für Werkzeugstahl und Schnellstahl benutzt werden. Hartmetallstähle dürfen auf diesen Scheiben nicht geschliffen werden, da sie ungeeignet sind, die harten Metallplättchen zu heiß werden und springen. Hartmetallstähle dürfen nur auf den dazugehörigen Schleifscheiben und von besonders ausgebildeten Leuten nachgeschliffen werden. Häufige Fehler beim Schleifen sind zu starkes Andrücken des Werkzeuges an die Schleifscheibe. Der Drehstahl wird zu heiß und glüht an den scharfen Kanten bis tief in den Drehstahl hinein aus. Dabei verliert er seine Härte und kann nur mit viel niedrigerer Schnittgeschwindigkeit verwendet werden. Ein sehr baldiges Nachschleifen ist erforderlich. Es muß dann die ganze Glühzone, oft mehrere Millimeter, fortgeschliffen werden. Da jedes Schleifen mit leichterem Druck langsamer geht, braucht man also für das Fortschleifen der Glühzone das 4···5fache an Zeit. Meist wird durch zu scharfes Andrücken auch die Drehzahl der Schleifscheibe herabgesetzt. Die Schleifscheibe schleift nur bei ihrer hohen Drehzahl richtig. Läuft sie ganz langsam, so beginnt der Drehstahl die Schleifscheibe zu bearbeiten und erzeugt Eindrehung in dieser, die wiederum ein richtiges Schleifen unmöglich macht. Der Kühlwasserstrom muß dabei sehr reichlich sein und genau auf die augenblicklich zu schleifende Schneide gerichtet werden. Setzt der Kühlstrom nur kurze Zeit aus, so findet eine örtliche Überhitzung des Drehstahles statt, und das oben geschilderte Ausglühen setzt ein.

10. Behandlung der Hartmetallstähle.

Bei Hartmetallstählen ist zu beachten, daß die Plättchen sehr spröde sind. Sie dürfen deshalb keine Stöße oder Schläge erhalten, sei es durch Fallenlassen des Werkzeuges oder hartes Anstoßen. Absolut zu vermeiden ist das Stillsetzen der Maschine, solange der Stahl in Eingriff steht, da dies beim Hartmetall sofort zum Bruch der teuren Plättchens führt. Es muß bei Hartmetall also bei jedem Stillsetzen der Maschine erst der Stahl außer Schnitt gebracht werden. Die Abstumpfung dieser Werkzeugschneiden äußert sich im feinen Ausbröckeln der Schneide. Bei ersten Anzeichen dieser Art sind die Werkzeuge sofort auszuwechseln, da beim Nachschleifen bis zu den ausgebrochenen Stellen geschliffen werden muß und bei langer Benutzung durch große Bruchstellen viel zu viel wertvolles Hartmetallmaterial fortgeschliffen werden muß. Ein Abziehen dieser Stähle mit dem Ölstein verlängert die Leistungsfähigkeit bis zum Doppelten. Die Ausführung muß aber sorgfältig und richtig erfolgen. Die Bewegung des Abziehsteines muß immer gegen die Schneide gehen, nie fortführen. Allgemein ist es gut, die scharfen Spitzen abzurunden, da diese eine besonders starke Belastung auszuhalten haben, die sich bei einer Rundung verteilt. Bei Gußeisen und Stahl sind besondere Plättchen entwickelt, wozu die Drehstähle eine Farbenmarkierung tragen.

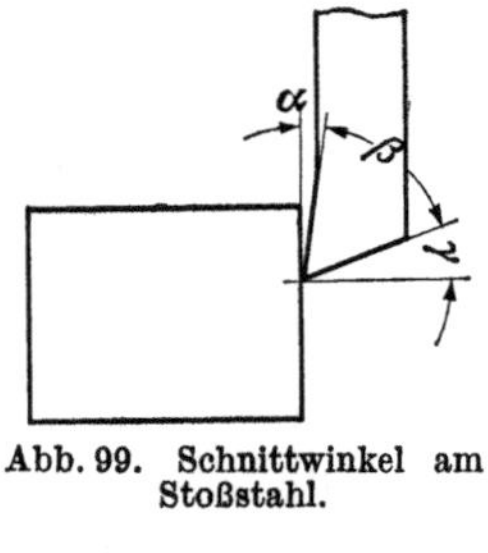

Abb. 99. Schnittwinkel am Stoßstahl.

11. Hobel- und Stoßstähle.

Für die Hobelstähle gelten sinngemäß die gleichen Angaben wie für Drehstähle. Eine Überhöhung beim Einstellen fällt natürlich fort.

Bei Stoßmaschinen findet eine ähnliche Spanabnahme wie beim Hobeln, also auch beim Drehen statt. Es gelten daher die gleichen Regeln, nur liegt hier der Spanwinkel γ an der Stirnseite, wie Abb. 99 zeigt. Es muß also die Stirnseite mit dem dem

Werkstoff entsprechenden Winkel aus Tabelle 12 versehen werden. Schnittgeschwindigkeiten sind aus Tabelle 10 zu nehmen.

12. Sonderstähle.

Zum Nachschlichten von Rundungen oder Hohlkehlen werden manchmal Handstähle verwendet. Es ist wichtig, daß dabei die Auflage „*w*" (Abb. 100) so dicht wie möglich an das Werkstück herangebracht wird, da sonst die Gefahr besteht, daß ein Einhaken des Werkzeuges hervorgerufen wird und zu Verletzungen führt. Der Schaber in Abb. 101 ist ein Werkzeug mit stumpfem oder negativem Spanwinkel. Er dient zum Glätten der Oberfläche durch Fortnehmen feinster hervorstehender Oberflächenteilchen.

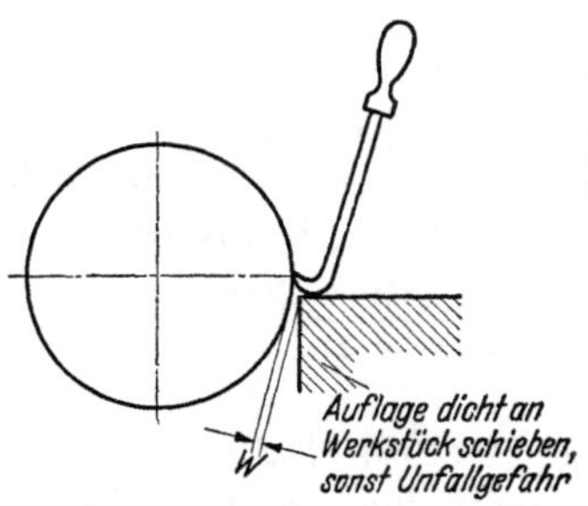

Abb. 100. Lage von Handstählen.

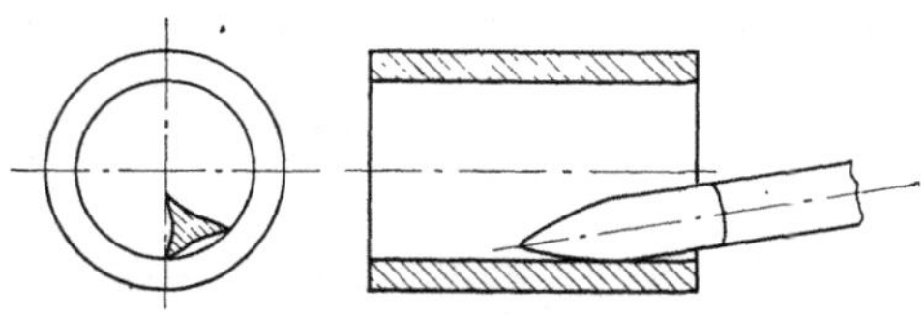

Abb. 101. Wirkungsart eines Dreikantschabers.

Für freihändig schwer herstellbare Profile werden Sonderstähle angefertigt, die genau senkrecht zur Werkstückachse einzustellen sind, da sonst das Profil schräg zu liegen kommt. Die Einstellung dieser Stähle genau auf die Mitte ist Voraussetzung für ein genaues Profil. Das Nachschleifen soll nur in der Werkzeugmacherei vorgenommen werden.

13. Bestimmung der Schnittgeschwindigkeit für Schnellstahl und Umrechnung in Umdrehungszahlen an der Maschine.

Die in der Tabelle 10 angegebenen Werte für Schnittgeschwindigkeiten und Vorschübe gelten stets für starre, kräftige Werkstücke bei einem mittleren Schnellstahl als Werkzeugstoff, günstige Werkzeugwinkel und gut geeignete Werkzeugmaschinen. Sie sind für Hobeln und Stoßen dieselben.

Wie stellt man die Schnittgeschwindigkeit fest? Zunächst stellt man auf der Zeichnung, der Stückliste oder der Begleitkarte den Werkstoff fest. Dann sucht man am Kopf der Tabelle 10 den Werkstoff auf. Die Schnittgeschwindigkeiten stehen jetzt in der gleichen Spalte senkrecht darunter. Auf der linken Seite stehen verschiedene Spanquerschnitte. Auf der gleichen Zeile geht man jetzt nach rechts, bis die Spalte für den Werkstoff erreicht ist und liest dort die Schnittgeschwindigkeit ab.

Da nun die Werkstoffe eine Toleranz in der Festigkeit haben, kann einmal eine höhere oder niedrigere Festigkeit vorliegen. Das ergibt sich dann beim Schnitt. Deshalb greifen die Werkstoffe manchmal über zwei Spalten hinweg. Man beginnt mit der höheren Schnittgeschwindigkeit und setzt diese bei zu schneller Abstumpfung der Werkzeuge herab, auf die der zunächst niedrigeren Spalte.

Wie wird die Umdrehungszahl an der Maschine berechnet? Wenn jetzt die Schnittgeschwindigkeit bekannt und der größte Durchmesser, von dem Späne abgehoben werden sollen, festgestellt ist, wird die Umdrehungszahl an der Maschine nach der Gleichung 9 ausgerechnet.

$$\text{Umdrehungszahl } n = \frac{\text{Schnittgeschwindigkeit } v \cdot 1000}{\underset{(=3{,}14)}{\pi} \cdot \text{Durchmesser } D}.$$

Einfacher ist es, die Umdrehungszahl aus der Abb. 102 abzugreifen. Dort geht man folgendermaßen vor. Man sucht den Durchmesser auf der linken Seite, geht dann parallel zu den Linien nach rechts oben, bis man auf die Schnittgeschwindigkeitslinie von oben links nach unten rechts stößt. Vom Schnittpunkt geht man waagerecht nach rechts und liest die Umdrehungszahl ab.

Beispiele für Abb. 102:

für $D = 160$ mm ⌀ und die Schnittgeschwindigkeit $v = 15$ m/min
wird $n = 30$ U/min,

für $D = 30$ mm ⌀ und die Schnittgeschwindigkeit $v = 45$ m/min
wird $n = \ldots$ U/min.

Auch aus Tabelle 13 kann die Umdrehungszahl entnommen werden.

Beispiele für Drehen. An obigem Beispiel wird jetzt die Ermittlung der Schnittgeschwindigkeit und der Umdrehungszahl durchgeführt.

Der Werkstoff StC 10.61 von 220 mm ⌀ soll mit dem Span 3×1 geschruppt werden. StC 10.61 steht in Tabelle 10 in der Spalte 15 und in der nächsten Hälfte der Spalte 16. Beide Spalten zusammen wieder ergeben für 3×1 Spanquerschnitt rund 55 m/min Schnittgeschwindigkeit. Aus der Gleichung (9) oder der Abb. 102 oder Tabelle 13 wird die Umdrehungszahl $n = 80$ festgestellt. Die nächste zur Verfügung stehende Spindeldrehzahl = 75 U/min wird eingestellt.

Dies gibt für einen Drehstahl mit $k = 45^0$. Bei anderen Einstellwinkeln ändern sich die Umdrehungszahlen auf

$$k = 30^0 \quad v_{(30^0)} = 125\,\% \text{ von } v_{(45^0)} = 1{,}25 \cdot 55 \text{ m/min} = \text{rund } 68 \text{ m/min}$$

oder = 1,25 · Umdrehungszahl $n = 1{,}25 \cdot 80 = 100$ Umdrehungen, eingestellt werden dann 95 U/min, soweit vorhanden sind.

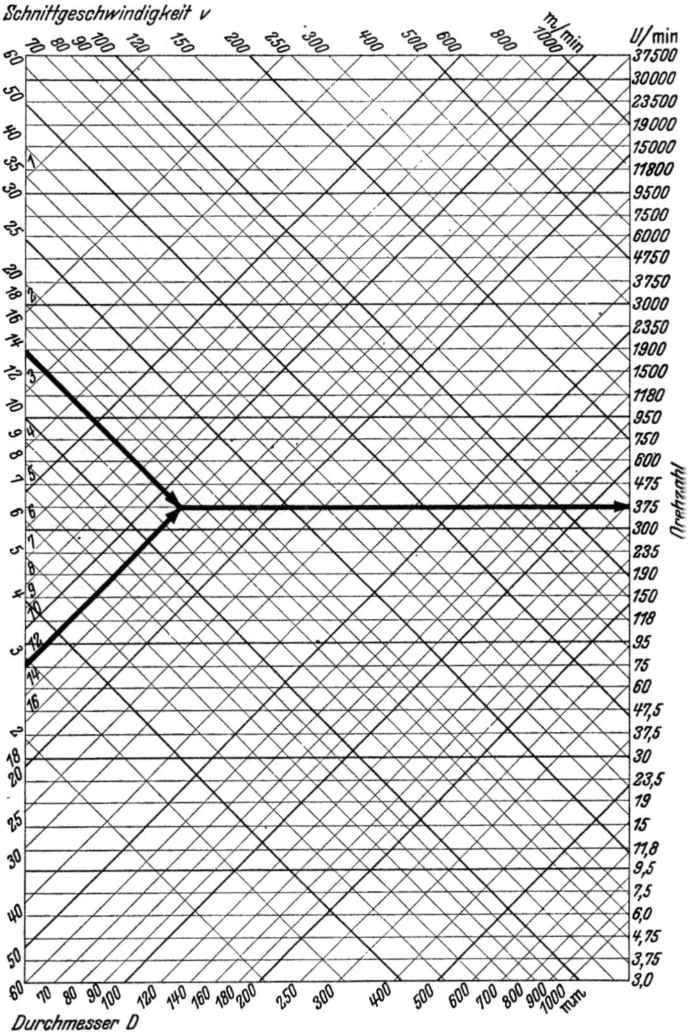

Abb. 102. Drehzahlschaubild.

Ebenso findet man für $D = 220$ ⌀ und $v = 68$ m/min in der Abb. 102, daß der Schnittpunkt etwas über 95 U/min liegt, die also zu nehmen sind.

$$k = 90^0 \quad v_{(90^0)} = 0{,}66 \cdot v_{(45^0)} = 0{,}66 \cdot 55 = 37 \text{ m/min}.$$

Tabelle 13. Drehzahltafel mit Schnittgeschwindigkeiten v in m/min.

Drehdurchmesser in mm																		Dreh-zahl
20	25	30	40	50	60	80	100	125	150	175	200	250	300	350	400	450	500	
						2,5	3,1	3,9	4,6	5,4	6,2	7,7	9,2	11	12,5	14	15,5	9,8
					2,5	3,5	4,1	5,1	6,1	7,1	8,2	10	12	14,5	16,5	18,5	20,0	13
				2,7	3,2	4,3	5,3	6,7	8,0	9,3	10,5	13,5	16	18,5	21	24	27	17
			2,5	3,1	3,7	4,9	6,1	7,7	9,2	10,5	12	15,5	18,5	21,5	24,5	27,5	30,5	19,5
		2,1	2,8	3,5	4,2	5,6	7,0	8,8	10,5	12,5	14	17,5	21	25	28	32	35	22,4
	2	2,5	3,3	4,1	4,9	6,5	8,2	10	12	14,5	16,5	20	24	29	33	37	41	26
1,9	2,4	2,8	3,8	4,7	5,6	7,5	9,4	12	14	16,5	19	24	28	33	38	42	47	30
2,1	2,7	3,2	4,3	5,3	6,4	8,5	10,5	13,5	16	18,5	21	27	32	37	43	48	54	34
2,5	3,1	3,7	4,9	6,1	7,4	9,8	12,5	15,5	18,5	21	24	31	37	43	49	55	62	39
2,8	3,5	4,2	5,7	7,1	8,5	11,5	14	17,5	21	25	28	35	42	49	56	64	70	45
3,3	4,1	4,9	6,5	8,2	9,8	13	16,5	21	24	29	33	41	49	58	65	74	82	52
3,8	4,7	5,7	7,5	9,4	11,5	15	19	24	28	33	38	47	56	66	75	85	94	60
4,3	5,3	6,4	8,5	10,5	13	17	21	27	32	37	43	54	64	75	85	96	105	68
4,9	6,1	7,4	9,8	12	14,5	19,5	24	31	37	43	49	62	74	86	98	110	120	78
5,6	7,1	8,5	11,5	14	17	23	28	35	42	49	56	70	85	98	115	125	140	90
6,6	8,2	9,8	13	16,5	20	26	33	41	50	58	66	82	98	115	130	150	165	105
7,5	9,4	11,5	15	19	23	30	38	47	56	66	75	94	115	130	150	170	190	120
8,5	10,5	12,5	17	21	25	34	42	52	64	74	85	105	125	150	170	190	210	135
9,7	12	14,5	19,5	24	29	39	49	60	72	85	96	120	145	170	195	220	240	155
11,5	14	17	20	28	34	45	56	70	85	98	115	140	170	200	230	250	280	180
13	16	19,5	26	32	39	52	64	80	96	115	130	160	195	230	260	290	320	205
14,5	18,5	22	29	37	44	60	74	92	110	130	145	185	220	260	290	330	370	235
17	21	25	34	42	50	68	85	105	125	150	170	210	250	300	340	380	420	270
19,5	24	29	39	49	58	78	92	120	145	170	195	240	290	340	390	440	490	310
22	28	33	45	56	66	90	110	140	165	195	220	280	330	390	450	500	560	355
26	32	39	52	64	78	105	130	160	195	230	260	320	390	450	520	580	640	410
30	37	45	60	74	90	120	150	185	220	260	300	370	450	520	600	680	750	475
34	42	50	68	85	100	135	170	210	260	300	340	420	500	600	680	760	850	540
39	49	58	78	98	115	155	195	240	290	340	390	490	580	680	780	880	980	620
45	56	66	90	110	135	180	220	280	330	390	450	560	660	780	900	1000		710
60	74	90	120	150	180	240	300	370	450	520	600	750	900	1050				950
78	98	120	155	195	240	310	390	490	580	680	780	980						1250

Schnittgeschwindigkeit v in m/min.

Aus Abb. 102 wird $n = 53$ U/min. Der Unterschied gegenüber $k = 30^0$ beträgt die Hälfte!

Wenn nun das Werkstück nicht starr und kräftig ist, sondern mittelmäßig, z. B. bei langen, dünnen Wellen, können nicht so große Schnittgeschwindigkeiten genommen werden, vor allem meist nicht so große Spanquerschnitte, oder man benutzt eine Hilfsstütze wie eine Lünette. Man wählt die Schnittgeschwindigkeit dann nur 0,8 so groß.

Mittleres Werkstück: $v_{(\text{Mittel})} = 0{,}8 \cdot v_{(45^0)} = 0{,}8 \cdot 55 = 44$ m/min
$n = 60$ U/min.

Leichte, sperrige Werkstücke. Diese können nicht mit großen Schruppspänen bearbeitet werden. Man wählt kleinere Späne und vermindert die gefundene Schnittgeschwindigkeit ebenfalls auf 80 %, also $v \cdot 0{,}8$ ausrechnen.

Beispiel für Langhobeln. Eine Grundplatte aus Ge 18.91 mit einer Länge von 5000 mm soll mit einem Span von 6×1 überhobelt werden. Wie groß ist die Schnittgeschwindigkeit und welche Hubzahl ist einzustellen?

Aus Tabelle 10 ist $v = 18{,}5$ m/min.

Wenn die Schnittgeschwindigkeit nicht direkt eingestellt werden kann, muß die Hubzahl nach Gleichung 2 ausgerechnet werden. Es ist bei einer Hublänge von 5200 für den Überlauf gerechnet nach Gleichung 5

$$\text{Hubzahl } n = \frac{\text{Schnittgeschwindigkeit } v \cdot 1000}{2 \text{ Hobellänge}} = \frac{18{,}5 \cdot 1000}{2 \cdot 5200} = 1{,}7 \text{ U/min.}$$

Je nach der Art der Arbeit wird der Spanquerschnitt zu wählen sein. Bei vielem Ansetzen und der Gefahr des Ausbrechens von Ecken oder Kanten muß ein kleinerer Spanquerschnitt genommen werden.

Beispiel für Kurzhobeln. Bei kurzen Hobellängen auf einem Schnellhobler wird die Gleichung 6 und 7 benutzt.

Bei Stg 52.81, einer Hobellänge von 200 mm und einem Spanquerschnitt von $3 \times 0{,}5$ wird aus Tabelle 10 $v = 41$ m/min. Dabei wird auf eine Hobellänge von 250 mm mit Überlauf

$$\text{Hubzahl } n = \frac{\text{Schnittgeschwindigkeit } v \cdot 1000}{3{,}14 \cdot \text{Hobellänge}} = \frac{41 \cdot 1000}{3{,}14 \cdot 250} = 52 \text{ Hübe/min.}$$

Beispiel für Stoßen. In eine Buchse aus Rg 10 mit der Länge von 100 mm soll eine Aussparung hinausgestoßen werden. Auf einen Span von etwa $1 + 0{,}5$ wird aus Tabelle 10 $v = 38$ m/min. Für 150 mm Gesamthub mit Überlauf wird dabei

$$n = \frac{v \cdot 1000}{3{,}14 \cdot L} = \frac{38 \cdot 1000}{3{,}14 \cdot 50} = 80 \text{ Hub/min.}$$

Es wird oft notwendig sein, zur besseren Verfolgung der Arbeit eine kleinere Hubzahl zu wählen, jedoch ist dann das Werkzeug nicht ausgenutzt.

14. Berücksichtigung der verschiedenen Schnellstahlqualitäten.

Es leuchtet ein, daß verschiedene Schnellstahlsorten verschiedene Qualitäten haben. Die eine Sorte wird besser halten, also höhere Schnittgeschwindigkeiten zulassen als die andere.

Die Tabelle 10 ist aufgebaut auf den Forschungsergebnissen aus Versuchen mit dem Schnellstahl *Böhler* Super Rapid Extra 214 (DRE 214). Es gibt Sorten, die nur $^3/_4$ so hohe Schnittgeschwindigkeiten vertragen, und solche, die bis zu $^6/_5$, also mehr vertragen. Es können wieder hier nur Werte für eine Sorte angegeben werden. Man muß bei der Arbeit feststellen, ob die angegebenen Werte erreicht werden können, dann stimmen alle Werte auch für die übrigen Werkstoffe, oder man stellt für einen bestimmten Spanquerschnitt einmal fest, wieviel die Schnittgeschwindigkeit darüber oder darunter liegt. Den Unterschied errechnet man sich als Faktor aus und nimmt dann alle Schnittgeschwindigkeitswerte mit diesem Faktor mal.

Für StC 10.61 und bei einem Spanquerschnitt 3×1 ist die Schnittgeschwindigkeit $v = 55$ m/min für den normalen Stahlanschliff. Es können aber nur 44 m/min genommen werden, weil sonst der Drehstahl sehr schnell abstumpft. Man teilt jetzt $44 : 55 = 0{,}8$. Der Faktor 0,8 muß jetzt mit allen anderen Schnittgeschwindigkeiten malgenommen werden.

Beispiel: Aus der Tabelle 10 ist $v = 30$ m/min, dann wird hier $v = 30 \cdot 0{,}8 = 24$ m/min. Mit $v = 24$ m/min ist die Umdrehungszahl auszurechnen.

15. Bestimmung der Schnittgeschwindigkeit für Hartmetall.

Für Hartmetall sucht man die Schnittgeschwindigkeiten auch aus der Tabelle 10 in der gleichen Art aus Werkstoff und Spanquerschnitt aus. Die Umrechnung in Umdrehungszahlen erfolgt nach Gleichung 9 oder nach der Tabelle 13.

Wichtig ist für das Arbeiten mit Hartmetall, daß unbedingt beim Stillsetzen der Maschine zuerst der Vorschub herausgenommen werden muß und dann erst die Maschine abgestellt werden darf. Es darf auch niemals der Drehstahl im Schnitt stehenbleiben und dann unter diesem Schnitt die Maschine wieder eingeschaltet werden. Hierbei bricht fast stets die Schneide aus.

16. Wie entstehen schlechte und unsaubere Oberflächen?

1. Der Spanwinkel ist ungeeignet.
2. Der Drehstahl steht nicht in richtiger Höhe.
3. Das Kühlmittel ist zu gering und kommt nicht mit kräftigem Strahl auf die Schnittstellen.
4. Das Werkstück ist nicht fest eingespannt und gibt nach.

5. Der Reitstock liegt mit der Körnerspitze nicht fest an, so daß das Werkstück nachgeben kann.

6. Der Reitstock liegt mit der Körnerspitze zu fest an, das Werkstück biegt sich durch. Bei längerem Schneiden findet durch Erwärmung eine Ausdehnung des Werkstückes statt, die durch Nachstellen des Reitstockes berücksichtigt werden muß.

7. Der Drehstahl ist nicht fest eingespannt.

8. Die Schnittgeschwindigkeit muß verändert werden, um die Resonanz auszuschalten.

9. Der Vorschub ist zu grob.

10. Die Bettführung ist nicht sauber, Späne klemmen sich unter den Schlitten und verändern so seine Lage beim Vorschieben.

Abschnitt 14.

Fräsen, Sägen.

1. Fräswerkzeuge.

Die verschiedenen Formen und Bezeichnungen von Fräsern sind als bekannt vorausgesetzt.

Abarten von Fräsern sind Messerköpfe mit festen und einstellbaren Messern, die zum Teil mit Schaft zum direkten Einspannen an den Frässpindelkopf ausgerüstet sind und ebenfalls genau rund laufen müssen. Auf satte Anlage des konischen Teiles ist die größte Sorgfalt zu legen.

Das Nachschleifen der Fräswerkzeuge kann nur auf Werkzeugschleifmaschinen erfolgen. Auch hier sind die Winkel am Fräser wichtig.

2. Welche Fräser verwendet man?

Sind bestimmte Nuten auszufräsen, so nimmt man Scheibenfräser oder Nutenfräser. Mehrere Scheibenfräser, nebeneinander durch genaue Zwischenringe in einem bestimmten Abstand gehalten, bilden einen Satz. Es können in diesen Satz auch Profilfräser eingefügt sein. Mit diesen Sätzen können Profile oder mehrere Operationen gleichzeitig gefräst werden.

Sägeblätter sind schmale Fräser und dienen zum Auftrennen oder zur Erzeugung schmaler Schlitze.

Zum Schruppen nimmt man Walzenfräser mit Spiralverzahnung oder besser Stirnfräser, weil mit diesen die höchste Schruppleistung erreicht wird.

3. Warum Spiralfräser?

Bei geradegezahnten Fräsern ist im ungünstigsten Fall nur ein Zahn im Schnitt. Tritt dieser aus dem Werkstück heraus, so findet eine plötzliche Entlastung statt. Der neu ansetzende Zahn bringt wieder eine plötzliche Belastung hervor. Durch das Spiel am Fräsdorn und der Maschine entstehen ruckartige Bewegungen, die eine erhöhte Beanspruchung des Fräsers bedeuten und seine Schnittgeschwindigkeit herabsetzen. Man muß deshalb solche Fräser wählen, wo mindestens zwei Zähne oder mehr immer gleichzeitig im Eingriff sind. Ein gerade verzahnter Fräser wird meistens rattern und unsaubere Oberflächen verursachen.

Die Überdeckung von mehreren Zähnen im Schnitt erreicht man nun leichter durch die Spiralverzahnung. Deshalb schneiden diese Fräser auch ruhiger und können einen größeren Vorschub erhalten. Die Oberfläche wird auch sauberer. Spiralsteigungen bis zu 40^0 sind günstig.

Sehr schmale Fräser kann man nicht mit zu hohem Drall ausführen. Der hohe Drall wirkt sich durch seitlichen Schub auf den Fräser aus. Nach Möglichkeit soll diese Kraft auf dem Frässpindelkopf hergerichtet sein, da die Spindelkopflagerung am besten Druckbeanspruchung aufnehmen kann.

4. Wie wirkt sich Fräserschlag aus?

Aus der Größe, der Form und der Güte des Fräsers ergibt sich die höchstmögliche Beanspruchung, damit auch die höchste Beanspruchung für den einzelnen Zahn. Es muß also erreicht werden, daß man jeden einzelnen Zahn gleichmäßig und hoch belasten kann. Sobald nun ein Fräser schlägt, stehen einige Zähne im Durchmesser mehr vor, d. h. bei der Spanabnahme heben diese Zähne mehr Werkstoff ab als die übrigen Zähne. Das bedeutet, daß der Vorschub so weit verringert werden muß, bis die vorstehenden Zähne gerade ihre Höchstspanleistung haben, die sie aushalten können. Die gesamte Fräszeit steigt aber, weil ein kleiner Vorschub notwendig wird gegenüber dem bei genau rundlaufendem Fräser. Es muß also stets Rundlauf der Fräserwerkzeuge zur Erzielung hoher Leistung angestrebt werden.

5. Wodurch entsteht Fräserschlag?

Der Fräserschlag kann durch eine oder mehrere Ursachen gleichzeitig entstehen.

1. Die Fräserzähne sind zur Bohrung nicht rundlaufend geschliffen.
2. Fräserbohrung paßt nicht zum Fräsdorn.
3. Fräsdorn läuft nicht rund und schlägt.
4. Fräsdorn läuft an sich rund, wird aber durch die nicht einwandfreien Zwischenringe verdrückt und schlägt in gespanntem Zustande.
5. Der Fräserkeil paßt nicht in Fräser oder Fräsdorn oder beiden. Fräser gibt ruckartig nach und erzeugt durch die plötzliche Belastungsschwankungen Schlag.

In den Fällen 1 und 2 sind andere Fräser zu nehmen. Fall 3, 4 und 5 sind durch die Behandlung der Hilfswerkzeuge durch den Arbeiter bedingt.

Man muß besonders auf den Dorn achten, daß er nicht durch Anfahren oder Fallenlassen verbogen wird. Meistens wird aber durch unsachgemäße Behandlung der Zwischenringe das Verziehen des Dornes bewirkt. Die Zwischenringe müssen genau parallele Stirnflächen haben. Befindet sich eine Kerbe oder ein Grat auf diesen Stirnflächen, so wird beim Zusammenspannen aller Ringe dieser Grat vorstehen und den Dorn zwangsläufig krumm drücken. Diese Zwischenringe müssen daher ganz sorgfältig aufbewahrt, abgenommen und nachgesehen werden. Erhöhungen sind durch Abfeilen oder Nachschleifen von Gratstellen jedesmal zu entfernen. Nur ein genau laufender Fräser kann Höchstleistungen erzielen und damit den Verdienst heben.

6. Was muß bei der Fräseraufspannung noch beachtet werden?

Die Drehrichtung ist normal immer nach Abb. 103a anzusetzen, nur auf besonderen Maschinen und auf Anweisung der Betriebsleitung nach Abb. 103b. Bei normalen Maschinen und Umlaufrichtung des Fräsers nach Abb. 103b klettert der Fräser auf das Werkstück, wenn der tote Gang in der Vorschubspindel nachgibt und geht zu Bruch. Oft wird auch das Werkstück dabei Ausschuß.

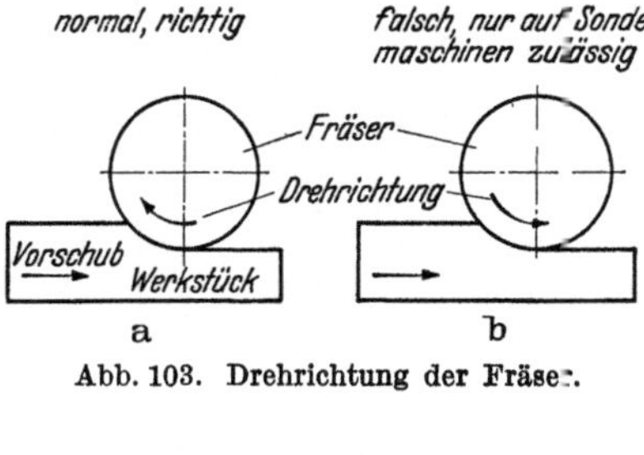

Abb. 103. Drehrichtung der Fräser.

Um ein erschütterungsfreies Laufen und geringe Durchbiegung des Dornes zu erhalten, spannt man die Fräser nicht wie in Abb. 104a mit den großen Abständen *a* und *b* zwischen Spindelkopf und Gegenhalter ein. Man schiebt den Gegen-

Tabelle 14. Fräserumdrehungszahle

m/min	500	600	150	200	60	80	40	60	20	40	20	26
	Leichtmetall				Rotmetall						Gu	
			Al-Mg-Mn					Ms 58···63				
	Elektron		Al-Mg-Si				Rg 4	Rg 8···10				Ge 18.91
	Al		Al-Cu-Mg		Cu		GBz 10	GBz 14	GBz 17		Ge 12.91	
Festigkeit					12	15	20	30	50	75	12	18
Lauf. Nr.	1	2	3	4	5	6	7	8	9	10	11	12
D	Schr.	Schl.	Schr.	Schl.	Schr.	Schl.	Schr.	Schl.	Schr.	Schl.	Schr.	Schl.
	Werkstoffgruppe für Vorschul											
D	*Fräserumdrehungszahle*											
4···6			8500	10500	3350	4200	2100	3350	1050	2100	1050	1500
6···9			5300	7500	2100	3000	1320	2100	750	1320	750	950
9···12	13200	17000	4200	6000	1700	2100	1050	1700	600	1050	600	750
12···15			3350	4200	1320	1700	850	1320	420	850	420	530
15···20	8500	9500	2350	3350	950	1320	670	950	335	670	335	420
20···25	6700	7500	1900	2650	750	1050	530	750	265	530	265	335
25···30	5300	6700	1700	2100	670	850	420	670	210	420	210	265
30···40	4200	4750	1180	1700	475	670	335	475	170	335	170	210
40···50	3350	4200	950	1320	375	530	265	375	132	265	132	170
50···65	2650	3000	750	1050	300	420	210	300	105	210	105	132
65···80	2100	2350	600	850	235	335	170	235	85	170	85	105
80···100	1700	1900	475	670	190	265	132	190	67	132	67	85
100···130	1320	1500	420	530	150	210	105	150	53	105	53	67
130···160	1050	1180	335	420	118	170	85	118	42	85	42	53
160···200	850	950	235	335	95	132	67	95	33,5	67	33,5	42
200···250	670	750	190	265	75	105	53	75	26,5	53	26,5	33,
250···300	530	670	170	210	67	85	42	67	21	42	21	26,
300···380	420	530	118	170	53	67	33,5	53	17	33,5	17	21
380···500	335	375	95	132	37,5	53	26,5	37,5	13,2	26,5	13,2	17
	Fräserumdrehungszahle											
130···160	3350	4200	600	850	235	335	190	265	170	190	132	190
160···200	2350	3350	475	670	190	235	150	210	132	150	105	150
200···250	1900	2650	375	530	150	190	118	170	105	118	85	118
250···300	1700	2100	335	420	132	170	95	132	85	95	75	95
300···380	1180	1700	265	335	105	118	75	105	67	75	60	75
380···500	950	1320	190	265	75	95	67	85	53	67	42	60
m/min	1500	2000	300	400	120	150	100	130	80	100	70	90

Schr. = Schruppen, Schl. = Schlichten.

für Schnellstahl und Hartmetall.

13	18	20	26	16	21	13	18	11,5	15	8	10	
eisen		Stahl und Stahlguß										
								SoSt 3	SoSt 4	SoSt 10(		
										NCT 3		
							EC 100 vgt	VMC 140 v		VCMo 240 v		
		Stg 38.81	Stg 45.81	Stg 52.81	Stg 60.81			EC 80				
					VCN 25	VCN 25 v		ECMo 80				
			EN15		ECN 35							
		St IV bis VII 23	St X 23		VCN 15	VCN 15 v		VCN 45	VCN 45 v			
			StC 25 61	StC 25.61 v	StC 45.61	StC 45.61 v			ECMo 100 v.			
Ge 30.91		StC 10.61	StC 16.61	StC 35.61	StC 35.61 v	StC 60.61		StC 60.61 v		VM 125 v		
22.91		St 00.11	St 37.11 St 42.11	St 50.11	St 60.11	St 70.11				VCMo 125 v		
25	30	30	40	50	60	70	80	90	100	110	120	kg/mm²
13	14	15	16	17	18	19	20	21	22	23	24	Lauf. Nr.
Schr.	Schl.	Schr.	Schl.	Schr.	Schl.	Schr.	Schl.	Schr.	Schl.	Schr.	Schl.	*D*
bestimmung I							*II*			*III*		
für Schnellstahl												*D*
750	950	1050	1500	850	1180	750	950	600	850	420	530	4···6
475	670	750	950	600	750	475	670	420	530	300	335	6···9
375	475	600	750	420	600	375	475	300	420	210	265	9···12
265	375	420	530	335	420	265	375	235	335	170	210	12···15
210	300	335	420	265	335	210	300	190	235	132	170	15···20
170	235	265	335	210	265	170	235	150	190	105	132	20···25
132	190	210	265	170	210	132	190	118	170	85	105	25···30
105	150	170	210	132	170	105	150	95	118	67	85	30···40
85	118	132	170	105	132	85	118	75	95	53	67	40···50
67	95	105	132	85	105	67	95	60	75	42	47,5	50···65
53	75	85	105	67	85	53	75	47,5	60	33,5	42	65···80
42	60	67	85	53	67	42	60	37,5	47,5	26,5	33,5	80···100
33,5	47,5	53	67	42	53	33,5	47,5	30	42	21	26,5	100···130
26,5	37,5	42	53	33,5	42	26,5	37,5	23,5	33,5	17	19	130···160
21	30	33,5	42	26,5	33,5	21	30	19	23,5	13,2	15	160···200
17	23,5	26,5	33,5	21	26,5	17	23,5	15	19	10,5	11,8	200···250
13,2	19	21	26,5	17	21	13,2	19	11,8	17	8,5	9,5	250···300
10,5	15	17	21	13,2	17	10,5	15	9,5	11,8	6,7	7,5	300···380
8,5	11,8	13,2	17	10,5	13,2	8,5	11,8	7,5	9,5	5,3	6,7	380···500
für Hartmetall												
105	118	118	170	105	118	85	105	53	67	42	53	130···160
85	95	95	132	85	95	67	85	42	53	33,5	42	160···200
67	75	75	105	67	75	53	67	33,5	42	26,5	33,5	200···250
53	67	67	85	53	67	42	53	26,5	33,5	21	26,5	250···300
42	53	53	67	42	53	33,5	42	21	26,5	17	21	300···380
33,5	37,5	37,5	53	33,5	37,5	26,5	33,5	17	21	13,2	17	380···500
50	60	60	80	50	60	40	50	26	33	20	23	

halter dicht heran (Abb. 104b) mit der kürzeren Entfernung *c* zum Fräser oder noch besser wie in Abb. 104c, man schiebt das Werkstück dicht an den Spindelkopf und lagert den Fräser mit den kurzen Abständen *d* und *e*. Hierdurch wird der ruhigste Lauf der Maschine erreicht.

a

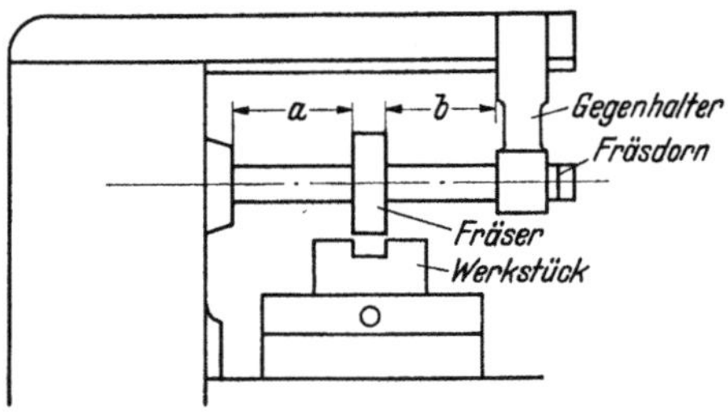

a) Schlechte Einspannung. Abstände des Fräsers von den Lagern zu groß.

b

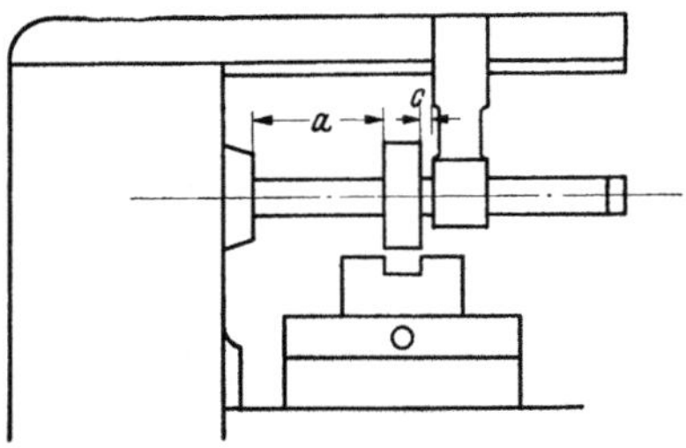

b) Bessere Lagerung.

c

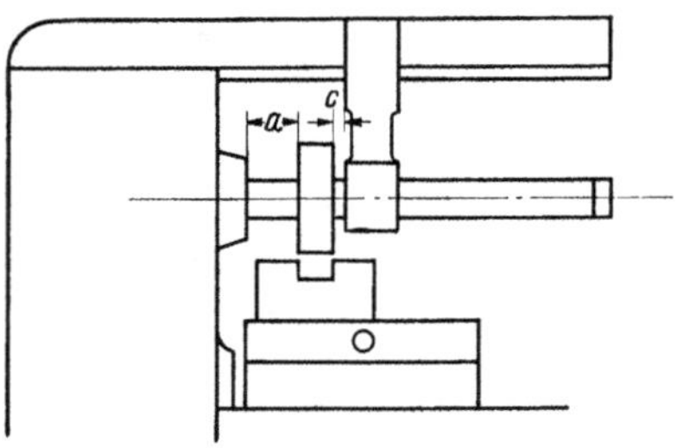

c) Richtige Aufspannung. Fräser dicht an Lagerstellen, keine Erschütterungen.

Abb. 104. Richtige Fräseraufspannung.

Für Fräser mit Hartmetallplättchen gilt schonendste Behandlung wegen der Sprödigkeit. Sie dürfen nicht angestoßen werden.

Eine Abnutzung oder beginnende Abstumpfung erkennt man an der unsauberen Oberfläche und blanken Stellen am Werkzeug. Es muß sofort ein neues Werkzeug eingespannt werden und das abgenutzte nachgeschliffen werden, sonst muß Bruch eintreten.

7. Ermittlung der Umdrehungszahl des Fräsers.

Die Umdrehungszahlen der Fräser sind aus den zulässigen Schnittgeschwindigkeiten für mittleren Schnellstahl errechnet. Sie gelten für kräftige und gut gespannte Werkstücke und werden aus Tabelle 14 entnommen. Zuerst stellt man aus der Zeichnung, der Stückliste oder der Arbeitsbegleitkarte den Werkstoff fest und sucht diesen im Kopf der Tabelle 14, z. B. steht VCN 45 in Spalte 21/22. Steht auf der Begleitkarte VCN 45v, ist der Werkstoff bereits vergütet und seine Lage ist in Spalte 22/23. Meist findet eine Vergütung erst nach der Bearbeitung statt. Es könnte auch möglich sein, daß während der Bearbeitung in einem Arbeitsgang vor dem Fräsen das Vergüten eingeschaltet ist. Dann steht auf der Begleitkarte nur VCN, die Vergütung liegt aber vor dem Fräsen, und für das Fräsen ist der vergütete Werkstoff einzusetzen. Mit dem Fräsdurchmesser D von z. B. 55 mm ⌀ findet man dann in Spalte 21/22 als Umdrehungszahl $n = 60$ U/min für Schruppen und 75 U/min für Schlichten. Diese Umdrehungszahlen stellt man an der Maschine ein.

8. Ermittlung des Vorschubes.

Bei der Bestimmung der Fräserdrehzahl wird gleichzeitig festgestellt, ob der Werkstoff zur Gruppe I, II oder III gehört. Aus den erfahrungsgemäß zulässigen Vorschüben je Zahn ist für die verschiedenen Zähnezahlen an Fräsern der Vorschub je Umdrehung in der Fräsvorschubtabelle 15 ausgerechnet. Diese Zahl ist der Faktor k, der mit der Fräserdrehzahl malgenommen den Vorschub/min ergibt.

Es ist also $$s = k \cdot n \qquad \text{(Gl. 9)}$$

Beispiel: 10 Zähne, Walzenfräser, schruppen, Werkstoffgruppe II, $n = 60$ U/min, ergibt $k = 1{,}8$. Vorschub ist dann

$$k \cdot n = 1{,}8 \cdot 60 = 108 \text{ mm/min.} \qquad \text{(Gl. 12)}$$

Als Schnittiefen dürfen für die Fräsvorschubtabelle 15 bis zu folgenden vorhanden sein:

bei Walzen und Walzenstirnfräsern	Frästiefe	3 mm,
„ Scheibenfräsern	„	gleich Scheibenbreite,
„ Schaftfräsern	„	gleich Fräserdurchmesser,
„ Messerköpfen	„	gleich 3···5 mm.

Bei größeren Schnittiefen muß der Vorschub vermindert werden.

Es ist durchaus möglich, in besonderen Fällen einen höheren Vorschub zu wählen bei Verringerung der Fräserdrehzahlen.

Die Schnittiefe hat auf die Standzeit, also auf die Fräserdrehzahl, geringen Einfluß. Sie hängt nur davon ab, ob die Maschine diese Leistung hergibt. Beim Schruppen nimmt man kleinere Fräserdrehzahlen und höhere Vorschübe, um schnell vielen Werkstoff abzuheben; beim Schlichten kleine Vorschübe und dafür höhere Fräserdrehzahlen, um saubere Oberflächen zu erzielen.

9. Wie lange dauert die Fräszeit?

Die Fräszeit ist leicht auszurechnen, da der Vorschub in m/min angegeben ist. Für den Anlauf des Fräsens rechnet man etwa $^1/_4$ Fräser-

Tabelle 15. Fräsvorschubtafel.

Zähnezahl Z	Werkstoffgruppe	Walzenfräser Walzenstirnfräser		Messerköpfe mit		Scheibenfräser / Schaftfräser Hinterdrehte Fräser	
		Schrupp	Schlicht	Schnellstahl	Hartmetall	Schrupp	Schlicht
s_z	I	0,2	0,05	0,3	0,1	0,07	0,04
	II	0,15	0,04	0,2	0,08	0,06	0,03
	III	0,1	0,02	0,1	0,05	0,04	0,02
4	I	0,8	0,2	1,2	0,4	0,28	0,16
	II	0,6	0,16	0,8	0,32	0,24	0,12
	III	0,4	0,08	0,4	0,2	0,16	0,08
5	I	1	0,25	1,5	0,5	0,35	0,2
	II	0,75	0,2	1	0,4	0,3	0,15
	III	0,5	0,1	0,5	0,25	0,2	0,1
6	I	1,2	0,3	1,8	0,6	0,42	0,24
	II	0,9	0,24	1,2	0,48	0,36	0,18
	III	0,6	0,12	0,6	0,3	0,24	0,12
8	I	1,6	0,4	2,4	0,8	0,56	0,32
	II	1,2	0,32	1,6	0,64	0,48	0,24
	III	0,8	0,16	0,8	0,4	0,32	0,16
10	I	2	0,5	3	1	0,7	0,4
	II	1,5	0,4	2	0,8	0,6	0,3
	III	1	0,2	1	0,5	0,4	0,2
12	I	2,4	0,6	3,6	1,2	0,84	0,5
	II	1,8	0,48	2,4	0,96	0,72	0,36
	III	1,2	0,24	1,2	0,6	0,5	0,24
14	I	2,8	0,7	4,2	1,4	0,98	0,56
	II	2,1	0,56	2,8	1,1	0,84	0,42
	III	1,4	0,28	1,4	0,7	0,56	0,28
16	I	3,2	0,8	4,8	1,6	1,12	0,64
	II	2,4	0,64	3,2	1,3	0,96	0,48
	III	1,6	0,32	1,6	0,8	0,64	0,32
18	I	3,6	0,9	5,4	1,8	1,26	0,7
	II	2,7	0,72	3,6	1,4	1,08	0,54
	III	1,8	0,36	1,8	0,9	0,7	0,4
20	I	4	1	6	2	1,4	0,8
	II	3	0,8	4	0,6	1,2	0,6
	III	2	0,4	2	1	0,8	0,4
24	I	4,8	1,2	7,2	2,4	1,68	0,95
	II	3,6	0,96	4,8	1,9	1,44	0,72
	III	2,4	0,48	2,4	1,2	0,95	0,5
30	I	6	1,5	9	3	2,1	1,2
	II	4,5	1,2	6	2,4	1,8	0,9
	III	3	0,6	3	1,5	1,2	0,6
40	I	8	2	12	4	2,8	1,6
	II	6	1,6	8	3,2	2,4	1,2
	III	4	0,8	4	2	1,6	0,8
50	I	10	2,5	15	5	3,5	2
	II	7,5	2	10	4	3	1,5
	III	5	1	5	2,5	2	1

Werkstoffgruppen I: Ge, Te, Rotmetall, Leichtmetall, St bis 60 kg/mm² Festigkeit.
II: St bis 85 kg/mm², III: St bis 110 kg/mm²

durchmesser (Abb. 105) hinzu und hat damit als gesamte Fräslänge $L + D/4$. Diese Länge wird durch den Vorschub geteilt und die Laufzeit in min errechnet wie in dem Beispiel 1 und 3.

Bei Messerköpfen ist die Länge des Überlaufes „U" (Abb. 106) vom Durchmesser des Messerkopfes und der Breite des Werkstückes abhängig. Jedenfalls wird die Fräslänge immer größer als die direkte Werkstücklänge.

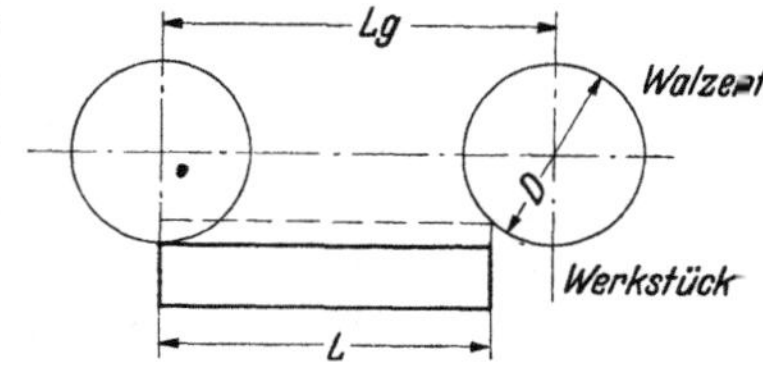

Abb. 105 Laufweg eines Walzenfräsers mit Anlaufweg.

1. Beispiel: Walzenfräser 120 mm ⌀, 10 Zähne zum Fräsen des Werkstoffes St 50.11. Schruppen mit 3 mm Frästiefe und 100 mm lang, Werkstoffgruppe I.

Tab. 14 $n = 48$ U/min der Frässpindel,
Tab. 15 $k = 2$
somit $s = 2 \cdot 48 = 96$ mm/min Vorschub des Frästisches,
Fräslänge $= 100$ mm $+ 120/4 = 130$ mm,
Fräszeit $T = 130 : 96 = 1{,}35$ min.

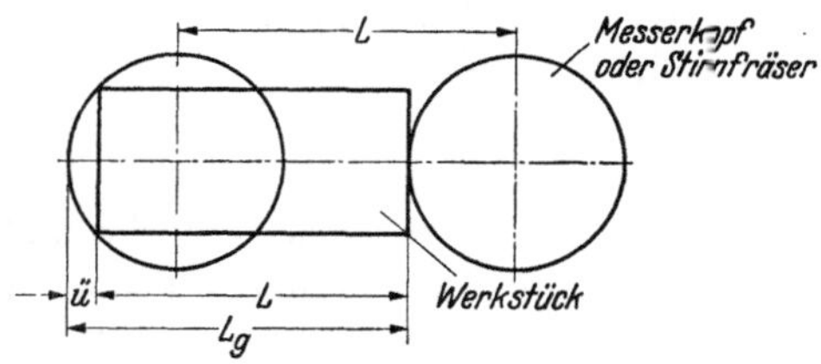

Abb. 106. Laufweg eines Messerkopfes.

2. Beispiel: Messerkopf mit Schnellstahlmessern 210 mm ⌀, 18 Zähne zum Fräsen des Werkstoffes VCN 45, Werkstoffgruppe III, schruppen mit 3 mm Frästiefe auf 370 mm Länge bei einer Werkstückbreite von 150 mm.

Aus Tab. 14 $n = 46$ U/min der Frässpindel,
„ „ 15 $k = 0{,}9$,
somit $s = 0{,}9 \cdot 46 = 41$ m/min Vorschub des Frästisches.
Fräszeit T etwa $410 : 41 = 10$ min.

3. Beispiel: Scheibenfräser 190 mm ⌀, Breite 15 mm, 12 Zähne zum Fräsen des Werkstoffes „Silumin", Werkstoffgruppe I; schruppen von 15 mm Frästiefe auf 250 mm Länge.

Aus Tab. 14 $n = 500$ U/min der Frässpindel,
„ „ 15 $k = 2{,}4$,
somit $s = 2{,}4 \cdot 500 = 1200$ mm/min Vorschub des Frästisches.

Dieser Vorschub kann aber nur genommen werden, wenn auch die Spindeldrehzahl vorhanden ist, sonst muß mit der geringeren Drehzahl über denselben Faktor 2,4 gerechnet werden.

Fräslänge $= 250 + 190/4 =$ rund 300 mm
Fräszeit $T = 300 : 1200 = 0{,}25$ min $= 15$ s.

10. Allgemeine Fräsregeln.

1. Der Fräser muß rundlaufen.

2. Kleiner Fräser — dicker Fräsdorn.

3. Fräser mit Spiralzähnen schneiden ruhiger und gleichförmiger.

4. Lieber zwei Schruppschnitte als wegen zu großer Schnittiefe den Vorschub herabsetzen. Nach dem Schruppen noch ein Schlichtschnitt.

5. Fräsen mit einem Schnitt: Vorschubgeschwindigkeit und Fräserdrehzahl wie schlichten.

6. Fräserbefestigung: Den Fräser so dicht wie möglich an den Spindelkopf heran; den Schaftfräser so kurz wie möglich spannen; das Fräsdornlager auf beiden Seiten so dicht wie möglich an den Fräser heran.

7. Werkstückbefestigung: Werkstück haltbar spannen und nicht verspannen. Schlecht spannbare Werkstücke mit kleinem Vorschub fräsen.

8. Fräserauswahl und -pflege: Achte auf die Winkel am Fräser und erhalte sie; du fräst sonst schlecht und falsch!

9. Gut und reichlich spülen schont das Werkzeug und gibt saubere Arbeit. Späne niemals mit Preßluft wegblasen.

10. Beim Fräsen über eine Gußhaut schneidet man erst vorsichtig an, am besten mit kleiner Schnittgeschwindigkeit und nach dem Durchbrechen der Haut mit voller Schnittgeschwindigkeit weiter.

11. Wie entstehen fehlerhafte Oberflächen?

Folgende Ursachen können vorliegen:

1. Fräser schlägt rund und seitlich, Aussparungen werden zu weit, die Oberfläche erhält Riefen.

2. Dorn schlägt, Fräser schneidet nur mit einigen Zähnen, Oberfläche wird wellig.

3. Kühlwasser ist zu wenig, Fräser ist abgestumpft und schneidet geringeres Maß aus. Kühlwasserpumpe reinigen und Fräser wechseln.

4. Werkstücke sind gegen Längsverschiebung nicht genügend gesichert und festgespannt.

5. Bei starkem Fräserdrall treten seitliche Kräfte auf, die durch entsprechendes Festspannen des Werkstückes aufgefangen werden müssen.

6. Die Fräserdrehrichtung zum Vorschub ist falsch, Fräser springt und erzeugt ungleiche Oberflächen.

7. Fräser hat im Keil oder dieser gleichzeitig im Dorn Luft und dreht sich ruckartig. Gefahr des Werkzeugbruches und schlechte Arbeit.

8. Die Gegenlager für den Dorn sind zu weit auseinander, der Fräsdorn federt und die entsprechenden Schwingungen übertragen sich als Rattermarken auf das Werkstück.

9. Die Vorschubspindeln für den Frästisch haben zuviel Luft und müssen nachgestellt werden.

12. Sägen.

Das Sägen kann erfolgen mit Bügelsägen, Kaltkreissägen und Metallbandsägen.

a) Bügelsägen. Für kurze Trennzeiten und lange Lebensdauer, hohen Bügeldruck und niedrige Schnittgeschwindigkeiten anwenden. Die Zahnteilung richtet sich nach Werkstoff und Werkstück und soll nach Tabelle 16 gewählt werden. Es müssen möglichst mehrere Zähne gleichzeitig auf einer Schnittstelle in Eingriff sein, daher müssen sehr feine Teilungen bei dünnwandigen Rohren, Drähten usw. benutzt werden.

Tabelle 16. Günstige Zahnteilung für Bügelsägeblätter.

Zahnteilung	Werkstoff	Werkstück
grob	hart	größer
fein	weich	kleiner
sehr fein		dünnwandiger Schnitt

Es treten auch große Qualitätsunterschiede der Sägeblätter auf, die entsprechend die Schnittgeschwindigkeiten vermindern. Die Schnittgeschwindigkeiten selbst können aus der Tabelle 10 „Schnittgeschwindigkeiten für Drehen“ folgendermaßen entnommen werden:

Zum Werkstoff sucht man sich am Kopf der Tabelle 10 die zugehörige Spalte, z. B. St 50.11 in Spalte 17 oder 18. Zulässig ist jetzt die Schnittgeschwindigkeit, wie sie für den Spanquerschnitt 12×1 empfohlen ist, also hier $V = 25\ mm/min$. Die Drehzahl muß dann, wie für das Hobeln, mit hin- und hergehender Bewegung ermittelt werden. Meistens wird jedoch ein kurzer Versuch am Werkstück erst die richtige Drehzahl ergeben.

b) Kaltkreissägen. Kaltkreissägen kann man wie dünne Scheibenfräser ansehen, mit sehr geringer Starrheit. Die zulässigen Schnittgeschwindigkeiten sind entsprechend dem Durchmesser auf Umdrehungszahlen in Tabelle 14 umgerechnet und können dort abgenommen werden.

Der Vorschub wird wie für Fräser Abschnitt 14 berechnet, und zwar aus Tabelle 15 nach der Spalte Scheibenfräser Schruppen. Bei 500 mm ⌀ und St 50.11 wird $n = 10{,}5$ U/min, und der Vorschub $s = 3 \cdot n = 60$ mm/min. Bei sehr guten Sägeblattqualitäten kann man bis zu doppelter Drehzahl gehen, muß aber dann den Vorschub etwas kleiner wählen.

Bei Verwendung von Werkzeugstahl-Sägeblättern sind nur die halben Schnittgeschwindigkeitswerte, aber gleichen Vorschübe anzuwenden. Es gibt auch Sägen mit eingesetzten Hartmetallzähnen, die bei kleineren Vorschüben bis zu 100% höhere Schnittgeschwindigkeiten zulassen. Ihre Drehzahl ist gleichfalls auf Tabelle 14 enthalten.

c) **Metallbandsägen.** Zuerst wurden nur weichere Werkstoffe bearbeitet, jetzt auch Stahl. Je härter der Werkstoff ist, desto schwieriger wird die Erzeugung von sauberen und genauen Schnitten. Die Schnittgeschwindigkeit bzw. die Drehzahl der Metallbandführungsrolle kann direkt nach Tabelle 14 eingestellt werden. Hat die Rolle 500 mm ⌀, so muß entsprechend dem Werkstoff die Drehzahl abgelesen und eingestellt werden.

Abschnitt 15.

Bohren, Reiben, Ansenken und Ausstechen.

Wenn eine Bohrung gerieben werden muß, ist stets vorher das Bohren und Aufbohren oder Aufsenken des Loches auf Reibmaß nötig, meist kommt dazu noch das Ansenken der Nabe. Diese drei Arbeitsverfahren müssen also gemeinsam betrachtet werden. Als Werkzeuge gehören zu den Gruppen:

A. *Bohrwerkzeuge*: Spiralbohrer, Spitzbohrer, Kanonenbohrer, Spiralsenker zum Aufbohren, Aufstecksenker zum Aufbohren.

B. *Reibwerkzeuge*: Feste und verstellbare Reibahlen, Aufsteckreibahlen.

C. *Ansenkwerkzeuge*: Zapfensenker, Aufstecksenker zum Anflächen, Messerstangen mit Senkmessern, Formsenker.

D. *Ausstechwerkzeuge*: Besondere Werkzeuge.

1. Bohrwerkzeuge.

Die Hauptbohrwerkzeuge, Spitzbohrer, Spiralbohrer, Kanonenbohrer, Spiralsenker und Aufstecksenker sind bekannt. Spitzbohrer werden seltener gebraucht, da sie ungünstigere Schnittverhältnisse haben als Spiralbohrer.

2. Spiralbohrer.

Am Spiralbohrer unterscheidet man (Abb. 107) die Hauptschneiden oder Lippen, die Querschneiden, die Fasenschneiden und den Drallwinkel δ für die Steigung der Spiralen. Der richtige Anschliff des Bohrers ist die Hauptsache, da sonst sofort Bruch eintritt. Folgendes ist zu beachten bzw. zu prüfen:

Die Lage der Querschneide (Abb. 107a) muß etwa 55° betragen, sonst ist der Bohrer falsch hinterschliffen. Der Spitzenwinkel muß gleichmäßig zur Achse nach rechts und links verteilt sein und soll für fast alle Werkstoffe 116···120° betragen. Die Spitze muß auch in der Mitte der Bohrerachse liegen. Abb. 108a···h zeigt verschiedene Fehlermöglichkeiten. Sehr wichtig ist das Freischleifen der Bohrerfreiflächen.

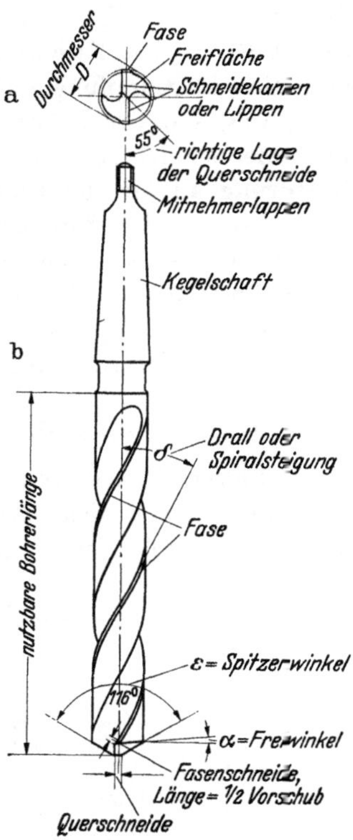

Abb. 107. Winkel am Spiralbohrer.

Beim Bohren dringen die Lippen stetig durch den Vorschub vorwärts. Wenn daher die Freiflächen des Bohrers gerade geschliffen wären, würden die hinter den Lippen nacheilenden Teile auf die Grundfläche des Loches drücken, zu Erwärmung und zu Bruch führen. Aus der Lage der Querschneide erkennt man, ob ein richtiger Freischliff vorliegt. Das Nachschleifen von Hand ist schwer, weil zu der Drehbewegung beim Schleifen noch zusätzlich eine Schwenkbewegung für den Hinterschliff ausgeführt werden muß. Es ist besser, das Nachschleifen auf Werkzeugschleifmaschinen vorzunehmen.

Die Bohrer haben an der Spitze das Nennmaß, das aufgeschlagen ist. Zum Einspannende hin verjüngt sich der Bohrer um ein geringes, damit die oberen Teile im Durchmesser nicht klemmen. Sehr kurz geschliffene Bohrer werden also beim richtigen Anschleifen kleiner als das Nennmaß bohren. Die Seelenstärke nimmt dagegen zum Einspannende etwas zu zwecks Verstärkung des Bohrers. Dadurch nimmt auch die Querschneidenbreite zu. Die ungünstigsten Schnittverhältnisse hat ohne Zweifel die Querschneide mit ihrem stumpfen Spanwinkel. Hier findet leicht eine Abstumpfung statt durch Verdrücken der Spitzen. Die größte Umfangsgeschwindigkeit und damit Schnittgeschwindigkeit, vgl. Abschnitt 10, hat die Fasenschneide am größten Durchmesser. Auch hier kann eine Abstumpfung stattfinden. Bei den ersten Anzeichen der Abstumpfung muß der Bohrer ausgewechselt oder nachgeschliffen werden, da immer so viel vom Bohrer fortgeschliffen werden muß, so weit die Zerstörung an der Querscheide oder den Fasenschneiden reicht. Sind die Ecken an der Fasenschneide nicht mehr maßhaltig, drückt der Bohrer mit seinen nachfolgenden Partien und führt zu Bruch. Bei Bohrer über 30 mm ⌀ kann ein richtiges Ausspitzen an der Querschneide gute Leistungssteigerungen bringen. Reichliche Kühlung ist bei allen Bohrarbeiten Vorbedingung für jede Leistung (vgl. Tab. 11).

3. Wie wirken sich Anschliffflächen des Bohrers aus?

1. Spitzenwinkel zu spitz (Abb. 108d). Die Schneidkanten der Hauptschneide sind von oben gesehen gekrümmt, die Lochwand wird rauh, der Bohrer rasch stumpf und bricht leicht.

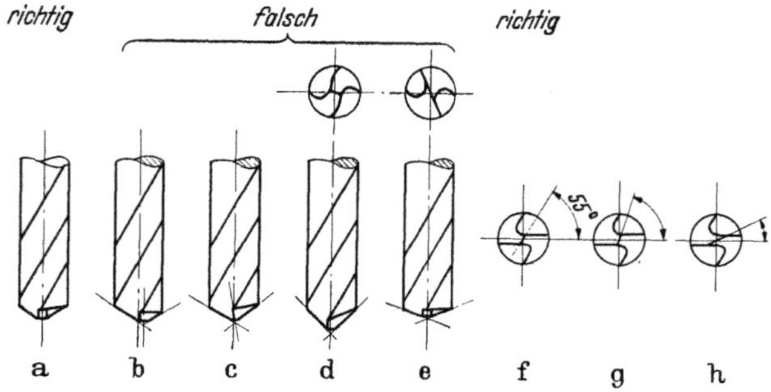

Abb. 108. Fehlermöglichkeiten am Spiralbohrer durch falschen Anschliff.

2. Spitzenwinkel zu stumpf (Abb. 108e). Die Schneidkanten sind wieder gekrümmt. Bohrer hakt leicht, Schneiden nützen sich rasch ab, Lochwand wird rauh, beim Austritt aus dem Werkstück erfolgt leicht Bruch.

3. Bohrerschneiden ungleich lang (Abb. 108b). Die Spitze liegt nicht in der Achse des Bohrers, die längere Schneide hebt größere Späne ab und wird einseitig beansprucht, Lochdurchmesser wird größer.

4. Bohrerschneiden mit ungleichen Winkeln zur Achse (Abb. 108c). Nur eine Schneidkante arbeitet, einseitige Beanspruchung, Loch wird ungenau.

5. Bohrerschneiden ungleich lang und ungleiche Winkel (Abb. 108f). Beide Fehler zusammen treten meist beim Schleifen von Hand auf. Einseitige Beanspruchung, Lochdurchmesser wird größer.

6. Zu kleiner Hinterschliff (Abb. 108g). Bohrerfreiflächen drücken auf Lochgrund. Der Bohrer kann nicht tiefer eindringen. Der Bohrdruck nimmt zu, starke Erwärmung kommt durch Reibung auf den Lochgrund dazu, dadurch bricht der Bohrer ab.

7. Zu großer Hinterschliff (Abb. 108h). Die Hauptschneiden sind zu wenig unterstützt. Nur geringere Drehzahlen zulässig, Bohrer hakt und bricht an der Schneide leicht aus. Aus der Lage der Querschneide erkennt man leicht den richtigen Hinterschliff.

8. Ausspitzen der Bohrer (Abb. 108). Nur bei richtigem Ausspitzen vorteilhaft. Sonst sind die Nachteile so bedeutend, daß eine wesentliche Herabsetzung der Leistung erfolgt und lieber nicht ausgespitzt werden soll.

4. Spitzbohrer.

Der Spitzbohrer ist das älteste Werkzeug. Auch hier gibt die Lage der Querschneide an, ob ein richtiger Hinterschliff vorliegt. Seine Leistung ist meist geringer als die der Spiralbohrer. Es müssen kleine Vorschübe unter 0,1 mm gewählt werden. Beim Ausbohren größerer Bohrungen auf Drehbänken mit Vollmessern wird das Prinzip der Spitzbohrer verwendet. Beginnende Abstumpfung ist am unruhigen Lauf der Maschine und starken Wärmeanstieg des Werkstückes erkennbar. Sofort auswechseln, da sonst unweigerlich Werkzeugbruch eintritt. Reichliche Kühlung ist Bedingung.

5. Kanonenbohrer.

Sie dienen zum Ausbohren langer Bohrungen und stehen still, während das Werkstück umläuft. Wichtig ist das richtige Freischleifen, da sonst durch Drücken Bruch erfolgt. Reichliche Kühlung ist zum Fortführen der Bohrspäne Bedingung.

6. Spiralsenker zum Aufsenken.

Spiralsenker sollen eine vorhandene Bohrung erweitern, meist bis auf Reibzugabe. Entsprechend haben sie keine Querschneide. Es kommen Dreilippen- und Mehrlippensenker vor. Die Abstumpfung erfolgt an der Phasenschneide, für die dasselbe wie bei Spiralbohrern gilt.

7. Aufstecksenker zum Aufsenken..

Diese haben dieselben Aufgaben wie Spiralsenker. Sie werden nicht direkt in der Maschine eingespannt, sondern durch eine Bohrstange aufgenommen. Beide müssen gut zueinander passen, um einwandfreie Arbeit zu erreichen.

8. Wie wird die Drehzahl und der Vorschub festgestellt?

Beides läßt sich direkt aus Tabelle 17 ablesen. Für Spiralbohrer, Spiralsenker, Kanonenbohrer (hierbei ist die Umdrehungszahl am Werkstück einzustellen) liest man zum Bohrerdurchmesser in der Spalte für den Werkstoff, der am Kopf der Tabelle 17 steht, Drehzahl und Vorschub ab.

Beispiel: Werkstoff ECN 35,
Lochdurchmesser 55 mm ⌀.

Der Werkstoff steht in Spalte 18/19. Man versucht zunächst

$n = 118$ U/min mit
$s = 0{,}45$ mm/U Vorschub.

Ist der Werkstoff jedoch härter, am Schnitt und schneller Abstumpfung erkennbar, muß nach Spalte 19 gewählt werden

$n = 95$ U/min mit
$s = 0{,}4$ mm/U.

Für Spitzbohrer und Aufstecksenker zum Aufsenken nimmt man etwa die Hälfte für die Drehzahl, wie sie Tabelle 21 angibt.

9. Wie groß ist die Laufzeit?

Aus der Bohrtiefe, der Drehzahl und dem Vorschub ergibt sich die Laufzeit T zu

$$\text{Laufzeit } T = \frac{\text{Bohrungslänge } L}{\text{Drehzahl } n \cdot \text{Vorschub } s} \qquad \text{(Gl. 13)}$$

oder

$$T = \frac{L}{n \cdot s}\,. \qquad \text{(Gl. 8)}$$

Beispiel: Bei einer Bohrlänge von 90 mm,
dem Bohrdurchmesser von 55 mm,
der Drehzahl n $= 118$ U/min,
aus dem Vorschub $s = 0{,}45$ mm/U

wird

$$T = \frac{90}{118 \cdot 0{,}45} = 1{,}7 \text{ min.}$$

10. Was ist beim Bohren wichtig?

Das Werkstück muß gut und fest gespannt sein (siehe Abschnitt 9). Wenn es federt, hakt der Bohrer beim Durchkommen ein und bricht. Wird das Werkstück nur von Hand gehalten, ist der Augenblick des Durchkommens des Bohrers am gefährlichsten. Es kann jetzt herumgerissen werden und zu Verletzungen führen. Zumindest muß gegen Herumreißen ein Anschlag auf dem Bohrtisch angebracht werden.

Beim Bohren in Vorrichtungen muß jedesmal die Anlage des Werkstückes frei von Spänen und sauber sein, sonst sitzen die Bohrungen an falschen Stellen oder in falschen Richtungen. Die Werkzeuge müssen leicht in den gehärteten Bohrbuchsen geführt sein. Bei Zwang und Erwärmung der Bohrer findet eine Abnutzung der Phase statt. Der Bohrdurchmesser wird hier kleiner und wenn der Nachschliff bis zu dieser Stelle kommt, drückt der Bohrer. Er wird bald zu Bruch gehen, ebenso durch Zwang in Bohrbuchsen. Gut Schmieren ist Bedingung, jedoch bei Elektron nicht mit Wasser! Eine beginnende Abstumpfung läßt sich bei Vorhandensein am Leistungsanzeiger beobachten. Steigt der Druck und damit die Leistung gegenüber dem frischen Bohrer um 30 %, muß der Bohrer nachgeschliffen werden. Ebenso beim Knirschen sofort Vorschub ausschalten und Bohrer wechseln. Ist selbsttätiger Vorschub vorhanden, wird dieser auch benutzt, weil damit eine höhere Leistung erreichbar ist als bei Handvorschub. Besonders beim Austritt aus schrägen Flächen (Abb. 109) ist Handvorschub sehr gefährlich. Hier nur mit selbsttätigem Vorschub arbeiten, desgleichen bei porösen Stellen oder Lunkern im Werkstoff.

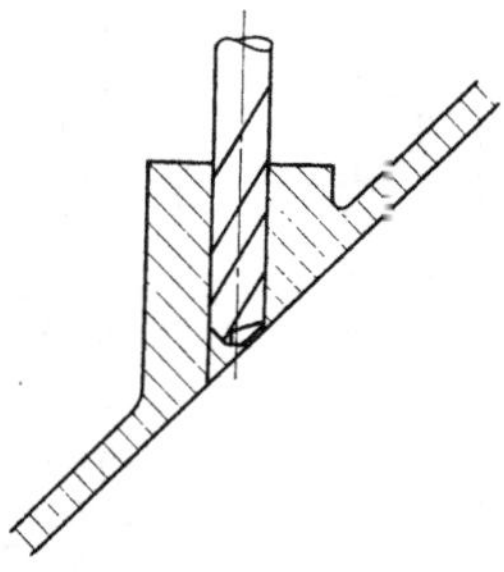

Abb. 109. Bohreraustritt an schrägen Flächen.

Bei allen Bohrwerkzeugen kommt es darauf an, daß sie genau in Richtung der Arbeitsrichtung, also Spindelrichtung sitzen und nicht

Tabelle 17. Umdrehungszahlen und Vorschüb

	Leichtmetall				Rotmetall						Gu	
			Al-Mg-Mn					Ms 58···63				
	Elektron		Al-Mg-Si				Rg 4	Rg 8···10				Ge 18.91
	Al		Al-Cu-Mg		Cu		GBz 10	GBz 14	GBz 17		Ge 12.91	
Festigkeit					12	15	20	30	50	75	12	18
Lfd. Nr.	1	2	3	4	5	6	7	8	9	10	11	12
D	*n*	*s*	*n*	*s*	*n*	*s*	*n*	*s*	*n*	*s*	*n*	*s*
1	42000	0,1	23500	0,1	15000	0,06	15000	0,04	10500	0,02	6000	0,0
2	23500		11800		7500		7500		6000		3000	
3	15000		8500		7500	0,08	6000	0,05	3750	0,04	2350	0,0
4	11800	0,15	6700	0,15	6000		4250		2650		1900	
5	9500		5300		6000	0,1	3350	0,08	2100	0,06	1500	0,1
6	7500		4200		5300		2650		1900		1320	0,1
7	6700		3750		4750	0,12	2350	0,1	1700	0,08	1180	0,1
8	6000		3350		4200	0,15	2100		1320		1050	
9	5300		2650		3750		1900	0,12	1180	0,1	950	0,2
10	4750	0,25	2650	0,25	3350	0,2	1700	0,15	1050		850	
11	4200		2350		3000		1500		950		750	0,2
12	3750		2100		2650	0,25	1320		850	0,12	670	
13	3750		1900		2350		1180	0,18	850		600	0,3
14	3350		1700		2350		1050		750		600	
15	3000		1700		2100	0,3	1050	0,2	750	0,15	530	
16	3000		1500		1900		950		670		475	0,4
18	2650		1320		1700	0,4	850	0,25	600	0,2	420	0,5
20	2350	0,4	1320	0,4	1500	0,5	750	0,3	530	0,3	375	
22	2100		1180		1320		750		475		335	0,6
25	1900		1050		1180	0,6	670	0,4	420	0,4	300	
28	1700		950		1050		600		375		265	
30	1500		850		950	0,7	530	0,5	335	0,5	235	0,8
35	1320		750		850		475		300		190	1,0
40	1180	0,5	670	0,5	750		420		265		170	
45	1050	0,6	600	0,6	670	0,8	375	0,6	235	0,6	150	1,2
50	950		530		600		335		210		132	1,3
55	850	0,7	475	0,7	530		300		190		118	
60	750	0,8	420	0,8	475	1,0	265	0,8	170	0,8	105	1,4
70	670		375		420		210		150		95	
80	600	1,0	300	1,0	375	1,0	190	0,8	132	0,8	75	1,5

u = Umdrehungen/min, *s* = Vorschub in mm/U.

für Spiralbohrer und Spiralsenker aus Schnellstahl.

eisen		Stahl und Stahlguß										
								SoSt 3	SoSt 4	SoSt 100		
										NCT 3		
							EC 100 vgt	VMC 140 v		VCMo 240 v		
		Stg 38.81	Stg 45.81	Stg 52.81	Stg 60.81			EC 80				
					VCN 25	VCN 25 v		ECMo 80				
			EN 15		ECN 35							
		St IV bis VII 23	St X23		VCN 15	VCN 15 v		VCN 45	VCN 45 v			
			StC 25.61	StC 25.61 v	StC 45.61	StC 45.61 v			ECMo100 v			
Ge 30.91		StC 10.61	StC 16.61	StC 35.61	StC 35.61 v	StC 60.61		StC 60.61 v		VM 125 v		
22.91		St 00.11	St 37.11 St 42.11	St 50.11	St 60.11	St 70.11				VCMo 125 v		
25	30	30	40	50	60	70	80	90	100	110	120	kg/mm
13	14	15	16	17	18	19	20	21	22	23	24	
n	*s*	*n*	*s*	*n*	*s*	*n*	*s*	*n*	*s*	*n*	*s*	*D*
4200	0,05	6000	0,05	6000	0,05	4750	0,03	3750	0,03	3000	0,02	1
2100		3000		3000		2650		1900		1500		2
1500	0,06	2350	0,06	2100	0,06	1700	0,05	1320	0,05	1050	0,03	3
1050	0,08	1900		1500		1180		950		750		4
850	0,1	1500	0,1	1320	0,1	950	0,08	750	0,08	600	0,05	5
750		1320	0,12	1200	0,12	850		670		530		6
670		1200	0,15	1050	0,15	750	0,1	600	0,1	475	0,08	7
600		1050		950		670		530		375		8
530		950		850		600	0,12	475		335		9
475	0,15	850	0,18	750	0,18	530	0,15	420	0,12	300	0,1	10
420		750		670		475		375		265		11
375		670	0,2	670	0,2	420		335		265		12
375	0,2	670		640		420		335	0,15	235		13
335		640		600		375	0,18	300		235	0,12	14
335		600	0,25	530	0,25	375		300		235		15
300		600		475		335	0,2	265		210		16
265	0,25	530		420		300		235		190		18
235		475	0,3	420	0,3	265	0,25	210	0,18	190	0,15	20
210		420		375		265		190		170		22
210	0,3	375		335		235	0,3	190	0,2	170		25
190		335	0,35	300	0,35	210		170	0,25	150		28
170		300		265		190	0,35	170		150	0,2	30
150		265		235		170		150		118		35
118	0,4	235	0,4	190	0,4	150		118	0,3	95		40
105		190		170		132		105		85		45
95	0,45	170	0,45	150	0,45	105		95		75	0,3	50
85		150		118		95	0,4	85		67		55
75	0,5	118	0,5	105	0,5	85		75	0,35	60		60
67		105		95		75		60		47,5		70
53	0,6	95	0,6	75	0,6	60	0,45	47,5	0,35	42	0,3	80

schlagen. Sie müssen ferner sehr fest sitzen; bei kegeliger Mitnahme soll nur der Kegel tragen, aber nicht die Lappen, da diese sonst abreißen. Größte Sorgfalt ist auf guten Sitz zu verwenden. Bei zylindrischen Bohrern muß der Sitz im Futter gut sein, das Futter muß schlagfrei laufen. Für alle Arbeiten, außer Bohren von Gußeisen und Leichtmetall, reichliche Kühlung anwenden (siehe Tabelle 11). Behandlung von Konushülsen siehe Abschnitt 9.

Müssen kleine Bohrer mit Kegelschaft in einem bedeutend größeren Kegel befestigt werden, dann nicht zwei oder mehr Konushülsen verwenden, sondern nur eine, die vom kleinen Kegel gleich auf den großen der Maschine übersetzt. Beim Lösen von Bohrern usw., die schwer von Hand zu halten sind, legt man einen weichen Gegenstand, z. B. Holz unter, damit beim Herabfallen die Bohrerspitze nicht verletzt wird. Normalerweise bohren die Bohrer größer als die angegebenen Durchmesser. Die angegebenen Richtwerte beziehen sich auf genau geschliffene und rundlaufende Bohrer. Die Übermaße betragen etwa bei gutgelagerten Maschinen

Übermaß $\ddot{u}$ in mm $= 0{,}006 \times$ Durchmesser für harte Werkstoffe
,, $\ddot{u}$ in mm $= 0{,}008 \times$,, ,, weiche ,,

Beispiel: Bei 50 mm Bohrerdurchmesser auf StC 45.61 bohrt der Bohrer größer um $\ddot{u} = 0{,}006 \cdot 50 = 0{,}3$ mm. Der Lochdurchmesser wird also $D = 50{,}3$ mm.

11. Wodurch entstehen schlechte Oberflächen?

1. Bohrer schlägt oder sitzt einseitig im Futter.

2. Bohrerspitzenwinkel ist zu groß, zu klein, einseitig oder schief aufgeschliffen.

3. Hinterschliff ist falsch, erkennbar an falscher Lage der Querschneide.

4. Kühlung zu gering, Bohrer ist ausgeglüht und hat keine Schnittleistung mehr.

5. Zu großer Vorschub.

6. Bei langen Bohrungen muß der Bohrer öfters aus der Bohrung herausgeholt werden, um die Späne zu entfernen. Diese verkratzen die Oberfläche, setzen sich in der Spiralnut fest, versperren somit dem weiteren Spanaustritt den Weg, was unweigerlich zum Bruch der sehr teuren Bohrer führt.

7. Auf den Rippen oder Phasen haben sich Aufbauschneiden, d. h.

Werkstoffteilchen festgesetzt. Entfernen, und Bohrer leicht aber richtig abziehen mit Ölstein.

8. Bei großen Bohrungen soll man etwa mit Seelenstärke des Bohrers ein kleines Loch vorbohren. Dadurch vermeidet man das Verlaufen und kann auf höhere Bohrleistung gehen, weil die Querschneide des großen Bohrers nicht mehr im Schnitt ist.

9. Bohrerspitze springt beim Anbohren aus der Ankörnung seitlich heraus, wird verdrückt und bohrt schräg. Bruchgefahr! Bei Wellen durch Verdrehen der Wellen im Prisma ausgleichen, z. B. Splintloch bohren.

12. Reibahlen.

Die Reibahlen dienen zur Herstellung genauer Bohrungen. Es gibt feste und nachstellbare Hand- und Maschinenreibahlen, sowie Aufsteckreibahlen. Durch ungleiche Teilung der Zähne werden unrunde Löcher und Rattermarken vermieden. Reibahlen können nur kleine Späne abheben, die von dem vordersten Teil, dem Anschnitt, genommen werden. Der zylindrische Teil glättet nur die Oberfläche. Zum Reiben werden die Bohrungen mit Reibzugabe vorgebohrt, die aus Tabelle 18 entnommen werden können. Je kleiner die Reibzugaben sind, desto sauberer und glatter wird die Oberfläche.

Tabelle 18. Untermaße für zu reibende Bohrungen.

Durchmesserbereich	Vorbohren mit Spiralbohrer zum Aufsenken auf Untermaß in mm	Aufsenken auf Untermaß in mm	
		Reibzugabe für St, Stg, Ge	Reibzugabe für Rotmetall Leichtmetall
0,8···1,2	—	0,05	0,2
1,2···1,6	—	0,05	0,3
1,6···3	—	0,05	0,4
3···6	—	0,1	0,5
6···10	—	0,1	0,6
10···18	1,0	0,15	0,7
18···30	1,5	0,15	0,8
30···50	2	0,2	0,8
50···80	2,5	0,2	0,8
80···110	3	0,3	0,8

Selbstverständlich dürfen beim Vorbohren mit geringen Reibzugaben keine zu tiefen Drehriefen in der Wandung sein, weil diese dann nicht mehr herausgerieben werden können, d. h. beim letzten Bohren oder Senken muß sorgfältig auf guten Schnitt geachtet werden.

Abziehen der Reibahlen sollte vermieden werden, nötigenfalls aber nur durch erfahrene Werkzeugmacher ausgeführt werden, da hierzu große Übung unerläßlich ist. Bei einem falschen Strich mit dem Ölstein ist die Reibahle verdorben, sie fängt an zu drücken, die Folge ist unweigerlich Bruch.

Ansätze von aufgeschweißtem Werkstoff müssen mit dem Ölstein entfernt werden, da sonst rauhe Oberflächen erzielt werden. Auch dies nur durch einen erfahrenen Mann. Bei Vorschubmarkierungen in der geriebenen Bohrung, abrunden der Schneidzähne gegen den Schaft, abziehen des Rückganges vom Anschnitt zum zylindrischen Teil. Wenn möglich, stets Pendelfutter benutzen. Bei verstellbaren Reibahlen durch leichte Schläge mittels Holzhammers auf weiche Auflage und auf sämtliche Messer für glatte Auflage auf den Grund der Schlitze sorgen. Meist schleifen notwendig. Ein Nachschleifen der Reibahlen ist nur auf Werkzeugschleifmaschinen einwandfrei möglich.

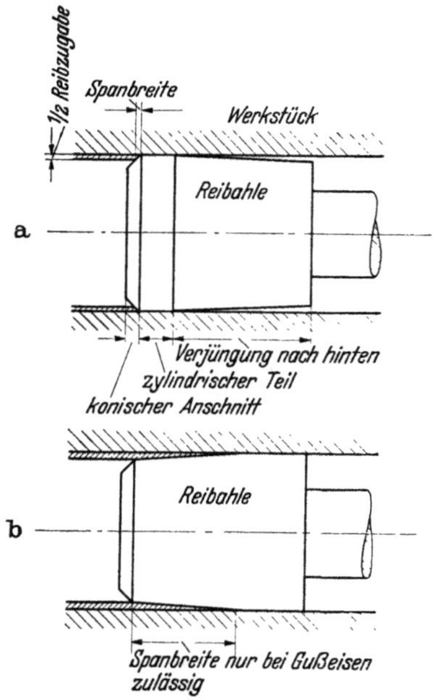

a) Richtiger Anschliff.
b) Falscher Anschliff. Reibahle fängt sich und geht zu Bruch.

Abb. 110. Anschliff von Reibahlen.

Der Anschnitt soll bei Stahl kürzer, bei Gußeisen länger sein. Fehlt bei Reibahlen (Abb. 110a/b) die hintere Verjüngung, so nutzt sich der vordere Teil ab und ein größeres Stück der Reibahle kommt in Eingriff. Durch die hohe Spanbreite wird die Beanspruchung sehr groß, so daß meist Bruch eintritt. Solche Reibahlen müssen rechtzeitig nachgeschliffen werden.

Neue Reibahlen haben meist einen feinen Grat an den Kanten und reiben die ersten Löcher größer. Man kann sich helfen durch Nachwetzen auf Maschinen oder Vorreiben auf Probestücken. Bei zu kleinen Reibahlen kann man durch Aufziehen mit einem harten Werkzeug, z. B. einem Drehstahl oder Schaber, etwa dreimal das Reibmaß um einige Hundertstel Millimeter erhöhen, aber nur durch einen erfahrenen Werkzeugmacher.

13. Wie werden geriebene Bohrungen erzeugt?

Bei der Herstellung von geriebenen Bohrern geht man üblicherweise wie folgt vor:

1. vorbohren mit Untermaß,
2. senken oder nachbohren (bis zu 18 mm ⌀ nicht üblich),
3. reiben.

Bei Fertigung auf Drehbänken oder Revolverdrehbänken muß mit der Bohrstange angebohrt werden, wenn die Bohrungen genau zum Außendurchmesser laufen sollen, weil der Spiralbohrer verläuft.

Die Unterwerte für das Vorbohren und Senken sind in Tabelle 19 zusammengefaßt. Bis zu dem angegebenen Untermaß muß mit den genannten Werkzeugen gearbeitet werden.

Bei Leicht- und Rotmetall wird direkt auf ein Untermaß entsprechend der Reibzugabe vorgebohrt, weil hier ein größerer Reibspan genommen werden kann.

1. Beispiel: Die Bohrung 5 H7 in Stahl ist herzustellen:

1. vorbohren mit Spiralbohrer auf $5 - 0{,}2 = 4{,}8$ mm ⌀,
2. senken auf $5 - 0{,}05 = 4{,}95$ mm ⌀,
3. reiben auf 5 mm ⌀ H7 $= 5\,{}^{+0{,}012}_{+0}$ mm ⌀.

2. Beispiel: Die Bohrung 60 H8 soll in Stahlguß hergestellt werden:

1. vorbohren auf 57,5 mm ⌀ mit Spiralbohrer,
2. senken auf $60 - 0{,}2 = 59{,}8$ mm ⌀,
3. reiben auf Maß 60 mm ⌀ H8 $= 60\,{}^{+0{,}046}_{+0}$ mm ⌀.

14. Wie werden Drehzahl und Vorschub bestimmt?

Aus Tabelle 19 werden zur Reibahle aus Werkzeugstahl oder Schnellstahl passend zum Werkstoff am Kopf Drehzahl und Vorschub abgelesen und eingestellt.

Hierbei ist die Güte der Oberfläche maßgebend, obgleich die Schnittgeschwindigkeit (siehe Abschnitt 12) der Reibahle höher sein könnte. Vor allem muß die Reibahle möglichst lange ihr Maß behalten.

15. Was muß beim Reiben beachtet werden?

Reiben stets mit Pendelfutter durchführen, durch das Pendeln wird das Nachschneiden der Reibahle verhindert. Eine Beeinflussung auf die Größe der Bohrung kann durch Verwendung verschiedener Schmiermittel vorgenommen werden.

Tabelle 19. Reibahlen-

m/min	10		6		10		5		2		4 ·	
	Leichtmetall				Rotmetall						Guß-	
			Al-Mg-Mn					Ms 58···63				
	Elektron		Al-Mg-Si				Rg 4	Rg 8···10				Ge 18.91
	Al		Al-Cu-Mg		Cu		GBz 10	GBz 14		GBz 17	Ge 12.91	Ge
Festigkeit					12	15	20	30	50	75	12	18
Lauf. Nr.	1	2	3	4	5	6	7	8	9	10	11	12
D	*n*	*s*	*n*	*s*	*n*	*s*	*n*	*s*	*n*	*s*	*n*	*s*
											Umdrehungszahlen von	
4···6	530	0,4	335	0,3	530	0,5	265	0,3	105	0,2	210	0,5
6···9	335	1	210	0,5	335	1	210	0,5	75	0,3	132	1
9···12	265		170		265		132		60		105	
12···15	210		132		210		105		42		85	
15···20	170	2	95	1	170	2	85	1	33,5	0,5	67	2
20···25	132		75		132		67		26,5		53	
25···30	105		67		105		53		21		42	
30···40	85		47,5		85		42		17		33,5	
40···50	67		37,5		67		33,5		13,2		26,5	
50···65	53		30		53		26,5		10,5		21	
65···80	42	4	23,5	2	42	4	21	2	8,5	1	17	4
80···100	33,5		19		33,5		17		6,7		13,2	
100···130	23,5		15		23,5		13,2		5,3		10,5	
											Umdrehungszahlen von	
4···6	670	0,4	420	0,3	670	0,5	335	0,3	170	0,2	265	0,5
6···9	420	1	300	0,5	420	1	210	0,5	132	0,3	210	1
9···12	335		210		335		170		75		132	
12···15	265		170		265		132		67		105	
15···20	190	2	132	1	190	2	95	1	47,5	0,5	85	2
20···25	150		105		150		75		37,5		67	
25···30	132		85		132		67		30		53	
30···40	95		67		95		47,5		23,5		42	
40···50	75		53		75		37,5		19		33,5	
50···65	60		42		60		30		15		26,5	
65···80	47,5	4	33,5	2	47,5	4	23,5	2	11,8	1	21	4
80···100	37,5		26,5		37,5		19		9,5		17	
100···130	30		21		30		15		7,5		13,2	
m/min	12		8		12		6		3		5	

n = Umdrehungen/min, s = Vorschub in mm/U.

umdrehungszahlen.

3		5		4		3		2,5		2		
eisen		Stahl und Stahlguß										
								SoSt 3	SoSt 4	SoSt 100		
										NCT 3		
							EC 100 v	VMC 140 v		VCM 240 v		
		Stg 38.81	Stg 45.81	Stg 52.81	Stg 60.81			EC 80				
					VCN 25	VCN 25 v		ECMo 80				
			EN 15		ECN 35							
		St IV bis VII 23	St X 23		VCN 15	VCN 15 v		VCN 45	VCN 45 v			
			StC 25.61	StC 25.61 v	StC 45.61	StC 45.61 v			ECMo 100 v			
Ge 30.91		StC 10.61	StC 16.61	StC 35.61	StC 35.61 v	StC 60.61		StC 60.61 v		VM 125 v		
22.91		St 00.11	St 37.11 St 42.11	St 50.11	St 60.11	St 70.11				VCMo 125 v		
25	30	30	40	50	60	70	80	90	100	110	120	kg/mm²
13	14	15	16	17	18	19	20	21	22	23	24	Lauf. Nr.
n	*s*	*n*	*s*	*n*	*s*	*n*	*s*	*n*	*s*	*n*	*s*	*D*

Reibahlen aus Werkzeugstahl.

n	*s*	*n*	*s*	*n*	*s*	*n*	*s*	*n*	*s*	*n*	*s*	*D*
170	0,3	265	0,3	210	0,3	170	0,2	132	0,2	105	0,2	4···6
132	0,5	210	0,4	132	0,3	132	0,3	105	0,3	75		6···9
67		132		105		75		67		60		9···12
53		105		85		67		53		42		12···15
42	1	85	0,6	67	0,5	47,5	0,4	42	0,3	33,5	0,3	15···20
33,5		67		53		37,5		33,5		26,5		20···25
26,5		53		42		30		26,5		21		25···30
21		42		33,5		23,5		21		17		30···40
17		33,5		26,5		19		17		13,2		40···50
13,2		26,5		21		15		13,2		10,5		50···65
10,5	2	21	1	17	0,8	11,8	0,6	10,5	0,4	8,5	0,4	65···80
8,5		17		13,2		9,5		8,5		6,7		80···100
6,7		13,2		10,5		7,5		6,7		5,3		100···130

Reibahlen aus Schnellstahl.

n	*s*	*n*	*s*	*n*	*s*	*n*	*s*	*n*	*s*	*n*	*s*	*D*
210	0,3	335	0,3	265	0,3	210	0,2	170	0,2	170	0,2	4···6
132	0,5	210	0,4	210	0,3	132	0,3	132	0,3	132		6···9
105		170		132		105		75		75		9···12
85		132		105		85		67		67		12···15
67	1	95	0,6	85	0,5	67	0,4	47,5	0,3	47,5	0,3	15···20
53		75		67		53		37,5		37,5		20···25
42		67		53		42		30		30		25···30
33,5		47,5		42		33,5		23,5		23,5		30···40
26,5		37,5		33,5		26,5		19		19		40···50
21		30		26,5		21		15		15		50···65
17	2	23,5	1	21	0,8	17	0,6	11,8	0,4	11,8	0,4	65···80
13,2		19		17		13,2		9,5		9,5		80···100
10,5		15		13,2		10,5		7,5		7,5		100···130
4		6		5		4		3		3		

Unter Reibüberweite versteht man das Übermaß des geriebenen Loches gegenüber dem Reibahlendurchmesser. Lochdurchmesser, Spantiefe und Vorschub üben keinen Einfluß auf die Reibüberweite aus, nur die Schmiermittel, d. h. die Reibüberweite ist bei kleinen und großen Löchern etwa gleich. Je geringer die Reibüberweite wird, desto besser wird die Oberfläche. Aber desto leichter ist die Gefahr des Festklemmens der Reibahle vorhanden. Sie geht dann leicht zu Bruch. Andererseits kann man bei frischen, also noch großen Reibahlen dünnflüssige Schmiermittel verwenden, die geringe Reibüberweite erzeugen, also gerade noch paßgerechte Bohrungen; dagegen bei Reibahlen mit kleinem Durchmesser Schmiermittel mit hohen Reibüberweiten benutzen. Dadurch können die Reibahlen länger benutzt werden. In der Tabelle 20 ist die Reibüberweite als Folge verschiedener Schmiermittel zusammengestellt. Mit ihrer verschiedenen Wirkung wird man sich öfter helfen können.

Tabelle 20. Reibüberweiten in mm bei verschiedenen Schmiermitteln.

Werkstoff	Terpentin	Mineralöl leichtflüssig	Rüböl dickflüssig	Bohröl	trocken
Gußeisen		0,009	0,007	0,005	0,020
Stahl		0,014	0,018	0,012	nicht möglich
Rotmetall		0,014	0,012	0,012	0,018
„ -Guß . .		0,010	0,007	0,006	0,014
Leichtmetall, weich	0,012		0,030	0,040	nicht möglich
„ hart	0,007		0,014	0,020	0,035

16. Fehlerhafte Oberflächen entstehen durch folgendes:

1. Zu hohe Schnittgeschwindigkeit.
2. Zu hoher Vorschub.
3. Zu große Spanabnahme.
4. Zu wenig Schmiermittel und ungeeignete Schmiermittel.
5. Starre Einstellung der Reibahlen statt Verwendung von Pendelhalter.
6. Zu großes vorgebohrtes Loch, Bohrriefen kommen nicht mehr heraus, kleiner vorbohren. Ebenso zu kleines Loch, da zu viel Spanabnahme.
7. Reibahle ist stumpf und drückt.

17. Senker zum Anflächen.

Senker sind Fräswerkzeuge, die auf Drehbänken, Bohrmaschinen und Bohrwerken zum Anflächen von Augen oder Warzen zwecks guter

Auflagefläche für Muttern oder Bolzenbunden Verwendung finden. Bei ihnen kommt es darauf an, daß sie keine Rattermarken erzeugen, was durch ungleiche Teilung der Zähne, Änderung des Vorschubes oder andere Drehzahlen erreicht werden kann. Auch sie müssen genau rund laufen.

18. Drehzahlen und Vorschübe.

Die Drehzahlen und Vorschübe stehen in Tabelle 21. Es ist zwischen Werkzeugstahl- und Schnellstahlwerkzeugen zu unterscheiden, die hauptsächlich vorkommen. Aufstecksenker haben dieselben Leistungen wie Zapfensenker. Auch wird man bei schwachen Werkstücken nur mit kleineren Vorschüben herangehen können als bei starken. Angenommen ist für die angegebenen Werte dieselbe Werkzeugqualität wie beim Drehen, also ein mittlerer Schnellstahl. Für Formsenker müssen zur Schonung des Werkzeuges die Werte wie für Messerstangen verwendet werden. Maßgebend für die Drehzahlen sind die äußersten schneidenden Werkzeugkanten, die als Durchmesser anzunehmen sind. Die Vorschübe werden direkt eingestellt.

Beispiel: Anflächen einer Nabe mit 50 mm ⌀ aus StC 45.61 mit Messerstahl und Schnellstahlmessern.

Aus Tabelle 21 $n = 422$ min
$s = 0{,}02$ mm/U.

19. Was muß beachtet werden?

Bohrstangen und Werkzeuge. Oftmals werden Werkzeuge, wie Senker, Reibahlen, Messer, Profilsenker und Profilmesser auf Bohrstangen aufgesteckt. Diese sind dann die Träger des Werkzeuges und selbst in der Maschine eingespannt. Voraussetzung für ruhigen Lauf ist bei Bohrstangen der Rundlauf, fester Sitz im Spindelkopf und genaues Zusammenpassen von Stange und Werkzeug. Folgende Ursachen können bei fehlerhafter Arbeit mit Bohrstangen vorliegen:

a) Bohrmaschinen.

1. Bohrstange schlägt.
2. Bohrstange sitzt nicht im Spindelkopf und gibt einseitig nach.
3. Bohrstange mit unterer Führung steht nicht senkrecht, sondern verdrückt und klemmt, nachrichten der unteren Führung oder des Auslegers bei Radialbohrmaschinen.
4. Werkzeuge sitzen nicht richtig auf Bohrstangen, Führung zu weit.

5. Bohrstange frißt in Führung, Bohrbüchse zu eng, Schmierung zu gering.

b) Bohrwerke.

1. Bohrstange schlägt, muß aber nicht immer der Grund für fehlerhafte Arbeit sein. Auch eine schlagende Bohrstange kann genaue und richtige Arbeit liefern.

2. Bohrstange liegt nicht in der Waage, das Gegenlager steht zu

Tabelle 21. Senkerumdrehungszahlen (zum Anflächen

	Leichtmetall				Rotmetall						Guß	
			Al-Mg-Mn					Ms 58···63				
	Elektron		Al-Mg-Si				Rg 4	Rg 8···10			Ge 18.91	
	Al		Al-Cu-Mg		Cu		GBz 10	GBz 14	GBz 17		Ge 12.91	G
Festigkeit					12	15	20	30	50	75	12	18
Lauf. Nr.	1	2	3	4	5	6	7	8	9	10	11	12
D	*n*	*s*	*n*	*s*	*n*	*s*	*n*	*s*	*n*	*s*	*n*	*s*
											Zapfensenker	*und*
25···30	300	0,2	85	0,2	300	0,2	210	0,2	85	0,2	132	0,2
30···40	235		67		235		170		67		105	
40···50	190		53		190		132		53		85	
50···65	150		42		150		105		42		67	
65···80	118	0,2	33,5	0,2	118	0,2	85	0,2	33,5	0,2	53	0,2
											Bohrstangen	*mit*
12···15	600	0,03	132	0,03	600	0,03	420	0,03	132	0,03	190	0,03
15···20	420	0,05	95	0,05	420	0,05	335	0,05	95	0,05	150	0,05
20···25	375		75		375		265		75		118	
25···30	300		67		300		210		67		95	
30···40	210		47,5		210		170		47,5		75	
40···50	170		37,5		170		132		37,5		60	
50···65	132	0,1	30	0,1	132	0,1	105	0,1	30	0,1	42	0,1
65···80	105		23,5		105		85		23,5		37,5	
80···100	85		19		85		67		19		30	
m/min	28		6		28		20		6		9	

n = Umdrehungen/min, *s* = Vorschub in mm/U.

hoch oder zu niedrig und muß nachgerichtet werden, sonst entstehen zwangsläufig schiefe Bohrungen.

3. Stets für ausreichende Schmierung in Gegenführungen sorgen.

4./5. wie unter a.

20. Wodurch entstehen schlechte Oberflächen?

1. Senker läuft nicht schlagfrei und ist schlecht befestigt.

für Werkzeuge aus Schnellstahl.

eisen		Stahl und Stahlguß										
								SoSt 3	SoSt 4	SoSt 100		
										NCT 3		
							EC 100 v	VMC 140 v		VCM 240 v		
		Stg 38.81	Stg 45.81	Stg 52.81	Stg 60.81			EC 80				
					VCN 25	VCN 25 v		ECMo 80				
			EN 15		ECN 35							
		St IV bis VII 23	St X 23		VCN 15	VCN 15 v		VCN 45	VCN 45 v			
			StC 25.61	StC 25.61 v	StC 45.61	StC 45.61 v			ECMo 100 v			
Ge 30.91		StC 10.61	StC 16.61	StC 35.61	StC 35.61 v	StC 60.61		StC 60.61 v		VM 125 v		
22.91		St 00.11	St 37.11 St 42.11	St 50.11	St 60.11	St 70.11				VCMo 125 v		
25	30	30	40	50	60	70	80	90	100	110	120	kg/mm²
13	14	15	16	17	18	19	20	21	22	23	24	Lauf. Nr.
n	*s*	*n*	*s*	*n*	*s*	*n*	*s*	*n*	*s*	*n*	*s*	*D*

Aufstecksenker zum Anflächen.

85	0,2	150	0,2	118	0,2	105	0,2	85	0,2	67	0,1	25···30
67		118		95		85		67		47,5		30···40
53		95		75		67		53		37,5		40···50
42		75		60		47,5		42		30		50···65
33,5	0,2	60	0,25	47,5	0,25	42	0,2	33,5	0,2	23,5	0,2	65···80

Messern und Formsenker.

132	0,03	170	0,01	150	0,01	132	0,01	105	0,01	85	0,01	12···15
95	0,05	132	0,02	105	0,02	95	0,02	85	0,02	67	0,02	15···20
75		105		95		75		67		53		20···25
67		85		75		67		53		42		25···30
47,5		67		53		47,5		42		33,5		30···40
37,5		53		42		37,5		33,5		26,5		40···50
30	0,1	42	0,03	33,5	0,03	30	0,03	26,5	0,03	21	0,03	50···65
23,5		33,5		26,5		23,5		21		17		65···80
19		26,5		21		19		17		13,2		80···100
6		8		7		6		5		4		

2. Rattermarken durch Umdrehungszahl und Vorschub ändern.
3. Saubere Ansenkflächen erhält man mit kleiner Schnittgeschwindigkeit.
4. Das Werkzeug muß fest und gerade aufliegen.

21. Ausstechwerkzeuge.

Bei großen Bohrungen in Blechen ist es vorteilhaft, eine Nut einzustechen und den Kern nicht zu zerspanen. Die Drehzahlen und Vorschübe für Aufsteckwerkzeuge sind halb so groß wie bei Spiralbohrern zu wählen. Reichliche Kühlung notwendig. Es müssen alle Messer schneiden.

Abschnitt 16.

Gewindeschneiden.

1. Allgemeines über Gewinde.

Das Gewinde ist eines der Grundelemente der Technik, ohne das unsere Entwicklung niemals hätte erfolgen können. Die dem Gewinde übertragenen Aufgaben kann es nur erfüllen, wenn ein genaues Zusammenpassen von Muttergewinde zum Bolzengewinde vorhanden ist. Dieses wiederum ist nur durch genaue und sorgfältige Fertigung möglich. Die Oberflächen der Gewinde sind meist ohne Bearbeitungszeichen versehen, weil stets höchste Güte entsprechend drei Bearbeitungsdreiecken oder zum Teil geschliffene Gewindeflächen, dann aber angegeben, notwendig sind.

2. Gewindearten.

Es gibt verschiedene Arten von Gewinden, die je nach Zweck vom Konstrukteur verwendet werden. Sie unterscheiden sich durch ihre Form und Steigung. In Abb. 111 sind vergrößerte Gewindeprofile gezeigt.

Beim metrischen Gewinde sind die Gewindespitzen fortgeschnitten, beim Withworth-Gewinde abgerundet. Der Außendurchmesser des Gewindes ist verständlich. Der Kerndurchmesser ist der Durchmesser des inneren vollbleibenden Bolzenmaterials. Beim Muttergewinde liegen die Verhältnisse umgekehrt. Dort stellt der Außendurchmesser den kleinsten vollbleibenden Muttermaterialdurchmesser dar. Wichtig ist, daß einer Gewindespitze auf der Gegenseite eine Rille gegenüberliegt. Dadurch kann man auf dem geraden Teil der Flanke an einer beliebigen

Stelle den richtigen Flankendurchmesser messen, allerdings nur bei symmetrischen Profilen. Ein ganzes eingeschnittenes Profil heißt Gang. Der Abstand von Spitze zu Spitze oder Rille zu Rille heißt Steigung. Diese wird angegeben in mm oder Gangzahl je Zoll. Bei einer Steigung von 2,5 mm beträgt also der Abstand von Gang zu Gang 2,5 mm. Man unterscheidet verschiedene Gewindearten, deren Maße in Normblättern festgelegt sind und aus denen auch die Bezeichnung ersichtlich ist.

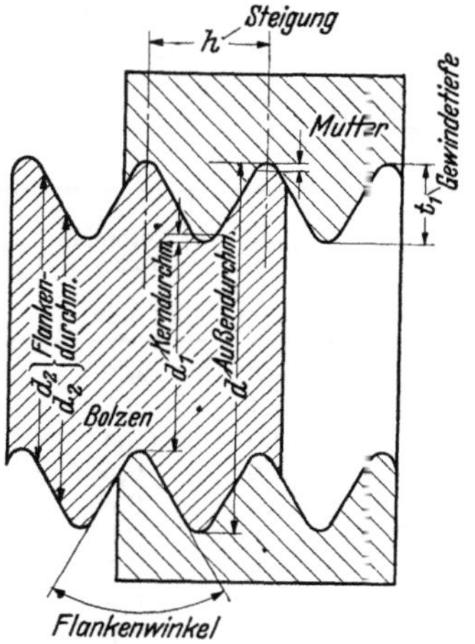

Abb. 111. Gewinde mit Vermaßung.

3. Gewindeherstellungsarten.

Aus Form und Schneidwirkung können folgende Verfahren nach ihren Werkzeugen unterschieden werden:

a) Gewindebohren mit Bohrern.
b) Gewindeschneiden mit Schneideisen.
c) Gewindefräsen.
d) Gewindedrehen mit Drehstählen und Strehlern.
e) Gewindedrücken.

Der letztere Fall interessiert hier nicht und ist nicht behandelt.

Bei den vier ersten Herstellarten ist eine vorhergehende Bearbeitung notwendig. Für das Fräsen und Drehen muß der Außendurchmesser bzw. bei Innengewinden der Kerndurchmesser vorher genau hergestellt sein.

Dagegen tritt beim Gewindebohren und Schneiden mit Schneideisen folgende Erscheinung auf. Durch die Art der Spanabnahme wird der Werkstoff außer Gußeisen an den Gewindespitzen etwas herausgequetscht. Würden hier die genauen Außen- oder Kerndurchmesser vorgearbeitet sein, so müssen die Werkzeuge den Gewindegrund oder die Spitzen mit ausschneiden. Das führt zu einer bedeutenden Mehrbeanspruchung und ist oft der Grund für das Ausreißen von Werkstoffteilchen. Man führt deshalb hierfür die Außendurchmesser kleiner und die Kerndurchmesser größer aus. Die Durchmesser sind für verschiedene Werkstoffe verschieden zu halten. In Tabelle 22 sind für die Hauptgewinde Vordreh- und Vorbohrdurchmesser angegeben.

1. Beispiel: Innengewinde M 18 ist bei Stahl vorzubohren auf 15,25 ⌀. Beachten, daß Bohrer größer bohren (Abschnitt 15, S. 120). Für gutgelagerte Maschinen also 0,006 × ⌀ = 0,006 · 15,25 rund 0,1 mm Übermaß zu erwarten. Daher Bohrer 15,15 ⌀ wählen.

2. Beispiel: Innengewinde M 18 × 1,5 ist vorzubohren. Vorbohrmaß aus Tabelle 22 für Steigung 1,5 = 16,4 mm. Somit Bohrer-⌀ = 16,3 mm wählen.

Tabelle 22. Vorbohrmaße zum Gewindeschneiden für metrische Feingewinde.

Steigung mm	Leicht-metall mm	Rotmetall Gußeisen mm	Stahl Stahlguß zähe Bronze mm	Steigung mm	Leicht-metall mm	Rotmetall Gußeisen mm	Stahl Stahlguß zähe Bronze mm
0,25	0,35	0,25	0,25	1	1,3	1,2	1,0
0,3	0,4	0,3	0,3	1,25	1,7	1,5	1,3
0,35	0,5	0,4	0,4	1,5	2,0	1,8	1,6
0,4	0,5	0,5	0,4	1,75	2,4	2,1	2
0,45	0,6	0,5	0,5	2	2,75	2,5	2,25
0,5	0,6	0,6	0,5	2,5	3,25	3	2,75
0,6	0,8	0,7	0,6	3	4	3,5	3,25
0,7	0,9	0,8	0,7	3,5	4,75	4,25	4
0,75	1,0	0,9	0,8	4	5,25	5	4,25
0,8	1,1	0,9	0,8	4,5	6	5,5	5
0,9	1,2	1,1	1,0	5	6,5	6	5,5

Vom Gewindeaußendurchmesser sind die angegebenen Werte abzuziehen, das errechnete Bohrungsmaß ist herzustellen. Z. B. für M 60×4 in Gußeisen ist das Vorbohrmaß 60 − 5 = 55 mm ⌀.

4. Gewindebohrer.

Bei Gewindebohrern wird das Ausschneiden der Gewinde durch den schrägen Teil des Bohrers, den Anschnitt, ausgeführt. Auch hier muß auf scharfe Werkzeuge geachtet werden. Die zugehörigen Vorbohrdurchmesser sind aus Tabelle 22 zu entnehmen. In Sacklöchern müssen Grundbohrer, d. h. Bohrer mit ganz kurzem Anschnitt, verwendet werden. Durchgehende Löcher können mit Mutterbohrern in einem Schnitt hergestellt werden. Die Gewindebohrer müssen genau senkrecht eingeführt werden, unter Umständen ist eine entsprechende Führung notwendig. Dabei ist besonders darauf zu achten, daß bei mehreren Bohrern der folgende Gewindebohrer genau in den Gang des durch den vorhergehenden Bohrer schon vorgeschnittenen Gewindeganges eingeführt wird. Sonst steigt beim Einführen des zweiten Bohrers derselbe gern auf den vorgeschnittenen Gang auf und macht das Gewinde bzw. das Werkstück zu Ausschuß. Der Schnittwiderstand hängt im hohen Maße vom richtigen Schmiermittel ab, das reichlich zugeführt werden muß. Vgl. Tabelle 11 Kühlmittel. Dieses hat vor allem auch die Aufgabe, die Späne abzuführen.

Vorschub und Drehzahl. Der Vorschub darf beim Gewindeschneiden niemals eingeschaltet werden, da sich der Bohrer selbst hineinzieht. Die Drehzahl ist $^2/_3$ so groß zu wählen wie bei Spiralbohrern. Wenn das Gewinde nicht sauber wird, allein die Oberflächengüte ist entscheidend, so muß die Drehzahl weiter herabgesetzt werden. Es kommen dann die Schnittgeschwindigkeiten und damit Drehzahlen wie bei Reibahlen in Frage. Zum Außendurchmesser nimmt man die Drehzahl aus Tabelle 19.

5. Fehlerhafte Oberflächen.

Sie können folgende Ursachen haben:

1. Die Gewindeschneideinrichtung ist nicht in Ordnung.
2. Die Kernlochbohrung ist zu eng.
3. Der Spanwinkel paßt nicht zum Werkstoff.
4. Werkstoffteilchen haben sich auf dem Gewindebohrer festgesetzt und müssen durch Abziehstein entfernt werden.
5. Der Anschnitt des Gewindebohrers ist stumpf, entweder durch ungleichmäßiges Nachschleifen oder durch Abnutzung.
6. Beim ersten Schneiden muß erst der am Gewindebohrerzahn durch Schleifen entstehende Grat entfernt werden, die ersten Gewinde fallen größer aus.
7. Gewindebohrer mit langem Anschnitt erzeugen engere Gewinde, mit kurzem Anschnitt weitere Gewinde.
8. Beim Nachschneiden mit 2. oder 3. Gewindebohrer sind die Gänge nicht richtig getroffen worden.
9. Die Schmierung war schlecht oder das Schmiermittel ungeeignet.

6. Schneideisen.

Schneideisen dienen zur Herstellung von Außengewinden. Größere Gewindedurchmesser, besonders solche mit hoher Steigung, müssen vorgefräst oder vorgeschnitten werden. Normale Gewinde können aus dem Vollen in einem Schnitt hergestellt werden, und zwar in

Stahl und Stahlguß	bis	M 16	oder	$^3/_8$″
Messing	,,	M 33	,,	$1^1/_4$″
Rotguß	,,	M 24	,,	1″
Leichtmetall	,,	M 20	,,	$^3/_4$″

Zum besseren Fassen des Schneideisens soll das Bolzenende angeschrägt werden. Das Einspannen der Schneideisen muß folgendermaßen vor sich gehen:

1. Stirnflächen des Schneideisens müssen genau anliegen.
2. Befestigung durch Druck- und Halteschrauben.
3. Einstellbare Schneideisen nach Musterstück einstellen.
4. Die ersten geschnittenen Werkstücke nachmessen.
5. Durchmesser nachstellen durch konische Spreizschrauben im Schlitz.
6. Druckschrauben nachrichten.

Vorschübe und Drehzahl. Auch hier niemals Vorschub einschalten. Als Drehzahlen können nur diejenigen wie bei Reibahlen (Tabelle 19) genommen werden. Man kann sich für Stahl und Ge ungefähr als Faustformel merken

$$\text{Drehzahl } n = \frac{1000}{\text{Durchmesser}}. \qquad \text{(Gl. 14)}$$

Bei M 20 wird dann

$$n = \frac{1000}{20} = 50 \text{ U/min}.$$

Die Schnittiefe der Einzelspäne ergibt sich aus der Länge des Anschnittes.

7. Fehlerhafte Oberflächen.

Unsaubere, ungenaue oder ausgerissene Gewinde können folgende Ursachen haben:

1. Das Profil kann nicht auf einmal geschnitten werden, weil zu groß.
2. Der vorgedrehte Außendurchmesser ist zu groß, Gewindegänge reißen aus.
3. Das Kühlmittel ist nicht geeignet oder war zu wenig.
4. Das Schneideisen sitzt nicht genau im Halter und steht schief zur Gewindeachse.
5. Der Rücklauf des Schneideisens ist zu schnell.
6. Das Schneideisen läuft zu weit vor und stößt hart gegen einen Bund. Gänge reißen aus.
7. Die Spanabfuhr ist nicht ausreichend und verstopft das Schneideisen. Andere Schnittwinkel anwenden.
8. Das Schneideisen schneidet einseitig, die Späne verstopfen einen Teil des Schneideisens.
9. Die Schnittgeschwindigkeit ist zu groß. Der Vorschub darf nie-

mals eingeschaltet sein. Ein richtiges Schneiden erkennt man an dem gleichmäßigen Herausquellen der Späne aus allen drei oder mehr Spanöffnungen.

8. Gewindefräser.

Für das Gewindefräsen gibt es Eingangprofilfräser, die den einzelnen Gewindegang herausfräsen oder Mehrganggewindefräser, die in einem Umlauf mit $^1/_6$ Überlauf für das Ansetzen des Gewindes dieses erzeugen. Der Einganggewindefräser muß entsprechend der Gewindesteigung schräg stehen, der Mehrganggewindefräser steht dagegen parallel zur Gewindeachse und kann für Flachgewinde nicht benutzt werden. Näheres ist den Anleitungsvorschriften zu den Maschinen zu entnehmen. Die Fräserdrehzahl ist aus Fräserdurchmesser nach Tabelle 14 zu nehmen, jedoch die niedrigere Drehzahl für das Schruppen. Fräserzähne ergeben sich aus der Zahl der quer zum Gewindeprofil eingeschnittenen Spanlücken. Mit dieser Zähnezahl z ist dann aus Tabelle 15 der Vorschub/min auszurechnen, das ist die Werkstückdrehzahl.

Beispiel: Fräser-⌀ = 85 mm — Werkstoff StC 45.61
Drehzahl aus Tabelle 14 — $n = 42$ U/min aus Werkstoff II
Zähnezahl $z = 8$ Zähne.

Somit aus Tabelle 15 (vgl. Abschnitt 14, Absatz 8) für hinterdrehte Fräser, also letzte Spalte, Werkstoff II

$$k = 0{,}24 \text{ mm/U}.$$

Der Vorschub wird dann nach Gleichung (12)

$$s = k \cdot n = 0{,}24 \cdot 42 = 10{,}1 \text{ mm/min}$$

für direkten Fertigschnitt.

Soll das Gewinde vor- und fertiggefräst werden, wird für das Schruppen

$$k = 0{,}48 \text{ und } s = 20 \text{ mm/min}.$$

Für das Schlichten die Drehzahl $n = 60$ U/min (Schlichten) aus

$$s = 0{,}24 \cdot 60 = 15 \text{ mm/min}.$$

Mit diesem Vorschub ist nun nach Anleitung zur Maschinenbedienung die Werkstückdrehzahl zu bestimmen und die Einstellung der Maschine vorzunehmen. Der Vorschub des Frässchlittens ist gleich der Steigung des Gewindes zu nehmen. Die Fräszeit kann aus Maschinentafeln abgelesen werden.

9. Gründe für fehlerhafte Gewinde.

1. Die Steigung stimmt nicht, die an der Maschine als Vorschub für den Bettschlitten eingestellt wird.

2. Die Mitnahme des Werkstückes ist nicht starr und hat nachgegeben.

3. Der Fräser sitzt nicht fest, er hat im Keil nachgegeben oder sich seitlich verschoben oder die Frässpindel hat seitlich Luft.

4. Der Fräser steht nicht parallel zur Gewindeachse und muß nachgerichtet werden.

5. Das Kühlmittel ist nicht geeignet oder zu wenig zugeführt und nicht auf die Schnittstelle.

6. Der Vorschub je Zahn ist zu groß und muß verkleinert werden, d. h. die Umdrehungszahl des Werkstückes muß herabgesetzt werden.

7. Die Schnittgeschwindigkeit ist zu groß. Der Fräser ist abgestumpft und schneidet nicht mehr voll aus.

8. Die Wechselräder am Spindelkopf zur Erzeugung des Bettschlittenvorschubes haben zuviel Zahnluft und geben unregelmäßig nach. Die Keile dieser Zahnräder passen nicht genau und lassen unregelmäßige Verdrehung während ihres Umlaufes zu.

9. Die Achse des Spindelkastens steht nicht genau in der Flucht des Bettes oder die Reitstockspitze ist verlagert, das Gewinde wird konisch aufgefräst. Nachrichten.

Dieselben Ursachen treten bei eingängigen Gewindefräsern sinngemäß auf.

10. Gewindedrehstähle und Strehler.

Gewindedrehstähle und Strehler sind als bekannt vorausgesetzt. Außer den allgemeinen Grundsätzen beim Drehen (siehe Abschnitt 11, 12 und 13) ist zusätzlich folgendes zu beachten:

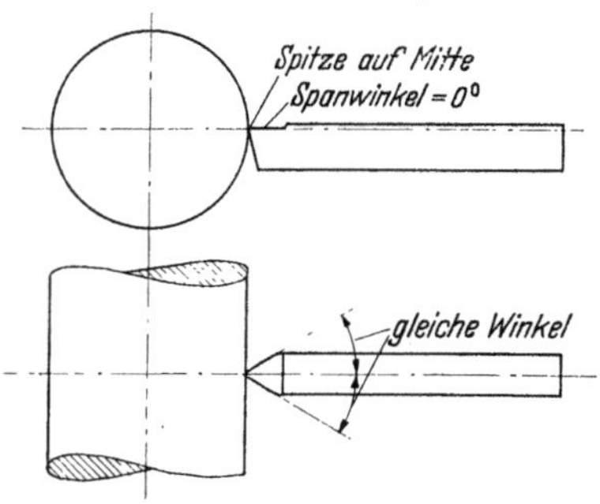

Abb. 112. Lage des Werkzeugprofiles zur Maschinenachse.

a) Gewindestähle und Strehler müssen auf Mitte stehen,

b) das Profil am Gewindestahl und Strehler muß senkrecht zur Werkstückachse liegen (Abb. 112), da in beiden Fällen bei Abweichungen ein falsches Gewindeprofil eintreten muß.

Zur Einstellung gibt es Einstellmikroskope. Das Schleifen des Profiles ist mit Lehren möglich und muß sehr genau durchgeführt werden, da die Gewindetoleranzen äußerst gering sind. Das Schneiden des Gewindes selbst erfolgt mit 10···30 Durchgängen, bei denen jeweils eine

Beistellung des Supportes vorgenommen wird. Dabei darf in den meisten Fällen das Drehbankschloß beim Rücklauf nicht herausgenommen werden, um den Gewindegang wieder zu treffen. Vorschub und Drehzahl ist maßgebend für den Vorschub, der am Räderkasten oder durch Wechselräder eingestellt werden muß.

Die Berechnung von Wechselrädern ist bei neueren Maschinen nicht notwendig, da ein direktes Einschalten der Steigungen möglich ist. Falls dies doch notwendig wird, sei auf die sehr gute und eingehende Darstellung in Heft 4 der Werkstattbücher verwiesen.

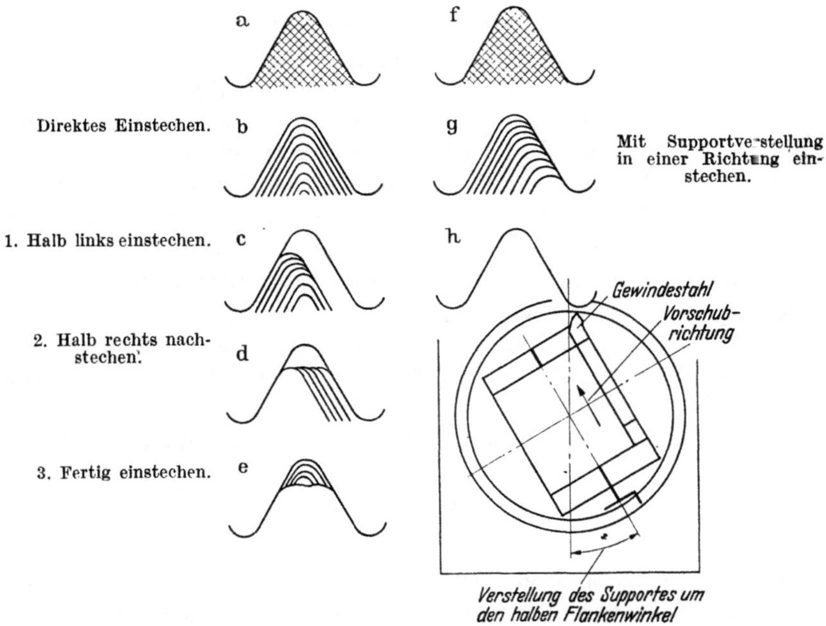

Abb. 113. Verschiedene Einstechverfahren beim Gewindedrehen.

Beim Gewindedrehen nimmt man zuerst Schruppspäne. Bei groben Gewinden kann man nicht direkt bis zum Spangrund hereinfahren, sondern man muß kleinere Späne abheben, wie in Abb. 113a···e oder wie in Abb. 113f···h. Zum Schlichten oder Feinen wird 0,1 mm draufgelassen. Das Fertigschneiden des Gewindes wird mit Strehlern am leichtesten genau.

Die Schnittgeschwindigkeiten sind nicht für Höchstleistungen des Werkzeuges, sondern nach Oberflächengüte zu wählen. Für Schruppspäne nehme man diejenigen aus Tabelle 10, wie sie für den Spanquerschnitt 2 × 1 angegeben sind. Zum Fertigdrehen oder Schlichten erhält man die besten Oberflächen mit Drehzahlen wie für Reibahlen aus Abb. 19. Reichlich schmieren! (Siehe Tabelle 11.)

Gewindestrehler sind Formmesser, die im Strehlerhalter auf Drehbänken und Revolverbänken verwendet werden. Ihr Vorschub wird auf Revolverbänken durch eine Gewindepatrone getätigt. Durch mehrfaches Ansetzen bei jeweils größerer Beistellung wird das Gewinde erzeugt.

11. Fehlerhafte Gewinde.

Folgende Ursachen können vorliegen:

1. Drehstahl steht nicht auf Mitte, Gewindeprofil ist verzerrt.
2. Drehstahl liegt nicht genau senkrecht zur Gewindeachse, sondern schräg. Dann stimmt der Winkel des Gewindes nicht.
3. Beim Prüfen müssen die scharfen Spitzen der Gewindegänge gebrochen sein. Bei Abrundung kann die Rundung nicht in der Mitte, sondern seitlich auf den Gangspitzen aufgebracht sein.
4. Eine Verstellung des Quersupportes hat stattgefunden, dadurch wird das Gewinde zu mager.
5. Die Anlage der Strehler in der Gewindepatrone ist nicht spielfrei.
6. Der Strehler steht nicht genau parallel zur Gewindeachse und kann in der Aufsicht und in der Seitenansicht schräg stehen.
7. Der Strehler steht nicht genau auf Mitte und verzerrt das Profil.

Abschnitt 17.
Räumen.

Die Werkzeuge sind sehr teuer und äußerst schonend zu behandeln. Sobald ein Zahn eine Abstumpfung an den Schneidecken zeigt, meist nur mit dem Vergrößerungsglas erkennbar, muß nachgeschliffen werden. Man erkennt eine Abstumpfung auch in der erhöhten Zugkraft der Maschine, die durch Manometer angezeigt sein kann. Bei einer Erhöhung um 30% dieser Zugkraft gegenüber dem ersten Zug soll ein neuer Anschliff erfolgen. Bei besonders hart anfallenden Werkstücken kann aber auch innerhalb einer Serie für ein oder mehrere Stücke eine Erhöhung der Zugkraft auftreten, die dann kein Kennzeichen der Abstumpfung bedeutet. Für größere Querschnitte sind oftmals zwei und mehr Räumnadeln vorgesehen. Die richtige Einführung der folgenden

Nadeln in das vorgeräumte Profil ist wichtig, weil sonst die Nadeln brechen. Beim Räumen von Nuten wird die Räumtiefe durch Beilagen unter den Räumnadeln ausgeglichen. Die Anlage der Werkstücke muß satt und frei von Spänen oder Schmutz sein. Reichliche Schmierung nötig für glatte Oberflächen und lange Lebensdauer des Werkzeuges.

Als Schnittgeschwindigkeiten (siehe Abschnitt 10 und 11) nimmt man für

Stahl und Stahlguß	hohe Festigkeit	1···2 m/min
,, ,, ,,	niedrige ,,	2···4 ,,
Leichtmetall		4···12 ,,

Maßgebend ist stets die Oberflächengüte des Werkstückes.

Abschnitt 18.

Schleifen.

1. Schleifscheiben.

Schleifscheiben müssen zur Erreichung ihrer Wirkung große Umfangsgeschwindigkeiten haben, und zwar zwischen 18 und 28 m/s, das bedeutet sehr hohe Drehzahlen. Für verschiedene Werkstoffe sind jeweils bestgeeignete Scheiben entwickelt und ausprobiert, die zur Unterscheidung die Bezeichnung Körnung und Korngrößen tragen und aus Tabelle 23 entnommen werden können. Es gibt natürliche und künstliche Korundscheiben (Elektrokorund), ferner Siliziumkarbidscheiben. Dies sind keramisch gebundene Scheiben, d. h. sie bestehen aus dem Schleifmittel und einem Bindemittel und werden vorgeformt im Ofen gebrannt, oder gummigebundene Scheiben, bei denen die Schleifkörnchen in Gummi eingewalzt sind und die Scheiben später vulkanisiert

Tabelle 23. Geeignete Härte und Körnung für Schleifscheiben.

Scheibensorte	Leichtmetall Siliziumkarbid	Rotmetall Siliziumkarbid	Gußeisen Siliziumkarbid	Stahl und Stahlguß Elektrokorund
Rundschleifen . .	30 bis 80 J bis K	24 bis 46 J bis K	36 J bis L	46 K
Innenschleifen . .	30 bis 40 H bis J	36 bis 60 J bis K	36 J bis K	46 bis 60 J bis M
Planschleifen . .	20 bis 40 H bis J	36 bis 60 J bis K	16 bis 30 J bis K	30 bis 60 H bis K

werden. Meistens finden die letzteren als Trennscheiben Verwendung. Die Scheiben sollen sich beim Schleifen selbst freischleifen, so daß durch Abnutzung und Ausbrechen abgenutzter Körner frische scharfe Körner zum Eingriff kommen. Findet dagegen beim Schleifen ein Verschmieren der Scheibe statt, so paßt die Körnung nicht für diesen Werkstoff und es muß eine andere Sorte gewählt werden.

2. Worauf muß geachtet werden?

Richtige Kühlung ist notwendig, da durch örtliche starke Erwärmung Spannungen in den Scheiben entstehen, die zu Rissen und zum Zerspringen führen. Es muß ferner auf ein genaues Auswuchten und richtige Flanschanlage der Schleifscheiben mit der Mitnahmewelle geachtet werden. Das Abziehen der Schleifscheiben erfolgt mit Abziehrädchen oder Diamanten. Als Grundsatz merke man sich, daß möglichst Punkt- oder Linienberührung der Schleifscheibe mit dem Werkstück, niemals Flächenberührung auftreten darf, weil sonst durch zu große Erwärmung einmal eine starke Abnutzung der Schleifscheibe stattfindet und ferner die geschliffene Fläche nicht gerade und unsauber wird.

3. Vorbedingungen für gute Schleifflächen.

Die Oberflächengüte beim Schleifen ist abhängig von der Schleifscheibe, also Bindung, Härtung, Körnung, der Umfangsgeschwindigkeit der Schleifscheibe und der Umfangsgeschwindigkeit der Werkstücke, reichlicher Kühlung. Die richtige Wahl dieser Einflußgrößen ist sehr schwer. In schwierigen Fällen müssen Versuche angestellt werden.

4. Schleifzugaben.

Geeignete Zugaben sind dem DIN-Blatt Kr 111, zu entnehmen.

5. Ursachen für schlechte Oberflächen.

1. Zu wenig Kühlwasser.

2. Scheibe verschmiert sich und schleift sich nicht selbst frei. Andere Körnung nehmen.

3. Schleifscheibe muß öfters abgezogen werden.

4. Umfangsgeschwindigkeit auf Scheibe und Werkstück passen nicht zueinander.

5. Bei verschmierten Scheiben oder zu großer Beistellung treten bei gehärteten Werkstücken durch örtlich starke Erwärmung Oberflächen-

risse auf, die die Werkstücke manchmal zu Ausschuß machen, also vorsichtig schleifen und Schleifscheibe öfters abziehen.

6. Oberflächenrisse können aber auch Härterisse sein, die durch falsche Behandlung des Werkstoffes oder durch Abweichung des Werkstoffes von sehr verschiedener Zusammensetzung herrühren.

7. Die Körnerspitzen laufen nicht rund, sind verschmutzt und geben dadurch ungleich nach.

Abschnitt 19.

Verschiedenes.

Tabelle 24. Zuordnung der Fliegwerkstoffe zu den Bearbeitungsspalten 1 bis 24 auf den verschiedenen Tabellen.

Fliegnorm	Bearbeitungsspalte	Fliegnorm	Bearbeitungsspalte	Fliegnorm	Bearbeitungsspalte	Fliegnorm	Bearbeitungsspalte
1000	15	1207.1	18 19	1456.4	21 23	1610.4	22 23
1010	15 16	.3	20 21	.5	23 24	1620.3	21 23
1040.7	17 18	1208.1	18 19	.6	24	.4	23 24
1042.7	19 20	.3	20 21	1458.1	19 21	1811.5	19 21
1050.2	18 19	1252.2	18 19	.5	21 23	.6	21 23
.7	19 20	.4	20 21	1470.1	18 19	1900.0	11 13
1100.2	16 19	1253.1	17 18	.3	21 23	1903.9	13 14
1101.2	15 16	.3	18 19	.4	22 24	1940	13 14
1110.2	16 17	.4	20 21	.5	24	2150.7	8 9
.7	18 19	.5	21 22	1471.4	20 22	2160.7	8 9
.8	19 20	1267.4	21 22	1545.4	21 23	.9	9
1111	17 18	1407.3	19 21	1550.5	18 20	2205.0	9 10
1120.2	17 18	1408.3	19 21	1552.4	20 21	2325	5 6
.3	18 19	1452.4	18 19	1554.2	20 21	2326	5 6
.5	19 20	.5	21 23	1556.2	19 20	2327	5 6
1130.2	18 19	1454.3	20 21	1562.5	20 22	2400.6	8 9
.4	19 20	.4	21 23	1570.4	19 21	2405.7	8 9
.5	20 21	1455.4	22 24	1604.2	18 19	2450.1	10
1150.2	19 20	1456.1	18 19	.4	18 20	alle Nr. 3000 u. darüber	1 bis 4
.5	22 23	.3	23 24	.5	21 23		

1. Werkzeugbruch.

Aus dem Werkzeugbruch erkennt man sofort, ob es sich um einen Werkstoffehler im Werkzeug oder Überbeanspruchung gehandelt hat. Daraus werden Schlüsse auf die Sorgfalt bei der Arbeit gezogen, so daß es im Interesse eines jeden liegt, möglichst schonend mit den teuren Werkzeugen umzugehen.

2. Feilen.

Falls bei der Bearbeitung eine kleine Nacharbeit durch Feilen vorgenommen wird, nimmt man feinere Schlichtfeilen. Setzen sich Späne in die Kerben, müssen diese mit einer Bürste oder einem weichen Blech entfernt werden. Feilen mit Kreide und Öl bestreichen, ergeben feinste Oberflächen.

Schlußwort.

Niemand kann verlangen, daß aus ihm bei einmaligem Durchlesen dieses Buches ein vollendeter Fachmann geworden ist. Das ist auch nicht der Zweck der Ausführungen. Wichtig ist zu wissen, wo finde ich Rat, um bessere und schnellere Arbeit leisten zu können. Wer sich dann an die Ratschläge und Beispiele hält, kommt sicher zu guter Leistung. Der Überblick weitet sich und aus dem im Dunkeln Tastenden wird der Sichere, der Beherrscher seiner Maschine und ihrer Leistungsfähigkeit. Doch dazu hilft nur eins: Ran an die Arbeit, immer wieder ran, zähe an sich selbst arbeiten und durchhalten. Dann kommt der Erfolg ganz von selbst und mein Wunsch für alle erfüllt sich:

Die Freude an der Arbeit
macht das Leben schön.

Weiteres Schrifttum.

Werkstattbücher, Springer-Verlag, Berlin, Preis RM. 2.—.

Heft 1. *Gewindeschneiden.* 3. Aufl. Von Ob.-Ing. O. M. Müller.

„ 4. *Wechselräderberechnung für Drehbänke.* 4. Aufl. (19. bis 24. Tausend). Von Betriebsdirektor G. Knappe.

„ 9. *Rezepte für die Werkstatt.* 3. Aufl. (17. bis 22. Tausend). Von Dr. Fritz Spitzer.

„ 15. *Bohren.* 2. Aufl. (8. bis 14. Tausend). Von Ing. J. Dinnebier u. Dr.-Ing. H. J. Stoewer.

„ 16. *Senken und Reiben.* 2. Aufl. (8. bis 13. Tausend). Von Ing. J. Dinnebier.

„ 22. *Die Fräser.* 2. Aufl. (8. bis 14. Tausend). Von Dr.-Ing. Ernst Brödner u. Ing. Paul Zieting.

„ 26. *Innenräumen.* 2. Aufl. (8. bis 14. Tausend). Von Ing. Leonhard Knoll.

„ 51. *Spannen im Maschinenbau.* Von Ing. A. Klautke.

„ 52. *Technisches Rechnen.* Von Dr. phil. V. Happach.

Druck von C. G. Röder, Leipzig.

Batch number: 10682421

Printed by Printforce, the Netherlands